Contents

Introduction to
Slovenia

Slovenia is a tiny country of endless variety, a magical landscape embracing imperious limestone mountains, sparkling lakes and a craggy coastline punctuated with historic coastal resorts. Add to the mix spectacular underground streams and canyons, sweeping vineyards and handsome Baroque towns, throw in a few theatrically sited castles and enchanting wayside villages, and it's clear to see why this nation of just two million people packs a mighty punch. But it is Slovenia's status as one of Europe's greenest and most environmentally sound countries that really sets it apart, something that becomes startlingly obvious the further you explore.

Dominated by Germanic and, to a lesser extent, Hungarian and Italian influences from the Middle Ages until the end of World War I, Slovenia spent the best part of the next seventy years locked into a less than harmonious **Yugoslav federation**. When the federation began to fracture in the late 1980s, Slovenia was the first to secede; save for the so-called **Ten-Day War** of independence in the summer of 1991, the country emerged more or less unscathed from the bloodbath that engulfed Croatia and Bosnia. While entry into the **European Union** in 2004 appears to have made little tangible difference to the lives of most Slovenes – always the most liberal and progressive of Yugoslavia's erstwhile republics, the country settled down to life in the new European order with ease – it did help raise Slovenia's profile in a big way.

Visitors will immediately be struck by the quality of the **tourist facilities** on offer, across the board – whether you're after a chic city break in a boutique hotel in Ljubljana or a restful stay on a rural tourist farm, an adrenaline-fuelled activity holiday or a slap-up feast of regional delicacies. Indeed, the standard of these facilities, allied to the country's excellent infrastructure – driving and cycling are an absolute joy – reflects an atmosphere of friendly order that wouldn't seem out of place in Scandinavia. And, much like Scandinavia, Slovenia's green credentials are impeccable, its pristine environment perfectly in keeping with a strong commitment to sustainable tourism.

ABOVE BLED CASTLE

THE ROUGH GUIDE TO
SLOVENIA

ROUGH
GUIDES

This fourth
Norm Lo

KT 2308702 1

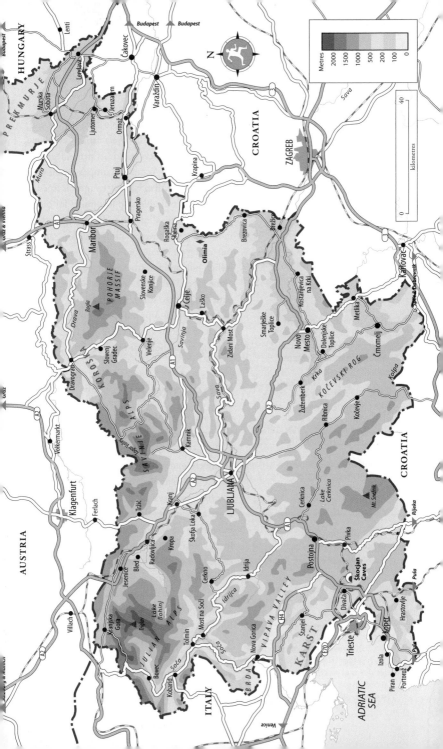

FACT FILE

- With an **area** of less than 21,000 square kilometres (roughly the size of Wales), and a **population** of two million, Slovenia is one of Europe's smallest nations.

- Forty percent of the country is covered by **mountains**, with three major mountain groups: the Julian Alps, the Kamniške-Savinja Alps and the Karavanke mountains. The highest peak is Triglav (2864m) in the Julian Alps. It's the third-most forested country in Europe, after Finland and Sweden, while its **coastline**, at 47km, is among the shortest – only Bosnia's is shorter.

- On June 25, 1991, Slovenia became an **independent republic** for the first time. The 1991 constitution set in place a **parliamentary system** of government, elected every four years, with the prime minister at its head. Elected every five years, the president is head of state. The country became a full member of the EU in 2004 and adopted the euro in 2007.

- **Tourism** is one of the fastest-growing sectors of the Slovenian economy, with alpine, coastal and spa resorts absorbing the bulk of the tourist traffic.

- Slovenia's most important **exports** are vehicles, electrical appliances and pharmaceutical goods, and its main trading partners are Germany and Italy.

- This is the only country in Europe to feature a mountain – Triglav – in its **coat of arms**.

- In 2000, **Davo Karničar** became the first man to ski down Mount Everest, and also the first man to ski down the highest summit in all seven continents.

This little country boasts a growing number of brilliantly conceived eco-resorts, while Ljubljana – named European Green Capital in 2016 – displays impressive forward thinking when it comes to eco issues.

As appealing as many of Slovenia's towns and cities are, especially the lovely capital, **Ljubljana**, the country's greatest asset is its magnificent natural heritage. As one of Europe's greenest nations – more than half the country is forested – Slovenia offers limitless opportunities for **outdoor pursuits**: skiing, climbing and trekking in the mountains, whitewater rafting, kayaking and canyoning on the many rivers, cycling through rolling hills and forests, or riding cross-country on a fine Lipizzaner horse, to name but a few. And with distances so small, in a single day you could be hiking in the Alps in the morning, downing a glass of wine in a local cellar over lunch and relaxing by the beach at the end of the day.

Where to go

Most visitors to Slovenia begin with a trip to the country's sophisticated capital, **Ljubljana**, whose engaging blend of Baroque and Habsburg architecture, not to mention its lovely riverside cafés and restaurants, could quite happily detain you for a few days. From here it is customary to make a beeline for the stunning alpine lakes and mountains northwest of the capital, namely **Lake Bled**, with its fairytale island church and clifftop castle, and the even more beautiful **Lake Bohinj**, less than 30km to the west. Both lakes lie on the fringe of the **Julian Alps**, whose magisterial peaks are as popular with climbers and hikers in the summer as they are with skiers in the winter. Most of the Alps are contained within **Triglav National Park**, which extends south to the sublime **Soča Valley**, whose eponymous green-blue river draws adventure-sports enthusiasts to its foaming waters each summer.

OPPOSITE FROM TOP LAKE BOHINJ; BEEHIVE PANELS; SOČA RIVER

SLOVENIAN WINE

Slovenian wine (*vino*) is little known beyond the country's borders, yet vineyards here cover roughly the same area as the Bordeaux region in France and produce about half the quantity of wine of that territory. In addition, much of what is produced is world class. There are three distinct wine-producing regions, each subdivided into separate districts (fourteen in total). The largest is **Podravje** in the northeast, where white wines such as Laški Rizling, Sauvignon and Šipon predominate; if you've only time to get to just one wine destination, make it the bewitching Jeruzalem–Ormož wine road.

Posavje, in the southeastern corner of Slovenia, is known for its reds, in particular the rich and velvety Metliška črnina from Bela Krajina and the blended, juice-like Cvicek from Dolenjska. Over to the far west of the country, **Primorje** has four quite distinct wine districts; by far the most celebrated is Goriška Brda, on the border with Italy, which yields a prolific number of both reds and whites, foremost of which are the excellent Merlot, the straw-yellow Zlata ("Golden") Rebula and the dry Tokaj. Further south, the wind-buffeted Vipava Valley boasts many outstanding vintners, while no visit to the neighbouring Karst region is complete without a drop of the full-blooded, ruby-red Teran wine.

By far the most enjoyable way to sample wine is to take a visit to one of the many **wine cellars** (*vinska klet*) that abound along the country's twenty or so **wine roads** (*vinske ceste*). Alternatively, most towns and cities have a *vinoteka* (wine shop) where you may be offered tastings, while any restaurant worth its salt will list a healthy complement of top-rate Slovenian wines.

South of the Soča Valley, beyond the captivating **Goriška Brda** and **Vipava Valley** wine-producing regions, you'll find the **Karst**. This rugged limestone plateau is scattered with ancient stone villages, including **Štanjel**, but is famed above all for its dramatic underground rivers, streams and depressions, seen most spectacularly in the **Škocjan Caves**. The Karst is also home to the world-famous **Lipica stud farm**, the original home of the Lipizzaner horse.

Although less than 50km long, Slovenia's **coast** packs in a multiplicity of appealing little resorts. Probably the most enjoyable are **Piran**, a town brimming with Venetian architecture, and **Portorož**, the country's major beach resort. A short way north of these, even the workaday port town of **Koper** conceals an appealing medieval centre.

RIGHT PIRAN

Returning inland, you will find more subterranean wonders to explore. Few can hold a candle to the breathtaking **Postojna Caves**, which lie within striking distance of another of Slovenia's remarkable natural phenomena, the "disappearing" **Lake Cerknica**. South of here, the dark forests and deep river valleys ranged along the Croatian border offer further opportunities for outdoor pursuits, while anyone seeking cultural diversions can take their pick from a rich tapestry of historical sites – churches, castles and ancient monasteries.

By comparison, the eastern part of the country is much less travelled, and though it might not possess the clear-cut attractions of other regions, there are some hugely rewarding places to visit. Chief among these is Slovenia's most historic and prettiest town, **Ptuj**, which is also the setting for the exuberant pre-Lenten Pust carnival. Just a short ride away is the country's vibrant, if underrated, second city, **Maribor**, and the sprawling **Pohorje massif**, a major summer and winter resort. Eastern Slovenia also abounds in **spas**, the most popular of which are the refined, Habsburg-era resort of **Rogaška Slatina** and the more modern, family-oriented **Čatež**. As you head further east, across the Mura River and towards the Hungarian border, the undulating hills of the **Podravje** wine-producing districts give way to the flat plains of **Prekmurje**, a lovely rural region of smooth fields interspersed with attractive villages distinguished by Hungarian-style farmhouses and little white churches.

When to go

Most visitors come to Slovenia during the **summer** high season (June to August), when the weather is at its most reliable, all the tourist sights are open and the country's numerous festivals are in full swing. However, many of Slovenia's attractions, including the capital, are just as enjoyable outside the summer months, and in particular during spring and autumn, when the countryside colours are at their most resplendent, hotel prices (at least in the resort areas) are slightly lower and the crowds are a little thinner.

Slovenia's **climate** follows three distinctive patterns. In the northwest, an **alpine** climate predominates, characterized by very cold winters, often with heavy rainfall and snow, and moderately warm summers, occasionally interspersed with short, violent storms. However, with the wide range of pursuits on offer in this region – skiing between December and March, and climbing, hiking and adventure sports between April and September – a visit to the mountains can be enjoyed at pretty much any time of the year. Aside from Kranjska Gora in the winter, and Lake Bled and Lake Bohinj in the height of summer, few resorts get so full that finding accommodation becomes a problem.

The **Primorska region** (from the Soča Valley down to the coast) has a typically **Mediterranean** climate – very warm summers with consistent sunshine, and pleasantly cool winters. This is the one part of the country that can feel a little pressured by crowds, particularly in August when hordes of holidaying Italians arrive from just across the border. Booking accommodation in advance around this time is recommended. Whatever the season, there's a good chance you'll experience the infamous **burja**, a vicious wind that whips down through the Karst on its way to the Bay of Trieste.

The remainder of the country subscribes to a **continental** climate of hot, dry summers – particularly in the south and east of the country – and bitterly cold winters.

AVERAGE MONTHLY TEMPERATURES AND RAINFALL

	Jan	Feb	Mar	Apr	May	Jun	Jul	Aug	Sep	Oct	Nov	Dec
ČRNOMELJ												
Temp °C/°F	1/34	4/40	7/46	11/52	16/61	19/66	21/70	20/68	16/61	11/52	6/43	2/36
Rain (mm)	30	25	30	40	50	70	50	58	35	25	40	40
KOPER												
Temp °C/°F	5/41	6/43	9/48	12/54	17/62	20/68	23/74	23/74	20/68	16/61	10/50	7/46
Rain (mm)	65	60	70	80	85	100	75	90	110	120	105	80
LJUBLJANA												
Temp °C/°F	-1/30	0/33	5/41	9/48	14/57	17/62	19/66	19/66	15/60	10/50	4/40	0/33
Rain (mm)	30	25	30	40	50	70	50	55	35	30	40	40
MARIBOR												
Temp °C/°F	-3/26	-1/30	4/40	9/48	14/57	17/62	19/66	18/64	14/57	9/48	3/37	-1/30
Rain (mm)	40	40	50	60	90	100	110	100	75	60	65	40

Author picks

Our author has scoured every inch of this fascinating country, from the highest mountain peaks and deepest caves to the most beautiful vineyards. Here he shares a few of his favourite experiences.

Plečnik-spotting The great architect's influence can be found throughout Slovenia, from his myriad projects in Ljubljana – such as the Triple Bridge (p.48), the National Library (p.56) and the Market Colonnade (p.49) – to the remarkable Church of the Ascension in Bogojina (p.290).

Handsome hayracks From single-stretch (*kozolec*) to double hayracks (*toplars*), the Slovenian countryside is littered with these vernacular structures, used for drying grain – the Studor group is the finest in the country (p.123).

Salty scenes The vast, hauntingly beautiful Sečovlje saltpans are still used today for harvesting salt, as well as being a haven for stunning birds and plant life (p.196).

Tough treks The Julian Alps abound with top trails. While Triglav may be the loftiest peak, there are other, more demanding, hikes to be tackled here, such as Jalovec, at 2645m (p.131).

Cosy stays A good night's sleep is guaranteed at Slovenia's many tourist farms, as is a warm welcome and delicious home-cooked food and wine; *Šeruga* (p.229) and *Lenar* (p.262) are two of the best.

Cool cave Don a helmet, flashlight and boots before descending into the forebodingly titled Bear's Corridor, and then venture beyond towards more than twenty shimmering underground lakes (p.212).

Spectacular drive Fifty hairpin bends, welcoming roadside huts and spectacular views at every turn will ensure that a trip over the snaking Vršič Pass will live long in the memory (p.133).

> Our author recommendations don't end here. We've flagged up our favourite places – a perfectly sited hotel, an atmospheric café, a special restaurant – throughout the Guide, highlighted with the ★ symbol.

FROM TOP MARKET COLONNADES, LJUBLJANA; SEČOVLJE SALTPANS; VRŠIČ PASS

things not to miss

It's not possible to see everything that Slovenia has to offer in one trip – and we don't suggest you try. What follows, in no particular order, is a selective taste of the country's highlights: outstanding architecture, natural wonders and historic sites. All highlights are colour-coded by chapter and have a page reference to take you straight into the Guide, where you can find out more.

1 ADVENTURE SPORTS ON THE SOČA
Page 142

This fabulous, foaming river is first rate for any number of adventure sports, from whitewater rafting and kayaking to canoeing and hydrospeeding.

2 PLANICA SKI-JUMPING
Page 130

Enjoy daring feats, beer and music at one of the world's great ski-jumping venues; and when they're not competing, have a go on the world's steepest zip-line.

3 THE KARST
Page 173

Explore intriguing dry-stone villages, including pretty hilltop Štanjel, and head underground to a mysterious world of rivers, streams and caverns.

4 LAKE BOHINJ
Page 117

Encircled by majestic mountains, Bohinj is the pearl of the alpine lakes, less visited and more serene than Lake Bled.

5 ŠKOCJAN CAVES
Page 177

Carved out by the thrashing Reka River, the world's largest underground canyon is a staggering natural wonder.

6 LENT FESTIVAL, MARIBOR
Page 275
Vibrant and entertaining summer spectacle, comprising music, theatre, dance, food, and loads more.

7 LAKE BLED
Page 107
This fairytale lake comes complete with island church and atmospheric castle. Take a dip or a stroll – or just kick back on a gondola.

8 LJUBLJANA
Page 40
Enjoy fabulous Baroque and Habsburg architecture, a hilltop castle and leafy riverside cafés in Slovenia's enchanting capital.

9 WINE
Page 8
From the sunny Goriška Brda hills in the west to the beautiful Ljutomer–Ormož vineyards in the east, Slovenia produces some surprisingly fabulous wines.

10 PIRAN
Page 189
The country's most alluring coastal town, strewn with gorgeous Gothic-Venetian architecture, pretty little churches and quaint squares.

11 KOČEVSKI ROG
Page 219
As well as being a terrific rambling spot, this thickly forested Karst plateau shelters one of Europe's largest populations of brown bears.

12 HIKING IN THE JULIAN ALPS
Page 119

Among the most stunning and least spoilt ranges in Europe, these mountain wilds are Slovenia's prime hiking region, with trails for walkers of all abilities.

13 PTUJ
Page 277

Slovenia's oldest and most appealing town is run through with more than two thousand years of history.

14 CHURCH OF THE HOLY TRINITY, HRASTOVLJE
Page 181

Acquaint yourself with the *Dance of Death* fresco, alongside many other terrific wall paintings, in this sun-baked Romanesque church.

15 PREKMURJE
Page 287

Lush green fields, picturesque villages dotted with storks' nests, and a distinct culinary tradition characterize Slovenia's intriguing easternmost region.

16 SKIING
Page 128

Take your pick from more than twenty ski resorts, with slopes and facilities to suit anyone from beginners to pros.

17 LOGAR VALLEY
Page 261

Impossibly picturesque glacial valley, carpeted with meadows and forests and hemmed in by the raw peaks of the Kamniške-Savinja Alps.

17

Itineraries

Small it may be, but Slovenia packs in an extraordinary number of cultural, natural and historical sites, many of which are covered in our Grand Tour. Visitors with energy to expend should follow the Great Outdoors itinerary – featuring everything from water to wildlife – while our Gastronomic Odyssey presents a feast of fabulous local delicacies and wines.

GRAND TOUR

Give yourself two weeks, and a car, to sample the very best of Slovenia.

❶ Ljubljana The captivating capital features sumptuous Baroque architecture, a handsome hilltop castle and plenty of leafy riverside cafés; two or three days is perfect. **See p.40**

❷ Lakes Bled and Bohinj Slovenia's twin pearls, the former celebrated for its cliff-bound castle and gorgeous island church, the latter more serene but no less resplendent. Stay in Bled and take a day-trip to Bohinj. **See p.107 & p.117**

❸ Soča Valley Sliced through by one of Europe's great alpine rivers, and littered with abandoned fortifications and World War I monuments, this is the Slovenian landscape at its most magisterial; the handsome town of Kobarid is an ideal base. **See p.141**

❹ Karst Dry, densely forested limestone plateau pockmarked by extraordinary cave systems and disappearing lakes. Stay at a tourist farm or in the pretty village of Štanjel. **See p.173**

❺ Piran and the saltpans Boasting glorious Gothic-Venetian architecture, Piran is the coast's most atmospheric town; spend two days here and visit the eerily beautiful Sečovlje saltpans. See p.189 & p.196

❻ Postojna With an underground train, wondrous formations and the enigmatic *Proteus*

anguinus – the "human fish" – this magical masterpiece of nature has been enthralling visitors for centuries. **See p.205**

❼ Ptuj Showcasing a raft of architectural and archeological treasures, Slovenia's oldest town also hosts the Kurent, the country's captivating pre-Lenten carnival. **See p.277**

❽ Prekmurje This region of lush green fields, little white churches and stork-populated villages receives relatively few visitors – stay in a tourist farm and enjoy the rural calm. **See p.287**

❾ Logar Valley Abutting the Austrian border, the serrated peaks framing this awesome valley offer superb outdoor activities, and wonderful farm accommodation. **See p.261**

THE GREAT OUTDOORS

Overground, underground or on the water, Slovenia offers incomparable opportunities for adrenaline sports – and more sedate pursuits. Allow ten days for this tour, and take in the country's most picturesque spots.

❶ Hiking the Julian Alps Extending across northwest Slovenia, these imperious limestone mountains present terrific hiking and climbing, not least the mighty Triglav. **See p.119**

❷ Rafting on the Soča It's a short drive to this awesome alpine river and its water-based activities; Bovec is the ideal base. **See p.142**

ABOVE SEASONAL GOURDS; DRAGON BRIDGE, LJUBLJANA

❸ Paragliding in the Vipava Valley Strap up and get soaring for bird's-eye views with the famous *bora* wind behind you. The wine village of Slap makes a great overnight stop. **See p.162**

❹ Caving Continue south to the Karst and a subterranean wonderland of fabulous caving experiences: Babji Zob, near Bled; Vilenica, near Lipica; and, best of all, the Križna water cave near Cerknica. **See p.113, p.177 & p.212**

❺ Coastal activities It's a short hop down to the sunny Slovenian coast, where Portorož offers fun-filled diversions, including stand-up paddling and sea kayaking. **See p.195**

❻ Bear-watching If you go down to the woods today… a rare opportunity to see these magnificent beasts up close in the wild, thankfully from the safety of a hideout. **See p.218**

❼ Mountain biking in Koroška Finally, head north to this mountain wilderness for some wonderfully scenic and challenging trails – you can even bike through a disused mine. **See p.260**

GASTRONOMIC ODYSSEY

You could spend ten happy days eating and drinking your way around Slovenia, where a new generation of innovative chefs and world-class wines are making their mark.

❶ Open Kitchen, Ljubljana Weather permitting, *Odprta Kuhna* is the perfect introduction to Slovenia's culinary delights, with many of the country's finest restaurants serving sample portions from their menus. **See p.71**

❷ Hiša Franko, Kobarid Between Ana's kitchen and Valter's cellar, you're assured an exquisite dining experience at *Franko's* – arguably Slovenia's best restaurant. **See p.150**

❸ Goriška Brda wine From *Franko's* it's an easy drive south to Slovenia's most celebrated – and picturesque – wine-growing region, producer of superlative reds. **See p.160**

❹ Pršut and teran, Karst Wherever you travel in the Karst you should sample a few slices of *pršut* (dry-cured ham) with a glass of Kraški Teran, a full-bodied tipple that takes its blood-red colour from the local iron-rich soil. **See p.173**

❺ Repnice, Brezovica Head to the other side of the country, where beautifully patterned sand caves, dug deep into the flint stone hills, make for a unique wine-tasting experience. **See p.236**

❻ Wine, Jeruzalem Further north you will find the lush, terraced vineyards of this lovely wine road. A leisurely drive will allow you to taste a host of sumptuous whites; sleep it off at a welcoming tourist farm. **See p.285**

❼ Prekmurje cuisine While *bograč* and *gibanica* are the region's staple dishes, few meals here are complete without a drizzle of deliciously nutty pumpkinseed oil. **See p.287**

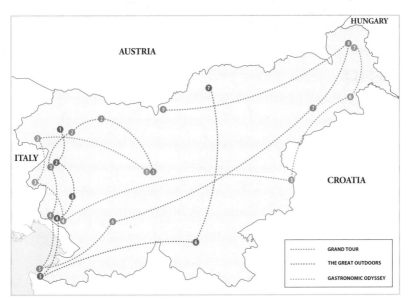

MOUNTAIN HUT, TRIGLAV NATIONAL PARK

Basics

Getting there

Flying is the easiest way to reach Slovenia, with several airlines now operating direct from airports in the UK. Flying from North America, Australasia or South Africa will entail one or more changes. Travelling overland from the UK is another option, though this inevitably takes longer and usually works out far more expensive.

If **flying**, you may be able to cut costs by going through a specialist flight agent, who in addition to dealing with discounted flights may also offer student and youth fares and travel insurance, rail passes, car rental, tours and the like.

Flights from the UK and Ireland

Flying to Slovenia from the UK takes approximately two hours. **Adria Airways** (ⓦadria.si/en), the Slovenian national carrier, operates flights from London Gatwick to the capital, Ljubljana; **easyJet** (ⓦeasyjet.com) from Stansted and London Gatwick to Ljubljana, and **WizzAir** (ⓦwizzair.com) from Luton to Ljubljana. Another possibility is to fly into one of the neighbouring countries, from where you can continue the onward journey by bus or train; options here include Venice and Trieste in Italy, and Zagreb in Croatia, all of which are close to the Slovenian border.

Prices depend on how far in advance you book, although **season** is also a factor. High-season flights (June–Aug, Christmas and New Year) will cost more than at other times, unless you book very well in advance; it is also generally more expensive to fly at weekends. Book far enough in advance with a low-cost airline and you can pick up a ticket for around £60–70 return, even in summer; book anything less than three or four weeks in advance and this could triple in price. **Flight search engines** such as ⓦskyscanner.net, ⓦkayak.co.uk or ⓦmomondo.com are invaluable for researching the best connections and prices.

Flights from the US and Canada

As there are **no direct flights** from North America to Slovenia you will need to fly into a major European hub and continue the journey from there. From the east coast of the **US**, expect to pay around US$700 low season and US$1000 high season; and from the west coast around US$1100 low season and US$1400 high season. From **Canada**, you're looking at around Can$1300 low season from Toronto (Can$1700 high season) and Can$1900 low season from Vancouver (Can$2300 high season).

Flights from Australia, New Zealand and South Africa

There are **no direct flights** from Australia or New Zealand to Slovenia. It is possible to change airlines, either in Asia or Europe, but the best option is to fly to a Western European gateway for a connecting flight. A return fare from eastern **Australia** is around Aus$2200 low season and Aus$2700 high season. From **New Zealand**, it's around NZ$2500 low season, and NZ$3000 high season.

It's not possible to fly direct to Slovenia from **South Africa**, so you'll have to change airlines at one of the main European gateways. A standard return fare from Johannesburg to Ljubljana, via Frankfurt or Vienna – with South African Airways (ⓦflysaa.com) or a leading European airline – is around ZAR9000 low season and ZAR11,000 high season.

Trains

Travelling by **train** to Slovenia is likely to be considerably more expensive than flying. The shortest journey from the UK takes about eighteen hours, with a standard second-class return ticket, incorporating Eurostar, costing around £200, if you book early. From London St Pancras International, take the Eurostar to Paris Gare du Nord, then walk over to Gare de l'Est for a train to Munich, where you change for Ljubljana.

A BETTER KIND OF TRAVEL

At Rough Guides we are passionately committed to travel. We believe it helps us understand the world we live in and the people we share it with – and of course tourism is vital to many developing economies. But the scale of modern tourism has also damaged some places irreparably, and climate change is accelerated by most forms of transport, especially flying. All Rough Guides' flights are carbon-offset, and every year we donate money to a variety of environmental charities.

Deutsche Bahn is the best option for making seat reservations on continental trains and its website is an excellent resource for checking timetables, while **The Man in Seat Sixty-One** is invaluable on most aspects of rail travel in Europe.

Rail passes

If you're taking in Slovenia as part of a more extensive trip around Europe, it may be worth buying a rail pass. **InterRail** passes are available to European citizens and residents only. They come in first- and second-class over-26 and (cheaper) under-26 versions.

The passes can cover a combination of countries for five days within a fifteen-day period (£225 second class, £170 under-26), seven days within one month (£268 second class, £210 under-26) and ten days within one month (£318 second class, £249 under-26); other options cover travel for fifteen consecutive days (£352 second class, £288 under-26), 22 consecutive days (£412 second class, £318 under-26) or one month unlimited (£533 second class, £408 under-26). Pass holders also receive a discounted rate on the Eurostar service.

Another InterRail scheme, the **One-Country Pass**, allows you to travel for a certain number of days during a one-month period. For Slovenia, eight days in one month costs £126 for over-26s/£91 for under-26s; six days in one month £107/£80; four days £81/£59; three days £67/£49.

Non-European residents qualify for the **Eurail Pass**, which must be bought before arrival in Europe, or from RailEurope in the UK. The pass allows unlimited first-class travel in 28 European countries, including Slovenia, and is available in various increments: for example, a fifteen-day continuous pass costs US$685 for over-26s/$449 under-26s, 22 days (US$883/$576), and one month (US$1084/$707). Other Eurail options include a One-Country Pass and a Select Pass, which allows you to travel in two-, three- or four neighbouring countries.

By car from the UK

Driving to Slovenia, a distance of some 1500km from London, is really only worth considering if you are planning to travel around Slovenia extensively (see p.24) or want to make stopovers en route.

Once across the channel – the easiest way being the drive-on drive-off shuttle services operated by **Eurotunnel**, or by **ferry** from Dover to Calais – the most direct route to Ljubljana (around 30hr at a leisurely pace with plenty of stops) is via Brussels, Stuttgart, Munich and Salzburg before crossing into Slovenia at the Karavanke Tunnel border.

Route plans can be obtained from the websites of Michelin (Ⓦ viamichelin.com), the AA (Ⓦ theaa .com) or the RAC (Ⓦ rac.co.uk).

Agents and operators

There are a good number of tour operators offering holidays in Slovenia, most of which are geared towards **adventure activities** and the outdoors. Hiking and cycling trips are the most sought after, though ski and spa breaks are also gaining in popularity.

RAIL CONTACTS

Deutsche Bahn Ⓦ bahn.de.
Eurail Ⓦ eurail.com.
European Rail UK Ⓣ 020 7619 1083, Ⓦ etrains4u.com.
Eurostar UK Ⓣ 08432 186186, international Ⓣ +44 (0)1233 617575, Ⓦ eurostar.com.
Interrail Ⓦ interrail.eu.
Man in Seat Sixty-One Ⓦ seat61.com.
Rail Europe UK Ⓣ 0844 848 5848, Ⓦ uk.voyages-sncf.com.

FERRIES/CHANNEL TUNNEL

DFDS Seaways UK Ⓣ 0871 522 9955, international Ⓣ +44 330 333 0245; Ⓦ dfdsseaways.co.uk.
Eurotunnel UK Ⓣ 0844 335 3535, international Ⓣ +33 (0)321 002061, Ⓦ eurotunnel.com.
P&O Ferries UK Ⓣ 0800 130 0030, Ireland Ⓣ +353 1 686 9467; Ⓦ poferries.com.
Stena Line UK Ⓣ 0844 770 7070, Ⓦ stenaline.co.uk.

TRAVEL AGENTS

North South Travel UK Ⓣ 01245 608291, Ⓦ northsouthtravel.co.uk. Friendly travel agency offering discounted fares worldwide. Profits are used to support projects in the developing world, especially the promotion of sustainable tourism.
STA Travel UK Ⓣ 0333 321 0099, Ⓦ statravel.co.uk; US Ⓣ 1800 781 4040, Australia Ⓣ 134782, New Zealand Ⓣ 0800 474400, South Africa Ⓣ 0861 781781. Worldwide specialists in independent travel; also student IDs, travel insurance, car rental, rail passes and more. Good discounts for students and under-26s.
Trailfinders UK Ⓣ 020 7368 1200, Ireland Ⓣ 021 464 8800; Ⓦ trailfinders.com. One of the best-informed and most efficient agents for independent travellers.
Travel CUTS Canada Ⓣ 1800 667 2887, US Ⓣ 1800 592 2887; Ⓦ travelcuts.com. Canada-based youth and student travel firm.
USIT Ireland Ⓣ 01 602 1906, Ⓦ usit.ie; Australia Ⓣ 1800 092499, Ⓦ usitaustralia.com.au. Student and youth travel specialists.

SPECIALIST OPERATORS

Balkan Holidays UK Ⓣ 0207 543 5555, Ⓦ balkanholidays.co.uk. Southeastern Europe specialists, offering package deals to Bled, Bohinj, Kranjska Gora and Portorož. Ski packages, too.

Crystal Holidays UK ☎ 020 8939 0739, Ⓦ crystalholidays.co.uk. Flight-only deals and summer and winter (ski) package deals to Bled, Bohinj, Bovec, Kranjska Gora and the Adriatic coast.

Eastern Eurotours Australia ☎ 1800 242353, Ⓦ easterneurotours .com.au. Week-long escorted tours taking in the country's star sights, and a biking/hiking tour of eastern Slovenia.

Explore Worldwide UK ☎ 01252 883967, Ⓦ explore.co.uk. Eight-day tours of the alpine lakes and an eight-day cycling trip from Venice to Porec (Croatia).

Just Slovenia UK ☎ 01373 814230, Ⓦ justslovenia.co.uk. UK's premier Slovenia specialist, offering tailor-made holidays, plus flights, accommodation (including tourist farms), sports and activity tours and car rental.

Thermalia Travel UK ☎ 01843 864688, Ⓦ thermaliaspas.co.uk. Spa holiday specialists offering a range of treatment programmes at the Laško, Rogaška Slatina, Šmarješke Toplice and Strunjan spas.

Vamos Travel UK ☎ 01926 330233, Ⓦ vamostravel.com. Excellent Central and Eastern Europe specialist offering tailor-made tours to Ljubljana and Bled, multi-activity adventure holidays, ski breaks and more.

ACTIVITY TOUR OPERATORS

Activities Abroad UK ☎ 01670 789991, Ⓦ activitiesabroad.com. Week-long multi-activity holidays in the Julian Alps and Soča Valley, including canyoning, caving, cycling, kayaking and rafting.

Exodus UK ☎ 0203 733 8382, Ⓦ exodus.co.uk. Wide range of eight-day tours, with multi-activity holidays in the Julian Alps, trekking and climbing trips (including an ascent of Mt Triglav), self-guided cycling holidays in the Alps and the Adriatic and family adventure holidays.

Headwater UK ☎ 01606 369418, Ⓦ headwater.com. Eight- and ten-day guided walking and cycling holidays (easy to moderate) in the Julian Alps and Adriatic.

Hooked on Cycling UK ☎ 01501 740985, Ⓦ hookedoncycling.co.uk. Seven- to ten-day guided cycling trips, including the Julian Alps, the spa and wine regions of eastern Slovenia and a road trip that takes in Croatia.

Inntravel UK ☎ 01653 617001, Ⓦ inntravel.co.uk. Seven- and fourteen-day walking holidays in the Julian Alps and lakes, plus trips that take in Italy too.

Saddle Skedaddle UK ☎ 0191 265 1110, Ⓦ skedaddle.co.uk. Twelve-day self-guided cycling tours of the Julian Alps and Croatia's Dalmatian coast.

Wilderness Travel US ☎ 1800 368 2794, Ⓦ wildernesstravel.com. Eleven-day hiking trip (moderate to difficult) through western Slovenia, taking in the Julian Alps, Logar Valley, Soča Valley and Piran.

Getting around

Whether you travel by train, bus or car, almost any journey you take around Slovenia will be wonderfully scenic, and the country's tiny scale means that you'll never have to travel long distances. On the whole, trains and buses are clean, reliable and inexpensive, the latter covering a far greater number of destinations. All that said, the country's overwhelmingly rural nature is perfect for driving, and brings the obvious advantages of allowing you to visit pretty much anywhere you please, and in your own good time.

By train

Slovene railways (*Slovenske železnice*) runs a smooth, efficient and inexpensive service, covering a modest 1200km, almost half of which is electrified. All the key lines, as well as international trains, run through Ljubljana.

Trains (*vlaki*) are divided into **slow trains** (*lokalni potniški*, abbreviated to "RG" or "LP"), which stop at every halt; **intercity trains** ("IC"), which are faster, more comfortable, and stop at fewer stations; and the very fast **Inter City Slovenia** ("ICS") three-carriage tilting trains, which run between Maribor and Ljubljana (1hr 50min), stopping at Pragersko, Celje and Zidani Most – at weekends between mid-June and August there is also a daily ICS service between Maribor and Koper. Inter City Slovenia trains are air-conditioned and wheelchair accessible, with buffet cars. To Most na Soči there is also the car train trom Bohinjska Bistrica (see p.114) and the museum train from Jesenice (see p.158). There are no domestic overnight trains.

Although there are no special carriages, **bicycles** (*kolo*) can be carried on all trains (except the ICS) for an extra €3.40.

Most **timetables** (*vozni red*) have translations in English; the yellow boards titled *Odhodi* are departures, the white boards titled *Prihodi*, arrivals. Timetable leaflets, which only indicate routes that trains from that particular station take, are often available from counters, but you can also check train information on the website Ⓦ slo-zeleznice.si, which has good English explanations.

There are **left-luggage lockers** (*garderoba*; typically €2–3 for 24hr) at all the larger stations.

Tickets

Tickets can be bought at the station (*železniška postaja*) up to two months in advance; staff invariably speak a high level of English. **Fares** are calculated by distance travelled, with a return ticket (*povratna vozovnica*) exactly double that of a single (*enosmerna vozovnica*). For example, a journey of 50km (on an Intercity train) costs around €7 (€10 first class), and a journey of 100km, €9.50 (€13.50 first class). ICS trains are more expensive; the second-class fare for the journey between Ljubljana and Maribor (156km) is around €16.50 (€24.50 first class). **Concessionary fares** on domestic services are available for children under the age of 6 (free), and for children aged between 6 and 12 (half-price).

Seat reservations (*rezervacije*; €3.60) are obligatory for services marked on a timetable with a boxed R (in effect all ICS trains and some international services), and optional for those designated by an R.

If you board a train without a ticket (for a good reason) you will have to pay a supplement of €2.50. Otherwise, fare dodging will cost you €40. Most stations now accept credit cards, though on trains, payment can only be made using cash.

By bus

Slovenia's **bus network** consists of a slightly confusing, but generally well-coordinated, array of small local companies. On the whole, buses are clean, comfortable and, except for some departing on a Friday evening, rarely crowded. They are able to reach significantly more destinations than trains, and services tend to be more frequent. That said, services, particularly those on rural routes, are dramatically reduced (or even nonexistent) at weekends, and especially on Sundays.

Towns such as Ljubljana, Maribor and Koper have large bus **stations** (*avtobusna postaja*) with computerized booking facilities where you can buy your tickets hours (if not days) in advance. Otherwise, simply pile onto the bus and pay the driver or conductor. If you need to store items of baggage in the hold you'll be charged a little extra. Like trains, **fares** are calculated according to distance travelled; typical fares are around €6 for 50km and €12 for 100km.

By car

All things considered, **driving** in Slovenia is a joy. Despite the country's high level of car ownership, Slovenia's well-surfaced roads often seem blissfully

traffic-free, and you'll be endlessly distracted by the scenery. Neither is driving likely to tire you out, such are the short distances between destinations. If driving in the **mountainous regions**, bear in mind that some of the higher passes, such as the Vršič Pass in the Julian Alps, are often closed for days or weeks at a time during periods of heavy snowfall.

The country is crossed by two **motorways** (*avtocesta*): the A1 which runs in an east–west direction from Šentilj, just north of Maribor, down to Koper on the coast, and the A2 which runs north–south from the Karavanke Tunnel on the Austrian border to Obrežje on the Croatian border (and continuing down to Zagreb); both these motorways pass through Ljubljana. There are three other, shorter, motorways: A3 (Divača to Fernetiči), A4 (Slivnica to Draženci) and A5 (Dragučova, near Maribor, to Pince, on the Hungarian border). Expressways, of which there are six, are the same as motorways but without emergency lanes. Lesser **highways**, linking the major centres, are numbered with a single digit, while secondary or tertiary roads are identified by two- or three-digit numbers. In order to travel on motorways and expressways, you need a **vignette** (sticker); these are supplied if you are renting a car within Slovenia, but if you rent a car in a neighbouring country (or are bringing in your own), you will have to buy one; they cost €15 for a week and €30 for a month, and are sold at petrol stations and post offices, and general stores at the border crossings. Stiff fines are levied for travelling on a motorway without one.

Petrol stations (*bencinska črpalka*) can be found everywhere, even in the most rural backwaters. Although most open from around 6 or 7am to 9 or 10pm, there are quite a few 24-hour service stations, usually located on the outskirts of larger towns and cities, and around resort areas. Lead-free fuel (*neosvinčen bencin*) currently costs around €1.25 per litre. Credit cards are accepted at most stations.

In cities, **parking** in white zones (marked with white lines) is permitted for up to two hours (typically €0.60/€0.80, though it will cost more down on the coast), while you can stay in a "blue zone" for thirty minutes or one hour for free. *Brezplačno* means free parking. Parking in car parks (*parkirišče*) normally costs around €1 per hour, slightly more in resorts like Portorož. Most hotels have free parking for guests.

For information on any aspect of driving within Slovenia, including up-to-the-minute information on traffic conditions, the website of the **Automobile**

BUS TIMETABLES

Bus timetables can be difficult to comprehend, as there's often little by way of English translation. The following letters indicate those days that buses operate: V (daily); D (Mon–Fri); D+ (Mon–Sat); SO (Sat); N (Sun); NP (Sun & holidays); ŠP (school days).

Association of Slovenia (Avto-moto zveza Slovenije or AMZS; ⓦ amzs.si) is excellent. They also publish a 1:270,000 tourist road map of Slovenia.

In the event of a **breakdown**, call AMZS's Assistance-Information Service (SPI) on the 24-hour emergency number ☎ 1987 or ☎ 386 1 530 5353. There are 24-hour technical centres in Celje, Koper, Kranj, Ljubljana, Maribor, Otočec and Postojna, with technical units (open 7am–8pm) in the other major towns; the addresses and telephone numbers of all centres can be found on the AMZS website. All accidents should be reported to the police on ☎ 113.

Rules of the road

Traffic drives on the right and **speed limits** for vehicles are 130km/h on motorways, 110km/h on expressways, 90km/h on secondary and tertiary roads, and 50km/h in built-up areas. Otherwise, the most important rules are the prohibitions against sounding the horn in a built-up area (unless to avert accidents) and using a hand-held mobile while driving. It is compulsory for driver and passengers to wear seatbelts, to use dipped headlights when travelling on all roads at all times, and to keep a triangular breakdown sign in the car. Between mid-November and mid-March you're required to carry snow chains.

If you are stopped by the police – you'll often see police vehicles on approaches to villages and built-up areas – you'll be required to show all your **documents**, so make sure you have them in the car at all times. The police are extremely hot on road traffic violations and any offence committed (speeding, not wearing a seatbelt, illegal parking and the like) is subject to a fine, which can be anything between €40 and €1200 depending on the offence; any fine must be paid at a post office or bank. It goes without saying that **drinking and driving** is a very bad idea; the permitted blood-alcohol level for drivers is 0.05mg per 100ml of blood, although you may still be liable to a €300 fine if caught with this amount. Any amount over this will incur a fine of anything up to €600.

Car rental

Renting a car is simple enough, provided you are 21 or older, and hold a valid national driving licence. The **cheapest deals** are almost always online: expect to pay around €35–40 for a day's rental and around €180 for a week.

Most of the major companies have an outlet in Ljubljana, including the airport, as well as in some of the major towns and cities. You may find that local companies, such as the excellent ABC Cars in Ljubljana (ⓦ europcar.si), offer better deals. You may be able to take the car into neighbouring countries, although most companies charge extra for this.

By bike

Slovenia's wonderfully varied topography presents endless opportunities for **cycling**. From the tough mountain climbs in Triglav National Park to the iron-flat landscapes of Prekmurje, there are a number of well-organized recreational routes and trails all over the country. Otherwise, cycling is permitted on all roads except motorways and expressways. Most urban centres have, to a greater or lesser degree, well-integrated cycle lanes or paths, though the traffic in towns and cities is rarely threatening. On a practical note, bikes can be taken onto trains, except ICS, for a small fee, while some buses might allow you to store your bike in the luggage compartment.

Accommodation

Slovenia has a terrific range of accommodation to suit all tastes and budgets; hotels abound and there is an increasing number of good-value pensions and guesthouses. Private rooms are also a good option, particularly along the coast and in star resorts like Bled and Bohinj, while a stay on a tourist farm provides an attractive, affordable and peaceful alternative. There's a decent spread of fabulous campsites, and some great hostels, many of which are distinctive and unusual.

Whichever kind of accommodation you choose, **reservations** are advisable during high season in the capital and more popular places (June–Aug, or Dec–Feb in the ski resorts), or if you're heading somewhere with limited possibilities. Details of all Slovenia's hotels, private rooms, tourist farms, hostels and campsites are listed at ⓦ slovenia.info.

Hotels and pensions

Generally speaking, **hotel prices** in the capital, along the coast and in the major resorts, such as Bled and Bohinj, are substantially higher than elsewhere, especially in high season (June–Aug); similarly, in ski resorts such as Kranjska Gora, prices are ramped up between December and February.

Slovenia's city **hotels** tend to be heavily geared towards business travellers – in Ljubljana, for example, budget or mid-priced hotels are few, a situation common to other places like Maribor, Celje and Nova Gorica. Many of the hotels in key resorts such as Bled, Bohinj or Portorož are aimed squarely at package tourists – the same goes for the many spa hotels in Slovenia. That said, there are an increasing number of **family-run hotels** and **pensions** (*penzion*) which, in most cases, offer much better value than a hotel of a similar price and invariably come with a more personal touch. Some pensions are more commonly known as **gostišče** (not to be confused with a *gostilna*, which is an eating establishment), but these are usually found in smaller towns and more rural areas.

Just about every hotel now has free wi-fi, and most hotels include **breakfast** in the price. This is not always made clear, however, so it's worth checking when you book.

Private rooms and apartments

Hostels aside, taking a **private room** (*zasebne sobe*) is the cheapest option, particularly if there are two of you sharing. Few towns and cities offer many private rooms, but there are plenty in the busier lake and coastal resorts. Rooms are usually **categorized** with either one or two stars; a one-star place is pretty basic and comes with shared shower and toilets – prices start at around €30 for a double in high season. A two-star (from €40 in high season) usually has private shower and toilet, and sometimes a television and air-conditioning. Breakfast, and tourist tax (around €1.50/person), are not included in the price, and in some places, prices are subject to a thirty percent surcharge if you stay fewer than three nights.

Rented out in the same way as private rooms, **apartments** (*apartmaji*) are a reasonably cheap alternative, particularly if there are a few of you. A standard two-bed apartment (sleeping four) in Bohinj or on the coast will cost in the region of €75–85.

With the odd exception, for example in Bohinj, very few tourist offices deal with bookings for private rooms; these are usually handled by local agencies. Larger agencies such as Kompas (ⓦkompas.si), represented in several towns and resorts, also take advance bookings – we've listed the major branches in the Guide.

Tourist farms

Farm tourism (*turističnih kmetji*) is a thriving sector in Slovenia, and if you're looking for a restful night, then these rural retreats are perfect. Note, though, that their very isolation means that they can often be difficult to reach if you don't have a car.

Despite a **classification system** (denoted by apples), there is often little distinction between the highest grade (four apples) and a lower grade, though most farms offer reasonably sized, modestly furnished rooms with bathroom. Farms with four apples invariably have larger, slightly better furnished rooms, sometimes with television. Although there are no hard and fast rules regarding **pricing**, as a guide a double room on a farm with three or four apples will cost around €50–60, two apples around €35–45, and one, or unclassified, farms around €30. All prices include breakfast, which is a wholesome affair, typically consisting of tea, coffee, juice, cereal, home-made bread, jam, cheese and ham; in some places you may also get a cooked breakfast. Most farms offer half board for about €8–10 extra, which is exceptional value given that the cooking is invariably superb – many also produce their own wine.

Activities, such as horseriding, cycling and tennis, are offered at some farms, while others allow you to help out – from baking bread or making jam to milking the cows or feeding the calves. The Association of Tourist Farms of Slovenia has an excellent website (Ⓦfarmtourism.si) that lists and describes every one of the country's tourist farms.

Mountain huts

There are some 175 **mountain huts** (*planinarski domovi*) scattered across Slovenia's hills and mountains, ranging from the most basic refuges with huge dorms and cold running water to more comfortable alpine villas offering cosier rooms, hot water and other amenities (see box, p.85). In any case, most huts are convivial places, where hikers share a beer or two and exchange information about trails or the weather before pushing on.

The majority of huts, especially those at higher altitudes, are open between June and September, while some are open a month or two longer than this, and a few year-round; if you're planning to spend any length of time in the more popular hiking areas, for example around Triglav, you'd be wise to book ahead. Depending on the type of hut and its location, you'll pay anything between €10 and €20 for a bed; UIAA-affiliated members are entitled to a discount. The website of the Alpine Association of Slovenia (Ⓦpzs.si) lists every hut, together with routes and approaches to the next lodge.

Hostels and dorms

Slovenia has a decent spread of **youth hostels** (*mladinski hoteli*), which are invariably excellent and offer comprehensive amenities. As well as several innovatively designed hostels in Ljubljana (see p.69), notably *Celica* and *Tresor*, there are some superb hostels elsewhere, such as *Hostel Soča Rocks* in Bovec, *Hostel Situla* in Novo Mesto and *Hostel Pliskovica* in the Karst, to name just three. Most charge around €15–20 per person, sometimes with breakfast included, with discounts for HI card holders. The website Ⓦyouth-hostel.si lists most, though not all, of Slovenia's hostels.

Another possibility is **student dorms** (*dijaški dom*), which are generally of a decent standard, but usually only open in July and August once the students have packed up. Quite a few keep some beds aside during the rest of the year, but these are usually available at weekends only. Expect to pay around €10–15 for a bed.

> ### TOP FIVE CAMPSITES
> **Adrenaline Check Eco Place**, Bovec. See p.143
> **Camp Koren**, Kobarid. See p.150
> **Lucija campsite**, Portorož. See p.195
> **Podzemelj ob Kolpi**, Metlika. See p.242
> **Ramšak**, Maribor. See p.274

Camping

Slovenia has a healthy spread of **campsites** (*kampi*) across the country, almost all of which, whatever their size, are clean and well appointed. Sites are categorized with between one and three stars; the better ones, such as those in Bled, Kobarid and Portorož, have excellent amenities – more often than not with restaurants, shops, sports facilities and children's play areas. In addition, there are now some superb **glampsites** around the country, variously incorporating wooden cabins, huts or pods, lean-tos (open-sided huts with bed and mattress inside) and treehouses.

Expect to pay around €8–12 per person per night (slightly more at better sites); more often than not, there is no extra charge for pitch or car, but where there is, expect to pay an additional €1–2. Prices are slightly higher in July and August. The majority of sites are open from April or May to September or October, with a handful open year-round. Note that **camping rough** is illegal.

Food and drink

Slovenia straddles several culinary cultures, absorbing Austrian, Balkan and Mediterranean influences. Despite increasing internationalization of restaurants and cafés, there remains a strong native Slovene tradition based on age-old peasant recipes, while a new generation of exciting young chefs is redefining modern culinary trends. You'll find a list of food and drink terms in our language chapter (see pp.316–319).

Types of restaurant

You'll find plenty of eating options in the larger towns and resorts – smaller towns, however, may have few places to eat, of any description. The most common type of eating establishment is a **restavracija** (restaurant), of which there are plenty

TOP FIVE RESTAURANTS

Gostišče Kapušin, Krasinec. See p.243
Hiša Franko, Kobarid. See p.150
Gostilna Krištof, Predoslje, Kranj. See p.97
Majerija, Slap. See p.165
Strelec, Ljubljana. See p.72

in the larger towns and cities, especially in Ljubljana and Maribor. Invariably more atmospheric is a **gostilna**, an inn-type place that is usually, but not always, located on the outskirts of town and in more rural areas; along the same lines, a **gostišče** serves food and also has some accommodation. At most of these places you'll come across *malica*, a filling two- or three-course meal with drink, usually served from 11am or noon until 3pm, and costing around €4–6.

If possible, don't pass up the opportunity to eat on a **tourist farm**, where you'll find Slovenian home cooking at its finest, with ingredients usually harvested on the farm itself; make sure to call in advance, as many only open for non-guests at weekends.

Generally speaking, wherever you eat you'll find **service** exceptional, with courteous and friendly waiting staff who can speak good English.

Breakfasts and snacks

Breakfast (*zajtrk*) in an average hotel typically consists of cereal, bread or rolls with jam or marmalade, cheese and salami, and coffee from a machine – only in the better places will you be offered a full buffet, with cooked food (sometimes to order), pastries or croissants, fresh fruit and yoghurt, and filter coffee. Breakfast on a tourist farm is invariably an enjoyable, wholesome affair, with everything from bread and milk to jams and cheeses prepared on site. If you've not been offered breakfast at your lodging, head for a **bakery** (*pekarna*), most of which sell a decent range of croissants and sandwiches, or a *slaščičarna* (patisserie).

The best places for **snacks** are *okrepčevalnice* (snack bars) and street kiosks, which dole out *burek*, a flaky and often very greasy pastry filled with cheese (*burek z sirom*) or meat (*burek z mesom*) and sausages – the latter come in various forms, by far the tastiest of which are *kranjska klobasa* (thick, spicy and slightly smoked).

Slovenia's **supermarkets** (*trgovina*) and delicatessens (*delikatesa*) are good places to stock up on sandwich and picnic ingredients, including local cheese (*sir*) and salami. You can buy fresh fruit and vegetables here too, but, if possible, try to get your produce from outdoor markets (*tržnica*) or roadside stalls, and to buy your bread at a bakery.

Slovenian cuisine

As a rule, menus are dominated by **meat** dishes (*mesne jedi*), mostly schnitzels (*zrezek*), beef (*govedina*), pork (*svinjina*) and veal (*teletina*). One Slovene **speciality** is horse steak (*žrebičkov zrezek*), and neither are Slovenes squeamish about offal – liver (*jetra*) and grilled or fried brains (*možgani*) are popular in cheaper restaurants. The majority of menus in classier restaurants will often feature game, with Slovenes particularly partial to bear (*medved*), venison (*srna*), pheasant (*fazan*) and rabbit (*zajec*). In addition, the tasty southern Balkan meats *čevapčiči* (grilled rolls of minced meat) and *sarma* (cabbage stuffed with meat and rice) frequently make their way onto menus.

Soup (*juha*) is a standard **starter** – in Primorska try *jota* (beans and sauerkraut), and in Štajerska, *kisla juha* (pigs' knuckles and head with sour cream) – while **pasta** dishes, including numerous variations of home-made *njoki* (gnocchi), appear on many restaurant menus. One of the most **traditional Slovene dishes**, and once the staple diet of rural Slovenes, is *ajdovi žganci*, a buckwheat or maize porridge seasoned with crackling and usually served with sauerkraut.

On the coast you'll find plenty of **fish** dishes (*ribje jedi*), in particular mussels (*školjke*), shrimps (*škampi*) and squid (*lignji*). If you're anywhere near the Soča Valley (and in particular Kobarid, which has some of the country's best restaurants), do try the fabulous freshwater trout (*postrvi*) from the local Soča River, the king of which is the superb, and much sought-after, marble trout. The **Karst**, too, has its own unique culinary traditions, and is renowned above all for its fantastic dry-cured meats, such as *pršut*, which goes down a treat with the local Teran wine.

In Prekmurje, near Hungary, the most prominent dish is, unsurprisingly, goulash (*golaž*), a variant of which is *bograč*, a thick, spicy stew served in the eponymous copper pot; *segedin* is goulash with lashings of sauerkraut. Other fantastically tasty local dishes to look out for include *žlikrofi* from Idrija, small, boiled dumplings filled with potato, onion and bacon; and *frika*, a deliciously gooey, fried potato and cheese pie, typically prepared in the Tolmin region.

The Primorska region has a rich history of harvesting **olive oil**. Its groves are among the furthest north in Europe, and the oils typically have a stronger, more pungent taste; producers regularly pick up awards from around the world. One of the most distinctive tasting olive oils, however, comes from northeastern Slovenia: pumpkin seed oil (*bučno olje*), whose rich, nutty taste and stunning dark green colour is quite something – it's delicious on ice cream.

The two most traditional Slovene **sweets** are *potica*, a doughy roll filled with nuts, tarragon and honey; and, from the Prekmurje region, *gibanica*, a delicious layered pastry that includes poppy seeds, walnuts, apples and cream. Otherwise, you'll find both strudel and *štruklji* (dumplings with fruit filling) on most menus; of the latter, the most delicious is the walnut-and-raisin-filled *Kobariški štruklji* from Kobarid. You're unlikely to leave Bled without wolfing down a portion of *kremšnita*, a substantial cream cake comprised of vanilla and whipped cream and topped with a layer of flaky pastry. Otherwise, you can't go wrong with *palačinke*, pancakes with a choice of fillings, or ice cream (*sladoled*), which is usually wonderful.

Vegetarian food

While still not hugely exciting, options for **vegetarians** in Slovenia have improved markedly in recent times, though it goes without saying that you'll have a far better time of it in the better restaurants. Slovenian salads can be exceptional, matching perfectly the country's exquisite range of olive oils; a firm favourite is *regrad*, dandelion salad, which is much tastier than it sounds. Otherwise, Slovenian specialities to look out for are *štruklji* (dumplings with cheese or fruit filling), *ocvrti sir* (cheese fried in breadcrumbs) and *gobova rižota* (mushroom risotto) – the last is usually excellent; in the better restaurants, you'll find upmarket variations on the above and usually one or two other dishes.

Drinking

When it comes to **drinking**, most Slovenes will head for a **café-bar**, or *kavarna*, where a range of cakes, pastries and ice cream is generally on offer, too. Coffee (*kava*) is usually served espresso-style – coffee with milk is *kava z mlekom* – though cappuccinos are invariably hit-and-miss, ranging from good to little more than a regular coffee with a dollop of whipped cream on top. A refreshing accompaniment, particularly on a hot day, is a glass of mineral water (*mineralna voda*), by far the most popular of which is Radenska, from the spa town Radenci. Tea (*čaj*) drinkers are in a minority here,

although there are a couple of fantastic little teahouses (*čajna hiša*) in Ljubljana and Maribor.

As well as café-bars, evening drinking also takes place in a more traditional *pivnica* (pub or beer hall) or *vinoteka* (wine cellar). There are an increasing number of dedicated wine bars (which often double up as shops), where you can taste and buy.

Slovene beer (*pivo*) has a good reputation. The two main breweries are Laško, based in the town of the same name and producer of Zlatorog (named after the mythical chamois), and the Ljubljana-based Union; once separate companies, these are now both owned by Heineken. Both also produce *temno pivo* (literally "dark beer"), a Guinness-like stout. More recently there has been a mushrooming of **microbreweries** throughout the country, which put out an exciting, and refreshingly original, range of craft beers, including pale ales, IPAs, stouts and so on; breweries to look out for include Pelican from Ajdovščina, Reservoir Dogs in Nova Gorica and Humanfish from Vrhnika just outside Ljubljana.

It is **wine** (*vino*), however, where Slovenia truly excels (see p.160, p.163, p.242 and p.273), and although it remains little known abroad – mainly due to the relatively small amounts produced, and limited amounts exported – it is superb. Any restaurant of decent standing will have a first-class wine list.

You shouldn't leave the country without trying one of the fiery **brandies**: *slivovka* (plum brandy), *viljamovka* (pear brandy), *sadjevec*, a brandy made from various fruits, and the gin-like juniper-based *brinovec*. And finally, look out for *medica*, a gorgeous honey liqueur from Carniola.

Festivals

The Slovenian calendar is studded with some marvellous festivals and events. While a good number take place in the larger cities such as Ljubljana and Maribor, there's an excellent spread of local events throughout the rest of the country. Neither are these entirely confined to the summer: Slovenia has several strongly rooted seasonal traditions, none more so than the Pust pre-Lenten carnival in February, which is perhaps the most uniquely Slovenian celebration.

Most cities, and many of the larger towns, stage some form of **summer festival**, which invariably incorporates a colourful mix of classical and contemporary music, art and theatrical performances. There is also a terrific range of **music**

festivals, from jazz and rock to classical, the last being particularly prominent, both in the capital and elsewhere; a number of the country's castles stage classical music concerts on summer evenings. The **mountains**, too, are the setting for a handful of splendid events, be they related to Slovenia's outstanding natural heritage or its local customs.

The country's strong wine-growing tradition is honoured in its many **wine-related events**, which occur throughout the major wine-producing centres, such as Brda and Jeruzalem, between May and September; the main collective wine celebration is St Martin's Day, on November 11. Aside from the festivals listed below there are dozens of other, more local, events across the country, as well as festivals for the LGBT community (see p.34) and children (see p.37); we've mentioned the best in the Guide.

A festival calendar

JANUARY TO MARCH

King Matjaž Snow Castle Festival Črna na Koroškem, last weekend Jan. Hugely popular ice-castle-building competition in the Koroška mountains. See p.260.

Kurentovanje Ptuj Sun before Shrove Tues, and Shrove Tues; Ⓦ kurentovanje.net. The most famous of Slovenia's pre-Lent Pusts, or carnivals, featuring riotous displays of masked revelry; the other major Pust carnivals take place in Cerkno and Cerknica. See p.171 & p.209.

World Ski-Jumping Championships Planica (Kranjska Gora), end March; Ⓦ planica.si. A high-octane weekend of top-class sport, music and lots of beer. See p.130.

APRIL AND MAY

Chocolate Festival Radovljica, third weekend April; Ⓦ radolca.si. This two-day gathering is a chocolate-lover's dream. See p.102.

Saltpans Festival Piran and Sečovlje, end April. Taking place in town and at the saltpans themselves, this action-packed festival features exhibitions, parades and guided tours of the saltpans to celebrate the start of the salt-making season. See p.183.

Druga Godba Ljubljana, end May for one week; Ⓦ drugagodba.si. Superb alternative/world music festival. See p.74.

International Wild Flower Festival Bohinj, end May for two weeks. Celebrating the wild flowers of the Julian Alps, this colourful event features exhibitions, workshops, a flower market, and tours of flowers in their natural habitat. See p.124.

JUNE

Ljubljana Jazz Festival Ljubljana, end June; Ⓦ ljubljanajazz.si. Five-day festival of world-class music. See p.74.

Festival Lent Maribor, end June for two weeks; Ⓦ festival-lent.si. Massive arts gathering, comprising everything from street theatre to ballet. See p.275.

Festival Seviqc Brežice Brežice and other venues across Slovenia, end June to end Aug; Ⓦ seviqc-brezice.si. Prestigious Baroque music festival, starring some of Europe's finest singers, orchestras and musicians. See p.234.

Ljubljana Festival Ljubljana, end June to mid-Sept; Ⓦ ljubljanafestival.si. Top-notch opera, classical music, ballet and theatre in the capital's key cultural happening. See p.74.

JULY

Ana Desetnica Street Theatre Ljubljana, early July. Colourful and enjoyable street theatre performances in the Old Town and around. Similar events take place in a dozen or so other towns and cities throughout Slovenia. See p.74.

Beer and Flowers Festival Laško, mid-July; Ⓦ pivo-cvetje.si. More beer than flowers, which is not surprising given that's it's home to the eponymous beer, plus good music to boot. See p.255.

Bled Days Bled, third weekend July. Fair and crafts stalls down by the lake, culminating in a spectacular fireworks display and thousands of candles on the lake. See p.111.

Okarina Festival Bled, last week July for two weeks; Ⓦ festival-okarina.si. High-class international and domestic folk and world music gathering. See p.111.

Metaldays Tolmin, end July; Ⓦ metaldays.net. Popular, small-scale, week-long metal-fest, starring bands from both home and abroad. See p.151.

Primorska Summer Festival Izola, Koper and Portorož, July to Aug. Open-air stage and street theatre performances, some of which take place in unusual locations such as a disused railway tunnel and the Sečovlje saltpans. See p.183.

AUGUST AND SEPTEMBER

TrnFest Ljubljana, throughout Aug. Cracking, small-scale arts festival. See p.74.

Festival Radovljica Early to mid-Aug; Ⓦ festival-radovljica.si. Well-regarded festival of ancient classical music. See p.102.

Days of Poetry and Wine Ptuj, end Aug; Ⓦ versoteque.com. Superb, week-long gathering of international poets, alongside musical performances and wine tastings.

Tartini Festival Piran, end Aug; Ⓦ tartinifestival.org. Two weeks of top-class classical fare in honour of the town's most famous former resident. See p.183.

National Costumes Festival Kamnik, second weekend Sept. Song, dance and colourful finery from Slovenia's multifarious regions. See p.81.

Kravji Bal (Cow's Ball) Lake Bohinj, second or third weekend Sept. Mass booze-up to celebrate the return of the cows from the mountains. See p.124.

OCTOBER TO DECEMBER

Festival of the Old Vine Maribor, early Oct until Nov 11. Superb gastronomic offerings in this lively affair celebrating the ceremonial harvesting of the world's oldest vine. See p.275.

St Martin's Day Countrywide, Nov 11. Nationwide wine celebrations.

LIFFe Ljubljana, mid-Nov; Ⓦ liffe.si. The Ljubljana International Film Festival is Slovenia's premier film gathering, showcasing domestic and international movies. See p.74.

Christmas Celebrations Countrywide. A month of yuletide celebrations kicks off on Dec 6 (St Nicholas's Day) with the giving of gifts to children.

Sports and outdoor activities

Given its small size and limited resources, Slovenia's sporting pedigree is impressive, many of its sportsmen and women having achieved notable successes in a number of sports since the split with Yugoslavia in 1991.

The most high-profile sporting event in the Slovenian calendar is the **World Ski-Jumping Championships** at Planica in March (see p.130), and the country has produced a legion of fine **skiers** and **ski-jumpers** – the Yugoslav national ski team was almost always made up exclusively of Slovenes, and today Slovenia rates a number of world-class exponents in this field. The current superstar of Slovenian skiing is double Olympic gold medallist Tine Maze, while the extraordinary Peter Prevc is currently the world's greatest ski-jumper.

Away from the slopes, the country's finest moment came at the 2000 Sydney Olympics, when it captured its first-ever gold medal courtesy of the rowers Iztok Čop and Luka Špik; indeed, **rowing** has been Slovenia's most prominent summer sport since the times of the former Yugoslavia, and now, as then, several major regattas are held on Lake Bled. The country's first ever track and field gold medallist was hammer thrower, Primoz Kozmuž, at the 2008 Beijing Olympics.

The most popular **team sports** are **basketball**, **handball** and **ice hockey** – all traditionally very strong sports in the former Yugoslavia – and while Slovenia has been left somewhat in the slipstream of Serbia and Croatia, its teams still manage to perform creditably at European level.

In spite of a desperately weak domestic league, Slovenia's **footballers** have massively overachieved in recent years, qualifying for the 2002 World Cup in Japan and the 2010 World Cup in South Africa.

Outdoor activities

There are few more **active** nations in Europe than Slovenia, most of whose inhabitants begin trekking, climbing and skiing at a very early age. The country's mountains, forests, hills, rivers and lakes offer unlimited potential to indulge in a wide range of **outdoor pursuits** – hiking and skiing in the Julian Alps, whitewater rafting or kayaking in the Soča Valley, cycling through the rolling hills of Dolenjska,

---

TOP FIVE ACTIVITIES

Hiking Julian Alps and Kamniške Alps. See p.119
Mountain biking Kranjska Gora. See p.130
Paragliding Vipava Valley. See p.162
Skiing Vogel, Krvavec and Maribor Pohorje. See p.128 & p.277
Whitewater rafting Soča River. See p.142

---

riding through the Logarska Dolina Valley, to name just a few. Moreover, just about any of these activities can be done as part of an organized group, usually with gear supplied.

Skiing

First popularized in Slovenia in the seventeenth century, **skiing** unequivocally remains the nation's number-one sport. Uniformly well equipped, efficient and safe, the country counts more than a dozen major resorts (and many smaller ones), the best and most popular of which are Kranjska Gora, a good family resort and international competition venue near the Austrian border, Krvavec, near Kranj (very popular with weekending Ljubljaniani), Vogel, near Bohinj, and Pohorje, on the outskirts of Maribor – this the country's largest skiing area. Most resorts also offer good **snowboarding** facilities, while **cross-country skiing** is another Slovene institution, the main venue being the Pokljuka Plateau near Bled. We've covered the practicalities of local skiing with individual accounts in the Guide.

Hiking and climbing

Slovenia is traversed by more than 7000km of marked paths; for the majority of **climbers and hikers** the main destination is the **Julian Alps**, at the heart of which is **Mount Triglav** (2864m), the country's highest peak. Along with the Julians, the **Karavanke mountains** and the **Kamniške-Savinja Alps** (both of which count numerous peaks topping the 2500m mark) offer the country's most varied and challenging climbs and hikes. For the less energetic, there's more moderate walking in the non-alpine tracts of the **Pohorje massif** near Maribor, and the **Snežnik hills** south of Postojna along the Croatian border. There's also gentler rambling territory south of Triglav National Park in the sub-alpine hills of Cerkno and Idrija, and in the deep forests of Dolenjska. There is more detail on the practicalities of hiking in Slovenia throughout the Guide.

Adventure sports

Slovenia is geared up in a big way for **adventure sports**, in particular on its rivers, which attract enthusiasts from all over Europe each summer. Without question, the major draw is the magnificent **Soča River**, whose fast, foaming waters offer the perfect setting for **whitewater rafting**, **canoeing** and **kayaking**, as well as more extreme pursuits including **canyoning** and **hydrospeed**. Both the Kolpa River, marking the border with Croatia, and the Sava River, are also terrific spots for rafting and kayaking. **Tandem paragliding** is another wonderful way to experience Slovenia's stunning mountain scenery, the most popular spots being the Soča Valley, Bohinj and the Vipava Valley.

Horseriding and golf

As the home of the Lipizzaner it's perhaps not surprising that Slovenia displays a deep-rooted attachment to all things equine. While the most obvious destination for equestrians is Lipica (see p.180), there are dozens more **horseriding centres** throughout the country, many in fabulously scenic locations. Most offer some form of recreational (trail) and arena riding, a range of classes and courses – and sometimes carriage rides, too; three of the most established centres are Pristava Lepena in the gorgeous Trenta Valley (there are Lipizzaner here too), the Kaval Centre at Prestranek near Postojna, and the Brdo estate just outside Kranj.

There are around a dozen **golf courses** in Slovenia, some of which, like those at Bled and Voljči Potok, can be played out against stunning alpine backdrops.

Fishing

Slovenia offers some of the finest freshwater **fishing** in Europe, its abundant rivers, streams and lakes richly stocked with many different species – indeed, more than ninety species have been catalogued, many of which are under permanent protection. The Soča River is renowned for its bountiful reserves of grayling and trout – brown trout, rainbow trout and, above all, the highly prized marble trout (*Salmo trutta marmoratus*). Elsewhere, the Kolpa, Krka, Sava Bohinjka and Unica rivers have healthy stocks of pike, perch, chub and eelpout. Of the lakes, fishing from boats is permitted at Lake Bohinj and the intermittent Lake Cerknica. The main fishing season lasts approximately from April to October. Permits are required (around €25–40 for a daily permit), details of which are listed throughout the Guide.

Watersports

Although a mere 46km long, the Slovene coast offers possibilities to indulge in a number of **watersports**: chiefly scuba diving (*potapljanje*) in the waters around Piran, along with sailing (*jadranje*) and windsurfing (*surfanje*). The coastal waters are perfectly safe for swimming (*plavanje*), but if you fancy something a little warmer you should be able to track down a local indoor pool in most towns of a reasonable size. Some of the better hotels, particularly those on the coast, have their own pools that can be used for a small fee by non-guests.

Travel essentials

Addresses

The Slovenian **address system** is not complicated. The most **common terms** are: *ulica* (street), *cesta* (road), *pot* (trail), *steza* (path) and *trg* (square). The street name always comes before the number. In some smaller towns and most villages throughout Slovenia there are no street names at all, just house numbers; where no street name is given in the Guide, you can assume it's because there isn't one.

Costs

Although Slovenia is by no means a bargain destination, it's still very **good value** on the whole, though prices in the capital, as well as in some of the more popular destinations like Bled, Bohinj and some of the coastal resorts, are higher than the rest of the country.

If you're on a tight budget, you could get by on around £30/€35/US$40 a day, staying in a hostel or private accommodation, eating in cheap diners and using public transport. Those on a moderate to mid-range budget (cheap to mid-range hotel, better restaurants, car rental) can expect to spend around £80/€95/US$105. If you want to splash out on the best hotels and restaurants and rent a car, count on spending upwards of £110/€130/US$145 per day. Food in supermarkets and convenience stores costs on a par with that in many Western European countries.

Museum admission charges are reasonable, typically around €2–4, although for some of the bigger attractions, major art galleries and castles for example, expect to pay in the region of €8–10. Premier attractions, such as the Postojna or Škocjan Caves, charge in excess of €15–20.

Crime and safety

Slovenia has a very **low crime rate** and it's extremely unlikely that you'll have any problems; violent crime against tourists is almost nonexistent and petty crime rare. Of course, the usual common-sense precautions apply: watching where you walk late at night, keeping an eye on valuables, particularly in crowded buses, and locking your car at all times when unattended.

In the unlikely event that you will have to deal with the police (*policija*), you'll generally find them easy-going, approachable and likely to speak good English. The only time you may be asked to provide some form of identification is if you're stopped while driving, which is possible. If you do have anything stolen while in Slovenia, you'll need to go to the police and file a report, which your insurance company will require before paying out for any claims made on your policy. Should you be arrested or need legal advice, ask to contact your embassy or consulate in Ljubljana (see p.75). To call the police dial ☎ 113.

Culture and etiquette

In common with all those countries from the former Yugoslavia, **smoking** is commonplace, although it is prohibited in restaurants and other public places. Although **tipping** is not obligatory, it is polite to round the bill up to a convenient figure in restaurants and taxis. **Public toilets** (*javno stranišče*), which can be found in most train and bus stations, are, on the whole, clean, though you'd do well to carry your own paper; most charge around €0.50. *Moški* means men and *Zenske* means women.

Electricity

Wall sockets in Slovenia operate at 220 volts and take round, two-pin plugs. A standard continental adaptor allows the use of 13-amp, square-pin plugs.

Entry requirements

Citizens of the EU, Australia, Canada, New Zealand and the US can enter Slovenia with just a passport and may stay in the country for up to ninety days, while citizens of some neighbouring countries, such as Italy and Austria, require only an identity card. South Africans require a visa. All the latest information can be obtained from the Slovene Foreign Ministry website at ⓦ mzz.gov/si.

SLOVENIAN EMBASSIES ABROAD

Australia and New Zealand 26 Akame Circuit, O'Malley, 2606 ACT, Canberra ☎ 02 6290 0000, ⓦ canberra.embassy.si.
Britain and Ireland 17 Dartmouth St, London SW1H 9BL ☎ 020 7222 5700, ⓦ london.embassy.si.
Canada 150 Metcalfe St, Suite 2200, Ottawa, Ontario K2P 1P1 ☎ 613 565 5781, ⓦ ottawa.embassy.si.
USA 2410 California St NW, Washington, DC 20008 ☎ 202 386 6610, ⓦ washington.embassy.si.

Health

Travelling in Slovenia should present few problems: standards of hygiene and health care are high, and **inoculations** unnecessary; that said, you may wish to consider being inoculated against tick-borne encephalitis if you're planning to spend time in the mountains or forested areas. **Tap water** is safe everywhere. Most problems tend to be **weather-related**; summers can be blisteringly hot, particularly in central, southern and eastern regions, so a high-factor sun cream is essential. Conversely, inclement weather in the mountainous regions, particularly at higher altitudes, is common, and can present potentially serious dangers – so the usual advice applies in regards to taking suitable clothing, sufficient provisions and equipment, and keeping a watchful eye on the forecast.

All towns and most villages have a **pharmacy** (*lekarna*), with highly trained staff, most of whom speak a good standard of English. Opening hours are normally from 7am to 7 or 8pm; signs in the window give the location or telephone number of the nearest all-night pharmacy (*dežurna lekarna*). In emergencies dial ☎ 112 for the ambulance service, which will whisk you off to the hospital (*bolnica*) where you should be attended to fairly rapidly.

Insurance

EU healthcare privileges apply in Slovenia, but citizens of the EU would still do well to take out an insurance policy before travelling to cover against theft, loss, and illness or injury. A typical travel **insurance policy** usually provides cover for the loss of baggage, tickets and – up to a certain limit – cash or cheques, as well as cancellation or curtailment of your journey. Most of them exclude so-called dangerous sports unless an extra premium is paid: in Slovenia this could mean, for example, skiing, scuba diving, whitewater rafting and trekking.

Internet

Wi-fi is widespread and invariably excellent. Nearly all **accommodation** – of any description – offers free wi-fi for their guests. Most **cafés**, even in the smaller towns, also have wi-fi, though you'll be obliged to make a purchase. There is also an increasing number of free wi-fi public locations in Ljubljana and some of the larger towns. With wi-fi so ubiquitous, **internet cafés** are now the exception rather than the rule, but where you do find one, expect to pay around €1 per hour.

LGBT travellers

Slovenia was always the most tolerant of the ex-Yugoslav republics, with an active gay and lesbian movement in existence since the mid-1980s, though that's not to say gays and lesbians have had an easy time of it. Indeed, the majority of the population remains largely unsympathetic towards the gay and lesbian community, and manifestations of gay life beyond the capital are almost nonexistent.

Ljubljana has a handful of gay bars and clubs, as well as being the only Slovenian city to stage any major LGBT events. The most prominent of these are June's **Ljubljana Pride** (ⓦ ljubljanapride.org), culminating in the Pride Parade, and the **Gay and Lesbian Film Festival** (ⓦ ljudmila.org) at the beginning of December, which has been running for more than thirty years and is the oldest such festival in Europe. Both are organized by the proactive gay association **Roza Klub**, itself just one wing of the autonomous, alternative cultural society Škuc, based at Kersnikova 4 (☎ 01 430 4740, ⓦ ljudmila.org/siqrd/magnus). Roza Klub also runs Galfon, a gay and lesbian advice line (☎ 01 432 4089; daily 7–10pm), organizes club nights and publishes magazines and fanzines.

Maps

The best Slovenia **road map** currently available is Kartografija's 1:270,000 edition, while the 1:100,000

Michelin road map of Slovenia, Croatia and Bosnia is particularly useful if you're thinking of combining either (or both) of these two countries with Slovenia. In addition to road maps, Kartografija (ⓦ kartografija.si) also produces a superb range of other maps – city, regional and themed – including 1:50,000 maps of Triglav National Park, the Kamniško-Savinjske Alps and the Karavanke mountains, and a 1:25,000 map of Mount Triglav. The Alpine Association of Slovenia (Paninska zveze Slovenije: PZS) also produces some good hiking maps.

Most tourist offices can give you a basic town or city map, but for more detailed ones, and regional maps, expect to pay around €5–6. If you haven't bought maps in advance of your trip, you're best off trying the bookshops in Ljubljana (see p.75), though most tourist offices have a good stock too.

Media

Despite 45 years of communism, the Slovene media always had the most balanced and pluralistic coverage of the ex-Yugoslav republics. Given its size, though, it's not surprising that the country has fewer daily **newspapers** in circulation than just about any other European nation.

Among the five major dailies, the most widely read by the urban population is the mildly pro-government *Delo*, which is also considered the most sophisticated read; this is followed by *Dnevnik* (daily), and the Maribor-based *Večer* (evening). Closest to Western tabloids in style is *Slovenske Novice*, full of the usual sensationalist trash stories.

Of the **English listings magazines**, *In Your Pocket* (ⓦ inyourpocket.com/slovenia) is by far the most informative and up to date, with print and online guides to Ljubljana and other towns and cities, as well as occasional spin-off guides to other parts of the country. Otherwise, the *Slovenia Times* (ⓦ slovenia times.com) is a straightforward English-language newspaper with daily news updates.

Slovenian **television** coverage differs little from that in any other central-east European country, with foreign cable and satellite TV supplementing domestic channels. National TV offers a rather bland, often unedifying diet of dull movies, game shows and soaps. The public service broadcaster, RTV Slovenija (Radio-Television Slovenia), transmits on two channels, while the chief commercial channels are Kanal A and Pop TV. RTV Slovenija also broadcasts the country's three major **radio** channels.

Most hotels have satellite TV, though most channels are German or Italian, while the better-quality hotels will usually have English-language channels such as CNN, Sky News and BBC World.

Money

Slovenia's currency is the **euro**, which officially changed over from the tolar in 2007. The euro is split into 100 cents. There are seven **notes** – in denominations of 5, 10, 20, 50, 100, 200 and 500 euros – and eight different **coins**, 1, 2, 5, 10, 20 and 50 cents, and 1 and 2 euros. At the time of writing, exchange rates were fluctuating widely, with £1 sterling equivalent to around €1.17 and US$1.20 – this is likely to change. See ⓦxe.com or ⓦoanda .com for current rates.

You're best off **changing money** in **banks** (*banka*), which are generally open from 8.30am to 12.30pm and 2 to 5pm on weekdays, and 8.30am to 11am or noon on Saturdays. Otherwise, you can change money at numerous small exchange offices (*menjalnice*), tourist offices, tourist agencies, post offices and hotels, though you may end up paying considerably more in commission.

Credit and debit cards are accepted in most hotels, restaurants and shops, and you'll have little trouble finding **ATMs** (*bančni avtomat*), even in the smallest towns.

PUBLIC HOLIDAYS

January 1 New Year
February 8 Day of Slovene Culture (Prešeren Day)
Easter Monday
April 27 Resistance Day
May 1 & 2 Labour Day Holidays
June 25 Slovenia Day
August 15 Assumption Day
October 31 Reformation Day
November 1 All Saints' Day
December 25 Christmas Day
December 26 Independence Day

Opening hours and public holidays

Most **shops** open Monday to Friday from 8am to 7pm and on Saturdays from 8am to 1pm, with some (usually the mall-type places in bigger towns and cities) open on Sundays between 11am and 5pm. There are also an increasing number of 24-hour food shops open throughout the country.

Museums are generally open from Tuesday to Sunday from 9 or 10am to 5 or 6pm, with shorter hours in winter, while some close down altogether during this period. There are, of course, exceptions to the above; all museum opening hours are given throughout the Guide.

Slovenia has **twelve public holidays**, a number of which celebrate important milestones in the country's history. Should any of these fall on a Sunday, then the Monday becomes the holiday.

Phones

Public phone boxes, found just about everywhere, use **phonecards** (*telekartice*; €4.25 or €14.85), which can be bought from post offices, newspaper kiosks

---

INTERNATIONAL CALLS

To **call Slovenia from abroad**, dial the international access code for your country (00 or 011 in most cases) then Slovenia's country code (386), before the rest of the number minus the initial 0.

CALLING HOME FROM SLOVENIA

Australia 00 + 61+ area code (minus initial zero) + number
Ireland 00 + 353 + area code (minus initial zero) + number
New Zealand 00 + 64 + area code (minus initial zero) + number
South Africa 00 + 27 + area code + number
UK 00 + 44 + area code (minus initial zero) + number
US & **Canada** 00 + 1 + area code + number

and tobacco shops. If making long-distance and international calls it's usually easier to go to the post office, where you're assigned to a cabin and given the bill afterwards. All Slovenian landline numbers have seven digits, and are preceded by two-digit **regional codes** – of which there are six (☎01 for Ljubljana, up to ☎07, but no ☎06). Mobile numbers start with three digits, for example, ☎030, ☎040, ☎031 and ☎070, and are followed by a further six digits. To make a direct call to somewhere outside the area you are in, you must use the regional code.

If you're staying any length of time, buy a **SIM card** from one of the main Slovenian mobile operators, which are Telekom Slovenije, Si.mobil and Telemach; these typically cost around €6, and include some starting credit.

Note that if you're travelling from the US, your cellphone may not work if it is not tri-band or from a supplier that has switched to GSM.

Post

The Slovene postal service (*Pošta Slovenije*) is a well-run, efficient organization. **Post offices** (*pošta*), rarely crowded, are orderly places and are usually open Monday to Friday from 8 or 9am to 5 or 6pm and until noon on Saturday, although in Ljubljana and some of the coastal resorts the main post offices may keep longer hours. **Stamps** (*znamke*) can be bought at post offices and at newsstands.

Shopping

Slovenia's rich **folk art** tradition – manifest most obviously in painted **beehive panels**, **woodenware** from Ribnica, **lace** from Idrija and **black pottery** from Prekmurje – is a great source of ideas for souvenir gifts; more often than not, such items can be found in the museums where they are actually exhibited, though there are occasional shops where you can pick up these things, as well as tourist offices within those regions – the one in Bohinj, for example, is excellent for locally produced souvenirs.

Slovenia's superb gastronomic tradition offers endless possibilities – whether buying for yourself or as a gift. First and foremost there is the **wine**, which is best bought from a wine cellar (*vinska klet*), but failing that, there are plenty of wine shops (*vinoteka*) where you can pick up a bottle or two. Schnapps – particularly *borovonica* (blueberry), *viljamovka* (pear) and *medica* (honey) – also make for terrific presents. Otherwise, olive oil, salt (from the saltpans in Piran) and chocolate will all go down a treat.

Flea markets are few and far between, though the Sunday morning one on the banks of the Ljubljanica, in Ljubljana, is definitely worth a browse, particularly for its Communist-era knick-knacks (see p.74).

Time

Slovenia is one hour ahead of GMT, six hours ahead of Eastern Standard Time and nine ahead of Western Standard Time. It is ten hours behind Australian Eastern Standard Time and twelve hours behind New Zealand.

Tourist information

The **Slovenian Tourist Board** (Ⓦslovenia.info) produces a fantastic array of free brochures and special-interest pamphlets, which are distributed throughout their excellent, and extensive, network of local-authority-run tourist offices within Slovenia. Almost without exception the staff, most of whom speak excellent English, are extremely knowledge-able and helpful. Tourist office opening times vary greatly, depending on both their location and the season; some keep impossibly convoluted hours, but as a rule you'll find most open between 9am and 6 or 7pm (8 or 9pm in more popular areas) over summer. We've included opening hours for those we list in the Guide.

Although there are exceptions, and these are listed throughout the Guide, tourist offices generally do not deal with booking private accommodation (see p.26); for this you're best off heading to local tourist agencies, which can be found in most towns and cities – again, these are listed in the Guide where relevant. Opening hours for these vary enormously, depending on the time of year; during high season, some stay open as late as 10pm, though may close an hour or so earlier, or later, than the scheduled time, depending on custom.

Travellers with disabilities

Although progress is being made, Slovenia remains dreadfully slow in acknowledging the needs of **disabled travellers**, and you shouldn't expect much in the way of special facilities. Few places are geared up for disabled travellers and, aside from the better ones, access to hotels and public buildings is generally poor, even in Ljubljana. Public transport is little better, although the Inter City Slovenije trains between Maribor and Ljubljana do have wheelchair facilities and specially adapted toilets, while an increasing number of train stations provide ramps for access to platforms. Similarly, most museums are ill equipped to deal with wheelchair users. The Slovene Disabled Association (Zveza Paraplegikov Slovenije) at Štihova ulica 14, Ljubljana (☎ 01 432 7138, ⓦ zveza -paraplegikov.si) can assist with any specific queries you may have about travelling in Slovenia.

Travelling with children

Slovenia is a wonderful destination for **families**, particularly if the outdoors is your, or their, thing. The mountains, lakes and rivers offer countless opportunities for kids to participate in activities such as cycling, horseriding, rafting, kayaking and so on, and there has been an explosion of summer-based pursuits like summer sledding and ziplining in resorts such as Bovec and Kranjska Gora.

Slovenia's myriad **showcaves** are always a hit with kids, but otherwise, the most obvious destination is the coast, whose **beaches** are, on the whole, clean and safe (most bathing areas are roped off), while many have grassy areas with sporting and play facilities; there are waterparks in Ljubljana, Bohinjska Bistrica and Čatež.

Another thing that might appeal to kids (and adults) is **puppetry**, a popular and well-regarded form of entertainment in Slovenia; there are particularly good theatres in Ljubljana and Maribor, details of which are given in the relevant sections of this Guide.

Beyond this, you'll find that many of the country's **festivals** incorporate elements specifically designed with children in mind; foremost among these is the excellent TrnFest, which takes place in Ljubljana in August (see p.74), and the Pippi Longstocking Festival in Velenje in late September (ⓦ festival -velenje.si), featuring music, cinema, theatre and dozens of workshops for kids.

From a practical point of view, travelling with children in Slovenia will present no obvious problems. Most of the better-quality hotels are well disposed to catering for children, while most restaurants should be able to provide highchairs. Most car-rental firms provide child or baby seats for a small extra charge. All supermarkets, and many smaller shops, are well stocked with the requisite nappies, baby food and so on.

Work, study and volunteering

Opportunities for **working in Slovenia** are few and far between, especially in the most traditional form of work abroad, **teaching English**. Mint International House (☎ 01 300 4300, ⓦ mint.si), is Ljubljana's main international private language school, though there are a few other, smaller, schools in the capital and Maribor.

For **studying Slovenian**, the well-established language centre at the Centre for Slovene as a Second Foreign Language, based within Ljubljana University's Faculty of Arts Department (☎ 01 241 8648, ⓦ centerslo.net), runs an excellent year-round programme of courses.

Voluntariat (☎ 01 239 1623, ⓦ zavod-voluntariat.si), working in conjunction with local organizations, coordinates a dozen or so **volunteer camps** throughout Slovenia, with projects as varied as working with Roma in Prekmurje to working on the saltpans near Portorož. In theory these programmes, which can last from two weeks to several months, are available year-round, but most volunteers work in the period between May and September. The only cost involved is a participation fee (around €80), payable on registration; thereafter all board and lodgings are paid for. If you are involved in a longer-term project (several months), you may also receive pocket money.

Ljubljana
and around

LJUBLJANICA CAFÉ

1

Ljubljana and around

Ljubljana is one of Europe's brightest and most engaging small cities, a destination that has managed to retain its low-key charm despite a recent increase in its profile. It's situated in the southern part of the Ljubljana River basin, at the juncture of the Alps and Dinaric mountain ranges, and pretty much everything converges here: all major transport links, industry and commerce, culture, politics and power. However, with a population of less than 300,000 – which easily makes it one of Europe's smallest capital cities – Ljubljana retains a distinctly languorous and provincial air.

As the former Yugoslavia imploded in the early 1990s, Ljubljana suffered few of the traumas that befell neighbouring Zagreb, its path smoothed by a relatively sound economic and political infrastructure. Now, more than 25 years later, as a European Union capital Ljubljana is a prosperous, self-assured place. Its slick veneer of sophistication masks a disparate number of outside influences – Austrian, Balkan and Mediterranean – subtly absorbed and tinkered with over the years.

While the city boasts a number of eminently enjoyable museums and galleries – the **City Museum**, **Ethnographic Museum** and **National Gallery** chief among them – its real charms lie outdoors. Ljubljana's central core is a showcase of princely Baroque and Secessionist edifices, while the legacy of magnificent buildings, bridges and pathways bequeathed by **Jože Plečnik**, Slovenia's greatest architect, is difficult to overestimate, transforming as it did the entire fabric of the city between the two world wars. Its **churches** too reveal dazzling artistry, from Francesco Robba's extraordinary altar sculptures to Quaglio's resplendent frescoes.

Fundamental to the city's layout and history is the slender **Ljubljanica**, a once navigable waterway, but now sprinkled with several fine-looking bridges. On both the left and right banks, vestiges of the city's Roman and medieval past can be detected, but it's the splendid Baroque townhouses and maze-like streets of the majestic **Old Town**, all wrapped around a regal **castle-topped hill**, that exert the greatest pull. The left bank too has more than its fair share of fine architecture, notably south of the main square **Kongresni trg**, beyond which are the delightful village-like suburbs of **Krakovo** and **Trnovo**.

Most of the city's key museums and galleries are concentrated within a compact area between **Slovenska cesta**, the busy main thoroughfare, and **Tivoli Park**, the city's engaging green pocket and something of a ramblers' paradise. There is a handful of further sights north and south of the centre, including fabulous churches and splendid natural heritage, notably the **Ljubljana Marshes**.

Above all, though, Ljubljana is a sociable city, a place to come and meet people, dip in and out of its enchanting riverside cafés and engage in the **nightlife**. Owing to both the country's size and the city's central location, you can take a day-trip from here to just about any of the country's principal attractions, be it the mountain lakes of Bled and Bohinj to the northwest, the Karst and coast to the south and west, or the castles and spas to the east.

KRIŽANKE

Highlights

① Jože Plečnik Stunning architecture at almost every turn from the nation's greatest architect. **See p.49**

② The Old Town With Baroque churches, elegant townhouses and cool cafés, the Old Town has charm in spades. **See p.50**

③ Ljubljana Castle The old castle looms high above the Old Town; visit the delightful Museum of Puppetry then climb the tower to enjoy the magnificent views of the Alps. **See p.52**

④ Križanke Take in a jazz or rock concert at the atmospheric, Plečnik-designed open-air theatre. **See p.56**

⑤ Trnovo Roman ruins, Plečnik oddities and riverside cafés in this green and peaceful suburb. **See p.58**

⑥ National Gallery Acquaint yourself with the biggest names in Slovenian art, such as Kobilca, Jakopič and Grohar, inside the country's finest gallery. **See p.59**

⑦ Tivoli Park The city's green heart, affording easy promenade strolls or more exerting hillside walks. **See p.62**

⑧ Drinking by the Ljubljanica Enjoy a beer at sundown in one of the many bars along the willow-fringed banks of the river. **See p.72**

HIGHLIGHTS ARE MARKED ON THE MAPS ON P.44 & P.46

1

Brief history

Though sources first mention Ljubljana in 1144, the history of settlement here goes as far back as 2000 BC, when lake-dwellers inhabited the marshy area to the south of the city. Following the **Illyrians** and **Celts** came the **Romans**, who engineered the first major commune, constructing a fortified military encampment, called **Emona**, on the left bank of the Ljubljanica around 50 BC. Emona was sacked in around 450 AD, though remnants of this period can still be seen in the form of several sections of the city walls, as well as archeological sites within the city itself. Next up were the **Slavs**, who settled here at the tail end of the sixth century in what is now Stari trg and Mestni trg.

Medieval Ljubljana and the Reformation

During the twelfth century this evolved into Ljubljana's **medieval** core, and was given the German name Laibach in 1144, before assuming its Slovenian name, Luwigana, in 1146. Following their arrival in the thirteenth century, the **Spanheim** family of **Carinthian dukes** granted the municipality city rights, and in 1243 the name **Ljubljana** first appeared; at around the same time, the city became the capital of the Carniola province, before falling under the jurisdiction of the **Habsburgs** in 1335.

A catastrophic **earthquake** in 1511, which left little of the city standing, coincided with Ljubljana becoming the leading centre of the **Reformation** in Slovenia. This period was marked by significant spiritual and cultural progression, thanks largely to leading reformers such as Primož Trubar, who sought to promote literacy among the populace and who published the first Slovene book – the primer, *Abecedarium* – in 1550; at this time the city also gained its first college and public library. The Reformation was successfully snuffed out at the end of the sixteenth century, a period that saw the arrival of the **Jesuits** (1597), who reorganized the city's educational system, and established many religious buildings.

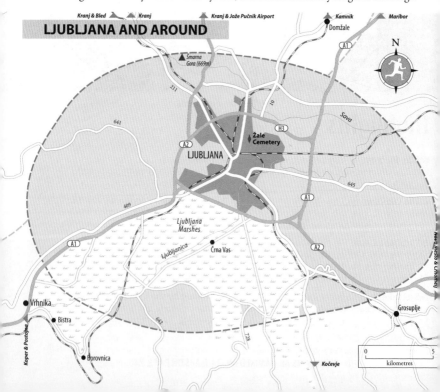

The city's cultural pulse quickened further with the establishment of the Academia Operosorum – the first society of scholars and intellectuals – in 1693, and the Academia Philharmonicorum in 1701, one of the first musical institutions in Europe. Alongside this new Catholic order, a distinct architectural style, **Ljubljana Baroque**, emerged, expressed most sublimely in the city's four principal churches: St James's (1615); the Annunciation (1660); St Nicholas' (1706); and Ursuline (1726), as well as Robba's outstanding Fountain of the Three Carnolian Rivers.

The nineteenth century

Between 1809 and 1814, Ljubljana was designated the capital of Napoleon's **Illyrian Provinces**, the city deemed a geographically convenient location for Napoleon in his attempt to prevent the Habsburgs accessing the Adriatic. During the mid-nineteenth century, and despite continued political repression, the city experienced something of an **industrial revolution** – the catalyst for which was the completion of the Vienna–Ljubljana–Trieste rail line in 1857. The city began to emerge from its provincialized cultural and political straitjacket in the 1880s, while a raft of cultural institutions, including the Opera House (1892) and National House (1896), were established. In 1895, a second destructive earthquake necessitated yet more wholesale reconstruction, though this time it was Vienna and the **Secessionist** school that provided the inspiration – the results of which are particularly outstanding along Miklošičeva.

The Kingdom of Serbs, Croats and Slovenes – and Yugoslavia

With the creation of the **Kingdom of Serbs, Croats and Slovenes** in 1918 – recast as the Kingdom of **Yugoslavia** in 1929 – power transferred from Vienna to Belgrade, though this left Ljubljana no better off than when under Habsburg rule. Nevertheless, the founding of the National Gallery (1918), University (1919) and Academy of Sciences and Arts (1938) was confirmation of the city's continuing cultural efflorescence. During this interwar period, Ljubljana also experienced an architectural revolution, thanks to **Jože Plečnik**, whose work completely transformed the city landscape. Following **World War II**, during which the city was occupied by both Italians and Germans before being liberated by the Partisans, it became the capital of the Republic of Slovenia, one of the six federal republics of the Federal People's Republic of Yugoslavia, and then, in 1963, the Socialist Federal Republic of Yugoslavia.

The 1980s and independence

After Tito's death in 1980, relations between Ljubljana and Belgrade gradually worsened, coming to a head in 1988 with the staging of the **"Ljubljana Four Trial"** (see p.304), a case many at the time regarded as the final denouement in Slovene-Serb relations (and by implication the end of Yugoslavia). At around the same time, Ljubljana was at the forefront of Yugoslavia's intoxicating **alternative cultural scene**, thanks in no small part to the controversial and provocative arts collective Neue Slowenische Kunst (NSK), or New Slovene Art, the core of which was the anarchic rock group Laibach. They, and other alternative movements, were fundamental in stimulating debate on social and political issues, prescient given the deepening tensions between Ljubljana and Belgrade.

On June 26, 1991, the day after Slovenia had officially declared its **independence**, thousands gathered on Republic Square to celebrate – somewhat prematurely as it turned out – unaware that Yugoslav Army (JNA) tank units were closing in on Brnik airport, just 23km away. However, the subsequent **Ten-Day War** had little direct effect on the city and on July 7 it was able, finally, to rejoice in its status as the capital of a new **republic**. Ljubljana has flourished in recent years, thanks in no small part to its outstanding green credentials – it was the first city in Europe to pioneer a programme of zero waste, while large parts are now cut off to traffic – which were rewarded with it becoming **European Green Capital** in 2016.

1

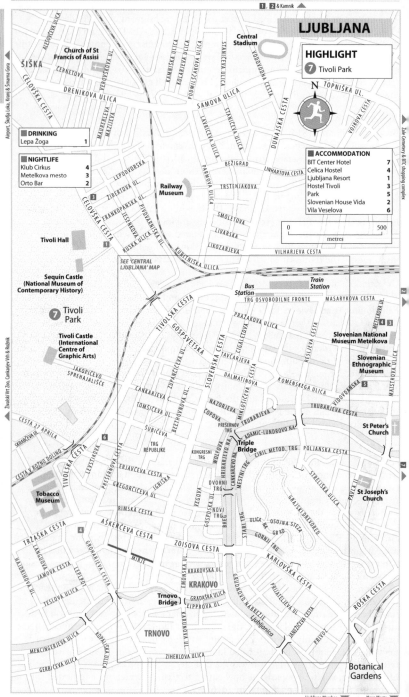

LJUBLJANA

HIGHLIGHT
7 Tivoli Park

N TOPNIŠKA UL.

DRINKING
Lepa Žoga — 1

NIGHTLIFE
Klub Cirkus — 4
Metelkova mesto — 3
Orto Bar — 2

ACCOMMODATION
BIT Center Hotel — 7
Celica Hostel — 4
Ljubljana Resort — 1
Hostel Tivoli — 3
Park — 5
Slovenian House Vida — 2
Vila Veselova — 6

0 — 500
metres

ŠIŠKA

Church of St Francis of Assisi

Central Stadium

Railway Museum

Tivoli Hall

Sequin Castle (National Museum of Contemporary History)

7 Tivoli Park

Tivoli Castle (International Centre of Graphic Arts)

JAKOPIČEVO SPREHAJALIŠČE

SEE 'CENTRAL LJUBLJANA' MAP

Bus Station

Train Station

TRG OSVOBODILNE FRONTE

MASARYKOVA CESTA

Slovenian National Museum Metelkova

Slovenian Ethnographic Museum

St Peter's Church

Triple Bridge

TRG REPUBLIKE

St Joseph's Church

Tobacco Museum

KRAKOVO

Trnovo Bridge

TRNOVO

Botanical Gardens

Prešernov trg and around

Flanked on three sides by distinguished buildings and busy streets, and on the other by the gently curving sweep of the Ljubljanica, cobbled **Prešernov trg** (Prešeren Square) is the city's geographical and social heart, a small but atmospheric space where open-air cafés do a cracking trade and street theatre performers and musicians keep the punters entertained in summer. Presiding over all this activity is the **monument to France Prešeren**, Slovenia's national poet (see box, p.113), after whom the square is named. Designed by Maks Fabiani and Ivan Zajec in 1905, the large, now rather scruffy-looking bronze monument has a straight-backed Prešeren standing beneath a naked muse holding a laurel wreath – the circular plinth underneath is a traditional meeting place for locals and tourists alike.

Frančiškanska Cerkev Marijnega oznanjenja

Prešernov trg 4 • Daily 10am–8pm • ⓦ marijino-oznanjenje.si

The striking red exterior of the Baroque seventeenth-century **Frančiškanska Cerkev Marijnega oznanjenja** (Church of the Annunciation) provides a marvellous backdrop to Prešernov trg. The first church on this site – this is the third – was erected in 1329 by the Augustins, but following the dissolution of the order by Emperor Joseph II in 1784, it was taken over by the Franciscans, who made several significant alterations to its structure and appearance. The centrepiece of a rather gloomy and weary-looking interior is Francesco Robba's eighteenth-century marble high altar, richly adorned with spiral columns and plastic figurines. The illusionist frescoes on the nave and presbytery vaults are by Matevž Langus and Matej Sternen.

Urbančeva hiša

Prešernov trg 5a

The **Urbančeva hiša** (Urbanc House), also known as **Centromerkur**, is Ljubljana's oldest department store, built in 1903 by Friedrich Sigmund of Graz. The focal points of this fine Secessionist building are the narrow clamshell-shaped glass canopy shading the entrance and the statue of Mercury, the Roman god of commerce, standing atop the narrow frontage. While the goods now on offer are unremarkable, it's worth having a look inside to view the superb Art Nouveau interior – the elegant staircase and gallery, the allegorical statue representing craft (fabric has long been sold here) and the beautifully polished wood furnishings, most of which are original.

Hauptmanova hiša and Mestna Hranilnica Ljubljanska

A few steps down Wolfova ulica to the left of the four-storey Secessionist **Hauptmanova hiša** (Hauptman House) you'll notice a terracotta window framing a relief of Julija Primic, gazing across to Prešeren, her life-long admirer. To the right of the Hauptman House is Čopova ulica, a lively pedestrianized shopping street. Few shops are actually worth venturing into, but do take a look at the street's one outstanding building, the **Mestna Hranilnica Ljubljanska** (City Savings Bank) at no. 3. Designed by the Croatian Josip Vancaš, it features a prominent glass and wrought-iron canopy, either side of which are allegorical statues symbolizing trade and commerce.

Miklošičeva cesta

The main street spearing north from Prešernov trg, **Miklošičeva cesta**, is strewn with a raft of marvellous **Secessionist buildings**, all of which were designed following the earthquake in 1895. Directly behind the Church of the Annunciation stands the

1

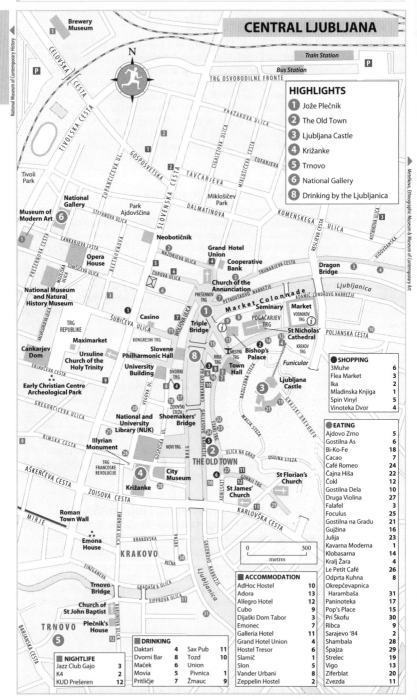

CENTRAL LJUBLJANA

Brewery Museum

Train Station

Bus Station

TRG OSVOBODILNE FRONTE

HIGHLIGHTS

1. Jože Plečnik
2. The Old Town
3. Ljubljana Castle
4. Križanke
5. Trnovo
6. National Gallery
8. Drinking by the Ljubljanica

● SHOPPING
3Muhe	6
Flea Market	3
Ika	2
Mladinska Knjiga	1
Spin Vinyl	5
Vinoteka Dvor	4

● EATING
Ajdovo Zrno	5
Gostilna As	6
Bi-Ko-Fe	18
Cacao	7
Café Romeo	24
Čajna Hiša	22
Čokl	12
Gostilna Dela	10
Druga Violina	27
Falafel	3
Foculus	25
Gostilna na Gradu	21
Gujžina	16
Julija	23
Kavarna Moderna	1
Klobasarna	14
Kralj Žara	4
Le Petit Café	26
Odprta Kuhna	8
Okrepčevapnica Harambaša	31
Paninoteka	17
Pop's Place	15
Pri Škofu	30
Ribca	9
Sarajevo '84	2
Shambala	28
Špajza	29
Strelec	19
Vigo	13
Žiferblat	20
Zvezda	11

■ ACCOMMODATION
AdHoc Hostel	10
Adora	13
Allegro Hotel	12
Cubo	9
Dijaški Dom Tabor	3
Emonec	7
Grand Hotel Union	4
Hostel Tresor	6
Slamič	1
Slon	5
Vander Urbani	8
Zeppelin Hostel	2

■ DRINKING
Daktari	4	Sax Pub	11
Dvorni Bar	8	Tozd	10
Maček	6	Union	1
Movia	5	Pivnica	
Pritličje	7	Žmauc	9

■ NIGHTLIFE
Jazz Club Gajo	3
K4	4
KUD Prešeren	12

0 — 300 metres

Labels within map:

CELOVSKA CESTA
TIVOLSKA CESTA
Tivoli Park
GOSPOSVETSKA CESTA
PRAŽAKOVA ULICA
CIGALETOVA ULICA
MIKLOŠIČEVA CESTA
ČUFARJEVA
TAVČARJEVA
National Gallery
Park Ajdovščina
Miklošičev Park
DALMATINOVA
KOMENSKEGA ULICA
Museum of Modern Art
ŠTEFANOVA ULICA
CANKARJEVA CESTA
Neobotičnik
Grand Hotel Union
Cooperative Bank
TRUBARJEVA CESTA
Dragon Bridge
Ljubljanica
Opera House
NAZORJEVA ULICA
Church of the Annunciation
PREŠERNOV TRG
Seminary
Market
VODNIKOV TRG
POLJANSKA CESTA
Market Colonnade
PETKOVŠKOVO NABREŽJE
ADAMIČ-LUNDROVO NABREŽJE
National Museum and Natural History Museum
ŠUBIČEVA ULICA
Casino
Triple Bridge
POGAČARJEV TRG
St Nicholas' Cathedral
KREKOV TRG
TRG REPUBLIKE
Maximarket
KONGRESNI TRG
Slovene Philharmonic Hall
MESTNI TRG
Bishop's Palace
Funicular
Cankarjev Dom
Ursuline Church of the Holy Trinity
University Building
RIBJI TRG
Town Hall
Ljubljana Castle
ERJAVČEVA CESTA
DVORNI TRG
Early Christian Centre Archeological Park
VEGOVA UL.
ŽIDOVSKA STEZA
GREGORČIČEVA ULICA
National and University Library (NUK)
Shoemakers' Bridge
RIMSKA CESTA
Illyrian Monument
NOVI TRG
THE OLD TOWN
ULICA NA GRAD
OSOJNA STEZA
TRG FRANCOSKE REVOLUCIJE
City Museum
St Florian's Church
AŠKERČEVA CESTA
ZOISOVA CESTA
Križanke
GORNJI TRG
St James' Church
KARLOVŠKA CESTA
Roman Town Wall
MIRJE
Emona House
KRAKOVO
KRAKOVSKA
GRADIŠČE NABREŽJE
Trnovo Bridge
GRADAŠKA ULICA
EIPPROVA ULICA
Ljubljanica
TRNOVO
Church of St John Baptist
Plečnik's House
BARJANSKA CESTA

handsome **Grand Hotel Union** completed in 1905 by Josip Vancaš, who designed the City Savings Bank (see p.45) – note the striking similarities.

Zadružna gospodarska banka and Miklošič parkirna

Opposite the *Grand Hotel Union* is the wildly colourful **Zadružna gospodarska banka** (Cooperative Bank). Designed in 1922 by the Slovene Ivan Vurnik, and painted by his wife Helena, the geometric folk-patterned decoration makes this one of the most outstanding buildings in the city; the interior, with a display of national motifs, is no less spectacular.

Some 200m further is **Miklošič parkirna** (Miklošič Park), laid out in 1899 by Maks Fabiani, a student of Otto Wagner and the Secessionist school of architecture in Vienna. Immediately after the earthquake, Fabiani was assigned the task of reshaping the entire area, a task he accomplished with astonishing speed. Formerly called Slovenski trg, it was renamed Miklošič Park in 1991 on the hundredth anniversary of the death of the philologist Fran Miklošič.

Bambergova hiša and Krisperjeva hiša

Built for the well-known Ljubljana printer Otomar Bamberg in 1907, the **Bambergova hiša** (Bamberg House) at Miklošičeva cesta 16 is one of Fabiani's more restrained pieces of work, consisting of a simple, rather plain design, but worth a glance for the ceramic reliefs of several eminent printers along the top.

On the opposite side of the road, at no. 20, is another, earlier, Fabiani building, the **Krisperjeva hiša** (Krisper House). Built in 1901, it was the first building to be designed within his overall concept of the square, and features garland-like, botanical decoration running along the entire length of the facade and a turret under a bell-shaped roof – note how, with the exception of the Bamberg House, all the buildings standing at the corners of the square have corner turrets, another Fabiani concept. Perhaps the most flamboyant example of Secessionist architecture in the area, though, is the **Čudnova hiša** (Čuden House) at Cigaletova ulica 3.

Neobotičnik

Running parallel to Miklošičeva cesta is the broad slash of **Slovenska cesta**, the city's busy main north–south thoroughfare. There's little to see here, save for the chunky 70m-high tower block, **Neobotičnik** (also known as "Skyscraper"), at the corner of Slovenska and Štefanova ulica. Commissioned by the Slovenian Pension Fund for the purpose of housing offices and apartments – and built in response to the American Art Deco skyscrapers of that period – it was, at the time of its completion in 1933, one of the highest residential buildings in Europe, and the first multistorey building in the Balkans. Inside, take a look at the impressive marble lobby and monumental spiral staircase; although this is roped off, you can take the lift to the rooftop floor café/restaurant (which is no great shakes) for the finest views in the city.

Trubarjeva cesta and Metelkova ulica

The area east of Prešernov trg is fairly low-key, but contains a few sights. East of the square is **Trubarjeva cesta**, a long, narrow, winding street packed with an eclectic mix of cafés, bars and shops. Midway along here, shortly after crossing Resljeva cesta, take a left up Vidovdanska cesta towards the *Park* hotel and carry on until you hit **Metelkova ulica**.

Metelkova

Metelkova ulica 10 • Ⓦ metelkovamesto.org

Metelkova – a kind of cultural complex – has a fascinating history: up until the moment the JNA (Yugoslav People's Army) withdrew in the autumn of 1991, Metelkova had

1

served as a barracks for more than one hundred years, having been initially commissioned by Vienna for the Austro-Hungarian army. In December 1990, on the same day that the plebiscite for independence was held, the Network for Metelkova – an organization born out of several student and cultural movements – was established, its express aim being to convert the barracks into Ljubljana's alternative cultural hub. However, after three years of frustrating negotiations with the authorities, the Network finally carried out their threats to squat. In the event, and after further crises, various groups and societies gradually established their own territories within the complex, and there now exists, among the still half-wrecked and rubble-strewn buildings, a cosmopolitan gang of bars, clubs (see p.73), galleries and independent societies.

At the entrance to the site is the **Hostel Celica** (see p.69), something of an attraction itself, having been converted from the gutted remains of the former military prison. Even if you're not staying, it's worth a look (daily tour 2pm; free) just to see the artistically designed "cells", which now function as rooms.

Slovenski Etnografski muzej

Metelkova ulica 2 • Tues–Sun 10am–6pm • €4.50 • ☎ 01 300 8700, ⓦ etno-muzej.si

The **Slovenski Etnografski muzej** (Slovenian Ethnographic Museum) holds a captivating collection of Slovene and non-Slovene exhibits. The first part of the museum is dedicated to the peoples of Asia, Africa and the Americas, with particularly enlightening expositions on the lives of the Mestizo peoples and the Meso-American Indians – don't miss the extraordinary, and really quite spooky, shrunken head, or *tsanta*, from Ecuador, now about a quarter of its original size – complete with some intriguing archive video footage.

The **Slovene collection** comprises a beautiful assortment of artefacts and treasures, from regional costumes and items representing prominent eighteenth- and nineteenth-century industries – such as pottery, blacksmithing, clockmaking and shoemaking – to the ever amusing beehive panels, as well as masks from the Kurent festival in Ptuj and Laufarija festival in Cerkno. In addition, different craftsmen (typically potters and weavers) often give demonstrations in the on-site workshops, while the lovely museum café is an enjoyable spot to rest up afterwards.

Narodni muzej Slovenije Metelkova

Maistrova ulica 1 • Tues–Sun 10am–6pm • €6 • ☎ 01 230 7030, ⓦ nms.si

The second, smaller, branch of the Slovenian National Museum, **Narodni muzej Slovenije Metelkova** (Slovenian National Museum Metelkova) – a fine glass-clad building on the former barracks site – offers a curious, occasionally stimulating, array of exhibitions. Among them are rooms dedicated to Applied Art, the Church, textiles and timepieces (the collection of pocket sundials is particularly lovely); most interesting are the two rooms given over to two of Slovenia's sporting greats (not that you'll have heard of them), namely fencer Rudolf Cvetko – who competed in the 1912 Olympics but was more feted as a coach – and gymnast Boris Gregorka, whose bronze medal at the 1928 Olympics is on display, along with his vault.

Tromostovje and around

Linking Prešernov trg and the right bank of the **Ljubljanica** is the enchanting **Tromostovje** (**Triple Bridge**), a brilliant piece of architecture and Ljubljana's most photographed landmark. In 1929, **Jože Plečnik** (see box opposite) decided to broaden the existing central bridge, which dates from 1842, with two lateral footbridges, in order to make access to the Old Town safer and more convenient for pedestrians;

JOŽE PLEČNIK

Jože Plečnik (1872–1957) was a world-class architect who transformed Ljubljana into an architectural and urban planning phenomenon. His immense body of work encompasses churches and their interior furnishings, town squares and parks, public buildings and a scattering of columns, pillars and obelisks.

Plečnik studied at the School of Architecture at the Vienna Academy of Fine Arts under the tutelage of **Otto Wagner**, with whom he would later work for a brief period. For the most part, though, Plečnik worked independently, renovating numerous buildings and concerning himself with interior design projects. Disillusioned with the growing tide of German nationalism, and the increasingly oppressive atmosphere in the Austrian capital, Plečnik moved to **Prague** in 1911, where his burgeoning reputation was further enhanced following the execution of several key projects, including the restoration of Hradčany Castle, the latter at the request of President Masaryk.

In 1921 the lure of a professorship in his home town compelled him to return to **Ljubljana University** to become head of the school of architecture; moreover, his return presented him with the opportunity to map out and implement his grand vision for the city. Over the next twenty years, despite extremely limited financial resources, Plečnik married classical architectural forms with his own richly imaginative ideas to create a series of monumental new buildings (including Market Colonnade, Žale Cemetery and the National and University Library), bridges (Triple Bridge, Shoemakers' Bridge) and churches (St Francis in Šiška, St Michael on the Marsh). A key component of his blueprint for this new cityscape was the redesign of large segments of Ljubljana, including numerous park areas, squares and streets.

Despite his extraordinary range and output, Plečnik's work was not appreciated by everybody, not least his contemporaries, most of whom were wed to the more traditional, functionalist principles of architecture. Indeed, it wasn't until some thirty years after his death that he received the recognition he deserved.

to top it off he added the Renaissance balustrades, based on the rising bridges of Venice's waterways, and rows of lamps, all of which gives the bridge a magical appearance at night.

Kolonada tržnice and Zmajski most

At the end of Plečnik's Triple Bridge, on Adamič-Lundrovo nabrežje, you're immediately confronted with another of the architect's masterpieces – the splendid **Kolonada tržnice** (Market Colonnade; Mon–Fri 7am–4pm, Sat 7am–2pm), an elongated, gently curving pavilion harbouring a galaxy of excellent food shops (see p.69) and a fish market. The colonnade runs along the length of the riverbank from the Triple Bridge to the **Zmajski most** (Dragon Bridge), a beautiful piece of Secessionist architecture completed in 1901 by the Croatian Jurij Zaninović, another student of the school of architecture in Vienna. Sitting atop the chunky pylons at each corner of the bridge are four carved, spitting, swirly-tailed dragons – the city symbol.

Pogačarjev trg

On the southern side of **Pogačarjev trg** – which, along with the much larger Vodnikov trg, lies adjacent to the Market Colonnade – the Renaissance-style **Škofijski dvorec** (Bishop's Palace) is one of the oldest buildings in the city. Dating back to 1512, and once a residence for distinguished guests – Napoleon stayed here in 1797, as did Tsar Alexander I in 1821 – its outstanding feature is the Baroque seventeenth-century arcaded courtyard.

On the eastern side of the square is the **Semenišič** (Seminary; for visits call ☎01 300 1953), built between 1708 and 1714 and used by theology students from the dioceses of

1

Koper and Ljubljana; the seminary houses the oldest library in the city, a quite stunning union of Baroque oak-wood furnishings and sky-blue ceiling frescoes representing Theology, Faith and Love by Giulio Quaglio. The stone portal on the southern side – by the flower market – is flanked by two lumbering giants carved by Angelo Pozzo.

Stolnica Sv Nikolaja
Pogačarjev trg • Daily 6am–noon & 3–6pm

Lording it over Pogačarjev trg, the Baroque **Stolnica Sv Nikolaja** (St Nicholas' Cathedral), easily spotted from all over town due to its enormous twin bell towers and 24m-high dome, is Ljubljana's most important and best-preserved ecclesiastical building. Dedicated to St Nicholas, the patron saint of fishermen and sailors – many of whom lived in the suburb of Krakovo – the present building, designed by Andrea Pozzo from Rome and completed in 1706, stands on the site of a thirteenth-century basilica. Entering through the weighty **bronze door**, designed in 1996 to commemorate Pope John Paul II's visit and bearing an impressive relief portraying over a thousand years of Slovene Christianity, you're presented with a riot of fine architecture, immaculate carvings and vibrant frescoes.

The cathedral really owes its reputation to the **frescoes** painted by Quaglio between 1703 and 1706, but restored in 2006; these vivid paintings illustrate the many sea-bound miracles of St Nicholas, such as the one depicting him steering a ship full of sailors to safety during a particularly nasty storm. Remarkably, Quaglio painted the presbytery vault, showing the scene of the Establishment of the Ljubljana bishopric, in just twelve days. The most impressive **altar** is in the northern wing of the transept, decorated by an oil painting of the Three Magi by Matevž Langus and further embellished with Robba's delightfully sculpted angels and cherubs. The southern wing has a copy of the *Virgin Mary of Brezje* (see p.104), held within a magnificent frame. Note, too, the fine Baroque choir seats with gilded reliefs of Christ and the Apostles, and the splendid pulpit, whose author is unknown. Inevitably, Jože Plečnik (see box, p.49) had a hand in the proceedings, designing the baptismal font and bishop's throne.

Peglezen and Cerkev Sv Jožefa
The area east of Vodnikov trg is fairly nondescript, though there are a couple of buildings that might be of interest, particularly to fans of Plečnik. At the beginning of Poljanska cesta, you'll pass Plečnik's **Peglezen** (Flat Iron Building), so named after its extraordinary tapered shape; originally constructed as a municipal building in 1934, it now accommodates a shop on the ground floor, and apartments and a winter garden on the floors above.

A few minutes further on, take a right turn down Ulica Janeza Pavla II towards the huge neo-Romanesque **Cerkev Sv Jožefa** (St Joseph's Church), completed in 1922 by the Jesuits. The vast interior is remarkably bare and, aside from Plečnik's monumental semicircular altar, there is literally nothing to see – which probably explains why it was used as a film studio from the end of World War II until its return to a monastery in 1996.

The Old Town
Defined by a tangle of narrow streets, handsome orange-and-red-roofed townhouses, and neat rows of compact pavement cafés and restaurants, Ljubljana's fabulous **Old Town** is for many the most enjoyable part of the city. Heavily fortified in the twelfth century by the Carinthian dukes, the Old Town extends from **Mestni trg**, across from the Triple Bridge, south down **Stari trg** to **Levstikov trg** and **Gornji trg**; the entire district is wedged between the Ljubljanica to the west and the **castle**-topped hill to the east.

Mestni trg and around

1

Elegant **Mestni trg** (Town Square) is the first of three medieval squares that form the backbone of the Old Town. Located on the square's northern fringe is a copy of Robba's majestic Baroque **Fountain of the Three Carniolan Rivers**, the original now residing in the National Gallery (see p.59). Mestni trg has many fine buildings: take a look at no. 24, the **Souvanova hiša** (Souvan House), whose frontage is the most outstanding example of Biedermeier anywhere in the city – note the stucco reliefs under the third-floor windows representing agriculture, art and trade.

Magistrat

Mestni trg 1 • Guided tours April–Sept Sat 1pm • €2

The white- and grey-brick **Magistrat** (Town Hall), dating from 1719, is one of the most identifiably Baroque buildings in the city. Sporting a gently protruding balcony and impressive clocktower, the building's most interesting features lie within, namely the arcaded inner courtyards adorned with *sgraffiti* and featuring two sculptures: the fountain of Narcissus by Robba, and a statue of Hercules, which previously stood in a fountain on Stari trg.

Ribji trg and around

Opposite the Magistrat a narrow passageway leads to **Ribji trg** (Fisherman's Square), a small, cobbled square where, in the sixteenth century, the fishermen of Krakovo would bring their freshly caught haul from the Ljubljanica to sell to the local inns and houses. Points of interest include the house (now a restaurant) at no. 2, which dates from 1528 (as indicated by its coat of arms), making it one of the oldest residences in the city, and the Neoclassical fountain in the centre, featuring a gilded statue of a girl pouring water from a pitcher. The square opens up onto **Cankarjevo nabrežje**, an engaging riverside parade home to some of the city's most vibrant bars and cafés, and site of the terrific Sunday flea market (see p.74).

Stari trg

Mestni trg gradually tapers southwards towards **Stari trg** (Old Square), Ljubljana's oldest medieval square, a slight misnomer for this narrow, gently curving street. With a sprightly assortment of cafés, restaurants and ice-cream parlours, it's the ideal place to re-energize before pressing on with sightseeing.

The expansive **Čevljarski most** (Shoemakers' Bridge) was so named after a group of local cobblers set up their trading booths here. Prior to their arrival, the bridge was settled by a group of butchers, but so troubled were the locals by the stench that the then emperor, Maximilian I, paid them all off to relocate elsewhere. Remarkably, there has been a bridge of sorts here since the thirteenth century, though this, the second of Plečnik's bridges, was built in 1932.

LJUBLJANA'S GHETTO

Židovska steža (Jewish Lane) and **Židovska ulica** (Jewish Street), immediately west of the Shoemakers' Bridge, together once comprised Ljubljana's small **Jewish ghetto**. Neither the synagogue, which once stood at Židovska steža 4, nor any other original tenements remain, although a new synagogue was opened in 2003; it's a ten-minute walk southwest of the centre at Tržaška cesta 2. Jews have played little more than a walk-on role in Slovenian history and it remains unclear as to when they first settled in the country, though it is believed that there was a Jewish presence here in the twelfth century. What is known is that, following an edict by Emperor Maximilian in 1515, all Jews were banished from Ljubljana, with the majority fleeing to neighbouring Italy and Hungary, and some being dispersed to Slovene villages. Today, it is estimated that somewhere between five hundred and a thousand Jews live in Slovenia, most of whom have settled in Ljubljana.

Levstikov trg and Gornji trg

Stari trg opens up into **Levstikov trg** (Levstik Square), in the centre of which is the **Hercules Fountain**, a 1991 copy of the original, now in the town hall. Arching eastwards from Levstikov trg, **Gornji trg** (Upper Square) is a lovely, gently inclining street whose dwellings, notwithstanding the Baroque elements, have retained medieval characteristics – three windows, wide with triangular gables, slightly set back from each other and separated by narrow passageways.

Cerkev Sv Jakoba

Gornji trg 18 • The church is usually closed, so try and visit during Mass (Mon–Fri 6.30pm, Sun 8am, 9.30m & 5pm) • ☎ 01 252 1727, ⓦ zupnija-lj-sv-jakob.rkc.si

During the Counter-Reformation, the Jesuits settled in and around the square. Their main legacy was **Cerkev Sv Jakoba** (St James's Church), the first Jesuit church in Slovenia, a bright lemon-yellow structure completed in 1615 and festooned with some outstanding sculptures. Retaining only the presbytery from the preceding Gothic church, the present layout is unusual, comprising a Baroque nave with rows of lateral chapels either side, each adorned with colourful Venetian-style stone altars designed by the local stonemason Luka Mislej, the author of most of the altar sculptures.

The **high altar**, by Robba, is a far more modest take on his other works, but no less impressive – he also made the marvellous sculptures in the Altar of St Anne, the third chapel on the left. The church's most significant addition, the octagonal **chapel of St Francis Xavier**, was completed in 1670, and features another marble altar with unusual statues of a "White Queen" and "Black King". Next to the church stands the slender column of the Virgin Mary, erected in 1682 in honour of victory over the Turks at Monošter (now Szentgotthard) in Hungary; the pedestal with four saints, underneath the bronze figure of Mary, was added by Plečnik when he redesigned the square between the two world wars.

Cerkev Sv Florijana

Crowning the upper end of Gornji trg is **Cerkev Sv Florijana** (St Florian's Church), built in 1672 following a fire twelve years earlier that wiped out the majority of houses along here – St Florian is the patron saint of firefighters and protection from fires. Above all else, the church has some intriguing external elements: in the 1930s Plečnik moved the entrance so that the statue of the Bohemian prelate St John of Nepomuk was placed in front of the original, now walled-up, portal. Robba's dramatic relief, in the niche under the pedestal, is of St John being thrown from the Charles Bridge into the Vltava in Prague. Look out too for the built-in head of an Emona citizen, thought to date from 2 AD; the two niches with badly damaged statues of Charles the Great and St Charles of Borromeo; and the fountain with a portrait of a mask from which water spouts.

Ljubljanski Grad

Daily: Jan–March & Nov 10am–8pm; April, May & Oct 9am–9pm; June–Sept 9am–11pm; Dec 10am–10pm • Grounds free; €7.50 (€10 including funicular) includes entry to the Museum of Puppetry, Exhibition of Slovene History, Virtual Castle and Viewing Tower • ☎ 01 306 4293, ⓦ ljubljanskigrad.si • The funicular from Krekov trg runs during castle opening hours (every 10min; €4 return)

Peeking out above lush woodland high above the Old Town on Castle Hill, **Ljubljanski Grad** (Ljubljana Castle), with its immaculate whitewashed walls and silky, manicured lawns, does little to give the impression of a residence dating back to the twelfth century, although much of what remains today is actually

CLOCKWISE FROM TOP LEFT METELKOVA (P.47); PLEČNIK COLUMN (P.49); TIVOLI PARK (P.62) >

1

sixteenth century, following the earthquake in 1511. Its first inhabitants were the Spanheim family of Carinthian dukes who settled here during the twelfth century, before the provincial lords of the Carniolan province, along with the Habsburgs, took over residence in the fourteenth century. Thereafter, the castle was used as a military fortress, a provincial jail and as a refuge for the poor. Although it was taken over by the municipal authorities in 1905, the castle continued to house convicts, including the writer Ivan Cankar who was imprisoned here for six weeks in 1914. Furthermore, the chronic housing shortage in the city meant that additional tenements had to be constructed, most of which remained occupied until the 1960s.

Today the castle complex accommodates a trio of enjoyable **museums** as well as two of the city's finest restaurants (see p.71). The vast courtyard, meanwhile, stages many of the city's principal **cultural happenings**, including the summer open-air cinema, and numerous events connected to the International Summer Festival (see box, p.74).

There is a **funicular** from Krekov trg, but if you fancy walking up you have a choice of three paths, each a stiff fifteen-minute climb: south of Vodnikov trg follow the path up Študentovska ulica; on Stari trg follow Reber Way and then Osojna steza; and from St Florian's Church on Gornji trg take Ulica na Grad.

Lutkovni muzej

The most rewarding of the castle's attractions – and the one to head to if time is short – is the sweet **Lutkovni muzej** (Museum of Puppetry), which documents the history of this much-cherished art form in Slovenia. The most prominent puppeteers were Milan Klemenčič, whose *Dead Man in a Red Coat* was the first puppet show in Slovenia, performed in Ajdovščina in 1910, and, later, Jože Pengov, who created the enduringly popular Speckles the Ball. More intriguingly, the Partisans formed their own puppet theatre on liberated territory during World War II, staging some wickedly satirical plays designed to mock the enemy, such as *Jurček and the Three Bandits*, featuring Hitler; there's some footage here. Children (and adults) can also fool around with all manner of shadow puppets, hand puppets, marionettes and so on.

Razstava Slovenska Zgodovina

Using several historical timelines, the **Razstava Slovenska Zgodovina** (Exhibition of Slovene History) attempts to cover the country's history. It's somewhat arbitrary, and most items are replicas, but the display does feature a few original gems, such as Peter Kozler's – of Union Brewery fame (see p.63) – pioneering *Map of Slovene Land and Regions*, published in 1853 and the first map to define the country's borders. You can also see youth relay batons used during Tito's time, and weapons and inscription boards from the Ten-Day War of Independence.

Virtualni Grad and Razgledni stolp

The **Virtualni Grad** (Virtual Castle) is an enlightening twenty-minute 3D visual presentation chronicling the city's urban and architectural development and its cultural and economic growth. Once you're done here, you can end your visit by climbing the landmark **Razgledni stolp** (Viewing Tower), built in 1848 but subsequently raised, and now affording wide and superlative views of the city and the Kamniške Alps to the north.

Left bank of the Ljubljanica

The **left bank of the Ljubljanica**, defined here as the area between **Kongresni trg** and **Zoisova cesta** to the south, holds magnificent architectural set-pieces, as well as vestiges from Roman Emona and some of Plečnik's greatest works. Its medieval heritage is most pronounced in **Novi trg** – the second-oldest square in the city – which was also surrounded by ramparts that extended as far south as Zoisova cesta.

Kongresni trg and around

A popular, grassy park shaded by leafy plane trees and fringed by venerable architectural gems, **Kongresni trg** (Congress Square) – also called Zvezda ("Star"), on account of its vaguely star-shaped path design – was laid out in 1821 to stage the Congress of the Holy Alliance, before which it was the site of a Capuchin monastery.

Kazina

Occupying the northwestern corner of Kongresni trg is the **Kazina** (Casino), a lovely Classicist mansion built in 1837 by the Kazina Society for the purposes of entertaining the Ljubljana elite, largely in the form of dances, evenings of song and other prestigious social events. Among the society's more distinguished patrons was France Prešeren, who spent many an evening here with his contemporaries; the Kazina is recalled in several of his poems. The building's present-day functions as bookshop and dance school are somewhat more prosaic. Between the two world wars, the Kazina also accommodated the posh *Café Zvezda* – its rather less refined modern-day equivalent, a little further down on the northeastern corner, serves up some of the best cakes and desserts in town (see p.70).

Slovenska filharmonija

The square's most prepossessing building is the buttermilk-coloured **Slovenska filharmonija** (Slovene Philharmonic Hall), whose orchestra, in its various guises, has been performing on this site for more than three hundred years; although this building only dates from 1892, it's one of the oldest musical institutions in Europe. Given its modest size, Slovenia's musical heritage is remarkably strong. The Academia Philharmonicorum, established in 1701, was the forerunner to today's Philharmonic, which subsequently became one of the foremost musical institutions in the Habsburg Empire.

Uršulinska Cerkev Sv Trojice

Slovenska cesta 21 • Daily 9–11am & 5–6.45pm

Completed in 1726, the **Uršulinska Cerkev Sv Trojice** (Ursuline Church of the Holy Trinity) is perhaps the most original Baroque statement in Ljubljana. Its fading coffee-coloured frontage, incorporating six thick columns and a graceful triangular

---

TREASURES OF THE LJUBLJANICA

The languid, muddy-green waters of the **Ljubljanica** have for centuries concealed one of Slovenia's most unlikely, and extraordinary, archeological sites. Over the past thirty years or so a remarkable number of ancient artefacts have been retrieved from the riverbed, including Bronze Age sickles and helmets, Iron Age spearheads, 2000-year-old Hallstatt bracelets, Roman pots and medieval swords and brooches, proof, if any were needed, that the river was a key centre of activity and movement long before its heyday in the seventeenth and eighteenth centuries. Some of these items, many of which have been superbly preserved owing to centuries of submersion, are held at the National Museum (see p.61), though many more have been gathered up by amateur archeologists, and reside in private collections.

ridged gable containing Gothic arches, is designed in Palladian style – its curved side wings serve as the entrances. The bright, airy interior, unpainted and completely white, is rather less elaborate, the exception being Robba's dazzling high altar; made from multicoloured African marble and adorned with the allegorical figures of Faith, Hope and Charity, it ranks alongside his most distinguished work.

Vegova ulica

Vegova ulica, the main street darting southwards from Kongresni trg, was once the westernmost boundary of the medieval city walls. It received its present appearance during the interwar period courtesy of Plečnik, who rearranged the entire street, punctuating it with several of his greatest monuments. The first building of note, on the right-hand side at no. 4, is the **Faculty of Engineering**, its stately neo-Romanesque facade and thrusting corner towers more than a match for the university building opposite. Across the road is the **Glasbena Matica** (Music School), distinguished by portrait reliefs on the facade, and busts of Slovene musicians – as well as a Croat and a Serb – lining the wall in front of the building; although Plečnik's idea, they were sculpted by his colleague Lojze Dolinar.

Narodna in univerzitetna knjižnica

Turjaška ulica 1 • Mon–Fri 8am–8pm, Sat 9am–2pm; reading room July to mid-Aug Mon, Tues & Thurs–Sat 3–7pm, Sun 11am–7pm • Free • ☎ 01 200 1209, ⓦ nuk.uni-lj.si

The **Narodna in univerzitetna knjižnica** (National and University Library; 1936–41), occupying the entire block between Turjaška ulica and the Križanke, is Plečnik's most lauded piece of work. Built on the site of a former palace, its extraordinary, variegated facade, consisting of rough grey stone quarried from Vrhnika and smooth orange brick from Podpeč, is one of the city's most outstanding, and conspicuous, landmarks. Upon entering the building – note the smart bronze horse-head handles on the copper-covered wooden door – you're confronted with a dark staircase ascending to a vestibule lined with black marble columns, the walk up symbolically meant to represent the journey from darkness to light, or from ignorance to knowledge. Beyond here, and filling the entire width of one wing of the building, is the grand **reading room**, with its "catherine wheel" chandeliers and industrial-style reading lamps. Note, though, that the reading room is off limits to non-library members, except for a short period in summer; otherwise, visitors are free to visit the main hall, information centre, exhibition room and basement café.

Trg Francoske revolucije

Vegova ulica winds up at **Trg Francoske revolucije** (French Revolution Square), whose main point of reference is the stern, square-shaped **Spomenik Ilirskim** (Illyrian Monument), designed by Plečnik in 1929 in belated recognition of Ljubljana's short-lived stint as the capital of Napoleon's Illyrian Provinces (1809–13). The obelisk, made from white marble from the island of Hvar in Croatia, is embellished with the Illyrian coat of arms – a crescent moon with three stars – and gilded bronze masks of Napoleon and Illyria. Retained within the core of the monument are the ashes of an unknown French soldier, killed in battle in 1813.

Križanke

Formerly the monastic complex of the Teutonic knights, the majestic **Križanke** is now the setting for the city's prestigious summer festival and other major concerts (see box, p.74). Its present appearance dates from the mid-1950s, when Plečnik, in his final contribution to the city – he was aged 80 upon its completion – set about transforming the abandoned monastery into an open-air theatre and festival space. The complex's original Gothic details were gradually usurped by Renaissance and Baroque elements, which can be most clearly seen in the main courtyard, which also features shallow archways and exuberantly coloured *sgraffiti*. Next door, the amphitheatre-like southern courtyard, with its vast retractable canopy, is a superb venue for classical, jazz and rock concerts. Plečnik also designed the **Peklensko dvorišče** (Devil's Courtyard), accessible through the restaurant and spotted with neat rows of weird-looking wall lamps.

Mestni muzej

Gosposka ulica 15 • Tues, Wed & Fri–Sun 10am–6pm, Thurs 10am–9pm • €4 • ☎ 01 241 2500, ⓦ mgml.si

For more than three hundred years, the splendid **Auerspergova palača** (Auersperg Palace) was home to the Turjak counts, a noble Slovene family with roots going back to the eleventh century; they eventually sold the palace to the city authorities who subsequently used the premises for what is now the excellent **Mestni muzej** (City Museum). The basement holds an impressive stock of archeological remains – including part of the original Roman road that once linked Emona to the port on the Ljubljanica – which were only discovered during the palace's decade-long renovation programme, which was completed in 2004. Also on display, unearthed in 2015, is a marvellous dark limestone votive altar dedicated to the Fons (God of Springs), and a gorgeous ceramic cradle, which was most likely a toy.

The main **permanent exhibition** is given over to the lives and the people (*ljubljančani*) who have inhabited the city over the course of time. An entertaining trawl, it begins with Ljubljana's role as a key trade route in the mid-nineteenth century, particularly following the inauguration of the Ljubljana to Trieste railway. There's comprehensive wartime coverage too, the most intriguing item being a radio concealed within a table; the property of local doctor Edvard Suhar, the radio – supposedly the first in occupied Europe to broadcast art programmes – was used in his waiting room to boost morale among visiting patients. Elsewhere, due deference is paid to Tito, in the form of portraits, busts and street signs, plus some rare archive footage of the former president giving a speech from the balcony of the nearby University building, while Slovene independence is celebrated in the form of Milan Kučan's pen, and, somewhat more excitingly, the wheel of a Yugoslav Army helicopter shot down hereabouts.

Up on the second floor, the protocol room holds a clutch of outstanding **paintings and sculptures**, notably Grohar's *Brna at a Wedding*, Jakopič's ever-colourful *Križanke* and Jurij Subič's *Saints Cyril and Metodius*; there's also a portrait of Ljubljana's most revered mayor, Ivan Hribar (1851–1941), by Croatian Vlaho Bukovac. It's always worth checking out the **temporary exhibitions**, which are usually the best in the city.

Novi trg and around

A rectangular, sloping space extending down to the Ljubljanica, **Novi trg** (New Square) is framed by some wonderful seventeenth- and eighteenth-century mansions, the best example of which is the **Lontovž** on the corner at no. 3; built in 1790, the Slovenian Academy of Arts and Sciences has been based here since 1938. Turning right at the bottom of Novi trg brings you to **Breg** (Embankment), a river wharf in the fourteenth century when the Ljubljanica was a navigable waterway. Indeed, the river remained the city's principal transport artery, with Breg as its chief port, until the end of the eighteenth century, when the widespread construction of the railways – and in particular the building of the Vienna–Trieste line – heralded its death knell. The boats and ships that used to dock here would sail up from Vrhnika, near its source 20km south of Ljubljana, laden with wood, salt and other goods from the Mediterranean. Today, Breg is a wide pedestrianized promenade, popular with strolling evening couples and families.

Krakovo

During the Middle Ages, the genteel southwestern suburb of **Krakovo** was largely settled by fishermen, many of whom supplemented their income by working as *pelajhtarji* (torch bearers), which entailed escorting the local citizens home late at night from the theatre or the inn. Horticulture is now the prime activity here; you'll notice the strips of carefully tended vegetable plots, the results of which sustain the market on Vodnikov trg (see p.69).

In parts, the area still retains a medieval-village-like character. This is especially true of **Krakovska ulica**, with its handsome, one- and two-storey squat houses; the street was once the haunt of prominent town artists, including the celebrated Slovenian Impressionist painter Rihard (1869–1943), who was born at no. 11.

Emonska hiša

Mirje 4 • Mid-April to Sept Sat & Sun 10am–6pm • €4 • ☎ 01 241 2506, ⓦ mgml.si

Among the most impressive of the city's many Roman ruins is the **Emonska hiša** (Emona House), the remains of which most likely date from around the turn of the fifth century. The house belonged to an owner of some wealth, as demonstrated by the two elaborate black-and-white floor mosaics and the complex underfloor heating system, or hypocaust (identifiable by the terracotta brick pillars), which would have had its own sewage channel feeding directly into the Ljubljanica.

West of the garden, across Barjanska cesta and spanning almost the entire length of Mirje, is a reconstructed section of the **Zimski zid** (Roman City Wall), topped with an incongruous-looking pyramid – one of Plečnik's less inspired concepts.

Trnovo

"A place of miserable name", the great Slovenian poet Prešeren once wrote of **Trnovo**, Krakovo's attractive neighbouring suburb. It can be reasonably assumed that the motive for this mildly apoplectic outburst was an unrequited love affair, for it was here in 1833 that Prešeren met his great love Julija Primic, who, tragically for him, never reciprocated his feelings.

Trnovski most and around

Facing the Church of St John the Baptist is the Plečnik-designed **Trnovski most** (Trnovo Bridge), completed in 1932 and incorporating several ungainly stone pyramids, a statue of St John the Baptist and rows of birch trees on either side. Leafy **Eipprova ulica**, the street running eastwards from the bridge along the Gradaščica canal's southern embankment, is worth checking out for its delightfully quirky cafés and bars (see p.72).

Plečnikova hiša

Karunova ulica 4 • Tues–Sun 10am–6pm; guided tours only, hourly • €6 • ☎ 01 280 1604, ⓦ mgml.si

Plečnikova hiša (Plečnik's House) was originally bought by his brother in 1915, before the great man moved in in 1921 following his return from Prague and where he lived until his death in 1957. It's actually a complex of houses, Jože Plečnik having purpose-built the cylindrical annexe to accommodate his studio before buying the neighbouring property.

The house exemplifies Plečnik's extraordinary commitment to modesty, each room practically yet creatively schemed: the ground-floor **studio** – with desks bearing numerous instruments, plans and models – conveniently doubled up as his bedroom, while the kitchen contained his special chair that enabled him to eat and work at the same time. Elsewhere, the spartan-looking bathroom comes complete with an ingenious wood-heated shower, and the small reception room, where he would receive friends and colleagues (he was fiercely protective of his space), features a stove with built-in copper kettle. The first-floor study, meanwhile, was also used by his students; note the model of his pavilion (his last project, in 1956) on Brioni, Tito's island retreat – in return, the Yugoslav president gave him the amphora which resides in the entrance hall. The **Winter Garden**, meanwhile, contains "leftovers", items that never got used for his projects.

A newly acquired space within the house accommodates an illuminating **exhibition** pertaining to Plečnik's life and work – not least his key projects in Vienna and Prague – courtesy of sketches, plans and models, including a wooden model of his unrealized Slovenian Parliament building. Despite his prolific number of large-scale works, his fondness for the everyday is evident in a series of beautifully crafted pieces, such as a pair of candlesticks and an ashtray. There are also some rare insights into Plečnik's personal life, about which very little is known, including letters to his long-term housekeeper, Urška Luzar.

West of Slovenska cesta

The neatly ordered district **west of Slovenska cesta** contains some of the city's most significant museums, most importantly, the revamped National Art Gallery, while both the **Museum of Modern Art** and the **National Museum** have sporadic highlights. Heading west along Cankarjeva cesta, you'll pass the horseshoe-shaped, neo-Renaissance **Opera House**, constructed in 1892 and home to the Slovenian National Opera and Ballet companies (see p.74).

Narodna galerija

Prešernova cesta 24 • Tues, Wed & Fri–Sun 10am–6pm, Thurs 10am–8pm • €5 • ☏ 01 241 5418, ⓦ ng-slo.si

If you weren't familiar with the work of Slovene artists before, then you certainly will be following a visit to the superb and thoroughgoing **Narodna galerija** (National Gallery). The collection, arranged chronologically and also featuring a smattering of European artists, is spread over two buildings: the Slovenski dom (National House), a grandiloquent, Habsburg-era pile facing Cankarjeva cesta, and a stark postmodernist extension around the corner on Prešernova cesta, which is where you'll find the main entrance.

Vodnjak treh kranjskih rek

Entering the gallery on Prešernova, you're confronted by Robba's **Vodnjak treh kranjskih rek** (Fountain of the Three Carniolan Rivers). Its removal from Mestni trg in 2006 (and placement here in 2009) has undoubtedly diluted its impact, though it remains a spectacular piece of work. Allegedly modelled on Bernini's Fountain of the Four Rivers in Rome's Piazza Navona (it is strikingly similar), the fountain, completed in 1751, symbolizes the meeting of the rivers Sava, Krka and Ljubljanica, as represented by three muscular tritons grasping oval jugs, with dolphins splashing at their feet.

1

Medieval art

The collection proper kicks off with **medieval art** and a superb display of Gothic statuary and frescoes, the most renowned piece being the exquisite, almost porcelain-like *Standing Madonna* (minus Jesus, who was cut off) from the Ptujska gora workshop, thought to date from around 1410. Other notable pieces here include the tympanum with the relief *Madonna on Solomon's Throne*, which once stood in Križanke, and the fragment of the fresco *Madonna and Child*, from the late fourteenth century.

Baroque and Neoclassical art

Heading up the splendid double staircase, you enter the grand main hall containing paintings from the **Baroque** and **Neoclassical** periods. The highlight here is the *Cardplayers* by Almanach, considered to be the most important seventeenth-century group portrait in the country; it is thought that the artist himself features in the picture (although Dutch, Almanach worked extensively in the former Slovene province of Carniola); indeed, there's a second *Cardplayers* by Almanach here – the players in this one considerably more worse for wear. There is also an impressive clutch of paintings by Valentin Metzinger and Franc Jelovšek, two of the country's foremost exponents of eighteenth-century church painting – the former was principally concerned with oils, whereas Jelovšek was almost entirely devoted to painting wall and ceiling frescoes.

Realists and Impressionists

One of the great Slovenian artistic movements was **Realism**, with a superb offering here by its leading representatives, Janez and Jurij Šubic, notably the fine *Before the Hunt* and the melancholic *Alone*, both by Jurij. One of the more curious pieces here is by Jožef Petkovšek, whose bleak *At Home*, where the family sit in gloomy silence, is notable for the missing arm and lower body of his mother – it's believed he'd gone mad by the time he painted this. There is also a wonderful collection by Ivana Kobilca (1861–1926), Slovenia's most celebrated female painter; among her finest works are the cheeky-looking *Woman Drinking Coffee* – the museum's signature piece – and the joyous *Summer*, featuring Kobilca's sister and nephews.

Fittingly, the best is saved until last, with an outstanding collection of work from Slovenia's highly revered **Impressionists**. This distinguished group of four painters was led by Ivan Grohar (1867–1911), renowned for investing such emotion in his dreamlike landscapes, such as the masterful *Sower* and *Škofja Loka in Snow*. Rihard Jakopič, a close colleague of Grohar, was a painter of bolder, more expressionist works, as shown in his paintings *Križanke in Summer* and *The Green Veil/Girl with Crown*. The third and fourth members of this quartet, Matej Sternen and Matija Jama, produced works of a brighter, more orthodox bent, for example Sternen's *The Red Parasol* and Jama's *Village in Winter*. Finally, look out for Plečnik's masterful sculpture, *The Second Chalice of Andrej*.

Moderna galerija

Cankarjeva cesta 15 • Tues, Wed, Fri & Sat 10am–6pm, Thurs 10am–8pm • €5 • ☎ 01 241 6800, ⓦ mg-lj.si

The **Moderna galerija** (Museum of Modern Art) takes over from where the National Gallery left off, kicking off with a clutch of paintings by Grohar and Jakopič, as well as numerous pieces by other Slovenian big-hitters like Tone Kralj, Veno Pilon, Miha Maleš and the sculptor Dolinar (*Hard Life*). Sculpture is a central theme here, with many more pieces in halls two and four, notably by Zdenko Kalin and Jakob Savinšek (*Female Torso* and *Nightmare*), as well as an intriguing wooden sculpture of Downing Street by Lojze Spacal.

Integral to the Partisan movement during World War II was art, as demonstrated here by a series of superb, often humorous, black-and-white prints and posters; two of the main exponents of Partisan art were Bozidar Jakac and France Mihelič, the latter represented here by the haunting *Deathly Bird*. Also worth taking a look at are the exhibits by the retro-avant-garde collective Irwin, who cofounded the controversial and influential Neue Slowenische Kunst or NSK (New Slovene Art) movement in the mid-1980s (see p.303); most striking are the posters of the Ten-Day War of Independence. The museum café is fabulous, too (see p.70).

Narodni muzej Slovenije and Prirodoslovni muzej

Prešernova cesta 20 • Tues, Wed & Fri–Sun 10am–6pm, Thurs 10am–8pm • €6, with Natural History Museum €8.50 • ☎ 01 241 4400, Ⓦ nms.si

Housed in a handsome Rudolfinum building since 1888 and graced at the entrance by four allegorical figures representing Art, History, Natural History and Labour, is the **Narodni muzej Slovenije** (National Museum). Inside, the standout feature is a magnificent double staircase with smooth sculptures of reclining muses, while the ceiling frescoes executed by the Šubic brothers are worth poring over.

While the collection itself is somewhat narrow, its extensive stockpile of archeological treasures is truly exceptional. Without question the museum's showpiece exhibit is the 60,000-year-old Neanderthal bone flute discovered at the Divje Babe Cave near Cerkno in 1995 (see p.172), though running it close are some stunning Bronze Age gold appliqués from Lake Bled (reputedly the oldest gold items found on the territory of Slovenia), and an Iron Age situla (bucket-shaped vessel) adorned with three beautiful bands of friezes depicting both humans and animals. Elsewhere, there is an exceptional hoard of finds excavated from both the Ljubljana Marshes (see p.64) and the more unlikely source of the Ljubljanica (see box, p.55): Celtic weaponry, Byzantine jewellery and a rich stash of grave goods, the most extraordinary of which are two incredibly rare ivory dolls, typically found in graves of young women who died before marriage.

Also housed within the building is the **Prirodoslovni muzej** (Natural History Museum), featuring an almost complete 20,000-year-old skeleton of a mammoth found near Kamnik in 1938, and a two-hundred-million-year-old fossilized fish skeleton found near Triglav.

Trg Republike and around

The vast concrete car park of **Trg Republike** (Republic Square) is the largest and, by some distance, the ugliest square in the city, embraced by unsightly postmodern buildings. It was on this square, on the night of June 26, 1991, that President Milan Kučan unfurled the new Slovene flag and pronounced, "This evening dreams are allowed, tomorrow is a new day" – the thousands celebrating on the square oblivious to the fact that, in a matter of hours, they would be at war (see box, p.305).

Arheološki park Zgodnjekrščansko središče

Erjavčeva cesta 16 • Mid-April to Sept Tues–Sun 10am–6pm • €4 • ☎ 01 241 2506, Ⓦ mgml.si

Discovered during excavations in 1969, the **Arheološki park Zgodnjekrščansko središče** (Early Christian Centre Archeological Park) originally began life as a house, but then during the fourth century converted into a centre for the local Christian community, as evidenced by the remains of part of a baptistery – with an octagonal baptismal pool – and portico, both of which feature some lovely multicoloured mosaics; the mosaic in the portico is notable for a well-defined dedication to its architect, Archdeacon Antiochus.

1

Tobačni muzej

Tobačna ulica 1 • Tues–Fri 11am–5pm • Free • ☎ 01 241 2500, ⓦ mgml.si

Housed inside the Tobacco 001 Cultural Centre, itself located on the premises of the Ljubljana Tobacco company building, is the enlightening **Tobačni muzej** (Tobacco Museum). The collection, neatly presented in gleaming glass cabinets, documents the processing and use of tobacco from the factory's establishment from 1871 to the present day, as well as the lives of those who worked in the factory. Prior to the introduction of machines at the beginning of the twentieth century, the factory employed mainly women (known as *cigarice* or "cigar ladies") as they were deemed to be more dexterous, a prerequisite for the delicate task of hand-rolling hundreds of cigars each day. Aside from photographs and documents there are some fascinating tobacco products, including a superb display of beautifully crafted pipes, cigar holders and snuff boxes.

Tivoli Park and around

If you're looking for a bit of peace and relaxation, you won't have to go far, thanks to **Tivoli Park**, a lush expanse of greenery carved up by broad promenades and backed by dense woodland and hills; it's also a major recreation and sporting centre. The park is accessible on a number of routes; the most direct is via the subway by the Museum of Modern Art.

Mednarodni Grafični Likovni Center

Tues–Sun 10am–6pm • €5 • ☎ 01 241 3800, ⓦ mglc-lj.si

At the top of Jakopič Promenade, laid out by Plečnik and split down the middle by a row of shabby lampposts, stands **Tivolski Grad** (Tivoli Castle). Since being transformed into a mansion by the Jesuits in 1713, it has been used as a military hospital and barracks, and as a residence for city officials. Local rumour has it that the creator of the cast-iron dogs by the staircase, Anton Fernkorn, was so disturbed by omitting their tongues that – in what might be construed as an over-reaction – he shot himself.

The mansion is now the permanent home of the **Mednarodni Grafični Likovni Center** (International Centre of Graphic Arts), an enterprising institution devoted to the promotion and printing of graphic art; the centre stages half a dozen or so exhibitions each year, though its chief activity is the organization of the International Graphic Arts Biennial (see box, p.74).

Muzej novejše zgodovine Slovenije

Čelovska cesta 23 • July & Aug Tues, Thurs & Sat 10am–8pm, Wed, Fri & Sun 10am–6pm; Sept–June Tues–Sun 10am–6pm • €3.50 • ☎ 01 300 9611, ⓦ muzej-nz.si

Up on the northern edge of the park is the brilliant-white Baroque mansion of the **Sequin Castle** (Cekinov Grad), which, since 1951, has been home to the enlightening **Muzej novejše zgodovine Slovenije** (National Museum of Contemporary History). Arranged chronologically, each room represents a period of twentieth-century Slovenia, starting with World War I, featuring several mock-up shelters and a remarkable display of photos and mementoes from the battlefields. The collection moves swiftly on to the interwar period, and illustrates the struggle to establish the country within the new Kingdom of Serbs, Croats and Slovenes. Among the more interesting exhibits in the World War II room are uniforms from the warring sides and a chess set made from bread and saliva by a prisoner of war. More startling, however, is a clutch of items (pocket watches, jewellery, gold false teeth) belonging to civilian and political prisoners who were dumped into mass graves such as Kočevski Rog (see p.219) after the war. The following rooms are devoted to war damage reconstruction and daily life in socialist Yugoslavia, with particular emphasis on the Slovenian economy. The last room documents events surrounding Slovenian independence in 1991, including the tail of a JNA gazelle shot down over Rožnik Hill during the Ten Days' War (see box, p.305), and the various landmark moments thereafter, notably EU accession in 2004 and the adoption of the euro in 2007.

Rožnik hrib

Bunched up behind Tivoli Park are a number of modest peaks, sewn together by a network of tidy, well-signposted tracks. The most popular short hike (approx 45min) is up to **Rožnik hrib** (Rožnik Hill), accessible via a number of paths, the best of which begins from behind Tivoli Castle. Having made it to the top, you can take a break and buy refreshments at the *Cankar Inn*, once periodically the home of novelist Ivan Cankar; opposite is a **memorial room** (April–Oct Sat & Sun 11am–6pm; free; ☎01 241 2500, ⓦmgml.si) containing a few of his personal effects (a wallet, tie and tickets) and some original furniture. The **Church of St Mary's Visitation**, just down from the inn, was built in 1740 – the high altar has a particularly fine painting by Jurij Šubic (visits during Mass only; May–Sept 10.30am).

Beyond the centre

There are some very enjoyable places to visit **beyond the centre** of Ljubljana. To the north are the **Brewery Museum**, the **Railway Museum** and a couple of **Plečnik**-related sights, while even further out, there's a terrific little walk to be had up **Šmarna Gora**. The two key sites south of the centre are the **Botanical Gardens** and the wonderful **Ljubljana Marshes**.

Pivnica muzej

Celovška cesta 22 • Tours Mon–Sat noon, 3pm & 5pm, Sun 3pm & 5pm • €7 (€5 without the tour) • ☎041 303 050, ⓦunion-experience.si

The **Pivnica muzej** (Brewery Museum) is located in the old malt-house of the sprawling Union Brewery – founded in 1864 by the cartographer Peter Kozler and his brother, and one of the two largest breweries in the country, the other being Laško (see p.255), though both were bought out by Heineken in 2015. Following a ten-minute video, you head through to the museum, whose many exhibits include century-old wooden barrels, carts for carrying crates, beer signs and plates, and a fine collection of beer mugs and tankards.

You can also take an optional **tour** of the production process, highlighting the brewing, filtration and bottling plants. The figures are impressive: forty thousand bottles (or 280 kegs) are produced an hour, with a warehouse that can store up to ten thousand pallets at any one time. The tour concludes with a pint of the brewery's finest in the *pivnica*, which is a great place for a bite to eat and a few beers (see p.72).

Železniški muzej

Parmova ulica 35 • Tues–Sun 10am–6pm • €3.50 • ☎01 291 2641

Sure to get rail buffs misty-eyed is the wonderful **Železniški muzej** (Railway Museum). Located in the splendid roundhouse are seventeen quite magnificent steam locomotives, the pick of which is an express loco built by the Austrian Southern Railway for the Ljubljana–Trieste line in 1914; somewhat dwarfed by these beasts is an ambulance carriage used to transport injured soldiers from the Soča Front to hospitals in Ljubljana.

Once you're done admiring these, pop across to the hut where there is an engaging exhibition on the history and development of the Slovenian rail network. Highlights include beautifully engineered signalling systems, track maintenance equipment,

1

old station clocks and an elegant, green-painted wrought-iron staircase from the old signal box at Ljubljana station; climb this to reach a gallery of delightful train paintings by Stane Kumar.

Cerkev Sv Frančiška Asiškega

Verovškova ulica, Šiška • Bus #22 to Drenikova ulica

Out in the suburb of Šiška is the first of the city's two Plečnik-designed churches, the **Cerkev Sv Frančiška Asiškega** (Church of St Francis of Assisi), distinguished by its double-storey, cylindrical belfry topped with a cone. Completed in 1931, this is the least conventional of Ljubljana's churches, its square main hall with a high, flat wooden ceiling and rows of square windows more reminiscent of a school gymnasium than your average place of worship. A colonnade of chunky, circular brick pillars forms a kind of inner square, in the centre of which is a pyramid-shaped altar; both this and the chandeliers are classic Plečnik.

Pokopališče Žale

Med hmeljniki 2 • Daily 7am–7pm • Buses #2 and #17 stop outside

Plečnik's **Pokopališče Žale** (Žale Cemetery), 1km northeast of the centre, is announced by a magnificent entrance in the form of a bright, two-storeyed arcade split by a graceful ceremonial arch – meant to symbolize the border between the city of the living and that of the dead. In the park beyond the entrance are a number of funeral chapels dedicated to patron saints, part of Plečnik's overall concept for the entire complex. The cemetery itself is immaculate, while **Plečnik's grave** – a typically modest effort – is to the left of the entrance in Plot 6.

Botanični vrt

Ižanska cesta 15 • Daily: April–June, Sept & Oct 7am–7pm; July & Aug 7am–8pm; Nov–March 7am–5pm • Free, glasshouse €2.80 • ☏ 01 427 1280, Ⓦ botanic-gardens-ljubljana.com • Bus #3 to Strelišče

Just under 1km south of the centre, and easily reached on foot (along busy Karlovška cesta or, more peacefully, along the banks of the Ljubljanica), are the university's **Botanični vrt** (Botanical Gardens). Established in 1810 by the Slovene botanist Franc Hladnik, which qualifies it as the oldest such institution in the country, there are now more than fifty thousand species of plants, shrubs and trees, representing every continent, in these colourful and beautifully tended gardens. The sparkling **tropical glasshouse** – built to celebrate the gardens' 200th anniversary – holds close to four hundred different species.

Ljubljansko barje

Covering an area of more than 160 square kilometres, the **Ljubljansko barje** (Ljubljana Marshes), some 5km south of the centre, originated two million years ago and are believed to have been the site of the first settlement in the city. The marshes are now a protected area, noted for their tremendously varied flora and fauna, with excellent opportunities for birdwatching, particularly around Kozlerjeva gošča, near the village of **Črna Vas** (Black Village) on the eastern extremes. The marshes are also a fertile hunting ground for archeologists, having yielded innumerable objects since extensive research began here soon after World War II – so much so that, in 2011, they were designated a UNESCO World Heritage Site, one of just three in Slovenia. The last significant find, in 2002, was a wooden wheel believed to be more than five thousand years old, making it the oldest such wheel ever discovered.

FROM TOP LJUBLJANA ROOFTOPS; STARI TRG (P.51) >

1

Cerkev Sv Mihaela na Barju

Bus #19 to the last stop, Barje; walk back across the junction and it's 500m ahead

In the centre of Črna Vas is Plečnik's **Cerkev Sv Mihaela na Barju** (Church of St Michael on the Marsh), built in 1938 – some ten years later than the Church of St Francis of Assisi (see p.64) but perhaps even more bewitching. The stone-built exterior, bridge-style staircase and detached hollow belfry are all instantly recognizable as Plečnik's work, as is the extraordinary, largely wooden interior, with its cupboard-shaped altar and Turkish-style lamps. The marshy ground necessitated construction on solid 8m-long oak piles, while the hall was elevated to the second floor because of the dangers of flooding. To be sure of getting a look, try and visit during Mass (Sat & Sun 10am).

Šmarna Gora

Bus #8 to Brod, from where it's a 5min walk to the start of the main trail

The isolated 669m-high hill of **Šmarna Gora**, 10km northwest of the centre, is extremely popular with locals, many of whom come here after work for a touch of exercise. At the summit, a partly preserved fifteenth-century wall is evidence that the hill was once a fortified camp providing protection from the rampaging Turks, though in the event it was never conquered. The **Pilgrimage Church of the Holy Mother**, first mentioned in 1314, was built on the old ruins in 1729 and has some lovely frescoes by Matevž Langus, though the only chance you'll get to see these is by visiting during Mass, each Sunday at 11am. Once you've reached the top, which takes around 45 minutes up one of the steep and bumpy tracks, give the bell-rope a sharp tug, partake in a cup of sweet tea from the hilltop hut, and take in the terrific views of the city and Sava Plain spread out below.

ARRIVAL AND DEPARTURE   **LJUBLJANA**

By plane Ljubljana's Jože Pučnik airport (☎ 01 206 1000, ⓦ lju-airport.si) is in Brnik, 23km north. The cheapest way to get into the city is by public bus; these arrive at and leave from bay 28 of the bus station (departures Mon–Fri 5.20am, then hourly 6.10am–8.10pm, Sat & Sun 6.10am, then every 2hr 9.10am–7.10pm; arrivals Mon–Fri 5am–8pm, Sat & Sun 7am, then every 2hr 10am–8pm). The trip to town takes 45min, and costs €4.10. A quicker, more expensive, option is the shuttle bus, which leaves frequently from (6.45am–11.45pm) and to (5.10am–10.30pm) the airport (30min; €9). A taxi from or to the airport will cost around €40.

By train The station (*železniška postaja*) is on Trg Osvobodilne fronte, from where it's a 10min walk south into the centre. You can get all information, and pick up timetables, at the information office (daily 5.30am–9.30pm); there are also 24-hour left-luggage lockers (€3).

Domestic destinations Bled-Lesce (hourly; 40min–1hr); Brežice (6–12 daily; 1hr 45min–2hr); Celje (every 30min–2hr; 1hr–1hr 40min); Črnomelj (Mon–Fri 9 daily, Sat & Sun 3 daily; 2hr 10min–2hr 30min); Divača (every 45min–1hr 30min; 1hr 30min); Kamnik (Mon–Fri hourly; 40min); Koper (3–5 daily; 2hr–2hr 30min); Kranj (every 30min–1hr; 20–35min); Maribor (every 30min–2hr; 1hr 50min–2hr 40min); Metlika (Mon–Fri 9 daily, Sat & Sun 3 daily; 2hr 30min–3hr); Novo Mesto (Mon–Fri every 45min–1hr 30min, Sat & Sun 4 daily; 1hr 30min–1hr 45min); Postojna (every 45min–1hr 30min; 1hr); Sežana (every 1–2hr; 1hr 40min–2hr); Ptuj (2 daily; 2hr 30min); Zidani Most (every 30min–1hr; 45min–1hr).

International destinations Belgrade (2 daily; 9hr); Budapest (1 daily; 8hr 45min); Munich (2 daily; 6hr 30min); Rijeka (2 daily; 2hr 45min); Vienna (1 daily; 6hr 10min); Zagreb (5 daily; 2hr 15min); Zurich (1 daily; 12hr).

By bus The bus station (*avtobusna postaja*) is next to the train station (ticket office daily 5am–11pm).

Domestic destinations Bled (every 30min–1hr; 1hr 20min); Celje (Mon–Fri 10 daily, Sat & Sun 3 daily; 1hr 45min); Idrija (Mon–Fri every 1–2hr, Sat & Sun 6 daily; 1hr 15min); Ivančna Gorica (hourly; 50min); Kamnik (every 15–30min; 40min); Kočevje (hourly; 1hr 30min); Koper (Mon–Fri 9 daily, Sat & Sun 4 daily; 2hr–2hr 20min); Kranj (every 30–45min; 40min); Kranjska Gora (hourly; 2hr); Maribor (Mon–Fri 7 daily, Sat & Sun 2 daily; 1hr 45min–2hr 30min); Nova Gorica (Mon–Fri every 30min–2hr, Sat & Sun 5 daily; 2hr 30min); Novo Mesto (Mon–Fri 7 daily, Sat & Sun 4 daily; 1hr 10min); Piran (Mon–Fri 4 daily, Sat & Sun 2 daily; 2hr 40min); Postojna (Mon–Fri every 30min–1hr 30min, Sat & Sun 8 daily; 45min–1hr); Radovljica (every 30min–1hr); Ribčev Laz (Lake Bohinj) (hourly; 2hr); Škofja Loka (every 30min–1hr; 40min).

International destinations Rijeka (1 daily; 2hr 15min); Trieste (5 daily; 1hr 35min); Zagreb (8 daily; 2hr 15min).

LJUBLJANA TOURIST CARD

1

If you're planning on staying in the city for a few days, consider investing in the **Ljubljana Tourist Card** (Ⓦ visitljubljana.com), valid for 24hr (€23), 48hr (€30) and 72hr (€35); this entitles you to unlimited travel on all the city's buses, free bike rental for four hours, a guided walking tour, a boat ride on the Ljubljanica, and discounted entrance fees to selected museums and galleries; it can be bought from the city's tourist information centres or online, which is slightly cheaper.

GETTING AROUND

The city's compact centre lends itself perfectly to walking and it's unlikely you'll need, or want, to use the refreshingly clean and efficient **public transport** system. Ljubljana's fabulous green credentials extend to the electrically powered golf-buggy-like vehicles called *kavalirs* (8am–8pm; free, order in advance on ☎ 031 666 331 or hail on the street) whizzing around the Old Town, which is otherwise closed to traffic.

BY BUS

City buses Buses run by Ljubljanski Potniški Promet (LPP; Ⓦ lpp.si), are clean, cheap and frequent. The majority of lines operate between 5am and 10.30pm, with the most important lines (#1, #2, #3, #6 & #11) – most of which run the length of Slovenska cesta – starting at 3.15am and running until midnight – each stop clearly indicates which buses stop there.

Fares and tickets To use the buses you need to buy an Urbana smartcard; these cost €2 and are available from the LPP office at Slovenska cesta 56 (Mon–Fri 7am–7pm), the main bus station, post office, kiosks, any of the tourist offices, or machines ("Urbanomats"), which can be found at most stops – you top them up in the same places. One journey, lasting up to 90min and allowing for unlimited transfers, costs €1.20.

Route map The useful, free fold-up LPP map, which clearly denotes the various bus lines and all the stops, can be obtained from the LPP office and the tourist offices.

BY TAXI

It's unlikely that you'll need to take a taxi, but if you do, expect to pay around €0.80–1.50 starting rate and then €0.80–1.70/km – calling a cab by phone will work out slightly cheaper, but taxis can also be flagged in the street or found at ranks by the train station, outside the *Slon* hotel (see p.68) and near Prešernov trg. Reliable companies include Laguna Taxis (☎ 031 492 299) and Rumeni Taxis (☎ 041 731 831).

BY BIKE

The excellent Bicike (LJ) bike rental scheme (Ⓦ en.bicikelj.si) has about thirty stations around the city. You must register online first (€1 for a week, €3 for a year), after which you can use bikes for up to 24 hours at any one time – rental is free for the first hour, €1 for the second hour, €2 for the third hour and €4 for each additional hour thereafter. From April to Oct, there's also the "Ljubljana Bike" rental programme run by the Slovenian Tourist Information Centre (April, May & Oct Mon–Fri 8am–7pm, Sat & Sun 9am–5pm; June–Sept daily 8am–9pm; €2 for 2hr, €8 for the day).

INFORMATION

Slovenian Tourist Information Centre (STIC) Krekov trg 10 (June–Sept daily 8am–9pm; Oct–May Mon–Fri 8am–7pm, Sat & Sun 9am–5pm; ☎ 01 306 4575, Ⓦ visit ljubljana.com). Can assist with information on any aspect of travel within the country.

Ljubljana Tourist Information Centre (TIC) Adamič-Lundrovo nabrežje 3 (daily: June–Sept 8am–9pm; Oct–May 8am–7pm; ☎ 01 306 1215, Ⓦ visitljubljana.com). Excellent centre offering a wealth of information including free maps; they can also book private accommodation (see p.68) and

sell tickets for most of the city's cultural and sporting events. There is also a TIC desk at the airport (daily: June–Sept 10.30am–7/7.30pm; Oct–May 10.30am–5/5.30pm).

Listings The monthly *Where To?* pamphlet, available at the information centres, lists museums and galleries plus monthly events and performances; another fabulous source of information is the entertaining and on-the-ball *Ljubljana In Your Pocket*, published bimonthly and available free from the information centres plus many hotels, hostels and bars.

TOURS

Official tours The TIC's standard tour includes a 2hr walk around the Old Town, a return ride on the funicular up to the castle and a bite to eat in a local restaurant (daily: April–Sept 10am; Oct–March 11am; €10). They offer a range of other tours, among them "Exploring Ljubljana by

Bike", "Ljubljana Beekeeping Trail" and "Žale Cemetery". Tickets for all should be bought in advance from the information centres or online.

Alternative tours Curiocity (☎ 051 640 750, Ⓦ curiocity .si) offers the best and most original options, a handful of

1

small-group tours that present an alternative slant on the city and its inhabitants. "From Ljubljana with Love includes visits to half a dozen socially responsible enterprises, such as the city's only Fairtrade shop and a restaurant partly staffed by the disabled and disadvantaged, which is where you also get to eat; other tours include "Express Your Selfie" and "Dragon's Tales".

Boat tours There are one-hour guided excursions along the Ljubljanica in summer, setting off from Ribji trg (daily: April–Oct noon & 4pm; €10). Tickets are available from the departure point or the information centres. Alternatively, Barka Ljubljanica offers 45min river cruises in a gorgeous wooden boat, which departs from Novi trg on the hour (11am–9pm; €8; ⓦ barka-ljubljanica.si) – just turn up.

ACCOMMODATION

The emphasis in Ljubljana is on quality not quantity, whether that's the crop of high-end **business hotels**, the fabulous selection of **boutique hotels** – a good number of which are in and around the cobbled streets of the Old Town – or the excellent spread of **hostels**. Another option is **private accommodation** – the information centres (see p.67) should be able to arrange something central, or you could try Tour AS at Mala ulica 8 (ⓣ 01 434 2660, ⓦ apartmaji.si), which, although it deals predominantly with apartments, has a handful of private rooms too. In the following reviews, **breakfast** is included in the price unless otherwise stated.

HOTELS AND GUESTHOUSES

★**Adora** Rožna ulica 7 ⓣ 082 057 241, ⓦ adorahotel.si; map p.46. This fine conversion of a bourgeois townhouse now conceals ten rooms with charm and style: polished teak furnishings and parquet flooring, chunky bedsteads and brass fitted showers and taps, not to mention some romantic touches like 1930s-style telephones and watercolours of old Ljubljana. The trim little courtyard is just the job for a sundowner. €115

Allegro Hotel Gornji trg 6 ⓣ 059 119 620, ⓦ allegrohotel.si; map p.46. The strong musical theme running through this superbly restored townhouse – the piano in reception and scores on the walls – is due to the fact that it was once home to a group of musicians from Bohemia; today it boasts seventeen gorgeous, variously sized and individually furnished rooms, each in a different colour scheme. To cap it off, there's a superb buffet breakfast in the brightly decorated cellar. €130

BIT Center Hotel Litijska cesta 57 ⓣ 01 548 0055, ⓦ bit-center.net; map p.44. Busy and lively sports hotel 2km east of the centre, which has freshly refurbished en-suite doubles, in addition to cleverly themed hostel rooms (doubles and multi-bedded) with shared shower facilities; guests get a fifty percent discount on use of sporting facilities (squash, badminton and fitness centre). Buses #5, #9, #13 and #22. Breakfast €3.50. Dorms €16, doubles €48

★**Cubo** Slovenska cesta 15 ⓣ 01 425 6000, ⓦ hotelcubo.com; map p.46. A graceful, refurbished white 1930s residential building fully deserves its many plaudits. The rooms – many with unencumbered views across to the castle – are finished in many shades of grey, with abstract wall art and glassed-in bathrooms with enormous walk-in showers and L'Occitane toiletries; then there's the rather splendid breakfast buffet to set you up for the day's sightseeing. €115

Emonec Wolfova ulica 12 ⓣ 01 200 1520, ⓦ hotel-emonec.com; map p.46. The best-value hotel in the centre and a brilliant location to boot, in a quiet off-street

spot near Prešernov trg (though there's no parking). The fetching brown and white rooms (including triples and quads) are simple, but fresh and modern looking, and the bathrooms are beautifully designed. €67

Galleria Hotel Gornji trg 3 ⓣ 01 421 3560, ⓦ hotelgalleria.eu; map p.46. The sixteen beautifully light, white-painted rooms in this wonderful, rambling boutique hotel feature gorgeous wooden beds, parquet flooring and sophisticated furnishings; rooms either have views up to the castle or looking over the pretty rose garden. €110

Grand Hotel Union Miklošičeva cesta 1 ⓣ 01 308 1270, ⓦ union-hotels.eu; map p.46. The preferred retreat of visiting celebrities and politicians, this splendid Art Nouveau building actually houses two hotels; the *Grand Union* itself has generously sized and handsomely furnished rooms, some with a balcony looking up to the castle. Rooms in the adjoining *Business* hotel are not dissimilar, though the colour scheme is somewhat less inspiring; the rather lovely indoor rooftop pool is also here. €140

Park Tabor 9 ⓣ 01 300 2500, ⓦ hotelpark.si; map p.44. Located amid a jumble of apartment buildings a few blocks east of the stations, this high-rise has better rooms than the exterior might suggest; a variety of standard, comfort and superior options, the latter two categories with a/c. It can get busy with large groups, but if you can put up with that, then this represents decent value. €60

Slamič Kersnikova ulica 1 ⓣ 01 433 8233, ⓦ slamic.si; map p.46. A delightful B&B just a stone's throw from the stations with seventeen smartly designed rooms divided between the main building and the more contemporary annexe on the other side of the rooftop terrace. Cool wrought-iron furnishings, panelled walls and waxed wooden floors come as standard, while breakfast is taken either on the terrace or in the quaint in-house café. €95

Slon Slovenska cesta 34 ⓣ 01 470 1100, ⓦ hotelslon.com; map p.46. The "Hotel Elephant" is so named after Archduke Maximilian who, with elephant in tow, allegedly stayed at an inn on this site en route to Vienna in 1552. Glass doors lead into sumptuous, parquet-floored bedrooms with chestnut-wood furnishings, combined flatscreen TV and DVD player, coffee- and tea-making facilities – and even a "pillow menu" to choose from. Fittingly, its magnificent breakfast room offers the best breakfast in town. **€150**

Slovenian House Vida Savlje 87 ☎040 475 426, ⓦ slovenianhouse.com; map p.44. Despite its location some 6km north of the city centre, this comely bed and breakfast is well worth the effort to reach, and in any case is easily accessed by bus (#14). The whole place manifests an easy-going countrified vibe (there are big open fields close by), though it's the handcrafted wine cellar – where breakfast is taken – that's the highlight. **€60**

Vander Urbani Krojaška ulica 6–8 ☎01 200 9000, ⓦ vanderhotel.com; map p.46. Possibly the coolest design hotel on the block, *Vander* occupies four conjoined townhouses, accommodating a total of sixteen rooms; the building's tight configuration necessitates modest, rather than spacious, rooms, but the fixtures and fittings are pure class, and you won't find more comfortable beds anywhere in the city. The rooftop infinity pool rounds things off perfectly. **€120**

HOSTELS

AdHoc Hostel Cankarjevo nabrežje 27 ☎051 268 288, ⓦ adhoc-hostel.com; map p.46. Super location in the heart of the Old Town for this sprawling, yet surprisingly quiet, hostel, with graffitied walls and large communal spaces. No breakfast, but there are kitchens. Dorms **€20**, doubles **€54**

Celica Hostel Metelkova ulica 8 ☎01 230 9700, ⓦ hostelcelica.com; map p.44. Brilliantly original hostel in a former military prison at the centre of artistic Metelkova, with bright dorms and two-/three-bed "cells", each designed by a different architect or artist – shower facilities are shared. There are also four- and five-bed rooms, and a seven- and twelve-bed dorm, all of which have bathrooms. There's a very decent café here, and you can also expect concerts, exhibitions and parties. Breakfast

included. Dorms **€22**, doubles **€60**

Dijaški Dom Tabor Vidovdanska cesta 7, entrance at Kotnikova ulica 4 ☎01 234 8840, ⓦ hostel.ddt.si; map p.46. Busy, central student hostel, with decent, very cheap beds on offer in July and August only. Breakfast included. Dorms **€11**, doubles **€38**

Hostel Tivoli Lepodvorska ulica 2 ☎059 160 974, ⓦ hosteltivoli.com; map p.44. Sweet little place on the ground floor of an apartment block a 15min walk from the stations; just two dorms (one lime green, the other orange), each with three-high bunks, and a double room, all with shared shower facilities. Breakfast included. Dorms **€21**, doubles **€60**

★**Hostel Tresor** Čopova ulica 38 ☎01 200 9060, ⓦ hostel-tresor.si; map p.46. This former bank building has been utilized to great effect: the spacious dorms are wonderfully bright and the old vaults now function as the breakfast room and games/chill-out area. Breakfast €3. Dorms **€12**, doubles **€36**

Vila Veselova Veselova ulica 14 ☎059 926 721, ⓦ vila veselovahostel.com; map p.44. Delightful, charmingly staffed hostel in a historic villa bordering peaceful Tivoli Park, with large, colour-themed dorms and one en-suite private room. Breakfast included. Dorms **€22**, double **€60**

Zeppelin Hostel Slovenska cesta 47 ☎059 191 427, ⓦ zeppelinhostel.com; map p.46. Bright, breezy and very sociable hostel just a 5min walk from the stations, with four-, six- and ten-bed dorms as well as doubles with or without bathroom. Breakfast included. Dorms **€22**, doubles **€64**

CAMPSITE

Ljubljana Resort Dunajska cesta 270 ☎01 589 0130, ⓦ ljubljanaresort.si; map p.44. Superbly equipped site 4km north of the centre in Ježica, which also has fully furnished chalets sleeping four – the resort's superb facilities include a water park, beach volleyball courts, play area, restaurant, bar and shop. Bus #6 or #8 from Slovenska cesta. Per person **€13.70**

EATING

As befits its sophisticated image, Ljubljana boasts a tight concentration of first-rate **restaurants**, including a dozen or so truly outstanding establishments, with the likes of *AS*, *Manna* and *Strelec* leading the way. Although the majority of places offer predominantly Slovene, Balkan and international food, there is the occasional very good Asian restaurant to be found. During the summer, **alfresco dining** is a big hit with locals, and many of the restaurants that we review offer outdoor seating in the warmer months. Although prices in Ljubljana are higher than in most other places in Slovenia, you can still eat tremendously well without breaking the bank: expect to pay around €18–20 for a two-course meal with a glass of wine in an average establishment, and around €25–30 in the more expensive places. If you're fending for yourself, head for Plečnik's splendid **Market Colonnade**, curving along the east bank of the Ljubljanica between the Triple Bridge and the Dragon Bridge, where you'll find excellent little food shops (Mon–Fri 7am–4pm, Sat 7am–2pm). Otherwise, the excellent **City Market** (summer Mon–Fri 6am–6pm, Sat 6am–4pm; winter Mon–Sat 6am–4pm), on Vodnikov trg, is the best place to stock up on fresh produce, and there are fish, meat and dairy products for sale down in the basement of the Seminary building on adjacent Pogačarjev trg. The best city-centre **supermarket** is in the basement of the Maximarket shopping centre on Trg Republike (Mon–Fri 9am–9pm, Sat 8am–5pm).

1

SNACKS AND FAST FOOD

Ajdovo Zrno Trubarjeva cesta 7 ☎ 040 832 446, ⓦ ajdovo-zrno.si; map p.46. Bright and cheerful veggie canteen in a pleasant off-street courtyard, with a self-service salad bar, soups, sandwiches and tortillas (€3–4), plus daily specials such as cannelloni and risotto. Sit down or takeaway. Mon–Fri 8am–5pm.

Falafel Trubarjeva cesta 40 ☎ 041 640 166, ⓦ falafel .si; map p.46. Popular little sit-down or takeaway joint offering delicious falafel-based snacks, as well as sand-wiches, kebabs, salads and baklava. Mon–Sat 10am–midnight, Sun 1–10pm.

Klobasarna Ciril-Metodov trg 15 ☎ 051 605 017, ⓦ klobasarna.si; map p.46. There's one item on the menu: sausage. But what a sausage it is – the mighty *kranjska klobasa* comes sliced and served with a roll and huge dollops of mustard and horseradish (€5.90). It's not sophisticated, but it does the job. Mon–Sat 10am–11pm, Sun 10am–3pm.

Paninoteka Jurčičev trg 3 ☎ 040 349 329; map p.46. With a cracking riverside setting by the Shoemakers' Bridge, this cool little sandwich bar serves up a range of piping hot panini and ciabattas, wraps, toasts and salads. Sit down or takeaway. Mon–Thurs 9am–11pm, Fri & Sat 9am–midnight, Sun 9am–10pm.

Ribca Adamič-Lundrovo nabrežje 1 ☎ 01 425 1544, ⓦ ribca.si; map p.46. Terrific fish snack bar on the lower floor of the Market Colonnade, serving generous plates of grilled and fried squid, sardines, seafood salads and soups (creamy crab), all for around €4–5. Sit down or takeaway. Mon 8am–4pm, Tues–Sat 8am–9pm, Sun 11am–8pm.

CAFÉS

Bi-Ko-Fe Židovska steza 2 ☎ 01 425 9393; map p.46. Artsy, colourful and chilled-out café attracting students, artists, designers and that ilk – the largely recycled furnishings make for a pleasing backdrop, while there's an imaginative range of drinks available, both alcoholic and non-alcoholic. Mon–Fri 7am–1am, Sat & Sun 10am–1am.

Cacao Petkovškovo nabrežje 3 ☎ 01 430 1772, ⓦ cacao .si; map p.46. Despite stiff competition, the general consensus is that this stylish riverside café-bar serves the city's best ice cream; take your pick from delicious flavours like pistachio, melon and forest strawberry (€1.80/scoop), or just kick back with a refreshing fruit juice or coffee. Daily 8am–midnight.

Čajna Hiša Stari trg 3 ☎ 01 421 2440, ⓦ cha.si; map p.46. Bijou teahouse manifesting a lovely dose of old-world charm and offering a divine range of teas from around the world, as well as excellent sandwiches and cakes and decent breakfasts. Invariably packed with locals, which tells you all you need to know. Mon–Fri 9am–8pm, Sat 9am–3pm, Sun 10am–2pm.

★ **Čokl** Krekov trg 8 ☎ 041 837 556, ⓦ cafecokl.si; map p.46. It's still pretty hard to find quality coffee in Ljubljana – but here you're on to a winner. Caffeine connoisseurs are well catered for in this cosy, happily careworn café, thanks to a fine selection of coffee made with single-estate beans; moreover, the genial owner, Tine, will delight in explaining every brewing method possible. On a warm day, try a cup of deliciously refreshing cold-pressed coffee. Mon–Fri 7am–11pm, Sat 9am–11pm, Sun 9am–8pm.

Le Petit Café Trg Francoske revolucije 4 ☎ 01 251 2575, ⓦ lepetit.si; map p.46. A small slice of Paris at this eternally busy and wonderfully atmospheric street-corner café opposite Križanke; perfect for a steaming *bela kava* and croissant for breakfast or a glass of wine in the evening. Daily 7.30am–1am.

Kavarna Moderna Cankarjeva cesta 15 ☎ 01 241 6800; map p.46. It's rare to find such a classy café inside a visitor attraction, but this place – part of the Museum of Modern Art (see p.60) – bucks that trend big-time. The contemporary, Scandinavian-style interior features cool grey sofas and lots of natural wood, while the coffee is brewed in all manner of ways: syphon, French Press, chemex and so on. They offer cakes, too. Tues–Sun 10am–10pm.

Vigo Stritarjeva ulica 4 ☎ 082 056 428, ⓦ vigo -icecream.com; map p.46. Running a very close second to *Cacao* – with many contending that this is actually *the* place to get your ice cream. Some of the flavours are simply divine: try mascarpone with chocolate, pistachio with hazelnut, or almond with coffee and amaretto (one scoop €1.50). Mon Sat 9am–11pm, Sun 9.30am–10pm.

★ **Ziferblat** Vegova ulica 8 ☎ 040 289 988, ⓦ ljubljana .ziferblat.net; map p.46. The concept is as simple as it is brilliant: the longer you stay, the more you pay (€0.50/min, €3/hr); and for that, all your drinks (sadly, none of the alcoholic variety) are free, as is use of the considerable space/facilities, amply filled with recycled and vintage furnishings, so you can read, paint, play an instrument or, if you fancy a kip, chill on a hammock. Daily 9am–10pm.

Zvezda Wolfova ulica 14 ☎ 01 421 9090, ⓦ zvezda ljubljana.si; map p.46. Named after the eponymous pre-World War II café in the Kazina building further up on Kongresni trg, this hugely popular hangout is the place to come for ices and pastries; the vaulted interior is lovely but the terrace is where most locals congregate. Mon–Sat 7am–11pm, Sun 10am–8pm.

RESTAURANTS

Gostilna As Čopova ulica 5a ☎ 01 425 8822, ⓦ gostilnaas.si; map p.46. Despite being a perennial favourite among local politicians and bigwigs, *As* is far from pretentious – nor is it extortionate, with dishes like home-made pappardelle with shrimps and cognac sauce (€19), baked Black Alaskan cod in miso (€23) and pannacotta with plum sauce in Teran wine (€6). Reservations essential. Daily noon–1am.

Café Romeo Stari trg 6 ☎040 706 070, ☜caferomeo .si; map p.46. Located opposite *Julija* (see below), naturally, *Romeo's* wide-ranging, if slightly less sophisticated, menu slants obviously towards Mexican – tacos, burritos and the like. Good for late-night munchies, and it also has a first-class cocktail menu. Daily 10am–1am.

★**Gostilna Dela** Poljanska cesta 7 ☎051 491 491; map p.46. The premise behind this bustling little daytime restaurant is to help those from disadvantaged groups, in a similar vein to Jamie Oliver's *Fifteen*. The daily menu is short, typically consisting of one soup, one meat (for example, roast veal with carrot mash) and one fish dish (maybe sea bream on barley risotto), and a dessert, but that matters little when the food tastes this good; each dish goes for around €7 a pop. Mon–Fri 8am–4pm.

Druga Violina Stari trg 21 ☎082 052 506; map p.46. Occupying an enviable Old Town spot, this delightful restaurant – part of a very laudable project to help people with disabilities assimilate into mainstream society – specializes in simple Slovenian classics like *jota* and *štruklji*, with mains typically around €5. Daily 8am–midnight.

Foculus Gregorčičeva ulica 3 ☎01 421 9295, ☜foculus .si; map p.46. Despite some strong competition, this long-standing and flamboyantly decorated pizzeria still ranks as one of Ljubljana's best, offering an exhaustive range of pizzas (including dessert pizzas) in lively surroundings, including a better-than-average vegetarian and seafood selection, and a generous salad buffet. Daily 11am–midnight.

Gostilna na Gradu Grajska Planota 1 ☎082 051 930, ☜nagradu.si; map p.46. The second of two superb restaurants located up in the castle grounds, "At the Castle" is run by the same team behind the wonderful *Hiša Franko* in Kobarid (see p.169), which gives you some idea of what to expect. While it's not quite in that league, the food remains a class above most places in town. Mon–Sat 10am–midnight, Sat noon–6pm.

Gujžina Mestni trg 19 ☎083 806 446, ☜prekmurska -gostilna.si; map p.46. If you don't manage to make it to Prekmurje in eastern Slovenia – and unfortunately few people do – then you'll have to content yourself with sampling some of the region's rather fine dishes here, which is generally heavier than elsewhere in the country. Perhaps try the *bograč*, a rich, spicy stew of pork with dumplings, garlic, onions and pepper served in a copper "goulash kettle" (€10.80), and don't leave without tasting the region's delicious pumpkin oil – it's terrific on ice cream. Daily 8am–midnight.

Julija Stari trg 9 ☎01 425 6463, ☜julijarestaurant .com; map p.46. A perennial Old Town favourite with both locals and visitors alike, this cheery restaurant serves up a tempting mix of Mediterranean inspired-dishes like

risotto with prawn tails and cherry tomatoes, and homespun Slovenian food such as grilled turkey with ceps and baked polenta. In summer, the tables strung along the cobbled street outside are enormously popular. Daily 11.30am–midnight.

Kralj Žara Trubarjeva cesta 52 ☎01 232 0990, ☜restaurant.kraljzara.si; map p.46. Hidden away down a cobblestone alley just off the main street, this cool, split-level smokehouse is the real deal when it comes to big hunks of meat; whether it's a burger or a steak you're after, you'll not find tastier or better cuts anywhere else in the city. Mon–Sat 11am–11pm.

Odprta Kuhna Pogačarjev trg ☜odprtakuhna.si; map p.46. Each Fri between mid-March and Oct, the locals flock to the terrific *Odprta Kuhna* (Open Kitchen), a buzzing open-air food market where some of the city's (and Slovenia's) very best establishments (including *Strelec* and *Gostilna As*) serve sample (and cheaper) portions of their restaurant dishes. There are also stalls selling many cuisines that you might not otherwise find in the city, with a phalanx of beer and wine sellers adding to the convivial atmosphere. Mid-March to Oct Fri 8am–10pm, weather permitting.

Okrepčevapnica Harambaša Trnovski pristan 4a ☎041 843 106, ☜harambasa.si; map p.46. Replicating a traditional Bosnian tavern, with low wooden tables and stools, and photos of old Sarajevo, this place is great fun; the menu features a handful of classic Bosnian dishes such as *pljeskavica* (oversized hamburger) and *čevapčiči* (rissoles of spiced minced meat) served with *kajmak* (creamy cheese) and *lepinja* (doughy bread), all for around €6–7. Round things off with a cup of Turkish coffee served in a *dzezva* (copper vessel) and a cube of Turkish delight. Mon–Fri 10am–10pm, Sat noon–10pm, Sun noon–6pm.

Pop's Place Cankarjevo nabrežje 3 ☎059 042 856; map p.46. You'll do well to grab a table in this tiny restaurant, but it's well worth the wait for the juiciest burgers and ribs in the city (€8–10); and to soak it all up, there's a terrific selection of craft beers. Daily noon–1am.

★**Pri Škofu** Rečna cesta 5 ☎01 426 4508; map p.46. Secreted away in a quiet residential street in Krakovo, this family-run restaurant is an absolute joy; the menu changes daily, but you're quite likely to see house specials like chestnut soup, home-made gnocchi with garlic, and pepper-encrusted tenderloin medallions (*biftek škof*) with fig sauce (€18) feature regularly. The small, warm terrace and simple, sunny interior round things off beautifully. Tues–Fri 10am–midnight, Sat & Sun noon–11pm.

Sarajevo '84 Nazorjeva ulica 12 ☎01 425 7106, ☜sarajevo84.si; map p.46. Decked out with sporting paraphernalia in homage to Sarajevo's staging of the winter Olympics, this fun bare-brick cellar restaurant serves, among other things, the classic Balkan grilled meats, *čevapčiči* and *pljeskavica* (€7). Mon–Wed 11am–midnight, Thurs & Fri 11am–1am, Sat noon–2am.

1

Shambala Križevniška ulica 12 ☎031 843 833, ⓦshambala.si; map p.46. A cut above any of the city's other Asian restaurants, this beautifully conceived place offers food from several countries; the dishes are simply stunning, both in their taste and execution, for example Vietnamese salad rolls with green papaya and sour mango, and miso-marinated back cod fillet with pineapple and snow peas (€15.50). Mon–Sat noon–10.30pm.

Špajza Gornji trg 28 ☎01 425 3094, ⓦspajza -restaurant.si; map p.46. One of Ljubljana's most enduringly popular restaurants. The elegant rustic trappings complement the expertly cooked Slovene food superbly; smoked trout with horseradish, *žlikrofi* with shrimp tails (€12) and (though perhaps not to everyone's taste) horse fillet with truffles (€24) are just some of the

treats on offer. First-class selection of wines, too. Daily noon–11pm.

★**Strelec** Grajska Planota 1 ☎031 687 648, ⓦkaval -group.si; map p.46. This place is secreted away in Ljubljana Castle's Archer's Tower – climb the elegant spiral staircase to emerge into an artfully designed room whose rust-red stone walls are painted with scenes of medieval battle. The super-talented young chef, Igor Jagodic, conjures up beautifully crafted and technically accomplished dishes such as veal tongue with smoked eel and horseradish mayonnaise, or buckwheat croquettes stuffed with duck liver, black walnuts and fir-tree foam. This is Ljubljana dining at its most exciting. Set menus from €28. Mon–Thurs 11am–10pm, Fri & Sat 11am–11pm, Sun 11am–5pm.

DRINKING

A drink on a warm summer's evening in one of the many convivial **cafés and bars** strung along the banks of the **Ljubljanica** is one of the city's great joys. Alternatively, a wander up and down **Mestni trg** and **Stari trg** will yield an interesting venue every 50m or so, and the clutch of energetic bars in **Knafljev prehod** (the courtyard area between Wolfova ulica and Slovenska cesta) are usually packed to the rafters.

Daktari Krekov trg 7 ☎059 055 538, ⓦdaktari.si; map p.46. It's the decor that really makes this convivial place special, with restored antique furniture, corner piano and shelves packed with books. Expect a regular programme of live music, cabaret and jam sessions. Mon–Sat 8am–1am, Sun 9am–midnight.

★**Dvorni Bar** Dvorni trg 2 ☎01 251 1257, ⓦdvornibar .net; map p.46. If you don't get to any of Slovenia's beautiful wine-growing regions, fear not; this classy bar, with tables spilling across the square and down to the river, has offerings from all over the country, be it the straw-coloured Rebula from Goriška Brda or the ruby-red Teran from the Karst (€3–4/glass); you can munch on a delicious selection of tapas-style bites, too. Mon–Sat 8am–1am, Sun 9am–midnight.

Lepa Žoga Celovška cesta 43 ☎01 432 3109; map p.44. Small, not too raucous sports café-bar near Tivoli Park, with shirts and other paraphernalia of the great and the good (mostly foreign sports stars) draped along the walls, and a constant diet of live TV sports, including most English Premier league football matches. Mon–Fri 6am–midnight, Sat & Sun 9am–midnight.

Maček Krojaška ulica 5 ☎01 425 3791; map p.46. The most popular of the string of hip cafés on the right bank of the Ljubljanica. The exuberant terrace is the place to see and be seen, and consequently always rammed; on cooler evenings, the brightly painted orange interior is a no less congenial spot to sup a beer. Mon–Sat 9am–12.30am, Sun 9am–11pm.

Movia Mestni trg 2 ☎051 304 590, ⓦmovia.si; map p.46. This snug little wine bar next to the Town Hall is second only to *Dvorni Bar* (see above) as a place to sample

Slovenian wines, though they do tend to lean towards those from their own winery in Goriška Brda (see p.160). Mon–Sat noon–11pm.

Pritličje Mestni trg 5 ☎040 204 693, ⓦpritlicje.si; map p.46. Dynamic cultural centre that functions as a café-bar by day and live music venue come dusk; expect all kinds of fun happenings on a daily basis. No less intriguingly, it's also home to the city's only comic book store. Mon–Wed & Sun 9am–1am, Thurs–Sat 9am–3am.

Sax Pub Eipprova cesta 7 ☎051 804 450; map p.46. The colourful, albeit now slightly faded, spray-painted *Sax* has been a fixture on the city's pub scene for years, popular for both its idyllic canal-side setting and live jazz (Thurs evenings). Mon–Sat 9am–1am, Sun 9am–10pm.

Tozd Gallusovo nabrežje 27 ☎040 699 453; map p.46. Down by the quieter, southern stretch of the river, this is a great spot to try some unusual coffees (they roast their own beans here) or cool off with a craft beer at sundown – they offer free tastings on Thurs afternoons. The hip brick and enamel interior – the centrepiece being a funky, retro-style kitchen counter – is plastered with all manner of random objects. Daily 8.30am–midnight.

★**Union Pivnica** Celovška cesta 22 ☎01 471 7335, ⓦpivnica-union.si; map p.46. Prepare for a rollicking good time at this cavernous, industrial-styled bar inside the brewery of the same name, selling a delicious range of pale, dark and amber ales – including some scrumptious unfiltered versions – alongside juicy beer sausages to soak it all up. Mon–Thurs 11am–midnight, Fri & Sat 11am–1am, Sun noon–5pm.

Žmauc Rimska cesta 21 ☎01 251 0324; map p.46. The graffiti-daubed exterior of this eternally popular, happy hippy dive gives some indication of what to expect – the small, buzzy terrace is packed with locals at pretty much any time of the day. Whether you're pitching up for a coffee or a beer, it's great fun. Mon–Fri 7.30am–1am, Sat 10am–1am, Sun 6pm–1am.

NIGHTLIFE

When it comes to **nightlife**, the city has always maintained a strong independent spirit, and many of its progressive **clubs** and venues double up as multicultural, arts-type centres. Festival seasons aside, Ljubljana offers a reasonable, if rather Balkan-centric, diet of **live music**, though it does suffer from having few decent **gig venues**; exceptions are Cankarjev Dom (see below) and the marvellous open-air Križanke complex, with bigger names playing at Tivoli Hall, in Tivoli Park.

Jazz Club Gajo Beethovnova ulica 8 ☎031 337 525, ⓦjazzclubgajo.com; map p.46. Named after its owner, this refined late-night jazz club triumphs with its stellar line-up of domestic and foreign acts. Jam sessions on Mon from 9pm. Between May and Sept, the club has performances at a fabulous outdoor garden on Cankarjeva cesta, across from the National Gallery. Mon–Sat 9am–midnight, Sun 9am–10pm.

K4 Kersnikova ulica 4 ⓦklubk4.org; map p.46. Stalwart of Ljubljana's alternative scene, offering some of the best music in the city – mainly electronic, but also rock, jazz, hip-hop and folk, plus gay nights. Student parties and performance art too. Days and hours vary.

Klub Cirkus Trg mladinskih delovnih brigad 7 ☎051 631 631, ⓦcirkusklub.si; map p.44. Occupying a former cinema-theatre building just a few minutes' walk from the centre, this vast two-storey space is currently the city's most popular straightforward clubbing experience; everything from R&B and house to electronica and disco. Wed, Fri & Sat 10pm–5am.

KUD Prešeren Karunova ulica 14 ☎01 283 2288, ⓦkud.si; map p.46. Superb, long-standing gig venue in the Trnovo district that also organizes regular literary events, workshops (including some for kids) and art exhibitions. There's a fine little café here too. Also stages the excellent *Trnfest* festival (see box, p.74). Mon–Sat 10am–1am, Sun 2pm–1am.

Metelkova mesto Metelkova cesta ⓦmetelkovamesto.org; map p.44. Ljubljana's legendary counter-cultural hub consisting of a cosmopolitan gang of left-field clubs, bars and NGOs (collectively entitled Metelkova) located in the former army barracks; venues include *Channel Zero* (dance), *Gala Hala* (punk/metal), *Mizzart* (lo-fi), *Klub Monokel* (lesbian only), *Tiffany* (gay) and *Gromki* (performance). Days and hours vary.

Orto Bar Grablovičeva ulica 1 ☎01 232 1674, ⓦorto-bar.com; map p.44. This good-time haunt a couple of blocks east of the train station has regular late-night club evenings; it's also the city's main small live-rock venue, and you can bank on finding at least a couple of gigs a week here. Tues & Wed 9pm–1am, Thurs 9pm–4am, Fri & Sat 9pm–5am.

ENTERTAINMENT

Ljubljana offers a surprisingly rich diet of **classical culture** for its size, with well-established orchestral, operatic and theatrical companies, and there's a good chance you'll catch something whatever time of the year you're here – although most of these institutions close down in July and Aug, by way of compensation there's plenty going on as part of the annual **Ljubljana Festival** (see box, p.74).

CINEMAS

Cankarjev Dom Prešernova cesta 10 ☎01 241 7299, ⓦcd-cc.si. Occasional screenings at this arts centre, which is also the principal venue for the two-week Ljubljana International Film Festival (LIFFe) in Nov.

Kinodvor Kolodvorska ulica 13 ☎01 239 2217, ⓦkinodvor.org. The best of the few remaining downtown cinemas, this excellent two-screen arthouse shows a diverse selection of domestic and foreign films; tickets are great value at €5.30 (€3.80 on Mon). There's also a fabulous bar for a pre- or post-film drink or two.

Kinoteka Miklošičeva cesta 28 ☎01 434 2524, ⓦkinoteka.si. Probably even more alternative than Kinodvor, this well-regarded, long-standing cinema shows premieres, cult classics and retrospectives; also a popular venue for festival screenings. Tickets €4.

CONCERT VENUES AND THEATRES

Cankarjev Dom Prešernova cesta 10 ☎01 241 7299, ⓦcd-cc.si. Enormous arts and convention centre staging major orchestral and theatrical events, folk and jazz concerts and art exhibitions. The box office is in the underpass of the Maximarket shopping centre. Mon–Fri 11am–1pm & 3–8pm, Sat 11am–1pm; also 1hr before each performance.

Križanke Trg Francoske revolucije 1 ☎01 241 6026, ⓦljubljanafestival.si. Plečnik's inspirational outdoor music venue (with a retractable roof) is *the* place to attend a concert, be it rock, pop, jazz or classical. Its main function, however, is as the principal venue for the Ljubljana Festival (see p.74). Festival box office Mon–Fri 10am–1.30pm & 4–8pm, Sat 10am–1pm; also 1hr before each performance.

1

FESTIVALS AND EVENTS: THE LJUBLJANA YEAR

MARCH

Slovenian Musical Days Mid-March. Four or five days of concerts performed principally by the Slovene philharmonic and RTV symphonic orchestras.

MAY AND JUNE

Druga Godba ("The Other Music") End May; ⓦ drugagodba.si. In the wonderful surroundings of Križanke, the ethno-alternative music festival is one of the year's most enjoyable music events, attracting a terrific line-up of domestic and international acts.

Ljubljana Jazz Festival End June; ⓦ ljubljanajazz.si. Slovenia's premier jazz festival features five days of world-class concerts, most of which are held in the atmospheric surrounds of the Križanke.

Ljubljana Festival End June to mid-Sept; ⓦ ljubljanafestival.si. The city's major annual event, taking in all genres of music, art, theatre and dance. Mostly takes place in Križanke and the castle courtyard.

JULY AND AUGUST

Film Under the Stars July. The castle courtyard is the setting for a nightly screening of blockbusters, classics and premieres in the open-air, weather permitting.

Ana Desetnica Festival of Street Theatre July. The streets of the Old Town burst into life with a seemingly nonstop programme of wonderful and often wacky street performances.

TrnFest Throughout Aug. A boutique summer festival, organized by *KUD* (see p.73), with gigs, exhibitions, workshops and screenings – plus a good programme for kids.

SEPTEMBER TO NOVEMBER

International Biennial of Graphic Arts Sept & Oct, every odd-numbered year. The city's foremost artistic event, held at Tivoli Castle – one of the premier exhibitions of its kind in Europe.

City of Women International Festival of Contemporary Art Mid-Oct; ⓦ cityofwomen.org. A fortnight of female artists' exhibitions, as well as theatre and performance.

Ljubljana International Film Festival (LIFFe) Mid-Nov; ⓦ liffe.si. Two weeks showcasing a selection of mostly European films at Cankarjev Dom.

National Drama Theatre Erjavčeva cesta 1 ⓐ 01 252 1511, ⓦ drama.si. Despite the unappealing muddy-green exterior, this is the city's premier theatre, staging performances since 1911. Box office Mon–Fri 11am–8pm, Sat from 6pm until the start of performance; also 1hr before each performance.

National Opera and Ballet Theatre Župančičeva ulica 1 ⓐ 01 241 5959, ⓦ opera.si. Slovenia's opera and ballet companies are housed in this grandiloquent Neoclassical building, with suitably high-class programmes to boot. Ticket office Mon–Fri 10am–1pm & 2–6pm, Sat 10am–1pm; also 1hr before each performance.

Philharmonic Hall Kongresni trg 10 ⓐ 01 241 0800, ⓦ filharmonija.si. This resplendent building is home to Ljubljana's energetic and highly regarded Slovenska Filharmonija, one of the world's oldest orchestras.

Puppet theatre (Lutkovno Gledališie) Krekov trg 2 ⓐ 01 300 0982, ⓦ lgl.si. Much-loved theatre company with a regular programme of shows throughout the year that will appeal even to non-native speakers. Ticket office Mon–Fri 9am–7pm, Sat 9am–1pm; also 1hr before each performance.

SHOPPING

There are few shopping areas of note within the city centre itself, although the streets and squares of the **Old Town**, particularly between Ciril-Metodov trg and Stari trg, yield some fabulous gift and food shops, variously specializing in chocolate, honey, salt, olive oil and brandy. Otherwise, most locals do their shopping out at the enormous **BTC shopping complex** (Mon–Sat 9am–8pm; ⓦ btc-city.com), 1.5km east of town on Šmartinska cesta (buses #2, #7 and #12).

3Muhe Stari trg 30 ⓐ 01 421 0715, ⓦ 3muhe.si; map p.46. The colourful "Three Flies" is the city's only Fairtrade shop, selling jewellery, ceramics, textiles and food items, among other things; they also stock products by Smetumet,

an innovative local company that produces a brilliant range of upcycled items, such as belts, handbags and notebooks. Mon–Fri 10am–7.30pm, Sat 10am–2pm.

Flea Market Right bank of the Ljubljanica, roughly

1

between the Triple Bridge and the Shoemakers' Bridge; map p.46. A great place to browse on a Sun morning; you can find just about anything and everything, from old records, books and stamps to furniture, musical instruments and Tito-era memorabilia. Sun 8am–1pm.

Ika Ciril-Metodov trg 13 ☎ 01 232 1743, ⓦ trgovinaika .si; map p.46. The pick of the many (classy) souvenir shops in the Old Town, *Ika* showcases handmade design products by local artists, typically art, clothing (including footwear) and pottery (the caricature mugs are ace). Look out, too, for the Funky Dragon products, in particular the postcards, the coolest in town. Mon–Fri 10am–7.30pm, Sat 9am–6pm, Sun 10am–2pm.

Mladinska Knjiga Slovenska cesta 29 ☎ 01 241 4684; map p.46. The city's largest bookshop comfortably has the largest selection of English-language books around (including what few books there are on Slovene history in English), plus an extensive travel section with all the maps you'll ever need on the country. Mon–Fri 8am–8pm, Sat 9am–3pm.

Spin Vinyl Gallusovo nabrežje 13 ☎ 01 251 1018, ⓦ spinvinyl.si; map p.46. If you're on the lookout for music – or just want to know what's happening on the local music scene – try this cult secondhand store; they have the best selection of music from Slovenia and the other ex-Yugoslav republics, on vinyl and CD, plus loads more. Mon–Fri 11am–7pm, Sat 11am–2pm, Sun 11am–1pm.

Vinoteka Dvor Dvorni trg 2 ☎ 01 251 3644, ⓦ kozelj.si; map p.46. The finest selection of Slovenian wines in the city, with genuinely helpful and knowledgeable staff. Mon–Fri 10am–8pm, Sat 10am–2pm.

DIRECTORY

Embassies and consulates Australia, Železna cesta 14 (☎ 01 234 8675); Canada, Linhartova cesta 49a (☎ 01 252 4444); Ireland, Poljanski nasip 6 (☎ 01 300 8970); UK, Trg Republike 3/IV (☎ 01 200 3910); US, Prešernova cesta 31 (☎ 01 200 5500).

Health For all emergency treatment go to the University Medical Centre Ljubljana at Zaloška cesta 7 (☎ 01 522 5050). For emergency dental treatment, contact the Central Ljubljana Community Health Centre at Metelkova ulica 9 (☎ 01 472 3718).

Internet WiFree Ljubljana (ⓦ wifreeljubljana.si) allows 1hr/day of free wi-fi throughout the city centre. Otherwise,

the Slovenian Tourist Information Centre (see p.67) has several terminals.

Pharmacies Central Pharmacy, Prešernov trg 5 (Mon–Fri 7.30am–7.30pm, Sat 8am–3pm; ☎ 01 244 2360 or ☎ 01 230 6100); Lekarna Ljubljana, Njegoševa 6 (☎ 01 230 230 6100), has a 24hr duty service.

Police For accidents and emergencies go to Trdinova 10 (☎ 01 475 0600).

Post offices The two main central offices are at Slovenska cesta 32 (Mon–Fri 8am–7pm, Sat 8am–noon) and Pražakova ulica 1 (Mon–Fri 8am–6pm, Sat 8am–noon).

Northwest Slovenia

VELIKA PLANINA

Northwest Slovenia

With by far the highest profile of any region in Slovenia, Gorenjska, the country's northwestern province, offers an outstanding synthesis of natural and cultural heritage, from dramatic alpine mountains, valleys and lakes to startlingly pretty medieval towns and villages. The defining feature here is the Julian Alps, a majestic limestone range packed with sawtoothed peaks, fantastical gorges and ravines, deep mountain lakes and dozens of waterfalls.

Most of the Slovene part of the **Julian Alps** – a small portion spills over into neighbouring Italy – falls within **Triglav National Park**. This is Slovenia's only designated national park, centring on **Mount Triglav**, which at 2864m is the country's highest and most exalted peak. Bordering Austria to the north are two further mountain ranges: the slender **Karavanke** chain, and, east of here, the **Kamniške Savinje Alps**, whose gloriously tapered peaks strongly resemble the Julians in parts. The tangle of well-worn paths furrowed across these three ranges heaves with hikers during the summer, though the crowds, rarely oppressive, are easily avoided. The region is also superb for adrenaline sports – typically, whitewater rafting, canyoning, hydrospeed and paragliding – as well as gentler pursuits including cycling, horseriding, fishing and swimming. Moreover, Gorenjska possesses the country's densest concentration of ski resorts, not least **Kranjska Gora**, in the north of the region, which is also a fabulous summer playground. At the tail end of the Alps are Slovenia's celebrated alpine resorts, the most popular of which is **Bled**, a once fashionable health resort whose enchanting lake is now one of the country's premier attractions. For many though, Lake Bled is surpassed by **Lake Bohinj** to the southwest, a fjord-like body of water settled amid gorgeous mountain scenery and bound by a huddle of sleepy villages.

The most engaging of Gorenjska's many small towns are the medieval settlements of **Kamnik**, sheltered under the Kamniške Alps north of Ljubljana, and **Škofja Loka**, northwest of the capital on the fringe of some delightful rolling countryside; meanwhile, **Kranj**, Gorenjska's largest city and its key commercial and industrial centre, masks a surprisingly endearing old core. Elsewhere, **Radovljica** is worthy of a stop-off thanks to its fascinating Beekeeping Museum, as is the exquisite iron-working village of **Kropa** and nearby **Brezje**, site of Slovenia's most important pilgrimage church.

ŠKOFJA LOKA

Highlights

❶ Velika Planina This alluring highland plain is spotted with herdsmen's huts, and offers wonderful walking opportunities. See **p.84**

❷ Škofja Loka Compact and elegant Škofja Loka is one of Slovenia's most beautifully preserved medieval towns. See **p.86**

❸ Kropa Comely one-street village with a rich and fascinating iron-forging heritage. See **p.103**

❹ Lake Bled A fairytale lake complete with a romantic island church and cliff-top castle. See **p.107**

❺ Lake Bohinj Fish, swim, take a boat ride – or simply enjoy a stroll around Slovenia's most stunning lake. See **p.117**

❻ Hiking in the Julian Alps Superb hiking and climbing, including, for the more adventurous, Mount Triglav, the country's highest peak. See **p.119**

❼ Planica Visit the cradle of Slovenian sport and marvel at the daring feats of the world's greatest ski-jumpers at the magnificent Planica Nordic Centre. See **p.130**

❽ Vršič Pass Slovenia's most spectacular mountain pass incorporates fifty hairpin bends, with dozens of attractions along the way. See **p.133**

HIGHLIGHTS ARE MARKED ON THE MAP ON P.80

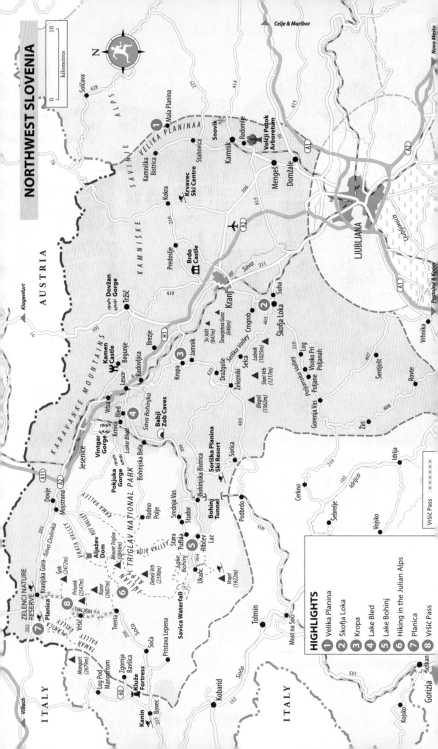

NORTHWEST SLOVENIA

N

0 — 10
kilometres

Celje & Maribor

Novo Mesto

AUSTRIA

Klagenfurt

ITALY

ITALY

Villach

Postojna & Koper

LJUBLJANA

HIGHLIGHTS

1. Velika Planina
2. Škofja Loka
3. Kropa
4. Lake Bled
5. Lake Bohinj
6. Hiking in the Julian Alps
7. Planica
8. Vršič Pass

Vršič Pass

Most places in Northwest Slovenia can be reached easily from Ljubljana, and, with the exception of the park interior, getting around the region is straightforward.

By car Save for a couple of key roads – notably the serpentine Vršič Pass, which forges a spectacularly scenic route across the mountains between Kranjska Gora and Trenta (in the Soča Valley) – access within Triglav Park is fairly limited, so having your own vehicle will make life much easier. There are quick and easy crossings into Italy and Austria, the former reached via the main road that bypasses Kranjska Gora, and the latter

via the Karavanke tunnel, under the mountains near Jesenice, and the Ljubelj tunnel north of Tržič.

By train Trains serve most key places, and a useful car train (see box, p.114) runs between Bohinjska Bistrica and Most na Soči.

By bus Buses offer faster and more frequent connections than trains in Northwest Slovenia.

Kamnik and around

Hemmed in by thick forests at the foot of the Kamniške Alps, **KAMNIK** – 23km north of Ljubljana – is one of Slovenia's prettiest medieval towns and a major staging post for hikers and skiiers heading onwards to the nearby alpine resorts. A market borough in the thirteenth century, the town established itself as a key trade and crafts centre during the Middle Ages, though the later creation of alternative routes left the town somewhat out on a limb. Industrialization and the construction of the Ljubljana–Kamnik railway in the nineteenth century played a part in its revival, as did the popularity of its thermal spas, frequented by both Ljubljančani and Austrians.

Nowadays, Kamnik is a sleepy, old-fashioned place that really only ever comes alive during its two major festivals: **Kamfest**, in August, constitutes three weeks of music and dance centred on Mali Grad, while the **National Costumes Festival** on the second weekend of September sees groups from Slovenia's many regions dress up in their most colourful gear. Nevertheless, the town's spruce, neatly preserved medieval old town, castles and museums warrant a trip any time. Most of Kamnik's attractions lie east and south of **Glavni trg** (Main Square), the town's focal point.

Frančiškanski samostan and Cerkev Sv Jakoba

Frančiškanski trg 2 • Contact the tourist office (see p.84) to visit • Free

Dating from 1495, the centrepiece of the **Frančiškanski samostan** (Franciscan Monastery) is its library, which holds some ten thousand volumes, including a fine collection of incunabula (books printed before 1501), a copy of Dalmatin's translation of the Bible (1584), and numerous editions by Stanislav Škrabec, former friar and Slovenia's most eminent linguist (see p.216).

Adjoining the monastery, **Cerkev Sv Jakoba** (Church of St Jacob) was also built in the fifteenth century but redesigned in Baroque style in the late seventeenth century. Otherwise unexceptional, the church is a must-see for Plečnik's extraordinary **Chapel of the Holy Grave**, positioned to the right of the high altar – charged with images of war, the great architect (see box, p.49) cast the altar in the shape of a bullet (actually meant to symbolize Christ's rock tomb), lined the walls with rows of studded lights (meant to represent helmets), and shaped the door knob into a dove's head, to symbolize peace.

Mali Grad

Chapel Daily: mid-June to mid-Sept 9am–7pm; mid-Sept to mid-June contact the tourist office (see p.84) • €2.50

Occupying a hillock south of Glavni trg, **Mali Grad** (Little Castle) is the town's most evocative building. At the summit, on the eastern tip of the ruins, sits the whitewashed, two-storey **Romanesque chapel and crypt**, parts of which date from the eleventh

2

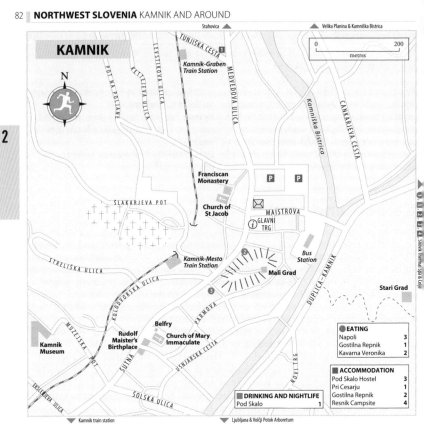

century, making it one of Slovenia's oldest surviving ecclesiastical monuments. The exquisite upper chapel, much strengthened and remodelled, contains remnants of some superb fifteenth-century late-Gothic frescoes illustrating several venerated saints, while the lower chapel is notable for some paintings by Janez Potočnik. From the balcony, the views of the Alps are fantastic.

Several decades of ongoing research have revealed some intriguing finds around the castle site, including the remains of a **Stone Age settlement** and some 27 graves from an Old Slavic burial ground believed to date from the tenth century – some finds are on display at the Kamnik Museum (see opposite). According to local myth, the castle is home to **Countess Veronika**, half-woman, half-snake, who is said to guard its hidden treasures jealously – whatever the truth, her legend lives on in the town seal.

Cerkev Marijinega brezmadežnega

Midway along **Šutna**, the town's attractive, crescent-shaped main street, lined with neat two-storey Baroque buildings, is the **Cerkev Marijinega brezmadežnega** (Church of Mary Immaculate), and next to it an enormous detached Gothic belfry. Preceded by two earlier churches, this eighteenth-century building features a Renaissance-style altar by Ivan Vurnik – well known for his decorative work in Ljubljana – while the frescoes on the presbytery walls, illustrating various feast days, are by Franc Jelovšek, and those on the nave by Matija Koželj. Note too the intricately cut relief above the portal entrance, which depicts a lamb with vine leaves.

Rojstna Hiša Rudolfa Maistra

Šutna 16 • Tues–Sat 10am–6pm • €2.50 • ☏ 059 097 580, ⓦ muzej-kamnik-on.net

Kamnik's most enjoyable museum, the **Rojstna Hiša Rudolfa Maistra** (Rudolf Maister's Birthplace), pays homage to one of Slovenia's most distinguished military officers, who was born here in 1874. It was under Maister's command that the city of Maribor was liberated on November 23, 1918, now a designated national holiday. Not just a military hero, the thickly moustachioed Maister was also a key cultural figure, writing several volumes of poetry, often under the pseudonym of Vojanov (a subtle play on *vojsko*, meaning soldier); an original copy of *Poezije 1904* is on display here, alongside a clutch of personal effects including his officer's cap and half-broken sabre.

2

Kamnik muzej

Muzejska pot 3 • March–Oct Tues–Fri 8am–2pm & 4–6pm, Sat 10am–1pm & 4–6pm, Sun 10am–1pm; Nov–Feb Tues–Fri 8am–3pm, Sat & Sun 10am–1pm • €2.50 • ☏ 01 831 7662, ⓦ muzej-kamnik-on.net

On a gently sloping hillside across the rail tracks stands the sixteenth-century **Grad Zaprice** (Zaprice Castle), later renovated into a Baroque mansion and now housing the **Kamnik muzej** (Kamnik Museum). The collection kicks off with some fascinating archeological and ecclesiastical finds, among them an exquisite statuette of Jupiter, an exceptional wood-carved Renaissance sculpture of two soldiers, entitled *Guard of God's Grave*, and weaponry and keys from Mali Grad. The Town and Country exhibition considers the many local trades and crafts in the region – typically pottery, millinery and goldsmithing – alongside displays on bourgeois Kamnik life in the nineteenth century. The real highlight, however, is the exhibition on **Velika Planina**. This is named after local architect and mountaineer Vlasto Kopač (1913–2006), who was instrumental in fighting to retain the original herdsmen's settlements on Velika Planina while simultaneously helping to establish tourism on the mountain. Aside from his personal effects, there's a lovely assemblage of *pisave* (wooden seals) used in the production of Trnič cheese (see p.85), thick-set clothing and, of course, cowbells. Elsewhere, there's an exhibition of bentwood furniture, whose pioneer, Michael Thonet, was the first person to use wood-bending techniques to craft chairs and tables.

On the lawn in front of the museum are four one- and two-cell *kašče* or **granaries** – squat, thatched-roof structures that served as storehouses for alpine herdsmen in the mountain valleys. Prevalent in the nearby Tuhinj Valley (from where these are taken), this particular form of peasant architecture is common throughout Slovenia.

Volčji Potok Arboretum

Near the village of Radomlje, 4km south of Kamnik • Daily: March & Oct 8am–6pm; April–Aug 8am–8pm; Sept 8am–7pm; Nov–Feb 8am–4pm • €7.50 • ☏ 01 831 2345, ⓦ arboretum-vp.si

Volčji Potok Arboretum is Slovenia's largest and most important horticultural park. The great Slovene polymath Janez Vajkard Valvasor (see box, p.223) once described the park – it translates as "Wolf's Brook" – as "a great and fertile place, boasting superb meadows and most fruitful fields". It is no less appealing today, home to more than three thousand species of plants, shrubs and trees, all sensitively assimilated into the surrounding woodland. Most people make a beeline for the neatly manicured **French Garden**; just as lovely is the landscaped **English Park**, with its silky, perfectly trimmed lawns, and the **beech forests**, which are ideal for a gentle ramble. Although a beautiful place to visit at any time of year, the best time to come is April or May, when the daffodils and tulips are in full bloom.

ARRIVAL AND INFORMATION   KAMNIK

By train Trains from Ljubljana (Mon–Fri hourly; 40min) arrive at the main train station on Kranjska cesta, a 5min walk south of the main street, Šutna, but you're better off alighting at the next stop, Kamnik-Mesto, a short

2

stroll west of Glavni trg on Kolodvorska ulica; Kamnik–Graben, a couple of minutes further down the line, is the last stop.

By bus The bus station is on Maistrova ulica, barely a 2min walk to Glavni trg.

Destinations Kamniška Bistrica (3 daily; 25min); Ljubljana (every 15–30min; 40min); Volčji Potok (Mon–Fri 5 daily; 10min).

Tourist office Glavni trg 2 (July & Aug daily 9am–9pm; Sept–June Mon–Sat 9am–6pm, Sun 9am–2pm; ☏ 01 831 8250, ⓦ kamnik-tourism.si); they also have bikes for rent (first hour free, €2.50/hr thereafter).

ACTIVITIES

Spa The Snovik Thermal Spa (Mon, Tues, Thurs & Sun 9am–8pm, Wed, Fri & Sat 9am–10pm; €10 for 2hr, €14 day-ticket; ☏ 01 834 4100, ⓦ terme-snovik.si), 9km east of Kamnik out on the road towards Celje, incorporates indoor and outdoor pools, saunas and steam baths. From Kamnik there are just three buses a day (and four return buses) on weekdays.

ACCOMMODATON

Pod Skalo Hostel Maistrova ulica 32 ☏ 01 839 1233, ⓦ podskalo.si. Despite its location on a busy main road, this is a fine and friendly family-run hostel with a guesthouse feel. There's an attractive, timber-beamed ten-bed dorm, but most rooms are en-suite doubles. Dorm **€18**, doubles **€56**

Pri Cesarju Tunjiška cesta 1 ☏ 041 629 846, ⓦ pricesarju.si. The eleven rooms here (including triples) lack a certain sparkle, but they're spotless and it's the best option if you wish to stay in the centre of town; the crowns on the doors are in tribute to the time when Emperor Franz Jozef allegedly stayed here. Breakfast €6. **€58**

★**Gostilna Repnik** Vrhpolje 186 ☏ 01 839 1293, ⓦ gostilna-repnik.si. Some 2km north of Kamnik, this fabulous *gostilna* holds nine gorgeous rooms finished in natural wood and raw concrete, each of which extends a playful nod to Slovenia's rich natural and man-made heritage – featuring a log-built headboard, for example, or a mini-climbing wall. **€75**

Resnik Campsite 500m east of the centre ☏ 01 831 7314, ⓦ kampresnik.com. Small and basic roadside campsite, well shaded by trees and handily located opposite *Pod Skalo*, Kamnik's best pub. Reception 6–10pm; when it's closed, find a pitch and pay later. May–Sept. **€13**

EATING

Napoli Sadnikarjeva ulica 5 ☏ 01 839 2744, ⓦ picerija napoli.com. A creditable Italian offering fresh pizzas (€7.50) straight from its large brick-fired oven, plus pastas and risottos; the outside decking area looking up to Mali Grad is a nice spot to while away an hour or so with a cold beer. Mon–Thurs 11am–10pm, Fri & Sat 11am–11pm, Sun noon–10pm.

Gostilna Repnik Vrhpolje 186 ☏ 01 839 1293, ⓦ gostilna-repnik.si. As accomplished as its rooms, this warm and welcoming inn offers exceptional regional specialities; start with a glass of *rušovc* (pine-cone liqueur) before tucking into spinach dumplings with Trnič cheese (see opposite) and a steaming bowl of venison goulash. Tues–Fri 10am–10pm, Sat noon–10pm, Sun noon–3pm.

Kavarna Veronika Glavni trg 6 ☏ 040 804 464. Tucked away in a fabulous spot underneath Mali Grad, *Veronika*, named after the town's mythological countess, is Kamnik's central meeting place. Come for good, strong coffee and a tempting selection of sweet-toothed goodies – lemon or pear cake, perhaps, or ice cream. Daily 8am–10pm.

DRINKING AND NIGHTLIFE

Pod Skalo Maistrova ulica 32 ☏ 01 839 1233, ⓦ podskalo.si. Nightlife in Kamnik is scant, but this fun, boisterous pub – part of the hostel of the same name – is worth seeking out; a cracking atmosphere, local craft beer (Mali Grad), and live music most weekends between Sept and May. Mon–Thurs 7.30am–midnight, Fri & Sat 7.30am–1am, Sun 9am–10pm.

Velika Planina

11km north of Kamnik • **Cable car** (*žičnica*) June & Sept daily every 30min 8.30am–6pm; July & Aug Mon–Thurs every 30min 8.30am–6pm, Fri–Sun every 30min 8.30am–8pm; Oct–May Mon–Thurs every 2hr 9am–4pm, Fri–Sun hourly 9am–5pm • €13 return, €15 including chairlift; bikes can be taken free of charge • ⓦ velikaplanina.si

In the heart of the Kamniške-Savinje Alps, **Velika Planina** is a broad alpine plateau comprising grassy slopes, sinkholes and clusters of dwarf pines – as well as being one of Slovenia's prime dairy farming regions, it's a hugely popular destination for skiers and walkers. Touching a height of 1666m, the plain, also known as the Great Highlands, was once a heavily forested area – as evidenced by the remaining clumps of trees

---

MOUNTAIN HUTS

Nearly a third of Slovenia's 175 **mountain huts** (*Planinarski Domovi*) lie within the National Park's boundaries, all managed and maintained by the **Alpine Association of Slovenia** (Planinska Zveza Slovenije or PZS; ☏ pzs.si), which has a full list on its website. Huts range from the most basic of refuges (*zavetišče*), often without accommodation or with very few beds and sometimes no running water, to more comfortable places, namely **huts** (*koča*) or **houses** (*dom*), which vary considerably in size, quality and sleeping capacity; expect to pay between €10 and €20 for a bed, depending on the size of the room. A thirty-percent discount is available to UIAA-affiliated members (International Mountaineering and Climbing Federation).

    Food, available at just about all huts, is usually wholesome, filling and cheap; staples include vegetable soup (*zelenjavna juha*), goulash (*golaž*), strudel and tea with lemon (*čaj z limono*). Owing to their high-altitude location, the majority of the park's huts are only **open** between June and September, though most of those along the Vršič Pass (see p.133) are open year-round. However, these dates aren't fixed and may deviate by a month either side depending on the weather. All huts take bookings.

2

scattered across the terrain – but is now given over to a group of small **settlements** (Velika Planina, **Mala Planina**, Tiha Dolina and others). Villages hereabouts are distinguished by dozens of silvery-grey **herdsmen's huts**, unique for their conical, shingled roofs which extend like witches' hats almost all the way down to ground level. The plateau is at its busiest in summer, when walkers, loaded with picnic supplies, trek the well-worn, marked paths between settlements, occasionally stopping off to buy cheese or milk from the shepherds; the most iconic product in these parts is **Trnič**, a hard and salty pear-shaped cheese imprinted with a pattern from a wooden seal (*pisave*). Produced in pairs, it's also known as "boob cheese"; tradition has it that a herdsman would bestow one of these cheeses on his beloved, and if she accepted, it meant that she agreed to courtship.

The most satisfying way to visit Velika Planina is to hike up and take the **cable car** down. The cable car starts 11km north of Kamnik and ascends to 1419m, from where there's a chairlift up to the top of the plateau – the area known as **Gradišče**; it's more fun, however, to walk up from the cable-car station, though it is a steep and fairly gruelling 45-minute climb – you will, though, be rewarded by the presence of the *Zeleni Rob* snack bar (see p.86). The main trail up to Velika Planina begins at the village of **Stahovica**, 5km north of Kamnik and 6km south of the cable-car station, a most enjoyable hike that takes around three hours at a steady pace; after about an hour, a sign diverts you to the fifteenth-century **Cerkev Sv Primoz** (Church of St Primoz), a convenient spot to pause and take in the glorious views, before pushing on towards Mala Planina. There's a good, and fairly demanding, **cycle track** on Velika Planina itself – pick up a cycle map from the tourist office in Kamnik (see opposite). **Mala Planina** has three **mountain huts** – *Jarški Dom* (☏ 041 676 254, ☏ jarski-dom.si; open all year), *Domžalski Dom* (☏ 051 665 665, ☏ domzalskidom.si; open all year) and *Črnuški Dom* (☏ 051 621 732; June–Sept daily; Oct–May Sat & Sun) – all of which offer multibedded rooms and hot food.

Preskarjev muzej

June–Aug daily 10am–6pm; Sept–May ask at the Zeleni Rob snack bar for the key • €2 • ☏ 01 832 7258

For some insight into how herdsmen used to live, wander over to the **Preskarjev muzej** (Preskar's Hut Museum), a ten-minute walk from the *Zeleni Rob* snack bar in the heart of the herdsmen's settlement. Named after its owner, who reconstructed this diminutive shingle-roofed oval cottage following World War II damage, it has an

2

HIKES FROM KAMNIŠKA BISTRICA

Kamniška Bistrica is a key starting point for **hikes** up into the central tract of the mountains. The two most popular hikes from here (note that these routes are all one-way), which should suit walkers of all abilities, are **Kamniško Sedlo** to the north (1884m; 3hr 30min) and **Kokrško Sedlo** to the northwest (1793m; 3hr 30min) – both have mountain huts open between June and mid-October. There are several longer and more demanding hikes just over 1km back down towards the cable-car station, beginning at a track just before the stone bridge; the track, which heads eastwards up the **Kamniška Bela Valley** (you must also cross the brook, which may be tricky if there has been rain), leads to **Presedelj** (1613m; 3hr), **Korošica** (1910m; 4hr 45min) – there's a hut here open between June and September – and **Ojstrica** (2350m; 6hr). If you don't fancy one of these hikes, take the same path for about 25 minutes until you come to a fork – the rocky path to the left will shortly bring you to the **Orglice Waterfall** (Slap Orglice), partly concealed but still an impressive sight.

---

exterior pen, which was used for keeping livestock, and within this, an interior living space – effectively a house within a stable. The latter comprises little more than a bunk bed (with hay for the mattress), a blackened fireplace, and shelves stacked with all the essentials for several months up in the mountains: tools, pots and pans, cheese-making implements and so on. Note the inner door, which was culled from the wreckage of a plane shot down hereabouts.

Kamniška Bistrica

Buses from Kamnik (3 daily; 25min)

Some 14km north of Kamnik, and just 3km north of the cable-car station, the tiny settlement of **KAMNIŠKA BISTRICA** is an idyllic recreation spot lying at the head of the Kamniške Alps. Just below the **mountain hut** *Dom v Kamniški Bistrici* (☏01 832 5544; open all year), which offers dorms and simple refreshments, is the source of the Kamniška Bistrica, a refreshingly cooling spot on a hot day; you can even have a dip. Less than 1km back down the road from the hut, a sign points the way to the contorted **Predaselj Gorge**, 30m high and just 5m wide in places, and defined by a series of natural bridges not dissimilar to Mostnica gorge (see p.126); a walk around it should take no longer than twenty minutes.

ACCOMMODATION AND EATING   VELIKA PLANINA

Kraljev Hrib Kamniška Bistrica 2 ☏041 816 477, ⓦkraljevhrib.si. A couple of hundred metres away from the cable-car station, in a secluded spot enveloped by high trees, the "King of the Hill" (so named because the area used to be a popular hunting ground for Tito and visiting presidents) is a guesthouse offering hostel-style accommodation (singles, doubles and a family room), a small camping area and a courtyard serving pizza from its brick oven; bike rental is available too. Breakfast €5. Camping €18, doubles €34

Zeleni Rob Gradišče ☏01 832 7258. Delicious home-cooked food such as cheese dumplings with *klobasa* and sauerkraut, and fruit-filled *štruklji*, await at this perennially busy snack bar located on Gradišče; alternatively, just kick back with a cold beer following the long hike up. Mon–Wed & Sun 8am–6pm, Thurs–Sat 8am–8pm.

Škofja Loka and around

ŠKOFJA LOKA (Bishop's Meadow), an easy 19km northwest of Ljubljana, lays fair claim to being one of the oldest and loveliest settlements in Slovenia. Lying at the confluence of the two branches of the Sora River, Škofja Loka was first documented in 973 AD, when the settlement of Stara Loka, along with the Selška dolina and Poljanska dolina valleys, was conferred on the bishops of Freising, who would oversee town rule for the next eight centuries. During the early fourteenth century the town was fortified with a five-gate wall – parts of which can still be seen – while the ancient core was "parcelled" into segments. However, despite being pillaged by both the counts of Celje and the Turks, the town layout has changed remarkably little.

Sights are reasonably well dispersed, from **Mestni trg** and the handsome **castle** in the centre to the southeastern suburb of **Puštal**; beyond town, in the villages of **Crngrob** and **Suha**, are two of the finest **frescoed churches** in Slovenia. Škofja Loka's major annual happening, usually on the third or fourth Saturday of June, is **Historical Škofja Loka**, a day of medieval-themed events.

Kapucinski most

Spanning the lively Selška River, the narrow **Kapucinski most** (Capuchin Bridge) is the town's most impressive architectural monument, its stunning stone arch reminiscent of the Mostar Bridge in Bosnia. It was built on the orders of Bishop Leopold in the fourteenth century, making it one of the oldest of its type in Europe, and later named after the Capuchin friars who settled here in the eighteenth century. Some years later, in a cruel twist of fate, the bishop plunged headlong into the river while riding across the bridge on his horse – an incident that probably would not have occurred had he also erected iron balustrades of the type that now line either side of the bridge. Perched on a pedestal in the centre of the bridge is a **statue** of a wistful-looking St John Nepomuk.

2

ŠKOFJA LOKA PASSION PLAY

Performed in 1999 for the first time in more than 270 years, and then again in 2009 and 2015, the **Škofjeloški pasijon** (*Škofja Loka Passion Play*) is one of Slovenia's most remarkable, albeit rarely seen, spectacles. Written by Friar Romauld Marušič in 1721, it was the first dramatic text in the Slovenian language, a form of medieval and Baroque theatre comprising biblical stories or allegories pertaining to the suffering of Christ – hence its staging around the Good Friday period.

The tone of the play (it's actually more of a procession) is set by the Starbearer – dressed in a red habit to symbolize the impending, bloody agony – followed by Death, Hell and a total of seventeen other scenes, or tableaux, such as the Last Supper, Judgement Day and the Crucifixion. Aside from its slight contemporary twist, and the introduction of a musical element, the play has otherwise remained faithful to its original eighteenth-century production, based on a similar order of events, an almost identical text and use of the original language.

Such is the organization and finance involved – some six hundred amateur actors, eighty horses and carefully constructed stage sets at various locations around town are all required – that the event is only staged every six years, with the next one scheduled for 2021.

Kapucinska samostan

Kapucinski trg • To visit call ☎ 04 506 3000

Built in 1709 and an otherwise rather ordinary building, the **Kapucinska samostan** (Capuchin Monastery) is singularly notable for its **library**, whose priceless collection of medieval manuscripts includes a copy of the celebrated *Škofjeloški pasijon* (*Škofja Loka Passion Play*), the oldest written dramatic text in the Slovene language, dating from 1721 (see box above).

Župnijska cerkev Sv Jacob

Cankarjev trg 13

Passing through the arch that once served as the town gate, you enter the old town, whose first major point of interest is the late-Gothic **Župnijska cerkev Sv Jacob** (Parish Church of St Jacob), most of which dates from 1471. Its untidy grey exterior contrasts sharply with the interior, which, though eerily dark, features a magnificent stellar rib-vaulted ceiling embellished with stone bosses showing portraits of church patrons and the town guilds. Other notable works include the black marble Renaissance altars dating from 1694, and the chandeliers and baptismal font by Plečnik. Note too the splendid late-Gothic tympanum above the main entrance.

Mestni trg

Mestni trg (Town Square) is the town's old medieval market place, an atmospheric, rectangular space framed by many-coloured three-storey burgher houses, many of them marked with a plaque denoting its historical significance. Baroque frescoes were revealed in 1972 on the facade of no. 35 – the former **Rotovž** (Town Hall) – which also possesses a fine Gothic portal and Renaissance-style arcaded courtyard. Opposite the town hall is the **Plague Pillar**, erected in 1751 by the townspeople in gratitude for their deliverance from fire and plague.

Homanova hiša

Occupying a prime spot at the north end of Mestni trg is the **Homanova hiša** (Homan's House), an exceptional amalgam of Gothic and Renaissance styles, featuring a turret-like corner projection and sixteenth-century frescoes of St Christopher and the bottom half of a warrior, only discovered in 1970. Its outdoor **café**, shaded by a magnificent linden tree, is the most popular meeting place in town (see p.91); Ivan Grohar, the outstanding Impressionist painter, was a regular at the inn and completed his celebrated *Loka in Snow*, now hanging in the National Gallery in Ljubljana, from here.

Kašča and Galerija Franceta Miheliča

Spodnji trg 1 • To visit the gallery contact the castle • Free • ☎ 04 517 0400, Ⓦ loski-muzej.si

Formerly a residential area for the poorer townsfolk, **Spodnji trg** (Lower Square) is now a rather downtrodden, traffic-filled thoroughfare. At its extreme northern end is the **Kašča** (Town Granary), a sturdy old building used during the Middle Ages for collecting taxes, which usually took the form of grain or cheese; the granary now houses a restaurant (see p.90) and the **Galerija Franceta Miheliča** (France Mihelič Gallery), featuring a superb exhibition of the artist's work from the 1970s. His apocalyptic themes of disintegration, decay and disappearance are embodied in a series of disturbing surrealist paintings of dismembered bodies and rotting organisms; of particular interest are his paintings of scenes from the Ptuj Kurent (see box, p.280).

2

Loški Grad

Grajska pot 13

Mounted on a low grassy hill, and reached via a couple of footpaths, Škofja Loka's majestic medieval **Loški Grad** (Town Castle) was first mentioned in 1215 as "castrum firmissimum Lonca" (strongly fortified castle), though most of what you see today dates from the beginning of the sixteenth century, following the earthquake of 1511. Today, its main interior feature is the **chapel**, which holds four spectacular Baroque gilded altars rescued from the church in the village of Dražgoše (see p.92), which was destroyed by the Germans during World War II.

Loški muzej

June–Sept daily 10am–6pm; Oct–May Tues–Sun 10am–5pm • €5 • ☎ 04 517 0400, Ⓦ loski-muzej.si

The castle is home to the comprehensive **Loški muzej** (Town Museum), whose first few rooms chart the rise of the town craftsmen and their guilds, set up in and around Škofja Loka in the fifteenth century in order to protect the interests of blacksmiths, tanners, tailors and other trades from local and foreign competition; the assemblage of deeds, chests and banners is very impressive.

Elsewhere on the ground floor are rooms dedicated to Ivan Grohar (albeit with just a couple of original paintings) and the highly regarded Slovene writer Ivan Tavčar; among his possessions is a beautiful bentwood cradle presented to him by the Karadordević Serbian royal family. You will also see some impressive painted peasant furniture belonging to the Kalan family, whom Tavčar wrote about in his acclaimed novel *Visoška kronika*, or *Visoko Chronicle* (see p.93). Upstairs, the **ethnographic collection** illustrates peasant life before industrialization, with a fine display of agricultural objects and models of buildings indigenous to the Loka region. Due prominence is also given to regional crafts such as lace-making, ironworking, millinery and dyeing, many of which have sadly long since disappeared. The last room is dedicated to the art of making honey bread using ornate wooden moulds, a practice known as "Mali Kruhek" ("Small Loaves"). You'll see a collection of the types of moulds – typically made from pear- or plum-tree wood and featuring motifs of a secular or figural design – used to shape the bread, which was traditionally baked for holidays and religious feasts.

Nacetova hiša

Puštal 74 • Call ☎ 040 500 791 to visit • €3.50

The peaceful suburb of **Puštal**, on the right bank of the Poljanska Sora River, is a lovely place for a stroll and is home to **Nacetova hiša** (Nace's House), one of the town's best sights. Named after its first owner, Ignacij "Nace" Homan, this almost perfectly preserved eighteenth-century Slovene homestead is predominantly of Baroque appearance, though its stone-vaulted cellar and two "black kitchens" (see p.123) are evidence of fifteenth- and sixteenth-century elements. The furnishings, including a fine maple-wood table, carved chairs and a ceramic heating stove featuring a motifed tile from 1417, are all original; take a look, too, at the skilfully crafted iron grilles (*gatri*) adorning the windows.

ARRIVAL AND INFORMATION   ŠKOFJA LOKA

Škofja Loka can easily be visited as a half- or full-day trip from Ljubljana or en route to Bled or Bohinj via Kranj.

By train The train station, 3km northeast of town, is connected to the centre by regular buses, though just a handful on Sun.
Destinations Bled-Lesce (every 1–2hr; 35min); Kranj (every 1–2hr; 10min); Ljubljana (every 1–2hr; 25min); Radovljica (every 1–2hr; 30min).
By bus The bus station is centrally located on Kapucinski trg.
Destinations Kranj (hourly; 25min); Ljubljana (every 30min–1hr; 40min); Železniki (Mon–Fri 6 daily, Sat & Sun 3 daily; 30min); Žiri (Mon–Fri 10 daily, Sat & Sun 3–4 daily; 45min).

Tourist office The main tourist office is a 5min walk east of the bus station at Kidričeva cesta 1a (May–June & Sept daily 9am–6pm; July & Aug daily 9am–7pm; Oct–April Mon–Fri 9am–4pm; ☎ 04 517 0600, ⓦ visitskofjaloka.si); they also have bikes for rent (€5 for half a day, €8 for a full day). There's another, less useful, branch at Mestni trg 7 (June–Sept Mon–Fri 8.30am–7.30pm, Sat & Sun 8.30am–12.30pm; Oct–May Mon–Fri 8.30am–7pm, Sat 8.30am–12.30pm; ☎ 04 512 0268).
Guided tours Free guided tours of the town start at 10am on Sat in July and Aug; meet at the bus station.

ACCOMMODATION

Garni Paleta Kapucinski trg 17 ☎ 04 512 6400, ⓦ hotel-skofjaloka.si. The only hotel in the centre of town is the quaint, family-run *Paleta*, by the Capuchin Bridge, which has six colourful rooms (doubles, triples and quads) overlooking the river; there's a lovely breakfast, and don't leave without trying Igor's home-made honey liqueur. **€65**
Mini Hotel Vincarje 47 ☎ 04 515 0540, ⓦ minihotel.si. Located 1.5km west of the centre, the eight rooms here are comfortable enough without being exciting, but the

views of the Alps are fabulous; there are also tennis courts, sauna and fitness facilities. From the bus station, cross the Capuchin Bridge, take a right turn and continue along the road. **€65**
Turizem Loka Stara Loka 8a ☎ 04 515 0986, ⓦ loka.si. Modern and very homely guesthouse a 10min walk north of the bus station, with a range of rooms, some of which sleep four and five people. **€60**

EATING

Jesharna Blaževa ulica 10 ☎ 04 512 2561. Warm and informal Italian restaurant perched above the river where you build your own pizza (€8) from a list of ingredients presented to you on a slip of paper. Locals love this place, which has to be a good sign. Mon–Sat

10am–11pm, Sun 11.30am–10pm.
Kašča Spodnji trg 1 ☎ 04 512 4300, ⓦ gostilna-kasca .si. Housed in the thick-set basement of the old granary, the emphasis at this perky restaurant is firmly on Austrian-style grub: schnitzels, sausages and stews,

---

HIKING AND CYCLING AROUND ŠKOFJA LOKA

The **Škofja Loka hills** to the west of town present some terrific opportunities for hiking and cycling. The most popular local excursion is the two-hour **hike** to **Lubnik** (1025m), reachable via footpaths from Vincarje or from Škofja Loka Castle, passing by the castle ruins and the hamlet of Grabovo. The *Dom na Lubnik* mountain hut at the summit has beds and serves hot food (☎ 04 512 0501; Jan & Feb Fri–Sun; March–Dec Tues–Sun). The further west you go, the higher the peaks, culminating in **Stari Vrh**, a small ski resort where you'll find the *Koča Stari Vrh* hut (☎ 041 682 082; open all year) and **Blegoš**, the region's highest peak at 1562m – where there's the *Koča na Blegošu* hut (☎ 051 614 587; May–Oct Tues–Sun; Nov–April Sat & Sun). The 1:40,000 map *Škofjeloško Idrijsko in Cerkljansko Hribovje* (€12), available from tourist offices, details all routes and has full guiding notes.

There's a superb network of **cycling tracks** in the hills, designed to suit riders of all abilities. The entire track covers an area of some 390km, divided into thirteen circular stages, with each trail clearly marked by green boards attached to posts. The excellent *Loka Cycle Route* (€2.50) map, available from tourist offices, details all stages, indicating elevation, degree of difficulty and sights along the way. **Bikes** can be rented from the tourist office on Kidričeva cesta (see above).

which augment the creditable wine list very nicely. Mon–Sat 11am–11pm.

Pr' Starman Stara Loka 22 ☎ 04 512 6490, ⓦ gostilna starman.si. Just down from the old castle north of the centre, this is Škofja Loka's best place to eat; wholesome, solidly traditional Slovene grub such as buckwheat porridge with mushrooms, and *klobasa* with black pudding. Mon–Thurs 7am–10pm, Fri & Sat 7am–midnight.

DRINKING

Homan's House Café Mestni trg 2 ☎ 04 512 3047, ⓦ kavarnahoman.si. Comfortably the best drinking spot in town, where the wood-decked terrace – enveloped by a huge linden tree – is a lovely place to relax, day or night. Mon–Thurs & Sun 8am–9pm, Fri & Sat 8am–11pm.

Cerkev Sv Janez Krstnik

Outskirts of Suha, 2.5km east of Škofja Loka • To visit, contact the tourist office in Skofja Loka (see opposite) • There is no public transport to the village (and buses do not stop on the nearby main road), so if you don't have your own transport rent a bike in Škofja Loka

Standing anonymously in a field 2.5km east of town near the village of **SUHA** is the diminutive **Cerkev Sv Janez Krstnik** (Church of St John the Baptist), acclaimed for its outstanding **medieval paintings**. On entering this small fifteenth-century church, you are immediately drawn to the stellar rib-vaulted presbytery, coated with stunning frescoes depicting scenes from the life of Christ and the Virgin Mary (surrounded by evangelists, angels and various Apostles peering through columns). The lower panels depict the sixteenth-century painter Jernej of Loka's images of the wise and foolish maidens and the holy martyrs. On the inner wall of the triumphal arch is a representation of the Last Judgement.

Cerkev Marijino oznanenje

Crngob, 4km north of Škofja Loka • To visit, contact the tourist office in Skofja Loka (see opposite) • The church can be reached via a monotonous, straggling road that extends northwards from Groharjevo naselje in Stara Loka (a 1hr walk); alternatively, take the Kranj bus and alight at the village of Dorfarje, from where it's a 20min walk to the church

In the tiny settlement of **CRNGOB** ("Black Grave") is the fourteenth-century pilgrimage church **Cerkev Marijino oznanenje** (Church of the Annunciation), regarded as one of Slovenia's most significant monuments and distinguished by some matchless **frescoes**. Completed in the seventeenth century, but originating in the thirteenth century, the church manifests a variety of styles – Romanesque, Gothic and Baroque – though its outward form is predominantly Gothic. The nineteenth-century neo-Gothic columned portico at the western end of the church reveals one of the finest frescoes in Slovenia, the partly effaced *Holy Sunday* (*Sveta Nedelja*), completed in around 1470 by the workshop of Janez Ljubljanski. More than forty scenes portray a series of tasks that good Christians are obliged to do on the Sabbath – pray, assist the sick, and so on – as well as what they should not be doing (gambling, drinking and the like). To the left is *The Passion of Christ*, an earlier work completed by the Friulian masters.

Inside, the shadowy tripartite nave gives way to a sumptuously light chancel supported by six octagonal columns and featuring a delightful pale red-, yellow- and blue-painted rib-vaulted ceiling. Completed by Ljubljana craftsman Jurij Skarnos in 1652, the profoundly ornate **high altar** – the largest Baroque gilded altar in the country – is festooned with almost one hundred statuettes and pillars and rounded off with an oil painting by Leopold Layer.

Selška Valley

Twisting its way north out of Škofja Loka, the narrow, flat-bottomed **Selška Valley** stretches for some 34km between the northern flank of the Škofja Loka hills and the southern ridge of the forested Jelovica plateau. The valley is often ignored in favour of the region's more obvious attractions a short way north, which is a shame, as there are several lovely **villages** here and some of the scenery is immensely rewarding. Although a few buses serve most of these places, having your own transport will enable you to see a lot more.

Železniki

ŽELEZNIKI is the valley's key economic centre, a spindly 3km-long town made up of several interconnected settlements. The town has been shaped by its centuries-old iron-smelting industry, which reached its peak in the seventeenth century when two blast furnaces and more than sixty workshops were operational. Technological advances throughout Europe at the end of the nineteenth century, coupled with the depletion of iron-ore stocks, brought about the demise of the industry, and the last **blast furnace** (*plavž*) was decommissioned in 1902. Situated on the attractively re-laid square at the western end of town, the furnace dates from 1826, replacing an earlier one on this site; records suggest that there is likely to have been a furnace here as early as the fourteenth century. The only preserved technical monument of its kind in the country, it's a magnificent specimen and stands as a fitting memorial to a bygone era.

Železniki muzej

Na Plavžu 58a • April–June & Sept Tues & Wed 9am–3pm, Thurs & Fri 9am–5pm, Sat 9am–3pm; July & Aug Tues & Wed 9am–3pm, Thurs & Fri 9am–5pm, Sat 9am–3pm, Sun 1–5pm; Oct–March Tues–Sat 9am–1pm • €2 • ☎ 04 514 7356

The town's impressive industrial heritage – notably blacksmiths, coopers, miners and sawyers – is thoroughly documented in the **Železniki muzej** (Železniki Museum), located opposite the furnace in the **Plavec house**, dating from 1637 and named after the former owner of the furnace. Despite the absence of English captions, the museum is an enjoyable affair, and includes a lovely collection of lace work from Železniki, the second-largest lace centre in Slovenia after Idrija. If you want to see what all the fuss is about, visit the town in mid-July during the **Days of Lace Fair**, a week-long series of lace-related events.

Dražgoše and around

If you have your own transport, you can enjoy a delightfully scenic ride from Železniki – and a good short cut to Kropa (see p.103) – up and over the **Jelovica Plateau**, a thickly forested highland plain that offered refuge to Partisans during World War II. That didn't, however, stop several ferocious battles taking place here, in particular in the hamlet of **DRAŽGOŠE**, 8km beyond Železniki on the plateau's southern fringe. Forty-one villagers were shot dead and the rest expelled as the village was razed by German troops in January 1942, an event belatedly commemorated by the erection of a brutal-looking concrete monument – though this can't detract from the superlative views of the surrounding lush countryside. Some 10km beyond Dražgoše, the diminutive fifteenth-century Church of St Primoz, perched on a slender ridge just outside the village of **JAMNIK**, hoves into view. On a clear day, you can easily identify a number of sights spread out below – including Kropa, Radovljica and the basilica in Brezje. From Jamnik, it's just 4km down to Kropa, by which time you're out of the valley.

Sorica

Some 9km west of Železniki, the road branches off to the right and winds steeply up to the extraordinarily picturesque alpine village of **SORICA**, its smooth undulating pastures spotted with small clusters of houses and dozens of hayracks. It's not difficult to see why this place was such an inspiration to Sorica's most famous son, the great Slovene Impressionist painter **Ivan Grohar**, a sculpture of whom – palette in hand – greets visitors at the entrance to the village.

Groharjeva hiša

Spodnja Sorica 18 • July & Aug Sat & Sun 2–5pm; Sept–June Mon–Fri 10am–2pm, Sat & Sun 2–5pm • €2 • ☎ 041 521 138

Beyond the church in the lower part of the village, **Groharjeva hiša** (Grohar's House) is where the painter was born and lived for the first three years of his life. Alas, there are no original works on display, just a few replicas, alongside a handful of personal effects. There's also an ethnographic exhibition documenting past life in the village and valley.

ARRIVAL AND INFORMATION SELŠKA VALLEY **2**

By bus In Železniki buses from Škofja Loka (Mon–Fri 6 daily, Sat & Sun 3 daily; 30min) drop passengers off in the centre of town by the church. The only buses from Sorica to Železniki (and vice versa) are the school (term-time) ones, with roughly four or five per day in both directions.

Tourist office Železniki Museum, Na Plavžu 58a (April–June & Sept Tues & Wed 9am–3pm, Thurs & Fri 9am–5pm, Sat 9am–3pm; July & Aug Tues & Wed 9am–3pm, Thurs & Fri 9am–5pm, Sat 9am–3pm, Sun 1–5pm; Oct–March Tues–Sat 9am–1pm; ☎ 04 514 7356).

ACCOMMODATION AND EATING

Gostišče Macesen Spodnja Sorica 16 ☎ 04 519 7060, ⓦ macesen.si. A few paces down from Grohar's house in Sorica, and named after one of his paintings (*Larch*), the inspiration for these thirteen bright and fresh-smelling rooms is the surrounding countryside, with simple peasant-style furnishings and wall paintings depicting scenes from Sorica. The food is delicious, too, with venison loin (€17) a house speciality. Restaurant daily 10am–11pm. **€80**

Poljanska Valley

Flanked by the Škofja Loka hills to the north and the slightly lower Polhov Gradec hills to the south, the **Poljanska Valley** extends for some 35km between Škofja Loka and the small town of Žiri.

Tavčarjev dvorec na Visokem

Visoko Pri Poljanah, 12km southwest of Škofja Loka • June–Sept Fri 9am–3pm, Sat & Sun 10am–6pm; at other times contact the tourist office in Škofja Loka (see p.90) • €2

Twelve kilometres southwest of Škofja Loka, in the village of **VISOKO PRI POLJANAH** (cross the bridge on the left just after the village of Log), stands the grand **Tavčarjev dvorec na Visokem** (Visoko Mansion). Once the property of the celebrated writer Ivan Tavčar (1851–1923), the mansion (also known as the Tavčar Manor) has been partially renovated to house a small exhibition on the author; there's a café, too, which is open in summer. The grounds themselves are a lovely place to wander; here you'll find an enormous bronze sculpture – completed in 1957 by Jakob Savinšek – of a cross-legged Tavčar gazing across the field, while you can't miss the magnificent double hayrack. Born in **Poljane**, the next village along, Tavčar, erstwhile Ljubljana mayor and politician, was considered one of the country's foremost prose writers, basing much of his work on his experiences of life in the valley. His most famous novel, *Visoška Kronika* (*Visoko Chronicle*), charted the lives of the Kalan family who lived in the same house some two hundred years before Tavčar. Tavčar is buried in the family tomb on the terrace above the mansion.

Žiri

ŽIRI, 12km south of Gorenja Vas, is a small, conservative town renowned for its lace and shoemaking industries. If you wish to have a look at, or buy, some lace, pop into the small **Lace Gallery** (Galerija čipke) at Jobstova 29 (Mon, Tues & Thurs–Sun 4.30–7pm, Wed 9–11am & 4.30–7pm; free; ☎ 04 519 2532).

2

THE RUPNIK LINE

Sequenced in an almost vertical chain between Soriška Planina in the north and the small town of Žiri some 50km further south are dozens of bunkers, tunnels, casemates and observation posts built by the Yugoslavs in response to border fortifications constructed by the Italians following the **Treaty of Rapallo** in 1920 (see p.300). Although proposals to fortify the border were initially submitted in the mid-1920s, construction work didn't begin until 1937, under the command of its chief architect **Leon Rupnik**, a Yugoslav army general who was later tried and shot in Ljubljana for treason. In the event, the line was neither fully completed – due to the onset of World War II – nor were its existing defences pressed into service.

Many of the fortifications have been cleaned up and it's now possible (with a guide) to visit some of them, an opportunity that will almost certainly appeal to adrenaline junkies; the descent into the bunkers and tunnels – some nearly 40m deep – is exhilarating. Moreover, the **hiking** in this region is terrific. The main organized visit (10am every first Saturday of the month; €5) is to the bunker at **Goli Vrh**, one of the largest and best-preserved fortifications along the line, and whose main gallery extends for some 200m; variously used as a hospital and storage space, it now holds an exhibition displaying remnants from the line – the tourist office in Škofja Loka (see p.90) can organize visits at other times, though these tend to be group-orientated. Alternatively, there are two self-guided trails (above ground only), both of which start in Gorenja Vas, 17km southwest of Škofja Loka: one is an easy two-hour circular hike, the other a more demanding five-hour jaunt winding up at Hrastov grič, some 6km distant.

Muzej Žiri

Tabor 2 • May–Oct Sun 3–6pm; other times by appointment – contact the tourist office in Škofja Loka (see p.90) • €2 • ☎ 031 532 798

The **Muzej Žiri** (Žiri Museum) stands 1km south of the centre in the dilapidated former mansion of the Freising bishops. Following World War II, the town's various shoemaking industries morphed into the Alpina factory, which now employs around eight hundred people manufacturing ski boots and sports footwear for some of the world's top climbers and athletes. Among those on display are the boots worn by Zejc Zaplotnik, the first Slovene to summit Everest. The museum's bobbin-lace collection, meanwhile, attests to the industry's importance in the town during the first part of the twentieth century. There's also coverage of the Rapallo Border, including boundary stones and a multimedia presentation – worth viewing if you're planning on visiting any of the fortifications (see above).

ARRIVAL AND DEPARTURE   ŽIRI

By bus Buses from Škofja Loka (Mon–Fri 10 daily, Sat & Sun 3–4 daily; 45min) drop passengers off in the centre of town.

ACCOMMODATION AND EATING

Gostišče Pri Županu Loška cesta 78 ☎ 04 505 0000 or ☎ 031 686 089. In the northern part of town, this is the sole central source of accommodation here, with a handful of neat, fresh-looking rooms. It's also the best place to eat, offering pizzas, salads and meat dishes. Mon 8am–3pm, Tues–Sat 9am–10pm, Sun noon–8pm. **€70**

Kranj and around

Despite its reputation as a hard-nosed and gritty industrial centre, **KRANJ**, Slovenia's fourth-largest city, possesses an attractive old core seriously at odds with its drab surroundings. Positioned on a steep, rocky promontory above the confluence of the Sava and Kokra rivers, between the foothills of the Julian Alps and the western spur of the Kamniške-Savinje Alps, Kranj has been the country's most important industrial city since the end of World War I. It is home to several of Slovenia's major **manufacturing industries**, which in total employ almost half of the city's population. However, beyond the grimescape of smoking chimneys, the **old town** possesses a clutch of fine late-Gothic buildings, and the city boasts strong associations with the poet **France Prešeren**. The two key events are **Festival Carniola** in mid-June (ⓦfestivalcarniola.si), a week of street theatre, concerts and workshops throughout the old town, and **Kranjfest**, a series of rock concerts at the end of July.

The best local excursion is to **Brdo Castle**, while the modest peaks of **Šmarjetna Gora** and **Sv Jošt** offer good walking.

Prešerenova hiša

Prešernova ulica 7 • Tues–Sun 10am–6pm • €2.50 • ☎ 04 201 3983, ⓦ gorenjski-muzej.si

Kranj's attractive medieval centre begins at **Maistrov trg**, formerly the site of the upper town gate and once enclosed by the northern section of the city walls. Liberally sprinkled with cafés, the square segues into Prešernova ulica where, at no. 7, a memorial plaque denotes **Prešerenova hiša** (Prešeren's House). This two-storey building, where France Prešeren spent the last three years of his life, is a fine example of a late-Gothic townhouse, its arcaded gallery uniting what were once two separate dwellings. The first floor has been turned into a superb **memorial museum**, chronologically presenting phases of Prešeren's life, with manuscripts, diaries and letters accompanied by excellent notes. There is also much original furniture, including the bed he died in and the desk and chair he used while working as a lawyer (see box, p.113).

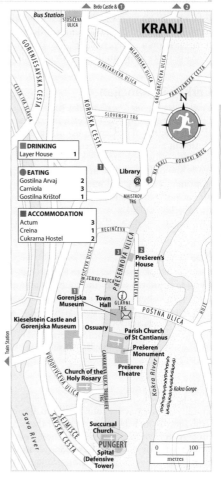

Prešeren is buried 500m north of the centre in **Prešernov gaj** (Prešeren Grove), a modest green space that functions as the city's main park. It contains just two other graves – those of his daughter, Ernestina Jelovšek, and another local poet, Simon Jenko.

Muzej Gorenjski

Glavni trg 4 • Tues–Sun 10am–6pm • €2.50 • ☎ 04 201 3980, ⓦ gorenjski-muzej.si

The heart of the old town is **Glavni trg** (Main Square), an elongated square framed by delightful Gothic and Renaissance buildings, the most prominent of which is the **town hall** (Mestna hiša), which now accommodates the enjoyable **Muzej Gorenjski** (Gorenjska Museum). Its trio of exhibitions kicks off with an above-average collection of archeological finds, notably some outstanding grave goods including ceramic jugs and vessels, and finely cut jewellery and figurines. Elsewhere, there's an interesting assortment of sculptures by Lojze Dolinar (a student of the eminent Croatian sculptor

Ivan Mestrovič), and an ethnological exhibition of folk art from Gorenjska, including beautifully crafted chests and cupboards, fifteenth-century frescoes, and a selection of Slovenia's famous beehive panels (see box, p.101). Note that there's a second branch of the Gorenjska Museum in **Kieselstein Castle** (see below).

Cerkev Sv Kancijan

Glavni trg • Daily: June–Sept 7.30am–7.30pm; Oct–May 8am–5pm

Dominating the square – indeed, the city skyline – is the glowering **Cerkev Sv Kancijan** (Parish Church of St Cantianus), the most outstanding example of a Gothic hall-church in Slovenia; supported by four immense octagonal columns, its stellar-vaulted central nave is decorated with the *Star of Beautiful Angels* fresco, attributed to the workshop of Janez Ljubljanski, while numerous detailed keystones adorn the arches, most notably Mary and infant Jesus in front of the Triumphal Arch. Other highlights are the modestly fashioned high altar by the church architect Ivan Vurnik, and the neo-Gothic stained-glass windows by Kregar. The tympanum above the main entrance incorporates a fine relief of Christ on the Mount of Olives.

Kostnica

Glavni trg • To visit, contact the Gorenjska Museum (see p.95) • €2.50 • ☎ 04 201 3980, ⓦ gorenjski-muzej.si

Outside the north side of the church is an early Slavonic **Kostnica** (Ossuary), containing thousands of bones and skulls of Kranj citizens thought to have been buried here between the fourteenth and sixteenth centuries but which were only discovered during intermittent excavations between 1953 and 1973. Uncovered at the same time were the foundations of a sixth-century baptistery and the remains of a cemetery chapel whose altar is still partially visible. It's all rather spooky, but quite fascinating.

Pungert

Beyond Jože Plečnik's **staircase** – on one side is a characteristic arcade, and in the middle, an unattractive fountain, both also by Plečnik – the old town winds up at Trubarjev trg and the southern tip of the promontory known as **Pungert**, which rises up over the confluence of the Sava and Kokra rivers; here, a circular glass ramp suspended high above the **Kokra Gorge**, an inaccessible 30m-deep canyon, offers marvellous views. The three-storey **Spital** (Defensive Tower), right on the tip, is the only entirely preserved tower within the ancient city walls; at one stage it was adapted for use as a prison and as lodgings – these days it's a children's play centre.

Grad Kieselstein

Tomšičeva ulica 44 • **Muzej Gorenjski** Tues–Sun 10am–6pm • €2.50 • ☎ 059 096 631, ⓦ gorenjski-muzej.si

Formerly a fifteenth-century stronghold, then a manor house, **Grad Kieselstein** (Kieselstein Castle) is now home to several cultural organizations and a second branch of the **Muzej Gorenjski** – the other branch is on the main square (see p.95). Entitled *Beautiful Gorenjska*, this enlightening exhibition charts the development of the region, more or less chronologically; among the more revealing items is a black-and-white coffin with painted skull and bones, recovered from the Parish Church of St Cantianus during excavations in the 1970s and which was found to hold the remains of a local priest. The economy is represented, in the main, by the region's iron-making industry, featuring some exquisite wrought-iron meshes and grilles from Kropa. Upstairs, war and politics are the dominant themes, from World War II and the horrors endured by those incarcerated in Begunje (see p.104), to life under Tito (there's a rare photo of him on display) and independence, with bullet casings and the ballot box used in the first multiparty elections.

Rovi pod Starim Kranjem

Entrance on Ljubljanska cesta • Guided tours (1hr) Tues & Fri 5pm, Sat & at 10am; meet in front of the tourist office • €3 • ☎ 04 238 0450

During World War II, the city authorities set about constructing a web of **underground tunnels** to be used as air-raid shelters, though in the event, most were never fully completed. Abandoned for years, the tunnels – officially called **Rovi pod Starim Kranjem** (Tunnels Under the Old Town Kranj) – were later used to cultivate mushrooms, before they fell into a state of ruin, only to be cleaned up a few years ago. Some 1300m in length, this is the longest of the tunnels and the only one open to the public; excellent guided tours conclude inside a mock-up shelter complete with simulated air-raid warnings and repeated (mild) reverberations.

ARRIVAL AND INFORMATION   KRANJ

By train The train station is on the west bank of the Sava, a 10min walk from town (bus #2).

Destinations Bled-Lesce (every 1–2hr; 25min); Ljubljana (Mon–Fri every 1–2hr; 35min); Radovljica (every 1–2hr; 20min); Škofja Loka (Mon–Fri every 1–2hr; 10min).

By bus The bus station lies 500m north of the old town on Stošičeva ulica.

Destinations Bled (hourly; 40min); Ljubljana (every 20–30min; 40min); Radovljica (every 30min; 25min); Škofja Loka (hourly; 25min); Tržič (hourly; 25min).

Tourist office Glavni trg 2 (Mon–Sat 8am–7pm, Sun 9am–6pm; ☎ 04 238 0450, ⓦ tourism-kranj.si); they have bikes for rent (€2 for 2hr, €5/day).

Internet Inside the superb town library at Gregorčičeva ulica 1 (Mon–Fri 8am–7.30pm, Sat 8am–3.30pm; 1hr free).

ACCOMMODATION

Actum Prešernova ulica 6 ☎ 059 082 400, ⓦ actum -hotel.com. This self-proclaimed car-themed hotel – Rolls-Royce parts are randomly scattered around the place – has seventeen differently configured rooms offering a tasteful, if slightly over-exuberant, mix of parquet floors and Persian carpets, sumptuously upholstered furnishings and the occasional Venetian chandelier or wall fresco. **€140**

Creina Koroška cesta 5 ☎ 04 281 7500, ⓦ hotelcreina .si. Designed by the eminent Slovene architect Edvard Ravnikar, and (hard though it is to believe) a historical and cultural monument, the brick-built *Creina* conceals surprisingly accomplished, if somewhat business-like, rooms. **€65**

Cukrarna Hostel Tavčarjeva ulica 9 ☎ 051 788 887, ⓦ cukrarna.si. Super-smart hostel occupying a seventeenth-century, rust-orange coloured building in an enviable spot alongside the Kokra Gorge, offering a range of impeccable dorms and doubles (including en suites), plus kitchen, chill-out room and outdoor terrace perched high above the river. Dorms **€12**, doubles **€30**

EATING

Gostilna Arvaj Kajuhova ulica 2 ☎ 04 280 0100, ⓦ gostilna-arvaj.si. A 10min walk north of the centre, *Arvaj* doesn't look much from the outside, and the busy roadside location is mildly off-putting, but the food, served on wooden platters, is terrific; the house staple is the gut-busting *Kranjska klobasa*, served with mustard and horseradish, but there's plenty more, including fillet of trout with polenta and spinach salad. Mon–Sat 8am–11pm, Sun 9am–4pm.

Carniola Gregorčičeva ulica 2 ☎ 04 202 5156. With two terraces, including one with a trampoline and other kiddie-friendly distractions, this café-cum-patisserie makes for a refreshing pit stop, and is especially good for ice creams

and sorbets (around €2.80 each). Mon–Fri 7am–10pm, Sat 8am–midnight, Sun 8am–10pm.

★**Gostilna Krištof** Predoslje 22 ☎ 04 234 1030, ⓦ gostilnakristof.si. A 10min walk down the road from Brdo Castle, this sublime roadside *gostilna* offers wonderful food and is worth making a special effort to get to; chef Tomaž Bolka conjures up fresh, stunningly crafted plates – beef carpaccio with crawfish and mango doused with orange olive oil, say, or trout fillet with pumpkin purée and roasted almonds – each accompanied by the finest of wines. Set menus from €25. Mon–Sat noon–midnight, Sun noon–5pm.

DRINKING

★**Layer House** Tomšičeva ulica 32 ☎ 031 379 237, ⓦ layer.si. The erstwhile residence of the eponymous Slovene painter is now Kranj's wonderfully creative cultural and social hub; aside from functioning as a multi-use arts space, it comprises a cool, low-vaulted café (offering craft

beers, cocktails and Turkish coffee), a wood-decked terrace with fine views across to Šmarjetna Gora, and a pretty cherry blossom garden, the perfect spot in which to kick back with a glass of wine. Mon–Thurs 9am–11pm, Fri & Sat 9am–midnight, Sun 4pm–midnight.

Grad Brdo

Near Predoslje, 4km northeast of Kranj • Castle €10 (must be booked at least a day in advance), grounds €3.50 • For any information regarding visiting the estate, contact the reception desk of the Brdo Hotel (☎ 04 260 1000, ⓦ brdo.si) • There's a designated, very pleasant, path from Kranj to Brdo, a walk of around 30min; otherwise take any bus heading towards Predoslje (hourly; 20min)

Grad Brdo (Brdo Castle) is Slovenia's most elite presidential residence. Surrounded by 11km of fencing, the estate is no longer reserved exclusively for visits by high-ranking officials and anyone can nose around the castle's stately rooms, ramble through the expansive parklands, or partake in various outdoor activities – there's a nine-hole **golf** course (€13); **horseriding** on Lipizzaner (€15 for 30min in the ring, €25 for a 45min jaunt around the estate); **carriage rides** (€15 for 20min), and **fishing** (€35 for 3hr) – indeed, the grounds even incorporate the National Football Centre.

As early as 1446, a manor house – owned by the noble Egkh family (Egkh is German for "brdo" which in English means "hillock") – existed close to, or on the site of, the present castle, though it didn't assume its present form until the sixteenth century. In the mid-eighteenth century, ownership was transferred to the munificent Zois family, who remained in custody of the estate until 1929, after which time it was owned for a short period by the Karadjordjevič Yugoslav royal family. At the end of World War II the estate was nationalized and became one of Tito's many summer retreats – he particularly liked Brdo for its fine hunting. During this period security was such that a soldier was positioned every 100m, whether the great man was in residence or not. In 1961 Tito issued a decree declaring the estate to the Republic of Slovenia, though this hasn't stopped various members of the Karadjordjevič clan from trying to reclaim the property; unsurprisingly, the Slovene authorities have rejected this out of hand.

A visit to the castle essentially comprises a brief **tour** around a handful of rooms – including the magnificent dining room and Tito's gift-laden trophy room – but the real appeal is a stroll around the **grounds** themselves, with their sweeping gardens, majestic lakes and elegant, tree-lined avenues: lime, linden and hornbeam to name but three.

Tržič

A small, somnolent market town slightly out on a limb 18km north of Kranj, **TRŽIČ** is little visited by tourists, but it holds a couple of very satisfying **museums** and is just a stone's throw away from a delightful **gorge**.

Although the town has a strong tradition in a number of trades and crafts dating back to the Middle Ages – and, unlikely as it may seem, has played a significant role in the development of **skiing** in Slovenia – it was **shoemaking** that really put Tržič on the map. At the end of the nineteenth century, almost every second house here accommodated a shoemakers' workshop, but a combination of increased industrialization allied to the loss of trade from those countries of the former Yugoslavia culminated in the closure of the local Peko factory (established in 1902) in 2016.

Tržič muzej

Muzejska ulica 11 • Tues–Sun 10am–6pm • €2.50, €3 with the Slovenian Ski Museum (see p.100) • ☎ 04 531 5500, ⓦ trziski-muzej.si

The town's history of shoemaking forms the centrepiece of the surprisingly compelling **Tržič muzej** (Tržič Museum). Aside from showing the various shoemaking techniques (typically pegging and sewing), there's a huge selection of footwear on show, including a wall of shoes belonging to Slovenia's most famous citizens – albeit few, if any, that most people will have heard of. The museum actually occupies an old town tannery, an industry that was second only to shoemaking; there were some sixteen tanneries in Tržič by the turn of the nineteenth century, with some two hundred skins tanned daily. The material's versatility is reflected in some fabulous products, including a fireman's belt and helmet, and a tobacco pouch crafted from a ram's scrotum.

FROM TOP CLIMBING TRIGLAV (P.121); PLEASURE BOATS, LAKE BLED (P.107) >

Slovenski Šmucarski muzej

Muzejska ulica 11 • Tues–Sun 10am–6pm • €2, €3 with the Tržič Museum (see p.98) • ☎ 04 531 5500, ⓦ trziski-muzej.si

In the same building as the Tržič Museum, on the ground floor, the wonderful little **Slovenski Šmucarski muzej** (Slovenian Ski Museum) celebrates Slovenia's most popular sport. Cleverly designed with an all-white interior resembling a downhill slope, the first part traces the development of skiing in general, with a forest of skis, from the earliest ones used on the Bloke Plateau (see p.214) to those belonging to the great and good, such as Hermann Maier – many of these were made by the Elan factory in Begunje, one of the world's foremost ski manufacturers. A cluster of slalom poles denotes the achievements of Slovenia's greatest skiers, by far the most successful of whom is Tine Maze, winner of gold medals in both downhill and Giant Slalom in Sochi. There's sobering coverage, too, of the 1937 Štoržič disaster, in which nine skiiers were buried under an avalanche and which led to the formation of the Tržič Mountain Rescue Division.

Kurnikova hiša

Kurnikova pot 2 • Tues–Sun 10am–6pm; contact the Tržič Museum (see p.98) before visiting • €2.50 • ☎ 04 531 5500, ⓦ trziski-muzej.si • Walk south from the Tržič Museum to the church, then along Partizanska ulica and across the bridge

The **Kurnikova hiša** (Kurnik's House) is a neatly preserved eighteenth-century Gorenjska peasant house named after its original owner, Vojteh Kurnik, who was born here in 1826. Although he was a wheelwright by profession, Kurnik's true passion was poetry; you can see a handful of wood shavings on which he wrote verses while working.

Dovžanova soteska

A 45-minute walk northeast of Tržič, beyond the tiny settlement of **Čadovlje**, is the fabulous **Dovžanova soteska** (Dovžan Gorge), a protected natural monument owing to its rich deposits of Palaeozoic fossils. Its most distinguishing features are the pyramidal limestone columns on the eastern slopes, and Borova Peč (Pine's bluff) on the western side, though the thrashing Tržiška Bistrica River, bisecting the gorge's steeply pitched sides, is no less impressive. At the gorge entrance you'll pass through a remarkable road tunnel, built at the end of the nineteenth century by Julij Born.

ARRIVAL AND INFORMATION   TRŽIČ

By bus The station, with services from Kranj (hourly; 25min), is handily located south of town on Cankarjeva cesta, from where it's a couple of minutes' walk north to the tourist office.

Tourist office Through the passageway at Trg svobode 18 (Mon–Fri 9am–6pm, Sat 9am–1pm; ☎ 04 597 1536, ⓦ visit-trzic.si).

EATING

Pizzeria Pod Gradom Koroška cesta 26 ☎ 04 596 2055. This tidy, colourful pizzeria, just down from the Tržič Museum, is the only place of note to eat in town, its big brick-fired oven doling out tasty pizzas at good prices (€6.50). Tues–Sun noon–10pm.

Radovljica and around

Often bypassed in the rush to get to Bled, **RADOVLJICA** is a likeable little town boasting a beautiful square stuffed with some superb Gothic and Renaissance architecture, and one of Slovenia's most surprisingly engaging museums. Built on a 75m-high outcrop above the Sava River, the town came into its golden period during the early Middle Ages when feudal lords, most importantly the Ortenburgs, settled here, building their vast estates. Although Radovljica suffered a lengthy period of stagnation in the eighteenth and nineteenth centuries, the subsequent development of both the highway and railway kick-started the town back into life, and today, despite a population of little more than six thousand, it's a significant administrative and educational centre.

The town makes a good base for a number of local excursions – if you've only time for one, the single-street village of **Kropa**, 10km southwest, is the place to aim for – you can get there relatively easily by bus. Other highlights are **Bazilika Marija Pomagaj**, an important pilgrimage site, and **Begunje**, with its excellent brace of museums.

Linhartov trg

Everything of interest in town is centred on **Linhartov trg** (Linhart Square), the old medieval core framed by a raft of fine Gothic and Renaissance buildings. The square was named in honour of the Slovene dramatist-historian Anton Tomaž Linhart (1756–95), whose **birthplace** at no. 7 bears a commemorative plaque and bas-relief of people at work and play.

Čebelarski muzej

Linhartov trg 1 • Jan & Feb Tues–Fri 8am–3pm; March, April, Nov & Dec Tues, Thurs & Fri 8am–3pm, Wed, Sat & Sun 10am–noon & 3–5pm; May–Oct Tues–Sun 10am–6pm • €3 • ☎ 04 532 0520, ⓦ mro.si

The **Thurnov Grad** (Thurn Mansion), built by the Ortenburg counts in the early Middle Ages, underwent several reincarnations before it acquired its current Baroque appearance in the eighteenth century. Inside, a magnificent double stairway leads up to the first floor and the splendid **Čebelarski muzej** (Beekeeping Museum), which charts the development and tradition of Slovenian **apiculture** from the eighteenth century to the present day. It begins with a collection of hives and wax presses, and by acknowledging the debt owed to the pioneers of beekeeping, such as master apiarists Anton Janša (1734–73), who published the first treatise on beekeeping, and Michael Ambrošič (1846–1904), the first Slovene to trade in the indigenous Grey Carniolan bee. The undoubted high point of the museum is its collection of more than two hundred **beehive panels** – wooden end panels painted with religious, satirical or humorous motifs and scenes – illustrated here in individually themed cabinets (deserters, bandits, hunters, craftsmen and so on); look out, too, for the marvellous

---

A NATION OF BEEKEEPERS

Beekeeping is one of Slovenia's oldest and most celebrated traditions, originating during the sixteenth century when honey was the principal sweetening agent available and wax an indispensable material for making candles. Bees, in particular the Grey Carniolan – affectionately known as the "Grizzly" owing to the lining of bright grey hair along its abdomen – have thrived in Slovenia for centuries, attracted to the rich forage in the country's abundant fields and forests. At the tail end of the nineteenth century **bee trading** became a hugely lucrative business, with the export of bees and their products of honey, wax and royal jelly to numerous European countries; today, the country's seven thousand or so beekeepers produce around two thousand tonnes of honey annually, just about sufficient for domestic requirements.

Bees were traditionally kept in wooden, oblong **hives** called *kranjiči* (Carniolans), neatly stacked together in rows that could be mounted onto carts and transported; the hives were particularly well known for their painted **front panels** (*panjske končnice*), a Slovenian folk art that emerged during the mid-eighteenth century, reaching its height a century later. Panels were illustrated with colourfully crafted motifs; older motifs typically portrayed biblical or historical happenings, while later paintings depicted moral or satirical, and occasionally profane, images, usually pertaining to peasant life. Many of these were deliciously humorous – such as the local gossip having her tongue sharpened on a grindstone by villagers, or the hunter being pursued by a gun-toting bear – many other panels feature Job, the patron of beekeepers. Panels had practical functions, too, their bright colours supposedly making orientation easier for bees, as well as enabling the beekeeper to distinguish between his many swarms.

2

RADOVLJICA FESTIVALS

Radovljica hosts two of Slovenia's most engaging annual events: on the third weekend of April, Linhartov trg is taken over by the wonderful **Chocolate Festival** (⚙ radolca.si), with tastings, demonstrations, sculpting and loads more from producers from all over Slovenia. For two to three weeks in August, it's the turn of the prestigious **Festival Radovljica** (⚙ festival-radovljica .si), one of Europe's foremost festivals of ancient classical music, featuring an international crop of artists.

---

figural beehives, namely a French soldier, a Turk and a Janissary. Elsewhere, there is an exposition on the **biology** of the aforementioned Carniolan bee, including a live hive and a reconstructed **apiary**.

Cerkev Sv Petra

A few paces east of the Thurn Mansion, in a pretty, irregularly shaped courtyard, stands the **Cerkev Sv Petra** (Parish Church of St Peter), a fine Gothic hall-church modelled on the parish church in Kranj (see p.96). The oldest part of the church, the presbytery, dates from the fifteenth century, while the church's Romanesque nave was replaced with its present, late-Gothic one in 1495. The Baroque high altar, from 1713, incorporates beautiful sculptural decoration by Angelo Pozzo, as does the white marble altar of St Mary, its sculptures completed by local stonemason Janez Vurnik.

Šivčeva hiša

Linhartov trg 22 • Tues–Sun: Jan–April, Nov & Dec 10am–noon & 4–6pm; May, June, Sept & Oct 10am–1pm & 4–7pm; July & Aug 10am–1pm & 5–8pm • €3 • ☎ 04 532 0523, ⚙ muzeji-radovljica.si

The most outstanding building on Linhartov trg is the muralled **Šivčeva hiša** (Šiveč House), an exceptional example of a Gothic-Renaissance house that was once the living quarters of a Radovljica burgher family but is now principally used for weddings. Otherwise unfurnished, it's noteworthy for its vaulted ground-floor hall, which hosts an **art gallery** with rotating exhibitions. The fine wood-panelled drawing room aside, the first floor also holds a kitchen and granary, while beyond the rearside balcony, another room holds a permanent exhibition on Slovenian illustrators; it's in Slovene only, but this doesn't detract from the warm and colourful books on display.

ARRIVAL AND INFORMATION
RADOVLJICA

By bus The bus station is in the centre of town on Kranjska cesta.
Destinations Begunje (hourly; 25min); Bled (hourly; 15min); Kranj (every 30min; 25min); Kranjska Gora (hourly; 55min); Kropa (Mon–Fri 8 daily; 20min); Ljubljana (every 30min; 1hr 5min); Ribčev Laz, for Lake Bohinj (hourly; 50min).
By train The train station lies a couple of minutes south of

the centre on Cesta svobode.
Destinations Bled-Lesce (every 1–2hr; 5min); Kranj (every 1–2hr; 20min); Ljubljana (every 1–2hr; 55min); Škofja Loka (Mon–Fri every 1–2hr; 30min).
Tourist office Linhartov trg 9 (daily: May–Sept 9am–7pm; Oct–April 9am–4pm; ☎ 04 531 5112, ⚙ radolca.si). Free guided walking tours every Tues at 10am.

ACCOMMODATION

Camping Radovljica Kopališka cesta 9 ☎ 04 531 5770, ⚙ camping-radovljica.com. A small, very basic campsite around a 10min walk north of the centre – campers get free use of the adjoining, championship-standard swimming pool. June to mid-Sept. **€11**
Pension Lectar Linhartov trg 2 ☎ 04 537 4800, ⚙ lectar.com. Nine homely rooms with pastel painted walls, lush red carpets and folksy, hand-painted furniture – gingerbread making has been an ongoing activity in

the house for more than 250 years, hence the gingerbread signs outside each room representing various trades and crafts. **€88**
Vidičeva Hiša Hostel Linhartov trg 3 ☎ 031 810 767, ⚙ vidichouse.com. Although it touts itself as a hostel, the rooms here – sleeping three to six people – are more like self-contained apartments, with kitchen and lounge areas. Nothing particularly special, but it's a top location and decent value. Breakfast €3. **€17.50**

EATING AND DRINKING

★ **Gostilna Kunstelj** Gorenjska cesta 9 ☎ 04 531 5178, ⓦ kunstelj.si. Rambling, convivial place a few paces west of Linhartov trg, whose strong, Slovene-crafted menu is the most accomplished in town. A mouthwatering meal might start with sautéed calf's liver (€10), followed by deer medallions with buckwheat and leeks, then ice cream with pumpkin seed oil and gingerbread; top-notch wines too. July & Aug daily noon–10pm; Sept–June Tues, Wed & Fri–Sun noon–10pm.

Gostilna Lectar Linhartov trg 2 ☎ 04 537 4800, ⓦ lectar.com. As amenable as the pension it's housed in,

this centuries-old restaurant offers an upscale take on meaty treats (rabbit, veal, pickled calf's tongue) as well as traditional Slovenian dishes like buckwheat, mushrooms and dumplings for vegetarians; end the meal with a slice of Linhart cake, comprising thick layers of biscuit, cream and caramel. Daily 11am–10pm.

Vidic House Linhartov trg 3 ☎ 031 810 767, ⓦ vidic house.com. Drop in at this retro café – the prime spot on the main square – for coffee and all things sweet, including cakes, ice cream and all manner of confectionery. Mon–Thurs & Sun 9am–9pm, Fri & Sat 9am–10pm.

Kropa

The comely hamlet of **KROPA**, 10km southwest of Radovljica, lies in a narrow valley below the Jelovica plateau, flanked by precipitously slanting hills. It's renowned for its **iron-mining** and **forging** industries, which reached their peak here during the early to mid-nineteenth century. Around 1.5km south of the village, up on the road to Železniki, stands a fourteenth-century **smelting furnace**, discovered as recently as 1953 when the mountain road to Jamnik was built. Nicknamed the "wolf", it could produce 200kg of iron in one day.

Kovaški muzej

Kropa 10 • Jan & Feb Tues–Fri 8am–3pm; March, April, Nov & Dec Tues, Thurs & Fri 8am–3pm, Wed, Sat & Sun 10am–noon & 3–5pm; May–Oct Tues–Sun 10am–6pm • €3 • ☎ 04 533 7200, ⓦ mro.si

The village's rich iron-forging history is relayed in the **Kovaški muzej** (Iron Forging Museum), part of the **Klinar House**, owned by the eponymous iron baron. As impressive as the assemblage of models, bellows and spikes is (there are, incredibly, more than one hundred varieties of spike), the work of master forger **Joža Bertoncelj** (1901–76) trumps all else here; already forging nails at the age of 11, Bertoncelj soon graduated to the village's Plamen factory before settling on a career as an artistic forger, resulting in a marvellous collection of wrought-iron gratings, chandeliers and sepulchral monuments. The second floor illustrates the economic and social conditions under which blacksmiths lived and worked; typically, the smiths and their families would squeeze into the attic, while the first floor was given over to the owner of the foundry. Looking at the salon and its coffered ceiling in the Klinar House, you can appreciate just how wealthy some of these owners were.

Umetnokovaška Obrt

Kropa 7a • July & Aug Mon–Fri 7am–6pm, Sat 9am–noon; Sept–June Mon–Fri 7am–3pm, Sat 9am–noon • ☎ 04 533 7300, ⓦ uko.si

A few paces north of the Iron Forging Museum is the **Umetnokovaška Obrt** (UKO Workshop), a decorative ironwork company set up in 1956 to preserve the tradition of manual forging; you can view the masters at work here and buy ironwork products from the neighbouring shop. Heading south towards **Plac**, the very small main square, have a look at the **Partisan monument**, comprising iron figures made at the aforementioned workshop.

Vigenjc and Cerkev Sv Lenarta

Running through the village is the **Kroparica**, a rapid, thrashing mountain stream that once propelled more than fifty water wheels for the bellows and sledgehammers of the foundries, most of which were decommissioned after World War I. A short way south of the bridge you'll find the **Vigenjc** (Vice Forge), the only preserved and operative workshop in Kropa; to view a demonstration, contact the Iron Forging Museum at least a day in advance (€2; ☎ 04 533 7200, ⓦ mro.si).

Just north of the forge, up the slope, is the Gothic **Cerkev Sv Lenarta** (Parish Church of St Leonard), whose cemetery contains beautifully crafted iron headstones, including the grave of Bertoncelj; there are lovely views of the village from the terrace.

EATING	KROPA
Pr' Kovač Kropa 30 • 04 533 6320. Just 50m south of Plac, the village's main square, this cosy place knocks up superb local specialities such as "Blacksmith's Plate"	(an assortment of meats), buckwheat omelette, and sour milk-and-bean soup – excellent wines too. Tues–Sun 10am–11pm.

Bazilika Marija Pomagaj

Brezje, around 6km southeast of Radovljica • Daily 7am–8pm • ☎ 04 537 0700, ⓦ marija.si • The easiest way to get to Brezje is by one of the four buses from Bled (see opposite) to the small village of Črnivec, from where it's a 10min walk to the village – four buses also make the return trip

A cluster of souvenir stalls, snack bars and an enormous car park (€2) welcome you to the small village of **BREZJE**, the setting for Slovenia's most important place of pilgrimage, the **Bazilika Marija Pomagaj** (Basilica of St Mary Help). Attracting some 300,000 visitors each year, the church began life in 1800 as a chapel, built as an extension to the fifteenth-century **St Vitus' Church**. It first became a site of prayer during Napoleon's occupation of northern Slovenia at the beginning of the nineteenth century, but it wasn't until the French departed that rumours of miracles occurring at Brezje began to spread, fuelling the arrival of tens of thousands of pilgrims from all over Europe. So great was the influx that, in 1900, it was necessary to construct a larger church, the results of which you see today. Around the same time, the Franciscans pitched up and proceeded to build an adjoining **monastery** and have remained the guardians of the church ever since.

Save for Janez Vurnik's stunning **high altar** – adorned with smoothly sculpted cherubs and instrument-playing angels – the interior is actually rather plain; still, this doesn't bother the majority of visitors, most of whom come here to pray at the **altar** of the Blessed Virgin of Help. This much reworked altar – in the fourth chapel on the right – contains the church's most renowned piece of work, Leopold Layer's painting *Mary Help*, framed by a dazzling gold mount designed by Tone Bitenc in 1977. There's also a contribution from Ivan Grohar, who completed the paintings in the third altars on the left and right. In the niche above the southern door is a statue by Boris Kalin, which previously stood at the nearby Otoče train station, and just across the way is a statue of Pope John Paul II, built to commemorate his visit here in 1996.

Begunje and around

In the tidy little village of **BEGUNJE**, 5km north of Radovljica, thousands of people – including many women and children – were detained, beaten and executed during the German occupation of Gorenjska (1941–45). During World War II the village's seventeenth-century **Katzenstein Castle** (now a psychiatric hospital) was used as a Gestapo prison; 849 prisoners were either executed or died here, while a further five thousand were sent to concentration camps in Austria, Germany and Poland.

Muzej Talcev

Katzenstein Castle, 200m north of the main bus stop • March, April, Nov & Dec Wed & Sat 9am–1pm, Sun 1–5pm; May, June, Sept & Oct Tues–Fri 9am–1pm, Sat & Sun 1–6pm; July & Aug Tues–Sun 1–6pm • €2 • ☎ 04 533 3790, ⓦ mro.si

Housed within a wing of the castle, the **Muzej Talcev** (Museum of Hostages) vividly documents Begunje's grim episode in Slovenian World War II history. Ten preserved cells illustrate the brutal experiences of the hostages confined here for months and years on end, most harrowingly in the form of farewell messages, which the Germans tried unsuccessfully to erase, etched into the walls as they awaited impending death. Many of those executed are buried in a **graveyard** in the park just across from the museum; beyond the graveyard stands a small **chapel**, unmistakably the work of Jože Plečnik (see box, p.49).

Muzej Avsenik

Begunje 21, opposite the main bus stop • Tues–Sun 11am–5pm • €3 • ☎ 04 533 3402, ⓦ avsenik.com

The **Muzej Avsenik** (Avsenik Museum) celebrates the life and work of local folk musician and national celebrity Slavko Avsenik (1929–2015), who was born in this very house. The walls are plastered with album covers (the Avsenik ensemble sold in excess of thirty million records), gold and platinum discs and innumerable awards, though pride of place goes to his costume (check out the knee-length boots) and two custom-made Hohner accordions.

One of the pioneers of the Oberkrainer sound – oompah-style folk music primarily employing accordion and various brass instruments – Avsenik was a bigger star in Germany than in Slovenia, so don't be surprised to see busloads of fans from the continent rocking up to pay homage to the great man. Today, his legacy lives on in the form of the Sašo Avsenik Ensemble, headed up by his grandson. The true fans make a beeline for the **Avsenik Festival**, held every odd-numbered year at the end of August – it doesn't take a genius to work out what that entails.

Grad Kamen

2km north of Begunje • Daily dawn to dusk • Free

The impressive, if slightly forlorn-looking, ruins of **Grad Kamen** (Kamen Castle) are all that is left of a structure established by the Ortenburg counts in the twelfth century as a means of defending the Radovljica Plain. Its most extensive period of development came in the fifteenth century, when the remarkably well-preserved tower and residential palace were constructed. In the early eighteenth century, no longer required to protect trade routes, ward off Turkish invaders and quell peasant revolts, the castle was abandoned. It remained in a state of decay until 1959, when work finally began to restore it; although there's nothing to see inside, it's a lovely, quiet spot with wonderful views down to the valley below.

ARRIVAL AND INFORMATION   BEGUNJE

By bus There are hourly buses to and from Bled and Radovljica.
Tourist information The Avsenik Museum functions as

the village's tourist information point (Tues–Sun 11am–5pm; ☎ 04 533 3402).

EATING

Avsenik Begunje 21 ☎ 04 533 3402, ⓦ avsenik.com. Begunje's sole restaurant is, inevitably, entwined with the Avsenik Museum, and all rather hammed up for the

tourists, with folk music most evenings – but this isn't such a bad thing, and neither is the traditional Slovene food. Tues–Sat 11am–10pm, Sun 11am–8pm.

Bled and around

BLED is by far the country's most popular destination, thanks to its placid fairytale **Lake Bled** and its island, a dramatically sited **castle** and the surrounding snow-tipped mountains. The town itself, which is most densely concentrated to the east of the lake, is unspectacular, with nothing specific to see; by way of contrast, the iconic lake is probably the country's single most photographed location.

Despite its status, Bled rarely feels overwhelmed, but if you do fancy a change of pace and a bit of solitude, there are some terrific attractions close by. Highlights include the hugely popular **Vintgar Gorge**, the less-visited but no less impressive **Pokljuka Plateau** and the fascinating **Babji Zob Caves**; to the northwest, in the village of **Vrba**, you can visit the birthplace of France Prešeren, Slovenia's greatest poet. Bled is also a good place to base yourself for hikes into the eastern tranche of the **Julian Alps**.

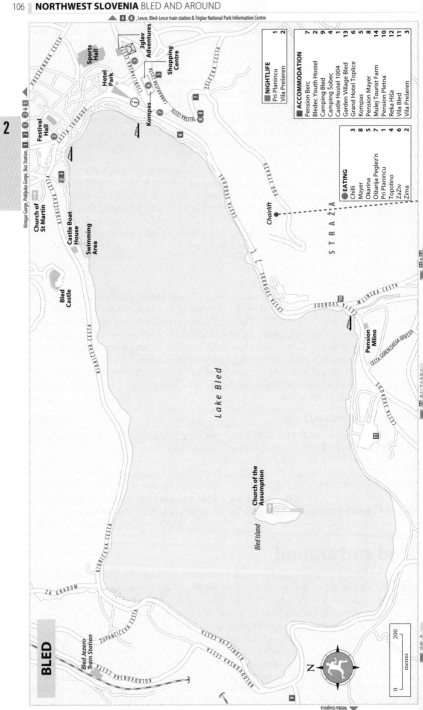

▲ 4 , 4 , Lesce, Bled-Lesce train station & Triglav National Park Information Centre

BLED

NIGHTLIFE
| Pri Planincu | 1 |
| Vila Prešeren | 2 |

ACCOMMODATION
Pension Berc	7
Bledec Youth Hostel	2
Camping Bled	9
Camping Sobec	4
Castle Hostel 1004	1
Garden Village Bled	13
Grand Hotel Toplice	6
Kompas	5
Pension Mayer	8
Mulej Tourist Farm	14
Pension Pletna	10
Reka Hiša	12
Vila Bled	11
Vila Prešeren	3

EATING
Chilli	3
Mayer	8
Okarina	5
Oštarija Peglez'n	7
Pri Planincu	1
Topolino	4
ZaZiv	6
Zima	2

Lake Bled

Bled Island

Church of the Assumption

STRAŽA

Chairlift

Pension Mlino

Bled Castle

Castle Boat House

Swimming Area

Church of St Martin

Festival Hall

Sports Hall

3glav Adventures

Shopping Centre

Hotel Park

Kompas

Bled Jezero Train Station

N

0 200 metres

Velika Osojnica

Brief history

The town dates from 1004, when the German emperor Henry II bestowed the castle, and the land between the two Sava rivers, to the bishops of Brixen – who would subsequently rule for the next eight hundred years. The first visitors to Bled were medieval **pilgrims** from Carniola and Carinthia, who came to pray at the island church, although mass **tourism** didn't take long to find its feet. This was in large part thanks to Arnold Rikli, a Swiss-born physician who opened a bathing resort and lodgings at Bled in 1855. Between the two World Wars the resort became a popular hideaway for politicians and royalty, with both the Yugoslav royal family, and later, Tito, spending much time here during the summer; even today, Bled is the one place high-ranking officials and diplomats are ushered to when visiting Slovenia.

2

Bled jezero

From a visitor's perspective, Bled is essentially the lake and all that happens on or around it. Created some 14,000 years ago when water flooded the depression left by a receding glacier, **Bled jezero** (Lake Bled) is a natural playground, bristling with rowing boats, gondolas and swimmers during the spring and summer. The best way to get your bearings is to take a circular walk, beginning at the *Hotel Park* and working your way round clockwise, which should take no more than two and a half hours.

Blejski otok

During the day, a continual relay of stretch gondolas (*pletnas*) glides back and forth across the water between the shore and **Blejski otok** (Bled Island), a magically picturesque islet crowned by the exquisite **Cerkev Sv Marija Božja** (Church of the Assumption; daily: April & Oct 9am–6pm; May–Sept 9am–7pm; Nov–March 9am–4pm; €6; ☎04 576 7979, ⓦblejskiotok.si). Findings support the theory that there was a settlement here in prehistoric times, while further excavations have revealed the remains of a pre-Romanesque chapel, as well as a large Slavic cemetery dating from around 9 AD. The present Baroque church dates from 1698, though its most outstanding features are from the preceding Gothic church, namely the remarkably well-preserved **frescoes** on the north and south presbytery walls, depicting scenes from the life of the Virgin, and a wooden statue of the Virgin with Child. The wishing bell, which keeps most visitors amused, was installed in 1534, though a larger bell hangs in the enormous freestanding belfry, itself a hybrid of Gothic and Baroque elements; inside, two opposite winding staircases allow access to the top, where you'll find a fine, late nineteenth-century **Pendulum Clock** made from forged iron, probably from Kropa (see p.103), and which chimes every fifteen minutes.

A few paces back down from the church, the **Provost's House** now hosts rotating exhibitions and, better still, a *potičnica*, a café specializing in **potica**, a traditional pastry-based nut roll, with flavours including walnut, hazelnut and almond; it'd be remiss to leave the island without trying a slice.

BOATING TO BLED ISLAND

If you fancy a boat trip to **Bled Island**, there are a couple of options. Thought to have derived from the German word "plateboot" (meaning flat-bottomed boat), **pletnas**, or gondolas (€14/person), depart from three locations: down below the *Hotel Park*, near the *Vila Prešeren* (both 30min to the island) and opposite *Pension Mlino* (15min). *Pletnas* leave only when full – which means you may have to sit idly for a bit while the *pletnar* solicits custom – and give you just thirty minutes on the island before returning, so you may prefer to rent a **rowing boat** from the Castle Boat House (below the castle) or *Pension Pletna* (€10/hr for a four-person boat). It may be harder going, but it's more fun and you won't feel rushed on the island. *Pletnas* and rowing boats operate year-round, depending on the weather.

2

ACTIVITIES IN AND AROUND BLED

Although far more challenging hikes can be had in Triglav National Park (see box, p.117), there are some very enjoyable **walks** near Lake Bled. Opportunities for other activities are rife, with a number of agencies specializing in **adrenaline sports**.

WALKING AND SKIING

Velika Osojnica, a 756m-high peak at the southwestern corner of the lake, offers the stiffest local walk but also the best views; take either the path from *Camping Bled* (via Ojstrica), or from the main road, Kidričeva cesta (via Mala Osojnica), and allow three hours for a return trip. For an excellent range of **hikes** in the Julian Alps, including two-day trips to Triglav (€200), and easy/moderate half-day hikes within the park (€65), contact **3glav Adventures** (☎ 041 683 184, ⓦ 3glav.com) in a small hut at Ljubljanska cesta 1.

A gentler alternative is to walk up to **Straža**, the 638m-high hill southwest of the *Grand Hotel Toplice*; this is also Bled's very modest **ski slope**, suitable for beginners only. Between December and February a chair lift operates from Pod Stražo, the road above Cesta svobode, to the summit; in summer the same hill becomes a 520m **toboggan run** (June–Sept daily 11am–7pm, plus night tobogganing July to mid-Aug Tues, Fri & Sat 9–11pm; €8 for one run, €14 for three; ⓦ straza-bled.si).

SWIMMING AND SKATING

Although **swimming** is permitted at various points around the lake (Mlino at the southern end, and Velika Zaka and Mala Zaka at the western end), you're better off sticking to the designated, roped-off, area on the north shore beneath the castle, which also has a grassy **beach** (Grajsko Kopališče; daily: June & early to mid-Sept 9am–7pm; July & Aug 9am–8pm; €7 for a daily ticket before noon, €6 after noon, €4 after 5pm); it's also got waterslides, changing rooms and lockers.

Sadly, the lake rarely freezes over these days; not quite as romantic, there's an indoor **skating rink** at the sports hall (Športna dvorana) east of *Hotel Park* (Oct–March Mon–Sat 9.30–11am & 4.30–6pm, Sun 4.30–6pm; €5, plus €4.50 for skate rental).

RIDING, FLYING, GOLF AND FISHING

There is **horseriding** at the Hippodrome in Lesce, 4km southeast of Bled (1hr trail ride, either cross-country or around the track, €25; €45/2hr; ☎ 041 675 482, ⓦ hipodromlesce.si); also in Lesce, the Alpine Flying Centre at Begunjska cesta 10 (☎ 04 532 0100, ⓦ alc-lesce.si) offers **panoramic flights** for €120. Slovenia's premier **golf** course, the Bled Golf Club (☎ 01 200 9901, ⓦ golfbled.si), is 2km east of town on the Bled–Lesce road, and comprises the eighteen-hole King's course (€80), and the nine-hole Lake course (€45). Licences for **fishing** (€30/day, €70 for three days), permitted on the lake between April and December, can be bought from the tourist office (see opposite).

ADRENALINE ACTIVITIES

Bled is overrun with outfits offering **adrenaline sports**, most of which are near the bus station; Mamut (☎ 040 121 900, ⓦ mamut-adventures.com) and Life Adventures (☎ 04 201 4875, ⓦ lifeadventures.si) are decent bets, as is 3glav Adventures (☎ 041 683 184, ☎ 3glav.com), which also leads organized hikes (see above). The agencies all offer pretty much the same thing, and at similar prices for roughly three to four hours – principally rafting (€38), canyoning (€60), kayaking (€55) and paragliding (€95).

Blejski Grad

North shore of the lake • Daily: April–Oct 8am–8pm; Nov–March 8am–6pm • €9 • ☎ 04 572 9782, ⓦ blejski-grad.si • Several paths (marked "Grad") wind up to the castle, each a reasonably stiff 15min climb; one from behind the swimming area (Grajsko Kopališče) on Kidričeva cesta, another from the youth hostel on Grajska cesta, and a third from Rikljeva ulica, near the Parish Church of St Martin (Cerkev Sv Martina)

Perched high up on a craggy bluff on the north shore of Lake Bled is **Blejski Grad** (Bled Castle), enclosed by a Romanesque wall and spotted with stout-looking parapets, towers and ramparts, just as a castle should be. Originally an eleventh-century fortification, the castle today dates from the seventeenth century (albeit with further renovations in the 1950s), and is characterized by a lower and upper courtyard. The outstanding feature of the neat upper courtyard is the lovely sixteenth-century **chapel**, decorated with frescoes from around 1700 but otherwise furnitureless.

The castle's neat and well-presented **museum** focuses primarily on local archeological finds, its most celebrated item being a stunning peacock brooch. The lake has yielded many extraordinary treasures, not least a bronze sword, dating from around 1300 BC; elsewhere there are Iron Age whorls and vessels, stone mortars and axes, bone harpoons and the like. Artistically, the most significant piece is a fine painting of Henry II conferring the property of Bled on Bishop Albuin. Don't miss the tiny, seventeenth-century box loo protruding over the rock face; there can't have been many more toilets in the world with more sensational views.

ARRIVAL AND DEPARTURE   BLED 2

By bus Bled's bus station is 5min northeast of the lake at the junction of Cesta svobode and Grajska cesta.
Destinations Kranj (hourly; 40min); Kranjska Gora (hourly; 1hr 15min); Ljubljana (hourly; 1hr 15min); Radovljica (hourly; 15min); Ribčev Laz, for Lake Bohinj (hourly; 40min).
By train The nearest train station to Bled is Bled Jezero (on the Jesenice–Nova Gorica line), on Kolodvorska cesta, a 10min walk northwest of the lake. If coming from Ljubljana, you'll alight at Bled-Lesce, 4km southeast of Bled and connected to the town by bus (every 30min).
Destinations (Bled Jezero) Bohinjska Bistrica (Mon–Fri 7 daily, Sat & Sun 4–5 daily; 20min); Most na Soči (Mon–Fri 7 daily, Sat & Sun 4–5 daily; 55min); Nova Gorica (Mon–Fri 7 daily, Sat & Sun 4–5 daily; 1hr 35min).
Destinations (Bled-Lesce) Jesenice (every 1–2hr; 15min); Kranj (every 1–2hr; 25min); Ljubljana (every 1–2hr; 1hr); Radovljica (every 1–2hr; 5min); Škofja Loka (every 1–2hr; 35min).

INFORMATION AND ACTIVITIES

Tourist office Cesta svobode 10, on the lakefront opposite *Hotel Park* (mid-April to June, Sept & Oct Mon–Sat 8am–7pm, Sun 10am–4pm; July & Aug Mon–Sat 8am–9pm, Sun 9am–5pm; Nov to mid-April Mon–Fri 8am–6pm, Sat & Sun 9am–4pm; ☎04 574 1122, ⓦbled.si).
Triglav National Park Information Centre Ljubljanska cesta 27 (daily: mid-April to mid-Oct 8am–6pm; mid-Oct to mid-April 8am–4pm; ☎04 578 0205, ⓦtnp.si). Get all the information you need on the national park, and on Bled and its surroundings, at this superb visitor centre.
Bike rental Numerous places offer bike rental; the tourist office and the Kompas agency in the shopping centre at Ljubljanska cesta 4 (Mon–Sat 8am–7pm; ☎04 572 7501, ⓦkompas-bled.si) charge the same (mountain bikes €6/3hr, €8/6hr; electric bikes €5/1hr, €10/4hr).
Tourist train This hop-on, hop-off train crawls around the lake clogging up the traffic; its starting point is the sports hall on the east shore (April–Nov; €4 for a day-ticket).
Horse-drawn carriages Parked near the Festival Hall, these carriages (*fijaker*) offer 30min jaunts around the lake (€40 for five people), with longer trips available.

ACCOMMODATION

As befits Slovenia's premier tourist destination, there is an abundance of accommodation in town, from top-class hotels to run-of-the-mill package-type places and homely pensions, the last offering a more satisfying and wallet-friendly stay. The area just up from the bus station is swarming with hostels. For **private accommodation**, contact the Kompas agency (see above).

HOTELS

★**Pension Berc** Želeška cesta 15 ☎04 574 1838, ⓦpenzion-berc.si. Overlooking pristine lawns, this gorgeous nineteenth-century farmhouse offers ten sumptuous rooms of sweet-smelling pine, marble and cut stone walls – the most restful, and best-value, option in town. Opposite, run by the same family, the *Garni Hotel Berc* offers similar comforts (and identical prices) but nowhere near the same level of charm. April–Oct. **€85**
Grand Hotel Toplice Cesta svobode 12 ☎04 579 1600, ⓦsava-hotels-resorts.com. Bled's most opulent – yet welcomingly unpretentious – hotel has magnificently appointed rooms, with antique furniture, large, handsome beds and gold-plated trimmings; the more expensive lakeside rooms have bed pumps, for that extra firmness. The stunning thermal pool and Finnish and Turkish saunas are free for guests; they also offer a bit of private beach and rowing boats. **€190**

Kompas Cankarjeva cesta 7 ☎04 620 5100, ⓦkompas hotel.com. On a small rise just above the shopping centre, this large, but far from impersonal, hotel offers an appealing mix of slickly furnished park and lakeside rooms, the latter affording smashing views; the terrace pool is the loveliest in town. **€140**
★**Pension Mayer** Želeška cesta 7 ☎04 576 5740, ⓦmayer-sp.si. In a similar style to the nearby *Berc*, this fine nineteenth-century building, set among lush lawns and flowerbeds, has thirteen stylishly understated rooms, all different colours but each with parquet floors, large, plump beds and spankingly clean bathrooms. Bikes for rent too. Top value. Mid-April to mid-Oct. **€82**
Mulej Tourist Farm Selo pri Bledu 42a ☎04 574 4617, ⓦmulej-bled.com. A welcome alternative to the town's hotels, this large, friendly and popular tourist farm, 1km south of the lake in the village of Selo, has eight simply furnished but

2

COMPETITIVE ROWING ON LAKE BLED

When the rowers Iztok Čop and Luka Špik claimed Slovenia's first-ever **Olympic gold medal** at the Sydney 2000 games (Čop also bagged Slovenia's first-ever Olympic medal – bronze – at the 1992 Barcelona games), Slovenian sport, and particularly rowing, at last gained the recognition it had craved since independence in 1991. **Rowing** has a long and distinguished history in Slovenia, with many of its rowers having formed the core of ex-Yugoslav teams before each republic went its separate way. Since then it has been a byword for Slovenian sporting achievement; its most successful rowers having been trained at the **Bled Rowing Club**, formed in 1949 and based at the western end of the lake, at Mala Zaka.

The lake is hugely popular as a practice arena with both Slovenian and international rowers, while its standing as a top-class international venue is manifest in the staging of four World Rowing Championships, in 1966, 1979, 1986 and 2011. Although several domestic regattas take place in Bled in spring and autumn, the best time to be here is in mid-June when the **Bled International Regatta** draws a world-class field.

---

very comfortable en-suite rooms, as well as four apartments. There's superb home cooking (€10/person for dinner), while the farm animals and pets will go down a treat with kids; free bike rental too. **€80**

Pension Pletna Cesta svobode 37 ☎ 04 574 3702, ⓦ pletna.com. Out towards the southern end of the lake in Mlino, the five rooms here are boxy but bright, with either lime green or gentle pink walls; despite being right on the noisy main road, they are well insulated and each has a balcony with superb lake views. Bikes, rowing boats and kayaks for rent too. Breakfast €6. **€70**

Reka Hiša Obrne 17, near the village of Bohinjska Bela, 4km west of Bled ☎ 04 576 0340, ⓦ rekahisa .com. Isolated, delightfully welcoming guesthouse beside the Bohinjska Sava River, offering four modest, cosy rooms with furnishings beautifully handcrafted by the owner; the host is a terrific cook, and rates include an evening meal. They also organize a range of activities (including kayaking and, in winter, skiing) and are able to arrange transfers from Bled or Bohinj. To get here from Bled, take any Bohinj-bound bus and alight by the bridge after the second exit for Bohinjska Bela, from where it's a 10min walk. **€90**

Vila Bled Cesta svobode 26 ☎ 04 575 3710, ⓦ brdo.si. Set in its own extensive grounds on the lake's southern shore, Bled's most historic establishment was rebuilt as yet another country retreat for Tito in 1947. The extraordinary socialist-era rooms have remained largely untouched since the president entertained world leaders here, retaining a uniquely time-warped appeal. The hotel also has a spa facility, its own private beach and boats. **€175**

Vila Prešeren Veslaška promenada 14 ☎ 04 575 2510, ⓦ sportina-turizem.si. Graceful nineteenth-century villa concealing six immaculate and supremely stylish rooms (two with lake view), decorated in cool pinks, greys and blacks, with wrought-iron furnishings, elegant bedside lamps, wood-framed mirrors, and a host of other neat touches. Wonderful terrace café and restaurant, too (see opposite). **€119**

HOSTELS

Bledec Youth Hostel Grajska cesta 17 ☎ 04 574 5250, ⓦ bledec.si. This high-quality, quiet, hostel has comfort-able dorms and doubles with traditional furniture – each has its own bathroom plus TV. There's a self-catering kitchen and a good restaurant, plus laundry facilities. Breakfast €5. Dorms **€22**, doubles **€56**

Castle Hostel 1004 Grajska cesta 22 ☎ 070 732 799, ⓦ hostel1004.com. The pick of the hostels near the bus station; small but immaculately kept dorms (four to twelve beds) and doubles, all with shared shower facilities, are complemented by a kitchen-cum-common area leading to a terrace with the best views in town. No breakfast, but there's a supermarket just a few paces away. Dorms **€14**, doubles **€40**

CAMPSITES

Camping Bled Kidričeva cesta 10 ☎ 04 575 2000, ⓦ sava-hotels-resorts.com. Beautifully located amid the pines at the western end of the lake, this family-friendly campsite has first-rate facilities. For glampers, there are superb wooden huts with double beds and hot tubs; the breakfast basket (€9) is fab. To get here, take any bus heading towards Bohinj and alight at the beginning of Kidričeva cesta. Easter–Oct. Camping **€27**, huts **€61**

Camping Šobec Šobčeva cesta 25 ☎ 04 535 3700, ⓦ sobec.si. Two kilometres east of Bled in the direction of Bled-Lesce, this is Slovenia's largest campsite, a vast area with its own lake and beach as well as sporting facilities (including tennis and mini-golf), playgrounds, a shop and restaurant; there are also bungalows sleeping up to six. To get here from Bled-Lesce station, walk north towards the crossing, take the second left down Finžgareva ulica for 100m, left again and continue behind the industrial zone for 400m before heading down a gravel track to the right. Mid-April to Sept. Camping **€28**, bungalows **€135**

Garden Village Bled Cesta Gorenjskega odreda 16 ☎ 083 899 220, ⓦ gardenvillagebled.com. In a secluded spot just 5min south of the lake, this is posh glamping and some. The sizeable wood-and-canvas glamping tents are furnished to a standard most upscale hotels would envy, and come with outdoor hot tub; more exciting are the surprisingly high treehouses (sleeping four). The cheapest options are the cosy two-person pier tents, perched on suspended platforms above a stream. Pier tents **€110**, treehouses **€290**, glamping tents **€340**

EATING

Bled's culinary offerings are decent rather than outstanding; the best restaurants are to be found in some of the better **pensions**.

Chilli Cesta svobode 9 ☎ 04 574 3027, ⓦ chillibled .com. Fun, contemporary establishment serving a stack of colourful and spicy Mexican and Mediterranean dishes from around €8; stuffed tortillas, burritos, enchiladas and so on, plus crisp salad platters (chilli, seafood, Greek). Its large wood-decked terrace is the ideal place for a beer or cocktail at sundown. Daily 9am–midnight.

★ **Mayer** Želeška cesta 7 ☎ 04 576 5740, ⓦ mayer-sp .si. Refined and extremely well-regarded restaurant in the pension of the same name, with a moderate to expensive menu using veggies and herbs sourced from their own garden. Fried cheese is a terrific starter, perhaps followed by fillet of venison (€23) or smoked trout fillet, with a buckwheat doughnut to finish. Daily 6–10pm.

Okarina Ljubljanska cesta 8 ☎ 04 574 1458, ⓦ okarina .com. Bled's most beautifully appointed restaurant is also its most intriguing, courtesy of its signature Tandoori dishes (€17) plus a heap of other treats such as wild boar cutlets or roe deer medallions (€22); the veggie options, too, are enticing, among them spinach pancake with soya steak (€13). Daily noon–3pm & 6pm–midnight.

Oštarija Peglez'n Cesta svobode 19a ☎ 04 574 4218. Warm, cottage-like restaurant whose seafood menu is the best in town, with smoked tuna steak with herbs, trout fillet with chard, and cuttlefish risotto (€12.50) all great options. The sunny yellow and blue interior, with its wicker chairs and walls happily cluttered with ceramics and household implements, looks great. Daily noon–10.30pm.

Pri Planincu Grajska cesta 8 ☎ 04 574 1613, ⓦ pri -planincu.com. This hugely popular and frenetic alpine inn-style place, just up from the bus station, has been serving hearty, meat-heavy dishes since 1903; notably the juicy Serbian specialities *pljeskavica* (oversized hamburger) and *čevapčiči* (rissoles of spiced minced meat). Daily 9am–11pm.

Topolino Ljubljanska cesta 26 ☎ 031 310 090, ⓦ restavracija-topolino.si. Just 400m east of the lake, this understated slow-food restaurant is Bled's most sophisticated outfit, gorgeously decorated, if possibly a little too stiff at times. The food and wine are of the highest order, so expect mouthwatering plates like goose prosciutto with pumpkin oil, or lamb fillet with aubergine purée and chocolate chilli (€20). May–Sept daily noon–10pm; Oct–April closed Tues.

ZaZiv Ljubljanska cesta 4 ☎ 041 643 531. Everything here – burgers, buns (spelt, corn, chickpea), juices and ice creams – is vegan, and jolly good it is too. Located inside the undistinguished concrete shopping complex, it's ostensibly a takeaway place, but they do have seating (and waiting service) a few paces away on the terrace. Daily 8am–9pm.

Zima Grajski cesta 3 ☎ 04 574 1616, ⓦ smon.si. Bled's most enduring café, near the bus station, has been doling out a prodigious selection of home-made pastries – notably the very creamy Bled speciality *Kremna Rezina* – since 1880; best enjoyed with a steaming mug of *bela kava* (white coffee). Daily 7.30am–9pm.

DRINKING

Pri Planincu Grajska cesta 8 ☎ 04 574 1613, ⓦ pri -planincu.com. Bled's most traditional pub-style venue, usually crammed with hikers and climbers following a hard day out in the mountains; a great spot for a beer. Daily 9am–11pm.

Vila Prešeren Veslaška promenada 14 ☎ 04 575 2510, ⓦ vilapreseren.si. Although principally a restaurant, *Preseren* has an unbeatable lakeside terrace that is just the spot (if you can find one) to sup an early morning coffee or tea; better still, head along at sundown and kick back with a glass of one of the many terrific wines on offer. Daily 7am–11pm.

BLED FESTIVALS

Bled's three major festivals all take place in July. The big one is **Bled Days** (Blejski Dnevi) on the third weekend of the month, with three days of fairs and concerts along the promenade at the eastern end of the lake; the event climaxes with the lighting of thousands of candles on the lake – a memorable sight – and fireworks. At the beginning of July, the **International Music Festival** (ⓦ festivalbled.com) is a two-week run of classical concerts staged at various venues, principally the Festival Hall and St Martin's Church; and at the end of July there's the fortnight-long **Okarina Festival** (ⓦ festival-okarina.si) featuring performances by an eclectic group of world musicians up at the castle and on the lakeshore promenade.

2

Soteska Vintgar

Near Podhom, 4km north of Bled • April–Oct daily 8am–7pm • €4 • ⓦ vintgar.si • From June to Sept there are buses to the gorge from Bled's bus station (June & Sept 10am; July & Aug 9am & 10am) with a return service at 12.30pm; the most enjoyable way to get here, however, is to walk, an easy and pleasant stroll along country roads and through a handful of pretty villages – from the bus station join the main road, Prešernova ulica, and head north until you come to Partizanska cesta; continue north along here, and after crossing the stream take the left fork (Cesta v Vintgar), continuing towards the village of Podhom, from where the gorge is signposted

2

The major attraction in Bled's immediate environs is the **Soteska Vintgar** (Vintgar Gorge), an impressive 1600m-long and 150m-high defile that makes a pleasant walk from town. The gorge was chanced upon by a local mayor and his cartographer colleague in 1891; so thrilled were they with their discovery that they set up a construction committee in order to seek ways of opening the gorge up to the public, an event that duly occurred two years later. It's since been accessible via a continuous chain of wooden gantries and bridges, suspended from the precipitous rock face, and running the entire length of the gorge to the **Slap Šum** (Slap Waterfall) at its northern end; from here you can either retrace your steps and return the way you came, or take the path on the right, returning to Bled via the pilgrimage **Cerkev Sv Katarine** (Church of St Catherine) and the village of **Zasip**. It can get very damp in the gorge, and if it's been raining, very slippery, so you'd do well to bring some waterproofs and good walking boots.

Vrba

VRBA, a tiny village 4km northeast of Bled just off the main road to Kranjska Gora, is famed as the birthplace of **France Prešeren**, Slovenia's most celebrated poet, who was sufficiently enamoured with his home village to write:

Vrba, happy village, my old home
My father's cottage stands there to this day
The lure of learning beckoned me away
Its serpent wiles enticing me to roam

Rojstna Hiša Prešerna hiša

Vrba 2 • Tues–Fri 9am–4pm, Sat & Sun 10am–5pm • €2.50 • ☎ 04 580 1503 • Take one of the hourly buses from Bled to Jesenice, which take a rather convoluted route via Radovljica

Rojstna Hiša Prešerna hiša (Prešeren's Birthplace), a solid whitewashed house on the right-hand side of the village as you enter, was built in the sixteenth century, but partly destroyed by a village fire in 1856. It contains a few original items of furniture, including the poet's cradle, but otherwise the exhibition about his life is disappointing, with little to get excited about beyond a couple of first editions; you'll learn more about the man and his work at the memorial house in Kranj (see p.95), where he lived and worked for the last few years of his life. Indeed, this house is actually more interesting as an architectural monument – most impressive is the traditional "black kitchen" (see p.123), preserved in its entirety.

Cerkev Sv Marko and around

Just up behind the birthplace on a small grassy hill, the Gothic **Cerkev Sv Marko** (Church of St Mark) is worth a look for its sixteenth-century frescoes by the prolific Jernej of Loka – including Christ's Passion and traces of St George doing battle with the dragon – and murals by Friulian masters. The wooden ceiling dates from 1991 when the latest renovation took place. A five-minute walk from here to the western edge of the village brings you to a sturdy 200-year-old **linden tree** encircled by sixteen large stones, one for each of the farmhouses that originally stood in the village – it was supposedly also the place where debates between the village representatives would take place.

2

FRANCE PREŠEREN

One of Slovenia's greatest nineteenth-century heroes and indisputably the country's greatest romantic poet, **France Prešeren** did more to advance the cause of the Slovene national consciousness in the nineteenth century than just about any other figure. Born in Vrba in 1800, Prešeren was educated in Ribnica and Ljubljana, before obtaining his law degree in Vienna. Although a lawyer by profession, Prešeren's true vocation was poetry. Underpinned by themes of unrequited love, homeland, friendships and other existential laments, Prešeren's poems combined classical, Renaissance and Romantic elements with traditional Slovene folk customs, resulting in a body of work considered to be the apotheosis of nineteenth-century Slovene language and culture. His most recognized piece of work was the epic *Krst pri Savici* (*Baptism at the Savica*), which explores themes of Christianization in Slovenia, though only one volume of his work, *Poezije doktorja Franceta Prešerna* (*Poems of Doctor France Prešeren*), was published during his lifetime, in 1845.

Through his writing, the liberal-minded Prešeren – along with his peers, in particular his mentor Matija Čop – attempted to create an **independent Slovene culture** oriented towards classical Western traditions, while he also sought to stimulate national awareness among the emerging Slovene middle class. However, he frequently clashed with the government in Vienna over his anti-German sentiments, as well as the Catholic Church, which considered his work immoral.

Prešeren's **personal life** was deeply unhappy: he was a melancholy character, a drunk and a philanderer, and he had three children out of wedlock. He was particularly depressed by an unrequited love affair with Julija Primič, whom he first met at the Church of St John in Trnovo, Ljubljana, and by the untimely death of Matija Čop.

From 1846 until his death, from cirrhosis of the liver, on February 8, 1849, Prešeren spent the last three years of his life working in Kranj, the city in which he is also buried. His writing aside, Prešeren's legacy is very much alive in other forms – the public holiday on February 8 is celebrated as **Prešeren Day** (the Day of Slovene Culture), while the seventh stanza of *Zdravljica* (*A Toast*), set to music by composer Stanko Premrl, was adopted as the national anthem of the republic in 1991.

Jama Pod Babjim Zobom

Near the village of Bohinjska Bela, 4km west of Bled • Tours (May–Oct) must be arranged in advance; usually a minimum of six people is required • €25, includes transport from Bled • ☎ 031 457 509, ✉ dzrbled@g-kabel.si

The **Jama Pod Babjim Zobom** (Babji Zob Caves) – beneath **Babji Zob** (Hags Tooth), a formidable-looking, tooth-shaped pillar poised atop a 1128m peak – couldn't be more different from your conventional cave visit. The caves can only be visited on a guided tour, which entails a not inconsiderable one-hour hike up to the cave entrance; thereafter it's a further hour's trek through the complex, before the steep descent back down the hill (approximately three hours in total).

At just 300m long it's not an expansive cave system, but it does possess some unique features, not least several groupings of rarely seen **helictites** – contorted, sometimes horizontal, calcite deposits, which grow in random directions seemingly defying gravity. Their existence has long confounded experts and remains one of the most vexing speleological questions, though one theory suggests that their form is caused by airflow within the cave. Bring warm clothing, waterproofs and a pair of older shoes, as it can get quite muddy.

Pokljuška soteska

7km west of Bled • Regular buses run from Bled to the village of Krnica, from where it's a 2km walk (follow the signs) to the gorge entrance; with your own transport it's possible to drive right to the entrance

As an antidote to the hordes that pile up to the Vintgar Gorge, the **Pokljuška soteska** (Pokljuka Gorge), a magnificent fossilized ravine, is perfect for anyone seeking solitude. Located on the northeastern margins of the **Pokljuka Plateau** – a thickly forested plain at the eastern extremes of the Julian Alps and a world-class venue for cross-country skiing – this dry and narrow trough-like ravine was hollowed out by the former course of the Ribščica River some ten thousand years ago, the retreating glaciers leaving behind the largest fossilized gorge in the country. It's characterized by peculiar dilations – known as *vrtci* (garden plots) – and a series of natural arches, although its most spectacular feature is the **Pokljuka luknja** (Pokljuka Window), a 15m-high subterranean hall with three natural windows hollowed out of its ceiling.

2

Bohinj and around

Some 20km long and 5km wide, **Bohinj** is the name given to the entire Sava Bohinjka basin southwest of Bled, a region of immense charm and beauty, embracing rugged valleys and mountains, alluring rustic idylls and, best of all, the magical **Lake Bohinj**.

The main train and bus connection points, and the tourist offices, are in Bohinj's two key settlements, **Bohinjska Bistrica** and **Ribčev Laz**. By way of contrast, the villages northeast of the lake in the upper valley – **Stara Fužina**, **Studor** and **Srednja Vas** – are a restful antidote to the often crowded lakeside, boasting fabulous indigenous rural architecture; the immensely popular **Savica Waterfall** and the beautiful **Mostnica Gorge** and **Voje Valley** are nearby. Although a fair proportion of visitors come to Bohinj to enjoy water-bound activities – on both the lake and the Sava Bohinjka River – many more come to trek in the mountains, with the major southerly approach to Triglav via the stunning **Valley of the Triglav Lakes** (also called the **Valley of the Seven Lakes**) starting here. Skiers, meanwhile, make a beeline for Slovenia's most spectacularly sited ski resort, in **Vogel**.

Brief history

Archeological finds have determined that Bohinj was settled in the late seventh century, a theory given further credence following the discovery of a handful of forges and foundries in the area. Indeed, for many centuries, the smelting of **iron** was the mainstay of the economy in the region, although eventually, as elsewhere in Gorenjska, competition from more sophisticated European foundries signalled an end to production. As a result, the natives turned to alpine dairy farming, and in particular the mass production of **cheese**, the quality of which was highly regarded throughout Central Europe. Although alpine farming is still practised by small pockets of the community, many more villagers are now becoming engaged in **tourism**.

Bohinjska Bistrica

Routinely given the cold shoulder by travellers keen to reach the star attraction a few kilometres further on, **BOHINJSKA BISTRICA** – 20km southwest of Bled – is Bohinj's

---

THE BOHINJ TUNNEL AND CAR-TRAIN

Built between 1901 and 1906, the **Bohinj Tunnel** extends for some 6327m (6.3km) between Bohinjska Bistrica and Podbrdo, making it Slovenia's longest railway tunnel. Introduced in 1999, the **car-train** transports vehicles (car, van or mobile home) through the mountains in a mere ten minutes – as opposed to the one hour it takes to drive across the tortuous road between Bohinj and Baška Grapa, via the village of Sorica. There are five daily trains between Bohinjska Bistrica and Podbrdo, three of which continue to Most na Soči, 25 minutes further on – the same number of trains run in the reverse direction (five daily trains from Podbrdo to Bohinjska Bistrica, three of which originate in Most na Soči). The trip from Bohinjska Bistrica to Podbrdo costs €9.10 one-way for car and driver, €2 for bikes; it's €14/€3 for the full journey to Most na Soči.

main, albeit rather nondescript, settlement. On the plus side, it does offer some decent accommodation, its train station is the closest to the mountains on this side of the Alps, and the **car-train** runs from here to Most na Soči further south (see box opposite). It also boasts a superb **museum**, and, for rainy days, there's an **Aquapark**, adjoining the *Bohinj Eco Hotel*, which has indoor pools with waterslides and climbing walls (daily 9am–9pm; €15.40 day-ticket; €12.70 for 3hr; ☎ 08 200 4140, ⓦ vodni-park-bohinj.si).

Muzej Tomaža Godca

Zoisova ulica 15 • Jan, Feb, Nov & Dec Fri–Sun 10am–noon & 4–6pm; March–Oct Tues–Sun 10am–noon & 4–6pm • €2.50 • ☎ 04 577 0142, ⓦ gorenjski-muzej.si

Located five minutes west of the post office, down Vodnikova cesta and across the stream, the **Muzej Tomaža Godca** (Tomaž Godec Museum) is well worth seeking out. Trained as a leather tanner, Godec was also a champion skier and mountaineer, but he was best known for his role as a founder member of the Slovene National Liberation Movement and as organizer of the 1941 Bohinj uprising, which is documented in brilliant fashion here. Around a thousand men from the region were recruited to the Partisans, but Godec was captured by the Germans in 1942 and carted off to Begunje (see p.104), before being transferred to Mauthausen where he was executed. The exhibition also recalls Bohinj's vital role during both world wars (for example, the railway was a major supply route to the Soča Front during World War I), with a display of brutal-looking weapons recovered from the Southern Bohinj mountains – particularly chilling is a collection of *buzdovan*, lethal spiked batons favoured by Bosnian soldiers – as well as some ingenious creations, such as a colander made from a helmet. Downstairs, in what was one of two early twentieth-century tanneries in Bistrica (the one here was owned by the Godec family), is a marvellous exhibition on tanning; the leather was primarily used for shoes and saddles, though the collection of bindings for skis and shoelaces for climbing boots reflected Godec's particular passion for those sports.

The building itself was party to a rather significant piece of history, for it was here, between March 15 and 18, 1939, that the **Central Committee of the Communist Party of Yugoslavia** (CKKPJ) was formed. Fittingly, Tito, who was present at the meeting, returned to open the museum some forty years later.

ARRIVAL AND INFORMATION

BOHINJSKA BISTRICA

By train Buses meet trains arriving at the station, which is 10min east of the centre, and link up to Ribčev Laz (see p.117).

Destinations Bled Jezero (Mon–Fri 7 daily, Sat & Sun 5–6 daily; 20min); Most na Soči (Mon–Fri 10 daily, Sat & Sun 6–7 daily; 35min); Nova Gorica (Mon–Fri 8 daily, Sat & Sun 4–5 daily; 1hr 15min).

By bus The main bus stop is a few paces north of the post office on Triglavska cesta.

Destinations Bled (hourly; 25min); Ribčev Laz, for Lake Bohinj (hourly; 15min).

Tourist office Mencingerjeva ulica 10, out on the road towards Bled (June and early to mid-Sept Mon–Fri 9am–noon & 2–6pm, Sat 9am–1pm, Sun 9am–noon; July & Aug Mon–Sat 8am–7pm, Sun 8am–1pm; ☎ 04 574 7600, ⓦ bohinj.si/ld-turizem.si).

ACCOMMODATION AND EATING

Bohinj Eco Hotel Triglavska cesta 17 ☎ 082 004 140, ⓦ bohinj-eco-hotel.si. Classy hotel applying numerous eco-initiatives, with a wide selection of rooms furnished in walnut or teak; depending upon the room type, hotel guests receive free or discounted access to the adjoining Aquapark (see above). **€110**

Camp Danica Triglavska cesta 60 ☎ 04 572 1702, ⓦ camp-danica.si. On the western fringe of the village, backing onto the Sava River, this is a calm, well-shaded site with clean, modern conveniences; also excellent sports

facilities including tennis courts (€7/hr), bike rental and a good restaurant. In summer, they run free guided biking and walking tours for camp guests. May–Sept. **€25**

Strud'l Triglavska cesta 23 ☎ 041 541 877. Unappealingly positioned by the central roundabout, this is nevertheless a lovely *gostilna*-type place with a folksy, alpine-style interior (note the fantastic cuckoo clock) offering scrumptious local dishes such as Bohinj sausages with minced lard (€8.50) and home-made noodles with apple and cinnamon. The honey-based breakfasts are a real treat, too. Daily 8am–10pm.

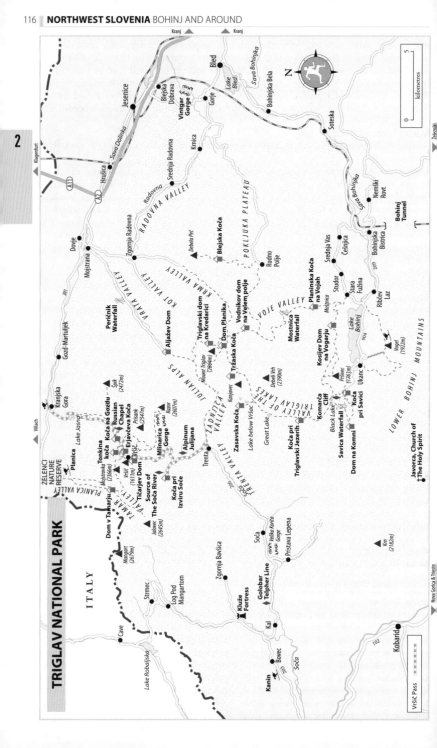

TRIGLAV NATIONAL PARK

ITALY

N

0   5
kilometres

Kranj

Kranj

Bled

Lake Bled

Sava Bohinjka

Bohinjska Bela

Soteska

Bohinj Tunnel

Žirmniki

Nemški Rovt

Češnjica

Bohinjska Bistrica

Jesenice

Blejska Dobrava

Vintgar Gorge

Gorje

Koritno

Srednja Radovna

Blejska Koča

POKLJUKA PLATEAU

Debela Peč

Rudno Polje

Planinska Koča na Veljem polje

Srednja Vas

Studor

Stara Fužina

Ribčev Laz

Vogel (1922m)

Hušica

Sava Dolinka

Zgornja Radovna

RADOVNA VALLEY

KRMA VALLEY

Triglavski dom na Kredarici

Vodnikov dom na Velem polje

VOJE VALLEY

Mostnica

Mostnica Waterfall

Kosijev Dom na Vogarju

Lake Bohinj

Dovje

Mojstrana

Zgornja Radovna

VRATA VALLEY

KOT VALLEY

Pericnik Waterfall

Aljažev Dom

Mount Triglav (2864m)

Dom Planika

Tržaška Koča

JULIAN ALPS

Debeli Vrh (2390m)

Ukanc

Komarča Cliff

Black Lake

Koča pri Savici

Gozd-Martuljek

Kranjska Gora

Lake Jasna

Špik (2472m)

Koča na Gozdu

Russian Chapel

Erjavčeva Koča

Prisank (2547m)

Mlinarica Gorge

Razor (2607m)

ZADNJICA VALLEY

Kanjavec

Zasavska Koča

VALLEY OF THE TRIGLAV LAKES

Lake below Vršič

Great Lake

Koča pri Triglavski Jezerih

Savica Waterfall

Dom na Komni

LOWER BOHINJ MOUNTAINS

Bovec

ZELENCI NATURE RESERVE

Planica

Tonkina koča (2336m)

Mojstrovka

Dom v Tamarju

Jalovec (2645m)

Vršič (1611m)

PLANICA VALLEY

TAMAR VALLEY

Tičarjev Dom

Source of The Soča River

Koča pri Izviru Soče

Trenta

TRENTA VALLEY

Alpinum Juliana

Soča

Zgornja Bavšica

Velika Korita Gorge

Pristava Lepena

Krn (2182m)

Klagenfurt

Villach

Mangart (2679m)

Log Pod Mangartom

Strmec

Cave

Lake Robanjska

Kal

Kanin

Bovec

Soča

Golobar Telpher Line

Kluže Fortress

Javorca, Church of † The Holy Spirit

Kobarid

Nova Gorica & Trieste

Vršič Pass

TRIGLAV NATIONAL PARK

Abutting the Italian border to the west, within touching distance of the Austrian border to the north, and embracing almost the entire Slovene part of the Julian Alps, **Triglav National Park** (Triglavski Narodni Park) comprises three distinct sectors: the **Bohinj district** – which incorporates Lake Bohinj and the greatest concentration of settlements; the **Sava Dolinka district** to the north, characterized by a series of glaciated valleys; and the **Soča district** in the west, extending southwards to Bovec and the Soča Valley (see p.141), and which accommodates the only road passing directly through the park.

The park is home to a wonderful array of **flora and fauna**; its most revered creature is the elusive **chamois**, of which some two thousand are believed to roam the grassy slopes. Other significant species include the recently reintroduced **marmot** and **ibex**, while sightings of the **golden eagle**, and encounters with **brown bear** – who stray up from the southern forests – are not unknown. However, the possibility of sighting any of these animals is slim, as they are all apt to steer well clear of humans. Many of the park's plant species are endemic to the mountains, such as the **Julian poppy** (*Papaver julicum*) and the purple **Zois' bellflower** (*Campanula zoysii*), named after the Slovene botanist Karl Zois – be warned that most alpine flora here is protected and picking them is an offence.

There are three dedicated **Triglav National Park Information Centres**: in Bled (see p.109), in Stara Fužina in Bohinj (see p.123) and in the Trenta Valley (see p.135).

Bohinjska jezero and around

The largest permanent body of water in Slovenia, **Bohinjska jezero** (Lake Bohinj) is utterly different from Lake Bled; its brooding, unerringly calm waters provide perfect theatre for the majestic, steeply pitched mountain faces that frame it. In his epic poem, *Baptism of the Savica*, France Prešeren eloquently described it thus:

The lake of Bohinj calm in stillness lies,
No sign of strife remains to outward sight;
Yet in the lake the fierce pike never sleep,
Nor other fell marauders of the deep.

More than 4km long, 1km wide, and reaching depths of 45m, the lake is fed by water from the Savica falls, which, in turn, feeds the Sava Bohinjka River at the southeastern corner of the lake. Mercifully, and unlike Bled, building has been forbidden along the entire lakeshore, resulting in a virtually unbroken sequence of trees and grassy banks. Nevertheless, and even more so than Bled, the lake is well geared up for a number of **activities**, with canoeing, kayaking and windsurfing along with the more traditional pursuits of swimming and fishing. The majority of Bohinj's amenities are in **RIBČEV LAZ**, which is where you'll also find the lake's outstanding monument, the tiny, brilliantly frescoed **Church of St John the Baptist**.

The best way to enjoy the lake is to take a leisurely circular walk around it, which should take around four and a half hours. Generally speaking, the **south shore** – alongside which the road to the hamlet of **Ukanc** runs – contains all the historical points of interest, but it's a bit of a grind, and the path is situated away from the lake, elevated above the busy main road. By way of contrast, the rocky, undisturbed **north shore** – accessible only by foot – is uplifting and possesses superior **views** of the lake.

Cerkev Sv Janez Krstnik

Ribčev Laz • July & Aug daily 10am–4pm; other times contact the tourist office

Opposite the stone bridge in **RIBČEV LAZ** – invariably clogged with walkers and traffic, but offering glorious head-on views of the lake – the chunky, evocative **Cerkev Sv Janez Krstnik** (Church of St John the Baptist) has origins dating back to the thirteenth century. Its exterior features a striking **wooden porch**, paved with round river stones in rhomboid style, the middle stones arranged to form the date – 1639 – when it was laid out. Most of

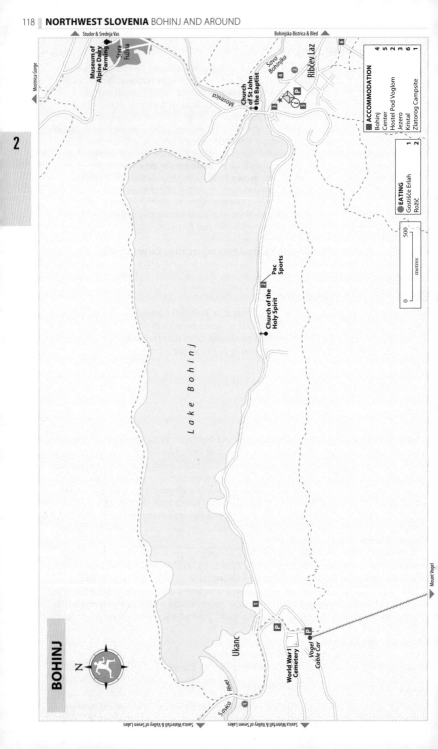

BOHINJ

N

Mostnica Gorge

Studor & Srednja Vas

Museum of
Alpine Dairy
Farming

Stara
Fužina

Bohinjska Bistrica & Bled

Sava
Bohinjka

Mostnica

Church
of St John
the Baptist

Ribčev Laz

ACCOMMODATION
Bohinj   4
Center   5
Hostel Pod Voglom   2
Jezero   3
Kristal   6
Zlatorog Campsite   1

EATING
Gostišče Erlah   1
Rožič   2

L a k e   B o h i n j

Pac
Sports

Church of the
Holy Spirit

0   500
metres

Mount Vogel

Ukanc

Sava River

World War I
Cemetery

Vogel
Cable Car

Savica Waterfall & Valley of Seven Lakes

Savica Waterfall & Valley of Seven Lakes

the exterior's sixteenth-century frescoes are barely discernible, save for those to the right of the entrance, one of which depicts St John, book in hand, baptizing kneeling people, and another of St Florian doing what he does best, dousing fires. The south exterior wall bears an oversized St Christopher with the Christ Child on his shoulder. Its Baroque **bell tower**, renovated several times over, features double windows framed with green stone from the Piračica stream, a material common to many church bell towers in the region.

Such is the sheer mass of interior **frescoes** – most of which were painted by the Master of Bohinj – that you may need a repeat visit just to take them all in, particularly if it's crowded. The Gothic presbytery, dating from around 1440, contains the densest concentration of frescoes, many of which were restored in 2016; working upwards, the lower walls are painted with singing angels holding up patterned curtains, while the next belt depicts bust-length pictures of holy figures in niches bearing a random selection of items (a lamb, a dragon, a pair of breasts); next up are the Apostles, standing against a background of stage scenery carrying various items of weaponry, above which, in the vaulted compartments, are angels playing instruments. The oldest layer of frescoes – dating from the fourteenth century – is on the north wall of the nave, featuring just about detectable fragments of scenes of St George and the Dragon, as well as St John the Evangelist blessing the poison (before drinking it and surviving); adjacent to this, on the north exterior of the arch, are some grisly scenes entitled *St John's Head to Herodius* and *Beheading of a Saint*, the latter featuring St John's headless corpse spewing blood.

HIKING IN THE JULIAN ALPS

The Julian Alps are a hiker's wonderland, its meadows, valleys and mountains carved up by a well-worn nexus of waymarked paths and trails. There are several key **starting points**.

FROM BLED

Bled, furthest from the park's mountainous heart, offers easy to moderate hikes around the eastern spur of the Alps; there are more demanding walks in the heavily forested **Karavanke** chain bordering Austria to the north.

FROM BOHINJ

The greatest choice of hikes emanates from **Bohinj** in the southeastern corner of Triglav National Park: the lush pastures of the **Fužine highlands** and the **Voje Valley** north of the lake; the **Lower Bohinj** mountains on the south side; the **Komna Plateau** to the west; and up through the **Valley of the Triglav Lakes** to the northwest (which continues towards Triglav), arguably the park's most scenic trek.

FROM KRANJSKA GORA

From **Kranjska Gora**, trails head off up into the **Planica** and **Tamar valleys**, as well as up the **Vršič Pass**, from where further tracks fan out in several directions. A short way east of Kranjska Gora, a trio of valleys – the most prominent being the **Vrata Valley** – provides the starting point for ascents towards Triglav itself (see box, p.121).

PRACTICALITIES

All paths in Slovenia are marked by a "target", that is, a red circle with a white centre, with intersections and forks indicated by arrows; however, some of the markings are a little inconclusive in places. The **best hiking months** are May, June and September, when the weather is at its most dependable and the crowds are somewhat thinner; bear in mind that the weather in the mountains can change with alarming rapidity and so the usual provisos apply – sufficient provisions and appropriate clothing and equipment – particularly if you plan to do any high-altitude hiking. A number of **agencies** in Bled and Bohinj (see p.108 & p.122) offer a full range of hikes, from easy to moderate half- or full-day trips such as Debela Peč and the meadows of Bohinj, to more difficult two-day trips up to Triglav (with an overnight stay in a hut). The best up-to-date **maps** are the 1:50,000 editions of *Triglavski Narodni Park* and *Julijske Alps*, published by the Alpine Association of Slovenia (see p.34). There's also *The Julian Alps of Slovenia* (see p.309), a pocket handbook that outlines key hikes from Bled, Bohinj, Kranjska Gora, Bovec and Kobarid.

Žičnice Vogel

Daily: mid-June to mid-Sept 7.30am–7pm, every 30min: mid-Sept to mid-June 8am–6pm, hourly • €10 one-way, €14 return • ☎ 04 572 9712, ⓦ vogel.si

Five kilometres beyond the stone bridge in Ribčev Laz is the turn-off for the **Žičnice Vogel** (Vogel Cable Car), which can accommodate up to eighty people as it cruises up to the *Ski Hotel* (1535m) in a speedy five minutes. The panorama gradually reveals itself, culminating in memorable views of the lake below and the serried peaks opposite – on cloudless days Triglav is visible. At the top, you can grab a bite to eat at the excellent, and cheap, *Viharnik* restaurant. If you fancy an easy to moderate walk, then you can always hike up; one route starts from the defunct *Hotel Bellevue* in Ribčev Laz, and another from Ukanc (both take around 2hr).

Ukanc and the north shore

After Ribčev Laz the lake's second main settlement is **UKANC**, which really only comes alive during September's wonderful **Kravlj Bal** (see box, p.124); otherwise, there's a smattering of accommodation, including a campsite, and a couple of restaurants here. Beyond the defunct *Hotel Zlatorog*, cross the bridge spanning the Savica River, after which the path splits – the left track heads towards the Savica Waterfall, while the other turns back towards the shore, opening up onto a pleasant grassy expanse popular with bathers and picnickers – the views across to the eastern end of the lake from here are splendid.

The initial part of the walk along the **north shore** is characterized by steep slopes of scree, a dry, boulder-strewn channel and densely forested woodland, which, for the most part, meanders tightly along the course of the shoreline. It then opens up into meadowland and a curving shallow bay, one of the best locations around the lake for **bathing** – if you can find a spot. Continuing along the path will bring you back to the bridge and the Church of St John the Baptist.

ARRIVAL AND INFORMATION   BOHINJSKA JEZERO

By bus Buses set down just before the lake by the *Jezero* hotel in Ribčev Laz.
Destinations Bled (hourly; 40min); Bohinjska Bistrica (hourly; 15min); Ljubljana (hourly; 1hr 55min); Stara Fužina (Mon–Fri 5 daily; 10min); Studor (Mon–Fri 5 daily; 15min).
Tourist office In the small complex at Ribčev Laz 48 (July & Aug Mon–Sat 8am–8pm, Sun 9am–7pm; Sept–June Mon–Sat 8am–6pm, Sun 9am–3pm; ☎ 04 574 6010, ⓦ bohinj.si). Bike rental available (€10/4hr, €15/day).

Bohinj Guest Card Between April and Oct, this card (€10) is available to anyone staying for two nights or more in one of Bohinj's hotels, rooms or apartments, and offers a number of discounts on local attractions, activities and restaurants, as well as on local transport, including the tourist boat (see p.122); you can get it at the tourist office as well as some hotels and campsites.
Internet There's free public wi-fi in the immediate vicinity of Ribčev Laz.

ACCOMMODATION

Lake Bohinj can count on just a handful of not particularly inspiring hotels, and although they are overpriced during the summer, prices do drop considerably out of season. Fortunately, there is plentiful **private accommodation** around the lake, particularly in Ribčev Laz and in the villages along the upper valley (Stara Fužina, Studor and Srednja Vas). During the summer expect to pay around €20/person/night for a room with bathroom, and an additional €7 should you require breakfast; an apartment for two people costs around €48–56/night – outside peak season, prices are around twenty percent less. Bookings can be made through the tourist office.

Bohinj Ribčev Laz 45 ☎ 04 572 0210, ⓦ hotel-bohinj .com. Pitched on a small rise across from the tourist office, this alpine-style building offers large and reasonably attractive pine-furnished rooms, some of which have glorious views overlooking the lake and across to Mt Triglav. **€100**
Center Ribčev Laz 50 ☎ 04 572 3170, ⓦ bohinj.si /center. In an uninspiring location facing the car park, the rooms here are fairly uniform and the colours are a little

jarring, but they are immaculately kept and do benefit from having a little lounge area and balcony or terrace. **€90**
Hostel Pod Voglom Ribčev Laz 60 ☎ 04 572 3461, ⓦ hostel-podvoglom.com. Rather old-fashioned, but very social, hostel occupying a prime lakeshore spot some 2km along the road to Ukanc; the mix of differently sized rooms come with both private and shared bathrooms. Buses to Ukanc stop right outside, and the excellent

CLIMBING TRIGLAV

It's said that every Slovene has to climb **Mount Triglav** at least once in their lifetime, but in no sense does this mean it's an easy outing. In fact it remained unclimbed until 1778, when a German doctor and three local guides made it to the 2864m summit. The mountain can be approached via several routes. The 1:25,000 *Triglav* **maps** published by the Alpine Association of Slovenia (see p.34) and Kartografija (Ⓦ kartografija.si) are currently the best available.

FROM THE SOUTH

The **most popular route** is from the **south**; from the defunct *Hotel Zlatorog* at the western end of **Lake Bohinj**, it's a forty-minute walk to the Savica Waterfall, where a path to the right begins the ascent of the formidable-looking Komarča Cliff, a tough climb of 700m but fitted with cables.

At the top, continue gently uphill in beech trees before arriving at the **Black Lake** (Črno jezero; 1294m) on your left. Soon after, turn left to pass around the lake to the north; after a couple of minutes go straight ahead at a junction, continuing on a slightly rocky path in pine trees, level and then rising for an hour in all.

From the top of the **White Cliff** (Bela skala) it's an easy fifteen-minute walk through limestone dykes to the *Koča pri Triglavskih Jezerih* mountain hut (1685m; ☎ 040 620 783; June–Oct), three to four hours from the *Hotel Zlatorog*. From the hut continue north up the valley and past the **Great Lake** (Veliko Triglavskih jezero), reaching the foot of an escarpment after an hour; the route leads steeply up to the right (following a red arrow to Hribarice), reaching the ridge in twenty minutes and the **Yellow Lake** (Želeno jezero; 1988m) soon after.

Continuing up to the right, you'll pass a turning to the *Prehodavici* hut (visible not too far to the left), and climb up, partly on scree, for half an hour. In another thirty minutes you reach the **Hribarice saddle** (2358m), from where the path is reasonably marked for a while; it descends and kinks to the left after about five minutes, then rises a little to reach the **Dolič saddle** (2164m) in another twenty minutes; from here the *Koča na Doliču* hut (2151m; ☎ 051 614 780; June–Sept) is also visible just to the left. The path swings sharply to the right here, and after an hour you'll reach the start of a fairly steep section, after which it takes just five minutes to reach the *Dom Planika pod Triglavom* hut (2401m; ☎ 04 828 0306; June–Sept), a good place to spend the night.

From here the route brings you, in thirty minutes, to the foot of a cliff, where a big red and white dot marks the start of the **final climb**. With the aid of pegs and cables you soon reach a shoulder, where a path leads left and down to the *Doliču* hut. The route to the **summit** turns right and climbs onwards, reaching the top after another forty minutes.

FROM THE NORTH

The **most dramatic approach** – and one not for the inexperienced or fainthearted – is from the **north**, as Triglav's north face is no less than 1200m high; its central part is for climbers only, but there are fairly tough hiking routes to either side, involving the use of fixed cables. From the *Aljažev Dom* hut (1015m; ☎ 04 589 1030; April–Sept) at the end of the Vrata Valley, continue past a monument to the Partisans, and after 45 minutes take the Prag path to the left. At the foot of the north face the Prag, or threshold (a rock cliff), is scaled with the help of metal steps and pegs; thereafter the path winds on up to a small spring, after which you fork right to reach the *Triglavski dom na Kredarici* (2515m; ☎ 04 531 2864; July–Sept), four or five hours from the *Aljažev Dom*. From the saddle above the hut, a huge painted marker denotes the start of the final ascent; with the aid of steel cables and pegs you should reach the summit in an hour or so. Here you'll find the Aljažev stolp, or turret, a tiny refuge erected in 1865 that looks like a small space rocket.

FROM THE EAST

The **shortest ascent** is from the **east**, from Rudno Polje (1340m); from here it's about two hours' hike to the Studorski preval (1892m), and another hour to the *Vodnikov dom na Velem polje* hut (☎ 051 607 211; June–Sept; 1817m), from where you continue to *Dom Planika pod Triglavom* (see above) and beyond to the summit.

2

ACTIVITIES IN BOHINJ

In addition to being a base for climbing Mount Triglav (see box, p.121), Bohinj presents some excellent opportunities for a range of activities.

WATER-BASED ACTIVITIES

On the lake itself, **tourist boats** (Turistična ladja; April–Oct daily 9.30am–6pm, every 40min; €9 one-way, €10.50 return) shuttle up and down between Ribčev Laz and Ukanc. It's also possible to **fish** on the lake (March–Oct) and in the Sava Bohinjka River (April–Oct), the latter well stocked with brown trout; permits (available at the tourist office) begin at €25 per day up to €155 for a week for the lake, and €42 (€259) for the river. **Swimming** is better here than in Bled due to the shallower waters close to the shore – the best areas are at the extreme western end of the lake and the bay-like area to the northeast.

BIKING AND HORSERIDING

For a shot of adrenaline-fuelled biking, there's the **Mountain Bike Park** (June–Sept; €22/day) at the top of **Vogel** (ⓦvogel.si), which offers trails for riders of all abilities. In winter, this area becomes the setting for one of Slovenia's premier ski resorts (see box, p.128). The **Bohinj Horse Centre** (Mrcina Ranč) in Studor, with its stable of Icelandic ponies, offers a varied programme of treks, with 1hr rides from around €20, half-day trips around €70 and full day-trips around €100 (ⓣ041 790 297, ⓦranc-mrcina.com).

AGENCIES

By far the best outfit is Pac Sports (ⓣ04 572 3461, ⓦpac-sports.com), based at the *Hostel Pod Voglom* and offering **rafting** (€29), **canyoning** (€49), **canoeing/kayaking** (€35) and **tandem paragliding** (€95 for a 15min flight), among other things; it also rents out **canoes and kayaks** (€7–9/hr) and **bikes** (€5/hr, €12/4hr, €16/full day) – as does the tourist office (see p.120). Similarly excellent is Hike&Bike (ⓣ031 374 660, ⓦhikeandbike.si), based in Bohinjska Bistrica, which offers a terrific range of dedicated cycling and **hiking** tours.

Pac Sports (see above) is on site. Breakfast included. Dorms **€18**, doubles **€44**

Jezero Ribčev Laz 51 ⓣ04 572 9100, ⓦhotel-jezero.si. Just 50m from the water, this is the lake's most prominent hotel, a slickly run place accommodating bright, if somewhat workaday, rooms; try and bag one of the lake-facing rooms, which cost the same as those with park views. Free indoor pool and fitness suite for guests. **€130**

Kristal Ribčev Laz 4 ⓣ04 577 8200, ⓦhotel-kristal -slovenia.com. Located at the entrance to the village, this popular and welcoming family-run pension provides simple but smartly furnished rooms, including triples and quads, plus two rooms for disabled people; the owner also produces her own delectable range of chocolate. **€60**

Zlatorog Campsite Ukanc 2 ⓣ059 923 648, ⓦcamp -bohinj.si. Extremely basic but splendidly located campsite on the lake's western tip; conveniently located for trips up the mountains. You can rent a tent here too (€5). May–Sept. **€22**

EATING

Gostišče Erlah Ukanc 67 ⓣ041 326 714, ⓦerlah.com. Good-value fish dishes such as fresh trout (€7), direct from their own farm, and grilled salmon feature on the menu at this friendly inn at the western end of the lake. Daily noon–9pm.

Rožič Ribčev Laz 42 ⓣ04 572 3393, ⓦpensionrozic -bohinj.com. In the pension of the same name, the very agreeable restaurant has a daily menu chalked up on a board featuring such delicious staples as deer steak, smoked sausages and Bohinj trout. Daily 11am–10pm.

Stara Fužina

One kilometre north of Ribčev Laz is **STARA FUŽINA**, the largest of the upper valley villages and the one with most amenities, including a **National Park information centre**. Thanks to its dense concentration of high-altitude meadows, Bohinj was for centuries the centre of alpine **dairy farming** in Slovenia, reaching its high point in the late nineteenth century when the introduction of cheese cooperatives substantially increased the lot of farmers and their families. The industry continued to prosper until the 1970s, but following the opening of a modern dairy in Srednja Vas, and the exodus of younger generations to the towns and cities, dairy farming slipped into decline and today it's barely sustained by a handful of older villagers.

Planšarski muzej

Stara Fužina 181 • Tues–Sun: Jan–June, Sept & Oct 10am–noon & 4–6pm; July & Aug 11am–7pm • €2.60 • ☎ 04 577 0156

Just across the bridge in the centre of the village, in the old dairy building, is the enjoyably old-fashioned **Planšarski muzej** (Museum of Alpine Dairy Farming), which, as its name suggests, relays the story of the valley's rich dairy-farming heritage. Among the plethora of exhibits on display are two huge copper rennet vats, some fine-looking *steči* (milk containers) and a herdsman's backpack, last used in 1961 and containing all the essential items (bed covers, pots and pans and so on) required for a season up in the mountains. There's also a lovely collection of butter moulds (*mušterc*) and some evocative black-and-white photos.

ARRIVAL AND INFORMATION

STARA FUŽINA

By bus Buses stop in the centre of the village just before the bridge.

Destinations Bohinjska Bistrica (Mon–Fri 5 daily; 15min); Ribčev Laz, for Lake Bohinj (Mon–Fri 5 daily; 10min).

Tourist office Just by the bridge in the centre of the village, at Stara Fužina 53, you'll find a small, seasonal tourist office (mid-June to mid-Sept Mon–Fri 8am–noon & 3–6pm; ☎ 04 572 3326).

Triglav National Park Information Centre Stara Fužina 37–38 (May, June, Sept & Oct daily 10am–6pm; July & Aug daily 9am–7pm; Nov–April Mon–Fri 10am–3pm, Sat & Sun 10am–5pm; ☎ 04 578 0245, ⓦ tnp.si). The newest of the park's three information centres, with plenty of information on all aspects of the park and exhibits focusing primarily on the Bohinj Valley, the lake and its associated flora and fauna.

EATING

Gostilna Mihovc Stara Fužina 118 ☎ 040 216 106, ⓦ gostilna-mihovc.si. Just down from the Museum of Alpine Dairy Farming, this friendly, warming restaurant offers good home-style cooking such as bean soup, buckwheat porridge and mushrooms, and Bohinj sausage in minced lard (€8). Tues–Fri noon–10pm, Sat & Sun 11am–10pm.

Studor and around

A couple of kilometres along the valley from Stara Fužina, the village of **STUDOR** is well known for its splendid double **hayracks**, called *toplars*. While the single stretch type of hayrack (*kozolec*) is more common – and can be found elsewhere in Europe – the double hayrack, consisting of two parallel single hayracks connected by a double-gabled roof (used for storage), is unique to Slovenia; those here, dating from the eighteenth and nineteenth centuries, are perhaps the most picturesque grouping of hayracks in the country.

   SREDNJA VAS, 1km beyond Studor, is the upper valley's central settlement, and though there's nothing specific to see, it's a pleasant enough place to stroll around, and there are a few good restaurants.

Oplenova hiša

Studor 16 • Tues–Sun: Jan–June, Sept & Oct 10am–noon & 4–6pm; July & Aug 11am–7pm • €2 • ☎ 059 226 774, ⓦ gorenjski-muzej.si

Hayracks aside, it's worth coming to Studor to view the marvellous **Oplenova hiša** (Oplen House), a typical nineteenth-century Bohinj farmhouse also known as a longhouse because of its unusual arrangement with living quarters and barn conjoined under one roof. In addition to the typical living room (*hiša*) and "black kitchen" – the latter so-called because its walls are blackened with smoke from the open cooking area – the dwelling area consists of a chamber (used primarily as a bedroom, as shown by the two impossibly small beds) and an attic.

ARRIVAL AND DEPARTURE

STUDOR

By bus Buses to and from Ribčev Laz, for Lake Bohinj (Mon–Fri 5 daily; 15min), stop on the main road 200m from the entrance to the village.

2

BOHINJ FESTIVALS

Bohinj sees several of Slovenia's most colourful festivals, most of which are connected to the valley's wonderful natural heritage: taking place throughout the last week of May and first week of June, the **International Wildflower Festival** (ⓦbohinj.si/alpskocvetje) showcases the region's flora with exhibitions, workshops, guided botanical and birdwatching tours and musical events. September sees three festivals: on the second or third weekend, the **Kravji Bal** ("Cows Ball") celebrates the return of the cattle from alpine pastures with folk events, live bands and a lot of drinking; also in mid-September, the two-week **Hiking Festival** (ⓦbohinj.si /pohodnistvo) offers a superb programme of themed guided walks; finally, the last week of the month is devoted to the **Fly Fishing Festival** (ⓦbohinj.si/ribolov).

ACCOMMODATION AND EATING

Gostilna pri Hrvatu Srednja Vas 76 ☎04 572 3670. The food in this solidly traditional *gostilna* has a reputation for being the best in the valley – buckwheat fritters; home-made sausages with mushrooms; wild boar with cranberry sauce and dumplings (€12) – all best savoured on the stone terrace above the Ribnica Creek. Daily except Tues 10am–11pm.

Pizzerija Ema Srednja Vas 73 ☎04 572 4126. The fabulous mountain views from the terrace and extensive menu of tasty pizzas and pasta more than justify the 4km hike from the lake to the pretty village of Srednja Vas. Mon–Thurs & Sun 8.30am–10pm, Fri & Sat 8.30am–midnight.

★**Rustic House 13** Studor 13 ☎031 466 707, ⓦstudor13.si. Exceptional guesthouse in a tastefully renovated historic house 3km from the lake, with two immaculate suites furnished in peasant style; each sleeps four, and one, with a bunk, is ideal for families. No breakfast, but there's a well-equipped kitchen for guests' use. Can offer free pickups from Bohinj. Two people €70, four people €110

Slap Savica

April–Oct 8am–6pm • €3

The number-one attraction around these parts is the majestic 78m-high **Slap Savica** (Savica Waterfall), a 45-minute walk along the path west of the defunct *Hotel Zlatorog* in Ukanc; you can also drive here by continuing along the road below the Vogel cable-car station. Once you've reached the entrance, it's a heavy-going twenty-minute climb up a series of zigzagging steps to the top of the gorge and a small observation hut, invariably crammed with people angling to get a photo. The falls themselves are spectacular: smooth photogenic ribbons of water tumbling into the circular pool below, before falling away to begin the long journey as the Sava River. To the left, emerging from the same fault, is the subsidiary fall, known as **Mali Savica** (Little Savica). Savica can get murderously busy on a summer's day, so to get the most out of it you're best off making an early start.

Dolina Triglavskih jezer

The car park at the entrance to the Savica Waterfall marks the starting point for several superb hikes into the heart of the Triglav National Park – and even an assault on Triglav itself (see box, p.121). One track forges westwards to the large *Dom na Komni* hut (1520m; 2hr 30min), open year-round (☎040 695 783), while another spears northwards via the formidable **Komarča cliff**, a tough and very steep route, aided by iron pegs and rungs. Both then carry on northwards, meeting at the *Koča pri Triglavskih Jezerih* (1685m; ☎040 620 783; mid-June to mid-Oct), which marks the beginning of the magical **Dolina Triglavskih jezer** (**Valley of the Triglav Lakes**), also known as the **Valley of the Seven Lakes**.

Lined with white limestone cliffs, and rich in alpine and karstic flora, the valley is famed for its beautiful tarns, the lowest and warmest of which is the **Črno jezero** (Black Lake), just above Komarča, while the highest, the **Jezero pod Vrsačem** (Lake below Vršac), lies at an altitude of 2000m. The largest and deepest of the seven lakes, the **Veliko jezero** (Great Lake), is approximately midway between these two. According to legend, the valley is also home to Zlatorog, the mythical chamois with golden horns.

Mostnice korita and Dolina Voje

April–Oct €2.50; Nov–March free

The journey up through the **Mostnice korita** (Mostnica Gorge), 1km north of Stara Fužina, makes a superb hike. Two trails – one just before the bridge in Stara Fužina, and one by St Paul's Church, at the eastern edge of the village – head towards the gorge entrance, before which you cross the stone **Hudičev most** (Devil's Bridge), built in 1777 in order to transport iron ore and charcoal from the surrounding hills to the ironworks that once lined the gorge; follow the path to the right for 400m, where you'll find the entry point, then take the path to the right. The ravine, 1km long and 20m deep in places, has been smoothly sculpted into all manner of extraordinary shapes, while hundreds of circular hollows, known as river mills, have been eroded into the riverbed, the result of stones spun by whirlpools in the stream; close inspection of the river is possible, as regular paths divert away from the main track, but be particularly careful if it has been raining.

At the end of the gorge (by the bridge), you can either return (via the other side), or continue northwards towards the **Dolina Voje** (Voje Valley) – scramble upwards through the trees for twenty minutes before arriving at the *Planinska Koča na Vojah* hut (☎041 234 625; May–Sept), a good place to stop for refreshments; thereafter, it's a pleasant forty-minute walk through open fields and meadows to the precipitous valley headwall and the modest 21m-high **Slap Mostnice** (Mostnica Waterfall). From here, you can continue to Velo Polje and the *Vodnikov dom na Velem polje* hut (see box, p.121) at 1817m (3hr 30min), or return the way you came.

Kranjska Gora and around

Tucked away in the extreme northwestern corner of the country, on the doorstep of Triglav National Park, the small town of **KRANJSKA GORA** is Slovenia's number-one winter playground. A remote settlement since the fourteenth century, the town merited little attention and was strategically unimportant until World War I when the nearby Vršič Pass (see p.133) was built to enable supplies to reach the Austrian army fighting along the Soča front. Kranjska Gora then developed into a major **winter sports** venue, with Slovenia's first ski jump and ski lifts constructed here in 1934 and 1950 respectively. Although skiing is undoubtedly the main draw –with the world-famous **Planica ski jumps** a further inducement to visit – it's arguably more exciting as a **summer destination** nowadays, with great mountain biking and hiking, among other things.

Liznjekova hiša

Borovška cesta 63 • May–Oct Tues–Sat 10am–6pm, Sun 10am–5pm; Nov–April Tues–Sat 9.30am–4pm, Sun 10am–4pm • €2.50 • ☎ 04 588 1999, ⓦ gmj.si

The one key site in town is the **Liznjekova hiša** (Liznjek House), a superbly preserved alpine homestead that was once the property of a wealthy local farmer. At the time the largest farm in the village (it also served as a pub), it mostly dates from the late eighteenth century, though its stone ground floor is of seventeenth-century origin. Its furnishings, including a lovely selection of folk-painted trousseau chests, a beautiful corner stove and a handsome, slender grandfather clock, are outstanding.

Opposite the house is the capacious barn, built in 1796 and originally used for storing food and housing livestock; it's now mostly empty, save for some battered old horse carts and grand-looking sleds. Downstairs in the small basement is an exhibition dedicated to the Slovene writer **Josip Vandot** (1884–1944), whose many stories about the clever shepherd boy Kekec endure to this day – many of these were made into films (see p.310).

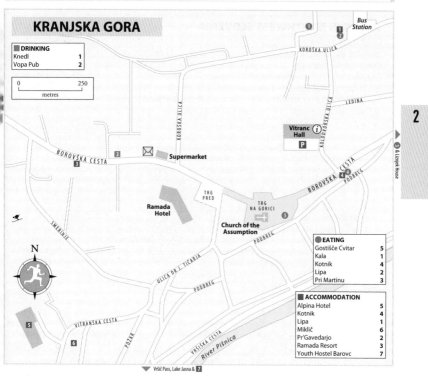

Vršič Pass, Lake Jasna & 7

Cerkev Sv vnebovzetje

Borovška cesta

The squat, late-Gothic **Cerkev Sv vnebovzetje** (Church of the Assumption) sits on the attractive, square-like portion of **Borovška cesta**, Kranjska Gora's central street. The only surviving part of the original structure is the stocky Romanesque bell tower; the church you see today dates from 1510. There's not an awful lot to see inside, though its exquisite interior does contain one of the most impressive **vaulted ceilings** in the region and a particularly fine organ, one of the oldest in Gorenjska.

Jezero Jasna

Just 2km south of Kranjska Gora, in the centre of a large gravel flood plain, **Jezero Jasna** (Lake Jasna) is a popular recreational spot with the locals in warmer months; at the entrance is a statue of the mythical gold-horned chamois, Zlatorog. The waters here are cold, but clean and wonderfully refreshing on a scorching day, and there are plenty of shallow, pool-like areas for kids to splash around in. A great place for a picnic, the shore also has a couple of wooden huts with outdoor seating, one selling coffee, beer and the like, and another selling ice creams.

Naravni rezervat Zelenci

Around 3km west of Kranjska Gora, sandwiched between the ski slopes of Podkoren and the main road to Italy, is the **Naravni rezervat Zelenci** (Zelenci Nature Reserve), home to an exceptional range of flora and fauna. Within the reserve is a marsh and a brilliant emerald-blue, crystal-clear lake below which cool springs spurt, volcano-like, from

2

SKIING IN NORTHWEST SLOVENIA

Given its predominantly mountainous terrain, it's not surprising that northwest Slovenia contains the greatest concentration of the country's **ski resorts**, and although you won't find the range of slopes that you would in Italy or France, the spectacular alpine scenery, thinner crowds and considerably lower prices are ample compensation. Moreover, Slovenia's ski resorts are invariably well equipped and extremely safe, and instruction is first-class.

Slovenia's largest and best-known ski resort is **Kranjska Gora**, its slopes best suited to beginners and intermediate skiiers, which makes it a great base for families – it is also one of only two resorts in the country to host international ski (and ski-jumping) competitions. Rated as one of the most fashionable centres in Slovenia – and the most popular resort among weekending *ljubljančani* – is **Krvavec**, some 25km north of the capital; located at a relatively high altitude, its extensive range of slopes is suitable for skiers of all abilities; moreover, it has a snowboard school, speed-skiing track and a freestyle mogul course. The country's highest-altitude skiing (over 2000m) is at **Kanin** near Bovec in the Soča Valley. Both this and **Vogel**, high above Lake Bohinj, offer the most dramatic scenery. An increasingly popular centre is **Cerkno**, a well-developed resort with some of the most challenging pistes in the country; this is covered in Chapter Three (see p.171).

The **season** typically lasts from December to March, though skiing on the higher pistes, such as Kanin, is often possible until well into April. Expect to **pay** around €30–35 for a day ski pass and €160–180 for a weekly pass; the **Ski Pass Slovenian Alps** (€62 for two days, and €183 for a week) covers Vogel, Krvavec and Kranjska Gora. Most centres have **ski schools** with English instruction (around €45 for a two-hour individual lesson, and €90 for five two-hour lessons as part of a group), and you can **rent equipment** (around €20 for skis, boots and poles). For more **information** on skiing in Slovenia, see ⓦ slovenia.info/ski.

limestone sediment called *kreda* – a phenomenon unique to Slovenia. The lake – which is also the source of the Sava Dolinka River, though technically this begins at the Nadiša karst spring up in the Tamar Valley (see p.130) – can be accessed via a series of carefully constructed walkways from either side of the reserve, while the observation tower provides some lovely overhead views.

As well as a dense concentration of vegetation – including pygmy willows, alder trees and common cottongrass – the reserve supports some unusual **fauna**, such as the whiskered bat, sand lizard, common viper snake and a rare bird species, the scarlet grosbeak, all of which have been placed on the "red list" – a list of Slovenia's most endangered species.

ARRIVAL AND INFORMATION   KRANJSKA GORA

By bus The bus station is a 5min walk north of the centre on Koroška ulica – head down Kolodvorska ulica to Borovška cesta, the town's main street.

Destinations Bled (hourly; 1hr 15min); Bovec (July & Aug 5 daily, plus June & Sept 1 on Sat & Sun; 1hr 45min); Ljubljana (hourly; 2hr); Mojstrana (hourly; 25min); Radovljica (hourly; 1hr 25min).

Tourist office Vitranc Hall, Kolodvorska ulica 1 (daily:

April, May & mid-Sept to Nov 8am–4pm; June to mid-Sept 8am–7pm; Dec–March 8am–6pm; ☎ 04 580 9440, ⓦ kranjska-gora.si).

Tourist bus In summer, a red bus shuttles between Kranjska Gora and a dozen or so other attractions throughout the area, including Mojstrana, the Peričnik Waterfall, the Zelenci Nature Reserve and Planica (July & Aug daily 9am–6pm; Sept Sat & Sun 9am–6pm; day ticket €9).

ACCOMMODATION

There's an abundance of hotels in town, though, inevitably, rates rise considerably during the **peak winter ski months** (Dec–March). Note, too, that some places sometimes close for a month or so post- or pre-ski season, often on a whim. Otherwise, there is plentiful **private accommodation** in the town centre and surrounding villages; contact the tourist office.

Alpina Hotel Vitranška cesta 12 ☎ 04 589 3100, ⓦ hit -alpinea.si. Ignore the portentous exterior – the rooms here are tasteful, albeit somewhat lacking in character, and many look straight out onto the ski slopes. Very popular with families. **€90**

Kotnik Borovška cesta 75 ☎ 04 588 1564, ⓦ hotel -kotnik.si. Housed in a luminous yellow building, this classy, family-run hotel offers fifteen beautifully kept rooms, including triples and quads, which puts it up there as the best-value place in town; there's also a very pleasant guest lounge with tea and coffee on tap. **€84**

★**Lipa** Koroška ulica 14 **☎**04 582 0000, **☻**hotel-lipa .si. Small, family-run hotel whose eleven rooms are by far the loveliest in town, each decorated in beige, mauve or grey, with soft grey carpets, gorgeous wooden bedsteads with drawers and, unusually, tea- and coffee-making facilities. A fine restaurant, too (see below). **€100**

Miklič Vitranška cesta 13 **☎**04 588 1635, **☻**hotelmiklic .com. Surrounded by baize-like lawns and neatly arranged flowerbeds, this pristine little hotel offers solid, as opposed to spectacular, rooms, but it does retain a more personal touch than most other places in town. **€100**

★**Pr'Gavedarjo** Podkoren 72, 2km west of town, just off the main road to Planica **☎**031 479 087, **☻**prgavedarjo.si. This magical four-room guesthouse – a 100-year-old homestead whose name translates as "At the Cattle Breeders" – is sublime in every respect, from the original frescoes under the ceiling rim and original larch

wood furnishings, to the embroidered cushions and organic linen embossed with the local carnation motif; the bathrooms are separated from the sleeping area only by a sliding glass partition, though there is a curtain for modesty. **€100**

Ramada Resort Borovška cesta 99 **☎**04 588 4100, **☻**hit-alpinea.si. Prominently sited between the main through road and the ski slopes, this is as luxurious as it gets in town; a slick establishment with ultramodern rooms. **€140**

Youth Hostel Barovc Naselje Ivana Krivca 22 **☎**04 582 0400, **☻**hostel-barovc.com. Located 1.5km south of town in a fabulous spot overlooking Lake Jasna, *Barovc* is a cut above your average hostel. Most of its vivid orange and lime-green rooms (all en suite) are doubles, though there are a few four-bed dorms and one with five beds. The hammocks strung between the pine trees are a nice touch. Dorms **€22**, doubles **€60**

EATING

Gostišče Cvitar Borovška cesta 83 **☎**04 588 3600, **☻**cvitar.com. A delightful 200-year-old tavern next to the church, whose informal stone terrace rates as the top spot to dine in town; the food doesn't deviate much from the usual schnitzels and steaks, but it's all well prepared and nicely presented, plus it's reasonably priced and the service is top-class. Daily 10am–10pm.

Kala Koroška ulica 13b **☎**04 588 5544. A sparkling little café/patisserie a 10min walk from the centre on the edge of a meadow, whose coffee and irresistible home-made cakes are worth the short trek; treat yourself to a wedge of forest fruit pie or *gibanica*, or, if it's hot, a scoop or two of ice cream. Daily 9am–9pm.

Kotnik Borovška cesta 15 **☎**04 588 1564, **☻**hotel -kotnik.si. Although the *Kotnik*'s restaurant is undoubtedly of some merit, it's the adjoining, pleasantly frenetic pizzeria

that people usually make a beeline for; a huge copper-clad oven spits out all manner of scrumptious pizzas (€8), but there's loads more besides. Daily noon–11pm.

Lipa Koroška ulica 14 **☎**04 582 0000, **☻**hotel-lipa.si. The menu in the *Lipa*'s polished restaurant is the most distinguished in town; veal cheeks with cheese dumplings and onion jam (€18), and crusted lamb shank with polenta are typical. Unusually, there are gluten-free possibilities too, including pizzas in the more informal adjoining winter garden. Daily noon–10pm.

Pri Martinu Borovška cesta 61 **☎**04 582 0300. Enjoyable, vaguely medieval-themed restaurant rustling up healthy portions of solid meat dishes – such as veal stew with buckwheat mush, or *kranjska klobasa* – as well as some sound veggie options, including dumplings and polenta. Daily 10am–10pm.

DRINKING

Knedl Borovška cesta 105 **☎**070 760 434. Activities completed, retreat to this buzzy café-cum-bar nestled at

the bottom of the chair lift, with its sun-trap terrace, and enjoy a coffee and a slice of strudel with ice cream, or sup

---

KRANJSKA GORA SKIING

The slopes of **Vitranc** and **Podkoren**, just west of Kranjska Gora town centre, offer some 20km of **ski runs** (with five chair lifts and numerous towbars). These are suitable for skiers of all abilities, though the proliferation of easy slopes makes it a popular destination for **families and beginners**. Kranjska Gora also has night-time skiing, and in early March the town welcomes international skiers for the men's World Cup Slalom and Giant Slalom races.

   Ski passes (Vozovnice; around €35 for a day pass, €180 for a weekly pass) are available from the ticket office at the Alpine Ski Club (Alpski Smučarski Klub), Borovška cesta 99 (**☎**04 588 5300, **☻**ask-kg.com). The club's school gives **ski and snowboard lessons** (around €32 for a 1hr individual lesson, around €80 for five two-hour lessons as part of a group). Both the Alpine Ski Club and Intersport Bernik offer **ski rental** (around €22 for skis or snowboard and boots). Between December and April the Julijana agency offers **sledding** (€15/2hr).

2

SUMMER ACTIVITIES IN KRANJSKA GORA

The area around Kranjska Gora offers some of the best **cycling** in the region. A cycling map (*Kolesarski izleti*) available from the tourist office details twelve excursions, ranging from gentle (Rateče) to very demanding (Vršič Pass, Belca); paths are clearly signposted at regular intervals, each one indicating relevant turn-off points, distances and length of time to the next destination. Plenty of places in town **rent bikes** – try Julijana (☎ 04 588 1325, ⓦ julijana.info) or Intersport Bernik, at Borovška cesta 88a (☎ 04 588 4780, ⓦ intersport-bernik.com), both of which charge €7 for two hours, €11 for half a day and €15 for a full day. For the more adventurous, there's the superb **Mountain Bike Park** (mid-April to Oct; ☎ 041 706 786, ⓦ bike-park.si; €7/single ticket, €20/4hr, €24/day; bike rental €45 for half a day) out by the ski slopes; several colour-coded trails – from green (easy) to black (difficult) – begin at the top of the chair lift and wend their way back down the slopes.

Also based next to the chair lift is the **summer toboggan** (€10 for one ride, €19 for three, €30 for five; price includes chair lift); 1500m long and with a drop of 293m, it's great fun for the whole family.

---

on a cool, crisp beer. Daily 9am–11pm.
Vopa Pub Borovška cesta 92 ☎ 04 588 2077. The town's central watering hole is guaranteed to be busy any time of the day, whether it's locals here for an early morning pick-me-up or a more raucous bout of beer drinking at sundown after a hard day on the slopes. Daily 7am–1am.

Planica

A little less than 1km beyond the Zelenci Nature Reserve, you come to the grassy lower part of the Planica Valley, the most westerly access point into the Alps. From here, the road ascends steeply up towards **Planica**, home to the extraordinary, and iconic, **Planica ski jumps**. The **Nordijski Center Planica** (Planica Nordic Centre) comprises eight ski-jumping hills – the largest such complex in the world – including one of the most revered hills in the sport.

If you've got the energy, hike up the 1191 steps located to the side of the jumps and enjoy the extraordinary views; if that's beyond you, take the **chair lift** up (€4) and walk down. For a real adrenaline rush, however, try the new **zipline** (€25; ⓦ planica-zipline.si), the world's steepest, which follows the course of the main hill at an average incline of 38 percent. Best of all, if you're around at the end of March, you shouldn't miss the annual **World Ski-Jumping Championships** (ⓦ planica.si); known as much for its drinking and music as for its sporting theatrics, it's the most celebrated of all Slovenia's annual events, sporting or otherwise.

Muzej Planica

Mon–Thurs 9am–6pm, Fri–Sun 9am–8pm • €6, €9 including a guided tour of the hills • ☎ 031 689 806, ⓦ nc-planica.si

The history of Planica, and the remarkable exploits of its daredevil athletes (see box opposite), is superbly relayed in the **Muzej Planica** (Planica Museum), housed in a stunning, wood-clad circular structure that's entirely in keeping with the inspirational surroundings. Having viewed some old footage on the ground floor, make your way upstairs where you can follow the growth of Planica as an international sporting venue, alongside the technical developments within the sport over the years, or at least since 1912 when Jože Pogačar jumped a modest 9m in a woolly hat. Look out, too, for the hoard of trophies, vests and medals, including the silver and bronze won by Peter Prevc in Sochi in 2014. Finally, head up to the third-floor terrace, which offers unrivalled views of the hills.

Tamar Valley

Re-entering the National Park beyond the Planica ski jumps, the road gives way to an untidy mess of gravel workings before continuing as a stony, gently inclining track (used as a cross-country ski track in winter) for about 3.5km up to a lush grassy glade and the *Dom v Tamarju* mountain hut (1108m; ☎04 587 6055; open all year). The walk up to this point, from the ski jumps, is tremendous, largely for the views of the mighty, razor-sharp peak of **Jalovec** (2645m), due south, and **Mojstrovka** (2366m) to the east. A ten-minute walk west of the hut is the **source of the Nadiža stream**, a powerful karstic spring which squirts through a small fissure in the rock face before disappearing into underground channels and re-emerging in Zelenci at the base of the valley. From the hut, one path heads south up the Tamar Valley to Jalovec (6hr), and another east to **Vršič** (1611m; 3hr); both contain some very exposed and difficult sections.

Mojstrana and the Vrata Valley

The small village of **Gozd-Martuljek**, 3km east of Kranjska Gora, is the starting point for hikes into the **Martuljek** group of mountains, a fierce, spectacular range which counts the imperious **Mount Špik** (2472m) among its number, regarded as one of the toughest climbs in the Alps.

A further ten kilometres east, just off the main road towards Jesenice, is the village of **MOJSTRANA**, where three parallel valleys fan out southwards into the core of the National Park, each furrowed with mountain paths heading towards Triglav itself. Mojstrana is the starting point for hikers attempting Triglav's north face (see box, p.121). The most direct road from the village heads southwest up into the **Vrata Valley** (Gateway Valley), the largest glacial valley in the northern tract of the Julian Alps and the most direct route to Triglav – consequently, it's often overflowing with hikers and motorists.

Slovenski planinski muzej

Triglavska cesta 49, Mojstrana • Daily: June to mid-Sept 9am–7pm; mid-Sept to May 9am–5pm • €6 • ☎ 08 380 6730, ⓦ planinskimuzej.si

Occupying a striking steel-clad building, designed as a rock mass, the **Slovenski planinski muzej** (Slovenian Alpine Museum) is an illuminating, and interactive, exhibition pertaining to Slovenian alpinism and those who have shaped its development. The story starts with **Jakob Aljaž** (1845–1927) – parish priest, composer and mountaineer – after whom both the hut at the end of the valley and the rocket-shaped turret (Aljažev stolp) at the top of Triglav are named; look out for his wood-carved walking stick. Other notable exhibits include the ice axe belonging to the world-class alpinist **Tomaž Humar**, who made more than 1500 ascents before his death, in Nepal, in 2009; and the skis used by **Davo Karničar** when he skiied down Everest in 2000, the first man to achieve the feat.

THE INCREDIBLE FLYING MEN

The world-renowned **Planica ski jumps** include one of the world's largest hills and have been the venue for some of the longest jumps in history. The first jump here was built in 1934, on the initiative of **Stanko Bloudek**, engineer, figure-skating champion and the man widely credited with bringing winter sports to a wider Slovenian audience. Not long after its construction (a mere 90m – today the longest is a breathtaking 225m), the first record at Planica fell, as the Austrian, **Sepp Bradl**, became the first man to jump beyond the magical 100m mark, in 1936. To this day, Planica proudly boasts of holding more ski-jump records than any other venue in the world, though the last one set here was in 2005.

Unsurprisingly, Slovenes have a fine pedigree in the sport, gaining their first Olympic medal (a team bronze) in the 2002 Salt Lake City games, which starred Robert Kranjec, one of the leading exponents over the years, along with Rok Benkovič and Primož Peterka. None, though, can hold a candle to the current superstar of the sport, **Peter Prevc**, who in 2015 became the first man to jump an astonishing 250m, in Vikersund, Norway – he also holds the current record at Planica, jumping 248.5m in 2015.

There's coverage, too, of the first mountain guides; the Alpine Association of Slovenia, formed in 1893; and the much-cherished Mountain Rescue Service, established in 1912 and whose reputation is second to none. The last exhibit is the original iron stove from Aljažev Stolp at the summit of Triglav, which climbers would use to stamp their cards.

ARRIVAL AND INFORMATION   MOJSTRANA

By bus Buses from Kranjska Gora (hourly; 25min) set down passengers on Triglavska cesta, the main street.
Tourist office In the centre of the village at Savska cesta

1, though in time they are likely to move to the Slovenian Alpine Museum (daily 10am–6pm; ☎04 589 1320, ⓦmojstrana.com).

ACCOMMODATION

Camping Kamne Dovje 9 ☎04 589 1105, ⓦcamping kamne.com. In the tiny village of Dovje, just above the main road heading down to Mojstrana, this decent, slightly hilly, site also has basic two- to five-bed bungalows (three-night minimum stay); other amenities include tennis courts, a small bar, bike rental and climbing gear. Buses stop on the road just outside the site. Camping €18, bungalows (three nights) €94

Hostel Pr' Jozlnu Triglavska cesta 50 ☎040 699 271, ⓦhosteljozl.com. Next door to the Slovenian Alpine Museum (indeed, it's in the old museum building), this is as much bar as hostel. The dorms, which have five to twelve beds, are no more than adequate, but they serve a purpose – it's a useful place to stop over if you're about to tackle Triglav. No breakfast; self-catering kitchen. €13

Slap Peričnik and Aljažev Dom

Four kilometres beyond Mojstrana, two paths branch off up a fairly steep and rocky forest slope (10min) to the **Slap Peričnik** (Peričnik Waterfall), which actually comprises an upper (16m) and lower (52m) fall. Unusually, the falls can be circled – via the narrow, sandy ledge – but wherever you view them from you're likely to get a good soaking. The best time to see the falls is in winter when the water freezes into thick curtains of ice.

Six kilometres further north, up an increasingly steep and rugged track (accessible by car), is **Aljažev Dom** (see box, p.121), named after the eponymous mountaineer, and the key lodge for hikers en route to Triglav. Ten minutes' walk north of the hut is a **memorial to World War II Partisan fighters**, which takes the form of climbing equipment (a carabiner and piton). From here, a couple of paths lead towards the summit. On a clear day, the views of Triglav's indomitable 1200m-high and 3km-wide north face are spectacular.

Kot and Krma valleys and Zgornja Radovna

From Mojstrana another road cuts south towards the second and third of the glens that forge into the belly of the National Park. Three kilometres beyond the **Kosma Pass** (847m), one road branches off into the secluded **Kot Valley**, while the main road continues through the hamlet of **ZGORNJA RADOVNA** and on to the **Krma Valley** which, at 7km in length, is the longest of the glacial valleys in the Julian Alps.

Pocarjeva domačija

Zgornja Radovna 25 • July & Aug Sat & Sun 11am–6pm; you need to contact the Mojstrana tourist office first (see p.132) • €2 • ☎04 578 0200

The **Pocarjeva domačija** (Pocar Farmhouse) is one of six farms believed to have existed in Zgornja Radovna during feudal times. This unusually large seventeenth-century farmhouse consists of a main living area, bedroom – note the date, 1775, inscribed onto the ceiling beam – a "black kitchen" (see p.123) and, upstairs, the attic and granary room – all furnishings and contents are original. The two-storey, part-stone, part-wooden **outbuilding**, previously used for housing livestock and storing hay, now displays farmers' implements and long wooden carts.

Radovna Valley

From Zgornja Radovna, the road east continues down through the **Radovna Valley** towards Bled, some 15km away. For cyclists there is a fairly sedate but attractive path (3hr) from the farmhouse to **Krnica** near Bled – regular information boards detail local points of interest. At roughly the midway point between Radovna and Bled, in the hamlet of **Srednja Radovna**, you'll come across the ruins of the Smolej farmhouse – the only building that remained following an attack on the village by Germans in September 1944, in retaliation for the ambush of two of their soldiers. At the road junction is a **monument to Jakob Aljaž**, which has the local hero pointing towards Triglav.

The Vršič Pass to the Soča Valley

Linking the Upper Sava and Soča valleys, the **Vršič Pass** – the highest mountain pass in Slovenia – is one of the most spectacular and scenically rewarding trips in the country. Constituting the stretch of road between Kranjska Gora and Trenta – a total of some 25km – the pass is defined by fifty hairpin bends, 24 on the Kranjska Gora side, 26 on the Trenta side (each bend is numbered and the altitude recorded).

GETTING AROUND   **THE VRŠIČ PASS**

Between June and Sept, four daily **buses** haul themselves up and over the pass and down to Bovec (44km south of Kranjska Gora), and while there are regular stops at all the huts and villages along the way, this limited service makes it extremely difficult to see much in one day. It's really only feasible to see many of the places described here if you have your own transport (the road is not suitable for caravans or trailers). The other alternative, of course, is to **hike** to or between various points. Due to snowdrifts and the threat of avalanches, the pass is periodically **closed** between Nov and April.

From Kranjska Gora to Vršič

Beyond Lake Jasna (see p.127), the road climbs steadily up past the 1000m point, reaching, at turn eight (1129m), the **Ruska kapelica** (Russian Chapel), probably the most poignant sight along the pass. Set back 100m from the road, the tiny wood-latticed chapel (which cannot be entered) was built between 1916 and 1917 to commemorate the deaths of more than three hundred Russian prisoners of war buried by an avalanche as they constructed the road; thousands more prisoners died from fatigue, starvation and torture during its construction, a few of whom are buried in the small **military cemetery**, set back 40m from the road just after turn 21.

Beyond this point the road becomes ever more sinuous, passing several mountain huts, including *Koča na Gozdu* (☎041 682 704; May–Sept daily; Oct–April Sat & Sun) and the delightful *Tonkina koča* (☎041 396 645; all year), serving the most delicious strudel this side of the Alps – before arriving at **Vršič**, the highest point along the pass at 1611m. There's another hut here – *Tičarjev Dom* (☎051 634 571; May–Oct) – and it's a good starting point for hikes into the surrounding mountains, including via Vratca (1108m; 3hr 30min), and **Prisank** (2547m; 4hr 30min), though both are hikes of some difficulty.

From Vršič to Trenta

The descent from Vršič to the **Trenta Valley** is every bit as dramatic as the ascent, with many an unscheduled diversion almost guaranteed – if you have wheels, that is. Stationed on an exposed ledge just after turn 48 is a fine-looking **monument** to Julius Kugy, the esteemed mountaineer and botanist who pioneered many new routes across the Alps, and whose biography *Alpine Pilgrimage* extolled the virtues of both the mountains and those who climbed them.

2

Izvir Soča and the Soška Pot

At turn 49, a road branches off towards the *Koča pri Izviru Soče* hut (☎04 586 6070; April–Oct), 2km away, and the **Izvir Soče** (source of the Soča River). From the hut, it's a short, twenty-minute climb up a very rocky and partially secured path to the source – care should be taken on approaching the latter part as it can get slippery; fed by an underground lake, the water emerges from a dark cave before streaking away on its long and eventful journey to the Adriatic, some 136km downstream.

If you don't fancy walking that far, you might like to tackle the 20km-long **Soška pot** (Soča Trail), a carefully tailored path (no bicycles) that follows the course of the river from its source down to Kišovec on the border of the National Park – information boards (marked "TNP") lining the route show points of interest. At 9am every Thursday in July and August there are **guided tours** (4hr; €6) from the source down to the lodge in Trenta (see opposite).

ACCOMMODATION   **IZVIR SOČA**

Kekčeva domačija pension ☎041 413 087, ⓦ kekceva-domacija.si. Secreted away in perfect rural isolation just a 10min walk west of the source, this wonderful rustic house is named after the legendary Slovenian children's character Kekec, the clever shepherd boy created by the Kranjska Gora-born writer Josip Vandot (see p.126) – the film *Good Luck, Kekec* was shot here in 1963. Each of the nine beautifully appointed apartments has an upstairs bedroom and a downstairs living area and bathroom. May–Sept. **€130**

Mlinarica Gorge and Alpinum Juliana

Less than 1km beyond turn 49 is the **Mlinarica Gorge**, another magical masterpiece of nature, which takes the form of immense, overhanging rock faces and an impenetrable ravine, at the head of which is another waterfall; to get here, cross the suspension bridge and follow the footpath to the right around to the gorge entrance, which is as far as you can go.

Grafted onto a picturesque hillside 2km south of the gorge is the **Alpski botanični vrt** (Alpinum Juliana; May–Sept daily 8.30am–6.30pm; €3; ☎01 241 0940), Slovenia's only alpine **botanical garden**. Founded in 1926 by Albert Bois de Chesne, a Trieste merchant and close colleague of the botanist Kugy (see p.133), the garden has a fine collection of flora from the country's various alpine regions, as well as samples from the Pyrenees and Caucasus; indeed, some six hundred species flourish here. The best time to visit is in May following the winter thaws.

Trenta

TRENTA marks the border of the upper part of the Trenta Valley, and is also the starting point for assaults on Triglav's massive west face, via the **Zadnjica Valley**. Otherwise, you will find the **Dom Trenta** (Trenta Lodge) here, which houses both the **Triglav National Park Information Centre** and the **Trenta Museum**.

Trenta muzej

Dom Trenta • Feb–April Mon–Fri 10am–2pm; May, June, Sept & Oct daily 10am–6pm; July & Aug daily 9am–7pm • €5 • ☎05 388 9330, ⓦ tnp.si

The **Trenta muzej** (Trenta Museum) is a mixed bag: exhibitions on the geology and geomorphology of the park, together with displays on its indigenous flora and fauna, are a little flat, though redeemed by a couple of beautifully produced video installations – *Mysteries of the Soča* and *The Forest – Time Triptych*. More interesting is coverage of the local mountain guides, including Kugy (see p.133), whose personal effects are on show, and Anton Tožbar, who sustained horrific injuries following a bear attack – as graphically illustrated in the photo showing his missing jaw – a rather unfortunate chap, he was killed twenty years later when felling a spruce tree.

Triglav National Park Information Centre Dom Trenta (Feb–April Mon–Fri 10am–2pm; May, June, Sept & Oct daily 10am–6pm; July & Aug daily 9am–7pm; ☎05 388 9330, ⊛tnp.si); information pertaining to most aspects of the park, with a comprehensive selection of maps.

ACCOMMODATION AND EATING

Camping Trenta Trenta 62a ☎031 615 966. A tidy campsite in a pleasant, cool riverside spot around 3km north of Trenta, which also has the most basic of bungalows sleeping two; a real bonus is the on-site pizzeria/bar. April–Oct. Camping **€11**, bungalows **€36**

Dom Trenta ☎05 388 9330, ⊛tnp.si. The lodge has a handful of apartments, each sleeping up to five people, with a kitchen and living space downstairs, in addition to private rooms (doubles) in *Hiša Trenta* some 300m away. Doubles **€44**, apartments **€60**

Velika Korita Gorge

Below the village of Soča, 10km beyond Trenta, the powerful current of the Soča River has hollowed out spectacular erosion and abrasion potholes in the limestone rock, creating the fantastic 750m-long, 15m-deep **Velika Korita Gorge** (also called the Soča Ravine), the best views of which can be had from the swing bridge at its upper end.

ACCOMMODATION AND EATING | VELIKA KORITA GORGE

Korita campsite Soca 38 ☎05 388 9322, ⊛camp -korita.com. A fabulous little eco-camp comprising half a dozen wood cabins – called lean-tos – sleeping two people and equipped with bedding, as well as hammocks complete with sleeping bag. There's also an open-air (roofed) kitchen with a chill-out area. Lean-tos & hammocks **€16**, camping **€20**

Pristava Lepena Lepena 2 ☎05 388 9900, ⊛pristava -lepena.com. An idyllic, self-contained complex incorporating ten wooden, cottage-style apartments at the edge of the forest, which also incorporates a fine restaurant and a riding school with Lipizzaners and Welsh ponies (€30 for 50min in riding ring, €25 for 1hr trail ride); rates include use of tennis, archery and whirlpool facilities. Mid-May to Sept. **€145**

Žicnica Golobar

The last point of interest before exiting the park is the **Žicnica Golobar** (Golobar Telpher Line), an odd-looking, but immensely powerful, roadside contraption that was once used to transport heavy goods via overhead cables. Telpher lines first appeared throughout the region during World War I as a means of supplying the front lines, though this one was built slightly later, in 1931, the cable running for more than 2000m to the upper station; it last saw service in 1968, but is one of the few remaining such monuments in Slovenia. Following the war, telpher lines were put to good use by farmers and foresters who used them to transport timber back and forth across the valley. From here the road descends through the lower Trenta Valley and exits the park just prior to Bovec (see p.141).

The Soča Valley to the Istrian coast

SEČOVLJE SALTPANS

The Soča Valley to the Istrian coast

While northwest Slovenia may possess the lion's share of the country's primary attractions, the thin wedge of land skirting the Italian border – known as Primorska – is unquestionably the country's most diverse region, constituting four geographically distinct areas, namely, from north to south, the Soča Valley, central Primorska, the Karst and the coast.

Crossing over from the Julian Alps or Triglav National Park, your first encounter with this region is likely to be the magisterial **Soča Valley**, whose rugged peaks were the setting for a sustained period of crushing mountain warfare between Italian forces and the Central Powers in World War I – events that are superbly relayed in the museum in **Kobarid**, situated close to many of the battle sites. The valley now ranks as the country's main **adventure-sports centre**, thanks both to its mountains, which embrace a continuous stream of hikers and skiers, and the amazing **Soča River**, one of Europe's most scenic, chock-full of rafters, canoeists and kayakers during the warmer months.

The valley's alpine peaks eventually give way to the more uniform topography of **central Primorska**, a region defined primarily by its fertile wine and fruit-growing regions – specifically the marvellous **Vipava** and **Brda** hills, located east and west respectively of the bland, modern town of **Nova Gorica**. Central Primorska also incorporates an attractive belt of subalpine countryside (with peaks still exceeding 1200m), sheltering the relatively little-known and under-visited towns of **Idrija** and **Cerkno**, handy bases from which to take in any number of local sights. Nature asserts itself in spectacular fashion a short way south of here with the **Karst** region, whose star attractions are the jaw-dropping **Škocjan Caves** and the world-famous **Lipica Stud Farm**.

Although the **Slovene coast** (all 46km of it) might lack some of the glamour of its more well-heeled Croatian cousin to the south – its beaches are, for the most part, rocky, concrete or grass affairs – there is still much to enjoy. Nearly five centuries of Venetian rule have endowed its towns with some fabulous architecture, not least in its prettiest and most popular resort, **Piran**, although both **Izola** and the coast's largest town and major port, **Koper**, possess a fine kernel of medieval buildings. Visitors seeking more self-indulgence should find **Portorož**, a stone's throw from Piran and the coast's brashest resort, more to their liking.

GETTING AROUND   **THE SOČA VALLEY TO THE ISTRIAN COAST**

Access up and down the Soča Valley is patchy, the rail line going no further than Most na Soči (midway between Nova Gorica and Kobarid), while bus services are fairly sporadic. Getting around the Karst and coastal areas is much easier, with a healthy stream of trains and buses serving both regions.

VINEYARDS, GORIŠKA BRDA

Highlights

❶ Whitewater rafting on the Soča This
magical alpine river provides some of the best
whitewater rafting, kayaking and canoeing in
Europe. **See p.142**

❷ Kobarid Museum Compelling and moving
museum documenting the region's World War I
mountain battles. **See p.147**

❸ Goriška Brda Trek down the cellars of these
gorgeous, vineyard-clad hills, which touch the
Italian border. **See p.159**

❹ Vipava Valley Whipped by the ferocious
bora wind, the lush Vipava Valley yields some
truly exceptional wines. **See p.162**

❺ Škocjan Caves Take a trip through this
breathtaking cave system, which features the
world's largest subterranean canyon. **See p.177**

❻ Lipica Stud Farm Visit the home of the
magnificent Lipizzaner horse and be wowed by a
display of the Classical Riding School. **See p.180**

❼ Church of the Holy Trinity, Hrastovlje A
Romanesque monument, smothered with
exceptional fifteenth-century frescoes including
the famous *Dance of Death*. **See p.181**

❽ Piran The coast's most beautiful resort has
Venetian Gothic-inspired architecture, Italianate
squares and pretty churches. **See p.189**

HIGHLIGHTS ARE MARKED ON THE MAP ON P.140

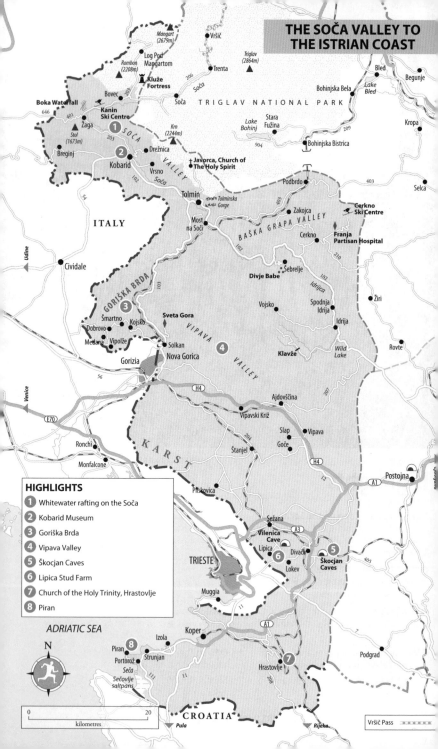

THE SOČA VALLEY TO THE ISTRIAN COAST

TRIGLAV NATIONAL PARK

Mangart (2679m)
Vršič
Triglav (2864m)
Log Pod Mangartom
Rombon (2208m)
Trenta
Bled
Lake Bled
Begunje
Kluže Fortress
Bohinjska Bela
Boka Waterfall
Bovec
Soča
Kanin Ski Centre
Žaga
Stol (1673m)
Krn (2244m)
Lake Bohinj
Stara Fužina
Kropa
Breginj
Drežnica
Javorca, Church of The Holy Spirit
Bohinjska Bistrica
Kobarid
Vrsno
Soča
Selca
Podbrdo
Tolmin
Tolminska Gorge
Zakojca
Cerkno Ski Centre
Most na Soči
BAŠKA GRAPA VALLEY
Cerkno
Franja Partisan Hospital
ITALY
Udine
Sebrelje
Divje Babe
Idrijca
Žiri
GORIŠKA BRDA
Vojsko
Spodnja Idrija
Cividale
Idrija
Rovte
Šmartno
Kojsko
Sveta Gora
VIPAVA VALLEY
Dobrovo
Vipolže
Medana
Solkan
Klavže
Wild Lake
Gorizia
Nova Gorica
H4
Venice
Ajdovščina
Vipavski Križ
Slap
Vipava
Ronchi
K A R S T
Goče
Štanjel
Monfalcone
H4
12
Postojna
A1
Pliskovica
Sežana
Vilenica Cave
A3
Lipica
Škocjan Caves
TRIESTE
Divača
Lokev
Muggia
Koper
A1
Podgrad
ADRIATIC SEA
Izola
Piran
Portorož
Strunjan
Seča
Hrastovlje
Sečovlje saltpans
CROATIA
Pula
Rijeka
N

HIGHLIGHTS

1. Whitewater rafting on the Soča
2. Kobarid Museum
3. Goriška Brda
4. Vipava Valley
5. Škocjan Caves
6. Lipica Stud Farm
7. Church of the Holy Trinity, Hrastovlje
8. Piran

0 ———— 20
kilometres

Vršič Pass

Soča Valley

Richly textured by history and nature, the **Soča Valley**, skirting Triglav National Park's western boundary and extending all the way down to the flatlands of Nova Gorica, is one of Slovenia's most captivating regions. Although not an immediately obvious destination, the valley has few peers when it comes to sheer, stark beauty; moreover, it boasts one of Europe's most dramatic alpine rivers, the **Soča**, which brings thousands of watersports enthusiasts to its milky blue-green waters.

During World War I the valley marked the front line – known as the **Soča Front** (or Isonzo Front) – between the Italian and Austro-Hungarian armies, which engaged in some of the most savage and relentless fighting in the history of mountain warfare. Consequently, the valley is strewn with memorial chapels, abandoned fortifications and dignified military cemeteries.

There are several key settlements sequenced vertically down the valley's spine. **Bovec** and **Kobarid**, in the upper part of the valley, are important tourist hubs: the former is one of the country's premier adventure-sports centres, the latter replete with poignant reminders from the battlefront and boasting a memorable museum. Further down the valley, the small town of **Tolmin** is worth investigating, not least because of its proximity to the fantastic **Tolminska Gorge** and stunningly situated **Church of the Holy Spirit** in Javorca, while a few kilometres south, **Most na Soči** holds some of Slovenia's most significant archeological sites.

Bovec and around

Lying in a broad basin in the shadow of the Kanin mountain range and the mighty Mount Rombon (2208m), the small alpine town of **BOVEC** is a major **watersports** centre thanks to its proximity to the **Soča River**. The town today has a distinctly youthful air in summer; for centuries, however, Bovec and its surroundings were an important centre for animal husbandry, the lofty alpine plateaus ideally suited for high-level pasturing, while the broad valley floor was used for growing hay. The twentieth century was particularly unkind to Bovec: it was burnt down in 1903, massive destruction followed during **World War I**, when the town was razed and much of the population deported, and, more recently, Bovec was struck by three earthquakes – two extremely powerful ones in 1976 and 1998, followed by a third, less destructive, quake in 2004.

Cerkev Sv Urh

Originally a Gothic construction, **Cerkev Sv Urh** (Parish Church of St Ulric), just up the hill from the main square, was rebuilt in neo-Romanesque style in 1734, and underwent substantial reconstruction following heavy World War I damage. Although the interior retains the odd Gothic flourish, notably the portals and triumphal arch, the highlight is the reddish-brown Baroque high altar, made from marble hewn from Mount Rombon, and framed either side by sculptures of St John Nepomuk and St Paul. Unusual features of the church are the niches on the front exterior, containing statues of Sts Peter, Paul and Ulric, and the headstones in the surrounding walls, which would indicate that this used to be a cemetery.

World War I collection

To arrange a visit call the tourist office (see p.143)

Visitors keen to learn more about the Soča Front (see box, p.148) can arrange to view a **private collection** of **World War I weaponry** and other objects retrieved from the battle sites. Amassed by a member of **Društvo 1313** (The 1313 Association) – an ardent group of local historians committed to honouring the men who fought on the Front – this extraordinary collection consists of a stash of weapons (grenades,

SPORTS AND ACTIVITIES ON THE SOČA RIVER

Between April and October, the **Soča River** draws watersports enthusiasts from many countries keen to test out one of the most challenging **whitewater** rivers in Europe. Sections of the river are **graded** according to the level of difficulty – from one, the easiest, up to six, the most difficult (which is open only to experienced competition rafters); most trips depart from **Boka**, 6km west of Bovec, and finish at **Trnovo ob Soči**, 10km further downriver.

AGENCIES

A huge number of agencies in Bovec offer rafting and a plethora of other river-bound activities. Most now also offer **mini-rafting** on two- to four-person rafts, either with a guide in the raft with you or accompanying you in a kayak. Also available are – roughly in order of popularity – canyoning (€50), **kayaking** (around €65 for a two- to three-hour course) and **hydrospeed** (€55). Whoever you go with, expect to pay around €45 per person, which also covers transfers to and from the river and all equipment – all you need is swimming gear and a towel. Good options include:
Aktivni Planet Trg golobarskih žrtev 19, and at *Hostel Soča Rocks* (see p.144) (☎041 653 417, ⓦaktivniplanet.si).
Bovec Rafting Team Mala Vas 106, on the edge of town opposite the *Mangart* hotel (☎041 338 308, ⓦbovec-rafting-team.com).
Sportmix Trg golobarskih žrtev 18 (☎031 871 991, ⓦsportmix.si).
X-Point Trg svobode 6, Kobarid (☎05 388 5308, ⓦxpoint.si).

FISHING

Between April and October, the river becomes prime **fishing** territory, richly populated with brown trout, rainbow trout, the famous marble trout (*Salmo trutta marmoratus*) and grayling. Fishing is permitted on two sections of the river; the upper part of the Soča down to Čezsoča (including Lepena and Koritnica), which costs €69 for one day and €172 for three days; and the lower part, from Čezsoča downwards, which costs €60 for one day and €162 for three days. Contact the tourist office in Bovec (see opposite) for information on obtaining permits.

shells, knives and so on), personal belongings (flasks, combs and toothbrushes) and illuminating photographs of some of the battle scenes.

Ravelnik and Vojaško Pokopališče Bovec

Following a signposted path 1km south of Bovec (500m before the turning towards Trenta) brings you to **Ravelnik**, an area containing a string of huts, caverns and trenches abandoned following the cessation of World War I fighting; many have been cleaned up and partly reconstructed but are, nevertheless, fascinating to look around. Two kilometres east of Bovec, at the crossroads of the Predel and Vršič roads, is the **Vojaško Pokopališče Bovec** (Bovec Military Cemetery), containing more than five hundred headstones of Austrian soldiers killed near Bovec and on Mount Rombon between 1915 and 1917.

Slap Boka

6km southwest of Bovec just before Žaga

The most popular local attraction is the thundering 106m-high and 30m-wide **Slap Boka** (Boka Waterfall), near the village of **Žaga** – indeed, Žaga itself was in the spotlight a few years back, as it was here that much of the 2008 Disney movie, *The Chronicles of Narnia: Prince Caspian*, was filmed. It's possible to see the waterfall from the main road (albeit at quite some distance), and close-up views can be obtained by scrambling along two trails by the **Most Boka** (Boka Bridge), each offering very different perspectives of Slovenia's highest permanent waterfall: the trail beginning at the west side of the bridge – which provides a head-on view – is the shorter and easier of the two paths, but does involve a fair amount of clambering over boulders; the far more difficult second route, beginning at the east side of the bridge, ascends to a spot above the head of the falls. Emanating from a deep karst spring in the Kanin mountains, the Boka is a stupendous sight, highly dependent on rain and snow-melt from the Kanin plateaus for its massive volume of water – so the best time to view it is in late spring.

Trdnjava Kluže

4km north of Bovec, in Triglav National Park (see p.117) • May & Oct Sat & Sun 10am–5pm; June & Sept Mon–Fri & Sun 10am–5pm, Sat 10am–6pm; July & Aug daily 9am–8pm • €3 • ☎ 05 388 6758

Inside Triglav National Park, on the road towards Log pod Mangartom and the Predel Pass, stands the formidable **Trdnjava Kluže** (Kluže Fortress). Strategically positioned on a steep rock face overlooking the impressive 60m-deep Koritnica Gorge, this heavily restored chunky grey fortress has seen more than its fair share of action over the years.

Although a wooden fortification was built here in the fifteenth century, it's believed that some kind of fortress existed on this site during **Roman** times, a theory based on the fact that a Roman road ran through the nearby Predel Pass, connecting the northern and southern parts of the Empire. The wooden fortification was supplanted by a stone construction in 1613, during which time it successfully repelled repeated Turkish attacks, before Napoleon's French marauders razed it in 1797. Its current appearance dates from 1882, though the upper part – named Fort Hermann after the hero of the 1809 Battle of Predel – was demolished by heavy and sustained shelling during World War I. Occupied by an Italian garrison during World War II, Kluže was then left in a state of disrepair, before a slow process of renovation began in the late 1980s.

The interior rooms now display a series of **exhibitions** on the fortress and, more interestingly, the **Soča Front**, with a hoard of items recovered from the battlefield, such as gas masks and helmets, pipes and tobacco, beer glasses and even a battered trumpet; the courtyard, meanwhile, makes a fitting venue for re-enactments of battle scenes performed by the 1313 Association (see p.141) during July and August. The ruins of Fort Hermann can be accessed via a path that begins across the road from Kluže, and should take no more than thirty minutes.

3

ARRIVAL AND INFORMATION   BOVEC

By bus The main bus stop is near the Cultural Centre, a few minutes' walk south of the main square, Trg golobarskih žrtev.

Destinations Kobarid (Mon–Fri 5 daily, Sat & Sun 2 daily; 30min); Kranjska Gora (July & Aug 5 daily, plus June & Sept 1 on Sat & Sun; 1hr 45min); Tolmin (Mon–Fri 5 daily, Sat & Sun 2 daily; 1hr).

Tourist office Just off the main square, at Trg golobarskih žrtev 8 (June–Aug daily 9am–8pm; Sept–May Mon–Fri 9am–4pm, Sat & Sun 9am–1pm; ☎ 05 384 1919, ⓦ bovec .si); it has a good stock of information about and maps of the Soča Valley.

ACCOMMODATION

There's plenty of varied accommodation in Bovec, including some six or so **campsites** in the vicinity; the two closest and best are listed here. Wherever you're staying, in July and Aug you'd do well to **book** in advance.

HOTELS

★**Dobra Vila** Mala Vas 112 ☎ 05 389 6400, ⓦ dobra -vila-bovec.si. A short walk east of the centre, the town's old telephone exchange building is now a supremely classy hotel, whose eleven handsome rooms – each one bearing a number relating to a local landmark (for example, 2300, the height of Kanin) – sport exquisite furnishings and big lush beds; bathrooms are dazzling, and some have clawfoot tubs. Breakfast is taken in the fabulous Art Deco styled winter garden overlooking the meadow. Closed Nov. **€140**

Mangart Mala Vas 107 ☎ 05 388 4250, ⓦ hotel -mangart.com. The location, just off the main roundabout, might not be anything to write home about, but the rooms

are beautifully appointed and all have a magnificent view of the mountains. **€100**

Stari Kovač Rupa 3 ☎ 05 388 6699, ⓦ starikovac.com. Low-key, and much cheaper than anywhere else in town, this pleasantly old-fashioned guesthouse, a few paces down from the main square, offers eight two- to four-bed rooms, plus a mix of small apartments in the neighbouring building. **€50**

HOSTELS AND CAMPING

★**Adrenaline Check Eco Place** Podklopca 4 ☎ 041 383 662, ⓦ adrenaline-check.com. Some 12km from Bovec, this self-styled sustainable outdoor hostel offers

MOUNTAIN ACTIVITIES AROUND BOVEC

Ranged high above Bovec to the west, the **Kanin mountains** offer superb adrenaline-fuelled activities, not least the highest-altitude skiing in Slovenia (around 2300m), with slopes for skiers of all abilities. If you're not here to ski, or have just come up to have a look around, then there are a number of excellent **hikes** to consider.

SKIING

The **Kanin ski centre** (☎05 389 6310, ⓦboveckanin.si), based in the hamlet of **Dvor**, 1km southwest of Bovec, is directly connected to the resort of Sella Nevea across the border in Italy. Four-seater **cable cars** transport passengers to the upper station, called **Podi** (station D; 2202m) in around thirty minutes (winter daily 8am–4pm nonstop; June & Sept Fri–Sun 8am–4pm hourly; July & Aug daily 7am–5pm hourly; €17 return), but be warned, this ride is not for the jittery. In summer, the sun-bleached rocks and boulders make for a rather bleak scene, but the views on a cloudless day are sensational – there's a basic restaurant at the top too.

HIKING

One of the easiest hiking paths **from Podi** is to **Prestreljenik** (2499m; 1hr 30min), with more demanding paths from Podi to **Visoki Kanin** (2587m; 3hr 30min) – on a clear day it's possible to see the Adriatic from here – and **Rombon** (2208m; 5hr). The one hut in these mountains is the *Dom Petra Skalarja na Kaninu* (July & Aug daily; June & Sept Fri–Sun only; ☎040 829 701), a 45-minute walk south of the upper station. All three hikes are doable from Bovec itself but, with the exception of Rombon (5hr from Bovec), you should count on an additional four hours at least for each. The excellent 1:50,000 **map** *Posočje*, available from the tourist office, will help you get your bearings. If you don't fancy going it alone, Aktivni Planet (see box, p.142) and Outdoor Galaxy (see below) organize a number of **guided hikes** and walks. Better still, in mid-September, the terrific, two-week long **Soča Valley Hiking Festival** comprises more than two dozen guided walks along various trails throughout the valley, as well as exhibitions and lectures.

ADRENALINE ACTIVITIES

There are two **zipline** parks in Bovec. The most dramatic is up in the Krnica Valley (ⓦzipline slovenia.com; €55 for three hours), which has five wires each between 500m and 700m long and some 200m above ground, so it's not for anyone without a head for heights – it's operated by Aktivni Planet (see box, p.142), whose office is the meeting point. The other park, operated by Soca Rafting at Trg golobarskih žrtev 14 (☎041 724 472, ⓦsocarafting.si), is up in the Učja Canyon and has eight ziplines (ⓦzipline.si; €55). Great fun, too, is the **Adventure Park** up in the beautiful Srnica Gorge, which combines a short hike with climbs along fixed steel cables and wooden bridges, and a couple of short zipwires; reservations must made through Outdoor Galaxy, at Kot 1 (☎040 605 325, ⓦoutdoor-galaxy.com; €27), which also organizes guided mountain bike tours and rents bikes (€15 for half a day, €20 full day). The mountains hereabouts make for wonderful **tandem paragliding**; Bovec Rafting Team (see box, p.142) or Aktivni Planet both charge around €145 for around 25 minutes in the air.

GOLF

For something a little less frenetic, there's **golf** at the nine-hole Bovec Golf Club (☎040 382 229, ⓦgolfbovec.si; €24 for nine holes, €36 for eighteen), 10km west of town, which, like most courses in Slovenia, plays out against a stunning backdrop.

spacious pitches for tents and lean-tos (a tent enclosed within a wooden hut, with double mattress), of which there are three deluxe versions with furnishings, terrace and hammock. Solar-powered showers and an open kitchen with fire pit complete this fabulous back-to-nature experience. Free pickups. Camping €26, rented tents €44, lean-tos €50

Hostel Soča Rocks Mala Vas 120 ☎041 317 777, ⓦhostelsocarocks.com. Rocks by name, rocks by nature, this cracking hostel – featuring colourful six-bed dorms

and doubles, along with lots of activities on offer – certainly lives up to its name; it also possesses an ace bar fashioned from stones from the Soča, which is as good a place as any in town for a beverage or two. Dorms €15, doubles €40

Kamp Polovnik Ledina 8 ☎05 389 6007, ⓦkamp -polovnik.com. Around 500m southeast of town, out by the road to Kobarid, this is by far the smallest campsite in the Bovec area, but it's a pleasant, well-shaded area and offers all the requisite amenities. April to mid-Oct. €18

EATING AND DRINKING

Črna Ovca Ledina 8 ☎051 397 882. If you come here during the day, as many locals do to sip coffee while the kids bomb around the playground, it's hard to believe that the excellent "Black Sheep" transforms into party central come sundown; they've also got tennis courts, boules and beach volleyball. June–Aug Mon–Thurs & Sun 10am–midnight, Fri & Sat 10am–3am; Sept–May Tues–Thurs & Sun 4pm–midnight, Fri & Sat 4pm–3am.

★**Dobra Vila** Mala Vas 112 ☎05 389 6400, ⓦdobra -vila-bovec.si. The town's one truly outstanding restaurant, whose food is every bit as sumptuous as the setting. Duck salad with sweet-and-sour sauce and almonds, lamb and mint risotto, and buckwheat mousse with burned butter ice cream and pine nuts are the sorts of treats you can expect to find on the daily four-course menu (€40); the wine pairings are tip-top too. Daily 7–10pm.

Letni Vrt Trg golobarskih žrtev 1 ☎05 389 6383. With its huge terrace, *Letni Vrt* has a reputation as a fantastic pizzeria, but this doesn't do justice to its fabulous assortment of local specialities, such as grilled trout; *čompe*, an appealing combination of potato, cottage cheese and hard cheese; and *buški krafi*, parcelled-up mashed pears flavoured with walnuts, raisins and cinnamon. Daily except Tues 11am–10pm.

Log pod Mangartom and around

3

Few people venture much further north than Bovec, which is a shame as the mountain scenery is as dramatic here as anywhere else in the country. Nestling under the Mangart mountain range is the pretty village of **LOG POD MANGARTOM**, which actually comprises the two adjoining settlements of **Spodnji Log** (Lower Log) and **Gorenji Log** (Upper Log).

Damaged in the 1998 earthquake, Log Pod Mangartom had to contend with an even greater catastrophe during the night of November 16–17, 2000, when a crushing **landslide** – believed to have been caused by a combination of torrential rainfall and significant seismological activity in the area – struck. The landslide began some 1000m further up in the Mangartski mountains and coursed down the valley slopes and along the bed of the Predelica River in a matter of seconds, before smashing into the upper settlement. Seven people died – one person was never found – and a number of houses and farm buildings were wiped out or irreparably damaged. At the reconstructed stone bridge in Gorenji Log, an information board documenting the history of the village illustrates the aftermath of the landslide, while the wide-open spaces around are testament to the devastation wrought. If you have your own transport, you can drive up to the top of the pass, and another reconstructed bridge, to see where the slide began.

Mount Mangart

Just beyond the bridge at the top of the pass, the main road continues onwards to Italy, while another – the country's highest mountain road – branches off towards the

---

WALK OF PEACE

The **Walk of Peace** (Pot Miru; ⓦpotmiru.si), is a 320km-long path/trail starting in Log Pod Mangartom and ending in Trieste; littered with cemeteries, fortifications and monuments from the World War I battlefield, the path is officially divided into fifteen sections, though the classic five-day hike is the 100km walk from Log Pod Mangartom to Tolmin. The staff at the Walk of Peace Visitor Centre in Kobarid (see p.149) organize a number of excellent **guided tours** – ranging from easy to medium three-hour walks to demanding day-long hikes; one of the most popular is the two-and-a-half-hour trip up to Kolovrat and the World War I outdoor museum. For all tours (around €25/hr) call at least one day, but preferably two or three, in advance.

Whether you're on a guided tour or hiking alone, the guidebook *The Walk of Peace, from the Alps to Trieste* (€14.90) is an invaluable aid, as is the 1:25,000 *Zgornje Posočje* (*The Walk of Peace, from the Alps to the Adriatic*) map, detailing all the major battle sites and areas of interest throughout the Soča Valley; both of these are available from the Walk of Peace Visitor Centre.

Mangart Saddle (2072m), below which is the *Koča na Mangrtskem sedlu* (☎041 954 761; June–Sept), the only hut in this group of mountains. Two hours' walk from the hut is the magnificent **Mount Mangart** (2679m), Slovenia's third-highest peak and known for its reddish-coloured sandstone.

Cerkev Sv Štefana and World War I Military Cemetery
The only site of note in Gorenji Log is the **Cerkev Sv Štefana** (Parish Church of St Stephen), which contains a ceiling fresco by Ivan Grohar, *The Stoning of St Stephen*, and a wooden Gothic statue of Queen Mary from the end of the fifteenth century. Midway between Upper and Lower Log, just behind the small civilian cemetery, lies a **World War I military cemetery** – one of the few in the region preserved in its original form. It has neat rows of black iron crosses on mounds denoting the final resting places of nearly nine hundred soldiers killed on Mount Rombon and Mount Čuklja, the majority of whom were from the fourth Bosnian-Herzegovinian Infantry. The monument in the centre of the cemetery features two soldiers, one an Austrian, the other a Bosnian, gazing up to the summit of Rombon.

Štoln
A few paces along from the church of St Stephen a path leads up to the entrance of the now disused **Štoln** (Mining Tunnel), alongside which an informative outdoor exhibition documents the tunnel's history from its opening in 1905 to its closure in 1991. The tunnel was used to supply the army with troops and materials during both world wars, as well as to transport injured troops away from the front; between 1916 and 1917 alone, some 34,000 trains made the journey through the 4km-long tunnel. Following World War II, villagers used it in order to reach the lead and zinc mines at Cave del Predil in Italy, particularly during periods of heavy snowfall when the journey by bus over the Predel Pass was not possible.

ARRIVAL AND DEPARTURE   **LOG POD MANGARTOM**

Unfortunately, there is **no public transport** from Bovec to Log pod Mangartom, so if you don't have your own vehicle you'll have to hitch or walk.

ACCOMMODATION AND EATING

Alpine No. 63 ☎08 205 4870, ⦿hotel-alpine.com. Up near the bridge, this spruce little hotel has solidly furnished, spotless rooms, most of which offer marvellous mountain views; they've also got a very creditable in-house pizzeria. April–Oct. **€60**

Kobarid
"A little white town with a campanile in a valley" was how American writer Ernest Hemingway described **KOBARID** in *A Farewell to Arms* in 1929, and though it has retained its pleasantly relaxed air, this handsome town, 21km south of Bovec, has had a pretty rum time of it over the years. In October 1917, the nearby Krn mountain range was the chief battleground for one of the war's most decisive military engagements – otherwise known as the **Twelfth Offensive** – in which the Italians were routed by the combined Central Powers of Germany and Austria, an event superbly documented in the town's gripping **museum**. The interwar years were defined by nationalist struggles on both sides, but Kobarid (then Caporetto) remained, as did much of the region, under Italian control until the end of World War II.

Although it retains a strong Italianate flavour – the border is just 9km to the west – much of Kobarid's present appearance dates from 1976, following the massive earthquake. The centre of town is essentially the small main square, **Trg svobode**, where the main roads from Bovec and Tolmin, and the road from Italy, converge. From the square, it's no more than ten minutes' walk to any of the town's attractions or facilities.

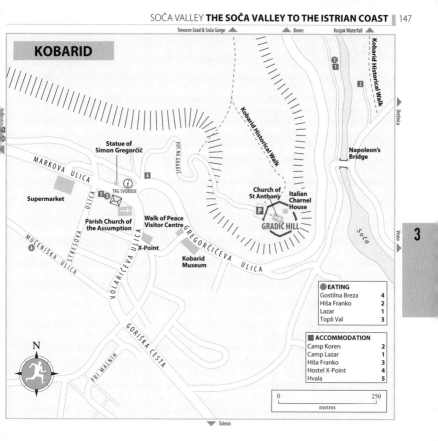

KOBARID

- Statue of Simon Gregorčič
- Supermarket
- Parish Church of the Assumption
- Walk of Peace Visitor Centre
- X-Point
- Kobarid Museum
- Church of St Anthony
- Italian Charnel House
- Napoleon's Bridge
- GRADIČ HILL

MARKOVA ULICA
TRG SVOBODE
POT NA GRADIČ
MUČENIŠKA ULICA
STRESOVA ULICA
VOLARIČEVA ULICA
GREGORČIČEVA ULICA
GORIŠKA CESTA
PRI MALNIH
Kobarid Historical Walk
Soča

Tonocov Grad & Soča Gorge ▲ | ▲ Bovec | Kozjak Waterfall ▲
Drežnica ▶
Vrsno ▶
▼ Tolmin

EATING

Gostilna Breza	4
Hiša Franko	2
Lazar	1
Topli Val	3

ACCOMMODATION

Camp Koren	2
Camp Lazar	1
Hiša Franko	3
Hostel X-Point	4
Hvala	5

0 ——————— 250
metres

3

Along with its museum, and a surfeit of brilliant **restaurants**, Kobarid's proximity to the **Soča River** and a stack of other historical and natural sights could quite easily detain you for a day or two.

Kobariški muzej

Gregorčičeva ulica 10 • Daily: April–Sept 9am–6pm; Oct–March 10am–5pm • €6 • ☎ 05 389 0000, ⓦ kobariski-muzej.si

Situated in a lovely two-storey Baroque house, the **Kobariški muzej** (Kobarid Museum) memorably evokes the horrors of the **Soča Front** (see box, p.148). First off you'll get to see a twenty-minute **film**, containing superbly shot footage of the battles along the Soča Front, and in particular the decisive Twelfth Offensive. The museum's rooms are thematically arranged: up on the first floor, the **Krn Range Room** is represented by a vast map-relief of the Krn mountain range, which illustrates the complex arrangements of the military positions confronting the warring sides. (As an interesting aside, the two rooms behind the Krn room hold a collection of local archeological finds, the most fascinating of which are some delicate bronze statuettes unearthed from Gradič Hill.)

The **Black Room** reflects upon the suffering of the combatants, graphically illustrated by the pictures of hideously disfigured soldiers; there is also a graffitied door from the military prison in Smast village near Kobarid. The other rooms on this floor – the **White Room** and **Rear Room** – are given over to themes of mobilization and civilian displacement, and the nightmarish struggle for survival in the mountains during the ferociously cold winter months. Exhibits include pick axes and jaw traps.

THE SOČA FRONT

When the Italians declared war on the Central Powers in May 1915, the Great War assumed a new and altogether more brutal dimension. This fresh battlefield, part of which extended for some 90km from Mount Rombon, north of Bovec, through Kobarid to a position a short way north of Trieste (Trst) on the Adriatic coast, was known as the **Soča Front** (Izonso Front).

Although the Austro-Hungarians, under the command of the "Soča Lion", General Svetozar Borojevič von Bojna, had already fortified the front, the Italians secured immediate success, capturing Kobarid and the nearby Krn range. More than two years and eleven debilitating and futile offensives later, the two heavily entrenched sides prepared for the denouement. With severely depleted troop numbers, Austrian Emperor Charles I approached the German Kaiser Wilhelm II for reinforcements, and together they formed the fourteenth Austro-German army. Their breakthrough plan, "Faith in Arms", was based on swiftly coordinated lightning strikes and the element of surprise; in this case, thousands of troops and armoury were quickly repositioned between Bovec and Tolmin.

Effected on October 24, 1917, this **Twelfth Offensive** – the first counteroffensive by the Central Powers – resulted in the Italian army being pressed all the way back to the Friulian Plain and the Piave River, an episode acknowledged as the greatest single breakthrough of the war and the first successful "blitzkrieg" in the history of European warfare. Fighting continued around the Piave River for another year, the outcome of which was victory for the Italians. With an estimated million fatalities on all sides, a significant number of whom were women and children, the human cost was catastrophic; moreover, many thousands more were forced to flee the region, only a fraction of whom returned at the war's end.

On the second floor, the room with the **map-relief** of the Upper Soča region clearly identifies both the positions of the warring troops throughout the valley prior to the Twelfth Offensive and the awesome volume of military machinery required for this attack; courtesy of a brilliant piece of technology, the room darkens and a clock begins to tick down as waves of blue (the Austro-Germans) sweep over the hapless Italian forces (in red), thereby illustrating the devastating speed at which the Twelfth Offensive occurred; pop down to the reception desk if you wish to see it in action. This room leads through to a mock-up **cavern**, in which a wistful young soldier pens one last letter to his father. The central **Breakthrough Room** considers the events pertaining to the critical operation of October 24–27, 1917, featuring a hoard of hellish-looking weaponry. Throughout, the photographs provide an exceptional, and frequently moving, supplement to the main exhibits.

Cerkev Marijino vnebovzetje
Trg svobode

The orderly **Cerkev Marijino vnebovzetje** (Parish Church of the Assumption) is home to some terrific artwork. The striking red-and-white marble high altar, designed by Lazzarini in 1716, features a handful of sculpted saints and angels, but it is actually more interesting for what you can't see. Concealed behind the altar picture is a late fifteenth-century statue of the Holy Mother, which is only revealed on special religious occasions or, if you're lucky, on request; ask at the priest's house opposite the church entrance. To commemorate Pope John Paul II's visit to Slovenia in 1996 (although he didn't actually visit Kobarid) the balcony was blanketed with a beautiful canvas, and is notable for its paintings of several eminent historical characters, including the pope himself. The stained-glass windows were installed in 1995 in order to lighten the church interior. Opposite the church is an oversized **sculpture of Simon Gregorčič**, the beloved Slovenian priest and poet who hailed from nearby Vrsno (see p.151).

Kobariška zgodovinska pot

For a real flavour of Kobarid's historical, cultural and natural heritage, you should follow the **Kobariška zgodovinska pot** (Kobarid Historical Walk), an enjoyable 5km stroll taking in wartime monuments, abandoned fortifications, bridges and waterfalls. A free leaflet outlining the route, and the key sights along the way, is available from the museum. A gently paced walk, including stops, should take between three and four hours.

Italijanska kostnica and Tonocov Grad

Beginning on the north side of Trg svobode, a winding road (Pot na Gradič) lined with the Stations of the Cross ascends to Gradič Hill and the **Italijanska kostnica** (Italian Charnel House), perhaps the valley's most evocative monument, especially when viewed from afar (it's possible to drive up to this point, but no further). The Charnel House – opened in 1938 with Mussolini in attendance – consists of three-tiered octagons tapering upwards towards the **Cerkev Sv Antona** (Church of St Anthony). Inside the huge ossuary lie the remains of more than seven thousand Italian soldiers killed during fighting on the Soča Front, the names of whom are engraved onto the slabs of greenish serpentine inside the large niches. From the Charnel House, take the path to the left which forks off into the woods – hereafter, the route is marked with red arrows and the museum logo – and onwards to the remains of the ancient fort of **Tonocov Grad**, unique in that it was occupied continuously from the middle Stone Age, through Antiquity to the Middle Ages.

Italian Line of Defence and Soča Gorge

From the fort, the path continues down towards the main road, which you should cross carefully, before a knee-jarring descent down to the Soča River – en route you'll pass a section of the **Italian Line of Defence**, one of three constructed by the Italians on the Soča Front during World War I; the trail then continues along a track in the direction of the *Koren* campsite, but you should take the path to the left which opens up into the **Soča Gorge** and a sturdy swing bridge, this one having replaced the original from World War I.

Slap Kozjak

From the bridge – where there are terrific views of the gorge and river – it's a twenty-minute walk to most people's favourite part of the circuit, the **Slap Kozjak** (Kozjak Waterfall), a graceful, 15m-high waterfall less impressive for its height than for its atmospheric cave-like hall carved out of the surrounding rock. From here, retrace your steps and take the path that forks left up to a **small fortress** and another **line of defence**, scattered with yet more caverns, shelters and observation posts.

Napoleonov most

The path then cuts inland, passing the *Koren* campsite and winding up at the **Napoleonov most** (Napoleon's Bridge), an elegant, stone-arched structure connecting the two banks of the river at one of the narrowest and most spectacular points of the gorge. The original bridge was built in 1750 and later named for the French leader after he marched across it en route to the Predel Pass. The day after World War I was declared, the bridge was blown up by retreating Austrians, though this didn't deter the Italians who first replaced it with a wooden, then an iron bridge; the one you see today was completed after the war.

ARRIVAL AND INFORMATION   KOBARID

By bus All buses stop on the main square, Trg svobode. Destinations Bovec (Mon–Fri 5 daily, Sat & Sun 2 daily; 30min); Tolmin (Mon–Fri 6 daily, Sat & Sun 2 daily; 30min).

Tourist office Trg svobode 16 (April Mon–Fri 9am–1pm & 2–4pm, Sat & Sun 9am–1pm & 4–7pm; May, June & Sept Mon–Fri 9am–1pm & 2–7pm, Sat & Sun 9am–1pm & 4–7pm; July & Aug daily 9am–8pm; Oct–March Mon–Fri 9am–1pm & 2–4pm, Sat 10am–2pm; ☎ 05 389 0490, ⓦ dolina-soce.com); they provide a good range of literature

and maps on the Soča Front, and can also book rooms both in the town and in local villages, especially Drežnica.

Walk of Peace Visitor Centre Next to the Kobarid Museum at Gregorčičeva ulica 8 (Mon–Fri 9am–12.30pm & 1.30–6pm, Sat & Sun 10am–1pm & 2–6pm; ☎ 05 389 0167, ⓦ potmiru.si). With an interactive exhibition on the Walk of Peace (see box, p.145), they offer information on all aspects of the path, including places to sleep and eat, and offer a great programme of guided walks.

3

ACCOMMODATION

★**Camp Koren** 500m east of town on the east bank of the Soča ☎05 389 1311, ⓦkamp-koren.si. Brilliantly located, *Koren* is a wonderful, rambling site with areas for campers, caravans and tents; it also has six stunning log cabins just above the main camping area, each sleeping up to six people (three-night minimum). You can pick herbs from the surrounding gardens, and superb on-site facilities include a kids' playground, bar and shop. Open all year. Camping €25, cabins (three nights) €190

Camp Lazar 500m east of town on the west bank of the Soča ☎05 388 5333, ⓦlazar.si. On the opposite bank to *Koren*, this is a smaller, flatter site with good, clean facilities, though somewhat surprisingly, its most appealing aspect is its restaurant (see below) – if you can't be bothered making your own, there's a terrific self-service breakfast in the restaurant (€8). April–Oct. €26

★**Hiša Franko** Staro Selo 1, 3km west of town ☎05 389 4120, ⓦhisafranko.com. *Franko's* simply oozes class. The original and idiosyncratic rooms (one with massage bath) are gorgeously furnished with finely cut drapes, bamboo, oak and other exotic materials, while the chrome-finished bathrooms feature luxurious rain showers. There's a handful of more modest rooms in the building opposite. €120

Hostel X-Point Reception at Trg svobode 6 ☎05 388 5308, ⓦxpoint.si. Clean, modern hostel run by the adventure-sports company (see box, p.142) with two- and three-bed rooms, shared bathrooms and a self-catering kitchen. Dorms €16, doubles €40

Hvala Trg svobode 1 ☎05 389 9300, ⓦhotelhvala.si. Kobarid's single hotel is this warm, family-run place whose clean-cut rooms are cosy enough if somewhat lacking in sparkle; there are also a handful of mansard rooms which, though much smaller and without a/c, are considerably cheaper. Good restaurant, too (see below). €112

EATING

Gostilna Breza Mučeniška ulica 17 ☎05 389 0040. While not as fashionable as *Hiša Franko* or *Topli Val*, this restful, homely place, secreted away 300m south of the main square, serves fine traditional Slovene food, including lamb and game; the interior's subtle green colour scheme, wood-beamed ceiling and ceramic stove are complemented by the smart summery terrace. Mon, Tues & Fri–Sun 11am–3pm & 6–11pm.

★**Hiša Franko** Staro Selo 1 ☎05 389 4120, ⓦhisafranko.com. Rated by many to be Slovenia's finest restaurant. *Hiša Franko's* chef, Ana Ros, contrives to create breathtakingly imaginative dishes – foamed trout liver with white asparagus and pink grapefruit, say, or caramelized roebuck fillet with apple purée and birch extract. The restaurant itself looks fantastic, from the bright orange interior though to the beautifully shaded terrace, a wonderful place to dine on a warm summer's evening; add to the mix charming staff and an extraordinary wine list (some 350 bottles), and you've got one very memorable dining experience. Five-course tasting menu €70. Wed–Sun noon–3pm & 7–11pm, plus Tues in summer.

Lazar Camp Lazar, 500m east of town on the west bank of the Soča ☎05 388 5333, ⓦlazar.si. If you don't mind a little walk (assuming you haven't got your own vehicle), take a trip down to this campsite's surprisingly accomplished restaurant, whose lovely rustic outdoor setting is perfect on a warm summer's evening. While not cheap, the food – for example, venison goulash with dumplings (€15), or roast lamb with red cabbage (€16) – is bang on; it'd also be remiss not to finish your meal with the delicious local speciality, *Kobariški Štruklji*, a sweet dumpling with walnut and raisin filling. April–Oct daily 8am–10pm; Nov–March Fri 6–10pm, Sat & Sun noon–10pm.

Topli Val Hvala hotel, Trg svobode 1 ☎05 389 9300, ⓦhotel-hvala.si. The classy "Warm Wave" restaurant is the town's most established place, with a freshwater and sea fish menu that would do the finest seafood restaurants on the coast proud; specialities include crayfish soup, trout salami, scampi *busara* with polenta, mussels and lobster. March–Oct Tues–Sun noon–10pm; Nov–Feb Sat & Sun noon–10pm.

Drežnica

Dramatically situated under the sunny slopes of the Krn mountain range 6km north of Kobarid, the peaceful little village of **DREŽNICA** (ⓦdreznica.si) is renowned for its **Shrovetide Carnival**, one of the most enjoyable local events in Slovenia. Taking place at the end of February, it's a kind of mini-Kurent (see box, p.280), starring a procession of masked figures (known as *psti*), who cut a dash through town, visiting houses and causing good-natured mayhem; the day concludes with much drinking and dancing. From the village it's a four-hour hike up to **Mount Krn** (2244m), the valley's most exalted peak and scene of some of the most ferocious battles of World War I. If you're not using your own transport to get to Drežnica you'll have to walk or hitch.

Cerkev Srca Jezusovega

Towering over Drežnica is the oversized neo-Romanesque **Cerkev Srca Jezusovega** (Church of the Sacred Heart), which, despite its prominent position, survived remarkably unscathed amid the fighting in these parts during World War I. Dating from 1911, this church replaced one pulled down a few years earlier and features a capacious, pastel-coloured tripartite nave smothered in frescoes, the most celebrated of which is *The Sacred Heart*, a dual effort by Avgust Černigoj and Zoran Mušič.

ACCOMMODATION   **DREŽNICA**

Tourist Farm Kranjc Koseč 7 ☎05 384 8562, Ⓦturizem-kranjc.si. Actually located in Koseč, the next village along from Drežnica, this super-friendly farm has simple but colourful, homely rooms, and, just below the house, two fabulous wooden glamping pods, each with a double bed, and with private shower facilities back up in the house. Exceptional home cooking too, which you can enjoy from the terrace looking out towards the Soča Valley. Doubles **€60**, pods **€70**

Vrsno

From Napoleon's Bridge in Kobarid, one road snakes up to Drežnica while the other winds steeply uphill for 7km to the village of **VRSNO**, known as the birthplace of nineteenth-century priest, poet and national revivalist **Simon Gregorčič** (1844–1906). His **birthplace** (Rojstna hiša; Vrsno 27a; March–Oct Wed–Sun 10am–5pm; €2; ☎05 389 1092) holds his cradle, original furnishings and some of his works, as well as a small museum downstairs. To visit the house in winter, contact the tourist office in Kobarid (see p.149). Gregorčič is actually buried in the village of Smast, back down on the road towards Kobarid. Note that there is no public transport to Vrsno.

Tolmin

South of Kobarid, the valley flattens out markedly before reaching **TOLMIN** some 14km further on. As the area's administrative centre it's not an especially appealing place, but it does conceal a handful of worthwhile sights, and also serves as an excellent jumping-off point for a couple of attractions just inside Triglav National Park (see p.117) a short way north, namely the fabulous **Tolmin Gorge**, and the **Church of the Holy Spirit** in Javorca.

Tolminski muzej

Mestni trg 4 • Tues–Fri 10am–4pm, Sat & Sun 1–5pm • €3 • ☎05 381 1360, Ⓦtol-muzej.si

Housed in the Coronini Mansion, formerly the home of the noble sixteenth-century Coronini family, the **Tolminski muzej** (Tolmin Museum) holds a quite astonishing, and beautifully presented, collection of **archeological finds**. Many were excavated from a grave in Most na Soči between 1999 and 2001 (see p.154); the most extraordinary is a clay skyphos (drinking cup) from Attica in Greece, an exquisite piece featuring one horizontal and one vertical handle, to the side of which is a painted owl. Look out too for the bronze handle of a patera in the form of a ram's head, the ornamented clay

---

TOLMIN MUSIC FESTIVALS

Tolmin has something of a monopoly on music festivals, with three in rapid succession in July and August. First up is the long-standing **Metaldays** (Ⓦmetaldays.net) in the last week of July, which takes place down by the banks of the Soča, 3km south of town. In August, the four-day **Punk Rock Holiday** (Ⓦpunkrockholiday.com), also down by the Soča, pretty much does what it says on the tin and is shortly followed by the **Overjam International Reggae Festival** (Ⓦoverjamfestival.com) – the only one of its kind in Slovenia – incorporating the family-friendly Overjam 4 Kidz festival.

pithos (a pottery urn) – which, when discovered, contained charred human remains – and the group of bronze fibulas (a type of clasp) worn by women in the Soča and Bohinj regions. Back up the valley, Gradič Hill, near Kobarid, has been just as forthcoming, its most impressive find being 28 exquisite bronze statuettes, mostly representing various gods.

Equally absorbing is the **ethnological collection**, relating to life in Tolmin from the time of the peasant uprisings of 1713. A mock-up village tavern precedes the grandest room in the building, appropriately staging an exhibition on the Tolmin Reading Society, one of the first in Slovenia, established in 1862. Thereafter, several rooms are given over to the region's various struggles for **identity** during the twentieth century, not least repression under Italian rule – you can't fail to miss Tone Kralj's typically provocative painting, the mocking *Nazi Cirkus*, which depicts the German soldier as a skeleton and the Italian as a clown. The postwar period charts the growth of tourism and industry within the valley under Socialist rule, featuring a rare bust of Tito.

Rounding things off in the basement is a valuable collection of fifteenth- to eighteenth-century **sacral art**, comprising wooden and sandstone sculptures, including a splendid one of St John the Baptist (minus hands and feet) found in the Soča River, along with paintings, religious relics and the wall painting *Our Lady of Mercy* (1886), rescued from a house in Breginj following the earthquake in 1976.

Kozlov Rob

1km northwest of town

Kozlov Rob (Goat's Edge) is a 426m-high hill topped with the substantial remains of a medieval fort. To get to the base of the hill it's a fifteen-minute walk along Brunov drevored, the road that forks left by the Church of St Ulric, itself a short way north of Mestni trg; from here it's a pleasantly exhausting forty-minute, zigzagging climb to the top, and, despite the thicket of shrubs and weeds smothering the fort, there are some tremendous views. Once fortified by four gigantic towers, Kozlov Rob is believed to have originated around the twelfth century, when it was fought over by various factions, including the Venetian and then the Habsburg monarchies. The last of several restorations occurred under the auspices of the Dornberg family at the beginning of the seventeenth century, after which time the Coronini family took control and the fort fell into long-term dilapidation, a state of affairs that pretty much remains to this day.

Nemška kostnica

2km south of town, down by the Soča River • Contact the tourist office (see below) if you wish to visit • To get here, walk past the tourist office and follow the tarmac road to the end, then take a right turn along the asphalt track

The tiny and undistinguished-looking **Nemška kostnica** (German Charnel House), completed in 1936 from German materials, contains the remains of nearly one thousand German soldiers killed during the Twelfth Offensive (see box, p.148). Beyond the forged grill that divides the space inside, the names of the dead are beautifully engraved mosaic-style on three walls.

ARRIVAL, INFORMATION AND ACTIVITIES   TOLMIN

By bus The bus station is in the centre of town on the main through road, Trg maršala Tita.

Destinations Bovec (Mon–Fri 5 daily, Sat & Sun 2 daily; 1hr); Cerkno (Mon–Fri 7 daily, Sat & Sun 2 daily; 50min); Kobarid (Mon–Fri 6 daily, Sat & Sun 2 daily; 30min); Most na Soči (Mon–Fri 10 daily, Sat & Sun 2 daily; 10min); Nova Gorica (Mon–Fri 7 daily, Sat 4 daily, Sun 2 daily; 50min).

Tourist office Just beyond Mestni trg at ulica Petra Skalarja 4, 300m southwest of the bus station (July & Aug Mon–Fri 9am–12.30pm & 1.30–8pm, Sat & Sun 9am–1.30pm & 3.30–8pm; Sept–June Mon–Fri 9am–12.30pm & 1.30–4pm, Sat 9am–1pm; ☎ 05 380 0480, ⓦ dolina-soce.com); they can book private accommodation in Tolmin and the surrounding villages.

Sports and activities A couple of kilometres west of town, down by the Soča River at Volče 87, the terrific, and extremely family-friendly, Maya Team (☎ 05 380 0530, ⓦ maya.si) runs a welter of water-based and land-bound activities, including rafting (€39), canyoning (€52) and kayaking (€42), plus hiking (from €26 for the day) and cycling (from €45 for the day); they also rent out bikes (€13 for 5hr, €18/day).

ACCOMMODATION AND EATING

Apartma Orhideja Brunov drevored 3 ☎ 051 438 949, ⓦ apartma-orhideja.com. Superbly located (aside from the racket created by the neighbouring church bells) a few paces from the main crossroads, and run by an extremely welcoming proprietor, the "Orchid Apartments" – actually a mix of rooms and apartments – are as bright and colourful as the name suggests. Fantastic value, even with breakfast costing an extra €7/person. **€45**

Labrca Volče 87 ☎ 05 380 0530, ⓦ maya.si. The restaurant inside Maya Team's Labrca sports centre (see above) is well worth a trip whether you're here to partake in an activity or not. Chomp on a plate of succulent *čevapčiči* and wash it down with a pint of craft beer; try the delicious, and deliciously titled, Cheating Tax Collector pale ale from the 1713 brewery in Kobarid. Mid-March to June & Sept daily 11am–9pm; July & Aug daily 11am–10pm.

Pension Rutar Mestni trg 7 ☎ 05 380 0500, ⓦ pension-rutar.si. Conspicuous lime-green building on the main square, with nine unspectacular but perfectly respectable rooms, all with a/c. **€72**

Tolminska korita

A 45-minute walk north of Tolmin, the **Tolminska korita** (Tolminska Gorge; open all year; €4 entrance fee April & Oct 9am–5.30pm, May & Sept 9am–6.30pm, June & July 9am–7.30pm) – at 180m the lowest point in Triglav National Park (see p.117), and its southernmost entry point – is as wild and spectacular as anything the park has to offer. From the entrance, just up from the snack bar, several rather confusing signs point to various sections of the gorge. The best way forward is to head straight along the road and through the tunnel to the vertiginous **Hudičev most** (Devil's Bridge), looming some 60m above the magnificent ravine. Approximately 500m beyond the bridge, just after the bend in the road, is the **Zadlaška Cave**, also known as **Dante's Cave**, for it was here that the poet supposedly found the inspiration for his terrifying inferno images in the *Divine Comedy*; unfortunately, the caves are currently closed to the public.

Backtracking 200m or so down the road will bring you to a set of steps. These lead down to a couple of paths that fork – take the left path down the **Zadlasišca gorge** and after 400m, where the path ends, you'll chance upon the gorge's most bizarre feature, **Medvedova Glava** (Bear's Head), a huge triangular-shaped boulder wedged between two rock faces. Be careful walking around here, as it can get very slippery. Retrace your steps back to the fork, where a couple of paths head down to the river; at this point you'll probably get lost among the twisting paths, secret tunnels and swing bridges, but it's all good fun and you're never far from the nearest way out.

Javorca and the Cerkev Sv Duha

From the Tolminska Gorge it's a twenty-minute drive (or a two-hour walk) up a mainly asphalt track that ascends to **Javorca** (571m) – coming by car, you'll have to walk the last 500m or so, as the road is too steep and narrow to continue. Perched on a panoramic terrace, with resplendent views across the Tolmin Valley, the half-stone, half-wooden **Cerkev Sv Duha** (Church of the Holy Spirit; mid-April to mid-June & Oct Sat & Sun 10am–5pm; mid-June to Aug daily 10am–7pm; Sept daily 10am–5pm; from Nov to mid-April contact the tourist office in Tolmin; €2) was built in 1916 by soldiers of the Austro-Hungarian army. Approaching via the stone staircase – which replaced the previous one damaged in the 1998 earthquake – the first thing you'll notice is the remarkably well-preserved coats of arms (22 in all) representing the various regions of the Austro-Hungarian Empire. The interior, meanwhile, is striking for its bold Secessionist-style decoration, painted in just four colours – black, blue, white and gold – and the wooden panels covering the walls, onto which the names of nearly three thousand soldiers have been scorched.

Čadrg

From Javorca it's a ninety-minute walk across to the elevated village of **ČADRG** (700m) where, uniquely, several houses are designated ecological (or organic) farms, making the settlement Slovenia's first **ecological village**. The villagers produce large quantities of cheese and other dairy products – made within their small cheese factory – as well as nuts, vegetables and brandy, all of which you can buy. To get here by car or bike, continue up the road that passes through the Tolmin Gorge, though be warned, it's very narrow – barely wide enough for one car – and not particularly well surfaced in places.

EATING   ČADRG

Letni vrt Pr' Jakču Zadlaz Čadrg 4 ☎ 051 438 949. This terrific snack bar – 2km up from the gorge and 3km shy of Čadrg itself – to all intents and purposes serves one thing: the local speciality, *frika*, a deliciously moreish fried-potato and cheese pie. Get the beer in and savour the glorious views. April–Oct daily 10am–8pm.

3

Most na Soči

Located on a rocky ledge at the confluence of the Soča and Idrijca rivers, 5km south of Tolmin, **MOST NA SOČI** (formerly St Lucija) was one of the most important prehistoric settlements in Slovenia, as evidenced by its exceptional hoard of **archeological finds** from the Bronze and Iron Ages through to the early Middle Ages. After the former rector of St Lucija, Tomaž Rutar, began excavations in the mid-nineteenth century, some seven thousand graves and architectural remains, including 35 Hallstatt dwellings, were discovered in the surrounding area; recent digs have unearthed yet more finds, including some one hundred Iron Age and Roman graves (5 BC to 2 AD) found in 2002 – many of these treasures are on display at the Tolmin Museum (see p.151).

Cultural and historical trail

If you've got time, the **Cultural and historical trail** is a most enjoyable stroll, marking the town's surprisingly rich tapestry of natural and cultural sights, such as burial grounds and settlements, and the extraordinary turquoise-coloured **lake**. The trail begins at the information point (Plac) next to the petrol station; thereafter all points are marked by information boards, denoted by an owl symbol (after the clay skyphos discovered here in 2001 and now on display in the Tolmin Museum).

Cerkev Sv Lucija

The former Gothic, but now Baroque, **Cerkev Sv Lucija** (Parish Church of St Lucy) is worth a glimpse for its exceptional range of artwork by Tone Kralj. He painted the allegory of St Lucy and the Apostles on the ceiling, but also the eight paintings in the presbytery representing the life and martyrdom of the same saint and the fantastically colourful oil pictures of the Way of the Cross in the nave. For good measure he completed the four wall statues.

ARRIVAL AND DEPARTURE   MOST NA SOČI

By bus Buses from Cerkno (Mon–Fri 7 daily, Sat & Sun 2 daily; 45min) and Tolmin (Mon–Fri 10 daily, Sat & Sun 2 daily; 10min) stop near the post office in the centre of town.

By train Most na Soči is on the train line between Jesenice and Nova Gorica, and is also the last stop for the car-train (see box, p.114) from Bohinjska Bistrica; the train station is across the river 1.5km southeast of town on the road to Idrija – there are sporadic buses into town, which continue to Tolmin.

Destinations Bled jezero (Mon–Fri 7 daily, Sat & Sun 4–5 daily; 55min); Bohinjska Bistrica (Mon–Fri 10 daily, Sat & Sun 6–7 daily; 40min); Nova Gorica (Mon–Fri 8 daily, Sat & Sun 4–5 daily; 40min).

FROM TOP PIRAN (P.189); LIPICA STUD FARM (P.180) >

ACCOMMODATION AND EATING

Jezero No. 52 ☎ 040 420 404. The town's go-to place (it's the only place *to* go), and not bad at all; (ridiculously cheap) pizzas and salads pretty much constitute the bulk of the menu, but otherwise, this is where the locals congregate for their daily coffee, beer and ice cream. Daily 6am–11pm.

Pension Šterk No. 55 ☎ 05 388 7065, ⊛ penzion-sterk .si. In a super location just across the bridge from town, and with head-on views across the lake, *Šterk* offers thirteen modern rooms with splashes of colour, a friendly welcome and a hearty breakfast that can be taken on the large summery patio. **€64**

Baška Grapa Valley

If you have your own transport, and an hour or two to spare, take a ride through the lovely **Baška Grapa Valley**, which meanders eastwards from Most na Soči, joining up with the Selščica Valley some 30km distant. Incised with deeply cut slopes onto which dozens of picturesque hamlets and lush vegetation have been neatly grafted, the road snakes along the valley floor in tow with the Bača stream and the scenic rail line.

At the narrow upper end of the valley, the village of **PODBRDO** was once an important frontier post, but is now significant as the southern entrance of the Bohinj tunnel and one of the stopping stations for the car-train (see box, p.114). A few kilometres east of Podbrdo is **PETROVO BRDO**, a tiny hamlet on the mountain-top pass linking the two valleys. The owner of the roadside hut *Planinski Dom na Petrovem Brdu* (☎ 05 380 8101; open all year), which serves limited refreshments and has a few beds, organizes local excursions along the **Rapallo Border Trail**, the one-time border between Yugoslavia and Italy (see box, p.94). Established in 1918, and confirmed by the Treaty of Rapallo in 1920 – which effectively annexed the Primorska region to Italy – the border is riddled with deserted fortifications, overgrown bunkers (there's one just metres from the hut) and bomb shelters constructed by the Italians between the two world wars. Walks, which take in a number of these extraordinary defences (many of which are in the process of being cleaned up), can be improvised to suit whatever time you have, from a short two-hour trip (€9) to a full-day excursion (€20). If you want to know more about visiting the trail, contact the hut or the tourist office in Tolmin (see p.152).

Petrovo Brdo is also an excellent starting point for ascents into the Lower Bohinj mountains; trails lead to **Kobla** (1498m; 90min) and **Črna Prst** (1844m; 4hr), where there's the *Dom Zorka Jeliniia na Črni prsti* hut (☎ 05 380 8609; mid-June to mid-Sept), and **Porezen** (1630m; 2hr 30min) and the *Dom Andreja Žvana-Borisa na Poreznu* hut (☎ 051 615 245; July & Aug).

Nova Gorica and around

The modern casino town of **NOVA GORICA**, 39km south of Tolmin and in the heart of **central Primorska**, was built following Gorica's (Gorizia) annexation to Italy at the end of World War II. Before then, and despite having been placed under Italian jurisdiction as part of the 1920 Treaty of Rapallo, it had been a predominantly Slovene-speaking community. Following the Paris Peace Treaty of 1947, however, the town was assigned to Italy, leaving the Slovenes without a centre of their own. Undeterred, local authorities pressed on with the construction of a nascent Slovene Gorica, based on plans drawn up by the prominent Slovene architect Edo Ravnikar, a keen disciple of Le Corbusier.

Although vestiges of antiquity remain, most notably in the northern suburb of **Solkan**, Nova Gorica's central hub is ultimately too modern to be anything other than charmless, and is dominated by the hotel **casinos** on which the local economy is almost entirely dependent. However, as well as being an important **transport** hub for destinations north into the Soča Valley and south towards the Karst and coast, Nova Gorica is also a key **crossing point** into Italy, so there's a good chance you'll wind up here at some point; luckily there are a few attractions in the outlying areas to occupy your time.

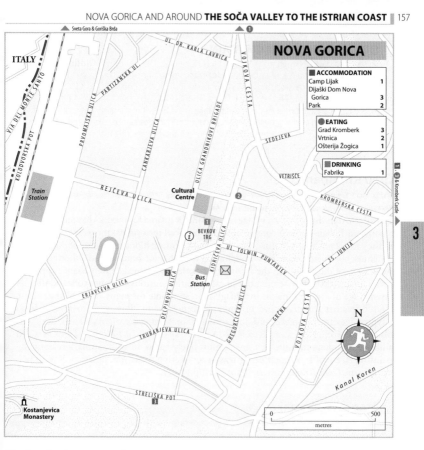

Kostanjevica samostan

Škrabčeva ulica 1 • Mon–Fri 9am–noon & 3–5pm, Sun 3–5pm • €2 • ☎ 05 330 7750, ⓦ samostan-kostanjevica.si

Fifteen minutes' walk south of town, atop a small green hill overlooking Gorizia, **Kostanjevica samostan** (Kostanjevica Monastery) was built in 1624. Its first custodians were the Carmelites, but following their expulsion in 1781 and a brief period of closure, the monastery was entrusted to the Franciscans, who have remained its guardians ever since.

Most visitors come here to view the tombs of the **French Bourbons**. Exiled from France following the 1830 Revolution in Paris, Charles X sought refuge in various countries, before eventually finding sanctuary in Gorizia under the protection of Count Coronini. His stay, however, was short-lived; barely three weeks after his arrival he died of cholera. The **crypt**, located along a narrow whitewashed passageway under the central aisle of the church, holds the sarcophagi of Charles X and five other members of the Bourbons, including his son Louis XIX (who also died in Gorizia) and his wife Marie Thérèse Charlotte, daughter of Marie-Antoinette (who was the granddaughter of Austrian Empress Maria Theresa).

Although usually only open to groups, it's worth enquiring about visits to the monastery's beautiful, sixteenth-century, completely renovated **library**, named after Stanislav Škrabec, one of Slovenia's greatest linguists and grammarians, who lived in Gorizia for more than forty years. The library's most priceless work is Adam Bohorič's delightful pocket-sized *Arcticae horulae* (*Winter Hours*), the first grammar book of Slovene, written in 1584.

> ## THE OLDTIMER MUSEUM TRAIN
>
> On selected days between mid-May and early November, the marvellous **Oldtimer Museum Train** (Muzej Vlak) puffs its way between **Jesenice** (departing at 8.53am), some 12km north of Bled, to **Nova Gorica**, stopping at Bled, Bohinjska Bistrica, Most na Soči and Kanal along the way (total journey time 3hr; return train from Nova Gorica departs at 4.46pm). A return fare costs €41; for an additional €34, you can partake in a full-day programme that includes a tour of the Goriška Brda wine-growing region, and lunch – bicycles can be taken on the train for no extra charge. Book tickets through the ABC Rent-a-Car office in Ljubljana (☎059 070 510, ⓦabc-tourism.si) or agencies in Bled and Bohinj.

Grad Kromberk

Grajska cesta 1, Kromberk, 3km east of town • May–Oct Mon–Fri 9am–7pm, Sun 1–7pm; Nov–April Mon–Fri 9am–5pm, Sun 1–5pm • €2 • ☎05 335 9811 • Take any bus towards Loke, Ljubljana or Ajdovščina

East of town in the suburban village of **KROMBERK** is **Grad Kromberk** (Kromberk Castle), a northern-Italian-inspired construction that replaced the original thirteenth-century castle in the early seventeenth century. Despite several reincarnations since – most markedly an almost complete reconstruction following the 1976 earthquake, and a thorough restoration of the interior in the 1990s – the castle has retained its Renaissance appearance.

The most worthwhile section of the castle's rather curious **museum collection** is its assemblage of art, with pieces by Quaglio – responsible for many of Ljubljana's finest church frescoes – and Tominc, but more excitingly Veno Pilon, whose *At the Café* is a typically expressive piece, and, in a similar vein, Avgust Černigoj's *Cirkus*; the ubiquitous Tone Kralj also gets a look-in, courtesy of *Self-portrait with Daughter*, and a lifesize wooden sculpture of a sower, most likely based on Ivan Grohar's celebrated painting (see p.60). A much better reason for visiting the castle, however, is to dine in the elegant *Grad Kromberk* restaurant (see opposite).

Svetogroska bazilika

Sveta Gora, just over 5km north of Nova Gorica • There are no buses to Sveta Gora so, unless you have your own transport, it's a very steep and exacting walk (roughly 1hr): after passing through Solkan, take the road marked Trnovo/Čepovan (it's a sharp right – the road straight ahead is the Tolmin road) for about 3km, before branching off up the steep and twisting road towards Sveta Gora

Positioned atop the 681m-high **Sveta Gora** (Holy Mountain), just over 5km north of Nova Gorica, the **Svetogroska bazilika** (Basilica of the Assumption) has been an important place of pilgrimage for centuries. Local legend has it that in 1539 a shepherd girl, Urška Ferligoj, was visited on several occasions by apparitions of the Virgin Mary, an occurrence that precipitated the building of the basilica two years later. A stone slab unearthed during its construction indicated that some form of religious centre has existed on this site since possibly as early as the eleventh century; however, it was most likely destroyed by the Turks in the late fifteenth century.

When the church was reduced to a pile of rubble during World War I, authorities initially considered employing Jože Plečnik to undertake a redesign, though, ultimately, the project was taken up by Silvano Barich from Gorizia, as it was ostensibly an Italian concern. The stained-glass windows aside, the church's high, dark and capacious interior betrays little in the way of ornamentation or colour. The high altar, too, is very simple, its only distinguishing feature a picture of the Virgin Mary; originally donated to the church in 1544, the painting (believed to be of Venetian origin) was taken to Gorizia during World War II, later found at the Vatican and returned to the basilica in 1951. Miraculously, the **Chapel of Appearance** – located to the rear of the high altar and containing the original gold wooden statue dating from 1541 – survived the bombing almost completely unscathed. As good a reason as any to visit, however, is for the superlative **views** south across to the Gulf of Trieste and the snow-tipped mountains of the Soča Valley to the north.

On the way from Nova Gorica, you'll see the magnificent **Solkan Railway Bridge**, which was, at the time of its construction in 1906, the largest stone arch bridge in Europe, some 85m high.

ARRIVAL AND INFORMATION
NOVA GORICA

By train A lovely Secessionist pile built in 1906, the train station lies 1.5km west of town on Kolodvorska pot, right on the Italian border.

Destinations Ajdovščina (Mon–Fri 2 daily; 45min); Bled jezero (5–7 daily; 1hr 40min); Bohinjska Bistrica (5–7 daily; 1hr 15min); Most na Soči (5–7 daily; 40min); Sežana (Mon–Fri 6 daily; Sat & Sun 1–2 daily; 1hr).

By bus The bus station is smack-bang in the centre of town on Kidričeva ulica.

Destinations Ajdovščina (Mon–Fri every 45min–1hr, Sat & Sun 4–5 daily; 40min); Bovec (Mon–Fri 5 daily, Sat & Sun 2 daily; 1hr 50min); Kobarid (Mon–Fri 5 daily, Sat & Sun 2 daily; 1hr 15min); Ljubljana (Mon–Fri 9 daily, Sat & Sun 4 daily; 2hr 30min); Postojna (Mon–Fri 10 daily, Sat & Sun 4 daily; 1hr 20min); Tolmin (Mon–Fri 8 daily, Sat 4 daily, Sun 2 daily; 50min); Vipava (Mon–Fri hourly, Sat & Sun 4 daily; 50min).

Tourist office Delpinova ulica 18 (May, June & Sept Mon–Fri 8am–6pm, Sat & Sun 9am–1pm; July & Aug Mon–Fri 8am–8pm, Sat & Sun 9am–1pm; Oct–April Mon–Fri 8am–6pm, Sat & Sun 9am–1pm; ☎05 330 4600, ⓦnovagorica-turizem.com); they rent out bikes for just €3/day, which can be useful if you want to explore Goriška Brda (see below).

ACCOMMODATION

Camp Lijak Ozeljan 8 ☎05 308 8557, ⓦcamplijak.com. Nestled under the formidable Nanos plateau 8km east of town, and popular with paragliders, the lovely *Lijak* offers straightforward camping alongside ten "hobbit holes" – diminutive huts with wooden bed (mattress, sheets and duvet provided) and electric lighting – plus bungalows sleeping up to six. Camping **€21**, hobbit holes **€32**, bungalows **€72**

Dijaški Dom Nova Gorica Streliška pot 7 ☎05 335 4800, ⓦhostel-ng.si. A 10min walk south of the bus station, this enormous hostel offers clean accommodation in single, double and triple rooms. Open daily in July and Aug and at weekends the rest of the year. Breakfast included. **€18**

Park Delpinova ulica 5 ☎05 336 2000, ⓦhit.si. The nicest of Nova Gorica's several HIT-owned hotels, though it's still firmly aimed at Italians here to make a quick buck at the casino. The rooms are as polished as you'd imagine, though without the pizzazz to really justify the prices. **€130**

EATING

Grad Kromberk Grajska cesta 1 ☎05 302 7160. On the ground floor of Kromberk Castle, this outstanding restaurant, with its tall-backed wooden chairs, lush red carpets and cast-iron chandeliers, is a suitably classy setting for a distinguished and thoroughly seasonal menu. Dishes might include smoked goose with pumpkin dumplings (€13) and poppy seeds, or *oves sčrno trobento* (oatgrain with black trumpet mushrooms); there's a fine wine selection, too. Wed–Sun noon–10pm.

Vrtnica Kidričeva ulica 11 ☎05 398 5555, ⓦrestavracija-vrtnica.si. Bright, functional and cheap self-service restaurant with very reasonable grub indeed, such as tagliatelle with salmon (€7) and gnocchi with venison ragout (€9); daily two-course menus from €7. Mon–Fri 7am–6pm.

Ošterija Žogica Soška cesta 52, 2.5km north of Nova Gorica ☎05 300 5240, ⓦzogica.com. Occupying a splendid spot on the Soča River, this cheery trattoria-style establishment has an atmospheric marquee-covered terrace and strong seasonal menus that might feature goose liver with red onion and mountain butter, followed by veal steak with spiced cottage cheese (€14) and, to finish, milk ice cream with figs and roasted hazelnuts (€4). Daily 11am–11pm.

DRINKING

Fabrika Bevkov trg 1 ☎041 535 148. Easily the most enjoyable spot among the clutch of cafés and bars on the main square, the "Factory", a vaguely industrial-styled café-cum-bar, makes for an ideal mid-morning coffee break, or a more vigorous bout of evening beer drinking. Daily 8am–1am.

Goriška Brda

Goriška Brda (often just referred to as **Brda**, which means hill), a small nub of land around 5km northwest of Nova Gorica, is a beautiful region of low, smoothly rounded hills, scattered villages and little white churches, best known for producing some of the country's finest **wines**. The hills are perfect for fruit growing, too, with the harvesting of

3

THE WINES OF GORIŠKA BRDA

Goriška Brda is the northernmost of the four wine-growing districts that constitute Slovenia's **Primorje** (coastal) region. Thanks to its favourable geographical location and Mediterranean climate and soil, Goriška Brda consistently yields a superlative range of both **red** and **white wines** – one of the few regions in Slovenia to harvest both, though whites account for roughly seventy percent here. Among the former, Cabernet Sauvignon and the lighter Merlot are pre-eminent, while of the latter, the ubiquitous Chardonnay (produced all over Slovenia), Beli Pinot, Sivi Pinot and the dry Briški Točaj (as opposed to the famous sweet Hungarian variety) prevail. The most distinctive white, though, is the golden-yellow Rebula, a widely cultivated, indigenous grape used in the production of *slamno vino* (straw wine). Some of Brda's best-regarded **vintners** include Edi Simčič, at Vipolže 39 (☎030 602 564, ⒲edisimcic.si), Ščurek, at Plešivo 44 (☎05 304 5021, ⒲scurek.com), Movia, at Ceglo 18 (☎05 395 9510, ⒲movia.si) and Prinčič, at Kozana 11 (☎05 304 1272, ⒲princic.si).

If you fancy a spot of **tasting**, there are dozens of cellars to choose from, all well signposted; expect to pay around €6–10 per person for four or five wines, with bread and cheese or *pršut*. You can either contact the cellars directly (a few hours' notice is usually appreciated), or call the tourist office in Dobrovo for further information (see opposite).

The most important of several wine-related events throughout Brda is **Martinmas (St Martin's Day)** on November 11, which is celebrated in grand style everywhere, topped off with a day of concerts and tasting aplenty within the grounds of Vipolže Castle (see p.162).

cherries, figs, peaches and apricots a major seasonal activity. From the wine aficionado's point of view, the most interesting villages are concentrated in the southernmost part of Brda, namely **Dobrovo** and **Medana**, while the villages of **Šmartno** and **Vipolže** attest to the region's position as an important frontier zone during the Venetian-Habsburg wars. Whether you're here for the wine or not, Goriška Brda is a wonderful place to explore, with a smattering of **accommodation** in several villages.

GETTING AROUND   **GORIŠKA BRDA**

Goriška Brda is really only accessible if you have your own car or bike – the latter can be rented in Nova Gorica (see p.159) – as there is only a limited, and poorly coordinated, bus service between Nova Gorica and Dobrovo. Buses only run on weekdays and often only during school term time, very early in the morning.

Kojsko

The comely little wayside settlement of **KOJSKO** is worth a brief stop to view the **Sveta Križna Taboru** (Church of the Holy Cross on Tabor), stationed just above the village. One of four watchtowers (the other three were burnt down) that once formed part of an ancient fortification here was later rearranged into the church bell tower, a feature common to many churches in these parts. Star of the interior is a beautifully preserved late-Gothic winged high altar, dating from around 1500.

Šmartno

A superb, fortified hilltop village, **ŠMARTNO** is girdled by partially preserved white-stone walls and watchtowers erected during the sixteenth century, its centre an attractive jumble of crooked, unevenly paved streets lined with crumbling stone houses. In the centre stands the **Cerkev Sv Martina** (Church of St Martin), whose fourteenth-century bell tower is another that was converted from a watchtower; take a look inside at the contemporary, and very colourful, frescoes by Tone Kralj.

ACCOMMODATION AND EATING   **ŠMARTNO**

Hiša Marica No. 33 ☎05 304 1039, ⒲marica.si. Renovated homestead with four prepossessing, wood-scented rooms with timber-framed ceilings and exposed patches of stone walls – alongside the building runs a *gank*,

a traditional wooden balcony common to many houses in the area. In the same vein is its gorgeous little restaurant, all stripped-down walls and elegantly laid tables; the wine selection is fabulous, as you'd expect, and ridiculously cheap. Restaurant daily except Tues noon–10pm. **€90**
San Martin No. 11 ✆05 330 5660, ⓦsanmartin.si.

Commanding a splendid, elevated spot at the entrance to the village, this modern, family-run establishment offers sunny, airy rooms, all of which have marvellous views of the surrounding vineyards – indeed, these are some of the finest views anywhere in Brda. If the sun's up, take breakfast out on the breezy terrace. **€75**

Dobrovo

DOBROVO is Goriška Brda's largest and most heavily populated town, which isn't really saying much. At its heart is **Grad Dobrovo** (Dobrovo Castle), a Renaissance-style structure built around 1600 on the site of an older castle (Tues–Fri 8am–4pm, Sat & Sun 1–6pm; €2; ✆05 395 9586) – it's not dissimilar to Kromberk near Nova Gorica (see p.158). The castle's **museum** offers an eminently missable cultural history section, though the gallery of graphic prints up on the second floor by internationally renowned local artist Zoran Mušič (1909–2005) is worth perusing; landscapes, including Brda, the Karst and Dalmatia in Croatia (where he spent many of his summers), dominate the collection, but there are also a number of haunting sketches inspired by Mušič's time in a concentration camp, part of a series entitled *We Are Not the Last.*

Klet Brda

Zadružna cesta 9 • Mon–Fri 10am–5pm, Sat 10am–3pm • Tours €6 • ✆05 331 0100, ⓦklet-brda.si
While you'll get much more out of visiting local wine cellars, if you're short of time, head to the **Klet Brda** (Brda winery), one of the largest wine production cellars in Slovenia. A guided tour entails some informative spiel about the region's wines, a walk around the cellar – where you'll see stunning four-hundred-year-old oak barrels from Bosnia – and a tasting session with snacks; lengthier, more advanced tours and tastings are also available.

ARRIVAL AND INFORMATION   DOBROVO

By bus What few buses that do head this way (mainly school buses) set down on the main square, Trg 25 maja.
Tourist office In the courtyard of Dobrovo Castle on Grajska cesta (April–Oct Mon–Fri 9am–5pm, Sat & Sun 10am–6pm; Nov–March Mon–Fri 9am–4pm, Sat & Sun

9am–noon; ✆05 395 9594, ⓦbrda.si); the office can assist with enquiries on any aspect of the Brda region, from wine tours and tasting to private accommodation. Bikes can also be rented from the castle courtyard (€3 for 1hr, €14 for the day).

Medana and Vipolže

MEDANA, 1.5km south of Dobrovo, is one of Brda's most prolific wine-growing villages, with several highly regarded wineries (see box opposite). From here, the road continues south towards the Italian border; after passing through the village of Ceglo, veer eastwards (continuing south will bring you to the border crossing) and

---

GORIŠKA BRDA FESTIVALS

Second only to the **St Martin's Day** wine festival (see box opposite), the biggest and brashest festival in Brda is the **Cherry Fest**, which takes place in Dobrovo during the second weekend of June. Marking the beginning of the cherry season, this lively spectacle entails concerts, tastings and general merriment, climaxing with the parade of the "Cherry Girl". In mid-April, the **Rebula and Olive Oil Festival** in the village of Višnjevik celebrates both the eponymous local grape and oil with lots of music and dancing – April also sees the start of the **Brda Spring Hiking Festival**, encompassing a dozen or so themed hikes on selected days until the end of May.

continue up the hill towards **VIPOLŽE**, which lies 3.5km south of Dobrovo. Located in the upper reaches of this quaint little village is **Grad Vipolže** (Vipolže Castle), originally an eleventh-century fortification, but later transformed into a handsome Renaissance-style manor house following its appropriation by the Venetians in the seventeenth century. Almost completely destroyed during World War I, when it was used as a military hospital, the house was recently renovated after years of neglect and now functions, rather prosaically, as a conference centre. Still, it's worth a quick stroll around the surrounding park, with its profusion of oaks and cypresses, for the marvellous **views** across the Friulian Plain. From Vipolže, you can return to Dobrovo via the road running parallel to Medana, or take the northeasterly road towards Šmartno.

ACCOMMODATION   **MEDANA**

Belica Tourist Farm No. 32 ☎ 05 304 2104, ⓦ belica .net. An upmarket establishment with eight decadently furnished a/c rooms overlooking a gorgeous lawn terrace and with views across to the Friulian hills; they also have tastings, as well as a fabulously classy restaurant, with an inevitable Italian slant, though the pick of the menu is a delicious range of home-made salamis, sausages and ribs. **€90**

Klinec Tourist Farm No. 20 ☎ 05 304 5092, ⓦ klinec.si. This beautifully located homestead has been producing vintages since 1918; its three modern and artfully styled guest rooms are in a building just down the road. **€80**

Vipava Valley

If the Brda region hasn't sated your thirst for wine, you might like to venture in the opposite direction towards the flat-bottomed **Vipava Valley** (Vipavska dolina), sandwiched between the thickly forested Trnovo Plateau to the north and the low-lying Karst region to the south, and raked by lush, rolling vineyards.

The valley's continental climate is epitomized by the **burja** (bora), a fiendishly cold and dry wind that whips down from the northern mountain peaks and batters its way through the valley, across the Karst, and down towards the Adriatic. For this reason many of the two dozen or so **wine villages** dispersed throughout the Vipava hills were built in relatively sheltered, south-facing locations, with neither windows nor doors positioned on sides exposed to the wind; as well as offering fantastic wines, these beautiful but little-known villages are replete with outstanding places to stay and eat. Otherwise, the main settlements are the small towns of **Ajdovščina** and **Vipava**, which are useful jumping-off points for the wine villages and for forays up onto the plateau. The valley is also ripe for a number of **outdoor activities**, not least hiking, cycling and paragliding – hugely popular hereabouts thanks to the strong winds.

Ajdovščina

The only centre of any significant size in the Vipava Valley, on the surface **AJDOVŠČINA** would appear to offer very little. However, it does hold some significant extant **Roman remains**, as well as a fine **gallery**, and one or two exciting places to stay and eat.

Roman remains

The compact ancient core of present-day Ajdovščina was once a military encampment called **Castra ad Fluvium Frigidum** (Fortress by the Cold River), built by the Romans around 270 AD as an important link in the defence line of the Empire. Its 4m-thick walls were perforated with fourteen circular towers, of which seven, either whole or partial, remain; the most tangible remnants, including an almost complete tower, lie east of the main square, **Lavričev trg** – other portions of the wall can be seen on the western side of the ancient quarter.

THE WINES OF THE VIPAVA VALLEY

Despite having one of the oldest wine-growing traditions in Slovenia, dating back to the Romans, the Vipava Valley is not generally as well recognized as some of the country's more fashionable **wine-growing** regions. This is changing, however. Like Goriška Brda, the Vipava Valley yields a superb quota of reds – notably Cabernet Sauvignon and Merlot – and whites, but it's most interesting for its indigenous varieties, namely the red Barbera and the beautifully light, crisp, dry whites Zelen and Pinela. There are dozens of first-class **vintners** throughout the valley; in particular look out for Rondič, at Slap 48 (❶05 364 5751, ⓦ rondic.si), Štokelj, Planina 9 (❶05 368 0203, ⓦ stokelj.si), Jamšek, Manče 9 (❶05 368 5136, ⓦ jamsek.si), and Batič, Šempas 130 (❶05 308 8676, ⓦ batic.si).

The handy *Vipava Wine Road* leaflet, available from the tourist office in Ajdovščina (see below), outlines a number of villages and cellars you can visit. Having your own **transport** is pretty much essential, as public transport is virtually nonexistent. If you don't fancy going it alone, contact Winestronaut (❶040 166 042, ⓦ winestronaut.com), whose winery tours typically entail a visit to a couple of cellars, with lunch or dinner if required; they can pick up and drop off from any location too, which gives you the obvious advantage of being able to drink as much wine as you like.

3

Pilonova galerija

Prešernova ulica 3 • Tues–Fri 9am–6pm, Sat & Sun 3–6pm • €2.50 • ❶05 368 9177, ⓦ venopilon.com

Housed in the old family bakery, the **Pilonova galerija** (Pilon Gallery) is dedicated to the life and works of **Veno Pilon** (1896–1970), one of Slovenia's most prolific and versatile twentieth-century artists. His portrait and landscape paintings – mostly motifs from the Vipava Valley, such as the rather fine *Stara elektrarna na Hublju* (*Old Power Plant Hubelj*) – represented the high point of Slovene expressionism in the 1920s, but the most eye-catching pieces here depict life in Montparnasse (where he spent the best part of forty years); his notorious, and rather saucy, *Kiki* is likely to raise a smile. Just as interesting is the room devoted to paintings of Pilon's family and friends; the most striking is *Moj Oče* (*My Father*), a typically eloquent piece, the subject's oversized hands a classic feature of the artist's work. Pilon's repertoire extended to graphic art and photography – note the poignant images of his father, and of his wife, Anne-Marie Guichard, before they married. You can also see sketches completed during his time as a prisoner of war in Russia during World War I.

Incidentally, as if all this weren't enough, Pilon also starred in Slovenia's first feature film, *Na Svoji Zemlji* (*On Our Own Land*), and translated a great deal of Slovenian poetry into French.

ARRIVAL, INFORMATION AND ACTIVITIES | AJDOVŠČINA

By bus and train From the bus and train stations, opposite each other on Goriška cesta, it's a 5min walk northeast to the centre of town.

Destinations (bus) Ljubljana (Mon–Fri 10 daily, Sat & Sun 4 daily; 1hr 30min); Nova Gorica (Mon–Fri every 45min–1hr, Sat & Sun 4–5 daily; 40min); Postojna (Mon–Fri 10 daily, Sat & Sun 4–5 daily; 45min); Vipava (Mon–Fri every 45min–1hr, Sat & Sun 4–5 daily; 10min).

Destinations (train) Nova Gorica (Mon–Fri 2 daily; 45min).

Tourist office Rather oddly, and inconveniently, located 1km north of town in the Youth Centre at cesta IV. Prekomorske 61 (May–Sept Mon–Fri 10am–6pm, Sat 8am–noon; Oct–April Mon–Fri 8am–4pm, Sat 8am–noon; ❶05 365 9140, ⓦ tic-ajdovscina.si).

Activities The excellent Wajdušna agency, near the train station at Zupančičeva ulica 1c (❶041 232 548, ⓦ wajdusna.com), can assist in organizing outdoor activities.

ACCOMMODATION

Gold Club Goriška cesta 25 ❶05 364 4700, ⓦ hotel goldclub.eu. Just 200m east of the stations, this oddly named hotel looks pretty unconvincing from the outside, but

it actually offers surprisingly smart, minimalist rooms. **€75**

Youth Hostel Ajdovščina Cesta IV. Prekomorske 61 ❶05 368 9383, ⓦ hostel-ajdovscina.si. Within the Youth

Centre 1km north of town, the cleverly designed dorms here (the largest has 24 beds, the smallest four – all with shared showers) feature boldly coloured, pod-like bunks;

there's a self-catering kitchen, plus bikes for rent. Breakfast €3. Dorms €18

EATING AND DRINKING

Domačija Lisjak ZALošče 40, 15km west of town ☎031 390 901, ⓦvinalisjak.si. Although quite a way away, the "Fox" homestead is well worth taking the time to visit. The split-level dining area is great, as is the food; homemade gnocchi with sausage, leek and smoked cottage cheese (€6), and roast veal prepared "Under the Bell" (ie, on hot coals under a clay or iron lid; €10) are typical house dishes. The home-harvested wine is terrific too; try the white Malvazia or red Barbera. Fri & Sat noon–10pm, Sun noon–5pm.

Faludur Lokarjev drevored 8 ☎040 232 987, ⓦfaludur.si. This sparkling little outfit – gourmet shop, tasting room and bar – offers the opportunity to try more than two hundred wines. They've also got an enticing range of beers from the local craft brewery, Pelican, the names of which are as intriguing as the beers themselves – *Yes, Boss!* (Indian pale ale) and *The 3rd Pill*, for example. Don't leave without trying the delicious coffee-flavoured stout. Tues–Fri 10am–10pm, Sat 9am–noon.

Vipava

A somnolent little market town lying under the towering slopes of the Nanos Plateau, **VIPAVA**, the valley's second centre, somewhat misguidedly styles itself as the Slovene Venice – for no good reason other than that it developed alongside the many karstic springs of the Vipava River. Of course, it's nothing like Venice, though it is endowed with a modicum of charm thanks to its generous spread of **Baroque architecture** and picturesque stone-block bridges; better still, there are many opportunities to sample the region's wines.

Vinoteka Vipava

Glavni trg 1 · July–Sept daily 9am–7pm; Oct–June Mon–Fri 9am–6pm, Sat 9am–2pm · ☎05 368 7041, ⓦizvirska-vipavska.si

The best place to familiarize yourself with the local **wines** – especially if you haven't got the time or means to get to the outlying villages – is the **Vinoteka Vipava**, adjoining the tourist office. The staff here really know their stuff, and as well as being able to sample, and buy, in excess of 150 wines, you can watch a multimedia presentation on the history of wine in the valley.

ARRIVAL AND INFORMATION   VIPAVA

By bus Buses from Ajdovščina (Mon–Fri 10 daily, Sat & Sun 4–5 daily; 10min) and Ljubljana (Mon–Fri every 1–2hr, Sat & Sun 4 daily; 1hr 20min) stop on the main square, Glavni trg.
Tourist office Glavni trg 1 (July–Sept daily 9am–7pm;

Oct–June Mon–Fri 9am–6pm, Sat 9am–2pm; ☎05 368 7041, ⓦizvirska-vipavska.si); this friendly little office has its own *vinoteka* (see above) and can help arrange visits to local wine cellars.

ACCOMMODATION AND EATING

Apartmaji Koren Glavni trg 2 ☎040 217 213, ⓦapartmaji-koren.com. Smart, well-appointed accommodation next to the tourist office, with a nice mix of rooms and apartments (some of which sleep up to five); cheaper rooms share bathroom facilities. Doubles €60, apartments €75
Gostilna pri Lojzetu Dvorec Zemono, around 2km west of Vipava ☎05 368 7007, ⓦprilojzetu.si. Located on the ground floor of Zemono Mansion, *Lojzetu* is one of the country's most celebrated slow-food establishments, excelling on just about every level, from the exquisite backdrop (a snug, romantic brick cellar) and the attentive (but not overbearing) waiting staff to the food itself. Chef Tomaž Kavčič creates playful, beautifully crafted dishes

such as citrus-cured beef on a cheese mousse with pea purée, and as you might expect, price-wise this is top end. Wed & Thurs 5–11pm, Fri & Sat noon–11pm, Sun noon–10pm.
★ **Gostilna Podfarovž** Ulica Ivana Ščeka 2 ☎040 232 090, ⓦpodfarovz.si. An absolute peach of a restaurant, whose terrace, perched above one of the springs of the Vipava River, is a delightful spot to kick back and enjoy a selection of house specialities. Try *šelinka*, a thick celeriac soup with potatoes, carrots and smoked pork, or a trout dish – smoked carpaccio of trout, maybe, or trout with polenta and fennel (€13). Wed–Sun noon–10pm.

Vipavski Križ

Rising out of the flat plain just 2km west of Ajdovščina, the scenic fortified medieval village of **VIPAVSKI KRIŽ** is one of the few settlements in the valley whose historical importance is greater than its viticultural significance. Its focal point is the **Capuchin Monastery**, built in 1637 and whose Church of the Holy Cross displays a beautifully carved dark-wooden high altar and a sublime painting of the Holy Trinity (1668), one of the largest Baroque canvases in the country. Its **library** contains an extensive assortment of books from the fifteenth century onwards. Visits to the monastery are best arranged through the tourist office in Ajdovščina (see p.163). Next to the monastery, on the eastern tip of the village, is the magnificent shell of the ruined fifteenth-century **castle**, erected on the orders of the bishop of Gorica so as to protect the village from Turkish and Venetian raids.

Goče and Slap

If just one wine village is your limit then make a beeline for **GOČE**, some 5km west of the main trunk road in the southeastern Vipava hills. With streets barely wide enough to squeeze a car through, the village is distinguished by its knot of tightly clustered eighteenth-century sandstone houses, ornamented with Karst-style courtyards and hewn stone portals. You'll have little difficulty tracking down somewhere to sample wine; there are more than sixty **cellars** here, which amounts to one for almost every house. It's a similar story in nearby **SLAP**, one of the valley's oldest, and loveliest, wine villages, whose narrow streets are lined with an endless supply of cellars.

ACCOMMODATION AND EATING   **GOČE AND SLAP**

★**Majerija** Slap 18 ☎05 268 5010, ⊚majerija.si. Stunning, and unique, subterranean guesthouse, whose ten rooms are named after the herbs from the garden beneath which they reside. They're refreshingly clutter-free, with no TVs, and pebble-floored bathrooms separated from the sleeping area by a frosted glass partition. Don't worry about being starved of natural light – there's a remote-controlled skylight. Breakfasts are fabulous (home-made jams – fig, elderberry, wild blueberry and more – plus fruit, salad and herbs picked fresh from the garden), but for a real treat, stay for dinner: crispy dandelion coated in honey and yoghurt, beef carpaccio with forest fruits, and vanilla ice cream with strawberries and pistachio foam are just some of the divine dishes you can expect. Breakfast €10. Thurs–Sat noon–3pm & 6–10pm, Sun noon–5pm. **€96**

Idrija and around

The history and development of **IDRIJA**, a town of some seven thousand inhabitants 36km north of Vipava, has been inextricably linked to its **mines** since the discovery of **mercury** here in 1490 – a fact acknowledged in 2012 when the town became Slovenia's third UNESCO World Heritage Site, jointly with Almadén in Spain. During the eighteenth century, the growth and success of the mines – which are now closed – spawned a number of other local industries, most importantly forestry and medicine; during this period, the town could justifiably claim to rival Ljubljana as a centre of scientific and technological advancement. **Lace-making** has also played a significant part in shaping Idrija's identity, from its origins as a seventeenth-century cottage industry to the establishment of Slovenia's first lace school in the late nineteenth century, an institution that still functions today.

Idrija is also renowned for its local delicacy, **žlikrofi**, distinctively shaped dumplings with a potato filling; there's even a festival (on the last Saturday of August) devoted to it, involving demonstrations, workshops and competitions, and a huge market on the main square.

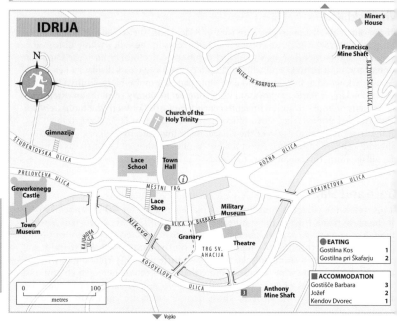

Despite its modest size, Idrija offers a handful of terrific **attractions**, all more or less associated with the mining and lace industries, and all of which are broadly contained within the attractive and compact **old core** on the western side of town. There's plenty more in the surrounding countryside, too, including the mysterious **Wild Lake** and, further afield, the immense **Klavže** water barriers and the fascinating **Partisan Printing Works**.

Anthonijev rov

Kosovelova ulica 3 • Tours: April–Nov Mon–Fri 10am & 3pm, Sat & Sun 10am, 3pm & 4pm; plus daily at noon in July & Aug; Dec–March Sat & Sun 10am & 3pm • €9 • ☎ 05 377 1142, ⓦ antonijevrov.si

The town's star attraction is undoubtedly the **Anthonijev rov** (Anthony Mine Shaft), which was sunk in 1500 and whose shafts extended for some 700km, its deepest point being 400m. Tours begin with a twenty-minute **audiovisual presentation** (in English) in the checking room – the place where miners would gather in the early morning to be allocated their duties by the Obergutman (a kind of foreman) before heading down into the mine. On the wall at the back of the room is the so-called death clock: before descending into the pit, each miner was obliged to take a number plate which, if not replaced at the end of the shift, indicated that he'd got lost or was in some sort of trouble. Having donned jacket and helmet, you walk along to the tiny underground **Chapel of the Holy Trinity**, where miners would pray before the statues of Sts Barbara and Acacius (patron saints of miners) for a safe return from their day's work; from here you're led along a series of lit galleries and laddered passageways, part of the Main Road that served as the main mine entrance for more than two hundred years. It's a total walk of around 1.2km, descending to a depth of 22m.

Several small alcoves, in which benches were placed for the miners to take their lunch, are now filled with items of equipment used to bore through the rock and various life-size models of miners. Look out for **Prekmandlc**, the pit dwarf, who in return for parcels of food would tap the walls to indicate to the miners where the richest sources of mercury lay.

Grad Gewerkenegg and Mestni muzej

Prelovčeva ulica 9 • **Town Museum** Daily 9am–6pm • €5 • ☎ 05 372 6600, ⓦ www.muzej-idrija-cerkno.si

Sited atop a small hill on the western fringe of town, and discernible from some distance thanks to its two cylindrical corner towers and oddly protruding central clock tower, **Grad Gewerkenegg** (Gewerkenegg Castle) was built by the Acacius Society of Mining Entrepreneurs around 1530 to house the mine administration and other official bodies. Though prevailingly Renaissance in form, the castle was embellished with Baroque appendages in the eighteenth century – including the arcaded courtyard and its rather lurid foliage-style frescoes.

The castle now hosts the comprehensive **Mestni muzej** (Town Museum), which, not surprisingly, dotes most heavily on the town's **mining** heritage. As an introduction to the Idrija mine, there's a depiction of the local tub-maker who kick-started the whole thing (see box below), before several rooms given over to all matters geological, starring a fine assemblage of fossils, minerals and cinnabar ore deposits. Similarly enlightening is the collection of mine maps, land registers, flasks and other objects gathered in the northern Rondel Tower, while the staircase in the southern Mercury Tower has been designed to symbolize the descent down the pit – at the bottom is a Plexiglas cube filled with droplets of mercury, though more evocative are the old black-and-white photos of miners at the coal face. Better still is the *Secrets of Mercury* exhibition, which highlights the importance of mercury production here and in Almadén; at their peak, the two mines together produced 48 percent of the world's mercury. One thing you can't fail to miss is the enormous hammer and sickle that used to adorn the entrance to the Francisca Mine Shaft (see p.168).

No less engaging is the exhibition charting Idrija's development in the twentieth century. Aided by some fascinating photographs, there is superb coverage of the town's involvement during the two world wars, including the first Italian occupation in 1918, which culminated in the Rapallo Treaty (see p.156), thereby annexing part of Slovenia and turning Idrija into a border town. World War II exhibits focus on the German occupation between September 1943 and April 1945, and its attendant Fascist denationalization policies.

The town's rich **lace** tradition is well documented, with exquisite samples of bobbin lace alongside dazzling designer laceware – the most interesting piece is a sprawling tablecloth made for President Tito's wife, Jovanka Broz, but which she never actually received.

MINING IN IDRIJA

In 1490, a local tub-maker, busy soaking his wooden vessel in a spring on the present-day site of the Holy Trinity Church, chanced on a hitherto unknown substance, **mercury**. He was unable to keep this secret to himself, and locals soon got wind of the discovery; some eight years later work began on the **Anthony Mine Shaft**.

Mercury appeared in the Idrija mine in two forms: as native mercury and cinnabar ore, the former as shimmering silver-grey drops dripping down on to the rock face, the latter a deep-red material from which the liquid could only be extracted after being burnt at temperatures of 800 degrees. At its peak the Idrija mine yielded thirteen percent of the world's total mercury output, second only to the Almadén mine in Spain, and employing around 1300 men. Working conditions were notoriously bad and, with prolonged exposure to this most toxic of substances, a miner could be expected to work for no more than six or seven years before becoming too ill to continue. Even with improved working practices in the early twentieth century, a miner could not reasonably expect to live much beyond the age of 40.

Several factors contributed to the mine's demise, namely the lack of rich ore, almost negligible prices on the world market and the increasing use of alternative, environmentally friendly substances. Moreover, the export of mercury is no longer permitted within the EU, with most production these days taking place in China.

Vojni muzej

Trg Svetega Ahacija 4 • Tues–Sun 10am–noon & 1–5pm • €3 • ☎ 041 407 651

The old town core boasts a couple of significant buildings, not least the former Mine Granary, part of which is now a **Vojni muzej** (Military Museum). This absorbing private collection features a welter of paraphernalia – mostly uniforms and weapons, in particular a remarkable hoard of submachine guns – from World War I right through to the 1991 Ten-Day War; intriguing photos include a couple of very rare images of Tito. There is no English captioning, but the exhibits speak for themselves.

Čipkarska šola

Prelovčeva ulica 2 • July & Aug Mon–Fri 10am–1pm & 3–6pm; Sept–June Mon–Fri 10am–1pm • €3 • ☎ 05 373 4570, ⓦ cipkarskasola.si

The most impressive building in town is the lovely Neoclassical **Stara šola** (Old School), which has been home to the town's **Čipkarska šola** (Lace School) since 1876 (see box below). The items on display here were completed by the students, all of whom attend voluntarily and are mostly aged between 6 and 14; if you ask, you may be allowed to see a lesson in progress. It's also one of the better places in town to buy lace gifts, selling beautiful products from brooches and bracelets to towels and tablecloths.

Jašek Frančiške and Rudarska hiša

Bazoviška ulica • Contact the tourist office (see opposite) if you wish to visit • €2

The former workshops of the **Jašek Frančiške** (Francisca Mine Shaft), which opened in 1792, now house a marvellous collection of carefully restored, nineteenth-century steam-driven pumps, drills, boilers and compressors, most of which were taken out of operation in the 1950s following the introduction of more modern working practices. The most impressive exhibit is the gargantuan Kley pump, built by the Škoda Pilsen factory in Austria, the largest such specimen in Slovenia and one of few such pumps preserved anywhere in the world.

Set against a gentle slope just behind the mine shaft is a typically striking, eighteenth-century **Rudarska hiša** (Miner's House). Defined by a high, slender frontage, a sharply pointed roof and neat rows of small, square windows, these houses were traditionally constructed from wood and stone, the external walls made of thick boards daubed with

---

LACE-MAKING IN IDRIJA

The art of bobbin **lace-making** first took off in Slovenia in the seventeenth century and, despite having been practised in many towns and rural areas throughout the country, its roots have remained strongest in Idrija, where the craft has been taught in the town's **Lace School** since 1876.

Traditionally, lace-making was practised by most women as a means of supplementing a miner's often very meagre wage – a state of affairs that became even more pressing following the decline of this and other traditional industries (such as iron smelting) in the late nineteenth and early twentieth centuries. The lace-making industry continued apace, with its products sold mainly to the Church, until World War II. After this, however, its popularity waned, only to be revived in the 1980s. Today's lace products are primarily made as gifts and souvenirs.

Idrija lace (*Idrijska čipka*) takes many forms, from simple flower-based patterns to intricately woven cloths featuring folk or peasant motifs, many of which are technically superb; you can view, and buy, many such specimens in several shops in town, though the best places to buy are the shops in the castle courtyard and the Lace School. This exquisite handicraft's ongoing importance and enduring popularity is celebrated in the annual **Lace Festival** (Čipkarski Festival) on the third weekend of June, involving lace-making competitions, arts and crafts exhibitions and evening entertainment.

lime-wash, and the rooftops protected with wooden shingles. A miner's house usually comprised three or four floors, so that several families could be accommodated in the same building – an important consideration during times of overpopulation; moreover, miners could rarely afford their own houses. It's now possible to visit the ground floor, where the cramped space – a living area with adjoining bedroom, a kitchen and a loo – illustrates just how tough living conditions were.

Kamšt

Vodnikova ulica, 1km southeast of the bus station • Contact the tourist office (see below) if you wish to visit • €3 • ☎ 05 372 6600, ⓦ muzej-idrija-cerkno.si

Concealed within a chunky stone-block building, the **Kamšt** is yet another reminder of Idrija's industrial pedigree. This magnificent wooden waterwheel is held to be the largest in Europe, measuring 13.6m in diameter, and for more than 150 years it pumped pit water from a depth of over 200m from the Joseph Shaft, which sits just above. Just below the Joseph Shaft, in the upper loading station of the old cableway, is a collection of mine railway engines.

3

ARRIVAL AND INFORMATION

IDRIJA

By bus The bus station is on Vodnikova ulica, from where it's just a few minutes' walk west to the centre.
Destinations Cerkno (Mon–Fri hourly, Sat & Sun 4–5 daily; 30min); Ljubljana (Mon–Fri 10 daily, Sat & Sun 5–6 daily; 1hr 15min); Tolmin (Mon–Fri 6 daily, Sat 2 daily, Sun 1 daily; 1hr 20min).

Tourist office Mestni trg 2 (April & Oct Mon–Sat 9am–5pm, Sun 9am–4pm; May–Sept Mon–Fri 9am–7pm, Sat & Sun 9am–6pm; Nov–March Mon–Fri 9am–4pm, Sat & Sun 10am–3pm; ☎ 05 374 3916, ⓦ visit-idrija.si).

ACCOMMODATION

Gostišče Barbara Kosovelova ulica 3 ☎ 05 377 1177, ⓦ barbara-idrija.si. Occupying the second floor of the Anthony Mine Shaft building, this decent guesthouse has four en-suite double/triple rooms with TV, and two hostel-style rooms, with shared shower facilities, each sleeping four. Dorms €25, rooms €60

Jožef Vojkova ulica 9a ☎ 05 375 0650, ⓦ hotel-jozef.si. Sparkling small hotel where almost every design aspect has been conceived with a nod to the local mining industry, from the copper-coloured steel cladding to the circular

windows. Inside, the twelve rooms have polished wooden furnishings and immaculately designed bathrooms. €110

Kendov Dvorec Na griču 2, Spodnja Idrija, 4km north of town ☎ 05 372 5100, ⓦ kendov-dvorec.com. This splendidly renovated fourteenth-century manor house, now a five-star Relais & Chateaux property, has eleven immaculate rooms, each named after a member of the Kenda family. Antique Baroque-style furniture and linen made from Idrija lace are standard, along with excellent service. €140

EATING

Gostilna Kos Tomšičeva ulica 4 ☎ 05 372 2030, ⓦ gostilna-kos.si. If you're looking for something quick and simple, *Kos* does the job; a lunchtime *malice* (€6) suffices for most visitors here. Mon–Sat 7am–3pm.

Gostilna pri Škafarju Ulica Svete Barbare 9 ☎ 05 377 3420, ⓦ skafar.si. Fairly plain-looking, but with a decent

menu, including *žlikrofi* prepared various ways – perhaps with mushrooms, pork or lamb (€10). Finish with the house speciality, *Rezi* cake, a strawberry and mascarpone mousse topped with glazed chocolate and finished with a delicate lace pattern. Mon–Thurs 11am–4pm, Fri & Sat 11am–3pm & 6–9pm, Sun 11am–8pm.

Divje jezero

Accessible on foot from Idrija, but If you have your own vehicle, take the Ljubljana road south and the lake is signposted after about 1.5km

From the Kamšt in Idrija (see above), a 3km-long trail (Pot ob Rakah) leads south to the brilliant blue-green **Divje jezero** (Wild Lake), an apposite name for this small body of water that has claimed the lives of several divers attempting to locate its as yet undiscovered source – to date, 164m is the deepest anyone has got, though dives are now forbidden. What is known is that water flows into the lake from an underground passage, or siphon, reckoned to measure approximately 200m long.

The lake itself is about 65m long and 30m wide, taking barely fifteen minutes to circle, unless, that is, you happen to be here following snow melt or extremely heavy rainfall, when massive volumes of water are discharged from its depths, flooding the lake to 3m above its normal level. Emanating from the lake is Slovenia's shortest river, the Jezernica, which discharges into the Idrijca after only 55m. Just as impressive are the precipitous, 100m-high **cliffs** encircling the lake, whose crevices and ledges shelter a galaxy of alpine **flora**, including several endemic species, such as the Carniolan primrose and hacquetia, the latter named after eminent local surgeon Baltazar Hacquet. Lurking in the lake's depths, and something you won't see, is **Proteus anguinus**, the "human fish" (see box, p.206).

Klavže

Twelve kilometres upstream from the Wild Lake on the Belca River (accessible via an increasingly rutted forest road) is the first of four remaining **Klavže** (Water Barriers) in the area. Known locally as the Slovene Pyramids, these superb technical monuments were constructed from wood in the sixteenth century, and replaced by sturdier stone structures in 1770. Their function was to accumulate enough water to enable vast quantities of timber to be floated downriver to Idrija, whereupon the logs would gather in front of a 412m-long dam (rake), at which point they would be carted off to the mines (where they were used as supporting structures for the galleries) and smelting plants (for fuel for burning iron ore). The rake remained operational until 1926, when road transportation was deemed more efficient, while the Klavže gradually fell into a state of disrepair. Restored in the 1980s, they now stand as a fitting memorial to a bygone era. There's another dam about 1.5km further upstream and another, also accessible by road, on the Idrijca River, which runs roughly parallel to the Belca.

The most impressive of the renovated dams is on the Klavžarica River, 8km west of Spodnja Idrija beyond the village of Kanomlja; 34m long and 8m wide, and constructed from sculpted lime rocks, the **Kanomeljske klavže** was built in 1813 and served the needs of the Idrija mine until 1912. To get here, take a left turn at the village of Spodnji Kanomlja and follow the signs – the final kilometre is not suited for cars, but it's a pleasant enough walk.

Partizanska tiskarna

About 2km north of the tiny hamlet of Planina (itself 14km west of Idrija) • Mid-April to mid-Oct 9am–4pm • €3 • ☎ 05 372 6600, ⊛ muzej-idrija-cerkno.si • It's a steep 20min walk to the printworks from the car park

Secreted away in an almost impenetrable forest ravine below the Vojsko plateau are several modest wooden cabins which, for a brief period during World War II, functioned as the **Partizanska tiskarna** (Partisan Printing Works). Operational between September 1944 and May 1945, and with some forty employees, the clandestinely run printworks rolled out between four thousand and seven thousand copies of *Partizanski Dnevnik* (*Partisan Daily*) per day, the only daily newspaper to be published by a resistance movement in occupied Europe during the war. Over the eight months more than a million copies of the paper were published, as well as stacks of other printed matter. Despite numerous German offensives in the vicinity – including one final major assault during the spring of 1945, in which more than three hundred Partisans were killed – the printworks was never rumbled. Owing to its extremely remote location, a visit requires a little organization and a degree of physical exertion.

Once you get there, you'll see the typesetting room (complete with printing moulds and dozens of original papers), the bindery, kitchen and dining room, the power plant and the printing room; a printing demonstration is usually given. Bought for a million lire, the still-functioning press was smuggled across from Milan, via Gorica, before being transported, piece by piece, to Vojsko.

Cerkno and around

Located somewhat out on a limb 19km north of Idrija (and 4km off the main Idrija–Tolmin road), the anonymous little town of **CERKNO** was a key centre of Partisan activity during World War II, when a number of military and political bodies, workshops and schools were stationed hereabouts. Life in Cerkno today is played out at a rather more languid pace, and there's little inducement to linger. That said, the **Laufarija carnival** in February is one of Slovenia's key events (see box below), while the annual three-day **Jazz Festival** (W jazzcerkno.si) in mid-May features a surprisingly impressive, and refreshingly diverse, roster of domestic and international artists.

The surrounding countryside offers some terrific sights, although unless you have your own transport or aren't averse to a reasonable amount of walking, reaching them will prove problematic. The best of these is the superbly evocative **Franja Partisan Hospital**; there's also the little-known **Divje Babe** archeological park a short way southwest of town, and the writer France Bevk's house in **Zakojca** to the north. Meanwhile, the town's **ski resort**, 12km northeast of the centre, is one of Slovenia's fastest developing winter sports centres.

3

Cerkljanski muzej

Bevkova ulica 12 • Tues–Fri 9am–3pm, Sat & Sun 10am–1pm & 2–6pm • €3.50 • ☎ 05 372 3180, W muzej-idrija-cerkno.si

The **Cerkljanski muzej** (Cerkno Museum) documents the history of the Cerkljansko region from the nineteenth century onwards, with a particularly interesting résumé of events hereabouts during World War II – exhibits include the wedding blouse of Franja Bidovec, founder of the Partisan Hospital (see p.172), and items belonging to writer France Bevk (see p.173), who served with the Partisans. The highlight, though, is an exhibition entitled *Pust Je Kriv!* (*Pust is to Blame!*), which relays the history of, and explores the characters involved in, the **Laufarija carnival** (see box below); around half of the masks displayed are the originals made by local folk artist Franc Kobal – the costumes, too, are fabulous, and you can cast your eye over some wonderful photos from carnivals past.

ARRIVAL AND INFORMATION   CERKNO

By bus Buses arrive at and depart from Glavni trg, the small main square around which everything revolves.
Destinations Idrija (Mon–Fri hourly, Sat & Sun 4–5 daily; 30min); Ljubljana (Mon–Fri 7 daily, Sat & Sun 3 daily; 1hr

40min); Tolmin (Mon–Fri 5 daily, Sat & Sun 2 daily; 50min).
Tourist office By the main square at Močnikova ulica 2 (Mon–Fri 9am–4pm, Sat & Sun 9am–3pm; ☎ 05 373 4645, W turizem-cerkno.si).

THE LAUFARIJA

One of Slovenia's more enjoyable **Pust** (Shrovetide) festivals is the **Laufarija**, staged each year on the Sunday before Ash Wednesday and on Shrove Tuesday in Cerkno's small town square. The carnival's origins are unclear, but what is known is that it ceased to be in 1914, following the onset of World War I, only to be revived in 1956 in its present form.

The central character is the horned *Pust*, adorned in a weighty costume of straw, moss and pine branches; as the personification of winter, the *Pust* is hauled up in front of a court and charged with a litany of barmy crimes – a poor harvest, inclement weather, dodgy roads and so on – before being found guilty and sentenced to summary execution (the indictment is read out on the Sunday and the execution takes place on the Tuesday). The two dozen other members of the Laufarija family – each of whom wears one of the distinctive **masks** (*larfe*) carved from soft lime-tree wood – represent either a local trade or craft, or display certain character traits or afflictions such as the drunk and his wife, the "scabby one" or the sick man with his accordion. To be honest, it's debatable whether even the locals quite know what's going on, but either way it's a great deal of fun.

ACCOMMODATION AND EATING

Cerkno Sedejev trg 8 ☎ 05 374 3400, ⓦ hotel-cerkno .si. The only accommodation in town is this unprepossessing concrete edifice just off the main square, whose rooms are comfortable, if not wildly exciting. There is a large pool, though. **€90**

Gostilna Gačnk v Logu Log, 6km along the road towards the Franja Partisan Hospital ☎ 05 372 4005, ⓦ cerkno.com. In the wayside hamlet of Log, this terrifically hospitable roadside tavern offers nine cosy, wood-furnished rooms; its restaurant, meanwhile, features a wide choice of exotic game (stag's back, chamois, boar and the like) and Serbian meats (*ćevapi* and *sarma*; €7–8). Franja Bojc Bidovec, of Franja Partisan Hospital fame (see below), got married here; hence the many pictures of her. Daily 9am–11pm. **€54**

Pr' Gabriel Prekomorskih brigad 1 ☎ 05 374 5333, ⓦ jazzcerkno.si. This garish, low-vaulted bar, just off the main square, is not only the town's chief drinking venue but also stages the occasional live concert (jazz, rock, post-punk) and hosts many of the Cerkno Jazz Festival gigs. Mon–Thurs & Sun 7am–midnight, Fri & Sat 7am–2am.

Želinc Tourist Farm Straža 8 ☎ 05 372 4020, ⓦ zelinc .com. Out on the Idrija–Tolmin road (at the junction of the Cerkno turn-off), and enveloped by thickly wooded hills, Želinc offers ten restful rooms, along with an outdoor pool, bikes for rent and super food. They've also a little field where you can pitch a tent, together with a modern hut with toilet/shower and cooking facilities. Camping **€9**, doubles **€60**

Partizanska Bolnišnica Franja

Dolenji Novaki pri Cerknem, 8km east of Cerkno • Daily: April–Sept 9am–6pm; Oct–March 9am–4pm • €5 • ☎ 05 372 3180, ⓦ muzej-idrija-cerkno.si

Dramatically sited in the heart of the spectacular **Pasica gorge** (7km northeast of Cerkno), the **Partizanska Bolnišnica Franja** (Franja Partisan Hospital) was built in December 1943 for wounded soldiers of the Ninth Corps of the Slovene Partisan Army. It was set up on the initiative of physician Viktor Volčjak, but was named after its chief physician **Franja Bojc Bidovec**, who was the hospital's chief administrator from January 1944 onwards. What you see today, however, is an almost complete – and practically perfect – reconstruction, after torrential floods in September 2007 tragically swept much of the original hospital away.

From the car park, a trail (10min) inclines up the forested gorge, bisected by the babbling Čerinščica stream and hemmed in by overhanging boulders. It was along this same path that prisoners were brought, after being blindfolded and spun around on the spot in order to disorientate them. As you walk, look out for a machine-gun nest pressed high up into the cliffs above, and, just before the entrance, the shattered half-remains of the memorial plate, testament to the damage wrought by the flood. Note that this last part up to the entrance has some steep steps.

The original hospital comprised thirteen camouflaged **wooden cabins** housing an operating room, isolation ward, kitchen, X-ray room and several recovery rooms, with the entire complex protected by bunkers, minefields and machine-gun nests. However, despite the area being shelled by Germans on several occasions, it was never captured. Indeed, its secrecy was such that the wounded were blindfolded before being admitted, food was lowered down the cliff face by neighbouring farmers and medical supplies were air-dropped in by Allied forces. Supplies notwithstanding, the hospital was remarkably self-reliant, making its own orthopaedic accessories, organizing cultural and educational activities for the wounded and even managing to publish its own bulletin, *Bolniški list* (*Patient's Bulletin*). The hospital remained in operation until May 1945, during which time it treated 578 severely wounded soldiers, mostly Partisans but also members of other Yugoslav nations, as well as soldiers from Italy, Russia and America.

Arheološki Park Divje Babe

Šebrelje, 12km west of Cerkno • April–Sept tours Sat & Sun 11am & 3pm, but check with the tourist office in Cerkno (see p.171) first; meet at St Ivan's church in Šebrelje, near the cave • €3.50 • ☎ 041 378 415, ⓦ divje-babe.si • It's easiest to get here with your own transport; otherwise, take a Cerkno–Tolmin bus and alight at the roadside hamlet of Stopnik, from where it is a steep 3km walk along the road up to Šebrelje

The **Arheološki Park Divje Babe** (Divje Babe Archeological Park) is one of the most important Paleolithic sites in Slovenia. While digging near the cave entrance in 1995, excavators stumbled across the femur of a young cave bear – nothing particularly revelatory in itself, but this one had been perforated with four holes (two complete, two partially worn away), giving it a flute-like appearance. Researchers in Canada calculated the 10cm bone to be around 45,000 years old, possibly more, thus dating from the Mousterian (Neanderthal) period. On the assumption that the holes were made by human hands – the most plausible explanation, given that no teeth marks were detected – it can lay fair claim to being the oldest known **musical instrument** in Europe. The flute now resides in the National Museum in Ljubljana (see p.61).

Zakojca and the Cerkno hills

The tiny village of **ZAKOJCA**, around 16km northwest of Cerkno, was the birthplace of children's novelist France Bevk (1890–1970). Today you can visit the immaculately restored **Domačija Franceta Bevka** (France Bevk Homestead) at Zakojca 10 (get the key from the Pri Flandru tourist farm at Zakojca 1; €3; ☎05 372 3180, ⊕muzej-idrija -cerkno.si), a fairly simple dwelling where the author spent much of his youth. The downstairs space comprises a living room (*hiša*), two small bedrooms, a "black kitchen" (see p.123) and a small stable for livestock, while the first-floor attic, where he wrote his earliest works, has been transformed into an exhibition space, with family photos, books and personal effects.

Bevk was also a formidable political activist. Following his stint as a soldier on the Eastern Front during World War I, he was one of the few Slovene authors to remain in Italian-controlled territory, but was imprisoned on several occasions owing to his antifascist stance. Having joined the Partisan movement, he was then part of the Yugoslav diplomatic delegation at the Paris Peace Conference at the end of World War II.

From Zakojca, you could tackle the highland area's highest peak, **Porezen**, which tops a very respectable 1630m (2hr); just below the summit is the *Koča na Poreznu* mountain hut (☎051 615 245; mid-June to mid-Sept). Porezen can also be attempted from the Franja Partisan Hospital (3hr). If you're considering any sort of **hiking** in the hills, consider buying the 1:50,000 *Idrijsko In Cerkljansko* map.

The Karst

A dry, rocky and thickly forested limestone plateau, scattered with ancient stone villages, the **Karst** is famed for its subterranean wonderland of rivers and streams, hollows, depressions and caves, which have fired the imagination of travellers for centuries – none more so than those at **Škocjan**. A few kilometres west of Škocjan is the Karst's second major draw, the world-famous **Lipica Stud Farm**, home to the magnificent Lipizzaner horses, and another fine cave at **Vilenica**. Of the villages, the obvious draw is **Štanjel**, with its bleached-white stone houses and wonderfully disparate range of sights.

While travelling in the Karst, make sure to sample the local **culinary specialities**, in particular the delicious air-dried *pršut* ham, which complements perfectly a glass of **Kraški Teran**, the spiky, cherry-red wine that acquires its deep aroma and colour from the iron-rich *terra rosa* soil peculiar to this region.

Štanjel

Contender for most picturesque village in the region, if not Slovenia, the medieval hilltop settlement of **ŠTANJEL**, 28km southeast of Nova Gorica, is the archetypal Karst village. Most likely the site of a Halstatt settlement, the prominent limestone hill was fortified around the twelfth century, gradually evolving across several gently curving, south-facing terraces, a layout modelled on the plans of the ancient Etruscan towns. Its striking stone houses are delightful, and there's more than enough to warrant a few hours' exploration.

Grad Štanjel and Galerija Lojzeta Spacala

Lojze Spacal Gallery April–Oct Thurs & Fri 11am–5pm, Sat & Sun 10am–6pm; Nov–March Sat & Sun 10am–4pm • €2.50, including entry to the Karst House (see below) • ☎ 041 337 422

The best place to start exploring Štanjel is the **Grad Štanjel** (Castle), located through the village's main **entrance gate**. Erected by the counts of Koblenz in the sixteenth century, on the foundations of an older, medieval castle, the structure today is little more than a battered shell following heavy pounding during World War II. That said, parts are slowly coming back to life, notably the renovated residential wing that now houses the **Galerija Lojzeta Spacala** (Lojze Spacal Gallery), a brilliant collection of abstract paintings, prints, woodcuts and tapestries by the Trieste-born artist. Spacal (1907–2000) was profoundly influenced by the surrounding landscape, as is evident in his extensive use of Karst motifs and colours – greys and whites representing stone (*Quarry in Karst*) and reds representing the soil (*Karst Fields*). Perhaps even more evocative are his coloured woodcuts, such as *Houses at Sunset* and *Moon above the Village*.

Cerkev Sv Danijela

100m from the castle • The church is usually closed, so contact the tourist office (see p.176) if you want to visit

Štanjel's most visible symbol, courtesy of its smooth steeple shaped like a bishop's hat, is the fifteenth-century **Cerkev Sv Danijela** (Church of St Daniel), a fetching amalgam of both Gothic and Baroque. Interesting features include a marble tomb etched with a relief of Daniel and the lions, a relief of the castle as it once supposedly looked, and paintings of interlocking crosses on the presbytery walls.

Kraška hiša

250m from the castle • April–Oct Thurs & Fri 11am–5pm, Sat & Sun 10am–6pm; Nov–March Sat & Sun 10am–4pm; to visit, contact the Lojze Spacal Gallery (see above) • €2.50, including entry to the Lojze Spacal Gallery • ☎ 041 337 422

The 600-year-old **Kraška hiša** (Karst House) is a superb example of vernacular architecture, constructed entirely from stone, including the roof and gutters. The downstairs space would have been used for keeping livestock, with a family of typically five or six members squeezed into the living quarters upstairs; both floors now hold a modest ethnological collection.

Ferrarijev vrt

In the southeastern corner of the village, a few hundred metres and a couple of terraces below the Karst House

The **Ferrarijev vrt** (Ferrari Garden) was designed by internationally renowned architect and town planner – and former mayor of Štanjel – Max Fabiani, but named after his nephew, Enrico Ferrari, a doctor in Trieste. This winsome little garden, designed as an adjunct to the now abandoned Ferrari Villa (which rises above its eastern edge), combines traditional Karst features – terraces, stone retaining walls and stairways – with foreign elements, such as a pavilion, oval pool and a delicate, balustraded stone bridge, the inspiration for which was undoubtedly the author's earlier work in Vienna. It had a utilitarian function, too; to counter chronic water shortages in the Karst region, Fabiani designed a water supply system using a series of ditches, storage tanks, pipes and irrigation channels to provide the villa and surrounding buildings with their own running water.

From the garden there are expansive views across the Karst towards Italy and the hills of the Vipava Valley. You can also follow a marked footpath (Fabiani Path) south towards the village of **Kobdilj**, Fabiani's birthplace – a walk of about fifteen minutes.

ARRIVAL AND INFORMATION   ŠTANJEL

By train Trains from Nova Gorica (Mon–Fri 5 daily, Sat & Sun 1–2 daily; 35min) and Sežana (Mon–Fri 5 daily, Sat & Sun 1–2 daily; 20min) stop in the village of Kobdilj, from where it's a 15min walk north into Štanjel.
By bus Buses from Divača and Nova Gorica stop on the main road opposite the main entrance to the village.

CERKVENIK BRIDGE, ŠKOCJAN CAVES (P.177) >

Tourist office Within the castle grounds, just above the courtyard (May–Oct Tues–Fri 9am–3pm, Sat & Sun 10am–6pm; Sept–April Tues–Fri 9am–3pm, Sat & Sun 10am–4pm; ☏ 05 769 0056, ⓦ stanjel.eu); they can organize private accommodation in Štanjel, and also offer guided tours (€4) of the village.

ACCOMMODATION AND EATING

While – other than private rooms or apartments – there's no formal accommodation in Štanjel itself, there are numerous possibilities in the surrounding **Karst villages**, all of which you'll need a car to get to.

Francinovi Tourist Farm Avber 21, 6km south of Štanjel ☏ 05 768 5120, ⓦ ukmar.si. This convivial farm offers simple but satisfying accommodation in double rooms (as well as an eight-bed room), with a breakfast terrace offering glorious views of the Karst; even if you're not staying here it's worth a trip for the wonderful food, in particular the roasted lamb. Sat & Sun noon–8pm. **€54**

Grad Štanjel Castle courtyard ☏ 05 731 0070. While the castle's café occupies a prime spot on the suntrap gravel courtyard, and undoubtedly looks great inside (lots of light and stone), it's nothing special – still, it suffices for a coffee or glass of wine once you've completed your tour of the village. Daily except Wed 9am–9pm.

Škerlj Tourist Farm Tomaj 53a, 12km south of Štanjel on the main road towards Sežana ☏ 05 764 0673, ⓦ tk-skerlj.si. One of the larger farms in the area, with homely rooms complemented by good food and hospitality – they've also got an outdoor pool and bikes for rent, and guests are welcome to help out on the farm, harvesting the grapes for example. **€60**

Youth Hostel Pliskovica Pliskovica 11, 10km southwest of Štanjel ☏ 05 764 0250, ⓦ hostelkras .com. In the small isolated village of Pliskovica, this beautifully restored 400-year-old farmstead – a preserved local heritage site – has six- to fourteen-bed dorms, all with shared bathroom, as well as double rooms and camping; they also offer bike rental and laundry and, best of all, a fabulous leafy patio where you can enjoy a glass of the local *teran* wine. Breakfast included. Camping **€10**, dorms **€16**, doubles **€40**

Divača

DIVAČA is a small, rather faceless town but, with its transport links and decent **accommodation**, it's a major jumping-off point for a number of local attractions and is itself home to the fabulous **Museum of Slovenian Film Actors**.

Muzej Slovenskih filmskih igralcev

Kraška cesta 26 • Tues, Wed & Fri–Sun: May–Sept 11am–6pm; Oct–April 10am–5pm • €4 • ☏ 05 731 0949, ⓦ muzejdivaca.si

The first building you see as you enter the **Muzej Slovenskih filmskih igralcev** (Museum of Slovenian Film Actors) complex is the **Škrateljinova hiša** (Škrateljinova Homestead), a superb example of vernacular architecture dating from the seventeenth century. One of the oldest houses in the Karst region, this was the birthplace of Slovenia's first major female film star, Ida Kravanja, better known under her pseudonym, **Ita Rina** (1907–79); photos, pictures and posters from her movies line the walls.

Behind here, the spectacularly renovated stables quarter an exhibition on the greatest **Slovenian actors**; while this will be of greater appeal to native audiences, there's much to enjoy, with English captioning. Exhibits include footage from the first Slovenian film, *Na Svoji Zemlji* (*On Our Own Land*; 1948), and costumes, scripts and posters, including some from what is arguably Slovenia's most enduring film, *Kekec* (see p.310). Every Friday evening between June and August, classic **films** (€3) are screened in the courtyard, weather permitting.

ARRIVAL AND DEPARTURE   DIVAČA

By train and bus Both the train station (with a handful of left-luggage lockers) and the main bus stop are on Trg 15 Aprila.
Destinations (train) Koper (4–7 daily; 50min); Ljubljana (Mon–Fri every 45min–2hr, Sat & Sun 6–7 daily; 1hr 40min); Postojna (Mon–Fri every 45min–1hr 30min, Sat & Sun 6–7 daily; 35min).
Destinations (bus) Koper (Mon–Fri 9 daily, Sat & Sun 2 daily; 1hr 15min); Ljubljana (Mon–Fri 7 daily, Sat & Sun 4 daily; 1hr 45min).

By bus to the Škocjan Caves If you're planning to visit the Škocjan Caves (see opposite) from Divača, and don't fancy walking the 3.5km, hop on one of the free buses from the train station (10am, 11.15am, 2pm & 3pm; return buses 10.45am, 11.45am, 2.12pm & 3.18pm).

ACCOMMODATION AND EATING

Malovec Kraška cesta 30 ☎ 05 763 3333, ⓦ hotel -malovec.si. Should you need to stay in Divača, this modern hotel has perfectly accomplished rooms, and a decent breakfast to see you on your way the next morning. **€80**

Orient Express Kraška cesta 67 ☎ 05 763 3010. Named after the legendary train that used to run through the town, this is a lively and colourful gaff serving up a slew of salads, pizzas and grills alongside a reasonable selection of light and dark beers brewed on site; it's across the road from the *Malovec*. Daily 11am–11pm.

Jama Vilenica

6km west of Divača, just beyond the village of Lokev • Tours April–Oct Sun 3pm & 5pm • €10 • ☎ 05 734 4259, ⓦ vilenica.com

The **Jama Vilenica** (Vilenica Cave) is a relative minnow in comparison to Slovenia's better-known and more glamorous show caves, but certainly no less attractive. Reputedly the first cave in the country open to the public, way back in 1633, it wasn't until 1963, when the local caving club took it upon themselves to clean up the galleries and install electric lighting, that tourism really made its mark here. The walk through, around 400m in length, takes in a wondrous array of weird and fantastically shaped stalagmites and stalactites, many of them stained a rich rust-red colour owing to the surrounding Karst soil. Each September, the largest hall in the system hosts the **Vilenica Festival**, a prestigious international literary gathering.

Vojaški muzej

Lokev, 5km southwest of Divača • Wed–Sun 9am–noon & 2–6pm • €3 • ☎ 05 767 0107, ⓦ vojaskimuzejtabor.eu

There's some delightful Karst architecture on view in the village of **LOKEV**; the most outstanding building here is the **Tabor Tower**, a cylindrical stone edifice built in 1485 by the Venetians as a defence against the Turks and which later served as the town granary. Its four floors are now home to the **Vojaški muzej** (War Museum), a voluminous – and quite illustrious – private collection with memorabilia from both world wars, as well as other conflicts up to and including the 1991 Ten-Day War (see box, p.305). Crammed into every conceivable space are medals, flags, busts and uniforms, including that of the commander of the Austrian forces on the Soča Front, Svetozar Borojević (aka the "Soča Lion"), and many more accoutrements from the various warring sides – most impressive is the hoard of weaponry from the Soča Front (see box, p.148). A fine display of photos includes a shot of Mussolini during his visit to the Postojna Caves in 1938.

Jama Škocjan

Škocjan Regional Park, 4.5km (3.5km if walking) southeast of Divača • Tours daily: Jan–March, Nov & Dec 10am & 1pm, plus 3pm on Sun; April, May & Oct 10am, 1pm & 3.30pm; June–Sept hourly 10am–5pm • €16, €21 with the "Following the Reka River Underground" tour (see p.179) • ☎ 05 708 2110, ⓦ park-skocjanske-jame.si • If travelling by bus, you may be able to get the driver to set you down by the access road (just off the Ljubljana–Koper highway), from where it's a manageable 1.5km walk to the caves; by train the nearest station is in Divača, from where you could catch a free bus (see opposite) or take a pleasant 45min walk (the caves are signposted from the station)

South of Divača, in the belly of the **Škocjan Regional Park**, the **Jama Škocjan** (Škocjan Caves) are the country's most memorable natural attraction, a breathtaking complex of passages, chambers, collapsed valleys and, reputedly, the world's largest subterranean canyon. Measuring around 5800m in length, the caves were formed by the **Reka River** (literally River River), which begins its journey from springs deep below Snežnik mountain 50km southeast of the cave near the Croatian border. At the village of **Škocjan**, not far from the cave entrance, the river sinks underground for the first time, briefly reappearing at the bottom of two collapsed sinkholes, before vanishing again into the mouth of the cave. It re-emerges some 40km later at the Timavo springs north of Trieste.

3

3

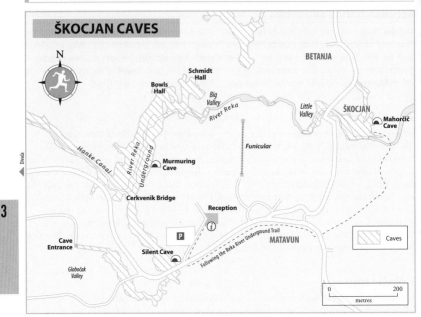

If you've got time and energy after exploring the caves you might want to **trek** the **Educational Trail** (Učna pot), a scenic 2km footpath that more or less circles the two collapsed valleys, **Velika dolina** (Big Valley) and **Mala dolina** (Little Valley); pick up a leaflet from the caves reception area, where the trail begins and ends. Alternatively, you could just do part of the walk, as far as Škocjan, which takes about ten minutes. The 1:6000 *Regijski park Škocjanske jame* map outlines further walks in the park.

Brief history

Little was known about the Škocjan Caves until the **sixteenth century**, when the first maps of the system were printed. After that, more thorough accounts were presented in several seminal seventeenth- and eighteenth-century works, most notably Valvasor's *Glory of the Duchy of Carniola* and Gruber's *Hydrological Letters from the Carniola*.

Although parts of the cave had already been discovered, and several paths cut, during the early nineteenth century, it wasn't until around 1840 that the first systematic explorations of the main cave took place, when Giovanni Svetina from Trieste managed to penetrate some 150m downstream. Other pioneering explorers followed, but the most important explorations were left to **Anton Hanke**, a Czech mining engineer, and two colleagues who, between 1884 and 1890, progressed to the fourteenth waterfall along what is now known as the Hanke Canal – in the process stumbling upon several more chambers. A few years later, four locals entered the cave proper for the first time. Electricity was installed in 1959 and the caves were given UNESCO World Heritage status in 1986, the first site in Slovenia to be bestowed with the honour.

The cave tour

From the reception area, you'll be escorted to the cave entrance down in the **Dolina Globočak** (Globočak Valley), some ten minutes' walk away. Heading along the 130m-long, artificially created tunnel, you enter the cave proper, the first part of which is called the **Tiha jama** (Silent Cave); at this point, you'll break off into different groups, depending on which language you speak.

Discovered in around 1904, and totalling some 500m, the Silent Cave comprises several smaller chambers, each modestly decorated with stalagmites and stalactites, though neither the first, the **Paradise Cave**, nor the second, the **Calvary**, is particularly well endowed, having been hit by earthquakes and floods aeons ago. More impressive is the 130m-long and 30m-high **Velika dvorana** (Great Hall), whose most celebrated formations are the 250,000-year-old Giant stalagmite and a ribbed dripstone stalactite dubbed the Organ because of its resemblance to a pipe organ and the sounds it emits when tapped.

Beyond here the cave widens, the temperature drops and the low rumbling of the **Reka River** can be heard; this marks your entry into the magnificent **Šumeča jama** (Murmuring Cave), a 300m-long, 60m-wide and 100m-high subterranean gorge carved out by the Reka – it is, quite simply, the most fantastic creation imaginable. From here you walk along a narrow ledge incised into the great shafts of limestone rock, towards the vertiginous 45m-high **Cerkvenikov most** (Cerkvenik Bridge), under which the Reka flows before continuing its course along the **Hanke Canal** towards further, larger chambers (accessible only to speleologists). The bridge was rebuilt in 2003, replacing the original Hanke Bridge – dating from 1933 – which itself replaced the **Cat's Footbridge**, the remains of which can be detected 20m higher, just below the ceiling.

From the bridge, the path continues upstream along the side of the gorge for several hundred metres, through the **Bowls Hall** – so-named because of its circular limestone troughs – and towards the **Schmidlova dvorana** (Schmidt Hall), the yawning, natural cave entrance that emerges into the collapsed **Velika dolina** (Big Valley); from here it's a short walk to the funicular, which transports you the 150m back to the top.

Ob Reki v podzemlje

Tours daily: April, May & Oct 11am & 2pm; June–Sept 10am–3pm • €11, €21 with the Škocjan Caves

In 2011, a new trail, **Ob Reki v podzemlje** ("Following the Reka River Underground"), was opened to visitors – note that this can either be self-guided (summer only) or visited on a tour. From the reception area, it's a fifteen-minute walk down to the entrance of the **Mahorčičeva jama** (Mahorčič Cave) – named after a local explorer (and one-time local mayor) – which sits directly beneath Škocjan village and is where the Reka River enters the cave system. Upon entering the cave you first cross a 40m-high bridge, where a plaque records the height at which floodwaters reached in 1965, which is scarcely believable as you look down into the chasm below. From here you descend to an atmospherically lit footpath which tracks the course of the twisting Reka through the cave. Emerging at the **Mala dolina** (Small Valley), you proceed under the natural bridge – in effect, what remains of the cave ceiling between the small valley and the **Velika dolina** (Big Valley). The trail ends at the Schmidt Hall, the exit point for the main cave tour (see opposite), from where it's a short walk to the funicular back to the top. If you're doing both tours, you take the regular cave tour first, before continuing on the trail; however, because it's in reverse (in effect uphill for much of the way), this is physically much more demanding.

Zgodovina od krivanja jam

Daily: Jan–March, Nov & Dec 9.30am–3pm; April, May & Oct 9.30am–5pm; June–Sept 9am–6pm • €4, free if visiting the caves

On the ground floor of the building housing the cave's information point (opposite the ticket office) is the absorbing **Zgodovina od krivanja jam** (History of Cave Exploration). There's some wonderful stuff on display here, including maps and sketches illustrating the discovery of the cave (one of which was drawn by Valvasor), a remnant of the original Hanke Bridge, and stacks of equipment, including gas and carbide lamps, hammers and harnesses and a steel ladder used for lowering cavers down into the depths. The collection of nineteenth-century plaques is particularly evocative; at one stage there were more than 150 of them here at Škocjan, though it's believed that fewer than twenty of them survived.

Škocjan museums

Škocjan • April, May & Oct Sat & Sun 11am–6pm; June–Sept daily 11.30am–7.30pm • €4, free if visiting the caves

There are two modest **museums** in the tiny Karst hamlet of **ŠKOCJAN**, each housed in a renovated stone barn. The old **J'kopinov skedenj** barn holds a gathering of ethnological implements, but more interesting is the stash of biological, geological and archeological artefacts a few paces away in the old **Delezova homestead**. Among the beautiful exhibits – for example, swords, axe heads and fibulas – is a delicate pin needle, found here in 2004 when the remains of an old wooden house were discovered on this site, and which now effectively forms part of the basement where this collection is held.

Lipica

6km south of Sežana, 2km from the Italian border • Tours Jan, Feb & Oct–Dec Tues–Sun hourly 10am–3pm, except noon; March daily hourly 10am–3pm, except noon; April–Sept daily hourly 10am–5pm • €16, includes admission to the grounds, stud farm and museums • **Classical Riding School** April & Oct Sun 3pm; May–Sept Tues, Fri & Sun 3pm • €23, includes admission to the grounds, stud farm and museums • **Carriage rides** Tues–Sun 10am–2pm & 4–6pm; €20/carriage for 15min, €30/30min, maximum four people • **Trail riding** Experienced riders only; €61 for 90min, which includes entrance to the stud farm • ☏ 05 739 1580, ⦿ lipica.org • Without your own transport, getting here will be difficult; the only other option is to hitch or take a taxi

After Postojna and Lake Bled, Slovenia's most emblematic tourist draw is **LIPICA**, birthplace of the famous white **Lipizzaner horse**. In 1580 the Lipica estates were acquired by the Austrian Archduke Karl (son of Emperor Ferdinand I); he established the stud here to breed horses for the Spanish Riding School in Vienna and the Royal Court stables in Graz. That the Lipizzaner has survived at all is remarkable; the breed was evacuated to southern Hungary during Napoleon's occupation in the late eighteenth century, divided by the Italians and Austrians during World War I and seized by the Germans during World War II. Today the horse is bred at half a dozen European stud farms and widely throughout the United States. Here at Lipica there are around 360 horses divided between show, competition and riding horses, with some three hundred more in private hands around the country – it's estimated that Slovenia is home to around one-fifth of the world's Lipizzaner.

Stud farm

You can visit the **stud farm** either solo or on a free guided tour – or you can do both – but whichever way you do it the real joy is being able to get up close to these magnificent creatures. The oldest of Lipica's stables is Velbanca, dating from 1704 and which retains many of its original features, including the vaulted ceiling ("velb" translates as "vault") and oak flooring; it houses the estate's breeding stallions, as it always has done. Only the adjoining manor house, now used for administrative purposes, is older.

THE LIPIZZANER

Despite competing claims from Austria and Italy over the geographical origin and lineage of the **Lipizzaner** (Lipicanec), the original stud was established at Lipica in 1580 by the then governor of the Slovene territories, Habsburg Archduke Karl. Horses of Spanish, Arabian and Berber stock were bred with the tough and muscular local Karst horse, thus creating the Lipizzaner strain. As a result of such fastidious breeding, Lipizzaner are comparatively small in stature – 14.3 to 15.2 hands – with a long back, short, thick neck and a powerful build. Born dark or bay coloured, they do not turn white until somewhere between the ages of 4 and 7, though their coat is in fact grey, a colour that only manifests itself when the horse sweats. These distinctive physical traits are complemented by a beautiful sense of balance and rhythm, a lively, high-stepping gait and an even temperament; schooling begins at the age of 3 and takes around five years to complete. With such qualities, it's little wonder that the Lipizzaner have for centuries excelled at **carriage driving** and as **show horses** – performing the perfect bows, pirouettes and other manoeuvres that delight dressage cognoscenti.

While experienced riders can go **trail riding** (see opposite), anyone can enjoy a **carriage ride** (from fifteen minutes up to an hour), which entails a gentle trot around the estate and its grand avenues, lined with linden, ash, chestnut and oak.

Classical Riding School

To really make your visit worthwhile, try and coordinate it with a presentation of the **Classical Riding School**. While nothing as grand as the shows put on at the Spanish Riding School in Vienna, it's still quite something, the riders toffed up in period costume while the horses perform their well-crafted exercises: extended trots, *pesade* (standing up on the hind legs with forelegs in the air) and the wonderful *capriole*, whereby the horse leaps into the air, kicking out its hind legs.

Lipikum muzej

For insights into the history of the horses and of Lipica, pop along to the **Lipikum muzej** (Lipikum Museum) in which the rooms progress from dark to light shades, mirroring the changing colour of the horse itself. The first couple of rooms trace the development of horses in general, before attention turns to the Lipizzaner itself, largely through interactive displays; there's even a full-size mock-up horse you can clamber up onto. Elsewhere, you can view fossil remains of horse teeth found in the area, spurs, stirrups and costumes as worn by the riders.

3

Hrastovlje

Some 31km south of Divača, in the upper Rižana River Valley – which roughly separates the Karst plateau from the coastal hinterland – **HRASTOVLJE** would be just another pretty, yet inconsequential, Istrian village were it not for the Romanesque **Cerkev Sv Trojice** (Church of the Holy Trinity), whose exceptional spread of late-medieval **frescoes** marks it out as a cultural monument of the highest rank.

Cerkev Sv Trojice

Daily 9am–noon & 1–6pm • €2 • ☎ 05 659 0050 • There are three daily buses (Mon–Fri) from Koper (see p.186) to Hrastovlje, though these are all in the afternoon, with four (morning) buses making the trip the other way, hence fairly useless for visitors; a return trip by taxi from Koper will cost around €35

Sited on an exposed, shallow rise and concealed within a thick, 10m-high, grey-stone wall, the **Cerkev Sv Trojice** (Church of the Holy Trinity) was built sometime between the twelfth and fourteenth centuries, although the wall was a sixteenth-century addition, erected to provide a place of refuge for the locals against marauding Turks. Constructed from stone-cut square blocks, with a typical Istrian stone-slab roof, this charmingly compact church is even smaller than you might imagine from outside the wall. The inside, comprising a simple tripartite nave, is completely unfurnished.

Taking almost ten years to complete, the **frescoes** were executed by the master Istrian painter Johannes de Castua (Janez Kastav) at the end of the fifteenth century, although they weren't discovered until the 1950s, concealed under several layers of whitewash. Far and away the most celebrated and complete painting is the **Dance of Death**, or *Danse Macabre* (see box, p.182), on the lower half of the south wall; with its powerful images alluding to the inevitability of death, this fresco pretty much surpasses any other specimen of medieval iconography in Slovenia. Cast your eye downwards and you'll see decorative **Glagolitic inscriptions**, an ancient Slav script that originated in the ninth century as a means of converting Slavs to Christianity.

The remaining frescoes, depicting numerous biblical scenes, take some digesting, so it's worth focusing on a select few: represented in fifteen scenes immediately above the *Dance of Death* is the cycle of Christ's Passion, while on the opposite, north wall, the Three Kings come bearing gifts for Mary, who is seated on a gold throne with the Infant Child. On the ceilings of the north and south aisles, the calendar year is represented by fourteen

3

THE DANCE OF DEATH

The **Dance of Death** is not unique to Hrastovlje and can be found in many countries throughout Europe, from England to Estonia – although the only other one in Istria is in the village of Beram, in Croatia. Thought to have derived from a thirteenth-century literary genre called Vado Mori ("I prepare myself to die"), the artistic genre of the Dance of Death originated as **La Danse Macabre** at the Cemetery of the Innocents in Paris around 1424. More often than not painted (or carved) on the outside walls of cloisters and ossuaries, or church interiors, the composition of the dance, and the number of characters involved, varies from place to place.

The *Dance of Death* in the **Cerkev Sv Trojice** in Hrastovlje has a cast of eleven human characters – including the pope, a king and queen, bishop, burgher, cripple and child – each being escorted by a skeleton towards the narrator (the twelfth skeleton), who sits on a stone throne, waiting with shovel and pick at his feet and hand poised on the coffin lid. There's some wonderful detail to admire, such as the painting of the usurer who – deciding it's not his time to go – tries to bribe the skeleton by offering a purse, seemingly impervious to the idea that not even the rich can circumvent a fate that awaits us all.

---

scenes of seasonal activities – hunting, harvesting and so on – and local customs, and is unique in that it is believed to be the only case of a secular cycle in a Slovene Gothic church. The apses are decorated with portraits of the Apostles, and scenes from the Crucifixion and the crowning of Mary. An English-language audio commentary can help you negotiate your way around this tangle of paintings.

The Istrian coast

Sandwiched between the Gulf of Trieste and the Croatian coast, Slovenia's **Istrian coast** packs a surprising amount into its short 46km stretch, with a rich complement of historical sights among the more traditional beach-related pursuits. While its proximity to Italy ensures that it receives a healthy number of vacationing Italians, this also means that certain places can get mobbed at the height of summer. Conversely, it's largely avoided by Slovenes, most of whom prefer to holiday along Croatia's Dalmatian coast. The **beaches**, such as they are, are invariably rocky or concrete affairs – though you might find the odd sandy spot if you're lucky – but that's not to say this coast is without charm. **Piran**, a protected cultural monument, is the most seductive spot; **Koper**, too, boasts a fabulously appealing old town, at odds with its prevailingly industrial backdrop. Down the coast, the pretty little fishing town of **Izola** is worth a minor diversion, while **Portorož** – the coast's main resort, just a stone's throw from Piran – offers a touch of hedonism.

Brief history

The basis for much of the coast's fabulous cultural legacy is overwhelmingly Italian – indeed, its handful of towns wouldn't look out of place on the other side of the Adriatic – thanks to nearly five hundred years of **Venetian rule** that preceded the region's incorporation into the Austro-Hungarian Empire, and, eventually, the Yugoslav Federation.

This northern part of Istria didn't actually become a part of Yugoslavia until the **1954 London Agreement**, which finally resolved the problem of post-World War II territorial boundaries between Italy and Yugoslavia. Until then, this bitterly disputed area of the Adriatic had been divided into two zones, known as the Free Territory of Trieste – Zone A (which included Trieste) and Zone B (which included Koper); the agreement subsequently assigned Zone A to Italy and Zone B to Yugoslavia. However, neither side was entirely appeased, as both lost what they considered to be historic pieces of territory, a fact recognized by the Italians who refused to ratify the agreement, at least

COASTAL FESTIVALS

Festival-wise, the coast has plenty to offer visitors, its temperate climate making it ideal for a year-round spread of events. The start of the salt-harvesting season at the end of April is celebrated in grand style with the **Saltpans Feast**, with a plethora of events, chiefly in Piran's Tartini Square and the Sečovlje and Strunjan saltpans; expect exhibitions, fairs and parades, as well as free guided tours of the various salt-related attractions. The coast is known for its film festivals, the best of which is the **Izola Film Festival** (ⓦ isolacinema.org) in early June, a five-day run of colourful and wide-ranging world movies, some of them screened alfresco. In early July, the **Mediterranean International Folklore Festival** (ⓦ miff.si) is a five-day jamboree featuring numerous ensembles, mostly from Eastern Europe, performing in the main squares of Koper and Piran, and on the beach at Portorož.

The **Primorsko Summer Festival**, a series of open-air theatrical performances (and occasionally dance and music), takes place throughout July and August in all the major coastal towns and some more unusual venues, such as a catamaran, a disused railway tunnel and the Sečovlje saltpans. The most prestigious happening, however, is the fortnight-long **Tartini Festival** (ⓦ tartinifestival.org), starting at the end of August in Piran, incorporating an impressive run of classical music concerts. Finally, there's the **International Festival of Desserts and Sweet Products**, which usually takes place on the third weekend of September, in Koper, and which really needs no explanation.

until the 1975 Treaty of Osimo, which did little more than review and reaffirm the original agreement. Although many Italians resettled in their homeland following the 1954 Agreement, many towns have retained significant communities.

GETTING AROUND   **THE ISTRIAN COAST**

Buses and ferries shuttle up and down the coast, and, if you're looking to push on to Trieste or the Croatian Istrian towns, there are frequent **bus** connections. Koper is the end of the line so far as trains go (and is pretty well served from Ljubljana), but there are plentiful onward connections from here.

Koper

Easily reached by train from Ljubljana, and just 20km from Trieste, **KOPER** (Capodistria in Italian) is the first major stop along the coast. At first glance it's an unenticing spectacle, little more than a messy jumble of cranes and tower blocks. However, within this gritty outer shell lies a beautifully preserved **medieval core**, embracing an attractive lattice of paved alleys, Italianate squares and a stack of fine cultural monuments. There's a small but tidy pebble and grass **beach**, too, between the pier and the Marina on Kopališko Nabrežje (daily 8am–8pm).

Believed to have originated as **Aegida** in around 3 BC, the town – at that time an island – acquired several identities before the **Venetians** assumed control in the late thirteenth century. Thanks to its maritime industries, the town's economy remained in rude health until the beginning of the eighteenth century, when both Trieste and Rijeka (in Croatia) were proclaimed free ports and an already bleak situation was further compounded by the opening of the Vienna–Trieste rail line in 1857. Following the 1954 London Agreement, the town experienced a surge of development, with the advancement of a new port and an extension of the rail line to Koper, thus reaffirming the town's status as the coast's most important economic and political centre, which it remains to this day.

Pretorska palača

Laid out in the fifteenth century, handsome **Titov trg** (Tito Square) was the one-time fulcrum of the old city. The square's stunning synthesis of Gothic, Renaissance and Baroque styles is superbly encapsulated in the **Pretorska palača** (Praetorian Palace), Koper's most enduring symbol, whose battlements look like a stage backdrop for a

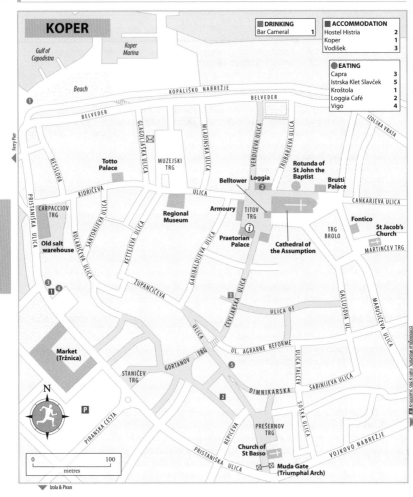

KOPER

Renaissance drama. Equally as impressive is its facade, plastered with reliefs and busts – the most striking of which is the black bust of Nicola Donato, praetor of Koper between 1579 and 1580. Although there was a building here in the thirteenth century (which was subsequently destroyed), the foundations for the current palace were laid down in the 1400s, when the Gothic left wing and the Renaissance right wing were constructed; its Baroque elements were added during further seventeenth-century renovations.

Loža

Opposite the Praetorian Palace, the fifteenth-century **Loža** (Loggia), with its striking Gothic-style lancet arches, has been the town's most popular meeting place ever since philosophers and artists gathered here in the seventeenth century – its first coffee house, *Caffe della Loggia*, established in 1846, is now the *Loggia*, which remains the most swish café in town; the statue of the Madonna in the corner pillar was placed there to commemorate the 1554 plague.

Stolnica Marija vnebovzetja

Cathedral Daily 7am–noon & 3–7pm • Free • **Bell Tower** Daily 9am–1pm & 4–8pm • €3

The **Stolnica Marija vnebovzetja** (Cathedral of the Assumption) on the east side of the square is believed to be the fifth or sixth church on this site, though much of this present structure has eighteenth-century origins. Its exterior is an odd amalgam of Gothic lower storey and Lombardy-style upper storey, the latter part completed a century later than the lower part. By way of contrast, its vast interior, endowed with some glorious works of art and furnishings, is mostly Baroque; note in particular the central nave's magnificent Rococo pulpit, designed by Lorenzo Ferolli in 1758, and, in the presbytery, the finely carved olive-wood choir pews and the gold-plate-encrusted bishop's throne, dating from 1730. The major works of art were completed by Vittore Carpaccio, the most outstanding of which is *The Enthroned Madonna with Child and Saints* from 1516.

Pressed into the cathedral's south side is the formidable **Mestni stolp** (Bell Tower), a fifteenth-century structure that once doubled as a lookout; climb the 43m to the top and you'll understand why – the views of the town, coast and hinterland are tremendous.

Trg Brolo and Čevljarska ulica

Trg Brolo, a leafy, triangular square just east of the cathedral, showcases some terrific Venetian-Baroque architecture, the most eye-catching of which is the **Brutti Palace** on the north side, whose facade is ornamented with relief images from the Old Testament – the building is now the town library. On the east side of the square at no. 4 is the several-times rebuilt **Fontico**, a former grain warehouse studded with rich heraldic decoration completed by Lombardian stonemasons.

Back on Titov trg, pass through the portico under the Praetorian Palace and take a stroll down **Čevljarska ulica** (Shoemaker's Street), which took its name from the profession that was practised here for several centuries. Probably the single prettiest street in the town, Čevljarska ulica preserves a happy ensemble of two- and three-storey shuttered tenements, shops and galleries.

Pokrajinksi muzej

Kidričeva ulica 19 • May–Aug Tues–Fri 8am–4pm, Sat 10am–2pm & 6–9pm, Sun 10am–2pm; Sept–April Tues–Fri 8am–4pm, Sat & Sun 10am–2pm • €5 • ☎ 041 556 644, ⓦ pokrajinksimuzejkoper.si

Housed inside the fine, sixteenth-century Mannerist-Baroque **Belgramoni-Tacco Palace** is the **Pokrajinski muzej** (Regional Museum), which, although pretty hit and miss, does have a strong archeological collection; highlights include a couple of stone-carved sarcophagi, a stone statue of Justice from the Praetorian Palace and, best of all, some fine marble (bird of prey clasping a hare) and Istrian stone (Madonna and Child) cut reliefs. The exhibition of contemporary history, describing Slovene Istria's role before, during and after the two world wars, is intermittently interesting, the most illuminating item being Tone Kralj's gruesome painting, *Rapallo*, in which a woman is savaged by hideous-looking creatures.

Kidričeva ulica and Carpacciov trg

As you continue down the gently sloping **Kidričeva ulica** from the Regional Museum, there's plenty of fine architecture to admire; initially, there's a splendid **Venetian-Gothic town house** – one of several such buildings in town – sporting a protruding upper floor and check-painted facade, though it looks like it's perilously close to collapsing. Opposite, the tatty facade of the **Totto Palace** bears a fine relief of a lion with an open book – traditionally, this was meant to symbolize peace, as opposed to a closed book, which symbolized war; similar reliefs adorn many other prominent buildings along the coast.

Kidričeva ulica eventually opens up onto **Carpacciov trg**, a peaceful little square named after the Venetian painter. Dominated by the old **salt warehouse**, the square also features the spindly **Column of St Justin**, erected to commemorate the famous naval victory against the Turks at Lepanto in 1571, in which a Koper galley participated.

Prešernov trg

In the centre of **Prešernov trg** (Prešeren Square), a pleasant, elongated space, stands **Ponte's Fountain**, built in 1666. The fountain is furnished with a small, Plečnik-style bridge – *ponte* is Italian for bridge – and, at the bottom, four masks which until 1898 spouted water. South of the fountain is the triumphal arch-style Muda Gate (Vrata Muda), built in 1516 and the last of the city's twelve town gates; note, on the inner arches, two reliefs of a blazing sun with the shape of a face, which is the city coat of arms.

Etnološki muzej

Gramšijev trg 4 • Tues–Sat 8am–4pm, Sun 10am–2pm • €3 • ☎ 05 663 3586, ⊛ pokrajinskimuzejkoper.si

Housed in an exceptional Venetian-Gothic building east of town is the hugely enjoyable **Etnološki muzej** (Ethnological Museum). For the most part, the collection focuses on the Istrian cultural landscape, with emphasis on stonecutting and stonedressing, industries which first took wing in the region during the seventeenth century. The pick of the collection is its assemblage of skilfully hewn stone-cut **portals**, commonly found at entrances to courtyards and houses; many portals were traditionally ornamented with floral patterns, sacral symbols and other motifs and reliefs, though few have been preserved.

More superb stonemasonry can be seen in a partial reconstruction of a **shepherd's hut**, typically used to store farming tools and arable crops but also useful as a form of shelter during extremes in temperature; and a portion of a **dry-stone wall**, a prevalent feature of the Istrian landscape. To round off this engaging collection, there is a presentation of a Koper **kitchen**, at the centre of which is a hearth, surrounded by some exquisite copper, glass and china food-preparation items garnered from the Veneto and Friuli regions, and which date from the nineteenth and twentieth centuries.

ARRIVAL AND INFORMATION   KOPER

By train and bus The stations are next to each other in a wasteland 1.5km southeast of town, from where it's a dull walk along Kolodvorska cesta to the centre; alternatively, regular buses shuttle passengers into town, and then on to Izola, Portorož and Piran.
Destinations (train) Divača (5–7 daily; 50min); Ljubljana (3–5 daily; 2hr 30min); Postojna (3–5 daily; 1hr 30min).
Destinations (bus) Hrastovlje (Mon–Fri 3 daily; 30min); Izola (every 20–30min; 10min); Ljubljana (Mon–Fri 9 daily,

Sat & Sun 4 daily; 2hr–2hr 20min); Piran (every 20–30min; 30min); Poreč, Croatia (2 daily; 1hr 15min); Postojna (Mon–Fri 8 daily, Sat & Sun 2–3 daily; 1hr 20min); Rovinj, Croatia (2 daily; 1hr 45min); Trieste, Italy (Mon–Fri 9 daily, Sat 5; 45min).
Tourist office Inside the Praetorian Palace on Titov trg (daily: June–Sept 9am–8pm; Oct–May 9am–5pm; ☎ 05 664 6403, ⊛ koper.si).

ACCOMMODATION

Hostel Histria Ulica pri velikih vratih 17 ☎ 070 133 552, ⊛ hostel-histria.si. Compact little neighbourhood hostel split between two buildings, the main one quartering six- and eight-bed dorms, each with a/c and a small kitchen attached, the other (just around the corner) with a mix of rooms, including doubles. Dorms €13, doubles €38
Koper Pristaniška ulica 3 ☎ 05 610 0500, ⊛ terme-catez

.si. The only hotel in the centre, this rather soulless concrete lump could do with some love and attention, but the rooms are decent enough, if not particularly exciting. Expensive, too. €150
Vodišek Kolodvorska cesta 2 ☎ 05 639 2468, ⊛ hotel-vodisek.com. Situated in a small shopping complex midway between the stations and the town centre, with neat, bright, a/c rooms; triples and quads, too. €88

EATING

Capra Pristaniška ulica 3 ☎ 041 602 030, ⊛ capra.si. Koper's best restaurant has a large covered terrace, a cool, grey-painted interior and the most interesting menu in town: cuttlefish salad, salted cod with truffles and home-made *fuži* with scampi (€15) are typical. Mon–Thurs & Sun 8am–10pm, Fri & Sat 8am–11pm.

Istrska Klet Slavček Župančičeva ulica 39 ☎ 05 627 6729. This warm and welcoming place has been going strong for the best part of fifty years, and the locals love it. Its simplicity is its charm, with wine straight from the barrel and filling domestic fare including *pršut* and cheese, calamari and fish goulash (€9). Daily except Sat 8am–10pm.

Kroštola Kopališko nabrežje 1 ☎ 05 627 8178. If you fancy a beachside rendezvous, you could do worse than head to this sprawling café doling out big mugs of *bela kava* (white coffee) and pastries. Daily 7.30am–10pm.

Loggia Café Titov trg 1 ☎ 030 691 608. Stalwart café that's been pulling in the punters for years, thanks in the main to its impressive raised terrace overlooking Koper's loveliest square.

The coffee's not bad either, and it's a good spot for a sundowner. Mon–Fri 7am–10pm, Sat & Sun 7am–5pm.

Vigo Pristaniška ulica 3 ☎ 051 740 777. In a town full of terrific ice-cream parlours, this bright, contemporary outlet takes some beating; flavours include Piemonte hazelnut or white chocolate and mango, all at a very reasonable €1.40 a scoop. Daily 10am–8pm.

DRINKING

Bar Cameral Čevljarska ulica 14 ☎ 041 323 380, ⓦ cameral.si. The most stylish bar in town, with a bare-brick interior harbouring a piano, shelves of books and other knick-knacks, and a funky soundtrack; as well as

quality local wines, there's a stellar selection of craft beers, including Brewdog from Scotland and Founders from the US. Mon–Sat 7am–11pm.

Izola

Jutting out to sea on a rounded promontory 6km south of Koper, **IZOLA** is a busy little fishing town and one of the country's fastest-growing tourist destinations. Though most visitors come here for the **beaches**, Izola possesses an endearing old town core, whose narrow, sloping streets and pastel-coloured tenements delight in their crumbling charm.

Brief history

Numerous local ruins bear testament to the long-standing presence of the **Romans** hereabouts, not least in Simon's Bay, where the ancient port of Heliaetum was located – it's said that, at very low tide, parts of the ancient pier are still visible. First mentioned in historical sources in 972 AD as Insula, the town enjoyed a brief period of autonomy before becoming a satellite of **Venice** in 1280, which it remained until the Republic's downfall in 1797; around the same time, both the town wall and its two gates were pulled down, and the town (hitherto an island) was finally connected to the mainland. Thereafter, the town acquired the northern Adriatic's largest **fishing fleet**, as well as a number of fish canneries, the first of which opened in 1879. While **tourism** has since supplanted the industry as the main source of income, the town's fishing tradition remains alive and kicking.

Ljubljanska ulica and Manziolijev trg

From the main square, Trg Republike, it's a short walk to **Ljubljanska ulica**, a pleasant, curling street accommodating a disproportionate number of **artists' workshops and galleries**. The end of Ljubljanska ulica opens up onto **Manziolijev trg**, Izola's loveliest square, and on which stands the **Cerkev Sv Marija** (Church of St Mary), whose oldest parts date from the ninth century. Directly opposite the church is the restored Venetian late-Gothic **Manzioli Palace**, now the town's Italian centre.

Besenghi degli Ughi Palace

Gregorčičeva ulica 76

The town's most important architectural set piece is the **Besenghi degli Ughi Palace**, distinguished by its pale blue, stucco-ornamented wrought-iron grilles, albeit now in need of a lick of paint. Its interior, too, is festooned with stuccowork, but is especially worth viewing for its first-floor salon, furnished with a fine wooden balcony and illusionist ceiling piece – the palace is now home to a music school.

Muzej Parenzana

Ulica Alma Vivode 3 • Tues–Sat 9am–noon & 6–8pm, Sun 9am–noon • €2.50 • ☎ 05 641 7357, ⓦ parenzana,net

The engaging **Muzej Parenzana** (Parenzana Museum) is named after the Parenzana Line, once the most important transport link between Central Europe and Istria;

built in 1902 by the Austrians, the line ran between Trieste and Poreč (in Croatia), passing through Koper, Izola and Portorož along the way, until 1937 when Mussolini pulled the plug and closed it. As well as a replica model of the railway, and other items pertaining to its heritage, the museum contains various collections related to Izola's main industries, notably lace and fishing; local sporting heroes get a look-in too. There's also a wonderful assortment of model boats, including several examples of a *batana*, a traditional flat-bottomed fishing vessel peculiar to this region.

Incidentally, the locomotive that used to chug up and down the Parenzana line is stationed at the town's eastern entrance by the *Jadranka* campsite. Meanwhile, the line – passing through settlements, hills, vineyards and all the old tunnels – has been transformed into a **walking and cycle track**; ask at the tourist office (see below).

Beaches

One of the coast's best **beaches** is at **Simonov zaliv** (Simon's Bay), 1.5km west of the centre; backed by pine trees and a large expanse of grass, this Blue Flag pebble beach has good facilities including water slides and a play area for kids, as well as sports activities (pedaloes €10 for 30min; €15/1hr; tubes €20 for 15min; stand-up paddles €7 for 30min, €10/1hr; kayaks €14/1hr). The other main strand is the slightly less developed, but no less popular, **Svetilnik beach**, a rocky and grassy affair just north of Veliki trg on the tip of the old town core.

ARRIVAL AND INFORMATION

IZOLA

By bus The town's main bus stop, with services from Koper (every 20–30min; 10min) and Piran (every 20–30min; 20min) is on Trg Republike, from where it's a 100m walk west to the old town core.

Tourist office Ljubljanska ulica 17 (daily: June–Sept 9am–8pm; Oct–May 9am–4pm; ☎ 05 640 1050, ⦿ izola.eu).

ACCOMMODATION

For **private accommodation**, head to the Bele Skale agency, next to the bus stop at Cankarjev drevored 2 (July & Aug Mon–Fri 9am–3pm & 4–7pm, Sat 9am–1pm; Sept–June Mon–Fri 9am–5pm, Sat 9am–noon; ☎ 05 640 3555, ⦿ beleskale.si); in summer, expect to pay around €45/night for a room.

Hostel Alieti Dvoriščina ulica 24 ☎ 051 670 680, ⦿ hostel-alieti.si. Sweet, tidily run hostel in a superbly renovated townhouse, holding four- and six-bed dorms, all with a/c and a shared bathroom on each floor; there's also a mansard room with seven mattresses. Breakfast, consisting of fresh croissants, juice and coffee or tea, costs just €2. **€20**

Marina Veliki trg 11 ☎ 05 660 4100, ⦿ hotelmarina.si. A cut above anything else in town, this congenial hotel can't be beaten for location (it's a stone's throw from the water), comfort or efficiency; variously sized, well-turned-out rooms have floor-to-ceiling windows, and there's a beautifully designed spa and superb restaurant (see below). **€110**

EATING AND DRINKING

Gušt Drevored 1 Maja ☎ 031 606 040, ⦿ gostilna-gust .si. Just south of Trg Republike, the almost pubby-like *Gušt* is the most convivial restaurant along this popular promenade, serving around two dozen varieties of pizza, steaming plates of pasta and spaghetti, soups, salads and surprises such as grilled beef with truffles. Daily 11am–10pm.

Manzioli Wine Bar Manziolijev trg 5 ☎ 05 616 2137. Occupying the ground floor of an erstwhile Venetian Gothic palace, this classy little bar on the square of the same name – all bare brick and wooden beams – is a delightful spot to sample wines from the Koper hinterland.

Daily 8am–midnight.

★**Marina** Veliki trg 11 ☎ 05 605 333, ⦿ hotelmarina .si. Like the hotel it's housed in (see above), this a cut above everything else in Izola, from the crisp, beautifully set tables on the vine-shaded terrace to the food itself; as you'd expect, fish is the order of the day (the daily catch is brought out on a trolley for you to select). Try sea bass carpaccio or marinated oysters steamed in *malvazia* wine (€4 each), or perhaps something from the land, like pork fillet with olive polenta and fresh truffles (€14). Daily noon–10pm.

NIGHTLIFE

Ambasada Gavioli Industrijska cesta 10 ☎ 031 255 706, ⓦ ambasadagavioli.si. Located out in the industrial zone east of town, this is, by general consensus, the coast's premier nightclub – indeed, it's one of the region's finest – attracting world-class DJs and electronica acts. Around €15. Fri & Sat.

Strunjan

A few kilometres along the coast from Izola is **STRUNJAN**, a small, widely dispersed settlement, part of which has been turned into a **nature reserve**. North of the large **Stjuža lagoon**, which backs onto the beach, a cobbled road trundles up to the top of the cliffs, passing the Church of St Mary and a small snack bar along the way. This stretch of coastline is unique along the Adriatic for its distinctive layers of Flysch sediment, composed of sandstone, marl and turbidite; its most prominent feature is **Cape Ronek** (Rtii Ronek) at its northernmost point, home to what few sub-Mediterranean species exist in the region, such as myrtle and strawberry trees. Below, in the **Bay of St Cross** (Zaliv Sv Križa), the large bed of seaweed shelters fan-mussels, sea dates and crabs. From the clifftop several paths wind down to the rocky beaches below, popular with naturists. Retracing your steps back to the abandoned saltpans, where the brackish water supports a wide range of fauna, and then walking north along the narrow path, brings you to another, busier, beach.

ARRIVAL AND DEPARTURE   **STRUNJAN**

All Koper–Piran **buses** (hourly) stop just off the main road.

Piran

Located on the tip of a long, tapering peninsula that projects like a lizard's tail into the Adriatic, **PIRAN** – the most Italianate of the coastal towns – is simply delightful. Having retained its compact **medieval** shape and character, the town is a tangle of arched alleys and tightly packed ranks of houses, fantastic Venetian-inspired architecture and exquisite little churches.

Brief history

Major urban development first occurred during the seventh century following the fall of the Roman Empire, when Piran became a heavily fortified "castrum". Under **Venetian** rule, which began here in 1283, the town's physical appearance changed considerably, as further town walls were erected to supplement the existing ones – which at that time encompassed the western Punta district at the end of the promontory. Economically, too, Piran was in good shape, thanks in no small measure to its three **saltworks** – in Sečovlje, Strunjan and Lucija, of which only the first is still operational. A prolonged period of decline ensued thereafter, first under the Habsburgs, and then, between the two world wars, the Italians. However, the development of nearby Portorož as a popular health resort, and the construction of the Lucija–Piran rail line, last operational in 1956, led to an increase in visitors to the town. While relations with Italy are today on a somewhat better footing, a prolonged dispute with Croatia over **fishing rights** in the Bay of Piran continues to cast a shadow.

Tartinijev trg

Piran's most obvious point of reference is the striking, marble-surfaced **Tartinijev trg** (Tartini Square), which features a bronze statue of the acclaimed violinist Giuseppe Tartini (1692–1770). The building on the square's west side is the old **courthouse**; adjacent is the **town hall**, dating from the late nineteenth century and distinguished by four graceful pillars, the lower parts of which are beautifully ornamented; in the central axis is the ubiquitous lion relief with an open book (see p.185). The oldest preserved

3

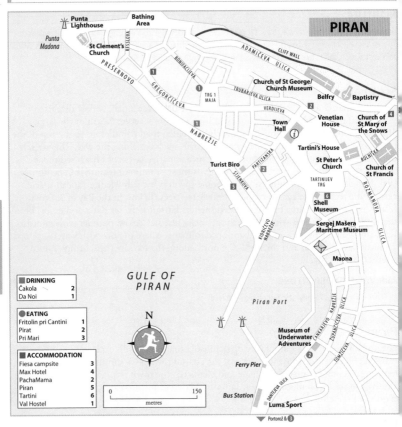

building here is the Gothic **Benečanke hiša** (Venetian House) at no. 10, a fifteenth-century edifice showcasing outstanding stonemasonry, exemplified by its superb corner balcony. The relief under the windows on the second floor bears the inscription "Lassa pur dir" ("Let them talk"), a retort to gossiping townsfolk disapproving of a wealthy merchant's romantic liaisons with a local girl.

Tartinijeva hiša

Tartinijev trg 7 • July & Aug daily 9am–noon & 6–9pm; Sept–May Tues–Sun 11am–noon & 5–6pm • €2 • ☎ 05 671 0040, ⓦ pomorskimuzej.si

The modest **Tartinijeva hiša** (Tartini's House) is where the eponymous musician was born in 1692. After being schooled in Koper, Tartini left Piran for Padua, in Italy, and remained there for the greater part of his life, composing, teaching and performing, before later devoting himself to theoretical and pedagogical issues. One room of the birthplace has been converted into a small memorial space containing one of his four violins – the whereabouts of the other three are unknown – his death mask, and scores of books, diaries and letters.

Cerkev Sv petra

On the square's north side, the early nineteenth-century **Cerkev Sv petra** (St Peter's Church) is fairly unremarkable save for the **Crucifix from Piran**, one of three such medieval masterpieces on the eastern Adriatic (the others are in Split, in Croatia, and

Kotor, in Montenegro). This much-restored polychrome sculpture, a beautifully mournful Christ nailed to a tree-shaped cross, is believed to have been completed some time in the fourteenth century, though its creator is unknown. Unfortunately, owing to previous theft and vandalism, the church can only be viewed through metal grilles – as can most of the churches in town.

Muzej Školjk

Tartinijev trg 15 • March–May, Oct & Nov Tues–Sun 11am–6pm; June–Sept daily 10am–8pm; Dec–Feb call in advance • €4 • ☎ 040 758 900, Ⓦ sveti-skoljk.si

The **Muzej Školjk** (Shell Museum) is a minor delight, a dazzling private collection of more than four thousand shells from all over the world. Represented are tropical land snails, freshwater snails, sea shells, cone shells, pearl shells, clams and so on. Standouts include a stunning albino shell from Morocco and some beautifully patterned polymita shells from Cuba; keep your eyes peeled, too, for the *Papustyla pulcherrima*, a rare, and extraordinary emerald-green coloured tree snail from Papua New Guinea. What you can't fail to miss is the world's largest clam, a magnificent specimen from the Indian Ocean weighing 150kg.

Trg 1 Maja

Trg 1 Maja (First of May Square), once the heart of the town, is now a pleasantly scruffy space framed by peeling Baroque edifices. Located under the square's vast elevated deck and guarded by allegorical stone statues of law and justice is a stone rainwater cistern, built in 1776 following a drought in order to conserve water; at the rear, the two statues of babies – one holding a pot, the other a fish – once connected surrounding gutters with the cistern.

Cerkev Sv Jurija

Museum Daily 11am–5pm • €1.50 • **Belfry** Daily 11am–5pm • €1

Crowning a commanding spot on a steep rise to the north of town is the temple-like **Cerkev Sv Jurija** (Church of St George), built some time around the twelfth century, but whose present appearance dates from 1637. It's a classic example of a simple Baroque hall-church, lined with seven mighty altars, each laden with paintings by Venetian and Dutch artists; the second altar on the left also incorporates a large sculpture of St George slaying the dragon. Take a look, too, at the cream and gold church organ, a magnificent specimen designed in 1746 by the Venetian master organ builder Peter Nakič. The unusually long and deep presbytery boasts the largest oil on canvas painting in the country, a colourful depiction of the martyrdom of St George (1844).

Between the church and **Baptistry** – where a large Roman sarcophagus can be viewed – is the monumental **belfry**, a fine-looking structure built in 1609 and modelled on the campanile in St Mark's Square, Venice – indeed, the bell was cast in Venice in 1477. If you thought the views from the church terrace were impressive, then you'll be wowed by the sensational vista of the Adriatic from atop the 46m-high tower.

Župnijski muzej

The small **Župnijski muzej** (Church Museum) displays a glittering hoard of church treasures, including bejewelled chalices, reliquaries and staffs – the most memorable piece is a marvellous silver-coated sculpture of St George and the Dragon. One floor below are some well-preserved archeological remains from an eighth-century Roman temple and a section of the church as it was in the fourteenth century; look out for the protruding bones in the corner. The sacristy, held in the basement, is especially interesting for its superb pictures illustrating the restoration process of the Crucifix from Piran, now in St Peter's Church (see opposite), and a 400-year-old wooden model of St George's Church thought to be the oldest of its type in the country.

Cerkev Marije Snežne and Cerkev Sv Frančiška

Among the tightly knit web of streets just below the Church of St George is a cluster of beautiful little churches. At the corner of Istrska and Bolniška, the delightfully named **Cerkev Marije Snežne** (Church of St Mary of the Snows) features a marvellous Baroque altar and two broad canvases depicting the Annunciation and other scenes from the life of the Virgin Mary.

Opposite is the fourteenth-century, but much remodelled, **Cerkev Sv Frančiška** (Church of St Francis), whose impressive gallery of paintings would be even more valuable had the most important one – *Mary with all the Saints* by Vittore Carpaccio – not been taken to Italy in 1940. It's an issue that still rankles with Slovenes, many of whom insist that this and other valuable Renaissance works be returned to Slovenia (these are collectively known as "Istria's Jewels", some of which are currently on display in Rome). The adjoining **Minorite Monastery** incorporates a bright atrium (*Križni Hodnik*, or *Passage of the Cross*), entered via a lovely stone-carved portal; the acoustics in the atrium are splendid, so try and catch one of the weekly chamber concerts (usually Thursdays), held between early July and early August.

Town walls

Daily: April–Oct 8am–9pm; Nov–March 9am–5pm • €1 (put a coin in the turnstile)

Ranged across the top of Mogoron hill (accessible via Ulica IX. korpusa or Rožmanova ulica) is a 200m stretch of the old **town walls**, completed between the late fifteenth and early sixteenth centuries and perforated with seven inspiring-looking towers; at the southern end of the wall stands the Gothic **Rašporska vrata** (Rašpor Gate). The walls, now connected by specially constructed walkways and stairs, offer spectacular views of the red-roofed townhouses below and the Bay of Piran stretching away in the distance.

Pomorski muzej Sergej Mašera

Cankarjevo nabrežje 3 • Tues–Sun: July & Aug 9am–noon & 5–9pm; Sept–June 9am–5pm • €3.50 • ☎ 05 671 0040, ⓦ pomorskimuzej.si

Occupying the splendid nineteenth-century **Gabrielli Palace** is the **Pomorski muzej Sergej Mašera** (Sergej Mašera Maritime Museum), named after the naval commander whose destroyer, *Zagreb*, was blown up off the Croatian coast during World War II. The highlight of this enjoyable collection, which charts Slovenia's seafaring exploits, is its outstanding ensemble of eighteenth-century model ships – built as teaching aids for future naval officers and nautical engineers – made in the Gruber workshop in Ljubljana; look out for the Austrian warship, *Emperor Charles VI*. On the ground floor there is a fine, and cleverly presented, display of underwater archeological finds from the Slovene Istrian coast, consisting mainly of Roman amphorae, fragments of earthen vessels and lead tiles and hoops; there's also an informative ethnological saltworks collection, which will especially appeal if you're thinking of visiting the saltpans in Sečovlje (see p.196).

Muzej podvodnih dejavnosti

Zupančičeva ulica 24 • June–Sept daily 10.30am–8pm; Oct–May Fri–Sun 11am–6pm • €3 • ☎ 041 685 379, ⓦ muzejpodvodnihdejavnosti.si

While it might not quite live up to its enthusiastic title, the **Muzej podvodnih dejavnostni** (Museum of Underwater Adventures) does an impressive job of charting the region's considerable contribution to underwater discovery. Diving takes centre stage, with a fine assemblage of apparatus from the Austro-Hungarian Imperial and Royal Navy, including helmets, boots and a rare back regulator. Following the collapse of the Austro-Hungarian Empire, the Royal Yugoslav Navy was established in 1921, and, conveniently, adopted many of the former's vessels, as well as its naval personnel, most of whom were of Slovene or Croatian origin anyway.

ARRIVAL AND INFORMATION PIRAN

By bus The station is on Dantejeva ulica, from where it's a pleasant 400m walk past the bustling little fishing harbour to Tartinijev trg.

Destinations Koper (every 20–30min; 30min); Ljubljana

(Mon–Fri 6 daily, Sat & Sun 4 daily; 2hr 40min); Portorož (every 15–30min; 10min); Sečovlje (Mon–Fri 10 daily, Sat 4 daily; 15min).

By car Only residents are allowed to park in Piran; visitors must park in the covered garage just outside town in Fornaci (about a 10min walk; €17/day, €7.50 if you are staying

overnight), though anyone staying the night can drop off luggage first. There are free shuttles (every 10min) back into Piran from the open-air car park just below the garage.

Tourist office Next to the town hall at Tartinijev trg 2 (daily: June & Sept 9am–7pm; July & Aug 9am–10pm; Oct–May 9am–5pm; ☎05 673 4440, ⓦportoroz.si).

ACTIVITIES

Beaches Piran doesn't have any conventional beaches, but the lively promenade east of the Punta lighthouse is the town's main (concrete) bathing area.

Bike rental Luma Šport, opposite the bus station at Dantejeva ulica 3 (Mon–Fri 9am–noon & 5–8pm, Sat & Sun 9am–1pm; €10/4hr, €15/day; ☎041 781 414, ⓦcyclingistria .com); particularly useful if you're thinking of heading to the

saltpans in Sečovlje. They also do repairs and servicing.

Boat trips The *San Frangisk* catamaran sails between Piran and Venice (May–Sept; departing Piran Sat 8.30am, Sun 7.30am, returning from Venice 5.15pm; €70 one-way).

Diving Sub-net, on the seafront at Prešernovo nabrežje 24 (☎05 673 2218, ⓦsub-net.si), offers a comprehensive programme; expect to pay around €35 for an hour's dive.

ACCOMMODATION

Piran has a surprisingly limited amount of accommodation, though what there is is pretty decent; note that **rates** drop dramatically outside the summer season. Another possibility is **private accommodation**, available through Maona, midway between the bus station and the main square at Cankarjevo nabrežje 7 (April–June, Sept & Oct Mon–Sat 9am–2pm; July & Aug Mon–Sat 9am–1pm & 3–6pm, Sun 9am–1pm & 4–6pm; ☎05 673 4520, ⓦmaona.si), or Turist Biro, opposite the *Hotel Piran* at Tomažičeva 3 (June–Sept Mon–Sat 10am–1pm & 4–6pm; Oct–May Mon–Fri 10am–1pm & 4–6pm; ☎05 673 2509, ⓦturistbiro.si); in high season expect to pay around €60 for a double room without breakfast.

Fiesa campsite Fiesa Bay, 1km east of Piran 59 ☎05 674 6230. Set back from the beach, this is a tidy, if somewhat basic and cramped, site with all the requisite facilities. The quickest way to get here by foot is to follow the coastal path that runs east from the Church of St George. May–Sept. **€24**

★**Max Hotel** Ulica IX korpusa 26 ☎05 673 3436, ⓦmaxpiran.com. Welcoming guesthouse in an eighteenth-century townhouse with six differently coloured rooms (sunflower yellow, mint green, sky blue, for example) with handcrafted wooden cupboards, intricately woven floor rugs and wall-mounted artwork; all rooms are triple-glazed, so bells from the neighbouring St George's church are not an issue. The cosy, brick-walled breakfast bar rounds things off nicely. Great value. **€65**

PachaMama Trubarjeva ulica 8 ☎059 183 495, ⓦpachamama.si. Named in honour of the owner's love of Inca mythology, this guesthouse has ample, smartly designed rooms in smooth natural woods, with splashes of grey and the occasional bit of exposed stone wall (one room even retains a segment of the original city walls), but

are otherwise unadorned save for the odd photograph of an Andean Indian tribe. Breakfast is taken on a pocket-sized stone terrace. **€70**

Piran Stjenkova ulica 1 ☎05 666 7100, ⓦhoteli-piran .si. Occupying a plum waterfront location, the *Piran* offers a level of comfort way beyond anything else in town, with supremely polished rooms. If you're lucky enough to bag a sea-facing one, you could quite happily spend all day on the balcony surveying the vista. **€140**

Tartini Tartinijev trg 15 ☎05 671 1000, ⓦhotel -tartini-piran.com. Superbly positioned, this moderately elegant establishment is ultimately a little disappointing; however, the a/c rooms feature colourful wood-furnishings and balconies, some with sea views, and there's a splendid rooftop terrace. **€135**

Val Hostel Gregorčičeva ulica 38a ☎05 673 2555, ⓦhostel-val.com. Secreted away among an atmospheric warren of alleys, this friendly, well-run hostel is actually more of a guesthouse; one-, two- and three-bedded rooms have colourful patchwork duvets, shared showers, laundry facilities and a good restaurant. Breakfast included. Doubles **€60**

EATING

Give the row of very touristy, very samey, and overpriced, seafood restaurants lining the **waterfront promenade** (Prešernovo nabrežje) a wide berth and explore the back streets for better food and atmosphere.

Fritolin pri Cantini Trg 1 Maja ☎041 873 872. Find a table, place your order at the vine-covered hatch and wait for the bell to ring before collecting your food, which could be squid and chips (€10), grilled tuna or gratin of mussels

with tomato and garlic, all of it delicious. There's also the added bonus of dining on the most appealing square in town. Daily noon–midnight.

Pirat Zupančičeva ulica 24 ☎05 616 488. A pleasant

antidote to the town's touristy restaurants, with terrific seafood (clams, fried squid, langoustine risotto) served in copper bowls and a good-value daily menu (soup, salad and main dish, though not seafood) for €7. Daily 10am–11pm. **Pri Mari** Dantejeva ulica 17 ☎ 05 673 4735, ⓦ primari

-piran.com. Just beyond the bus station, this homely, Italian-style trattoria offers some terrific dishes such as spicy squid pasta or fillet of tuna on a bed of rocket salad (€12); with its understated maritime decor, it looks fab too. Tues–Sat noon–4pm & 6–10pm, Sun 2–6pm.

DRINKING

Čakola Partizanska ulica 2 ☎ 051 694 110. Endearing little corner café-bar that's much frequented by locals enjoying a natter over a morning coffee and croissant or, later on, a glass or two of the excellent local wine. Daily 8am–midnight.

Da Noi Prešernovo nabrežje 4 ☎ 041 226 885. The town's best drinking spot, whose cool, breezy seafront terrace is complemented by a swinging, cellar-style bar that hosts live rock music most Thursdays. Mon–Thurs & Sun 8am–1am, Fri & Sat 8am–3am.

Portorož and around

3

Situated in its own sunny sheltered bay just 2km south of Piran, **PORTOROŽ** (Port of Roses) is Slovenia's major beach resort. While it may feel like stepping into a cold shower after Piran's charm, it's a likeable enough place, and despite possessing all the customary trappings of your average seaside resort, it's by no means brash; moreover, the **beaches** are clean, safe and well maintained, and there's enough going on here to keep activity-seekers happy. Pretty much everything of note is located on **Obala**, the main strip running through town.

Brief history

The town's modern appearance belies a history dating back to the **thirteenth century**, when Benedictine monks from the nearby Monastery of St Lawrence cured a range of diseases using the local mineral-rich brine and mud from the saltpans, the same health-inducing properties that led to the development of Portorož as a popular **resort** in the nineteenth century. The resort's first hotel – originally intended to accommodate the military – went up in 1830, followed by the once magnificent *Palace Hotel* in 1912, built in expectation of a visit by Emperor Franz Jozef. While Portorož remains a popular health and treatment centre, most visitors today come here for the more traditional **beach** diversions.

ARRIVAL AND INFORMATION

PORTOROŽ

On foot It's a gentle 30min walk from Piran to Portorož via a seafront footpath running through the Bernadin complex.

By bus The main bus stop is midway along Obala, though most buses stop at regular intervals along the street.

Destinations Koper (every 20–30min; 25min); Piran (every 15–30min; 10min).

Tourist office Across the road from the bus stop at Obala 16 (daily: June & Sept 9am–7pm; July & Aug 9am–10pm; Oct–May 9am–5pm; ☎ 05 674 2220, ⓦ portoroz.si).

Bike rental Atlas Express agency, Obala 55 (Mon–Fri 9am–4pm, Sat 9am–noon; ☎ 05 674 5078; €12/6hr, €18/day).

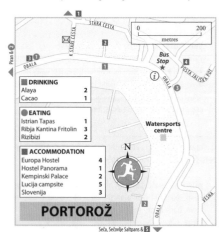

DRINKING
Alaya	2
Cacao	1

EATING
Istrian Tapas	1
Ribja Kantina Fritolin	3
Rizibizi	2

ACCOMMODATION
Europa Hostel	4
Hostel Panorama	1
Kempinski Palace	2
Lucija campsite	5
Slovenija	3

PORTOROŽ

ACCOMMODATION

As befits Slovenia's major beach resort, Portorož is awash with hotels, though most are characterless establishments managed by small groups of companies and are very expensive, in summer at least; there are, though, some decent **hostels**, a fabulous **campsite**, and plentiful **private accommodation**, for which you should head to Turist Biro at Obala 57 (March–May,

PORTOROŽ BEACHES AND ACTIVITIES

Portorož's main **beach**, an incongruous mix of sand, grass and concrete, is clean and well maintained, with lifeguards along the shore and a wide range of facilities available, including parasols and sunbeds for rent (€5/day). Inevitably, it can get tremendously crowded, though there's usually enough space to go around; otherwise you could head to one of several **private beaches** (around €5) – in effect those owned by the hotels – the best of which is the one in front of the *Slovenija*. All these designated beaches are roped off and it is forbidden to swim outside the boundary. There are other spots along the beachfront (essentially concrete banks) where you can bathe without restriction.

ACTIVITIES

There are activities aplenty to be had on the main beach and nearby. In addition to those listed below there is also a good pool opposite the *Metropol Hotel* (daily 9am–6pm; €5), next door to which are **tennis** courts (€12 for 1hr).

Laguna Waterpark Bernardin Complex, out towards Piran (☎ 05 695 8902, ⓦ bernardingroup.si). A fabulous swimming pool (Mon–Fri €13 for the day, Sat & Sun €16/day), with a great section for kids, and Turkish and Finnish saunas (Mon–Fri €12 for 2hr, Sat & Sun €14). Daily 7am–8pm.

Lepa Vida Thalasso Spa In the heart of the Sečovlje saltpans (see p.196) ☎ 05 672 1360, ⓦ thalasso-lepavida.si. Something a little special. Making the most of the natural ingredients, this small but stunningly conceived open-air complex (€18 for two hours, €30 for four) comprises a main sea-water swimming pool plus several smaller brine and pebble pools; various treatments are also available, including the popular saltpan mud wrap (€20 for 30min). Once done, enjoy a coffee or a cocktail in the beach bar. May–Sept daily 10am–6pm.

Watersports centre Central kiosk, main beach ☎ 070 348 480, ⓦ vodnisporti.eu. A variety of activities including kayaking (€10 for 1hr), standup paddling (€12 for 1hr; €40 for a two-hour course), water-skiing (€45 for 15min), jet-skiing (€40 for 15min) and tubes (€17 for 10min). June to mid-Sept.

Oct & Nov Mon–Fri 10am–1pm & 4–6pm; June–Sept daily 9am–1pm & 4–7pm; ☎ 05 674 1055, ⓦ turistbiro.si); they have a comprehensive stock of rooms and apartments, all of which are priced according to category and distance from the sea.

Europa Hostel Senčna pot 2 ☎ 05 903 2574, ⓦ ehp.si. Brilliantly located right behind the main bus stop, the dorms – variously three- to ten-bedded, some en suite – are named and themed after a particular country; they're a little boxy but very clean. Breakfast included. Dorms €22

Hostel Panorama Šentjane 25 ☎ 031 678 767, ⓦ hostelportoroz.si. Large hostel with a range of dorms and apartments, high up in the hills halfway between Portorož and Piran, with fine views of the Istrian coast. There's no public transport, so expect a stiff 30min walk. Breakfast included. Dorms €23, doubles €48

Kempinski Palace Obala 45 ☎ 05 692 7000, ⓦ kempinski.com. Fronted by tall palms and silky lawns, this is the coast's most opulent hotel. Built in 1912, it has had a majestic restoration, resulting in stunningly appointed rooms and first-rate facilities, including a gorgeous pool and a wonderful breakfast terrace – which is worth (an expensive) coffee even if you're not staying here. €250

★ **Lucija campsite** Seča 204, 2km south of the main bus stop in the suburb of Lucija ☎ 05 690 6000, ⓦ camp-lucija.si. Large, superbly equipped site with three categories of pitch priced according to location – terrace, standard and seaside – the last of which affords marvellous water views. Facilities include a shop, playground, tennis and mini-golf, a restaurant and a superb beach bar. €24

Slovenija Obala 33 ☎ 05 692 9001, ⓦ lifeclass.net. From the outside, this looks like pretty much any other hotel along the main strip, but of all the resort's luxury hotels it's the most appealing, its lavishly appointed rooms offering ultimate comfort. It's by no means cheap, but you do also get access to the hotel's complex of indoor pools as well as its own bit of beach. €210

EATING

Istrian Tapas Obala 33 ☎ 05 692 5010, ⓦ lifeclass.net. Tapas is a refreshingly new concept hereabouts and one that this modern, shiny place – attached to the *Slovenija* hotel – manages to pull off with style. Sea bass tartar, truffle omelette and lamb ravioli are typical dishes, each costing around €2.50; you're better off paying €5 for three plates, €8 for five or €12 for seven. Daily noon–11pm.

Ribja Kantina Fritolin Obala 55 ☎ 05 674 0210. Cheap

and cheerful fish restaurant with nautical regalia hanging from the walls and ceilings and simple bench seating inside and out. The food is uncomplicated and terrific; anchovies and cheese, smoked mackerel, scallops (€3.50 each) and squid (€8.50), plus just about whatever other type of fish you can think of. Daily 11am–11pm.

Rizbizi Vilfanova 10 ⓣ05 993 5320, ⓦrizibizi.si. Roughly midway between Portorož and Piran, this sublime restaurant has an elevated position and fabulous sea views from the dining room and the tidy stone terrace. Food, meanwhile, is mouthwateringly light and fresh, with dishes such as octopus with asparagus, and cornflake-encrusted sea bass with black and white polenta (€14). Daily noon–11pm.

DRINKING AND NIGHTLIFE

There are plenty of places to **drink** in Portorož, with an array of upbeat cafés, bars and clubs along Obala. Also look out for films and concerts at the **open-air theatre** (Avditorij Portorož), behind the bus station at Senčna pot 8 (ⓣ05 676 6777, ⓦavditoriji.si).

Alaya Obala 22 ⓣ051 332 233, ⓦalaya.si. The most popular of the open-air beach bars, this sprawling, tropically themed hangout at the southern end of the beach has regular live music and party nights, ranging from Latin and salsa to house and dance. Mon–Sat 9am–3am.

Cacao Obala 14 ⓣ05 674 1035, ⓦcacao.si. This laidback bar sports a cool, loungey interior and L-shaped deck terrace facing the beach; best of all, perhaps, it serves the finest ice cream anywhere along the coast. Mon–Thurs & Sun 8am–10pm, Fri & Sat 8am–midnight.

3

Seča

If you want to leave the crowds behind, take a stroll over to **Seča**, 2km south of town. Dispersed among thick rows of olive trees throughout the western end of this knobbly peninsula is the **Forma Viva Sculpture Park** (accessible either via the road behind the campsite or a set of steps within the campsite), one of several such sculpture parks in Slovenia. Each park displays works of art made from a different material; this grouping, opened in 1961, consists of more than one hundred greying, weather-worn pieces carved from stone. Though the odd piece might be of interest, even better are the **views** back to Portorož and the sea.

Sečoveljske soline

Daily: April–Oct 8am–9pm; Nov–March 8am–5pm • €7 including bike rental • ⓣ05 672 1350, ⓦkpss.si • There's no public transport directly to the saltpans, so if you haven't got your own transport, getting here is a little tricky: travelling to the Lera part, get the bus driver to drop you off by the road down to the entrance; if heading to Fontanigge, the nearest you can get by bus is the village of Sečovlje itself, around 1km before the border crossing, though you might be able to jump on a Croatia-bound bus and get off at the border crossing (either way, take your passport, as you will have to pass through Slovenian customs) – 100m beyond the crossing (but before the Croatian border – you are now in "no man's land"), a sign on your right points to the museum

Running along the border with Croatia, some 3km south of Portorož, are the **Sečoveljske soline** (Sečovlje saltpans), once the most extensive saltpans in Slovenia, but now part of the **Krajinski park Sečoveljske soline** (Sečovlje Salina Nature Park). Although salt is still harvested in the northern section of the park (Lera), the larger southern part (Fontanigge) – traversed by vast grids of canals, dykes and pools – has been out of commission since the late 1960s.

Among the most important heritage sites in the country – it is, along with the Škocjan Caves, on the Ramsar List of internationally protected wetlands – the rich, salt-impregnated soil supports a wide variety of saltwater (halophytic) **flora**, sheltering more than forty species of plant, many of which feature on the "Red List" (Slovenia's list of endangered plant and animal species), and a range of land vertebrates, including *Suncus etruscus*, a tiny shrew alleged to be Europe's smallest mammal. **Birdlife**, too, is prominent; the warm, sub-Mediterranean climate and abundance of food in the basins attracts large numbers of migratory birds, such as the common coot and great cormorant, while herons, gulls and egrets have established themselves as permanent residents.

SALT OF THE EARTH

Salt harvesting has been practised along the Slovenian coast since the first saltpans were introduced in Piran some time in the fourteenth century. Although the pans remain at Strunjan, Sečovlje is now the only place where harvesting still takes place, albeit on a much smaller scale than in its heyday during the first half of the twentieth century, when more than forty thousand tonnes of salt were yielded annually – today around five thousand tonnes are harvested each year.

The **saltpans** are supplied by seawater funnelled along several large channels, before settling in dammed crystallization basins lined with "petola" (artificially grown crust consisting of algae, gypsum and clay), a method used so as to prevent the salt mixing with sea mud and other sediments. The water is then slowly removed with the aid of large wind-powered pumps, while the remainder evaporates in the sun as the salt crystallizes. After being drained and washed, the salt would be carted off to large warehouses (*skladišča soli*) sited along the coast, before being distributed; there's a good example of one of these (now disused) warehouses in Portorož, near the Bernardin complex.

Saltpanners' (*solinarji*) dwellings – inhabited by the entire family, but only during the harvesting season (April to September) – were extremely modest, comprising a large downstairs storage room and, upstairs, living quarters, divided into a couple of bedrooms and a joint living and kitchen area; the most important aspects of the building, however, were the windows and doors, positioned on both sides of the house so that changes in the weather could be carefully observed.

Visiting the park

There are two official **entrances** to the park; the main one is at Lera, reached via a road which branches off in the village of Seča. On reaching the hut, it's an 800m walk to the park's souvenir shop, which stocks beautifully packaged, salt-related paraphernalia, then another 800m to the **visitor centre**, which gives detailed explanations of the salt-making process via a multimedia presentation and relief maps. The second entrance is at Fontanigge; from the main road (see opposite), a long, dusty track runs alongside the Dragonje River, which marks the border between Slovenia and Croatia. After the first kilometre or so (by which point, if you're not driving, you'll probably have despaired at the monotony of the walk), you'll reach the entrance, which is also as far as cars can go; here you can rent a bike, which is included in the entrance fee. Continuing along the track, dozens of deserted saltpanners' houses slowly inch into view; it makes for an eerie sight, these stark, crumbling, grey-stone houses randomly strewn across the pancake-flat landscape.

A further 2km down the track, it comes as some relief to see the **Muzej Solinarstva** (Saltworks Museum) – the only two intact buildings in the park, having been completely renovated in order to house the museum. As interesting as the exhibits are, including a store of salt-making equipment and techniques and, upstairs, a mock-up of a saltpanner's living quarters, more fascinating is the detailed explanation of the salt-making process given by the helpful guide.

Note that the saltpans are very **exposed** and it can get very hot, so bring a hat, sun cream and water.

Southern Slovenia

KRIŽNA WATER CAVE

Southern Slovenia

The three regions comprising southern Slovenia – Notranjska, Dolenjska and Bela Krajina – offer an attractive mix of darkly forested hills, karstic rock formations, river valleys, castles, monasteries and spas, not to mention several outstanding wine-producing regions. Unsurprisingly, there are opportunities aplenty for hiking, cycling and other leisure pursuits.

The province of **Notranjska** encompasses an expanse of terrain extending south from the Ljubljana marshes to the Croatian border, bound by Primorska and the Karst to the west and by the Velika Gora hills to the east. Characterized by karst fields, underground rivers and thickly forested limestone hills and plateaus pocked by innumerable cave systems, its most celebrated attractions are the astonishing **Postojna Caves** and the majestically sited **Predjama Castle**. Largely ignored by most travellers, Notranjska's lesser-known sites include **Lake Cerknica**, Europe's largest intermittent lake, the wonderful **Križna Water Cave** and the **Snežnik mountains**, which offer some of the country's best non-alpine hiking. And for history buffs, there's the wonderful **Park of Military History** near Pivka.

The thick forests of Notranjska extend eastwards into the neighbouring province of **Dolenjska**, the largest of the three regions and the one possessing the lion's share of southern Slovenia's historical sites. Its westernmost flank centres around the low-key towns of **Ribnica** and **Kočevje**, close to both the massive forests of Velika Gora and **Kočevski Rog**, and the idyllic **Kolpa River Valley** on the Croatian border. The only town of any real size is **Novo Mesto**, a handy base from which to take in any number of local attractions, foremost of which is the beautiful **Krka River Valley**, which extends northwest to the village of **Muljava**, itself just a few kilometres from the ancient **Stična Monastery**. Following the course of the Krka River eastwards from Novo Mesto brings you to **Otočec Castle**, the secluded **Pleterje Monastery** and the sleepy island town of **Kostanjevica na Krki**. Beyond here the road and river continue to **Brežice**, setting for one of the country's most celebrated classical music festivals; **Čatež**, the country's largest spa centre; and the **Bizeljsko wine region**, perhaps the most appealing of the area's four wine-growing centres.

Quietly tucked away in the far southeastern corner of the country and bound by the forests of Kočevski Rog to the west and the Croatian border to the south and east is **Bela Krajina**. This is the smallest of southern Slovenia's regions, a gentle landscape where hilly slopes raked with lush vineyards descend to flatlands strewn with the region's famous white birch trees. Neither of the province's two main towns, **Črnomelj** and **Metlika**, are particularly exciting, but they do lie close to some significant cultural and natural sites, not to mention some lovely **wine villages**.

GETTING AROUND   SOUTHERN SLOVENIA

Getting around by **public transport** is more difficult here than in any other part of the country, so it's the one region where having your own vehicle is particularly advantageous, especially if you wish to visit more than one place on the same day; trains serve relatively few places outlined in this chapter, while local bus services are patchy at best.

LAKE CERKNICA

Highlights

❶ Postojna Caves Vast chambers and dazzling formations in one of the world's great cave systems. **See p.205**

❷ Park of Military History, Pivka Explore one of Europe's finest military history collections, including a gripping exhibition on the Ten-Day War. **See p.208**

❸ Lake Cerknica Europe's largest intermittent lake is one of Slovenia's great natural wonders. **See p.210**

❹ Križna Water Cave Discover cave-bear bones and more than a dozen lakes in one of Europe's finest water caves. **See p.212**

❺ Walking in Kočevski Rog Explore Slovenia's finest expanse of forest, and catch some wildlife along the way – mind the bears, though. **See p.219**

❻ Kayaking on the Kolpa River The beautiful, twisting Kolpa River is a great spot for kayaking and other watersports. **See p.221**

❼ Pleterje Monastery Visit the atmospheric church and grounds of Slovenia's only functioning Carthusian monastery. **See p.230**

❽ Repnice wine cellars Down a few glasses of wine in unique cellars hewn from sand. **See p.236**

HIGHLIGHTS ARE MARKED ON THE MAP ON P.202

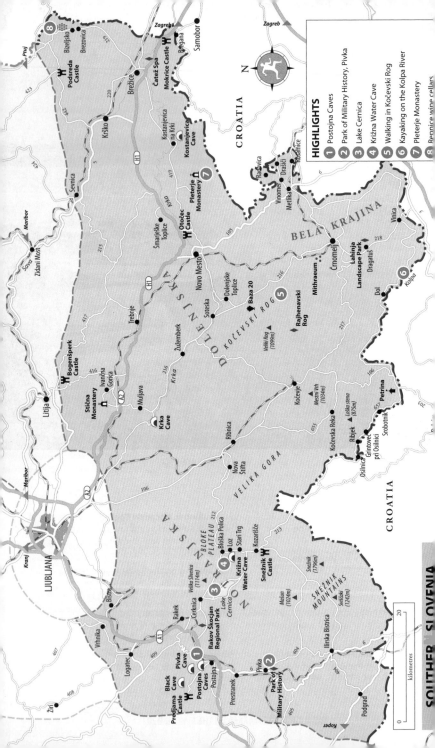

HIGHLIGHTS

① Postojna Caves
② Park of Military History, Pivka
③ Lake Cerknica
④ Križna Water Cave
⑤ Walking in Kočevski Rog
⑥ Kayaking on the Kolpa River
⑦ Pleterje Monastery
⑧ Repnice wine cellars

CROATIA

CROATIA

Zagreb

Zagreb

Maribor

Maribor

Maribor

Ptuj

Kranj

LJUBLJANA

Koper

BELA KRAJINA

DOLENJSKA

KOČEVSKI ROG

NOTRANJSKA

VELIKA GORA

BLOKE PLATEAU

SNEŽNIK MOUNTAINS

SOUTHERN SLOVENIA

Žiri
Logatec
Vrhnika
Bistra
Rakek
Cerknica
Velika Slivnica (1114m)
Bloška Polica
Loz
Stari Trg
Kozarišče
Snežnik Castle
Snežnik (1796m)
Mašun (1024m)
Snežnik (1242m)
Ilirska Bistrica
Podgrad
Prestranek
Postojna
Postojna Caves
Predjama Castle
Black Cave
Pivka Cave
Park of Military History
Pivka
Rakov Škocjan Regional Park
Lokev
Cerknica
Križna Water Cave

Litija
Zidani Most
Sevnica
Krško
Brežice
Bizeljsko
Brezovica
Podsreda Castle
Samobor
Bregana
Mokrice Castle
Čatež Spa
Kostanjevica na Krki
Kostanjevica Cave
Pleterje Monastery
Otočec Castle
Šmarješke Toplice
Novo Mesto
Dolenjske Toplice
Soteska
Žužemberk
Krka
Muljava
Ivančna Gorica
Stična Monastery
Bogenšperk Castle
Krka Cave
Ribnica
Nova Štifta
Kočevje
Mestni Vrh (1034m)
Kočevska Reka
Ribjek
Grintovec pri Osilnici
Srobotnik
Oslnica
Baza 20
Rajhenavski Rog
Veliki Rog (1099m)
Soteska
Metlika
Vinomer
Radovica
Drašiči
Rosalnice
Mithraeum
Črnomelj
Lahinja Landscape Park
Dragatuš
Vinica
Dol
Kolpa
Petrina
Loška stena (875m)

kilometres
0   20

Notranjska

Most visitors to **Notranjska** head straight to Slovenia's number-one tourist attraction, the **Postojna Caves**, and follow that with a visit to the nearby **Predjama Castle**, perched miraculously halfway up a cliff. Other, less-visited subterranean delights come in the form of the **Pivka and Black caves**, a stone's throw from their more famous counterparts. East of Postojna, **Rakov Škocjan Regional Park** is an enjoyable place for a walk; from here it's a short distance to one of Slovenia's most extraordinary geographical features, **Lake Cerknica** – by winter a lake, by summer a field. Permanent, though underground, lakes can be explored at **Križna Water Cave**, where skeletons of prehistoric cave bears have been discovered. Pressed up hard against the Croatian border, the **Snežnik mountains** offer tremendous hiking and opportunities to spot some of Slovenia's most spectacular wildlife, not least bears; tucked away under the shadow of these mountains is the Renaissance **Snežnik Castle**.

Tehniški muzej Slovenije

Bistra 6, 22km southwest of Ljubljana • March–June & Sept–Nov Tues–Fri 8am–4pm, Sat 9am–5pm, Sun 10am–6pm; July & Aug Tues–Fri 10am–6pm, Sat 9am–5pm, Sun 10am–6pm • €4.50 • ☎ 01 750 6670, ⊕ tms.si • Regular buses run from Ljubljana to Vrhnika, from where it's a 3km walk along a winding country road to the museum; there's a good chance of hitching a ride

Near the small settlement of **Vrhnika** in the hamlet of **BISTRA**, the former **Bistra Monastery** is a large complex that's now home to the **Tehniški muzej Slovenije** (Technical Museum of Slovenia). The museum is divided into several sections, though such is the size of the place you're best off making a beeline for a select few, particularly if time is short. As interesting as the voluminous displays of textiles, forestry, agriculture and engineering are, it's the massive road vehicle exhibit – largely comprising a magnificent collection of pre-World War II automobiles, carriages (including a fine Ljubljana tram from 1901), bicycles and tractors – that demands greatest attention.

The highlight of the collection is some two dozen **cars** given as gifts to Tito by various government offices and heads of state, which were used for his many travels throughout Yugoslavia and abroad, including India and Burma; there are some splendid models on display, notably a magnificent Rolls Royce Silver Wraith, a Mercedes Benz (from the Croatian Home Office) and an armour-plated 1937 Packard Twelve presented to Tito by Stalin in 1945 – ironically, just three years before Yugoslavia's expulsion from Cominform. There's also a 1953 Fiat Zastava, just one of Tito's many hunting vehicles.

The newest section, entitled *Our Beloved Car*, celebrates a century of motoring in Slovenia and embraces fifteen vehicles, ranging from a gorgeous red, two-seat Piccolo from 1906, to the rather less glamorous Zastava 101, an iconic – though not particularly well-performing – car popular throughout Yugoslavia in the 1970s, which had its base in Kragujevac, Serbia.

Postojna

POSTOJNA, 66km south of Ljubljana, would be eminently forgettable were it not for its location near one of Slovenia's most popular tourist attractions, the amazing **Postojna Caves**, whose vast chambers and dazzling formations have been pulling in the punters for nearly two centuries. Located on the main road and rail routes to the coast, the caves are easily managed as a half-day trip from Ljubljana, or as a stop-off en route to the coast itself. Stopping a while in Postojna is no problem, however; there's a fine **museum** here, along with some choice accommodation and good restaurants.

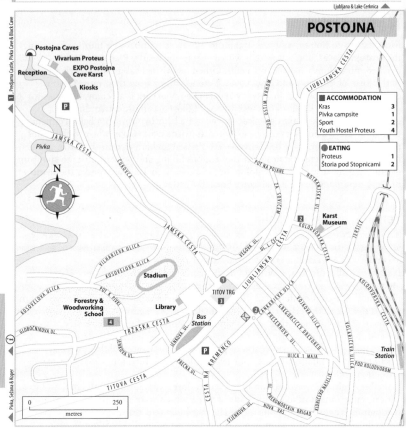

Ljubljana & Lake Cerknica ▲

POSTOJNA

Postojna Caves
Vivarium Proteus
Reception
EXPO Postojna
Cave Karst
Kiosks

Pivka

JAMSKA CESTA

ČUKOVCA

N

POD OSTIM VRHOM

POT NA POJANE

LJUBLJANSKA CESTA

NOTRANJSKA UL.

LA SOVIČEM

JAMSKA CESTA

VILHARJEVA ULICA

KOSOVELOVA ULICA

Stadium

KOSOVELOVA ULICA

POT K PIVKI

Forestry &
Woodworking
School

Library

GLOBOČNIKOVA UL.

TRŽAŠKA CESTA

JENKOVA ULICA

JENKOVA UL.

Bus
Station

TITOV TRG

TITOVA CESTA

VEGOVA UL.

UL. L. ČEČA

LJUBLJANSKA CESTA

Karst
Museum

KOLODVORSKA CESTA

CANKARJEVA ULICA

GREGORČIČEV DREVORED

PREŠERNOVA UL.

PRESERNOVA UL.

CESTA NA KREMENCO

PREČNA UL.

ULICA 1 MAJA

KIDRIČEVO NASELJE

UL. PREKOMORSKIH BRIGAD

NOVA VAS

STJENKOVA UL.

VOLKOVA ULICA

KOLODVORSKA CESTA

TERSKE

JERŠICE

VOLARIČEVA ULICA

POD KOLODVOROM

Train
Station

 █ **ACCOMMODATION**
Kras   3
Pivka campsite   1
Sport   2
Youth Hostel Proteus   4

● **EATING**
Proteus   1
Štoria pod Stopnicami   2

0 ———— 250
metres

Muzej Krasa

Kolodvorska cesta 3 • Tues–Sun: May–Oct 10am–6pm & 5pm; Nov–April 10am–5pm • €5 • 📞 041 313 179, 🌐 muzejkrasa.si

The **Muzej Krasa** (Karst Museum) sheds fascinating light on this beguiling landscape. The key theme on the ground floor is the **geology** of the Karst, with lucid explanations on the peculiarly unique Karst landforms, such as *dolines* (sinkholes), *poljes* (Karst fields) and dripstones, which, you will learn, grow between 0.1 and 0.3mm per year. Karst **architecture** gets a look-in too, with heavy emphasis on the importance of stonemasonry hereabouts, manifest in the dry-stone walls, wells and, above all, the stone houses that litter the local landscape – look out for a splendid *voussoir* (an arch of stone blocks) from a portal dated 1614, one of the oldest known inscription stones anywhere in the region. The first floor, meanwhile, delves deep into the Karst underworld, examining the incredibly diverse **cave fauna** lurking (or that once lurked) within, from cave crickets and slenderneck beetles to larger predators like cave bears and hyenas; a skull of the former and the jaws of the latter are on show. Cave **exploration** also features prominently, the most resonant exhibit being a preserved section of a winch used by Anton Hanke, Škocjan's most celebrated explorer, in 1889 (see p.178).

For all that, the museum's star turn is the **Predjama Cache**, an extraordinary assemblage of ten objects found wrapped in rotting linen in the castle cellar in 1991. It's believed that these precious finds – including goblets, candlesticks, a chalice, windmill cup (used for drinking games) and a salt cellar – were of German origin, dating from the late sixteenth century and probably buried at the beginning of the seventeenth century.

Postojnska jama

Jamska cesta 30 • Tours (1hr) daily: Jan–March, Nov & Dec 10am, noon & 3pm; April & Oct 10am–4pm, except noon; May, June & Sept hourly 9am–5pm; July & Aug hourly 9am–6pm • €23.90 plus €4 to park; €31.90 including entrance to Predjama Castle (see p.207); €37.90 including entrance to Predjama Castle, Proteus Vivarium and EXPO Postojna Cave Karst • ☎ 05 700 0100, ⦿ postojnska-jama.eu

Located an easy 1.5km walk northwest of town along the road to Predjama, the 24km of tunnels, chambers and passages that constitute the **Postojnska jama** (Postojna Caves) lie under the slopes of a broad karstic limestone plateau on the eastern fringes of the Postojna basin. Millions of years of erosion and corrosion by the Pivka River, coupled with abundant rainfall seeping through the cave's permeable limestone ceilings, have created a fantastic jungle of stalactites and stalagmites, Gothic-like chiselled columns and translucent stone draperies.

Although parts of the cave had been continually visited since the Middle Ages, it was the brilliant seventeenth-century polymath **Valvasor** (see box, p.223), inevitably, who first reported upon this immense grotto, commenting, "in some places you see terrifying heights, elsewhere everything is in columns so strangely shaped as to seem like some creepy-crawly, snake or other animal in front of one". The caves were pronounced open to tourists on the occasion of a visit by **Emperor Franz Ferdinand** in 1819, the first in a long line of distinguished visitors to Postojna. Within six years, the caves had been illuminated with oil lamps and professional guides had been employed. The famous **cave train**, meanwhile, entered service in 1872, a rather crude model in which tourists were shunted along in hand-pushed wagons. These carriages were superseded by gas-powered trains in 1914, themselves replaced by the electric version (used today) in 1959.

The cave tour

The **cave tour** begins with a ride on the iconic **cave train**, which whisks you along 3km of preliminary systems before the tour proper begins. As the train hurtles forth, keep an eye out for several interesting features: a shaft of blackened walls, the result of a Nazi fuel dump blown up by Partisan saboteurs during World War II; the **Congress Hall**, a beautifully lit chamber so-named following the staging of a Speleological Congress here in 1965; and the **Curtain**, a transparent, wafer-thin formation precariously angled on a sloping wall.

Alighting at the **Velika Gora** (Great Mountain), you'll break off into the group of your chosen language before the guided tour begins. The most impressive formations in this vast hall – a 45m-high stone-block mound formed when the ceiling collapsed and which, in time, became smothered in calcite – are the so-called **Natural Curtains**, whose shape and colour is akin to that of dried tobacco leaves. Crossing the **Russian Bridge**, built in 1916 by Russian prisoners of war, you enter the most enchanting part of the system, a series of chambers collectively known as the **Lepe jame** (Beautiful Caves), whose names are suggestive of some of the lustrous formations and colours on display, such as the **Spaghetti Hall**, with its dripping, needle-like formations, the calcium-rich **White Hall** and the **Red Room**, stained a rich ochre by iron oxides.

Continuing in a circuitous route, you pass back under the Russian Bridge through several more chambers, one of which, the **Zimska dvorana** (Winter Chamber), is home to the two formations that have become symbols of the cave: one called the **Pillar**, and another dubbed **Brilliant**, the latter on account of its dazzling snow-white colour and peculiar shape, which resembles something like a stack of giant cauliflowers. The main attraction in the next gallery has less to do with the formations on display and more to do with the contents of the large tank located in the centre, which contains **Proteus anguinus**, the largest permanent cave-dwelling vertebrate known to man (see box, p.206). The tour concludes a little further on in the **Koncertna dvorana** (Concert Hall), the largest open space in the system, and which, you are told, can hold some ten thousand people – the odd concert is still held here.

PROTEUS ANGUINUS – THE HUMAN FISH

There are an estimated two hundred animal species in Slovenia's caves, but none is as enigmatic, or evokes such fascination, as **Proteus anguinus**, the **human fish**. This peculiar-looking creature – officially called an olm – is a 25cm-long amphibian with pigment-less skin, bright red gills and atrophied eyes; it is snake-like in appearance, with two tiny pairs of legs (the front ones have three digits, the rear two – hence the "human" part of its name) and a flat, pointed fin to help propel itself through water. The fact that the human fish is completely blind matters little, as the creature spends almost all of its 100-year life entirely in the dark. While it usually consumes insect larvae, it's not uncommon for Proteus to indulge in a spot of cannibalism; conversely, it can go years without food, leaving researchers stumped. The most vexing questions, however, concern its habits of reproduction, which remain a mystery. In 2016, something quite remarkable happened; between January and February, a total of 64 eggs were laid in the cave's aquarium (see p.205), the first of which hatched at the end of May, to be followed over the next few weeks by 21 more hatchlings, or baby dragons as they've affectionately become known; the remainder sadly perished. The plight of these newborns attracted the attention of much of the world's media keen to learn more about this extraordinary, and incredibly rare, occurrence.

To get the most out of your visit, try and make one of the first or last tours of the day to avoid the **crowds**, which can be overwhelming in summer. Dress **warmly**, as it can get quite chilly.

Vivarijem Proteus

Daily: Jan–March, Nov & Dec 9.30am–3pm; April & Oct 9.30am–4pm; May, June & Sept 8.30am–5pm; July & Aug 8.30am–6pm • €8.90 • ☎ 05 700 0100, ⓦ postojnska-jama.eu

You can see *Proteus anguinus*, as well as other cave flora and fauna – such as crickets, beetles and spiders – in the Speleobiology Station, or **Vivarijem Proteus** (Vivarium Proteus), a short walk from the cave entrance by the kiosks. You'll do well, though, to spot more than a handful of these tiny creatures, as most are apt to hide themselves away. The exhibition is housed inside the Gallery of Signatures, so-called because of the many signatures scrawled over the cave walls, the oldest of which (no longer visible) is thought to date from 1213.

EXPO Postojnska Jama Kras

Daily: Jan–March, Nov & Dec 10am–3pm; April & Oct 9.30am–4pm; May, June & Sept 9am–6pm; July & Aug 9am–7pm • €8.90 • ☎ 05 700 0100, ⓦ postojnska-jama.eu

In the pavilion a few paces along from the Vivarium, the illuminating **EXPO Postojnska Jama Kras** (EXPO Postojna Cave Karst) is a worthwhile supplement to visiting the caves themselves. Largely presented through interactive means, including a clever 3D model-projection and a simulator mimicking the Postojna train, the history of Postojna is relayed in clear and colourful fashion, with archeological displays, exhibits on how stalactites and stalagmites are formed and a section devoted to cave fauna, not least the mysterious "human fish" (see box above).

Pivka jama and Črna jama

4km north of Postojna • Both caves May, June & Sept by prior arrangement; July & Aug daily 9am & 5pm • €11.90 for both

If you'd rather avoid the Postojna crowds, head for the final two caves along the underground Pivka River – the **Pivka jama** (Pivka Cave) and **Črna jama** (Black Cave) – which make low-key subterranean alternatives. The entrance to the former is via a spectacular 60m-deep collapsed chasm; descending nearly three hundred steps, you then follow a route along a specially constructed walkway cut into the wall just above the level of the Pivka River.

Beyond an iron door and a short tunnel – built in 1922 by the Italians for military purposes, but never actually used for these means – you enter the Black Cave (also known as the Magdalena Cave), a modestly sized, dry gallery that takes its name from the large amount of black calcite present. Here, too, you'll find signatures scrawled into the walls, some highly visible, including one dating from 1820 signed *Eygenhoffer*. Due to the higher temperatures in these two caves, there are fewer formations present here, but what you may get to see in the Black Cave are olms – *Proteus anguinus*, or the **human fish** (see box opposite) – in their natural environment, which is really quite something. From the end of the Black Cave, a 1km-long passage joins up with the Postojna Cave, though this is not accessible to visitors.

ARRIVAL AND INFORMATION   POSTOJNA

By bus The bus station is on Titova cesta, from where it's a 5min walk to the main square, Titov trg.
Destinations Ajdovščina (Mon–Fri 10 daily, Sat & Sun 4–5 daily; 45min); Cerknica (Mon–Fri 7 daily; 30min); Koper (Mon–Fri 8 daily, Sat & Sun 3–4 daily; 1hr 20min); Ljubljana (Mon–Fri every 30min–1hr 30min, Sat & Sun 8 daily; 45min–1hr; 1hr); Nova Gorica (Mon–Fri 10 daily, Sat & Sun 4 daily; 1hr 20min); Piran (Mon–Fri 4 daily, Sat & Sun 2–3 daily; 1hr 40min); Pivka (Mon–Fri hourly; 30min).
By train The train station is 1km southeast of town on Kolodvorska cesta – from the station exit, take the stairs down to Pod Kolodvorom, then walk along Ulica 1 Maja until you reach the main square.

Destinations Divača (every 45min–1hr 30min; 35min); Koper (3–5 daily; 1hr 30min); Ljubljana (every 45min–1hr 30min; 1hr); Pivka (every 30min–1hr 30min; 15min); Pula, Croatia (1 daily; 3hr 30min); Rijeka, Croatia (2 daily; 1hr 45min); Sežana (hourly–every 1hr 30min; 45min).
Tourist office The tourist office is located, somewhat oddly and inconveniently, on the main road heading west out of town, at Tržaška cesta 59a (daily: April–June & Sept 10am–6pm; July & Aug 8am–8pm; Oct–March 10am–3/4pm; ☎ 05 720 1610).
Bike rental Bikes can be rented from the *Proteus* hostel and the *Sport* hotel (see below).

ACCOMMODATION   4

Kras Tržaška cesta 1 ☎ 05 700 2300, ⓦ hotelkras.si. The town's principal hotel, a flashy glass structure facing Titov trg, concealing well-sized and extremely stylish rooms in various shades of brown and with floor-to-ceiling windows. €90
Pivka campsite Veli Otok 50 ☎ 05 720 3993, ⓦ camping -postojna.com. Scenically located in a pine forest 4km north of the caves, this large, superbly equipped site also has simple four-bed bungalows with bathrooms, some with a kitchen. Amenities include good sports facilities and a restaurant. Mid-April to Oct. Camping €21, bungalows €42
Sport Kolodvorska cesta 1 ☎ 05 720 2244, ⓦ hotel -sport.si. A simple, colourful and welcoming place offering

singles, doubles and triples, as well as four-bed family rooms – they also rent out bikes (€9 for 4hr, €15/day). €85
Youth Hostel Proteus Tržaška cesta 36 ☎ 05 850 1020, ⓦ proteus.sgls.si. Hidden away in a small park, and part of the Forestry and Woodworking School, this outwardly dull-looking building conceals a cool and colourful hostel; the three-bed dorms feature brilliantly conceived, inter-locking wooden beds designed by students from the school. A designer-styled kitchen, laundry and bike rental (€15/day) complete this fine ensemble. Shower facilities are shared. Breakfast €3. Dorms €23, doubles €34

EATING

★**Proteus** Titov trg 1 ☎ 081 610 300, ⓦ postojna-jama .eu. This gorgeous restaurant, with tables separated by white, spaghetti-like curtains meant to resemble the cave's geo-logical formations, offers a sublime fine-dining experience. Mouthwatering dishes include marinated Cerknica trout with lemon mousse (€9) or dry-cured Karst ham with red polenta in Teran wine sauce (€10), and the wine list is top drawer. Five-course menu €35. Daily 8am–11pm.

Štorja pod Stopnicami Ulica 1 Maja 1 ☎ 05 992 7898, ⓦ storja.si. Elegant little trattoria with green wood-panelled walls and red-checked tablecloths. The food is right on the money – grilled liver in a red wine sauce with polenta (€7.50), for example, or pork fillet with bacon and rosemary (€15). Super service, too. Mon–Fri 7am–11pm, Sat & Sun 8am–11pm.

Predjamski Grad

9km north of Postojna • Daily: Jan–March, Nov & Dec 10am–4pm; April & Oct 10am–5pm; May, June & Sept 9am–6pm; July & Aug 9am–7pm • €11.90, or €31.90 with Postojna Caves (see p.205) • ☎ 05 700 0100, ⓦ postojnska-jama.eu • In July & Aug a free shuttle bus runs between the caves and Predjama for those with a combined ticket

The fabulously dramatic setting of **Predjamski Grad** (Predjama Castle) – pressed into a huge cavern hollowed out of the high, flat rock face, above the karstic swallow hole of

---

THE DEATH OF ERASMUS LUEGER

The beginning of what proved to be a rather sticky ending for **Erasmus Lueger**, fifteenth-century knight and brigand, began after he killed one of the Austrian emperor Frederick III's kinsmen in revenge for the decapitation of a friend. Hot on his heels as he fled to Predjama was the governor of Trieste, Caspar Ravbar, whose mission it was to capture him. For more than a year Ravbar and his men laid siege to Predjama, attempting to starve out its defenders. However, Ravbar hadn't reckoned on a **secret natural passage** beyond the castle walls, through which came a constant supply of fresh food that Erasmus would occasionally hurl down into the valley to taunt his besiegers. Finally betrayed by a double-dealing servant, Erasmus died an ignoble **death** – the poor fellow was blasted to bits by a large projectile while settling down to answer nature's call. Local legend has it that he is buried under the linden tree, supposedly planted by his lover, next to the **Church of Our Lady of Sorrows**, just down from the castle.

---

the Lokva stream – is as unforgettable as it is improbable. Stopping here in 1802 en route to Italy, the German architect Karl Schinkel recalled, "it was with the wildest bravery that man was ordered to settle in this place. There is nothing more stirring than to look upon the castle, wondrously composed of tower-like structures which, built under the dark vault of the cavern, need not their own ramparts, as the dark cavern's huge bulk hangs far beyond them." Among its many aristocratic residents, the most infamous was the castle's last owner, **Erasmus Lueger** (see box above), who lived here during the second half of the fifteenth century, and whose life – in particular the manner of his death – has intrigued historians for centuries.

Dating back to around the twelfth century, the castle manifests a number of styles, from Romanesque through to Gothic, although its predominant form is **Renaissance** following heavy renovation in the sixteenth century. With some fifteen rooms, as well as numerous passageways, galleries and alcoves, all condensed into five floors, there's much to see, though little of what's on display is original. On the second floor, keep an eye out for a portrait of the suitably gruff Erasmus (one of the few pictures of him known to exist), and the cupboard in the dining room – made by an inmate of a local prison using just his pocket knife. On the third floor – where Erasmus came to grief – you can see the tiny castle **chapel**, containing a fifteenth-century Gothic pietà. Next door is the chaplain's room, from where he could witness the punishments being meted out in the torture chamber one floor below. Natural apertures on each floor afford fine panoramas of the flower-speckled Vipava Valley ahead.

Jama pod Predjamskim gradom

Tours May–Sept daily 11am, 1pm, 3pm & 5pm • €8.90, or €13 with the castle

At the very top of the castle – across the drawbridge and up some uneven steps – lie the ruins of the Cave Castle, beyond which is the **secret natural passage**; tours of the latter are possible during the summer, but you should call the castle a couple of days in advance. Easier to visit is the **Jama pod Predjamskim gradom** (Cave under the Castle), which extends for some 14km (much of it still unexplored) to the Vipava Valley, though only around 700m of walking is possible for the casual visitor. Bar the odd stalactite, there's not an awful lot to see, but it's one of the few caves around that hasn't been artificially lit, so it's quite good fun wandering around with headlights.

Park vojaške zgodovine muzej

Kolodvorsja 51, Pivka, 14km south of Postojna • Jan–April, Nov & Dec Sat & Sun 10am–6pm; May, June, Sept & Oct Mon–Fri 10am–4pm; Sat & Sun 10am–6pm; July & Aug daily 10am–6pm • €11.90, plus €5 to enter the submarine • ☏ 031 775 002, ⊕ parkvojaskezgodovine.si • From Postojna, hourly trains and buses run to Pivka, from where it's 2km south to the park

Just outside the small town of Pivka the absorbing **Park vojaške zgodovine muzej** (Park of Military History) is well worth making the time and effort to get to. It was from these former barracks – built by the Italians in 1930 and home to the Yugoslav People's Army from 1945 to 1991 – that, on June 26, 1991, Yugoslav army tanks departed en route to confront Slovene troops following Slovenia's declaration of independence. From the Komanda building (the former command centre and now the reception), you head out to **pavilions B and C**, which, respectively, hold a mightily impressive line-up of armoured vehicles and artillery, mostly Partisan tanks but also both Soviet and American-built machinery, Yugoslavia being one of the few countries to use both country's armament during the Cold War.

The most illuminating part of the park is in **Pavilion A**; entitled "Road to Independence", it documents civil and military life in **Socialist-era Slovenia** (and by implication Yugoslavia) and the increasingly fractious nature of relations between the republics, before the eventual descent into the Ten-Day War (see box, p.305). Exhibit-wise, pride of place goes to the pistol belonging to Anton Krkovič, the commander of the Slovenian Territorial Defence, and the gleaming sabre used by President Kučan at the declaration of independence ceremony on Trg Republike in Ljubljana. Passing through a mocked-up home from 1991 (complete with television footage of the war), you enter the vast hall, replete with aircraft and armoured vehicles, including a T55 tank captured at Rožna dolina and the battered turret of an M84 catapulted into a ditch when the tank exploded.

For all the fantastic military hardware on display, the museum's showstealer is a P-913 pocket, or commando, **submarine**, one of six constructed in Split (Croatia) in the 1980s. The last submarine to be taken out of operation, in 2003, *Zeta* was gifted to the Slovene authorities by the Montenegrin government in 2011, though it had to be taken through Italian waters to prevent it from being seized by Croatian authorities. For an extra fee it's possible to descend into the bowels of the submarine, where you can experience the extraordinarily claustrophobic conditions submariners had to endure, often for months on end. Once done, grab a bite to eat in the museum's excellent, militarily themed restaurant, *Kantina Pivka*.

Rakov Škocjan krajinski park

A couple of kilometres north of Postojna, the secondary road running parallel to the A1 Ljubljana–Koper highway breaks off sharply to the right towards the **Rakov Škocjan krajinski park** (Rakov Škocjan Regional Park), a small, lush karst valley popular with local walkers. There's an easy, well-marked, circular trail around the park, which should take no more than a couple of hours.

The focal point here is the short, well-defined **Rak Gorge**, which begins at the **Mali naravni most** (Small Natural Bridge) – the first of two stunning natural rock bridges sited at either end of the gorge – just below which lurks the **Zelške jama** (Zelške Cave) and the Rak Spring, from where the babbling **Rak River** emerges. The river, which carries water from Cerknica Polje to the Planina Polje, winds its way down the gorge to the immaculately cut arch of the **Veliki naravni most** (Great Natural Bridge), beneath which is the **Tkalca jama** (Tkalca Cave). On the far side of the bridge a crumbling heap of stone ruins, including parts of a stone altar, is all that remains of the **Church of St Kancijan**. During periods when the river is low, or completely dry, it is possible to explore both cave entrances, but take care, as it's likely to be slippery.

Cerknica

CERKNICA, around 4km east of Rakov Škocjan, is a small, fairly drab town. It's enlivened, however, during the February **Pust** – one of Slovenia's better-organized carnivals – and it does offer a handful of places to stay and eat, which is useful if you're planning to spend a day or two near Lake Cerknica (see p.210).

The town is also the starting point for trails to the **Slivnica Plateau**, ranged across the lake's northern shore. If the water looks impressive from ground level, the views from atop its highest peak, **Velika Slivnica** (1114m; 2hr from Cerknica), are superlative; Velika Slivnica is also known as witch mountain, owing to its associations with witchcraft in the Middle Ages. At the top, you can enjoy refreshments at the *Dom na Slivnici* (☎01 709 4140; beds May–Sept Sat & Sun only) just below the summit.

ARRIVAL AND INFORMATION   CERKNICA

By bus The bus station is on Čabranska ulica, in the centre of town.
Destinations Ljubljana (Mon–Fri hourly–every 2hr, Sat & Sun 4 daily; 50min–1hr 15min); Postojna (Mon–Fri 7 daily; 30min); Stari Trg (Mon–Fri 7 daily, Sat & Sun 2 daily; 25min).

By train The nearest train station is in Rakek, 4km northwest.
Destinations Ljubljana (every 30min–2hr; 50min); Postojna (every 30min–2hr; 10min).
Tourist office Inside the fine medieval tower at Tabor 42, 200m north of the bus station (Mon–Sat 8am–4pm, Sun 8am–noon; ☎01 709 3636, ⌨notranjska-park.si).

ACCOMMODATION AND EATING

Gostilna Glažk Partizanska cesta 17 ☎01 709 3344, ⌨glazk.si. Cerknica's one worthwhile place to eat looks pretty down at heel from the outside, but the food is actually very creditable; pizzas and schnitzels aside, there's some delicious local dishes on offer, such as *jota*, and *štruklji* with veal (€11.50). Daily 7am–11pm.

Pri Ancki Casermanova ulica 9 ☎031 644 279. On a quiet residential street across the Cerkniščica, 500m south of the centre, this sweet, attentively run B&B has a handful of simple, colourful and immaculately prepared rooms, and a warming communal breakfast table. **€50**

Cerkniško jezero

There are several ways to approach a visit to the mysterious **Cerkniško jezero** (Lake Cerknica), about 2.5km south of Cerknica, but what you see, and how you see it, will largely be determined by which time of the year you come, and which mode of transport, if any, you use. The most direct route across the lake (or field) is via an unsurfaced north–south road that shaves the lake's western shore. Beginning at **Dolenje Jezero**, a small village 2km south of Cerknica, the road bisects a group of sinkholes

---

THE DISAPPEARING LAKE

Although the so-called **"disappearing lake"** of Cerkniško jezero had been the subject of much postulation and fascination on the part of researchers and explorers long before Valvasor's time, it was left to the great polymath himself to unravel the lake's eccentricities, concluding as he did: "I think there is no lake so remarkable either in Europe or in any other of the three corners of the world…no lake has as many exceptional features." As a result of his efforts, which included publishing a map of the lake in 1689, Valvasor was granted honorary membership of the Royal Society in London. There were other significant contributions, too, most notably from the botanist Balthazar Haquet and the Jesuit Tobijas Gruber, both of whom offered thorough accounts of the lake's extraordinary hydrological functions.

The lake's behaviour, while mysterious, can be explained: once water from the Slivnica and Bloke plateaus to the east, and the Javornik mountains to the west, enters the permeable limestone surface of the lakebed, it begins to percolate through the many sinkholes into the subterranean area, and when more water enters the lake than can be depleted, the waters of the main channel, the Stržen (itself fed by a number of tributaries and streams), overflow to create the shallow lake in a matter of days. At its fullest, the lake can extend for some 10km in length and nearly 5km in width – that's roughly three to four times the size of Lake Bohinj, Slovenia's largest permanent body of water. The disappearing act takes a little longer, usually between three and four weeks. There have been numerous, thus far unsuccessful, attempts at **human intervention** over the years – either to prevent the lake filling (in order to grow more hay for livestock), or, conversely, to preserve a permanent body of water (in order to prolong the fishing season and encourage tourism).

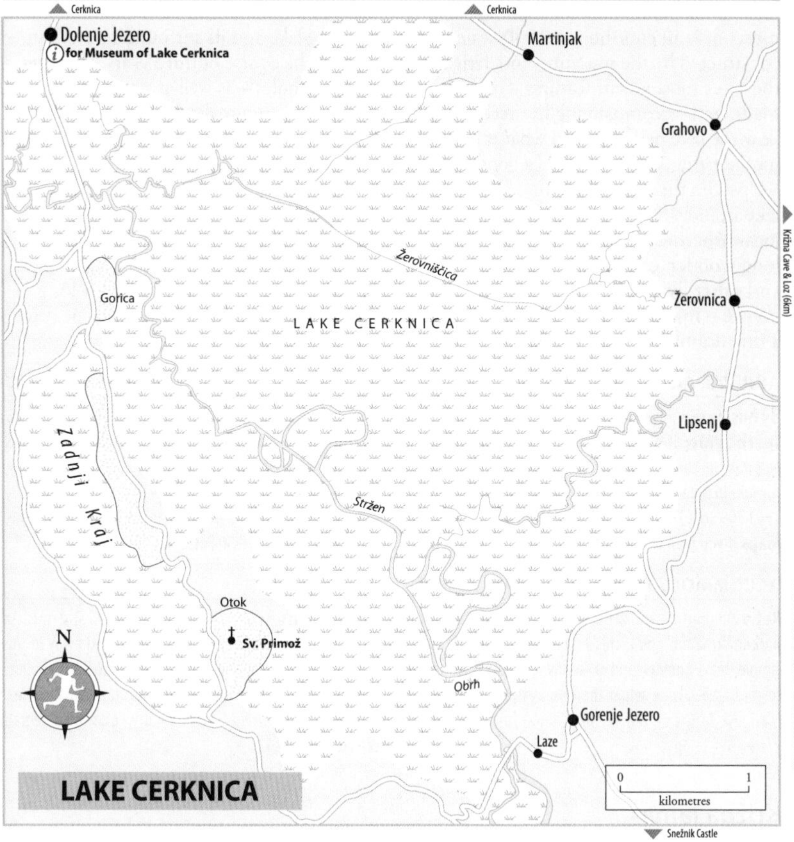

before passing the small wooded island of Gorica and continuing southwards to **Otok** (Island), which, when the lake is full, magically becomes the country's sole inhabited island. From Otok you can either head back in a northerly direction via the forest road that skirts the western shore of the **Zadnji kraj inlet**, or take the longer route along the lake's eastern shore through the settlements of Laze, Gorenje Jezero, Lipsenj and Žerovnica, winding up at Grahovo on the main road.

As a rule this "disappearing lake" (see box opposite) is usually present between October and June, and at its most voluminous during spring, following snowmelt from both the Snežnik and Slivnica plateaus. During this period, Cerkniško jezero becomes a vast playground for a multitude of **water-based activities**, the most popular of which is fishing – pike, tench and chub are the main stock here – as well as swimming, rowing and windsurfing. With more than two hundred species of **birds**, including corncrakes, red-necked grebes, lapwings and field larks, either migrating or nesting among the wide expanse of reeds, the lake is something of a haven for birdwatchers. You may even catch sight of a bear sniffing around for fish.

Muzej Cerkniškega jezera

Dolenje Jezero 1e • Guided tours only (45min): Mon, Wed & Fri 11am, Tues & Thurs 2pm, Sat 3pm, but do check in advance; outside these times, call to arrange a visit • €7 • T 01 709 4053, W jezerski-hram.si

For a better understanding of the lake's peculiarities, pay a visit to the family-run **Muzej Cerkniškega jezera** (Museum of Lake Cerknica). The centrepiece of this enlightening little museum is an enormous 1:2500-scale **map-relief** of the lake and its surrounding features, constructed by the museum's indefatigable owner over the course of three years. Showing the lake's most salient features – tributaries, springs, sinkholes – as well as settlements and roads, with accompanying live recordings of birds and other animals, the map illustrates how the lake performs and what it looks like during both dry and wet periods. Strangely mesmerizing, the relief takes a good thirty minutes to fill with water.

Upstairs there's a 25-minute slide show, featuring some beautifully shot images of the lake in its various guises, and a collection of tools and implements traditionally used by local fishermen – wooden skates, nets, baskets and the like – as well as models of the long wooden canoes (*drevak*) that were used, until the 1970s, for transporting cattle and other livestock across the lake. There's a superb example of a life-size (12m-long) *drevak* – made from a fir tree – in the owner's workshop outside, which stands next to a fine double hayrack, or *toplar*.

ARRIVAL AND INFORMATION   CERKNIŠKO JEZERO

By bus There is no public transport to the lake.

Tourist office There's an information point (it's actually a *lojtarnik*, or carriage) in the car park at the entrance to the lake in Dolenje Jezero (May–Sept Sat & Sun 9am–4pm; ☎ 01 709 3636).

Maps If you plan to spend any length of time around the lake, arm yourself with a copy of the 1:25,000 *Notranjska Cerkniško jezero* map, which outlines a good range of walks and cycle routes in the area.

Bike rental The most enjoyable way to see the lake is by bike, and while there's nowhere in Cerknica to rent one, you'll find a few places in Postojna (see p.207).

ACCOMMODATION AND EATING

Kebe Dolenje Jezero ☎ 01 709 4053. Opposite the car park/information point, this homely roadside café offers simple refreshments and a sunny terrace looking out towards the lake – when the lake is there. July & Aug Mon–Fri 1–11pm, Sat & Sun 9am–11pm, Sept–June Wed–Sun 1–6pm.

Miškar House Žerovnica 66 ☎ 040 839 425, ⓦ miskar .si. Welcoming guesthouse peacefully tucked away in the forests just outside the village, on the road to Bloška Polica. There are three tidy rooms and decent communal facilities, including kitchen/diner and laundry, plus bike rental. Breakfast €5. **€46**

Križna jama

Bloška Polica 7, 12km southeast of Cerknica · **One-hour tours** April–June Sat & Sun 3pm; July & Aug daily 11am, 1pm, 3pm & 5pm; Sept daily 11am, 1pm & 3pm; outside these times, call to arrange a visit · €8 · **Four-hour tours** (must be booked in advance): July–Sept €65/ person for two people, €55/person for three people, €45 for four; Oct–June €42/€35/€30 · ☎ 041 632 153, ⓦ krizna-jama.si

Utterly different from Postojna and its ilk, the 8km-long **Križna jama** (Križna Water Cave) is one of the world's great lake caves, and *the* cave to visit if it's an authentic caving experience you're after. Entering – helmet, flashlight and boots are supplied – via a small aperture hollowed out of the rock face, you immediately descend into a rocky, dry gallery, known as **Medvedji rov** (Bear's Corridor) owing to the many **cave bears** (*Ursus spelaeus*) that sheltered here thousands of years ago. The first cave-bear excavations – carried out in the late nineteenth century – uncovered around two thousand fossil remains from more than two hundred animals, mainly mandibles, skulls and other bone fragments; you'll see shards, typically part of a jaw or a tooth, still embedded within the rock. There's also an almost-complete cave-bear skull on display, next to a much smaller skull of a **brown bear**; the difference in size is striking, though this will be of little comfort should you have the misfortune to encounter one of the latter in the surrounding forests, which is by no means improbable (see box, p.218). Less alarmingly, the cave is home to a large number of **bats**, drawn here by the relatively warm temperature of around 8°C.

First explored in 1926, the chain of 22 lakes that comprise the **Jezerski rov** (Lakes and Stream Passages) is the undeniable high point of a visit to Križna. Separated by calcite barriers, the lakes are fed with water from the nearby Bloke Plateau, via a number of springs in the eastern part of Lake Cerknica. On the one-hour tour, you get to cross the first lake only, but the four-hour tour takes you as far as the thirteenth and most decorative of all the lakes, the **Kalvarija** (Calvary), a wonderful grotto comprising a huge mound of collapsed material and a shimmering array of stalactites and stalagmites, many of which lie submerged under water.

Grad Snežnik

Kozarišče, 7km south of Križna jama • Guided tours only, on the hour: April–Sept daily 10am–6pm; Oct–March Tues–Sun 10am–4pm • €5 • ☎ 01 705 7814, ⊕ nms.si • The closest you can get by bus is the village of Stari Trg, 4km north of Kozarišče, from where the only option is to hitch or walk

Sitting in the middle of a luscious landscaped park of chestnut trees and silky lawns, just beyond the village of **KOZARIŠČE**, is **Grad Snežnik** (Snežnik Castle), a handsome, three-storey Renaissance building impressively girdled by ramparts, towers and a high grey wall.

Entered via a graceful stone-arch bridge spanning a small brook, Snežnik was originally the thirteenth-century domain of the Aquileian patriarchs, and their subjects the Snežniški lords, after which time it changed hands on many occasions. As a result of a court assessment in 1832 the castle was recovered from the heavily-in-debt Lichtenberg family and declared a lottery prize; however, its winner, a Hungarian blacksmith, opted for cash instead, leaving the entire estate up for grabs. Snapped up by **Prince Oton Schönburg** at an auction in 1853, the castle remained under the ownership of the family until World War II, when it was appropriated by the state. Unlike many other castles in Slovenia during World War II, Snežnik was fortunate enough to retain most of its original nineteenth-century bourgeois furnishings and other works of art, most of which is on display in a dozen or so rooms, through which you're ushered in rather speedy fashion. The pick of the items on display is an exotic hoard of deities, sphinxes and pharaohs in the **Egyptian Room**, gifted to the owners by Egyptian officials in 1906 in return for a stay here.

Snežnik Castle is also the main starting point for **hiking trails** and **cycle routes** up into the Snežnik plateau/mountains (see below); visitors with a car can take the mountain road that winds its way across the plateau to Ilirska Bistrica.

Lovski Polharski muzej

May–Sept Sat 11am–6pm, Sun 10am–1pm & 3–6pm • €2 • ☎ 01 705 7516

Housed in one of the former dairy buildings across from the castle is the **Lovski Polharski muzej** (Dormouse Hunting Museum), where you can learn more about one of Slovenia's more unusual customs. A unique tradition in Notranjska, the dormouse (*polh*) has long been hunted for commercial purposes – its fur is used for caps and its fat for machine oil – though it's also something of a culinary speciality in these parts. The first Saturday in October, known as **Dormouse Hunting Night** (Polharska noč), is given over to a frenzied night of hunting activity. The grounds around the castle are a lovely spot for a picnic, with or without dormice.

The Snežnik mountains

The wonderful **Snežnik mountain range** is a densely forested karst plateau cloaked in spruce, beech, fir and dwarf pine, and sheltering numerous large mammals, including lynx, wolf and a significant bear population. The plateau is traversed by a number of well-marked trails, including a section of the European footpath E6.

The best approach is from the small market town of **Ilirska Bistrica**, 33km south of Postojna and just 11km shy of the Croatian border; from here it's a good three-hour walk to **Sviščaki** (1242m), where you'll find the *Planinski Dom na Sviščakih* (☎051 219 799; June to mid-Sept daily; mid-Sept to May Sat & Sun), and then a further two-hour trek to the cone-like **Mount Snežnik** (1796m) and the *Koča Draga Karolina* *na Velikem Snežniku* (☎050 615 356; May–Oct Sat & Sun; Aug daily). Usually topped with snow until late spring, Snežnik, Slovenia's highest non-alpine mountain, offers fantastic views of the Alps to the north and the Croatian seaboard, dotted with its many islands, to the south.

From here the path continues to **Mašun** (1024m; 4hr), and down through the Leskova Valley towards Snežnik Castle (see p.213). If you have a car, you could drive to Sviščaki and walk to Snežnik from there – from Sviščaki, the deteriorating mountain road continues to Mašun (13km), before descending to Snežnik Castle. If you're doing this route in reverse – from Snežnik Castle – you could drive to Mašun and walk to Snežnik from there.

Western Dolenjska

Western Dolenjska has just a couple of very low-key towns: **Ribnica**, renowned throughout Slovenia for its woodenware tradition, and **Kočevje**, once home to the country's German-speaking minority and containing Slovenia's first parliament building. It's the region's **natural heritage** that is the big draw, in particular the stunning virgin forests of **Kočevski Rog** and, straddling the Croatian border south of Kočevje, the beautiful **Kolpa Valley**. The valley is Dolenjska's centre for river-based activities, which can be organized from its main village, **Osilnica**.

Bloke Plateau

From Lake Cerknica the road heads eastwards across the **Bloke Plateau** – a flat, wide and largely featureless karst plateau whose name gave rise to one of Slovenia's most enduring cultural symbols, the **Bloke skis**. These short, fat skis, made of beech or birch wood and bound to the foot by a leather strap, were used principally as a means of transportation across the snowy plateau in winter. Valvasor, for one, was suitably impressed, proclaiming: "they descend into the valley with incredible speed … one such strip of wood is strapped under each foot, they take a stout cudgel into their hands and push it into their armpit, and use it as if it were some sort of a rudder to slide off … no less swift than those who use skates in Holland to glide on ice." Although downhill skiing as a sport all but died out here after World War I, the plateau is now a popular place for **cross-country skiing**.

Ribnica

Pitched in the centre of a lovely flat-bottomed river valley, between the pine- and beech-covered ridges of Velika Gora and Mala Gora 40km south of Ljubljana, the idyllic small town of **RIBNICA** is famed in Slovenia for its delightful **woodenware** and pottery, and its witchcraft legends. Like many other towns and villages in Dolenjska, Ribnica suffered mercilessly at the hands of the Turks during the fifteenth century: records recount 27 raids in all; ironically, it was as a result of these incursions that the town's woodenware, or *suha roba* (dry goods), industry flourished. In order to kick-start the local economy, Emperor Frederick III issued a decree allowing peddlers from Ribnica, Kočevje and surrounding areas to trade freely throughout the Austrian territories. Such was their aptitude for a good sell, however, that these indomitable characters began to trade as far afield as Africa and Asia.

The best time to see the full array of products is at the **Ribnica Fair**, on the first Sunday in September, which entails much trading of wares – wicker baskets, wooden spoons, ceramic bowls and so on – along the main street. It's also worth taking a look at the **Ribnica Handicraft Centre**, just beyond the castle at Cesta na Ugar 6 (Mon–Fri

PREDJAMA CASTLE (P.207) >

9am–5pm, Sat 9am–1pm; ☎01 836 1104, ⓦrokodelskicenter-ribnica.si). The centre, which also houses the tourist office, displays exquisite examples of woodenware and pottery, with frequent demonstrations of both.

Muzej Ribnica
Grad Ribnica • May–Oct Mon–Thurs & Sun 10am–1pm & 4–7pm • €2 • ☎01 836 1104, ⓦrokodelskicenter-ribnica.si

Running parallel to Škrabčev trg – the town's main thoroughfare – is the slender **Bistrica River**, spanned by three exquisite stone bridges, each of which crosses over to the **Grad Ribnica** (Ribnica Castle) on the left bank. Originally built around the tenth or eleventh century, it later assumed a Renaissance form, though all that remains now – two defensive towers linked by a residential passageway – is the result of the building having been occupied, and subsequently wrecked, during World War II.

Occupying what's left of the castle is the **Muzej Ribnica** (Museum of Ribnica), worth a visit to view its **woodenware** collection. The activity of creating woodenware was traditionally split into nine or ten branches, each branch – for example, vessel making, sieve making, wickerwork and plaiting – linked to a particular household, village or type of wood (typically pine, beech or lime). Although somewhat haphazardly arranged, there's much to admire here, from wicker baskets, drinking vessels and farm tools to less orthodox items such as mousetraps, ski-shoes and backpacks, every single one of which was handmade. There's also a tidy little collection of **ceramics** from the nearby pottery villages of Dolenja Vas and Prigorica, the latter particularly known for its clay figurines. Along the gantry, in the castle tower, there's an exhibition on **witchcraft**, featuring a group of mocked-up implements and nasty contraptions – gallows, spiked chairs and the like – used in the torture and killing of witches between the fifteenth and eighteenth centuries.

More commonly known as the **Cultural Activists' Park**, the surrounding grounds feature busts and memorial stones of prominent local achievers such as composer Jakob Gallus and the linguist Stanislav Škrabec (see below).

Cerkev Sv Štefan
Škrabčev trg 15 • If the church is closed, call in at the priest's house next door (no. 15) for the key

Built in 1868, the otherwise dull-looking **Cerkev Sv Štefan** (Parish Church of St Stephen) was given a sharp contemporary twist shortly after World War II by Jože Plečnik (see box, p.49), who designed the crown-like steeples atop the twin bell towers – an odd, but effective, amalgamation of triangular arches, spiked cones and pillars. Originally designed for an unnamed cathedral, this was Plečnik's last ever project, though it was actually completed by one of his students after his death. Its interior stars a ceiling painting of the Holy Trinity, a couple of sculptures of St Peter and St Paul, and some terrific paintings by the likes of Langus and Koželj.

The **Štekliček House**, opposite the church at no. 26, is where Slovenia's most esteemed poet, France Prešeren (see box, p.113), was schooled between 1810 and 1812.

Škrabčeva Domačija
Hrovača 42, 1km south of town • No set hours; call in advance • €2 • ☎01 581 6308, ⓦskrabceva-domacija.com

Located in Hrovača, a prim, village-like suburb of Ribnica, is the enjoyable **Škrabčeva Domačija** (Škrabec Homestead), ancestral home of the Škrabec family for more than two centuries. Widely regarded as the country's premier nineteenth-century linguist, Stanislav Škrabec (1844–1918) published his first work in 1870 – a text on the vocal properties and dialect of Slovene literary language and writing – followed by a number of other important treatises, critiques and religious texts. He also taught several languages at a monastic school in Gorizia. The renovated house comprises the traditional setup of "black kitchen" (see p.123), living room and bedroom, each room having retained its outstanding original furnishings. Across the road, a beautifully renovated **smithy** now functions as a gallery and exhibition space.

ARRIVAL AND INFORMATION

By bus Buses from Kočevje (Mon–Fri hourly, Sat & Sun 6 daily; 30min) and Ljubljana (Mon–Fri every 30min, Sat & Sun every 1–2 hr; 1hr) stop outside the church on Škrabčev trg.

Tourist office The office, such as it is, is inside the Ribnica Handicraft Centre (see p.214), Cesta na Ugar 6.

ACCOMMODATION AND EATING

Gostilna Harlekin Gorenjska cesta 21 ☎01 836 1532, ⓦharlekin.si. Located 500m northwest of the centre back out on the road to Ljubljana, this crisp, clean *gostilna* doubles nicely, and conveniently, as somewhere both to bed down and to eat. There are five fragrant rooms with natural wood furnishings, while the restaurant doles out scrummy pizzas from a brick-fired oven, and filling daily *malice* for just €6. Mon–Fri 10am–10pm, Sat noon–11pm, Sun noon–10pm. **€50**

Škrabčeva Domačija Hrovača 42, 1km south of town ☎01 836 4515, ⓦskrabceva-domacija.com. This renovated barn – which forms part of the Škrabec Homestead complex (see opposite) – houses four stunning rooms (two upstairs, two down) painted in beautiful pastel shades with oak furnishings. The odd, playful design feature pays homage to the local woodenware industry (sieves on the ceilings, for example), while the original "black kitchen" remains *in situ* between the two ground-floor rooms. **€60**

Vnebovzetje Device Marije

Nova Štifta, 6km west of Ribnica • Outside Sun Mass the church is usually kept locked, but there should be someone with the key in the adjacent monastery building • You will need your own transport to get here

In the hamlet of **NOVA ŠTIFTA**, in the foothills of Velika Gora, the **Vnebovzetje Device Marije** (Church of the Assumption) is one of Slovenia's most important pilgrimage churches, a fine-looking Baroque structure built between 1641 and 1671 and noteworthy for its unorthodox octagonal form and unusual arcaded portico embracing the south and east facades.

Its interior would be unremarkable were it not for the blisteringly colourful, gold, red and green wood-carved **altars**, ornamented with dazzling spiral columns. Around a century after the church was built, the **Holy Steps** (Sancta Sanctorum) were constructed on the north side in order to allow greater numbers of pilgrims into the church; unless you're here for Sunday Mass, the steps are usually out of bounds, though you can just catch a glimpse of them, and the frescoes lining the side walls, through the windows.

Kočevje

Sixteen kilometres southeast of Ribnica is **KOČEVJE**, whose first inhabitants, way back in the fourteenth century, were German settlers, the result of a systematic colonization policy introduced by the ruling Ortenburgs. (The name Kočevje is actually derived from the German word Gottschee, the name of the region – and the German-speaking, Slovene, minority – during the interwar years.) Historically, **Kočevska** (the name of the region) has always been sparsely populated, the legacy of poor transportation links, a programme of mass resettlement of the majority ethnic German population towards the end of World War II, and the closure of a large part of the region for military purposes following the end of the same war – a regulation that was lifted following independence in 1991. In truth, apart from its excellent **regional museum**, Kočevje is not particularly appealing, and tourist facilities are negligible, but its proximity to both Kočevski Rog and the Kolpa Valley means that there's a good chance you'll pass through if you're heading to those places.

Pokrajinski muzej Kočevje

Prešernova ulica 11 • Mon–Fri 9am–3pm, Sat 10am–1pm • €3 • ☎01 895 0303, ⓦpmk-kocevje.si

The rewarding **Pokrajinski muzej Kočevje** (Kočevje Regional Museum) stands a ten-minute walk east of the main square, Trg zbora odposlancev. Of particular interest – indeed, of some historical importance for Slovenes – is the building itself:

4

BROWN BEARS

The majority of Slovenia's estimated six hundred or so **brown bears** are to be found in the heavily forested regions of southern Slovenia, and, in particular, those forests surrounding Kočevje and Snežnik.

The country's **indigenous brown bear population** was almost decimated during the nineteenth century, thanks to intensive farming, deforestation and excessive hunting. But stricter environmental protection standards since the end of World War II have contributed to a sharp increase in their number over the past few decades, numbers that were boosted during the wars in Bosnia in the early 1990s when many bears sought to escape their disturbed habitats. Today, between seventy and one hundred bears are culled each year, while small numbers are regularly transferred to France, Spain and other European countries in order to repopulate certain areas.

The most likely time to **see bears** is from April to June and in October and November. Organized **bear-watching** trips (usually April to mid-Oct) can be arranged at the tourist information office in Lož, 6km east of Lake Cerknica (☎081 602 853, ⓦloskadolina.info) – expect to pay around €90 per person, or less in bigger groups. At any time of year, you'd do well to follow the cardinal rules: store food and rubbish properly; watch out for fresh tracks, diggings and droppings; make sure bears know you're there (make lots of noise as you're walking); and, clearly, do not approach them.

built in 1937, the portentous Socialist-style **Šeškov House** (Šeškov dom) staged the Assembly of the Delegates of the Slovene Nation in October 1943, the first elected parliament in Slovenia's history. The only remaining original feature of the hall is the heavily pockmarked bright red insignia above the stage, which reads "Narod si bo pisal Sodbo Sam" ("The people will make their own judgement").

Božidar Jakac collection

The walls of the hall are now framed with a fine selection of sketches and drawings by Dolenjska native **Božidar Jakac**, an artist whose work you'll come across time and again in this region; completed during the sessions of the 1943 assembly, his black and brown chalk drawings depict local landscapes, portraits and the lives of the Rog inhabitants – notably the Partisans (*Singing by Fire at Baza 20* and *In a Shelter During German Offensive*), for whom he acted as pictorial chronicler.

Kočevje Germans

The museum's core exhibition deals with the plight of the **Kočevje Germans** who, until the Italian occupation during the winter of 1941–42, had been the region's majority population for some six hundred years – in fact, they were one of the earliest German ethnic groups outside Germany and Austria. The effect of the occupation was catastrophic; most of the population (nearly twelve thousand) was relocated into homes of previously deported Slovenes in the lower Posavje region (which was then under German control), more than half of the 175 or so German-speaking settlements in the region were abandoned, demolished or renamed, and nearly one hundred churches were razed. One of the most intriguing items on display is a church bell buried by a priest before the forced relocations, which was dug up in 1990.

ARRIVAL AND INFORMATION   KOČEVJE

By bus The bus station is on Reška cesta, 200m south of the main square, Trg zbora odposlancev (abbreviated to TZO on signs).
Destinations Ljubljana (Mon–Fri hourly, Sat & Sun hourly–every 2hr; 1hr 30min); Ribnica (Mon–Fri hourly, Sat & Sun 6 daily; 30min).

Tourist office Just off the main square at Trg zbora odposlancev 47 (Mon–Fri 8am–7pm, Sat 8am–1pm; ☎083 829 000, ⓦkocevska.net); staff here can organize bear-watching trips, and you can also rent bikes (€12 for 6hr, €16/day).

ACCOMMODATION AND EATING

Kočevje Cultural Centre Trg zbora odposlancev 62 ☏ 082 009 485, ⊛ kck.si. The town's enterprising cultural hub, comprising a cute little café – easily the town's best place for a drink, be it a daytime coffee or an evening beer – and cinema. Concerts are also staged here, too, and there's an open BBQ in the garden every Thurs in summer. Mon–Thurs 7am–10pm, Fri 7am–midnight,

Sat 10am–midnight, Sun 10am–10pm.
Veronika Ljubljanska cesta 35 ☏ 01 895 3017, ⊛ artplet.si. This highly conspicuous, rather overblown Art Nouveau villa 800m north of the centre is pretty much the best place in Kočevje to bed down for the night, even if the rooms are like something from the 1970s; still, they're clean and a good size, with triples and quads available, too. **€65**

Kočevski Rog

One of the country's most secluded karst landscapes, **Kočevski Rog** is a massively forested 35km-long mountain range bordering Kočevje to the east, and extending in a northwest–southeast direction (a typical Dinaric range) towards the Kolpa River and Croatian border. During World War II Kočevski Rog offered perfect sanctuary for **Partisan** activities, sheltering military and political offices, workshops, hospitals, printing presses and schools.

It was in these forests, too, that several thousand anti-communist forces – mostly members of the notorious Slovene Home Guard (Domobranci) returned by British military authorities at the war's end – were summarily executed and dumped into limestone pits. The existence of these **mass graves** remained a secret until 1975, when the dissident writer and politician Edvard Kocbek revealed the grim details in an interview with a Trieste newspaper. It was only recently, however, that the victims of these "silent killings" were acknowledged, with the passing of the 2003 War Graves Act, which effectively made provision for the management and marking of burial sites at the appropriate spots.

4

Baza 20

On the eastern ridge of Kočevski Rog • To visit, contact the tourist office in Dolenjske Toplice (see p.225) • It's easiest to get here from Dolenjske Toplice, at the foot of Rog; take the road south for 1km to Podturn, then head up the mountain road to the car park, a further 7km distant; from here it's a 15min walk through the forest

The centre of Partisan operations in Kočevski Rog was **Baza 20** (Base 20), some 26 wooden shacks occupied by members of both the Central Committee of the

---

HIKING IN KOČEVSKI ROG AND THE VIRGIN FORESTS

Kočevski Rog offers some of the best **non-alpine hiking** in the country and, though not especially demanding, the walks here are very enjoyable. You'd do well, however, to stick closely to the trails; not only are you likely to get completely lost if you stray, but it's not inconceivable that you'll encounter a brown bear (see box opposite), a large number of which inhabit these parts – as do lynx, wolves, boars and red deer (not surprisingly, Kočevksi Rog is popular with hunters). The 1:50,000 *Kočevsko* map is an essential aid if you plan to hike anywhere in these forests.

The circular **Rog Footpath** (Roška pešpot) – somewhat ominously marked out by bear paws – totals some 60km. While it's unlikely you'd want to tackle the whole thing – it would take around three days – you can easily do parts of it; one possibility is to drive to the highest point, **Veliki Rog** (1099m), where's there's a viewing tower, and hike a section of the trail from there. Three kilometres south of Veliki Rog is **Rajhenavski Rog**, one of Kočevski's six **virgin forests** – there is a total of fourteen in the whole country. The trees here are higher, thicker and older (400- and 500-year-old trees are not uncommon) than those of your average forest, and strictly administered rules forbid the cutting or removal of any of them, dead or alive. As protected and preserved areas, virgin forests are strictly off limits to the general public, though trails are laid out around the periphery. The best known of the trees, and the symbol of Kočevski Rog, is the **Queen of Rog**, a magnificent 50m-high, 500-year-old fir 2km south of Rajhenavski Rog itself.

Communist Party of Slovenia and the Executive Committee of the Liberation Front. At the height of operations, nearly two hundred people were ensconced here. As an attraction, Baza 20 can't compare with the Franja Partisan Hospital near Cerkno (see p.172), but it is possible to look inside a couple of the huts (save for some bunk beds and a small exhibition there's not much to see).

Kolpa Valley

The main Ljubljana–Ribnica–Kočevje road continues south towards the stunning **Kolpa Valley**, a contorted, gorge-like river valley named after the beautiful 120km-long **Kolpa River** (Kupa in Croatian), which forms the border with Croatia. For the most part, the valley remains well off the main tourist track, thanks both to the popularity of more established destinations further north and the paucity of public transport hereabouts. This is, though, wonderful driving and cycling country, and if you have wheels or are prepared to hitch then you could do a lot worse than spend a day taking in the scenery, enjoying any number of **water activities**, or just resting up at one of the many delightful **riverside picnic** spots. Although quite different in character and temperament from the Soča River, the Kolpa, with its picturesque rapids and dams, is a big draw for **adventure-sports enthusiasts**, with swimmers and bathers flocking to its warm waters in summer.

Upper Kolpa Valley

The valley is at its most impressive between the hamlet of **Dol** – some 26km east of the Petrina border crossing – and the village of **Osilnica**, 20km west of the same crossing, a stretch known as the **Upper Kolpa Valley** (Zgornja Kolpska dolina).

Approximately 10km west of the border crossing, just beyond the village of **Srobotnik** (stop off at the small parking bay), a short gravel path sneaks its way up to the redundant **Cerkev Sv Ana** (Church of St Anne); the church is closed but the stupendous views are more than ample compensation. Back on the road, shortly after the church, the entrance to the uppermost part of the valley – **Osilniška dolina** (Osilnica Valley) – is marked by a hulk-sized **wooden statue** of the local mythological folk hero **Peter Klepec**, whose feats of strength and daring against the Turks are the stuff of legend in these parts. A further 4km on from here, the village of **Grintovec pri Osilnici** is the starting point for an energetic hike up to the formidable bluff of **Loška stena** (875m; 5hr).

Ribjek

The first building you see on entering the village of **RIBJEK**, some 2km beyond Grintovec and sited almost directly beneath Loška stena, is the preposterously pretty roadside **Cerkev Sv Egidija** (Church of St Egidius), the valley's most important historical monument. Built around 1680 but renovated a few years ago, this dinky Renaissance structure manifests some absorbing detail: whitewashed walls, painted window frames, shingled gable roof and portico and a flat bell tower. Its interior, meanwhile, stars a wood-coffered ceiling and elaborately carved wooden altars dating from around the same time. When the church is locked the key can be obtained from no. 2, just a few paces away.

Osilnica

At the confluence of the Kolpa and Čabranka rivers, 3km beyond Ribjek, **OSILNICA** is the valley's largest settlement, and pretty much the end of the line as far as things to see and do are concerned. Aside from harbouring most of the valley's practical facilities, it's also the centre for local sports and activities.

SPORT AND ACTIVITIES ON THE KOLPA

Between April and October, there's a whole range of **activities** available on the Kolpa. **Kolpa Sports** (☎01 894 1508, ⓦkolpa-sports.com), linked to the *Kovač* hotel in Osilnica (see below), is a good place to start, offering rafting, kayaking and canoeing (all around €25/person for 3hr), and paintballing (€19 for 3hr); there's also an Adrenaline Park (€19 for 3hr) within the *Kovač* hotel grounds. Guided hikes are possible on request, and there are bikes for rent (€10 for half a day, €15/day). Call at least a day in advance to organize any of these activities.

If you prefer to go it alone, you could also hike to the **source of the Kolpa** in Croatia, which should take around five hours (round trip; take your passport).

ACCOMMODATION AND EATING   OSILNICA

Kovač Sela 5 ☎01 894 1508, ⓦkovac-kolpa.com. Busy, family-run affair a 5min walk from the main square, where pretty much everything in the village happens. Accommodation-wise, they've got comfortable hotel rooms, apartments sleeping from four to six people and a tidy little campsite. The classy restaurant offers superb home-style cooking; its terrace is a splendid place to eat in summer. Daily 7am–10pm. Camping **€20**, dorms **€50**

Eastern Dolenjska

The majority of the sights in **eastern Dolenjska** are ranged along the picturesque **Krka River Valley**, whose river emanates from a cave near the village of the same name and flows eastwards for 94km towards the Croatian border, joining up with the mighty Sava River near Brežice. Approximately midway between Ljubljana and the beginning of the Krka, both **Stična Monastery** and **Bogenšperk Castle** are well worth visiting.

From its source, the Krka – distinguished by its attractive calc-tufa falls and rapids, step-like waterfalls composed of porous rock formed from calcium carbonate – continues east towards the ruins of **Žužemberk Castle** and **Soteska Manor**, before turning north just prior to the atmospheric little spa town of **Dolenjske Toplice**. A little further on is **Novo Mesto**, southern Slovenia's largest town and worthy of a day's exploration. East of Novo Mesto, the river continues past the beautifully set **Otočec Castle**, and the delightfully slumberous town of **Kostanjevica na Krki**, itself close to another of Slovenia's ancient monasteries, **Pleterje**. The region's easternmost attractions are the small market town of **Brežice**, and the country's largest spa centre in **Čatež**.

Cistercijanski samostan Stična

Near Ivančna, 30km southeast of Ljubljana • Guided tours only, taking in the Slovene Museum of Christianity, the Abbey church and cloister: Tues–Sat 8.30am, 10am, 2pm & 4pm, Sun 2pm & 4pm • €5 • ☎01 787 7100, ⓦmks-sticna.si • Trains run from Ljubljana to Ivančna Gorica (Mon–Fri every 30min–1hr, Sat & Sun 4 daily), from where it's about 2.5km to the monastery

Just off the Ljubljana–Novo Mesto highway, near the village of **Ivančna Gorica**, **Cistercijanski samostan Stična** (Stična Monastery) is Slovenia's oldest monastery, established in 1132 as part of the European network of Cistercian monasteries. Within a few years Stična had assumed the role of Dolenjska's chief centre of culture and learning, with several important religious manuscripts drawn up in the monastery's scriptorium; these are now kept at the NUK library in Ljubljana and the Austrian National Library in Vienna.

The thick walls and towers you see today were erected as a result of repeated Turkish raids during the fifteenth century, a period of otherwise relative prosperity for Stična. Dissolved by Emperor Joseph II in 1784 as part of his sweeping reforms, the monastery remained defunct until 1898, at which point it was revived by Cistercians from the monastery at Bodensee (Lake Constance). It is currently home to eleven monks (including the abbot), and while not as asocial as those at Pleterje Monastery (see p.230), the monks here remain strictly governed by the motto of Saint Benedict, *"Ora et labora"*

("Pray and Work"), devoting themselves to between six and eight hours of prayer each day, with all meals taken in complete silence.

Muzej krščanstva na Slovenskem

On the north side of the courtyard (to the right as you enter), the two-storey, Renaissance-era **Old Prelature**, formerly the monastery's administrative centre, now houses the **Muzej krščanstva na Slovenskem** (Slovene Museum of Christianity). Its first floor is a treasure-trove of monastic riches – antique furniture, liturgical vessels, vestments and so on – while the second floor (titled "Christianity in Slovenia") chronicles the many disparate groups and movements that have shaped the development of the Slovene Church throughout the centuries, including Protestants, Jesuits, Capuchins and Ursulines. The impressive art and cultural history section has fresco remains by the renowned fifteenth-century artist Janez Ljubljanski, paintings by Langus and Metzinger, and a typically exuberant chalice designed by architect Jože Plečnik as a gift for Simon Ašič, a former abbot who happened to be one of Slovenia's most eminent herbalists; you can buy some of his medicinal herbs and teas from the shop by the entrance.

Abbey church and cloister

Adjacent to the Prelature, the twelfth-century **Abbey church** betrays few signs of its Romanesque origins, having been extensively reworked in Baroque style during the seventeenth and eighteenth centuries. Its vast, white tripartite nave is fairly naked, save for a larger than usual number of side altars – one for each priest to pray to – although there are some fine artistic treasures to admire. Look out for the fourteen Stations of the Cross painted by Fortunat Bregant in 1766; a marble tabernacle by Plečnik; and some beautifully worked tombstones – in particular the red stone tombstone of Abbot Jacob Reinprecht, the chief architect of the church's present Baroque appearance.

Abutting the church at the heart of the complex is the thirteenth-century Gothic **cloister**, a splendid rib-vaulted space complete with lancet windows and several layers of just about discernible frescoes, the best of which are those by master painter Janez Ljubljanski in the north wing. Elsewhere, note the figural keystones in the western wing depicting human faces, and the two superbly restored bifora (double-arched windows), the cloister's most obvious Romanesque remains. On the south side of the cloister, the **refectory**'s pink vaulted ceiling is decorated with some marvellous stuccowork (it's forbidden to enter, but you can see it from the doorway), as is the ceiling of the **Upper Tower**, located on the opposite side of the Prelature; the compositions on the latter depict scenes from the Crucifixion and Last Judgement, as well as images of the four Church Fathers.

Grad Bogenšperk

Bogenšperk, 7.5km south of Litija • March & Nov Sat & Sun 10am–5pm; April–June, Sept & Oct Tues–Fri 9am–4pm, Sat & Sun 10am–6pm; July & Aug Tues–Sat 9am–5pm, Sun 10am–6pm • €4.50 • ☎ 01 898 7664, ⓦ bogensperk.si • Trains run from Ljubljana to Litija (every 30min; 30min), from where you should be able to hitch to the castle

Surrounded by the densely forested Dolenjska hills, **Grad Bogenšperk** (Bogenšperk Castle) is a descendant of a twelfth-century medieval fortification, though the present structure dates from around 1511. Built by the lords of Wagen (Wagensperg is German for Bogenšperk), the castle is synonymous with the great polymath Janez Vajkard Valvasor (see box opposite), who lived and worked here between 1672 and 1692, during which time he compiled his immense opus *The Glory of the Duchy of Carniola*.

The building is a classic Renaissance-era chateau featuring three cylindrical towers and a partly arcaded inner courtyard. The interior, meanwhile, has been refurbished – the castle's entire contents were plundered at the end of World War II – so as to evoke the atmosphere of Valvasor's day. His **library** is now used as a wedding venue, while the old hunting room contains an odd, and rather mundane, mishmash of exhibits: hunting

JANEZ VAJKARD VALVASOR

Arguably Slovenia's greatest scholar, **Janez Vajkard Valvasor** (1641–93) – historian, topographer and ethnologist – was born in Ljubljana to a noble family from Bergamo in Italy. Following extensive travels throughout Europe and North Africa, Valvasor bought Bogenšperk in 1672, assembling a rich library and establishing important graphics and printing workshops within the castle. Having devoted his entire life to research, he spent the next fifteen years compiling and writing his monumental Baroque topography *The Glory of the Duchy of Carniola*, four illustrated encyclopedic volumes weighing in at 3532 pages. In it, Valvasor offered the first thorough presentation of the then province of Carniola, as well as several neighbouring provinces, expounding on the region's extraordinary natural phenomena, such as the caves at Postojna and Škocjan, and the disappearing Lake Cerknica, as well as extolling the virtues of the people who shaped these lands. Following publication, Valvasor lectured at the Royal Society in London on the miraculous workings of the lake, an occasion that saw him rewarded with a fellowship. However, such was the debt he accumulated while compiling and publishing the book that Valvasor was eventually forced to sell the castle and all its contents. He died, destitute, in the town of Krško, aged 52.

trophies, geological and folk-costume displays, along with an exposition on seventeenth-century witch trials, a subject Valvasor wrote about in *The Glory*. Of greater interest are the two rooms packed with fascinating maps and sketches, including original works by Valvasor and eminent Slovene cartographer Peter Kosler, and a cylinder printing press of the type Valvasor used – the original is in Mainz, Germany. Valvasor's **study** contains the museum's principal exhibit, an original copy of *The Glory of the Duchy of Carniola*.

4

Muljava

South of Ivančna Gorica, on the other side of the highway, **MULJAVA** is an attractive little village known throughout the country as the birthplace of popular Slovene novelist and journalist **Josip Jurčič** (1844–81), the man credited with writing Slovenia's first full-length novel *Deseti Brat* (*The Tenth Brother*), in 1866. The village also marks the starting point for the scenic and popular **Jurčičeva Pot walk** (3–4hr), which winds up at the lovely little medieval settlement of Višnja Gora (550m) 15km north.

Jurčičeva Domačija

Muljava 11 • March–Nov Tues–Sat 8am–noon & 2–5pm • €3 • ☎ 01 787 6500 • Trains run from Ljubljana to Ivančna Gorica (Mon–Fri every 30min–1hr, Sat & Sun 4 daily), from where it's a 4.5km walk or hitched ride to Muljava

Jurčičeva Domačija, the house in which Josip Jurčič was born and where he lived until the age of 12, was built by his grandfather in 1826 and is as interesting for its architectural detail – a traditional "black kitchen" (see p.123), living room, bedroom and cellar – as it is for the Jurčič memorabilia on display. In the garden stands a beehive, furnished with the traditional painted panels, while to the rear of the house there's a granary and a *krjavelj* hut, a timber shack dwelling usually inhabited by a *bajtar* – a poor villager.

Each year, on two or three consecutive weekends at the end of June/beginning of July, several of Jurčič's works are staged in the fabulous natural **amphitheatre** at the edge of woodland behind the house; tickets (around €10) can be bought one hour before each performance.

Krška jama

Opening times can be erratic but usually open for guided tours April–Oct Sat & Sun 2–4pm; it's best to call in advance to make sure • €3 • ☎ 041 276 252

One section of the Jurčičeva Pot walk (see above) takes in the village of **Krka**, 2km south of Muljava, and the **source of the Krka River** (Pri Izviru), another 2km further on.

The source (a 17m-deep siphon lake) is actually located inside the small, 200m-long **Krška jama** (Krka Cave), a low-key spectacle compared to Slovenia's much grander showcaves, but which does hold a specimen of *Proteus anguinus*, the human fish (see box, p.206). Although the cave was recorded by Valvasor in the seventeenth century, it wasn't until 1887 that the first plans were drawn up, and another hundred years or so before the caves were opened up to visitors.

Žužemberk

ŽUŽEMBERK, the Krka River Valley's major settlement, is a tranquil market town whose position on the Krka allowed for the extensive development, during the sixteenth and seventeenth centuries, of water-powered iron foundries and sawmills. At one stage there were around forty of the latter lining this stretch of river, though by the end of the twentieth century most had ceased functioning. In the centre of the **main square** is a fine little cast-iron fountain, forged at the ironworks in the nearby village of Dvor and worth a look for its splendidly crafted animal heads, from which water still spouts.

Grad Žužemberk

May, Sept & Oct Sat & Sun 8am–6pm; June–Aug daily 8am–8pm • Free

The formidable bulk of **Grad Žužemberk** (Žužemberk Castle) is dramatically located on a steep bank high above the Krka River, buffered by a thick clump of trees that slopes down to the water. The original structure dates from the thirteenth century, with further, piecemeal development – including the defensive walls, arcades and vaulted cellars – over the ensuing centuries. Much of the castle was razed during World War II, since when a painfully slow renovation programme has restored the five huge towers and bastions, but little else. For the best views of the castle, walk down to the river and across to the opposite bank; standing on the bridge gives you head-on views of the calc-tufa falls.

Today, the castle's large inner courtyard is an atmospheric venue for summer concerts and plays, all of which are usually free; the key event is the **Market Town Days Festival** (Trški dnevni) in mid-July, a boisterous weekend of medieval jousting, exhibitions and food and craft stalls.

ARRIVAL AND ACTIVITIES   ŽUŽEMBERK

By bus Buses from Dolenjske Toplice (Mon–Fri 4 daily; 30min) stop on the main square, Grajski trg.

Canoeing The Krka River is popular with watersports enthusiasts; canoes (€7/hr) can be rented from the *Koren Tourist Farm*.

ACCOMMODATION AND EATING

Koren Tourist Farm Dolga Vas 5 ☎07 308 7260, ⓦturizem-koren.com. Perfectly sited on the opposite bank to the castle, this convivial place offers six one- to five-bed rooms (all en suite), with campers welcome to pitch tents (for free) in the adjoining field. The restaurant serves decent food, such as home-made cheese dumplings, or buckwheat with *klobasa* sausage and porcini mushrooms (€9), best enjoyed out on the stone terrace overlooking the water. Daily 10am–11pm. **€52**

Dvorec Soteska and Hudičev turn

Some 9km downriver from Žužemberk Castle are the less complete ruins of **Dvorec Soteska** (Soteska Manor), built between 1664 and 1689 by Duke Jurij Gallenberg but which, for the greater part of its existence, was the domicile of the Auersperg counts. Today, a fairly unbroken outer shell incorporating two of the four original corner towers and the entrance gate are all that remain of the manor following its destruction in 1943 by Partisan units, an act of deliberate sabotage carried out in order to prevent

German troops from appropriating it. The former storage depot has been opened up to accommodate a small collection of random **vintage vehicles** (Sun 1–5pm; €1.50), mostly from the 1920s, including a deep-green Citroën, several Fiats from Italy and a fire engine.

From the former entrance to the manor, a path cuts across the main road towards a field (formerly a walled-in park) in the centre of which stands the park pavilion, otherwise known as the **Hudičev turn** (Devil's Tower). Its empty interior – if you wish to see it, contact the tourist office in Dolenjske Toplice (see below) – is illuminated with murals of mythological figures, pillared architecture and other fantastical compositions painted by the Almanach workshop in the seventeenth century. Before the manor's destruction, the path was lined with three stone portals, one of which – and it's a particularly fine piece of craftsmanship – now marks the entrance to the field.

Dolenjske Toplice

Just where the river turns sharply in the direction of Novo Mesto is **DOLENJSKE TOPLICE**, a classic, neat and orderly **spa town** whose elegant Habsburg-era buildings give it an authentic *fin-de-siècle* ambience. Exploited since medieval times for curative purposes, the town's springs were first channelled into a bathhouse by Ivan Vajkard, a member of the Auersperg family, in the seventeenth century, although it wasn't until the late nineteenth century that Dolenjske Toplice (then called Strascha Toplitz) prospered as a fashionable, modern spa resort, utilized to treat a wide range of disorders and illnesses. During both World Wars the resort was pressed into action as an emergency military treatment centre and hospital.

ARRIVAL AND INFORMATION

DOLENJSKE TOPLICE

By bus Buses stop along Zdraviliški trg, the main street; from here nothing is more than a 10min walk away.
Destinations Novo Mesto (Mon–Fri hourly, Sat 5 daily; 20min); Žužemberk (Mon–Fri 4 daily; 30min).
Tourist office From the bus stop, it's a short walk beyond the *Kristal* hotel and across the bridge to the (rather useless) tourist office in the Cultural Centre at Sokolski trg 4 (June–Aug Mon–Fri 9am–noon & 2–7pm, Sat 9am–3pm, Sun 9am–noon; Sept–May Mon–Fri 9am–3pm, Sat & Sun 9am–noon; ☎ 07 384 5180, ⓦ dolenjske-toplice.si).

ACCOMMODATION AND EATING

Camping Potočar Podhosta 48 ☎ 040 466 589, ⓦ camping-potocar.si. The town's small campsite is picturesquely located at the foot of the wooded slopes by the Sušica stream, around 500m north of Zdraviliški trg. Hemmed in by tall spruce and fir trees, this long, narrow site has limited but modern facilities including a shower/toilet block and laundry, plus bikes for rent (€5 for 3hr, €10/ day). Mid-April to Sept. **€22**

Oštarija Sokolski trg 2 ☎ 051 262 990, ⓦ ostarija.si. As smart as the rooms are – warmly decorated in browns and oranges – it's the restaurant, with its brilliantly graffitied walls and splashes of artwork, that sets this place apart. The accent is firmly on regional ingredients and dishes, hence the likes of smoked catfish; cheese *štruklji* with

---

BATHING MATTERS

Dolenjske Toplice's main **thermal pools** are part of the supermodern Balnea Wellness Centre, Zdraviliški trg 7 (Mon–Thurs & Sun 8am–9pm, Fri & Sat 8am–11pm; Mon–Fri €8 for 3hr, €10/day, Sat & Sun €11 for 3hr, €13/day; ⓦ terme-krka.com), which has both indoor and outdoor (May–Sept) thermal pools, complete with water massages, waterwalls and geysers, as well as a pool for kids. In the same complex, the **Oasis sauna centre** (Mon, Wed & Thurs 11am–9pm, Tues & Sun 9am–9pm, Fri 11am–11pm, Sat 9am–11pm; Mon–Fri €15 for 3hr, €17/day, Sat & Sun €17 for 3hr, €19/day) comprises, among other things, a whirlpool, herbal sauna, Turkish steam bath and Japanese sweat bath. Elsewhere, the modern complex inside the *Vital* hotel, Zdraviliški trg 1, houses three pools (daily 7am–8pm; Mon–Fri €7, Sat & Sun €9). Note that guests staying at any of the three spa hotels (*Balnea*, *Vital* and *Kristal*) are permitted free entry to all the town's thermal pools.

morel sauce (€7); and venison in juniper sauce with grilled *cepes* and vegetable souffle (€19). Tues–Sat noon–11pm, Sun noon–4pm. **€60**

Pri Mostu Pionirski cesta 2 ☎ 051 388 388, ⓦ primostu .si. Opposite *Oštarija* and not quite as classy, this lively

hotel/pub represents terrific value. There are seven super-modern rooms, one with four beds including a bunk, plus a lounge-like bar and cheery terrace overlooking the river. Breakfast €5. **€49**

Novo Mesto

Dolenjska's cultural and religious centre since the Middle Ages, **NOVO MESTO** (New Town) is the largest town in southeastern Slovenia. Continuously settled since the Bronze Age – as attested to by the numerous **archeological sites** hereabouts – Novo Mesto was granted city rights in 1365, thereafter evolving into a prosperous market town and trade centre and, following the establishment of a collegiate chapter around the same time, a centre of ecclesiastical importance. In recent times, Novo Mesto has established itself as one of the country's leading **industrial** power bases, home to the major pharmaceutical enterprise Krka and the highly productive vehicle manufacturer Revoz (a subsidiary of Renault), formerly the largest plant in Yugoslavia.

Novo Mesto's sights are few, but its personable **old core**, attractively sited on a rocky promontory in a hairpin bend of the Krka River, does possess a couple of noteworthy monuments, and its **museum** keeps a first-rate collection of archeological treasures. The town is also a handy springboard for the many attractions – rivers, castles, spas and monasteries – close at hand.

Glavni trg

The focal point of Novo Mesto is cobbled **Glavni trg** (Main Square), actually more street than square. Once the haunt of merchants and craftsmen, today the square is lined with handsome townhouses, shops and cafés, though its most striking feature is its elegant arcades. The most prominent building, midway down the left-hand side at no. 6, is the grey, mock-Renaissance **Town Hall** (Rotovž), built in 1905.

Frančiškanska cerkev Sv Lenarta

Frančišk trg • Visits by prior arrangement only; contact the tourist office (see p.228)

Lurking just behind the Town Hall stands **Frančiškanska cerkev Sv Lenarta** (St Leonard's Franciscan Church), whose elegant, mustard-coloured neo-Gothic gabled facade, dating from around 1880, was just one of the church's many piecemeal additions following a fire in 1664. From the original church, built in 1472 as a place of refuge for Franciscan monks from Bosnia – who had initially sheltered at the Tri Fare Parish in Metlika (see p.243) – only the Gothic presbytery was retained, although its wooden altars were lost and replaced with the current neo-Gothic additions. The adjoining **monastery** boasts a fine library with some superb manuscripts, a tiny prayer book from 1450 and a psalm book made from animal skin, which features Gothic and Baroque text from 1418.

Cerkev Sv Miklavža

Kapiteljski hrib • Daily 7am–7pm • Free • ☎ 07 384 4408

Commanding the summit of Kapiteljski hrib, the **Cerkev Sv Miklavža** (Chapter Church of St Nicholas) is the town's oldest monument, encompassing a chequered mix of Gothic, neo-Gothic and Baroque elements. The most striking thing about the church is its fifteenth-century presbytery, constructed at a peculiar seventeen-degree angle to the nave, possibly the result of the awkward terrain upon which it was built. Inside, the church has some outstanding works of art, most notably the high-altar painting *St Nicholas* by Tintoretto, one of the country's most celebrated church paintings and, allegedly, one of only two of the Venetian master's works in Slovenia. Elsewhere, look out for the copy of *Maria Pomagaj* (*Mary Help*) in the first altar on the left and several works by Metzinger adorning other altars.

To the right of the presbytery a flight of steps leads down to a chilly, Gothic-vaulted **crypt**, the only one of its kind in the country and somewhat unusual in that there's actually no one buried here – it was built as a support for the presbytery, which was constructed on a slight downwards slope. At opposing ends of the crypt are two contrasting altars, one a white neo-Gothic tabernacle, the other a superb grey-black stone-cut Renaissance altar depicting Christ on the cross and a skull and bones.

Dolenjski muzej

Muzejska ulica 7 • Tues–Sat: April–Oct 9am–5pm; Nov–March 9am–4pm • €5 • ☎ 07 373 1130, ⊛ dolenjskimuzej.si

Housed in a complex of several buildings a few paces down from the church, the **Dolenjski muzej** (Dolenjska Museum) boasts one of the finest stockpiles of archeological treasures in Slovenia. The core of the collection comprises grave finds unearthed from hundreds of burial sites on the slopes of Marof and Mestne njive, two modest rises a short way north of the town centre. The earliest artefacts, from the late Bronze Age (the so-called Urnfield culture), comprise a superb display of large ceramic urns, into which the remains of the deceased, together with their personal belongings – bronze needles, jewellery, beads and the like – were placed.

The **Hallstatt** period (the early Iron or late Bronze Age, approximately eighth to fourth centuries BC) is represented by more vessels and jewellery, including earrings, bracelets and anklets, as well as several pieces of armour – the star exhibits are a beautifully well-preserved Bronze Age helmet and breast plate. The most impressive items, however, are the specimens of **Situla Art**, bronze buckets, or pails, ornately embossed with festive or hunting scenes, a collection that represents the greatest achievement in prehistoric art in Slovenia. The larger grave urns from the Celtic period were somewhat more sophisticated, suggesting that the deceased were from a higher social rank. Rounding off this veritable treasure-trove is a hoard of **Roman grave goods**, typically cups, coins, wine pitchers and oil lamps, as well as a stash of Roman legionary weapons. The remainder of the museum, comprising ethnological and modern history collections, is, by comparison, distinctly underwhelming.

Jakčev dom

Sokolska ulica 1 • Tues–Sat: April–Oct 9am–5pm; Nov–March 9am–4pm • €3 • ☎ 07 373 1130, ⊚ dolenjskimuzej.si

At Glavni trg's southern end, perched just above the picturesque **Breg** embankment, the **Jakčev dom** (Božidar Jakac House) holds the artist's largest collection of sketches and drawings outside Kostanjevica (see p.232); there's also a terrific selection of watercolours, oils and pastels depicting town scenes and local landscapes, such as the lovely *Novo Mesto with a Cloister*. Formerly a hotel, this building was actually the house of his father – Jakac was born 100m further up the street at Cvelbarjeva ulica 9. Crossing the **Kandijski most** (Kandijski Bridge) gives you some lovely views back to Breg and the bright orange-tiled rooftops of the Old Town.

ARRIVAL AND INFORMATION   NOVO MESTO

By bus The bus station is on Topliška cesta, a 10min walk southwest of the town centre.

Destinations Brežice (Mon–Fri 4 daily, Sat & Sun 3 daily; 1hr); Dolenjske Toplice (Mon–Fri hourly, Sat 3 daily; 20min); Kostanjevica na krki (Mon–Fri 4 daily, Sat & Sun 3 daily; 40min); Ljubljana (Mon–Fri 7 daily, Sat & Sun 3–4 daily; 1hr 10min); Otočec (Mon–Fri 7 daily, Sat 3 daily; 15min); Žužemberk (Mon–Fri 1 daily; 45min).

By train There are two train stations – the main one, Novo Mesto, is 800m west of town on Ljubljanska cesta; the second, Center, is on the north side of the Šmihelski Bridge,

just a 5min walk into town. All trains stop at both stations; make sure to alight at Center.

Destinations Črnomelj (Mon–Fri 10 daily, Sat & Sun 2–3 daily; 40–50min); Ljubljana (Mon–Fri 12 daily, Sat & Sun 4–5 daily; 1hr 40min–2hr); Metlika (Mon–Fri 10 daily, Sat & Sun 2–3 daily; 1hr–1hr 10min).

Tourist office Near the town hall at Glavni trg 11 (April–Oct Mon–Fri 8am–7pm, Sat 9am–3pm, Sun 9am–1pm; Nov–March Mon–Fri 9am–5pm, Sat 9am–2pm; ☎ 07 393 9263, ⊚ visitnovomesto.si).

ACCOMMODATION

Krka Novi trg ☎ 07 394 2100, ⊚ terme-krka.com. If you don't mind paying over the odds, then the town's one hotel will more than suffice; the place retains a distinct business-like feel, though the rooms are as polished as you'd expect (and hope) when forking out this much. **€114**

Ravbar Apartments Smrečnikova ulica 15–17 ☎ 07 373 0680, ⊚ ravbar.net. This family-run place, a 15min walk east of the bus station, is a decent bet, with apartments sleeping two to six people as well as single

and double rooms. All are large, modern and immaculately kept. Breakfast €7. Doubles **€35**, apartments **€46**

★ **Situla Hostel** Dilančeva ulica 1 ☎ 07 394 2000, ⊚ situla.si. In the heart of the Old Town, *Situla* is a fabulously conceived lodging whose artfully designed rooms – three- to eight-bed dorms, singles, doubles and a family room – offer a playful nod to the town's archeological heritage. It also has a very respectable restaurant (see opposite). Breakfast included. Dorms **€19**, doubles **€44**

CVIČEK

While in Novo Mesto, it would be remiss not to try the local speciality, **Cviček** (pronounced tsveechek), one of the country's most distinctive and unusual wines. Cultivated only here in southeast Dolenjska, Cviček is produced from a blend of red and white grapes – said to be more than a dozen, but this is considered an exaggeration – giving it a cranberry-juice-like appearance. Despite its dry, rather sour, taste, it's a surprisingly refreshing wine, made all the more drinkable thanks to its low alcoholic content of around nine percent. Although most Cviček is produced for home consumption, it's the first drink you'll be offered in the local restaurants and bars. The wine also plays a starring role in the **Cviček Week** festival at the end of May, which takes place in a different town each year.

EATING

Gostišče Loka Zupančičevo sprehajališče 2 ☎07 332 1108, ⓦgostisce-loka.si. The pick of the town's restaurants, both for its breezy waterside location – close to the Šmihelski Bridge – and fresh, Mediterranean-influenced food, such as risotto with prawns and courgettes (€8). You could also pop along for coffee and cake in the restaurant's adjoining *kavarna*. Mon–Fri 8am–11.30pm, Sat 9am–11pm, Sun 9am–9pm.

Situla Dilančeva ulica 1 ☎07 394 2000, ⓦsitula.si. The surprisingly sleek-looking restaurant in this hostel (see opposite) is just the job for a lunchtime *malica* (€4.50), which could be, for example, grilled cheese or vegetable soup followed by fried chicken with buttered carrots; wash it down with a glass of Cviček from the cellar (see box opposite). Mon–Fri 10am–2pm.

DRINKING

Lokal Patriot Glavni trg 6 ☎07 337 4371, ⓦlokal patriot.si. Long-standing, and very enterprising, student/ youth club serving up a varied mix of club nights, film screenings and rock and jazz concerts, occasionally starring some of Slovenia's top acts. Mon–Thurs 9am–11am, Fri 9am–2am, Sat 5pm–2am.

Pri Slonu Rozmanova ulica 22 ☎07 332 1495. "At the Elephant" is an old-style café-cum-bar that's been around for aeons; it's still a firm favourite with locals seeking a strong early-morning cup of coffee or a bout of more vigorous late-night drinking. Mon–Thurs 7am–11.30pm, Fri 7am–2am, Sat 6pm–12.30am.

Grad Otočec

Picturesquely sited on an elongated, tree-covered island in the middle of an attractive stretch of the Krka River, 7km east of Novo Mesto, is **Grad Otočec** (Otočec Castle). Surrounded by dozens of tiny islets and the Krka's distinctive calc-tufa falls, the country's only **island castle** was originally occupied by the knights of Otočec during the thirteenth century, thereafter passing through the hands of various noble families. Fortified with high walls and four chunky towers during persistent fifteenth-century Turkish raids, the castle was purchased in 1560 by Ivan Lenkovič, commander of the Austrian Empire's Vojna Krajina region, during which time it acquired its current, largely Renaissance, appearance (albeit heavily renovated following extensive World War II damage). The castle now functions as a **five-star hotel**, though anyone is welcome to have a nose around. Otherwise, the surrounding **woodland** is a lovely spot for a ramble and a picnic, or you could go for a paddle with a **canoe** rented from the campsite (see below).

ACCOMMODATION AND EATING

GRAD OTOČEC

Hotel Grad Otočec ☎082 050 310, ⓦgrad-otocec .com. Expensive, but not pretentious, this superb castle hotel offers ten rooms and six suites, each one beautifully fitted out in walnut wood and with enormous bathrooms with spa bath or rain shower. The elegant and inevitably pricey restaurant serves up wonderfully creative dishes, such as thyme-marinated rabbit fillet with black garlic and zucchini carpaccio (€19), but if your wallet can't stretch to a meal, then settle for an (expensive) cup of coffee in the suntrap courtyard café. Daily 7am–10pm. **€260**

Kamp Otočec 500m east of the castle ☎040 466 589, ⓦcamping-potocar.si. On the river's south bank, this small site has few facilities beyond a shower and toilet block, but it's spotlessly clean and well shaded, and also has canoes (€5/hr) and bikes (€5/3hr, €10/day) for rent. April to mid-Oct. **€22**

★ **Šeruga Tourist Farm** Sela pri Ratežu 15 ☎07 334 6900, ⓦseruga.si. Secreted away in an isolated wooded area 3km south of Otočec (just off the main road to Kostanjevica), this is Slovenian farm tourism at its finest. The ten gorgeous, homely, wood-furnished rooms – and a fabulous wooden cottage (the old granary) in the field beyond – are complemented by exceptional home cooking (buckwheat *štruklji*, roast rabbit, grilled trout) and local wines. **€70**

Gostilna Vovko Ratež 48 ☎07 308 5603, ⓦgostilna -vovko.si. A popular roadside inn 2km east of *Šeruga*, with a handful of good-value rooms. Even if you're not staying, but you're in the area, don't miss its terrific restaurant. The lengthy, locally influenced menu typically features the likes of Doljenski dumplings with forest mushrooms, and Krško pork trotters with buckwheat (mains €9–10). Tues–Sat noon–10pm, Sun noon–4pm. **€56**

4

Pleterje samostan

Presentation €4, €6 including a visit to the Skansen (see below); buy tickets in the shop or at the Skansen • **Shop** Mon–Sat 7.30am–5.30pm • ☎ 07 308 1219, ⓦ kartuzija-pleterje.si • Buses run to Šentjernej (6km west of Kostanjevica along the road to Novo Mesto), from where it's a 3km walk south to the monastery

Beautifully set in a secluded valley at the foot of the Gorjanci forests, **Pleterje samostan** (Pleterje Monastery) is Europe's easternmost Carthusian monastery, and the only one of Slovenia's four charterhouses still functioning. Shut off from the outside world by a formidable 2600m-long, 3m-high enclosure wall, the monastery has endured a chequered history not that dissimilar to that of Stična (see p.221). Founded in 1403 by Count Herman II of Celje, Pleterje was fortified during the fifteenth century in advance of Turkish raids, before its dissolution and subsequent appropriation by the Jesuits at the end of the sixteenth century. Following the reforms of Emperor Joseph II, the monastery was disbanded again in 1784, only to be repurchased and rebuilt by the Carthusian order in 1899.

While the **main church** is open to visitors, the rest of the monastery is strictly out of bounds. Rooted in the anchorite traditions of Early Christianity, the eleven monks at Pleterje live according to a precisely defined schedule, entirely devoted to prayer and work.

Cerkev Sv Trojice

Rated as one of the best-preserved examples of early French Gothic in Central Europe, the single-nave **Cerkev Sv Trojice** (Church of the Holy Trinity), built in 1420, is astonishingly simple and, though almost completely devoid of furniture or ornamentation, has some wonderfully subtle detail. Entering through the low, stone rood screen that separates the nave and chancel, take a look up at the splendid cross rib-vaulted ceiling, embellished with numerous bosses bearing a range of motifs, and the seventy or so clay vessels (also known as acoustical pottery) spotted along the walls. You can't really miss the high altar, a smooth slab of grey stone placed on two stone stools. On the exterior the badly pockmarked wall was the result of heavy shelling during World War II.

You can learn more about the Carthusian order by watching the informative, 25-minute **presentation** in the sacristy to the side of the church. The monastery **shop**, just down from the church, has a terrific stock of brandies from their own distillery – try juniper (*brinovec*), pear (*hruška*) or plum (*slivovka*) – as well as wines, honey and propolis.

Skansen

April–Oct daily 10am–5pm • €4, €6 including the presentation at the monastery (see above) • ☎ 07 043 4241, ⓦ skansen.si

Spread out across a lovely green field at the bottom of the road leading up to the monastery is a fabulous little **Skansen**, or open-air museum, whose handful of buildings, representing a typical farmyard from this region, were relocated here partly in order to draw visitors away from the monastery itself. As well as its classic thatched wooden house, dating from 1833 and fully equipped with authentic domestic furniture and a "black kitchen" (see p.123), the complex includes a threshing floor, fruit and flax dryer, and a superb double hayrack; you can also buy pottery and ceramics.

Time and energy permitting, you can walk along the **Pleterje Way**, a circular footpath that skirts the hills above the monastery, and which affords views of the complex you wouldn't normally get to see; allow around ninety minutes to complete it.

Kostanjevica na Krki and around

Compacted into a tight loop of the Krka River, the island settlement of **KOSTANJEVICA NA KRKI** is one of the country's smallest towns, a once thriving commercial centre with its own Mint but now a rural backwater possessed of a ghostly charm. From the main bus stop on Ljubljanska cesta, it's a five-minute walk north to the **bridge**, which in turn leads you onto the tranquil, palette-shaped island. Here you will find two main streets

CLOCKWISE FROM TOP LEFT BREŽICE CASTLE (P.233); KOLPA RIVER (P.220); PARK OF MILITARY HISTORY (P.208); PIVKA CAVE (P.206) >

that join to form a circle around a cluster of buildings variously spruced up or in an advanced state of decay. Aside from a couple of small Gothic churches sited at either end, there's actually very little to see or do on the island, but if you've got an hour to spare following a visit to the out-of-town attractions, it's worth taking a leisurely stroll around. In warmer weather the waters of the Krka at the north end of the island become a popular **bathing** spot; stand-up paddle boards can also be rented here.

Cistercijanski samostan

Grajska cesta 45

A fifteen-minute walk southwest of town (head down Ljubljanska cesta and follow the signs) is the former **Cistercijanski samostan** (Cistercian Monastery), founded in 1234, disbanded in 1786, largely destroyed during a fire in 1942 and all but completely renovated now. There are some interesting masonry fragments – vaulted ribs, keystones and so on – from the previously damaged church in the **lapidarium**, in the eastern arcaded passage of the monastery's immense three-sided cloister. The monastery gardens are dotted with around one hundred oak-wood **sculptures**, otherwise known as the **Forma Viva** (Living Form); this is one of several such sculpture parks in Slovenia, each of which demonstrates works of art made from a different material.

Galerija Božidar Jakac

Tues–Sun: April–Oct 9am–6pm; Nov–March 9am–4pm • €3 • ☎ 07 498 8150, ⓦ galerija-bj.si

The monastery cloister today accommodates the **Galerija Božidar Jakac** (Božidar Jakac Gallery), which, with the works of eight of Slovenia's most prominent artists to plough through, requires no little stamina. The first few rooms feature the fabulously creative, Surrealist bronze sculptures of **Janez Boljka**, whose work evolved from sculpting simple motifs to more adventurous subject matter, including the animal kingdom (*A Monkey, Two Rhinos Mating*) and the human form. He was noted for his sculptures of eminent Slovenes (*Ivan Cankar and his Muse, Rihard Jakopič Seated*); indeed, there's a whole room devoted to his sculptures of Cankar. From here, you head through the empty church (which usually has a multimedia display of some sort) up to the most recently renovated arcade, which holds an exhibition on the monastery church itself. You'll see some impressive remnants: tracery, capitals, a few sections of rib vaulting and the one remaining preserved boss.

Up next is **Tone Kralj**, a key figure in the interwar Slovene avant-garde but whose later works veered towards the realm of Socialist Realism. His later work, in particular, is biased towards themes of war, revolt and daily peasant life (*Shrovetide Procession*). Family portraits feature heavily too, such as the disturbing *My Mother*, which depicts his mother standing over his dead pilot brother's body; his etchings and illustrations are worth poring over too, especially those of the fictional folk hero, Martin Krpan. Room four is devoted to the versatile **Božidar Jakac**, whose prolific stock of prints and graphics, many of which document his time spent with the Partisans, is complemented by some exquisite pastels and oils. On display are land- and townscapes from Slovenia (*Hayrack*) and Prague, where he studied – keep an eye out for the lovely *Midnight Mass on Hradčani*. The most extensive collection, though, is given over to **France Kralj**, Tone's brother. The volume here of his paintings and sculptures takes some digesting; look out for the delightful *Penguins* sculpture, and the painting *Young Club*, which depicts many of Slovenia's heavyweight artists (including Pilon, Spacal and, of course, his brother) posing as if for a photograph.

Kostanjeviška jama

Guided tours (45min): mid-April to June, Sept & Oct Sat & Sun 10am, noon, 2pm, 4pm & 6pm; July & Aug daily 10am, noon, 2pm, 4pm & 6pm • €8 • ☎ 041 297 001, ⓦ kostanjeviska-jama.com

Around 1.5km southeast of town, in a small wooded area bound by a stream, is **Kostanjeviška jama** (Kostanjevica Cave), the largest and most impressive of Dolenjska's cave systems. Speleologists were first drawn to the possibility of the cave's existence following a flood in 1937, after which systematic exploration uncovered numerous other shafts, chambers and lakes.

Guided tours of the old part of the cave take in approximately 250m of the 1800m discovered to date, beginning at the 60m-long entrance tunnel. Beyond here a series of tight passages and staircases wend their way through several chambers, past two lakes, the **Razvodna dvorana** (Watershed Cavern) and the **Presihajoče jezero** (Intermittent Lake), and up to the **Križna dvorana** (Cross Cavern). The tour winds up at the **Kapniška dvorana** (Stalactite Cavern), a relatively narrow hall that, true to its name, is replete with dozens of shimmering stalactites, the tallest of which, the pillar, stands 12m high. The remainder of the cave is accessible only to experienced cavers. There are bats here, too, lots of them, including the southern horseshoe bat, which is found only in this cave.

ARRIVAL AND INFORMATION KOSTANJEVICA NA KRKI

By bus The main bus stop is opposite the *Green Bar* on Ljubljanska cesta, from where it's a 5min walk to the island.
Destinations Brežice (Mon–Fri 5 daily, Sat & Sun 3 daily; 30min); Novo Mesto (Mon–Fri 5 daily, Sat & Sun 3 daily; 40min).

Tourist office The tourist office, such as it is, is at the entrance to the Božidar Jakac Gallery, Grajska cesta 45 (Tues–Sun: April–Oct 9am–6pm; Nov–March 9am–4pm; ☎ 07 498 8150).

ACCOMMODATION AND EATING

Vila Castanea Ulica talcev 9 ☎ 031 662 011, ⓦ vila castanea.com. Restful B&B occupying a handsome nineteenth-century townhouse, whose nine rooms variously feature beautifully designed, low wooden beds with thick mattresses, parquet flooring and glass partitioning between the bedrooms and bathrooms. **€60**

Gostilna Žolnir Krška cesta 4 ☎ 07 498 7133, ⓦ zolnir.eu. Around 500m north of St James Church, across the bridge, this agreeably old-fashioned *gostilna* has twelve fairly standard rooms, all with three beds, as well as a worthy restaurant whose locally renowned house speciality is venison with dumplings and juniper berries. Daily 7am–10pm. **€50**

Brežice

A moderately important regional economic and cultural centre, **BREŽICE** sits at the confluence of the Krka and Sava rivers in the middle of the hill-fringed Krško Plain 15km east of Kostanjevica na Krki. Granted its town charter in 1354, Brežice retains a distinctive, small-town atmosphere, its single concession to grandeur a fine Renaissance **castle** now housing a good **museum**. Beyond this, there's little else to see or do here, but if you want to make good use of a night's stopover you could consider several nearby trips; the **Čatež Spa** and **Mokrice Castle** a few kilometres to the south, and the **Bizeljsko wine region** to the north, though the last is served by just a few buses.

Grad Brežice

Cesta prvih borcev 1

Prominently positioned at the extreme southern end of the town's long and attractive main street, the foundations of present-day **Grad Brežice** (Brežice Castle) were laid in 1529, when it was also fortified with robust, red-tiled conical towers. Following its purchase by the counts of Attems in the seventeenth century, the castle underwent a major style renovation – the courtyard was arcaded with Tuscan columns and several of its most important spaces, such as the stairway, chapel and, most famously, the Knight's Hall, were decorated with splendid Baroque frescoes.

Posavski muzej

April–June, Sept & Oct Tues–Sat 10am–6pm, Sun 2–6pm; July & Aug Tues–Sat 10am–8pm, Sun 2–8pm; Nov–March Tues–Sat 8am–4pm, Sun 1–4pm • €3 • ☎ 07 466 0517, ⓦ pmb.si

The castle is now home to the comprehensive **Posavski muzej** (Posavski Museum). The first half a dozen or so rooms are given over to archeological and ethnological collections; highlights from the former include ancient skeletons, weapons, jewellery and equine equipment extricated from more than four hundred Celtic graves at Dobova on the Croatian border, while the latter documents life in the Posavje region, and in particular wine-making.

Occupying two small vaulted rooms in the northeastern tower, a small **medieval history** section documents Slovene and Croatian peasant struggles. You can also see items and literature related to the Reformation in Dolenjska; the key exhibit, albeit only a copy, is the Dalmatin Bible from 1584, the first complete translation of the Bible from German into Slovene. Of the 1500 copies originally printed, only around eighty survive.

The museum's centrepiece is the magnificent **Viteška dvorana** (Knight's Hall). Awash with typically florid Italian Baroque paintings featuring scenes from classical myth and legend – Aurora and Apollo in a dove-drawn chariot, Europa and Zeus as a bull – the arts and sciences, and portraits of the Attems family, the hall is now used for weddings, high-level state functions and as one of the principal venues for Brežice Festival concerts (see box below).

The rooms at the opposite end of the hall (up the stairs) are given over to themes of **war and occupation**, with illuminating, and occasionally harrowing, coverage of life in Posavje during World War II, when more than 17,000 people were deported from the Lower Sava Valley. One poignant display is the bullet-riddled prison door from Kunejav Hram, near Podsreda, where fifteen young resistance fighters from the Brežice Company were killed or executed in 1941.

Finally, and if you've got any energy left, there's some fine **sacral art** to admire, in particular wooden sculptures, paintings by Metzinger and, best of all, a magnificent eighteenth-century wooden **sled** made in Vienna and donated to Brežice by Empress Maria Theresa.

ARRIVAL AND INFORMATION   BREŽICE

By bus From the bus station, around 800m east of town on Cesta svobode, it's a 10min walk to the centre: heading south, take a right down Bizeljska ulica, then past the Water Tower to the main street, Cesta prvih borcev.
Destinations Bizeljsko (Mon–Fri 3 daily; 30min); Kostanjevica na Kri (Mon–Fri 5 daily, Sat & Sun 3 daily; 30min); Ljubljana (3–4 daily; 2hr 15min); Novo Mesto (Mon–Fri 5 daily, Sat & Sun 3 daily; 1hr).
By train The train station is 2.5km north of town on Trg Vstaje in the village of Šentlenart; buses depart from the station forecourt (roughly Mon–Fri every 45min–1hr,

Sat every 2hr 5.45am–2.20pm). If walking into town, leave the station, turn left and follow the road around until you get to Cesta prvih borcev.
Destinations Ljubljana (Mon–Fri hourly, Sat & Sun every 2hr; 1hr 45min–2hr).
Tourist office Inside the old town hall at Cesta prvih borcev 22 (daily: July & Aug 8am–noon & 6–10pm; Sept– June Mon–Fri 7am–6pm, Sat 8am–2pm; ☏ 064 130 082, ⓦ discoverbrezice.com). It's as much a shop as a tourist office; they also offer wine tastings – which is good if you can't get to the Bizeljsko region.

ACCOMMODATION

Gostilna Les Rimska cesta 31 ☏ 07 496 1100, ⓦ pension.si. South of the river in Čatež ob Savi, *Les* is a respectable, if unexciting, out-of-town option, offering

a range of variously sized double rooms in the main inn, as well as apartments (three to six beds) in the building across the road. Breakfast €5. Doubles €64, apartments €70

THE BREŽICE FESTIVAL

One of the country's most celebrated musical and cultural events, the **Brežice Festival** (end June to end Aug) is an outstanding series of ancient and Baroque music concerts, featuring some of Europe's finest singers, orchestras and musicians. Although the majority of concerts are staged here in Brežice – some in the superb Knight's Hall – many events take place in other castles and churches throughout Slovenia, such as St Leonard's Church in Novo Mesto (see p.227), the Church of St Jacob in Kamnik in northwest Slovenia, and the National Hall in Celje in the east – though these do change each year. Tickets (€8–25; ☏ 01 242 0812, ⓦ seviqc-brezice.si) usually go on sale at the beginning of May.

MC Hostel Brežice Gubčeva cesta 10a ☎059 083 790, ⓦmc-hostel.si. Pleasantly located in the city park opposite the castle, *MC* is an integral part of the large youth and cultural centre of the same name, with spacious, smart-looking six-bed dorms and doubles, with and without showers. Breakfast €3. Dorms €15, doubles €36

Splavar Cesta prvih borcev 40a ☎07 499 0630, ⓦsplavar.si. Accommodation in the centre of Brežice is extremely limited, but this enthusiastically run small hotel bang in the middle of the town's main street fits the bill; the rooms are a little on the small side, but the intricately handcrafted beds combined with a number of other personal touches make for a very pleasant stopover. There's a good restaurant, too (see below). €75

EATING AND DRINKING

Aquarius Bizeljska cesta 4 ☎051 252 440. Brežice's most distinctive landmark, the 46m-high salmon-pink Water Tower, now houses four small circular floors of fun in the guise of this energetic café/bar; there's even an elevator to transport drinks up to the fourth floor. Mon–Thurs 7am–midnight, Fri & Sat 7am–1am, Sun 8am–midnight.

★**Ošterija Debeluh** Trg izgnancev 7 ☎07 496 1070, ⓦdebeluh.si. One of Slovenia's most highly rated restaurants, the wonderfully named "Fatso" offers a marvellous array of dishes such as smoked trout on poached pear with horseradish (€12) or duck with peaches and balsamic vinegar (€20) – for something a little cheaper, try one of the delicious morsels

from the charcoal-grill menu. The wine pairings are top-notch, with only the very best vintages from the nearby Bizeljsko region. The restaurant's countrified interior, with its pastel-painted walls and elegantly set tables, looks fabulous. Mon–Sat noon–10pm.

Splavar Cesta prvih borcev 40a ☎07 499 0630, ⓦsplavar.si. In the hotel of the same name, *Splavar* doubles up as a fine little patisserie serving home-baked goodies and ice cream, as well as the town's most congenial restaurant; the food – for example, pork tenderloin with porcini mushrooms and home-made *štruklji* (€14) and a superb choice of thick-crust pizzas – is really very good. Daily 7am–1pm.

Čatež

Three kilometres southeast of Brežice across the Sava River, **ČATEŽ** is Slovenia's largest and most popular **spa centre** (Terme Čatež). Hot springs were first discovered at Čatež in 1797, only to be flooded by the Sava, then rediscovered some fifty years later, around which time the first private spa – a basic wood cabin and pool – was built by Father Edvard Zagorc. A fledgling resort in the 1920s, offering numerous therapies and treatments for a wide variety of disorders, Čatež only really began to develop as a serious spa centre in the 1960s when the first large pools and hotels were built.

Today this more or less self-contained village, incorporating restaurants, shops, a bank and post office, is as much a recreational park as it is a therapeutic and treatment centre, offering **activities** including indoor (€15/hour) and outdoor tennis (€7/hour), badminton (€8/hour) and squash (€9 for 45min).

Water and sauna parks

Summer Thermal Riviera Daily: mid-April to May & Sept 9am–7pm; June–Aug 8am–8pm • Mon–Fri €11, Sat & Sun €15 • **Winter Thermal Riviera** Mon–Fri & Sun 9am–9pm, Sat 9am–midnight • Mon–Fri €13, Sat & Sun €16 • **Sauna Park** Mon–Fri 11am–9pm, Sat & Sun 10am–9pm • Mon–Fri €13, Sat & Sun €17.50 • ⓦterme-catez.si

The huge **Summer Thermal Riviera** comprises some ten thermal pools and bathing areas (average temperature 30°C), with a fantastic array of wave machines, waterfalls and slides, and dedicated water parks for kids. For cooler days, there's indoor action at the *Hotel Toplice*'s **Winter Thermal Riviera**, which has a multitude of slides, wave pools, whirlpools and water massage machines – and night swimming each Saturday.

If you fancy sweating off a few pounds, head for the **sauna park**, also inside the *Toplice*, which incorporates eight saunas – the Indian sauna, Salt sauna and Finnish Aroma sauna, to name but three.

ARRIVAL AND INFORMATION   ČATEŽ

By bus There are hourly buses (5min) from Brežice to Čatež.

Tourist office Opposite the *Hotel Toplice* at Topliška cesta 35 (daily: Feb–April & Nov 9am–3pm; May, June, Sept &

Oct 9am–5pm; July & Aug 8am–noon & 6–10pm; Dec & Jan 10am–2pm; ☎07 620 7035, ⓦdiscoverbrezice.com); they've got bikes for rent (€3.50/hr, €17/day).

ACCOMMODATION AND EATING

The complex incorporates three pricey hotels and various, more attractive, camping options. There are numerous snack bars and cafés sprinkled around, none of which particularly stands out.

Camp Terme Čatež ☎07 620 7810, ⓦterme-catez.si. At the eastern end of the complex, this vast site has all the requisite five-star amenities, with a choice of a standard field pitch or a slightly more expensive lakeside pitch; rates include two one-time tickets to the Summer Thermal Riviera. Open all year. **€44**

Indian village Topliška cesta 35 ☎07 620 7810, ⓦterme-catez.si. A great deal of fun – a cluster of some 25 tepees, each equipped with four beds, kitchenette and other furnishings; modern bathroom facilities are shared. On-site activities include archery and, if you really must, Indian dancing. May–Oct. **€90**

Bizeljsko-Sremič

Tracking the Croatian border, the road heading north out of Brežice heads up through the **Bizeljsko-Sremič wine region**, renowned for its characteristic blended wines, such as the dry whites Bizeljian and Sremičan. Although the odd bus trundles this way (Mon–Fri 3 daily), it's difficult to get the most out of the region unless you've got your own transport. Wine can be sampled anywhere where you see the sign **vinska klet** (wine cellar), of which there are many – however, to be sure of getting a visit in, it's best to call a few hours, if not a day, in advance. You should reckon on paying around €5 for three or four wines, a little more for sparkling varieties. The wine road doesn't really begin until the village of **Stari Vas**, some 10km north of Brežice.

Brezovica

From the *Istenič* wine cellar (see below) in Stari Vas, a footpath (Pot k repnicam) winds its way across the shallow hills up to the village of **BREZOVICA**, some 5km distant. Dotted around this area are some 150 unique cellars called **repnice**, small sand caves hewn from the surrounding flint-stone hills, their walls and ceilings wonderfully patterned with obliquely laid layers of sand. *Repnice* were traditionally used for the storage of turnips (*repa* means turnip) and other produce, before local vintners discovered that the caves' climatic conditions (a constant 7–11°C) and humidity were ideal for the maturing and storage of wine. Around thirty *repnice* are still in use today, though it's only possible to visit a handful of these, the greatest concentration of which are in Brezovica itself. Particularly worth trying are *Kovačič* at no. 29 (☎07 495 1091), *Kelhar* at no. 31 (☎07 495 1551), which was dug out in 1825, and, most impressively, *Najger* at no. 32 (☎07 495 1115) – all three are located approximately 1.5km from the main road up the hill. The next village along is **Bizeljsko**, the region's main settlement.

Grad Podsreda

Podsreda • April–Oct Tues–Sun 10am–6pm • €3 • ☎03 800 7100, ⓦkozjanski-park.si

Beyond Bizeljsko the road gently ascends to Bistrica ob Sotli, whereupon a branch road cuts west to the village of **PODSREDA**, above which looms the resplendent **Grad Podsreda** (Podsreda Castle). Originally a thirteenth-century fortification, its fine Romanesque core remains splendidly intact, although systematic and comprehensive renovation work on the interior has left few visible traces of its former state, with just the old medieval kitchen and single-cell jail remaining from the original building. Its empty rooms are now used almost exclusively as exhibition and gallery spaces. The castle can be reached by road (5km from Podsreda) or, if you're walking, via a steep trail (45min) beginning south of the village – look for the signs to Levstikov mlin (Levstikov Mill) and the trail starts there.

ACCOMMODATION, EATING AND DRINKING   BIZELJSKO-SREMIČ

Istenič Stari Vas 7 ☎07 495 1559, ⓦistenic.si. One of Slovenia's premier sparkling wine producers, and the one vintner to make tracks for if time is short, Istenič produces

a fantastic range, including whites made from chardonnay, muškat and laški rizling, and a couple of sumptuous rosés made from pinot noir; three tastings with nibbles and a cellar tour costs €7. They've also got a comfortable little pension on site, accommodating eight double rooms with balconies overlooking the vineyards. **€54**

Gostilna Šekoranja Bizeljsko 72 ☎07 495 1310. Wonderfully old-fashioned, and very well regarded, inn serving up heavy home-made Slovene food such as smoked bacon, chunky sausages and black pudding, with buckwheat cake to finish things. Main dishes start at around €8. Tues–Sun 8.30am–11pm.

Bela Krajina

Bela Krajina acquired its name – meaning "White Carniola", derived partly from the ubiquitous birch tree, and partly from the white costumes worn by its inhabitants, the **Bela Kranjci** (White Carniolans) – during the fifteenth century, when the lands were incorporated into the province of Carniola. Its frontline position ensured that, around the same time, the region's towns and villages suffered a fair battering at the hands of the Turks, whose unremitting drive up through the Balkans also led to an influx of Croat and Serb refugees and renegades (Uskoks) from Bosnia. A period of cultural and economic efflorescence eventually gave way to regional decline, as the closure of many important industrial plants was compounded by a catastrophic bout of phylloxera at the end of the nineteenth century, which destroyed almost all the region's vineyards. Much of the local population was forced to emigrate, mainly to North America, while those who remained continued to engage in traditional cottage industries as a means of eking out a living. Its two main towns, **Črnomelj** and **Metlika**, are low-key places, convenient for the more interesting sites close at hand.

The best of Bela Krajina is to be found in the surrounding countryside, amid the birch trees and vineyards. History and culture buffs can get their kicks at the **Mithraeum shrine** at Rožanec, and the **Three Parishes Pilgrimage Centre** at Rosalnice, near Metlika. Visitors seeking something more relaxing should make a beeline for the **Lahinja Landscape Park** or the numerous wine villages sprinkled around the region, such as **Drašiči** with its pleasant vineyard-clad surroundings.

Črnomelj

Sitting plumb in the geographical centre of Bela Krajina, **ČRNOMELJ** is the capital, and the largest, of the province's towns. Frankly, it's not much to get excited about, but that said, the town does stage two cracking festivals, namely the marvellous **Jurjevanje folklore festival** in June (see box, p.238), and August's two-week **Črnfest**, which brings a welcome urban vibe to the place in the form of stand-up, theatre and concerts staged in the castle atrium and many other venues. What there is of interest is centred on an elongated promontory in a tight loop of the Dobličica and Lahinja rivers to the south of town.

Unlike many settlements in the region, Črnomelj was spared widespread

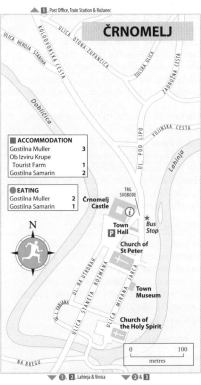

ČRNOMELJ

1, Post Office, Train Station & Rožanec

■ **ACCOMMODATION**
Gostilna Muller	3
Ob Izviru Krupe Tourist Farm	1
Gostilna Samarin	2

● **EATING**
Gostilna Muller	2
Gostilna Samarin	1

Črnomelj Castle

TRG SVOBODE

Town Hall

Bus Stop

Church of St Peter

Town Museum

Church of the Holy Spirit

N

0   100
metres

1, 2, Lahinja & Vinica   2 & 3

> ## JURJEVANJE
>
> Bela Krajina's rich folk-music heritage is joyously celebrated in Črnomelj during the annual **Jurjevanje** (St George's Day Festival; ⊛ jurjevanje.si), which features a tremendous, and usually very accomplished, line-up of local and international folkloric groups and dance troupes, along with a host of other cultural happenings. Usually held in the last week of June, it's a great opportunity to see rarely used folk instruments – such as the *tamburica*, *bisernica* (lute) and *berdo* (contrabass) – being played live.

devastation by the Turks, owing to its naturally strong fortifications, although its strategic importance was stripped away in the mid-sixteenth century following the erection of a fort and the relocation of the command of the military frontier across the border in Karlovac, Croatia. Its decline continued for several centuries thereafter, though its fortunes were partially revived following the opening of the Novo Mesto–Karlovac rail line in 1914.

Grad Črnomelj
Trg svobode

The rather low-key **Grad Črnomelj** (Črnomelj Castle) consumes the western side of the main square, **Trg svobode**. Built in the twelfth century, the castle was rebuilt, modified and tinkered with by numerous owners over the years, the result being that it doesn't look much like a castle at all now. It does, however, house the tourist office, and its atmospheric atrium is used as a performance space.

Mestna muzejska
Ulica Mlrana Jarca 3 • Tues, Wed & Fri noon–4pm, Thurs noon–6pm, Sat 11am–3pm • €4 • ☎ 07 620 0897, ⊛ muzej-crnomelj.si

To learn more about the town, and region's, rich history, pop along to the small but surprisingly enjoyable **Mestna muzejska** (Town Museum). The ground floor's gleaming cabinets display rare and important finds from antiquity, including a stunning comb made from dog bone, while much of the first floor is given over to the Middle Ages – check out the magnificent two-handed sword recovered from the Lahinja River – as well as celebrating the town's long-standing Jurjevanje festival (see box above). There's very little in English, but the helpful curator will happily show you around and explain what's what.

Cerkev Sv Petra and Cerkev Sv Duha
Uljca Staneta Rozmana

A few paces south of the Town Museum, at the beginning of Ulica Staneta Rozmana – the main thoroughfare – the Baroque **Cerkev Sv Petra** (Church of St Peter) is fairly standard, but look out for an oversized fresco of St Christopher on the exterior west wall. Perched above the confluence of the two rivers at the end of Ulica Mirana Jarca, the street running parallel to Ulica Staneta Rozmana, is the late fifteenth-century **Cerkev Sv Duha** (Church of the Holy Spirit), now restored to something like its former glory.

ARRIVAL AND INFORMATION ČRNOMELJ

By train The train station is 1km north of the centre on Železničarska cesta, from where it's a 20min walk south to the core of the old town.
Destinations Ljubljana (Mon–Fri 9 daily, Sat & Sun 2–3 daily; 2hr 10min–2hr 45min); Metlika (Mon–Fri 9 daily, Sat & Sun 2–3 daily; 20min); Novo Mesto (Mon–Fri 9 daily, Sat & Sun 2–3 daily; 40–50min).

By bus Buses stop on the main square, Trg svobode.
Destinations Metlika (Mon–Fri 5 daily; 25min); Novo Mesto (Mon–Fri 3 daily; 50min); Vinica (Mon–Fri hourly– every 1hr 30min, Sat & Sun 5 daily; 35min).
Tourist office The super-helpful tourist office is inside the castle at Trg svobode 3 (Mon–Fri 8am–4pm, Sat 9am– noon; ☎ 07 305 6530, ⊛ belakrajina.si).

ACCOMMODATION

Gostilna Muller Ločka cesta 6 ☎ 07 356 7200, ⊛ gostilna-muller.si. The most convenient (in fact just about the only) spot to stay in the centre of town, *Muller* has three large, spotless and reasonably priced rooms with all the standard amenities, including a/c, and a good restaurant (see below). €50

Ob Izviru Krupe Tourist Farm Krupa 9 ☎07 306 8012, ⓦturisticna-kmetija.cerjanec.si. Named after the source of the Kolpa just a few hundred metres away, this large and popular tourist farm, 11km north of Črnomelj, near Semič, promises a wonderfully restful stay; good-sized, en-suite rooms are complemented by

wholesome food and home-harvested wine. €50

Gostilna Samarin Kočevje 10c ☎07 305 4026, ⓦgostilna-samarin.si. It's worth making a little extra effort to get to this homely establishment 1km south of the centre out on the road to Vinica. The six contemporary rooms exude warmth, from the oakwood floors and handcrafted beds and wardrobes to the patterned walls and soothing lighting. There's a good restaurant, too (see below). €60

EATING

Gostilna Muller Ločka cesta 6 ☎07 356 7200, ⓦgostilna-muller.si. Rustically decorated restaurant offering a generous choice of seafood, game and vegetarian dishes (mains €8–12); the vine-shaded summer terrace overlooking the Lahinja is a nice spot to linger over a drink on a warm summer's evening. Tues–Fri 9am–11pm, Sat 11am–11pm, Sun 11am–9pm.

Gostilna Samarin Kočevje 10c ☎07 305 4026, ⓦgostilna-samarin.si. Balkan-sized (ie enormous) portions of food are the order of the day at this bustling inn, especially the charcoal-grilled lamb (€10) and suckling pig, both of which are huge favourites with the locals. Otherwise, it's a great place to rock up for a beer or a glass of the local wine. Daily 7am–11pm.

Mitrej

Just beyond the village of Lokve, beyond a couple of Romany settlements, a left turn takes you up to the smaller village of **Rožanec**; from the parking place, a signposted path leads you up to and across the rail track, then into a chestnut forest, at the edge of which is a small, picturesque hollow. Hewn into the rock face of one wall is the **Mitrej** (Mithraeum), a second-century **Roman shrine** dedicated to the invincible sun god Mithras (see box, p.284).

The centrepiece of the rock-cut relief (first excavated in 1921) is the sacrifice of the bull, which has Mithras kneeling on, and plunging a dagger into, its back. The spilling of the bull's blood supposedly gave rise to the plant kingdom, while its semen gave rise to the animal kingdom, the latter represented here by the presence of a dog, a snake and a scorpion. The sacrificial scene is accompanied by personifications of the sun and the moon (light and darkness), as well as two priests, Cautopates and Cautes. The inscription, meanwhile, is an address to Mithras from three brothers (Nepos, Prokulus and Firminus), appealing for health and prosperity. The Mithraeum's presence at this particular site is unsurprising given that a Roman road once ran from Črnomelj to Semič, a small town some 5km further north. At Semič it divided, with one road continuing to Emona (Ljubljana), the other heading towards present-day Novo Mesto. A copy of the relief is held in the Bela Krajina Museum in Metlika (see p.241).

Krajinski park Lahinja

A couple of kilometres south of Črnomelj – along the road to Vinica and the Kolpa River – you'll pass another Romany settlement, 7km beyond which is the **Krajinski park Lahinja** (Lahinja Landscape Park), a protected area of fields, marshy groves, streams and karstic springs. There's birdlife here, too, not least kingfishers (the park symbol), though you'll do well to spot these shy birds. The park can be accessed from any one of several hamlets clustered in or around its boundary, though there are two main entry points. The first is **Pusti Gradac**, the park's northernmost settlement, which lies up a gravel track 1.5km south of the village of **Dragatuš**; if you're travelling by bus, get the driver to set you down on the main road, from where it's a twenty-minute walk. The second entry point is 2km further along the same road from Dragatuš, at **Veliki Nerajec**; here, one of the late eighteenth-century stone-built dwellings – still fully furnished with a "black kitchen" – has been turned into a small exhibition space/information hut (May–Oct Thurs–Sat 11am–6pm; ☎07 305 7428).

Pusti Gradac

Pusti Gradac (which literally means "Leave the Castle") is the park's most culturally well-endowed patch: not only have several extremely important archeological finds been unearthed here – including a remarkable gold coin featuring an imprint of Hungarian King Matthias Corvinus (which dates from around the fifteenth century) – but it's also the site of one of the country's few remaining working **water mills** (Klepčev mlin). The mill still operates according to traditional methods, its grinders powered by an impressively large water wheel, itself propelled by waters from the nearby Lahinja River. Demonstrations of the mill are organized by the Klepec family, who live in the house next door at no. 10 (☎07 305 7660, ✉klepec@siol.net). They can also arrange two- to four-hour-long **guided tours** of the park (from around €3); in theory, these tours are only available to groups, but arrangements can be made for individuals as long as you contact the family at least a day or two in advance. A leisurely circular walk around the park takes around three hours.

ACCOMMODATION	KRAJINSKI PARK LAHINJA
Malerič Podlog 3 ☎040 300 676, ⊕turizemmaleric.si. Bela Krajina is becoming something of a glamping hot spot, typified by this gorgeous little site 2km north of Pusti Gradac. Each of the four white-framed wooden pods has two	bedrooms – with a couch for another two people if required – floor-to-ceiling windows, a kitchen-cum-lounge area and its own wood-decked terrace fronting a biological pond. The views across to the Bela Krajinci hills are fabulous. **€100**

Vinica

The small fishing village of **VINICA**, 10km south of the Lahinja Landscape Park, right on the Croatian border, is the birthplace of the poet, playwright and essayist **Oton Župančič** (1878–1949). Along with Ivan Cankar, Župančič was regarded as the principal exponent of the so-called **Moderna** movement, a Slovene literary trend that appeared at the end of the nineteenth century, and which was closely aligned to the tenets of Slovene national and sociohistorical identity; his principal contribution was a collection of poetry entitled *Caša opojnosti* (*Intoxicating Cup*). A prolific wordsmith, Župančič also wrote and translated numerous plays (including Shakespeare), composed poems for the Partisan press, and wrote many children's stories; above all, he is known to every Slovene as the creator of the children's character, *Ciciban*. In his **birthplace**, on the main road in the centre of the village (Tues–Sat: May–Oct 9am–4pm; Nov–April 9am–3pm; €2; ☎07 306 4343, ⊕belokranjski-muzej.si), you can see copies of his work, his death mask and a beautiful sketch portrait completed by Božidar Jakac just two years before the writer's death. Župančič is buried at Žale cemetery in Ljubljana.

ACCOMMODATION	VINICA
Kamp Kolpa-Vinica Vinica 19a ☎031 513 060, ⊕kamp -kolpa.si. Down by the river on the southern fringe of the village, close to the border crossing, this clean, green and	spacious site ticks all the boxes, and also has tidy four-person chalets. May–Sept. Camping **€18**, chalets **€60**

Metlika

Pressed up hard against the Croatian border just 15km northeast of Črnomelj, **METLIKA** is Bela Krajina's second centre of population. It's a mellow town, palpably more interesting than its neighbour thanks to a couple of fine **museums**, some lovely **architecture** and a strong **viticultural tradition**.

Founded in the thirteenth century when the province (then an important frontier region) was known as Metlika March, Metlika acquired its town rights and developed into a prosperous medieval centre the following century. However, as one of Austria's border strongholds it found itself at the sharp end of Hungarian, then Turkish, attacks – it was razed no fewer than sixteen times. Almost entirely gutted by fire in 1705, its historic centre was swiftly rebuilt, although it received another battering at the hands of its Italian occupiers during World War II, which makes the survival of its attractive old core all the more remarkable. Everything of interest in Metlika is located within the confines of the **Old Town**, sited on a low elevation between the main thoroughfare, **Cesta Bratstva in Enotnosti**, and the River Obrh, and reached via Ulica na Trg, opposite the *Bela Krajina* hotel.

The town's principal annual event is the **Spring Wine Festival** (Vinska Vigred) on the third weekend of May, a booze-fuelled three days of wine-related events taking place throughout the Old Town's three squares.

Belokranjski muzej

Trg svobode • Mon–Sat 9am–5pm, Sun 10am–2pm • €4 • ☎ 07 306 3370, 🌐 belokrajnski-muzej.si

On the north side of Trg svobode, the largest and most central of the three irregularly shaped squares which form the backbone of the Old Town, stands the neat, triangular **Grad Metlika** (Metlika Castle), whose vaulted tracts house the engaging **Belokranjski muzej** (Bela Krajina Museum). Following an informative fifteen-minute film about the region, the collection kicks off with an impressive haul of Bronze and Iron

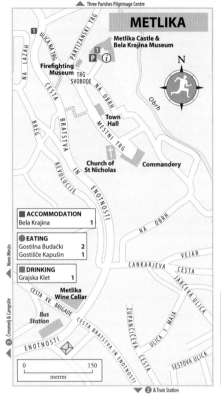

Age artefacts – vessels, armour, jewellery and the like – and a stash of Roman finds, many of which were unearthed from Pusti Gradac, south of Črnomelj (see opposite); there's also a copy of the Mithraic relief at Rožanec (see p.239). The most enjoyable section is devoted to the region's inhabitants, **Bela Kranjci**, and features a fine display of homespun attire, as well as items and artefacts pertaining to the local traditional cottage industries, typically pottery, spinning, weaving, cart- and barrel-making and an exhibition of one of the more delicate Slovenian folk-arts, *Pisanice* (egg-painting).

The development of **viticulture** – as important to the local economy today as agriculture was prior to World War II – is given due prominence, as is the role of local societies and associations in Bela Krajina during the nineteenth and twentieth centuries. To a backdrop of patriotic anthems, the collection winds up documenting the activities of the **Partisans** during World War II, the region's first unit having been formed near Semič in 1941; the most arresting of an otherwise outstanding group of photos is one of the unit's commissioner, Jože Mihelič, with a group of Italian soldiers prior to being sentenced to death.

Slovenski gasiliski muzej

Trg svobode 5 • Tues–Sat 9am–2pm • €2 • ☎ 07 305 8697

The locals are tremendously proud of the fact that Slovenia's first firefighting brigade was formed here in Metlika, in 1869, and their heroics are superbly documented in the **Slovenski gasilski muzej** (Firefighting Museum) in the building next to the castle. Opened on the occasion of the brigade's centenary in 1969, the museum proudly displays an assortment of photographs, awards, helmets and uniforms, klaxons and other memorabilia. Best of all, though, are the old firefighting machines – the oldest of which, a model from Cerknica, dates from 1836 – located in both this building and the pavilion opposite.

Mestni trg

Trg svobode segues into **Mestni trg**, an elongated square bound by an attractive blend of beige-, cream- and mint-coloured buildings, the most distinguished being the neo-Gothic **Town Hall** at no. 24. Positioned atop the building is a slightly askew town coat of arms, featuring two ravens perched either side of a castle tower – no doubt on the look-out for rampaging Turks. The bottom end of the square is consumed by the box-like **Cerkev Sv Nikolaj** (Church of St Nicholas), a uniform Baroque structure resurrected in 1759 following a fire some fifty years earlier. The statues of St Nicholas and the pope adorning the high altar were carved by an unknown sculptor, while the frescoes were executed by the Friulian Domenico Fabrio.

ARRIVAL AND INFORMATION   METLIKA

By bus The bus station is on the main crossroads at the southern entrance to town, from where it's a 15min walk to the Old Town.
Destinations Črnomelj (Mon–Fri 6 daily; 25min); Novo Mesto (Mon–Fri 3 daily; 25min).
By train The train station is on Kolodvorska ulica, 1km southeast of town near the Croatian border.

Destinations Črnomelj (Mon–Fri 8 daily, Sat & Sun 2–3 daily; 20min); Ljubljana (Mon–Fri 8 daily, Sat & Sun 2–3 daily; 2hr 40min–3hr 10min); Novo Mesto (Mon–Fri 7 daily, Sat & Sun 2–3 daily; 1hr–1hr 15min).
Tourist office In the castle courtyard (June–Aug Mon–Fri 8am–5pm, Sat 9am–1pm; Sept–May Mon–Fri 8am–4pm, Sat 9am–noon; ☎ 07 363 5470, ⓦ belakrajina.si).

ACCOMMODATION

Bela Krajina Cesta Bratstva in Enotnosti 32 ☎ 07 305 8123, ⓦ hotel-belakrajina.si. The town's only hotel (hence slightly overpriced) won't set the pulse racing, but at least the rooms are spotlessly clean and cheerily colourful. **€76**
Podzemelj ob Kolpi 7km southwest of town just off the main Črnomelj–Metlika road ☎ 07 306 9572, ⓦ kamp-podzemelj.si. Superbly located on the banks of the Kolpa River, this excellent campsite also accommodates

a couple of eco-cottages each with a double bed. It's great for families, as not only are the waters ideal for swimming, but also there's an adrenaline (treetops) park, play area and sporting facilities, plus a fab restaurant, all of which means there's very little reason to leave the site at all. Buses can drop you off on the main road, from where it's about 1km to the site. May to mid-Sept. Camping **€21**, pods **€69**

EATING

Gostilna Budački Ulica Belokranjskega odreda 14 ☎ 07 363 5200. Awkwardly located in a residential area out near the train station, this is really the only restaurant

worth considering in Metlika itself, featuring a decent grill menu and fish from the nearby Kolpa. Mon–Thurs 8am–10pm, Fri & Sat 8am–11pm, Sun noon–5pm.

WINE VILLAGES

The triangle of land between Metlika and the pretty **wine villages** of Drašiči, Vinomer and Radovica to the northeast is classic Krajina countryside, with swathes of copse-like *steljniki* – birch tree and fern – set against the backdrop of soft, gently sloping vineyards. The majority of wines cultivated here are blends, the best-known being Metliška Črnina, a dry, velvety and very dark red; others worth trying include the lighter reds, Modra Portugalka and Modri Pinot, and, if you're prepared to spend that little extra, the sparkling white Metliška Penina.

Of the villages, **Drašiči** (6km northeast of Metlika) offers most for wine connoisseurs, with a number of cellars providing tastings: a good option for starters is the *Simonič Tourist Farm* at no. 56 (☎ 07 305 8185). *Prus*, in nearby Krmačina, at no. 6 (☎ 07 305 9098, ⓦ vinaprus.si), is also very highly rated; otherwise, take your pick from the many cellars advertised. You can approach them direct or, alternatively, contact the tourist office in Metlika (see above), who will happily fix something up for you. The 1:50,000 *Bela Krajina* map, available from the tourist offices in Črnomelj and Metlika, will help you navigate your way around.

★**Gostišče Kapušin** Krasinec 55, 8km south of Metlika ☎07 369 9150, ⓦgostilna-kapusin.si. Bela Krajina's one truly outstanding restaurant. A typical four-course tasting menu (€24) might feature tuna carpaccio, home-made *žlikrofi* with porcini sauce and veal medallions with dumplings, before ending with a trio of wickedly enticing desserts – which may well include vanilla ice cream with roasted pumpkin seed oil. Both the setting and the service are exemplary. Wed–Sat 8am–11pm, Sun 1–10pm.

DRINKING

Grajska Klet Trg svobode 3 ☎07 305 8999. If you don't manage to get to any of the wine villages, then the sophisticated little "Castle Cellar" bar inside the castle courtyard is the next best thing, with dozens of regional wines available by the glass (€2–3.50) and bottle, best sampled with some cheese and *pršut*. Mon–Thurs 7.30am–11pm, Fri & Sat 7.30am–1am, Sun 8am–noon.

Tri Fare

Rosalnice, 2km east of Metlika • To visit, call the tourist office in Metlika (see opposite) • Free • To get here, walk along Cankarjeva cesta, which begins from a point some 100m north of the main crossroads in the south of town (on Cesta Bratstva in Enotnosti) and winds its way to the village

The **Tri Fare** (Three Parishes Pilgrimage Centre) – comprising three fourteenth- and fifteenth-century Gothic churches – is the region's most outstanding ecclesiastical monument. From the few historical documents that existed, it was ascertained that the original churches were likely to have been built by the Knights Templar some time during the twelfth century. Following the arrival of a group of refugee Franciscan monks from Bosnia shortly after the completion of the middle church in the fifteenth century, the complex evolved into an important pilgrimage site. It reached its apogee a century or two later when followers of many different faiths, including Orthodox, journeyed here regularly.

Žalostna Mati božja

The largest and oldest of the three churches, and the only one where Mass is still held, the **Žalostna Mati božja** (Lady of Our Sorrows) features a superb Gothic interior with Baroque appendages, decorated with a splendid array of frescoes: the presbytery is covered with scenes from the New Testament, the side walls with images of the Apostles and, on the triumphal arch, scenes representing the Ten Commandments. The main altar is ornamented with a fine statuette of Mary with Seven Swords (the Seven Sorrows), the story of which is relayed in the middle church, while the Rococo side altars – dedicated to St John Nepomuk and St Francis of Paola – are no less impressive.

Glej Človek

Next to Our Sorrows, the **Glej Človek** (Ecce Homo Church) is the smallest of the three and the only one with a bell tower. It, too, boasts a marvellous Gothic presbytery and high altar, but the show-stealer is its cupola ceiling, painted with wildly colourful frescoes depicting the story of Mary's Seven Sorrows.

Lurška Devica Marija

Completing the trio of churches is the poorly preserved **Lurška Devica Marija** (Church of Our Lady of Lourdes), almost completely devoid of colour or ornamentation. Its singular highlight is the neo-Gothic high altar featuring a statue of Mary of Lourdes, while it's just about possible to detect the fragments of a fresco of the Crucifixion, from around 1500.

4

Eastern Slovenia

MARIBOR

5

Eastern Slovenia

Eastern Slovenia receives relatively few visitors, which is a shame – with enticing countryside and a wealth of interesting sites to explore, along with a number of excellent festivals and carnivals, the region should not be overlooked. The main centres of population are Maribor and Celje, the second- and third-largest cities in Slovenia respectively, though neither can match the historic resonance of Ptuj, the country's oldest and most appealing town, which is a short ride away from the stunning Gothic Church of the Virgin Mary in Ptujska Gora.

Located in the heart of Štajerska, the country's largest province, Maribor sits on the doorstep of some of Slovenia's finest **wine roads**, as well as the **Pohorje massif**, a broad, arcing plateau which extends some 50km west from the foothills of Maribor, and offers recreational opportunities including two of the country's largest and best-equipped **ski resorts**. Just north of Celje, **Velenje** merits a visit by virtue of its strangely appealing Socialist-era architecture. Eastern Slovenia is also renowned for its spas, not least **Rogaška Slatina**, the country's quintessential spa town.

Lying to the west of the Pohorje massif and bordering Austria to the north, **Koroška** was once the centre of the oldest Slovene state, Karantanija, from the seventh century, and later part of the former Habsburg duchy of Carinthia; like Štajerska, it came under the sway of the Austrians during World War II. Slovenia's smallest region, Koroška marks a return to the alpine peaks of the west, its former mining and iron-working towns now acting as useful bases for forays into the surrounding hills and mountains, which are crisscrossed with excellent hiking and cycling routes. Of the region's few towns, by far the most appealing is **Slovenj Gradec**. To the west of Koroška, the extraordinarily picturesque **Logar Valley** is among the most scenic spots in all Slovenia and another superb area for cycling and walking.

Spread across the edge of the Pannonian basin, bordering Austria, Croatia and Hungary, **Prekmurje** is, in many ways, the country's most distinctive region. Subject to around a thousand years of Hungarian rule before being divided between Hungary and the new Yugoslav state in 1920, it's the polar opposite of mountainous western Slovenia. This is Slovenia's least visited region, yet its mellow tranquillity offers an enchanting mix of neat, flower-bedecked villages, such as **Bogojina**, **Filovci** and **Beltinci**, ancient churches, as at **Martjanci** and **Selo**, and lush, green countryside where the wide, flat open spaces provide ideal terrain for cyclists with an aversion to hills.

GETTING AROUND   **EASTERN SLOVENIA**

Transport links in this part of the country are pretty good: the main rail line spears northeast towards Celje and Maribor, with important junctions at Zidani Most (for the southeast and Zagreb) and Pragersko (for Ptuj, Prekmurje and onwards

KURENT CARNIVAL PARADE, PTUJ

Highlights

❶ **Mountain biking, Koroška** Grab a bike and take to these mountain wilds for some of the country's most exciting, and challenging, trails. See p.260

❷ **Logar Valley** Gorgeous alpine valley in the heart of the Kamniške-Savinja Alps, ideal for a number of leisure pursuits. See p.261

❸ **Pohorje massif** Skiing, cycling and hiking are just three sporting possibilities on this thickly wooded plateau. See p.277

❹ **Kurent carnival, Ptuj** Slovenia's oldest and prettiest town, stuffed with remnants of its

Roman and medieval past, is famed for its lively spring carnival. See p.280

❺ **Church of the Virgin Mary, Ptujska Gora** Sublime Gothic church featuring the masterful *Virgin with Mantle* relief. See p.285

❻ **Ljutomer wine road** Spend the day cycling through the rolling, stepped vineyards of this beautiful wine road. See p.286

❼ **Prekmurje** Quaint villages, churches, charming farmhouses – and numerous storks – characterize Slovenia's distinctively flat northeastern region. See p.287

HIGHLIGHTS ARE MARKED ON THE MAP ON P.248

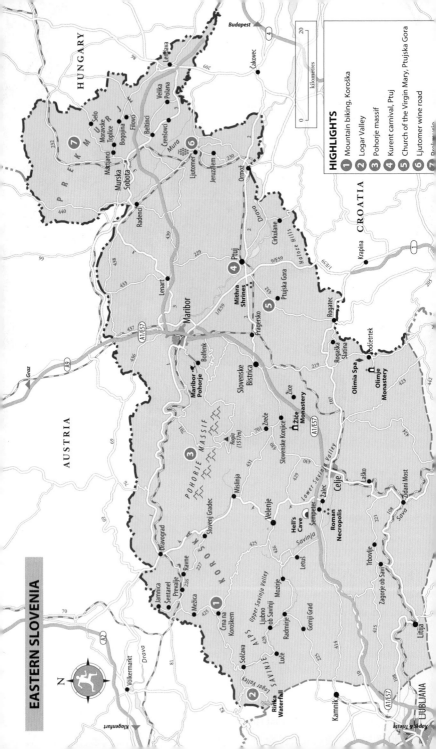

EASTERN SLOVENIA

HIGHLIGHTS

1. Mountain biking, Koroška
2. Logar Valley
3. Pohorje massif
4. Kurent carnival, Ptuj
5. Church of the Virgin Mary, Ptujska Gora
6. Ljutomer wine road
7. Prekmurje

Graz
AUSTRIA
Völkermarkt
Klagenfurt
Koper & Trieste
LJUBLJANA
Kamnik

HUNGARY
PREKMURJE
Budapest
Lendava
Velika Polana
Moravske Toplice
Selo
Bogojina
Filovci
Beltinci
Matjanci
Crensovci
Murska Sobota
Mura
Ljutomer
Jeruzalem
Ormož
Radenci

CROATIA
Čakovec
Krapina
Rogatec
Podčetrtek

Lenart
Maribor
Ptuj
Cirkulane
Haloze Hills
Drava
Mithra Shrines
Pragersko
Ptujska Gora
Rogaška Slatina
Olimje Monastery
Olimia Spa

Maribor Pohorje
Bolfenk
Slovenske Bistrica
Žreče
Žiče Monastery
Rogla (1517m)
POHORJE MASSIF
Slovenske Konjice
Mislinja
Velenje
Laško
Zidani Most
Celje
Žalec
Lower Savinja Valley
Roman Necropolis
Šempeter
Hell's Cave
Trbovlje
Zagorje ob Savi
Sava
Litija

Dravograd
Slovenj Gradec
KOROŠKA
Ravne
Prevalje
Mežica
Jamnica
Šentanel
Črna na Koroškem
Upper Savinja Valley
Ljubno ob Savinji
Mozirje
Radmirje
Gornji Grad
Letuš
Luče
Solčava
SAVINJE ALPS
Rinka Waterfall
Logar Valley

N

kilometres
0   20

to Hungary). Bus routes are comprehensive enough on the main routes, with a fairly well-integrated bus system linking more remote towns and villages; however, services are severely depleted at weekends just about everywhere. But as anywhere in Slovenia, having your own vehicle will enable you to reach the more rural spots far more easily, not least the region's many wine roads.

Celje and around

CELJE, Slovenia's third-largest city after Ljubljana and Maribor, though with a population that still just barely tops the forty thousand mark, lies at the heart of the **Lower Savinja Valley** (Spodnja Savinjska dolina), a predominantly flat, fairly densely populated landscape raked with vast hop plantations and wheat fields. Despite its heavy industry, Celje is not unattractive, and worthy of a full day's sightseeing thanks to its rich history, clutch of impressive museums and huge **castle**. Nearby, the main attractions are the impressive **Roman necropolis** in Šempeter and the forebodingly titled **Hell's Cave**.

Brief history

Celje derives its name from the **Roman** settlement, Celeia, a key administrative centre of the Roman province of Noricum. Economically and culturally the town peaked in the **Middle Ages** under its overlords, the counts of Celje, who, for three centuries, staked their claim as one of Central Europe's foremost ruling dynasties – one of their last acts before the Habsburgs assumed control was to award Celje its town rights in 1451. As in much of the Štajerska region, Celje faced formidable Germanizing pressures during the late nineteenth and early twentieth centuries, culminating in **German occupation** during World War II, during which time the town was heavily bombed by Allied planes.

Fotografski atelje Josip Pelikan

Razlagova ulica 5 • Tues–Sat 9am–1pm, Sun 2–6pm • €3 • ☎ 03 428 6410, ⓦ fotopelikan.si

The **Fotografski atelje Josip Pelikan** (Josip Pelikan Gallery) holds an extensive number of the pioneering photographer's studio portraits, mountain landscapes (he was a mountaineer himself) and pictures of Celje and surroundings. The gallery is actually part of the late nineteenth-century glass photo studio – the only surviving such studio from this period in Slovenia – in which Pelikan (1885–1977) worked from 1920, so there's plenty of his original equipment on display too.

Muzej novejše zgodovine

Prešernova ulica 17 • Tues–Fri 9am–5pm, Sat 9am–1pm, Sun 2–6pm • €3, includes Herman's Den • ☎ 03 428 6410, ⓦ muzej-nz-ce.si

The former town hall now accommodates the **Muzej novejše zgodovine** (Museum of Modern History), an enjoyable and imaginatively presented trawl through twentieth-century Celje. Numerous items from different fields, such as education, work and war, are presented through the eyes of three fictitious characters, each from a different generation. The most illuminating period covered is **World War II**, and in particular the annexation of Slovene Styria (effectively northeastern Slovenia, which included Celje) to the Third Reich, resulting in a catastrophic programme of Germanization; the main themes are deportation – some eighty thousand Slovenes were expelled from the region – and resistance, and in particular the Celjska ČETA, the area's first Partisan association. Among the many sobering exhibits is a Gestapo whip from Stari Pisker (see p.251) and many chilling photos, including an unbearably grim image of a group of hostages moments before their execution. On a lighter note, you'll find the travel chest, as well as books and letters, belonging to **Alma Karlin** (see p.251), while, upstairs, the

5

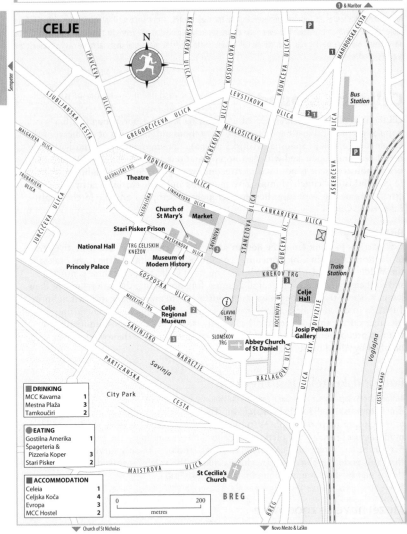

DRINKING
MCC Kavarna	1
Mestna Plaža	3
Tamkoučiri	2

EATING
Gostilna Amerika	1
Špageteria & Pizzeria Koper	3
Stari Pisker	2

ACCOMMODATION
Celeia	1
Celjska Koča	4
Evropa	3
MCC Hostel	2

"Streets of Craftsmen" show mock-up workshops representing goldsmiths, clockmakers, milliners, tailors and so on, who thrived here during the interwar period.

Hermanov brlog

Tues–Fri 9am–5pm, Sat 9am–1pm, Sun 2–6pm

Hermanov brlog (Herman's Den), in the same building as the Museum of Modern History, is the country's only dedicated children's museum. Although primarily aimed at local schoolchildren, there's an exquisite collection of more than three hundred toys to admire, from Slovenia and the rest of the world, including a horse whistle from 1925 (the oldest item in the collection) and a puzzle elephant from Turkey. Elsewhere, there are plenty of gadgets and gizmos to keep the kids entertained, as well as a small play area to mess around in.

Stari Pisker

Prešernova ulica 20 • Tues–Sat 9am–1pm; to visit, first contact the Museum of Modern History across the road • €3 • ☎ 03 428 6428, ⓦ muzej-nz-ce.si

Located on the site of the former Minorite monastery, **Stari Pisker** (whose literal translation is "Old Pot") is the old city prison where, between September 1941 and August 1942, 374 prisoners were executed by occupying German forces. The courtyard where the shootings took place is now a **memorial yard**, with the names of those killed identified on one wall alongside a bronze relief, while the old torture chamber now contains various items from that time, including clothing, shackles and objects made by prisoners – particularly moving are the many farewell letters, though more shocking are the photos of the shootings, which were taken by Josip Pelikan (see p.249). A large number of Yugoslav army soldiers were briefly held here during Slovenia's Ten-Day War of independence in 1991; today the prison functions as a young offenders' centre.

Knežji dvor Celje

Trg celjskih knezov 8 • March–Oct Tues–Sun 10am–6pm; Nov–Feb Tues–Fri 10am–4pm, Sat 9am–1pm • €4 • ☎ 03 428 0962, ⓦ pokmuz-ce.si

A large, irregularly shaped space dominated by the late nineteenth-century, neo-Renaissance **Narodni dom** (National Hall), the grandly named **Trg celjskih knezov** (Dukes of Celje Square), is also the site of the **Knežji dvor Celje** (Princely Palace), almost exclusively used for military purposes during the twentieth century. Excavations of the underground site began in 1992, revealing some extraordinary **Roman** and, to a lesser extent, Gothic remains. Running through the heart of the site is a Roman road (part of which has wheel tracks embedded), while there are also extensive foundations of two houses, one of which bears some remarkable wall frescoes. Best of all, however, is a stunning white marble statue (minus head and arms), believed to be the figure of an aristocratic woman.

Most of the upstairs rooms are given over to the deeds of the **counts of Celje** (see box, p.252). Among the highlights are three coins (sixteen are known to still exist) minted by the counts in the fifteenth century; most people, however, are drawn to the room holding eighteen of the counts' grisly skulls, including that of its last ruler Ulrich II, easily identifiable as it's the one with the jaw missing.

Pokrajinski muzej Celje

Muzejski trg 1 • March–Oct Tues–Sun 10am–6pm; Nov–Feb Tues–Fri 10am–4pm, Sat 9am–1pm • €4 • ☎ 03 428 0962, ⓦ pokmuz-ce.si

The arcaded, Renaissance **Stari Grofija** (Old Count's Mansion) is now home to the **Pokrajinksi muzej Celje** (Celje Regional Museum), which holds a rather strange mishmash of a cultural history collection, though that's not to say it's not without merit. Exhibits aside – look out for the 35,000-year-old bone needle, the oldest in Europe – there's some sublime ornamentation to admire. One room is plastered with Dutch black and blue ceramic wall tiles depicting peasant scenes, while the Garden Room is so-named after its parkland wall paintings, rendered in a style known as fresco-secco.

The museum's defining feature – one of Slovenia's most important works of art – is the **Celje Ceiling**, a dramatic, illusionist tempera painting discovered under another wooden ceiling in 1926. Completed around 1600 by an unknown artist (the piece has been attributed to Almanac, although this is disputed), this splendid Renaissance composition comprises eleven panels featuring the four seasons, four gods, two battle scenes and, in the central panel, a tangle of pillars and columns rising upwards to an imaginary sky.

Downstairs, don't miss a wonderful exhibition dedicated to the writer and polyglot **Alma Karlin** (1889–1950). This remarkable, but little-known, woman spent eight consecutive years (1919–27) travelling alone (with Erika, her typewriter) – quite a feat for anyone, let alone a woman, at that time; she chronicled her extraordinary journey

5

> ## THE COUNTS OF CELJE
>
> For more than three hundred years the **counts of Celje** ranked among the great Central European ruling dynasties. The dynastic line began with Gebhard I de Saun in 1130, before it morphed into the lords of Žovnek in the thirteenth century and the counts of Celje in 1341. As their status and wealth grew, the counts established their own court system, minted their own money and built castles and churches around the Savinja region. They reached the zenith of their powers under the reign of Hermann II around the end of the fourteenth century, a period during which they extended their sphere of control outside Slovenia into neighbouring lands, at the same time establishing important ties with other European ruling aristocratic houses. Raised to the rank of dukes of the province in 1436, the counts were, for a short period, the equal of their great adversaries and former feudal overlords, the Habsburgs. Their sudden demise followed Ulrich II's assassination by his long-time Hungarian adversary, László Hunyadi, in Belgrade in 1456.

in *The Odyssey of a Lonely Woman*. On display are numerous items gathered from that trip, including fans from the Far East, shells from Australia and wooden dolls from Africa. In the centre of Krekov trg, there's a bronze statue of the diminutive Karlin with trusty suitcase in hand.

Slomškov trg and Glavni trg

One of Celje's loveliest squares, **Slomškov trg** is named in honour of the saint Anton Slomšek (see box, p.271), a statue of whom stands nearby. This small, cobbled space is dominated by the fourteenth-century **Cerkev Sv Danijel** (Abbey Church of St Daniel), the town's most impressive ecclesiastical monument. Invested with some outstanding Gothic architecture, including a fine rib-vaulted ceiling and a towering arch at the entrance to the presbytery, the church also features numerous high-quality wall frescoes, most notably in the **Chapel of Our Lady of the Sorrows**, which also keeps a fifteenth-century pietà of the Madonna cradling the dead body of Jesus. The chapel dedicated to Slomšek was added in 2000, one year after his beatification in Maribor.

A narrow path leads from Slomškov trg through to **Glavni trg**, a handsome square flush with Baroque and Renaissance buildings, and a convivial place to enjoy a drink during the warmer months. In the centre stands **St Mary's Column**, adorned with statues of saints Rok, Joseph and Florian.

Stari Grad

Cesta na grad 78 • Daily: Jan & Dec 10am–4pm; Feb & Nov 9am–5pm; March, April & Oct 9am–6pm; May & Sept 9am–8pm; June–Aug 9am–9pm • €4 • ☎ 03 544 3690, ⓦ grad-celje.com • By foot, head through the underpass by the train station and follow the signs; beyond the old football stadium, the quickest walking route is to cut through the woods and rejoin the road at the top, from where it's a further 1km or so

Once the largest fortification in the country, the windswept ruin of Celje's **Stari Grad** (Old Castle) sits atop a 400m rise 2km southeast of town. Originally a twelfth-century structure, the castle acquired its present layout in the fourteenth century during the rule of the counts of Celje (see box above), who reinforced the walls and invested the interior with residential quarters; ad-hoc additions followed, before its eventual demise and descent into ruin during the seventeenth century. Although there are vestigial Romanesque and Gothic remains, years of renovation have quashed much of the structure's historical charm; nevertheless, it remains an impressive sight, particularly when viewed from afar. A programme of **medieval themed events** runs here throughout the summer; the principal happening takes place on the last Saturday in August.

In truth, there isn't a whole lot to see within the castle, but it would be remiss not to climb the enormous, 23m-high **Friderikov Stolp** (Friedrich Tower). This four-storey defence tower, built by the counts in the fourteenth century, is now a roofless structure offering stupendous **views** of the town's rust-red- and orange-tiled rooftops and the humpback hills of the Lower Savinja Valley.

The castle is also a good starting point for several short to medium-length **hikes**, with signposted trails to Celjska koča (651m; 1hr 30min or 2hr 30min), Svebotnik (700m; 2hr) and the delightful little hill village of Svetina (679m; 2hr 30min). If you are planning to do some walking, pick up a copy of the 1:50,000 *Celjska Kotlina* map, available from the tourist office.

ARRIVAL AND INFORMATION   CELJE

By train The train station is smack-bang in the centre of town, just across the road from Krekov trg.

Destinations Laško (every 30min–1hr; 10min); Ljubljana (every 30min–2hr; 1hr–1hr 40min); Maribor (every 30min–2hr; 45min–1hr 10min); Podčetrtek (Mon–Fri 2–3 daily; 45min); Rogaška Slatina (Mon–Fri 7 daily; 45min); Velenje (Mon–Fri 10 daily, Sat 3 daily; 50min).

By bus The bus station lies 400m north of the train station.

Destinations Laško (Mon–Fri hourly, Sat 3 daily; 15min); Ljubljana (Mon–Fri 9 daily, Sat & Sun 3 daily; 1hr 45min); Maribor (Mon–Fri 6–7 daily, Sat & Sun 2–3 daily; 1hr 15min); Rogaška Slatina (Mon–Fri 7 daily, Sat & Sun 3–4 daily; 40min); Slovenske Konjice (Mon–Fri hourly, Sat & Sun 2 daily; 25min); Velenje (Mon–Fri hourly, Sat 5 daily, Sun 2 daily; 25min).

Tourist office Glavni trg 17 (Mon–Fri 9am–5pm, Sat 9am–1pm; ☎ 03 428 7936, ⓦ celje.si).

ACTIVITIES

There are several activities to be had behind the *Celjska Koča* hotel (see below), including a **bobkart** (April–June Sat & Sun 10am–6pm; July & Aug Mon–Thurs 9am–noon & 4–8pm, Fri–Sun 10am–8pm; Sept & Oct Sat & Sun 2–6pm; €4 for one run, €15 for five runs) and an **adventure park** with a trio of tree-top trails of varying difficulty (April–June Sat & Sun 10am–6pm; July & Aug Mon–Thurs 9am–noon & 4–8pm, Fri–Sun 10am–8pm; Sept & Oct Sat & Sun 2–6pm; €15); the hotel also has mountain bikes for rent (€4/4hr, €8/day) and is the starting point for several excellent hikes.

ACCOMMODATION

Celeia Mariborska cesta 3 ☎ 03 426 9700, ⓦ hotel -celeia.si. Modest high-rise just across from the bus station with a business-like feel. While its rooms won't set the pulse racing (and are a little overpriced), they are competent enough. **€110**

Celjska Koča 10km south of Celje ☎ 05 907 0400, ⓦ celjska-koca.si. This superb alpine-style lodge (located at 650m) offers double and triple rooms as well as two attic dorms, most of which afford fabulous views of the Savinja Valley; there's also a wellness centre, a good restaurant and a raft of activities available (see above). To get here, take the road east towards the castle, before continuing south along Cesta na Grad, from where there are signs. **€65**

Evropa Krekov trg 4 ☎ 03 426 9000, ⓦ hotel-evropa.si. A hotel since 1875, the *Evropa* remains Celje's most prominent lodging, its generous rooms smartly decorated in chocolate brown and cream. **€96**

★**MCC Hostel** Mariborska cesta 2 ☎ 03 490 8742, ⓦ mc -celje.si. Ideally located near both the stations and the centre of town, this cracking, eco-conscious hostel has a range of four-, six- and eight-bed dorms, as well as eleven brilliantly themed en-suite doubles – "The Red House", for example, representing Socialism, and "Subculture", illustrating Celje's anarchic spirit. Free bike rental. Good café/bar, too (see p.254). Dorms **€16**, doubles **€44**

EATING

Gostilna Amerika Mariborska cesta 79 ☎ 03 541 9320, ⓦ gostilna-amerika.si. Despite its inconvenient and unappealing location 1km north of the centre, opposite the City Center shopping complex, this oddly named *gostilna* is worth trekking to for its huge portions of southern Balkan specialities such as bean stews, *čevapčiči* (rissoles of minced meat and onion) and *ražnjiči* (skewered meats). Mon–Fri 10am–11pm, Sat & Sun 11am–11pm.

Špageterija & Pizzeria Koper Krekov trg 4 ☎ 059 071 380, ⓦ pizzeria-koper.si. Strange name aside (there's no link to Koper whatsoever), there's much to enjoy about this affable restaurant, not least dishes that are a touch more creative than your average pizzeria. Try pasta with tuna,

rocket and capers, or risotto with radicchio, pancetta and pine nuts (€8); there are gluten-free options, too. Daily 10am–10pm.

Stari Pisker Savinova ulica 9 ☎ 03 544 2480, ⓦ stari -pisker.com. A good all-rounder, the "Old Pot" offers a meat-fest of a menu, featuring gourmet burgers (€9), BBQ skewers (prawns, tenderloin) and steaks, among other things. Between 11am and 5pm they offer a good selection of *malica* (two- or three-course set meals) for €6. The beer selection is top-notch, with craft varieties from Slovenia (Mali Grad and Pelicon) and the UK (Brewdog). Mon–Thurs & Sun 10am–10pm, Fri & Sat 10am–midnight.

5

DRINKING

MCC Kavarna Mariborska cesta 2 ☎ 03 490 8742, ⓦ hostel-celje.com. The hostel's creatively run café/bar is a super little hub; the playful interior features paint-splattered walls, art installations and upholstered armchairs – oh, and a fish tank – while the small grassy terrace out back (with hammocks) invariably hosts the most interesting happenings in town. Mon–Thurs 6–10pm, Fri & Sat 8am–1am, Sun 8am–10pm.

Mestna Plaža ☎ 031 804 213. In summer, the grassy riverbank area in front of the Regional Museum becomes the City Beach, a coolly shaded, open-air café-cum-bar with deckchairs, bench sofas and swing seats, and hammocks strung between the trees; there's also a daily programme of fun events staged here, such as dancing, theatre and puppetry. A lovely spot to while away an hour or two in quiet contemplation. June–Sept daily 7am–11pm.

Tamkoučiri Gosposka ulica 1a ☎ 041 329 261. The name aside, which translates as "the same place as yesterday", this is easily the most desirable drinking venue in town, an artsy, laidback brick-vaulted bar with tall wooden tables and stools and a sweet little garden terrace; better still, the beer's superb, with Humanfish pale ale on tap. Mon–Thurs & Sun 7am–11pm, Fri & Sat 7am–1am.

Rimska Nekropola

Ob Rimski Nekropoli, Šempeter, 12km west of Celje • April daily 9am–3pm; May, June & Sept daily 9am–5pm; July & Aug daily 10am–6pm; Oct Sat & Sun 10am–4pm • €5 • ☎ 03 700 2056, ⓦ td-sempeter.si • To get here, take one of the hourly buses from Celje, alight in the centre, and backtrack 100m to the traffic lights; from here walk up Ob Rimski Nekropoli towards the church, opposite which is both the necropolis and tourist office (April–Oct Tues–Sun 10am–6pm; ☎ 03 700 2056, ⓦ td-sempeter.si)

Reached along the main road running parallel to the A1 highway, the small urban settlement of **ŠEMPETER** is the setting for the **Rimska Nekropola** (Roman Necropolis). One of the most important archeological sites in this part of Europe, the necropolis, excavated and reconstructed over a fifteen-year period during the 1950s and 1960s, served as a burial ground for the nobles of Celeia (Roman Celje) until it was swamped by floodwaters from the Savinja River around 270 AD. Four marble mausolea, emblazoned with relief portraits of the families they commemorate, as well as scenes from classical mythology, were re-erected, and dozens more plinths, columns and fragments were unearthed.

The largest and grandest of the four monuments is the 8m-high **Spectatii** family tomb, its members represented by three headless statues; the funerary plinths are arrayed with mythical figures and various seasonal scenes, while the head of Medusa juts out over the gable. The most arresting tomb is that of the **Ennii** family, depicted here by three shallow relief portraits of the mother, father and daughter, Kalendina, though curiously there's not one of the son, Vitulus. On the front-facing plinth there's a fine relief of *Europa Riding the Bull* and, on the Baldachin ceiling, sculpted caskets bursting with rosettes. The other two mausolea are less fanciful: the altar-shaped tomb of **Vindonius** – understood to be the oldest of the four – features reliefs of *Hercules and Alcestis* and, on the side panels, two hunters, one with a hare draped around his neck, the other carrying a shepherd's staff and a basket of birds. Built in the form of a chapel, the tomb of **Secundinii** is largely devoid of ornamentation.

Pekel jama

Podlog, 5km north of Šempeter • Hourly tours March & Oct Sat & Sun 10am–5pm; April daily 10am–5pm; May–Sept daily 10am–6pm • €8 • ☎ 03 700 2056, ⓦ td-sempeter.si

If you don't manage to get down to the Karst region (see pp.173–182), you can content yourself with a visit to the fearsomely titled **Pekel jama** (Hell's Cave), an atmospheric little cavern that takes its name from the devilish figure carved into the rock face above the entrance. The cave was one of the first in Slovenia to be opened to visitors – around 1860 – as testified by the signatures on the walls. Inside, it's split between two levels; the first, lower, gallery tracks the Peklenščica (Hell Stream) past several small lakes towards a 4m-high waterfall, which, though modest in size, is the highest subterranean waterfall (that can be viewed) in Slovenia. Thereafter it's a steady climb to the stalactite-infested upper gallery, and then onwards to the exit, some 40m higher than the entrance; the total walk is around 1200m.

Laško

Straddling the Savinja River, 11km south of Celje, the small town of **LAŠKO** is synonymous with **beer** and **spas** – the former has been brewed here since 1825, and thermal springs are known to have existed hereabouts since Roman times. A pleasant but sedate place, the town really only comes to life during the **Beer and Flowers Festival** (w pivo-cvetje.si) in mid-July; one of the most enjoyable provincial events in the Slovene calendar, it comprises four manic days of music, sports and games, flower displays and, of course, lots of beer.

Pivovarna Laško

Trubarjeva ulica 28 • Tours (2hr 30min) Mon–Fri 8am–5pm, Sat 9am–noon • €8 • ☏ 03 734 8000, w pivo-lasko.si

Established by gingerbread baker, Franz Geyer, in 1825, **Pivovarna Laško** was formerly one of the largest breweries in Yugoslavia and today ranks as one of the two largest in Slovenia – the Union brewery in Ljubljana being the other – albeit both are now owned by Heineken. **Tours** of the *pivovarna* (brewery) take in the filtration and bottling plants, a museum and a generous spot of sampling with nibbles; tours normally run only if there is a minimum of ten people, so you'd do well to call in advance.

Thermana Laško

Zdravilišče cesta 6 • **Thermana Park Laško** Daily 9am–9pm • Mon–Fri €9 for 3hr, €12/day; Sat & Sun €11 for 3hr, €14/day • ☏ 03 423 2000, w thermana.si • **Zdravlišče Laško** Mon–Sat 9.30am–9pm, Sun 7am–9pm • Mon–Fri €9 for 3hr, €11/day; Sat & Sun €10 for 3hr, €12/day • ☏ 03 734 5771, w thermana.si

The town's thermal springs have been pulling in the punters since 1854 when the first formal baths were built. Today, the **Thermana Laško** (Laško Spa), a ten-minute walk north of the tourist office, is a thoroughly modern affair, incorporating two complexes. With its huge glass cupola, the **Thermana Park Laško** has a myriad of indoor and outdoor thermal baths, comprising whirlpools, massage pools, water slides and wave machines, in addition to a sauna centre and a smart hotel; next door the **Zdravlišče Laško** complex also has a wide range of indoor and outdoor baths and generally attracts a slightly older crowd.

ARRIVAL AND INFORMATION LAŠKO

By train The town's train station, with services from Celje (every 30min–1hr; 10min), is on Trg svobode on the west bank of the Savinja River.

By bus Buses from Celje (Mon–Fri hourly, Sat 2 daily; 15min) pull into the station next door to the train station.

Tourist office Across the bridge from the stations at Valvasorjev trg 1 (Mon–Fri 8am–6pm, Sat 9am–2pm; ☏ 03 733 8950, w lasko.info); they rent bikes (€5 for 3hr, €9 for the day).

ACCOMMODATION AND EATING

Nemec Tourist Farm Sedraž 3 ☏ 03 573 6549. High up in the hills in the village of Sedraž (430m), around 8km east of Laško, this gem of a tourist farm has six rooms, each with glorious views of the surrounding countryside. As ever on these farms, there's terrific home-cooking, too. €56

Pavus Cesta na Svetino 23 ☏ 03 620 0723, w pavus.si. Posh, though eminently affordable, restaurant inside Tabor Castle, beautifully set on the slopes of Mt Hum (583m) 1km north of town. The superbly conceived menu lists such dishes as zander fillet with nettle risotto and vegetable ragout (€19), or marinated veal with raspberries and foie gras, alongside intriguing local specialities including dark beer sorbet (€6.50). Wed–Sat noon–10pm, Sun noon–8pm.

Savinja B&B Valvasorjev trg 1 ☏ 03 734 3030, w lasko .info. Located above the tourist office (which acts as the reception), this restful, and remarkably good-value, B&B offers ten large rooms with floor-to-ceiling windows, low wooden beds and sofas. €60

Velenje

Opened with great ceremonial pomp in 1959, **VELENJE** is Slovenia's youngest town. Formerly known as Titov Velenje – the Yugoslav president Tito visited here no fewer than four times, on one occasion with Brezhnev – modern-day Velenje was designed as a model industrial workers' town, characterized by a uniform series of grim high-rise apartments and wide streets broken up by the odd splash of greenery. Today, Slovenia's fifth-largest city is still sustained by industry, including coal mining and the major domestic appliances producer, Gorenje. Its oddly appealing **Socialist Realist** aesthetic makes it worth a visit, as does its rich mining heritage and, more surprisingly, a **lake** that doubles up as the town beach.

Titov trg

Titov trg is a vast concrete square littered with Socialist-era buildings and monuments, the most conspicuous of which is an oversized **monument of Tito**, one of very few statues of the former Yugoslav president remaining in Slovenia – indeed, this is the largest known statue of him anywhere in the world. On the opposite side, and just beyond a bronze statue of a miner, is the **Speechless Rifles** monument, comprising a cluster of upturned rifles merging into people, through which a fountain emerges. Nearby a more sobering monument commemorates some 668 victims of fascist oppression during World War II.

Muzej Velenje

Velenjski Grad, Ljubljanska cesta 54 • Tues–Sun 10am–6pm • €3 • ☎ 03 898 2630, Ⓦ muzej-velenje.si

Sited on a high, rounded hill above Velenje's small, almost forgotten, Old Town quarter is the beautifully renovated **Velenjski Grad** (Velenje Castle), most of which dates from the sixteenth century. The castle now houses the **Muzej Velenje** (Velenje Museum), which comprises several disparate but interesting exhibitions: most enthralling is the collection of **African art** donated to the museum by Czech-born sculptor František Foit, who spent more than twenty years living in and travelling around the continent. During this time he accumulated some terrific stuff, most of which is on display here, including jewellery, furniture, musical instruments, tribal masks and puppets, as well as some of his own wood-carved sculptures. The worthwhile exhibition covers twentieth-century **Slovene art**, featuring big-hitters such as Pilon, Kralj, Mihelič and Tisnikar.

Velenjska Plaža

Cesta Simona Blatnika

In summer, Velenje's lake becomes the unlikely setting for **Velenjska Plaža**, the town **beach**. This extensive grass and gravel bank comes complete with water-bound inflatables, showers and lifeguards; it's also possible to rent windsurf equipment and stand-up paddles. The water itself is clean and warm, and shallow enough in places for kids to paddle – there's a terrific beach bar here, too (see opposite).

Muzej premogovništva slovenije

Koroška cesta, Škale, 1.5km north of Velenje • Tues–Sat 9am–4.30pm; guided tours (90min) 9am, noon & 2.30pm • €10 including guided tour, €3 for coal mining exhibition only • ☎ 031 752 418, Ⓦ muzej.rlv.si • It's a 30min walk from the centre; head north up Cesta talcev, cross the rail tracks and continue along Kidričeva cesta, which loops round and becomes Koroška cesta

Coal has been excavated at the Velenje Coal Mine in Škale since 1875, although it was the drilling of the main lignite layer around a century later that really put the town on the map. Although the mine remains operational, it's possible to visit certain parts, defined as the **Muzej premogovništva slovenije** (Coal Mining Museum of Slovenia), on an organized **tour**. Descending 160m in the original elevator, the tour – enlivened by audiovisual presentations and models of assorted mine characters – takes in sections of both the old and new mine shafts, the latter first used after World War II; you also get

5

to eat a typical miner's lunch, comprising a chunky *Kranjska* sausage, bread and juice, in the old canteen. The complex includes an illuminating **coal mining exhibition**, which documents the history of the mine, including a miner's apartment.

ARRIVAL AND INFORMATION

VELENJE

By bus The bus station is in the centre of town on Šaleška cesta.

Destinations Celje (Mon–Fri hourly, Sat 5 daily, Sun 2 daily; 25min); Črna na Koroškem (Mon–Fri hourly, Sat & Sun 4 daily; 50min); Ljubljana (Mon–Fri 3 daily, Sat & Sun 1 daily; 1hr 30min); Slovenj Gradec (Mon–Fri 8 daily, Sat & Sun 4 daily; 25min).

By train The train station lies 1km northeast of the centre, just off Cesta talcev near the industrial zone.

Destinations Celje (Mon–Fri 11 daily, Sat 2 daily; 50min).

Tourist office Inside the Villa Bianca at Start trg 3, 300m west of the bus station (Mon–Fri 7am–7pm, Sat & Sun 9am–5pm; ☎ 03 896 1860, ⓦ velenje-tourism.si); they've got bikes for rent (€3 for 3hr, €10/day).

ACCOMMODATION AND EATING

Camping Jezero Cesta Simona Blatnika 27 ☎ 031 455 977, ⓦ camp-jezero.si. Flat, green and well-shaded site superbly positioned out by the lake 2km west of town, which also has tents, windsurfers and stand-up paddles for rent, and an on-site bar – and of course, there's the lake to swim in. May–Oct. **€18**

Plaža Mia Mia Cesta Simona Blatnika 26 ☎ 051 621 146. Although a bit of a schlep to reach – unless you're staying at the nearby campsite (see above), or spending an afternoon bathing in the lake – this funky little wooden beach bar is worth taking the time and effort to get to; by day a relaxing chill-out zone with locals sipping coffee and eating ice cream, it morphs into quite the party place come sundown. May–Sept daily 9am–1/2am.

Ražgoršek Stari trg ☎ 03 898 3630, ⓦ hotelrazgorsek .si. Occupying one of the more appealing spots in Velenje, in the small Old Town area just below the castle, with brazenly colourful – almost museum piece – rooms in Baroque style, with plush carpets, oversized paintings and gold trimmings. **€76**

Youth Hostel MC Velenje Efenkova cesta 61a ☎ 05 923 4600, ⓦ mc-velenje.si. Continuing the trend across Slovenia for newly built hostels-cum youth centres, this large, modern hostel, 500m east of the centre, has immaculate dorms (three or six beds) and doubles, some with bathrooms and TVs; there is also a large and well-equipped self-catering kitchen. Dorms **€18**, doubles **€40**

Koroška

From Velenje, two roads forge their way into the heart of **Koroška**, a mountainous, heavily forested region crossed by three river valleys and scattered with isolated highland farmsteads and small valley settlements. One road heads north up the Mislinja Valley to the pretty town of **Slovenj Gradec**, and beyond to **Dravograd**, while the other road straggles across a mountain pass northwest to the ex-mining towns of **Črna na Koroškem** and **Mežica**; the former is also a key starting point for forays into the heart of the Koroška mountains.

Slovenj Gradec

In stark contrast to Velenje, the spruce little town of **SLOVENJ GRADEC**, 27km further north in the Mislinja Valley and the largest settlement in Koroška, preserves a delightful medieval core. The town is renowned for its rich cultural heritage, thanks to the likes of prominent Slovene artists Bogdan Borčič and Jože Tisnikar, and the Austrian composer Hugo Wolf, all of whom were born here. Everything of interest is spread out along **Glavni trg**, a wide, smoothly curving street that forms the heart of the town's beautifully preserved medieval core.

Koroška galerija likovnih umetnosti

Glavni trg 24 • Tues–Fri 9am–6pm, Sat & Sun 10am–1pm & 2–5pm • €2.50 • ☎ 02 882 2131, ⓦ glu-sg.si

On the first floor of the town hall is the **Koroška galerija likovnih umetnosti** (Koroška Gallery of Fine Arts), one of the largest and most progressive art centres in

5

the country. The gallery focuses almost exclusively on the works of three of Koroška's most prominent artists: avant-garde painter Valentin Oman, represented here by a series of enormous vertical images, mostly of the human form; Bogdan Borčič, painter of brightly coloured abstract pieces (though several darker works were influenced by his time spent in Dachau); and, most prominently, **Jože Tisnikar**, whose overwhelmingly bleak and moody paintings, defined as "dark modernism" – for example *In the Morgue* and *Horsemen of the Apocalypse* – undoubtedly owe much to the time he spent in a hospital pathology department. His fondness for crows (he kept one as a pet) is evident in several of his paintings, such as *The Procession of Crows*; here too is the painting he was working on when he was killed in a car crash in 1998.

Muzej Slovenj Gradec

Glavni trg 24 • Tues–Fri 9am–6pm, Sat & Sun 10am–1pm & 2–5pm • €2.50 • ☎ 02 625 2122, ⓦ kpm.si

On the second floor of the building that holds the Gallery of Fine Arts, the **Muzej Slovenj Gradec** (Slovenj Gradec Museum) is a random assortment of treasures bequeathed by local priest and cultural ambassador Jakob Soklič. The undoubted highlight is a quartet of stunning Egyptian statuettes, each representing various deities, which would typically be placed in tombs – most striking are the gilded wooden statue of a mummified Osiris, and another representing the goddess Taweret, bearing the head and body of a hippopotamus, the paws of a bear and a woman's breasts. There's also a memorial room dedicated to Soklič's fellow priest (and poet) and acquaintance, Franc Ksaver Meško – you can see thousands of books from his library as well as his travelling bag and cane, jacket and death mask.

Cerkev Sv Elizabete and Cerkev Sv Duha

Situated on Trg svobode directly opposite the town hall, the thirteenth-century, but several times rebuilt, **Cerkev Sv Elizabete** (Parish Church of St Elizabeth) honours the Hungarian princess Elizabeth. Although the exterior is largely of Gothic appearance, the interior showcases an abundance of Baroque extravagances, most notably a sumptuously overblown high altar – the central painting of *Elizabeth Amongst the Beggars* was executed by the Baroque workshop of Franz Strauss – and a richly gilded pulpit. Also look out for numerous liturgical items, Gothic knights' tombstones and, to the right as you enter, a painting of St Anton Slomšek (see box, p.271), completed in 1999.

Standing in its shadow is the lovely wood-shingled **Cerkev Sv Duha** (Church of the Holy Spirit), beautifully ornamented with a fine array of fifteenth-century frescoes – note, too, the fragment of a Roman tombstone embedded into the exterior wall on the north side. The church is usually closed, so contact the tourist office to arrange a visit.

ARRIVAL AND INFORMATION   SLOVENJ GRADEC

By bus The bus station is on Pohorska cesta, from where it's a 10min walk south to Glavni trg.
Destinations Črna na Koroškem (Mon–Fri hourly–every 1hr 30min, Sat 5 daily, Sun 3 daily; 50min); Velenje (Mon–Fri hourly, Sat & Sun 5 daily; 25min).

Tourist office On the ground floor of the old town hall at Glavni trg 24 (May–Sept Mon–Fri 8am–6pm, Sat & Sun 10am–5pm; Oct–April Mon–Fri 8am–4pm, Sat & Sun 10am–1pm; ☎ 02 881 2116, ⓦ slovenjgradec.si).

ACCOMMODATION AND EATING

Čajnica Pec Glavni trg 24 ☎ 041 906 629. In the arcaded courtyard just beyond the passageway separating the tourist office and the museum entrance, this happy, hippy dive is the most sociable spot in town, and the atmospheric little courtyard is often used for concerts and exhibitions.

Mon–Thurs 8am–11pm, Fri & Sat 9am–midnight, Sun 10am–9pm.
Hostel Slovenj Gradec Ozare 18 ☎ 02 884 6290, ⓦ spotur.si. Anonymously located in a light industrial area a 10min walk north of the centre, this is yet another

> **UNDERGROUND ADVENTURES**
>
> For something adventurous, and certainly different, you can participate in guided **underground bike rides** through a section of the **Mežica mine**, along 5km of illuminated tunnels constructed for the transportation of lead ore and waste materials (Tues–Sun 10am & 2pm; 2hr 30min; €25 for two to three people, €22 for four to seven people; bike rental €10). Even more thrilling are the **underground kayaking tours** (Tues–Sun 9am & 11am; 4hr; €40), taking in a section of the submerged part of the mine – these involve around ninety minutes on the water (in two-seater kayaks), followed by a light miner's lunch. Both these tours can be booked through the mine itself or at the *Ecohotel* in Jamnica (see p.260).

youth centre-based hostel, and a good one it is too, with a mix of single, double, triple and quad rooms, all en suite; there's a colourful café attached, too. Dorms €17, doubles €40

Rotovnik-Plesnik Tourist Farm Legen 134a • 02 885 3666, Ⓦ rotovnik-plesnik.si. If you have your own transport, by far the best option is this delightful homestead 4km east of town on the road up to the Kope ski resort; on offer are six warm rooms – furnished in beech, cherry or maple wood – a common area for self-catering, super home-cooked food (the organic breakfast is delicious) and a working 1970s jukebox. €64

Mežica

Glančnik 8 • Tours (90min) April–June & Sept–Nov Tues–Sun 11am; July & Aug Tues–Fri 11am, Sat & Sun 11am & 3pm; Dec–March Sat 11am • Mine tour €9, €10 including mine museum • 02 870 0180, Ⓦ podzemljepece.com

Up until a few years ago, lead and zinc had been mined in **MEŽICA** for more than three hundred years. Although mining began here back in 1665, it wasn't until Napoleon's arrival in 1809 that intensive, heavy-duty production began. Further modernization during the early twentieth century saw the introduction of electricity and pneumatic drilling, but the gradual depletion of ore reserves after World War II led to a decline in production and the mine finally closed in 2000. Part of the excellent **information centre** inside Glančnik, one of three former forges, is given over to a blacksmith's exhibition; there's a café, too.

Mine tour

Kitted out with jacket, helmet and torch, you begin the **mine tour** by clambering aboard the very small and rickety mine train (not for the claustrophobic), which transports you 3.5km through the Glančnik tunnel into the heart of the mine complex, known as Moring. Then, walking through twenty large galleries on two levels, each approximately 30m apart, you'll see the calling room, where miners would gather at the beginning of the shift before dispersing to their stations, various mining equipment and machinery preserved *in situ* and a series of audiovisual demonstrations.

Mine museum

Tues–Sun: April–Oct 9am–5pm; Nov–March 9am–3pm • €3

The **mine museum** displays a fine collection of minerals and fossils, mine survey maps and mapping instruments; don't miss the mocked-up miner's home, a typically cramped living space which would be expected to accommodate up to eight members of the same family.

Črna na Koroškem

ČRNA NA KOROŠKEM, a sedate little town 7km south of Mežica in the Upper Meža Valley, has a few useful tourist facilities and is a key springboard for onward ventures into the **mountains**. There are a couple of minor collections to nose

5

CYCLING AND HIKING AROUND ČRNA NA KOROŠKEM

The mountains encircling Črna na Koroškem, also known as King Matjaž Park, offer some of the best **cycling** in the country, with twelve circular routes adding up to around 1000km of marked trails – each of which is marked out by yellow animal footprints. Everything you need to know about cycling in the region can be obtained from the *Ecohotel Koroš* cyclists' hotel in Jamnica (see below), where you can also **rent bikes** (€25/day) and get repairs done; they also organize a superb range of guided mountain **bike tours** (€40/half-day, €70/day; reduced prices if there are more people), in addition to underground cycling and kayaking trips in the Mežica mine (see box, p.259).

There are a number of good **hiking** possibilities from Črna. The most popular is the trek northwest up to **Mala Peca** (1731m; 3hr 15min), just below which is the *Dom na Peci* hut (April–Oct daily; Nov–March Sat & Sun; ☎02 823 5378); fifteen minutes' walk from the hut is the **cave of King Matjaž** (Matjaževa jama), the alleged sleeping place of the mythological folk hero named after the Hungarian king, Matthias Corvinus – there's a bronze statue of Matjaž inside the cave entrance. From the hut, you can continue via one of two paths towards Kordeževa glava (2125m; 1hr on easier path, 2hr on more challenging path) on the Austrian border. From Črna, there are shorter hikes, too, including a ninety-minute trail north to the year-round *Koča na Pikovem* hut (992m), which has just a handful of beds (☎02 823 8525), and another trail south to **Najevska Lipa** (1hr 45min), the site of an enormous linden tree, alleged to be one of the largest trees in Slovenia. Whatever activity you plan to undertake, you'll find the 1:50,000 *Koroška* **map** useful; it's available from the tourist office in Črna (see below).

around, if you have time to kill; contact the tourist office (see below) if you with to visit either. Opposite the bus stop, the **ethnological museum** (€2) comprises a modest assortment of everyday household items and farming implements used by local peasants. Hewn into the rock face a few metres from the bus station, the **mining museum** (€2) presents mine trucks, drilling equipment and tools used in the Mežica mine before its closure.

ARRIVAL AND INFORMATION

By bus Buses stop near the main roundabout in the centre of town.
Destinations Maribor (3 daily; 1hr 50min); Slovenj Gradec (Mon–Fri hourly, Sat 7 daily, Sun 3 daily; 50min); Velenje

(Mon–Fri 8 daily, Sat & Sun 4 daily; 50min).
Tourist office A few paces from the bus stop at Center 101 (Mon–Fri 8am–4pm, Sat 9am–noon; ☎02 870 4820, ⊛crna.si).

ACCOMMODATION AND EATING

Ecohotel Koroš Jamnica 10 ☎02 870 3060, ⊛bike nomad.com. As well as being the main cycling centre for the region (see box above), this cyclists' hotel offers simple, warm and comfortable double en-suite rooms, as well as delicious home-cooked food. Facilities include bike storage, with space to wash and dry clothes and boots. **€70**

Kavalir Center 109 ☎02 621 4300, ⊛kavalir.in. It comes as a welcome surprise to find this gorgeous, if

expensive, boutique hotel here in Črna. The five luxurious rooms are named/themed after local characters or trades – including a metallic silver-and-black miner's room, a Baroque-furnished count's room and a hunter's room with aged wood furnishings, oak flooring and animal prints. Each is beautifully conceived, with sliding glass walls separating the bedrooms from the bathrooms, L'Occitane toiletries and a free minibar. The on-site café is a similarly classy affair. Daily 9am–9pm. **€150**

THE SNOW CASTLE FESTIVAL

Črna is known throughout Slovenia for its **King Matjaž Snow Castle Festival**, held 6km from town at Pod Peca on the last weekend of January. More than a hundred teams compete to design the highest, grandest or most dazzling ice castle; how long these constructions remain intact is, naturally enough, dependent on the weather, though most are still standing about a week or so after the event.

Upper Savinja Valley

Named after the **Savinja River**, which flows from the heart of the Kamniške-Savinja Alps, down through Celje and beyond to Zidani Most, where it joins the Sava River, the **Upper Savinja Valley** (Zgornja Savinjska dolina) is a pristine landscape of towering alpine peaks, river valleys and undulating slopes. The region's settlements are mainly large villages and a couple of small towns; picturesque as some of them are, they're not really worth a special visit. In any case, chances are that you'll be keen to push on to the surrounding hills and mountains.

Logarska dolina and around

The region's siren draw is the extraordinarily beautiful **Logarska dolina** (Logar Valley), a 7km-long alpine valley situated along the western margins of the Upper Savinja in the cradle of the Kamniške-Savinja Alps. Formed during the Ice Age, the U-shaped glaciated valley features a level, green valley floor covered with flower-speckled meadows and beech woods, enclosed by step-like cliff sides riddled with glacial boulders, waterfalls, springs, streams and a majestic wreath of jagged grey peaks, most of which top 2000m.

From the entrance to the valley, it's about 2km to the information hut (see p.262) and a couple of hotels (see p.262), beyond which point the road continues for a further 5km up to the head of the valley and Logarska's most popular site, the 90m **Slap Rinka** (Rinka Waterfall). There's a walking trail (6km) to the waterfall beginning approximately 1km along the road after you've entered the valley.

Although the mountains look formidable, they can be traversed via a trail that starts at Rinka and climbs to **Okrešelj** (1396m) and the *Frischaufov dom* hut (☎03 838 9070; May–Oct), before continuing to **Kamniško Sedlo** (1864m) and the *Kamniška koča* hut (☎051 611 367; mid-June to mid-Oct); from here the trail continues down to Kamniška Bistrica (see p.86).

The one major approach to Logarska is via the road from **Ljubno ob Savinji**, a small town 34km east of Kamnik and 26km northwest of the Ljubljana–Celje highway. Logarska can also be reached from Črna na Koroškem (see p.259), via a relatively short (20km), but difficult and mostly unsurfaced, mountain road – the road actually emerges in Solčava, from where it's a short drive to the valley.

Robanov Kot and Matkov Kot

Although most cars and buses pile into Logarska, the two glaciated valleys flanking Logarska dolina – **Robanov Kot** to the east and the narrower, more heavily forested **Matkov Kot** to the west (a couple of kilometres from the Austrian border) – are no less magnificent, and should appeal to anyone seeking more solitude. They have some beautifully situated accommodation, too.

Center Rinka

Solčava 29 • Daily: July & Aug 8am–7pm; Sept–June 8am–5pm • ☎03 839 0710, ⓦ solcavsko.info

The nearest settlement en route to Logarska is the pretty roadside village of **SOLČAVA**, 4km to the east. It's well worth stopping off here to visit the **Center Rinka** (Rinka Centre), whose lovely, wood-clad facade – meant to resemble a mountain peak – holds an information centre, permanent exhibition and café. The main theme of the engaging little exhibition is mountain wood; around eighty percent of the valley is forested, mostly with larch and spruce, but also beech, red pine and ash, samples of which, in various guises, are present here. Larch is particularly prominent in the construction of houses hereabouts, owing to its durability. These steeply forested slopes also shelter the indigenous Jezerkso-Solčavka sheep, a hardy alpine breed from which felt is produced to create a beautiful range of items, such as slippers, hats and bags.

5

Felt-making remains an important local craft; if you ask at the information centre they'll be happy to show you around the workshop across the road.

ARRIVAL AND INFORMATION LOGARSKA DOLINA

By bus Although there are a handful of (weekday) buses from Celje and Velenje to Luče and Solčava (the nearest settlements to Logarska), only two of these continue to Logarska, and even then, that's only on Sat and Sun between April and Oct (departing Celje 7.10am & 1.10pm). During this same period, there are two buses at weekends (10am & 6pm) departing Logarska for Celje, plus one bus on weekdays at 12.46pm.

By car Between April and Oct, a one-time fee of €7/car is payable at the entrance to the valley; you have to pay for this even if you're staying here.

Tourist information From the entrance to the valley, it's about 2km to the information hut (April–June, Sept & Oct Sat & Sun 10am–4pm; July & Aug daily 9am–6pm; ☎ 03 838 9004, ⍉ logarska-dolina.si).

Activities The staff at the information hut organize three-hour guided walks of the valley (€3.50/person for a group of up to ten) plus rock climbing (€25 for 1hr), archery (€10 for 1hr) and tandem paragliding (€60); you can also rent bikes (€5 for 1hr, €15/day).

ACCOMMODATION AND EATING

Gradišnik Tourist Farm Logarska dolina 18, Matkov Kot ☎ 03 838 9012, ⍉ gradisnik.si. Stunningly situated in the next valley along, and slightly more peaceful, this welcoming farm offers two pine-furnished en-suite rooms and two apartments; the farm is particularly well known for its archery (€13/person), which is available to non-guests too. **€50**

Kmečka hiša Ojstrica Logarska dolina 13a ☎ 03 838 9051, ⍉ logarska-ojstrica.si. Opposite *Lenar*, the cottagey, pine-clad interior of this charming and perennially busy farmhouse restaurant is a wonderful spot in which to tuck into the likes of buckwheat porridge with chanterelle mushrooms, or meat dumplings with crackling (€9). In summer, the barbecue is invariably on the go, offering spicy grilled sausages and the like – great with a beer on the terrace. Daily 12.30–4pm & 6–10pm.

★**Lenar Tourist Farm** Logarska dolina 11 ☎ 041 851 829, ⍉ lenar.si. Sitting in a colourful meadow 500m from the information hut, this convivial homestead offers gorgeously furnished rooms, each with terrific views of the valley; more fun is the adjoining hay barn (sleeps six), complete with (remarkably comfortable) straw mattresses, downstairs bathroom and a covered open-air kitchen. While enjoying breakfast, check out the photo of Tito with the family, snapped on the porch back in the 1970s; look out, too, for Mica, the pot-bellied pig. Hay barn for two **€36**, doubles **€60**

Plesnik Logarska dolina 10 ☎ 03 839 2300, ⍉ plesnik.si. Opposite the information hut, the valley's one conventional hotel is an extremely comfortable alpine-style lodge with big windows offering tremendous mountain views, plus an outdoor pool. Directly opposite, the hotel's homely *Vila Palenk* has some rooms with a fireplace, lovely in winter. Plesnik **€72**, Vila Palenk **€90**

East of Celje

The region **east of Celje** is dominated by its spas. Best known are **Rogaška Slatina**, once one of Europe's grandest resorts, and **Olimia**, a relatively recent addition to the scene. There is also a brace of cultural diversions to enjoy – the Skansen-like **Rogatec open-air museum** near Rogaška Slatina, and **Olimje Monastery**, not far from the Olimia spa. Northeast of Celje, the charming little town of **Slovenske Konjice** is the jumping-off point for the enchanting ruins of **Žiče Monastery**.

Rogaška Slatina and around

Thirty kilometres east of Celje, **ROGAŠKA SLATINA** was built around three mineral-rich springs (Donat, Styria and Tempel) discovered during the sixteenth century, and was once one of the most fashionable spa resorts in Central Europe – illustrious visitors included the Habsburg ruler Franz Jozef, the French Bonapartes and King Karadordevič of Serbia. Despite the addition of a couple of beastly-looking hotels, the town has managed to preserve its quintessential spa ambience, which is particularly true around its central square, **Zdraviliški trg**, a broad, immaculately kept landscaped park neatly framed by gravel walkways and grand buildings. The pick of these is the stately **Zdraviliški Dom** (now the *Grand Hotel Rogaška*), one of the finest Neoclassical buildings in the country.

5

Pivnica mineralnih vod

Zdraviliški trg • Daily 7am–1pm & 3–7pm • €1.50

Although its curative properties have long been used to treat a wide range of disorders – typically gastrointestinal complaints and metabolic problems – the water is tapped first and foremost for commercial purposes. You'll find many bottled waters from Rogaška in bars and restaurants throughout the country; in its purest form, however, it is incredibly metallic and barely drinkable. You can sample the magnesium-laden Donat Mg, the spa's most famous water, and others, in the large **Pivnica mineralnih vod** (Pump Room), at the northern end of Zdraviliški trg near the **Temple**, an oval pavilion sitting on top of the spa's main spring; head towards reception, grab a cup and away you go.

Steklarska šola

Ulica talcev 1, 2km south of town • Tours (1hr) Mon–Fri 10.30am–1.30pm; shop Mon–Fri 8am–7pm, Sat 8am–1pm • €8 • ☎ 02 818 0205, Ⓦ steklarna-rogaska.si

Thermal waters aside, Rogaška is also known for its crystal **glassware**, which has been produced in the region since 1665, and on the current site since 1927. Tours of the **Steklarska šola** (Glass Factory) – which today employs some nine hundred people – are not wildly exciting, but you do get to view the master glassblowers at work in the furnace, as well as the supremely skilful cutters and painters applying finishing touches to the dazzling array of bowls, cups and vases. Inevitably, the tour winds up in the shop, packed full of glittering, and mostly quite expensive, products.

ARRIVAL AND INFORMATION | ROGAŠKA SLATINA

By train The train station is on Kidričeva ulica, 500m south of town.

Destinations Celje (Mon–Fri 6 daily; 50min); Rogatec (7 daily; 10min).

By bus The bus station is closer to the centre on Celjska cesta, from where it's a 5min walk to the main square, Zdraviliški trg.

Destinations Celje (Mon–Fri 8 daily, Sat 5 daily, Sun 3 daily; 40min); Podčetrtek (Mon–Fri hourly, Sat & Sun 4 daily; 20min); Rogatec (Mon–Fri 9 daily, Sat 4 daily, Sun 3 daily; 15min).

Tourist train Between May and Oct, the tourist train (*turistični vlak*) runs to the Olimia spa and onwards to Olimje Monastery (€12); check schedules with the tourist office.

Tourist office Zdraviliški trg (July & Aug Mon–Fri 8am–7pm, Sat & Sun 8am–noon; Sept–June Mon–Fri 8am–4pm, Sat 8am–noon; ☎ 03 581 4414, Ⓦ rogaska-tourism.com). Private accommodation can be arranged here.

Activities The Rogaška Riviera swimming complex, Celjska cesta 5 (April–Oct daily 9am–8pm; Mon–Fri €8 for 3hr, €10/day, Sat & Sun €9 for 3hr, €12/day; ☎ 03 818 1950, Ⓦ rogaska-resort.com), has several indoor and outdoor thermal pools, with an average temperature of 30°C; guests of some hotels receive free entry, so check with yours.

ACCOMMODATION

★**Kmetija Marjanca** Spodnji Kostrivnica 5 ☎ 03 581 4264, Ⓦ tk-marjanca.net. Perched atop a low hill 5km west of Rogaška Slatina, the rooms – floor-to-ceiling windows offering exciting views; beautiful wood furnishings ingrained with bold colours; snappily designed bathrooms – are several notches above what you'll find on most tourist farms. There's even a small wellness centre. Breakfast consists of delicious goodies cultivated in the garden. **€54**

Slatina Celjska cesta 6 ☎ 03 818 4100, Ⓦ hotel-slatina.si. The most realistically priced hotel in town, the *Slatina*

offers a mix of en-suite rooms (including triples) and apartments; they're well furnished, if not very inspiring decor-wise, and there's a rather lovely basement pool. **€90**

Slovenija Celjska cesta 1 ☎ 03 811 5000, Ⓦ hotel-slovenija-net. A large, square yellow building 100m north of the tourist office on the town's main promenade, the smart *Slovenija* is immediately recognizable for its Plečnik-designed facade, with its distinctive columns and pillars; inside, plush rooms are complemented by a gorgeous, pillar-framed pool. **€100**

EATING AND DRINKING

Mia Mia Celjska cesta 3 ☎ 051 621 146. Cosy, colourful hangout inside the rather incongruous-looking cultural centre midway along the promenade, serving good strong coffee plus cookies and pastries, and a selection of beers

and wines. There's pleasant outdoor seating underneath pop-up gazebos. Mon–Fri 7am–10pm & 6–10pm, Sat 8am–11pm, Sun 8am–10pm.

Sonce Celjska cesta 9 ☎ 03 819 160, Ⓦ restavracijasonce

5

.com. A short walk beyond the Riviera swimming complex, the pick of the restaurants offers a menu heavily skewed towards fish from the Dalmatian coast, plus rare delicacies such as horsemeat and ostrich – they've got a fine stock of wines, too. Mains from €10. Mon–Sat 9am–10pm, Sun 11am–9pm.

Muzej na prostem Rogatec

Ptujska cesta 23, Rogatec, 10km east of Rogaška Slatina • April–Oct Tues–Sun 10am–6pm; Nov–March Sat 10am–4pm • €3 • ☎ 03 818 6200, ⓦ rogatec.si • From Rogaška Slatina train station, head north using the church as a marker; at the main road turn right and walk to another road junction where you should turn left following the signs for Ptuj – the museum is about 1km along the road from here; buses from Rogaška (Mon–Fri 9 daily, Sat & Sun 3–4 daily) stop at the *Gostilna Jelša*, from where you must backtrack until you reach the road junction – again, from here, follow signs to Ptuj

The ancient little market village of **ROGATEC** is known for its delightful **Muzej na prostem Rogatec** (Rogatec Open-Air Museum), a modest gathering of vernacular architecture from Štajerska's sub-Pannonian plain. The museum's central space is taken up by the early nineteenth-century wooden **Šmitova hiša** (Šmit's house), which once belonged to local poet Jože Šmit from the nearby village of Tlake. Comprising a traditional setup of *lojpa* (entrance hall), *kuhna* ("black kitchen") and *hiša* (living room), this type of house had unusual sleeping arrangements – while young, the children would sleep with their parents in the larger bedroom, but once grown up, the girls would move to another bedroom, which had smaller windows barred with an iron cross, in case of any unwanted male visitors; the boys, meanwhile, had to make do with the barn.

There's also a single-room **forge**, built from sandstone in 1930, and stuffed with tools and semi-finished products, and a typical Rogatec **general store** (*lodn*), with a counter surrounded by weighing and measuring machines, containers and jars full of goodies. The double **hayrack**, meanwhile, is of the type found all over Slovenia, though, curiously, this one comes from Croatia; there are some lovely old photos of the Šmit family inside. You can also see a working well, a beehive and a thatch-roofed pigsty, which doubles as a storage rack for turnip and carrot leaves, used as fodder for the swine in winter. Finally, the old **winegrower's house** holds excellent workshops in summer; you can watch, or participate in, such pursuits as bread making, corn braiding, stonecutting and nail forging.

Samostan Olimje and around

Olimje 82, 18km southwest of Rogaška Slatina • Daily 9am–noon & 12.45–6pm • Free • ☎ 03 582 9161, ⓦ olimje.net

From the village of **PODČETRTEK** (14km south of Rogaška Slatina), a smooth, winding valley road snakes through some gorgeous countryside to the **Samostan Olimje** (Olimje Monastery), 4km southwest. Built as a castle in 1550, on the site of a former fortification possibly dating from the eleventh century, the building was acquired by Pauline monks from Croatia in 1663. They converted it into a monastery, enlarging the premises and augmenting it with a church before the order's dissolution in 1782 – the Minorite order returned here in 1990.

Tacked on to the left-hand side of the monastery, the **Cerkev Sv Marije Vnebovzete** (Church of the Assumption) was completed in 1675 by the monks as part of the monastery's rebuilding programme. Preceded by two jet-black and gold marble altars – the one to the left holds a painting of Christ's Passion, the one to the right honours St Paul the Hermit, regarded as the founding father of the monastery – the small presbytery is almost entirely filled with an immense three-tiered golden altar, finished with several paintings and a dozen statues of saints. The side-chapel, dedicated to St Francis Xavier and featuring a majestic, caramel-coloured late Baroque altar, was a later addition (1766) to the church. Note, too, the fine upright organ in the choir loft.

FROM TOP VINEYARD, JERUZALEM (P.286); LENT FESTIVAL, MARIBOR (P.275) >

5

Stara Lekarna

Reputedly the third-oldest preserved pharmacy in Europe – Paris and Dubrovnik lay claim to the oldest and second-oldest – the **Stara Lekarna** (Old Pharmacy), on the ground floor of the left round tower as you face the monastery, was founded in the mid-eighteenth century, functioning until 1782 when the monastery was disbanded. There's little left in the way of fittings and fixtures or pharmaceutical goods (these were all removed when the monastery was dissolved), but its frescoes – executed around 1789 by local painter Anton Lerchinger, and depicting Sts Cosmas and Damian, patron saints of physicians and pharmacists, eminent physicians Aesculapius and Paracelsus and scenes of Christ healing – are certainly worth viewing. There's also a shop where you can buy myriad herbal teas and brandies, honey, oils and creams; most of the ingredients are cultivated in the surrounding gardens.

Čokoladnica Olimje

Mon–Fri 9am–6pm, Sat & Sun 10am–6pm • ☎ 03 810 9036, ⓦ cokoladnica-olimje.si

Just behind the monastery is the fantastic **Čokoladnica Olimje** (Chocolateria Olimje), where you can indulge your wildest sweet-toothed fantasies with an eye-popping selection of the finest chocolates – all of which are produced in the factory at the back of the shop. Slovenia is replete with boutique chocolatiers, but this remains one of the best and most original.

ARRIVAL AND DEPARTURE · SAMOSTAN OLIMJE AND AROUND

There's no public transport to Olimje, but if you don't have your own vehicle, it's an easy and enjoyable trek from **Podčetrtek**.

By train Confusingly, there are three train stations in Podčetrtek: for Podčetrtek itself – with services from Celje (Mon–Fri 5 daily; 50min) – alight at the station of the same name; for the spa it's Atomske Toplice (the old name for the spa); and for the campsite and water park, it's Podčetrtek Toplice.
By bus Buses stop near the supermarket by the main roundabout in Podčetrtek.

Destinations Bistrica ob Sotli (Mon–Fri 6 daily; 25min); Celje (Mon–Fri 2–3 daily; 45min); Rogaška Slatina (Mon–Fri hourly, Sat 4 daily; 20min).
Tourist office The very useful office at Škofja Gora 1, Podčetrtek (Mon–Fri 8am–3pm, Sat 8am–noon, Sun 9am–noon; ☎ 03 810 9013, ⓦ turizem-podcetrtek.si) has copies of the 1:18,000 *Podčetrtek* map, which details several local walks (1–4hr), including the walk to Olimje.

ACTIVITIES

Spas The Terme Olimia resort (☎ 03 829 7000, ⓦ terme-olimia.com), 1km northeast of Podčetrtek, incorporates the Wellness Centre Termalija (Mon–Thurs 11am–10pm, Fri 11am–midnight, Sat 10am–midnight, Sun 10am–10pm; Mon–Fri €10 for 3hr, €13/day; Sat & Sun €12 for 3hr, €15/day); the stunningly designed and super-luxurious Wellness Orhidelia (Mon–Thurs & Sun 9am–10pm, Fri & Sat 9am–midnight; Mon–Fri €24 for 3hr, €27/day; Sat & Sun €31 for 3hr, €35/day); and the World of Saunas (same

hours as Termalija; Mon–Fri €14 for 3hr, €18/day; Sat & Sun €17 for 3hr, €21/day).
Water park Less than 1km north of the spa, the Thermal Park Aqualuna (May–Sept daily 9am–8pm; Mon–Fri €15, Sat & Sun €12; ☎ 03 829 7700, ⓦ terme-olimia.com) features slides bearing names like King Kobra and Kamikaze.
Golf There's a short but tight nine-hole golf course next to *Gostišče Amon* (☎ 03 810 9066; €30 for eighteen holes, €20 for nine holes; €6 for set of clubs).

ACCOMMODATION AND EATING

Camp Natura Next to the Thermal Park Aqualuna ☎ 03 829 7836, ⓦ terme-olimia.com. This large site has level, grassy pitches, plus a restaurant, shop and excellent sports facilities; there's also easy (and discounted) access to the water park. Open all year; tents May–Sept only. €29
Domačija Haler Olimje 6 ☎ 03 812 1202, ⓦ haler-sp.si. Roughly midway between Podčetrtek and the monastery, this roadside restaurant/pub brews its own beer (Haler Pivo) on the premises, the perfect match for its *pivska klobasa*

(beer sausages; €7) and other juicy grilled meat dishes. Mon–Thurs & Sun 11am–10pm, Fri & Sat 10am–11pm.
Gostišče Amon Olimje 24 ☎ 03 818 2480, ⓦ amon.si. Just down from the monastery, *Amon* was one of the first private wineries in the country, and its fine wines complement well the exceptional food. Specialities include roast duck (lovely with baked apples and steamed red cabbage; €15) and fresh oyster mushrooms. The interior looks great; chunky oak tables and chairs recycled from old

wine presses and bench seating culled from barrels. Mon–Thurs & Sun noon–10pm, Fri & Sat noon–11pm.
Jelenov Greben Olimje 90 ☎ 03 582 9046, ⓦ jelenov-greben.si. In a superbly isolated hillside spot up behind the monastery, and with deer roaming freely around the valley below, *Jelenov* (meaning deer) offers classy accommodation in its two pensions, as well as a decent restaurant; the family also cultivate their own foodstuffs, such as mushrooms, jams, fruits and nuts, all available in its capacious, well-stocked shop. **€108**
Ortenia Škofja gora 36, Podčetrtek ☎ 03 582 4197, ⓦ ortenia.com. Secreted away at the northern end of the village, this restful eco-estate takes its name from the hortensias that grow on the surrounding hillside. The six apartments have been fitted with natural materials – granite sinks, pebble-floored showers and oiled oak tables – and are utterly inspiring. A breakfast basket is delivered to your room. Not cheap, but worth it. **€198**

Slovenske Konjice

Nineteen kilometres northeast of Celje, just off the main highway to Maribor, is **SLOVENSKE KONJICE**, the self-styled town of "wine and flowers", owing to triumphant efforts in Europe-wide floral competitions and a strong tradition of wine-making. The centre of town is shaped by Stari trg, a lovely, gently inclining street framed by a neat kernel of two- and three-storey yellow, apricot and lime-green townhouses, and bisected by the Gospodična (Miss) stream, itself straddled by a series of tiny wooden bridges.

Mestna galerija Riemer

Stari trg 15 • Contact the tourist office (see below) if you wish to visit • €3
The **Mestna galerija Riemer** (Riemer Gallery) is a small private collection of art and period furniture amassed by wealthy local businessman Franc Riemer. It's an impressive yet curious mixture, with pieces by Cézanne, Klimt and Rodin, as well as prominent Slovenes Ivana Kobilca and Rihard Jakopič. The show-stealer, however, is a fourteenth-century fresco (albeit substantially effaced) of the Crucifixion, retrieved from Žiče Monastery in 1996, and held to be the only fresco from the monastery still in existence.

Dvorec Trebnik

Grajska cesta 4 • Mon–Fri 10am–2pm • ☎ 03 757 4832, ⓦ trebnik.com
Located up beyond the Church of St George stands the renovated **Dvorec Trebnik** (Trebnik Manor House), which originally hosted the medieval court of the Trebniks, before control passed to the Tattenbachs, who were responsible for its current, largely Renaissance, appearance. One part of the house has been transformed into a herbal shop and gallery, displaying and selling a range of products such as honey, oils, creams, shampoos and brandies; ingredients have been cultivated from the beautifully tended herb garden. From behind the manor house, it's a two-hour walk up a marked path to **Konjiška Gora**, from where there is a superlative panorama of the town and vineyards below and the Pohorje massif in the distance.

ARRIVAL AND INFORMATION   SLOVENSKE KONJICE

By bus The bus station is on Liptovska cesta, from where it's a couple of minutes' walk north to Mestni trg and beyond (across the bridge) to the centre of town, which is essentially the main street, Stari trg.
Destinations Celje (Mon–Fri hourly, Sat & Sun 2 daily;
25min); Ljubljana (Mon–Fri 4 daily, Sat 1 daily; 2hr 15min); Maribor (Mon–Fri 3 daily, Sat & Sun 1 daily; 50min).
Tourist office Stari trg 27 (April–Oct Mon–Fri 8am–5pm, Sat 10am–noon; Nov–March Mon–Fri 8am–4pm; ☎ 05 759 3110, ⓦ tic.konjice.si).

EATING AND DRINKING

★ **Gostilna Grič** Škalce 80 ☎ 03 758 0358, ⓦ gostilna-gric.si. Set among the impossibly lush Škalce vineyards, a 15min walk north of the centre (it's well signposted), this outstanding restaurant offers food and wine of the highest
order – venison with fried buckwheat cubes and cream of carrot and star anise (€19), say, and chocolate fondant with lime crumble (€5.50). Really, though, it's a place to come and enjoy the setting – there are few finer backdrops

5

anywhere in the country. Weaving its way through these same vineyards is a gorgeous nine-hole golf course (March–Nov; nine holes €23, eighteen holes €28). Mon–Fri 10am–9pm, Sat 10am–10pm, Sun 10am–7pm.

Patriot Bar Žička 4 ☎ 03 759 1320. At the top end of Stari trg, just behind the fire station, the focal point of the town's youth club (Mladinski Center) is this groovy, grungey bar with occasional live music at weekends. Mon–Thurs

7am–11pm, Fri & Sat 7am–3am, Sun 3–10pm.

Tattenbach Stari trg 15 ☎ 03 750 0339. Of the several cafés lining this side of the main street, the laidback *Tattenbach*, next to the Riemer Gallery, retains the most character; it's a lovely spot to linger with a coffee and cake as the gentle waters of the Gospodična trickle by behind you. Daily 7am–11pm.

Žička kartuzija

Špitalič pri Slovenskih Konjicah 9, 12km southwest of Slovenske Konjice • April–Oct Tues–Sun 10am–6pm; Nov–March Thurs–Sun 10am–4pm • €5, includes audio-guide • ☎ 03 752 3732 • Buses (Mon–Fri 3 daily) from Slovenske Konjice go as far as the village of Špitalič, 2km shy of the monastery, from where it's a gentle walk

The mist-swathed ruins of **Žička kartuzija** (Žiče Monastery) lie fringed by ancient woodland in the isolated splendour of the Valley of St John. Founded around 1160 by Otakar III of Traungau, the margrave of Styria, Žiče was the first of four Carthusian monasteries to be chartered on Slovenian territory – and the first outside France – fairly prospering until its dissolution under the reforms of Joseph II in 1782. Although part of the complex has been renovated, the rest is pretty much as it was, including the twelfth-century Romanesque **Church of St John the Baptist**, now hollowed out – its vaults and roof collapsed around 1840 – but still exuding a befitting sense of authority. Standing proud within the only remaining section of the monastery's once-formidable defence wall is the **defence tower**, a fine cylindrical Gothic structure topped with a steeply pitched, cone-like roof. Below here, in the midst of the old cemetery, or Holy Ground – where monks were buried without a coffin and with an unmarked cross – is the equally impressive, and still very whole, Gothic **chapel**.

A healing place of repute during the thirteenth century, Žiče remained an important medicinal centre for locals and travellers alike until the monastery's dissolution; there's now a reconstructed **apothecary** on the site of the old one, where you can sample powerful home-made herbal brandies. The small, grass-covered mounds just behind the pharmacy were the former monks' cells.

In one restored wing, there's a small **museum** where you can view a fine collection of thirteenth- and fourteenth-century keystones, consoles and other stone fragments from the original building; look out for the keystone with a beautiful engraving of the infant Jesus holding Mary's chin. Here too are some beautifully illustrated ancient texts and manuscripts, and clothing, including a consecrated habit from Pleterje (see p.230).

Maribor and around

Located on the easternmost foothills of the Pohorje massif, **MARIBOR** is Slovenia's second city of culture, commerce and education. Despite this, the city remains small, with a modest population of around one hundred thousand. Although it lacks Ljubljana's sophistication and cultural appeal, Maribor offers much to enjoy; the prevailing industrial sprawl is countered by an incoherent, yet appealing, Austrianate **old core**, patchworked with an elegant confection of architectural styles, colourful squares and streets, monuments and churches. There's plenty to see and do on the outskirts too, including several **wine roads** and the **Pohorje massif**, where it's possible to ski, hike or enjoy any number of other adventure activities.

Brief history

The seeds of present-day Maribor were sown around the **twelfth century**, when the Carinthian duke, Spanheim, instructed a fort to be built (known as Marchburg, later

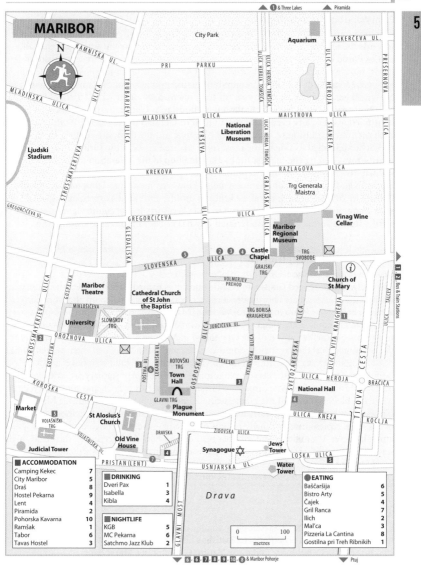

MARIBOR

ACCOMMODATION	
Camping Kekec	7
City Maribor	5
Draš	8
Hostel Pekarna	9
Lent	4
Piramida	2
Pohorska Kavarna	10
Ramšak	1
Tabor	6
Tavas Hostel	3

DRINKING	
Dveri Pax	1
Isabella	3
Kibla	4

NIGHTLIFE	
KGB	5
MC Pekarna	6
Satchmo Jazz Klub	2

EATING	
Baščaršija	6
Bistro Arty	5
Čajek	4
Gril Ranca	7
Ilich	2
Mal'ca	3
Pizzeria La Cantina	8
Gostilna pri Treh Ribnikih	1

0   100
metres

Marburg and eventually Maribor) on Piramida, a low hill to the north of town, in order to protect it from Hungarian raiders from Pannonia. In the **fourteenth century**, a large Jewish population established important commercial ties with Milan, Prague and Dubrovnik; unfortunately their expulsion from the city in 1497, in addition to Hungarian and Turkish sieges, fires and recurrent plague epidemics, led to a sudden and long-term decline in the city's fortunes. The key to its revival in the **nineteenth century** was the arrival of the rail line from Vienna in 1846 (which would later be extended to Ljubljana and Trieste), together with the relocation of the seat of the Lavantine diocese from St Andraz in Austria to Maribor. The establishment of a raft of major cultural and financial institutions further heightened the city's importance.

5

From World War I to Independence

Ongoing nationalist struggles between the city's German and Slovene populations towards the end of the nineteenth century culminated in outright warfare at the tail end of **World War I** following German attempts to incorporate the city into Austrian lands. However, a resounding defeat for the Germans at the hands of the Slovenes, led by General Rudolf Maister, resulted in the incorporation of Slovenian Styria into Slovene lands, and the establishment of the present-day border with Austria. Despite Maribor's assimilation into the **Kingdom of Yugoslavia**, German expansionist tendencies continued and the city eventually succumbed to German forces during **World War II**, with the mass expulsion of thousands of Slovenes and the demolition of nearly half of the city's buildings. As one of the most industrialized cities in the former Yugoslavia, Maribor was among the hardest hit by the **break-up of the federation** in 1991, the sudden loss of important inter-republic trade resulting in tremendous economic hardship and high levels of unemployment. However, its stint as **European Capital of Culture** in 2012 did much to raise Maribor's profile, and thanks to a booming local **wine trade**, its proximity to one of the largest **ski resorts** in the country and some terrific **festivals**, this vibrant, underrated city has undergone a real transformation.

Pokrajinski muzej Maribor

Grajska ulica 2 • Tues–Sat 10am–6pm • €3 • ☎ 02 228 3551, ⓦ pmuzej-mb.si

The lively, wedge-shaped **Grajski trg** (Castle Square) is named after the fifteenth-century town **castle** on the square's northeastern corner, which today is taken up almost exclusively with the exhaustive **Pokrajinski muzej Maribor** (Maribor Regional Museum). Displays start with an outstanding **archeological** collection whose star exhibit is a gorgeous clay skyphos from Starše, a smaller version of the type found in Most na Soči (see p.156). Highlights of the **ethnographical** display include some fine rafts and cargo boats – of the type that would dock along the Drava waterfront in the nineteenth century – guild cash boxes and a beehive fascia board. There's also an extraordinary assemblage of statuary art, not least the original (1743) statue of Mary from the Plague Column (see p.272), and some marvellous white marble tomb slabs of the Herberstein Counts from Betnava, just outside Maribor. No less absorbing is the **cultural history** section, and in particular its voluminous collection of costumes representing the many regions of Slovenia – the most celebrated piece of attire, however, is a military uniform that belonged to Tito. Architecturally, the castle's high spot is a wonderfully fanciful Rococo staircase, ornamented with fourteen sculptures by **Jožef Straub** (1721–83), Slovenia's leading exponent of Baroque sculpture, while the ceiling is strewn with stuccoed swirls and vines.

Trg svobode

Otherwise nondescript, **Trg svobode** is notable only for a bizarre (some might say ugly), bulbous-shaped bronze **memorial to Partisans** killed during World War II. Across the way stands the massive red-brick **Cerkev Sv Marija** (Church of St Mary; daily 7am–8pm), commissioned by Viennese architect Richard Jordan in 1903 and built at the same time as the Franciscan monastery complex behind. The only concession to grandeur inside the capacious and gloomy interior is the high altar, featuring four statues in niches and some contemporary, almost cartoonish, wall paintings. These are the work of Catholic priest and artist Stane Kregar, one of Slovenia's foremost post-World War II church painters.

Muzej narodne osvoboditve

Ulica heroja Tomšiča 5 • Mon–Fri 8am–5pm, Sat 9am–noon • €3 • ☎ 02 235 2605, ⓦ mnom.si

Housed in a handsome late nineteenth-century terracotta and grey villa, the **Muzej narodne osvoboditve** (National Liberation Museum) is fairly limited in scope but does an excellent job of documenting the fate of the city (and the region of Styria as a whole) during and between the two world wars. Coverage focuses heavily on the achievements of General Rudolf Maister (see p.83) – a statue of whom stands just across the road on Trg generala Maistra – and especially his attempts to stifle Germanizing pressures following the end of World War I, as well as the efforts of local resistance groups during World War II. Among the more sobering objects are items retrieved from the graves of people killed at Buchenwald and Mauthausen, including a ring, pocket watch and wallet, and a handkerchief on which a prisoner has written his farewell words. The museum also puts on some excellent temporary exhibitions.

Mestni park, Trije ribniki and Piramida

A broad, lamp-lined promenade marks the entrance to the **Mestni park** (City Park), a large, well-groomed expanse of greenery laid out in 1872 and carved up by concrete strips of pathway – beyond here, the park tapers towards the slender chain of the **Trije ribniki** (Three Lakes), another popular spot for a Sunday morning stroll. If you fancy a slightly more strenuous walk, take the path that peels off from Ribniška ulica (the road skirting the park's eastern side), and continue uphill through the almost vertically pitched vineyard to **Piramida** (386m), at the top of which is a tiny chapel; from here there are fine views of the bright red and terracotta-coloured rooftops of the city, and the broad slopes of the Pohorje mountains in the distance.

Slomškov trg

Named after St Anton Slomšek (see box below) – a large bronze statue of whom stands in its centre – **Slomškov trg** is the largest, greenest and grandest of the city's three squares, endowed with some venerable buildings. Foremost among these is the **university building** (former City Savings Bank), a neo-Renaissance bulk at the square's western end. Similar, but appreciably smaller, is the splendid, pea-green-coloured **Pošta Slovenije** (post office) building at no. 10 on the square's south side. Although aesthetically less pleasing, the other building of note is the **National Theatre** (see p.276), next to the university on the north side.

The square is also the site of Maribor's premier ecclesiastical monument, the lumpish **Cerkev Sv Janez Krstnik** (Cathedral Church of St John the Baptist). Built as a single-naved Romanesque structure in the twelfth century, it took on its present, predominantly Gothic and Baroque, appearance due to later modifications. The highlight of what is otherwise a rather plain interior is the splendid, and unusually long, Gothic presbytery, featuring exquisitely carved choir stalls inlaid with reliefs showing scenes from the life of the patron saint. Other notable detail comes in the form of three rather grand chandeliers, each

---

ANTON SLOMŠEK

Bishop, poet and scribe, **Anton Martin Slomšek** (1800–62) was born in the small parish of Ponikva, near Celje. Ordained in 1824, just three years into his theological studies, Slomšek took his first Mass in Olimje that same year, before returning to his studies in Celovec. He devoted the next few years to the development of Slovene schooling – in particular Sunday schools – in rural areas, and writing prayer and hymn books; by the time of his death, Slomšek had published some fifty books. His greatest achievement, however, was to transfer the seat of the Lavantine diocese from St Andraz, in Austria, to Maribor, thus uniting all Styrian Slovenes in one diocese, as well as effecting an upgrade in the status of the parish church to a cathedral. Slomšek was also instrumental in setting up the Catholic Society of St Hermagoras (Družba Sv Mohorja), a publishing house established in 1851 in order to help Slovenes read and write. His second great contribution was the establishment of Maribor's Theological High School in 1859, the forerunner to today's university. Slomšek was beatified by the pope in September 1999.

5

donated by a local trade in the eighteenth century in thanks for those who were saved from the plague; the one with the cast of the pretzel was given to the church by the association of bakers, the one with the ring by the jewellers and the one with the bull by the butchers.

The north-side **Chapel of the Holy Cross** holds the tomb of Slomšek, while the stained-glass windows depicting images of Pope John Paul II were crafted on the occasion of his second visit to Maribor, in 1999 – his first was in 1996.

Glavni trg

Bounded on one side by a sweep of elegant buildings, and on the other by one of the city's busiest thoroughfares, cobbled **Glavni trg** is a fine-looking Renaissance square that functioned as the city's market area during the Middle Ages. In the centre, and arguably one of the finest monuments of its type in Central Europe, the **Plague Monument** was originally raised in 1681 as a memorial to the thousands that perished during the great plague. This second version was erected in 1743, its smooth column topped with a gold-leaf statue of Mary, and its base with six saintly intercessors, the entire project masterfully sculpted by **Jožef Straub**. Opposite, at no. 9, the Renaissance **town hall** was built in 1515, though reworked several times over before it attained its present appearance, featuring an exquisite Venetian stone balcony emblazoned with a two-lion relief and the city coat of arms – note the slightly off-centre bell tower.

Sinagoga and around

Židovska ulica 4 • Mon–Fri 8am–4pm • €1 • ☎ 02 252 7836, ⓦ sinagogamaribor.si

Židovska ulica (Jewish Street) was the centre of the Jewish ghetto in the Middle Ages, its focal point the now beautifully restored **synagogue** (Sinagoga). The first Jewish presence in the city was recorded around 1290, at around the same time the synagogue was built, but, following a decree in 1496 banishing Jews from Maribor, the synagogue was converted into a Catholic church. It was closed down under the reforms of Emperor Joseph II at the end of the eighteenth century; thereafter it functioned variously as a factory, warehouse and residential quarters. A decade-long renovation programme, during which four wooden boxes containing the remains of ancient skeletons were unearthed, has restored the synagogue to something like its former glory, and it's now used as a cultural centre and exhibition venue. Erected in 1465, the **Židovski stolp** (Jews' Tower), a few paces away at Židovska ulica 6, was once an integral part of the city's defence walls – it's now a photography gallery (Tues–Fri 2–6pm, Sat 10am–1pm; free).

Lent

From the busy main street, Koroška cesta, several alleyways slope down to the **Drava River** and the **Pristan** (Pier) district, or, as it's more commonly known, **Lent** (Port). Until the construction of the railways in the 1860s, the Drava was the city's principal transport artery, and Lent the main docking station for the hundreds of rafts and small cargo vessels that would stop here en route to the Danube and the Black Sea. Today, it's a bustling promenade and *the* place to kick back with a beer on summer evenings.

Hiša stare trte

Vojašniška ulica 8 • Daily: May–Sept 10am–8pm; Oct–April 10am–6pm • ☎ 02 251 5100

Lent's star attraction, and the city's most celebrated symbol, is the four-hundred-year-old **Stara trta** (Vine), which runs along the facade of the **Hiša stare trte** (Old Vine House). Reputedly the world's oldest vine, it still yields the evocatively titled Žametna Črnina (Black Velvet), around 20 litres of which are harvested each year, although, unfortunately (or fortunately, judging by those who have tasted it), this is usually bottled up for visiting

MARIBOR'S WINE ROADS

Maribor is one of the **Podravje** wine region's six wine-producing areas, and counts three **wine roads**; the easiest to get to is the **Maribor** wine road itself, where, among others, you'll find the excellent *Joannes Tourist Farm* (the Protner winery) at Vodole 34a (☏ 02 473 2100, ⊚ joannes.si), where you can also sample grilled blood sausages with sauerkraut. Southwest of Maribor is the **Podpohorje** road – one to visit here is the superb Frešer winery at Ritoznoj 17 (☏ 02 803 4215, ⊚ freser.si); while, to the north along the Austrian border, the **Upper Slovenske gorice** wine road has some of the finest wine producers in Slovenia, such as Gaube, at Špičnik 17 (☏ 02 656 3511, ⊚ vino-gaube.si) – it lies next to the heart-shaped road familiar from scores of posters and promotional materials – and Valdhuber, at Svečina 15a (☏ 041 346 895, ⊚ valdhuber.si). Although a couple of reds are produced in this region (Žametna Črnina and Modri Pinot), this is overwhelmingly white wine territory – you'll see Laški and Renski Rizling, Chardonnay and Sauvignon, as well as the blended Mariborčan. Although having your own vehicle is certainly an advantage, it is feasible to walk at least part of these routes from Maribor. The 1:50,000 *Podravje* **map**, available from the Maribor tourist office (see below), should help you navigate your way around.

If you have neither the time nor the means to head out into the countryside, make your way to the **Vinag Wine Cellar** in Maribor at Trg svobode 3 (☏ 030 203 527, ⊚ vinag.eu), with a massive 2.2km of tunnels; wine is no longer stored down here, but you will see some 150 wooden, concrete and aluminium barrels, the oldest of which dates from 1862, and the largest of which holds 176,000 litres – so big you can climb inside it. **Tours** include a tasting of three wines (Mon–Thurs 11am & 2pm, Fri–Sun 11am, 2pm & 4pm; €5).

dignitaries. It's quite a sight in full bloom around mid-September, just before harvesting. The house itself – dating from the sixteenth century when it was part of the southern defence wall – holds a small exhibition relaying the history of the vine.

More interesting is the marvellous floor **mosaic**, completed in 2014 and which took artist Igor Orešič eighteen months to complete; comprising 1.3 million pieces, it's meant to represent the Drava but is also replete with other city symbols and events. Really, though, the house is a place to come and sample some wine, with more than forty local winemakers represented; expect to pay around €4 for three wines (there's no need to reserve). Two of the city's main events, the pruning of the vine, and its ceremonial harvesting, take place here (see box, p.275).

Sodni stolp and around

At the westernmost point of Lent stands the rotund, whitewashed **Sodni stolp** (Judicial Tower), though this is something of a misnomer given that it was erected as a defensive bastion in 1310; the present structure dates from 1830. Up behind the tower, Vojašniška ulica (Army Street) and Vojašniški trg (Army Square) – essentially one and the same – are scattered with a shabby fusion of half-wrecked buildings, one of which, the former **Minorite Church and Monastery**, once functioned as a barracks and warehouse, though it's now defunct and decaying. Just beyond is Vodnikov trg and the city's open-air market place. The best views of Lent are from **Glavni most** (Main Bridge), an elegant, rich-red structure completed in 1913.

ARRIVAL AND INFORMATION   MARIBOR

By bus and train The bus and train stations are just 400m apart on Partizanska cesta, from where it's a 5min walk into the city centre.

Destinations (bus) Celje (Mon–Fri 7–8 daily, Sat & Sun 4 daily; 1hr 15min); Ljubljana (Mon–Fri 6 daily, Sat & Sun 3 daily; 1hr 45min–2hr 30min); Ljutomer (Mon–Fri 3 daily, Sat & Sun 1 daily; 1hr 20min); Murska Sobota (Mon–Fri hourly, Sat 5 daily; 1hr 10min); Ptuj (Mon–Fri every

45min–hourly, Sat hourly, Sun 6 daily; 30min); Slovenske Konjice (Mon–Fri 6 daily, Sat & Sun 3 daily; 50min).

Destinations (train) Celje (every 30min–2hr; 45min–1hr 10min); Ljubljana (every 30min–2hr; 1hr 45min–2hr 45min); Ptuj (Mon–Fri hourly–every 2hr, Sat & Sun 4–5 daily; 40–50min); Graz (4 daily; 1hr 15min); Vienna (2 daily; 4hr).

Tourist office Partizanska cesta 6a (April–Oct Mon–Fri 9am–7pm, Sat & Sun 9am–5pm; Nov–March Mon–Fri

5

9am–7pm, Sat 10am–3pm; ☎02 234 6611, ⓦmaribor
-pohorje.si); they rent bikes (€5 for 3hr, €10/day).
Tours Between June and Oct, the tourist office runs guided

tours on Fri at 5pm and Sat at 10pm (€5).
Internet There's free wi-fi in some public spaces and
excellent access at *Kibla* (see p.276).

ACCOMMODATION

Surprisingly, the city centre is not hugely well served with places to stay, but there are other – often more appealing –
possibilities in Zgornje Radvanje, at the foot of the **Maribor Pohorje** ski resort 7km southwest of town (bus #6 from the
train station). There are also some hotels at the top of Pohorje itself (see p.277). Moreover, the tourist office can book
private accommodation, from around €20/person.

HOTELS

City Maribor Ulica kneza Koclja 22 ☎02 621 2500,
ⓦcityhotel-mb.si. The town's most expensive option, but
this determinedly conspicuous hotel does occupy a prime
position facing the Drava, and offers a high level of comfort;
rooms (standard and superior) are decorated in shades of
grey, with cool wood furnishings, sumptuous beds and
enormous walk-in showers. The terrace bar perched high
above the river is perfect for a sundowner. €180
Draš Pohorska cesta 57, Zgornje Radvanje ☎059 076
600, ⓦdras.si. Don't let the fact that this modern hotel is
part of a large sports complex (often accommodating
national teams from all over the world) put you off; one
bonus is that the beds are longer than usual, while the
attractive rooms also sport partially wood-clad walls,
glassed-in bathrooms and tremendous mountain views. €85
Lent Dravska ulica 9 ☎02 250 6769, ⓦhotel-lent.si.
This small, family-run hotel tucked away behind the main
street represents the best value for money in the centre;
the seventeen almost identical rooms are a little boxy, but
immaculately kept and tastefully decorated. €79
Piramida Ulica heroja Šlandra 10 ☎02 234 4400,
ⓦtermemb.si. The city's premier business hotel, this is
very much in the mould of your typical *Best Western*. What
it lacks in character it makes up for in cleanliness and
competence, and the rooms do have tea- and coffee-
making facilities. €120
Pohorska Kavarna Ob ribniku 1, Zgornje Radvanje ☎02
614 1500, ⓦpohorska-kavarna.com. About 500m before
the cable car, this clean, bright and modern pension has nine
two- and three-bed, a/c, en-suite rooms painted in fetching
peachy colours. Chances are that you'll spend most of your
time in the fabulous downstairs coffeehouse/patisserie. €63
Tabor Ulica heroja Zidanška 18 ☎02 421 6410,
ⓦhoteltabor-maribor.si. The most appealing option on
the south side of the river, with en-suite rooms (two to five

beds) decorated/themed according to the seasons (blue
representing winter, green for spring and so on) and enhanced
with wall-length, mood-reflecting prints. Bus #6. €70

HOSTELS, CAMPING AND GLAMPING

Camping Kekec Pohorska ulica 35, Zgornje Radvanje
☎040 665 732, ⓦcck.si. Small, very neat, and superbly
well-maintained campsite a few hundred metres shy of the
cable-car station in Radvanje. Facilities boil down to a large
hut incorporating showers, toilets and a washing-up area,
and a children's play area; there are bikes for rent and the
supermarket is 200m away. Bus #6 will drop you on the
main road nearby. €19
★**Hostel Pekarna** Ob železnici 16 ☎059 180 880,
ⓦmkc-hostelpekarna.si. Housed in one part of an old
bakery complex, which now also accommodates Maribor's
foremost alternative cultural centre, this sparky hostel offers
boldly coloured four-bed dorms – all en suite and with a/c –
as well as studio rooms and apartments; guests are free to use
herbs and vegetables from the balcony garden, which they
can then put to good use in the fabulous kitchen. Breakfast
and free bike rental included. Dorms €21, doubles €54
★**Ramšak** Počehova 35 ☎031 692 886, ⓦchateau
ramsak.com. Just 2km north of the centre, this wonderfully picturesque vineyard resort comprises six glamping
tents, each sleeping either two or four and with its own
substantial wood-decked terrace and jacuzzi, as well as a
splendid treehouse tent sleeping four. Breakfast can be
taken in the main house, or you can have a basket brought
to your tent. With an outdoor bar and wine tasting aplenty,
there's really very little reason to leave the site at all.
Glamping tents €200, treehouse €390
Tavas Hostel Vetrinjska ulica 5 ☎040 894 492. Small,
very basic, very clean hostel bang in the centre of the city,
with a ten-bed dorm and one apartment (sleeping two or
three), shared bathroom facilities and kitchen. Dorm €17

EATING

Baščaršija Poštna ulica 8 ☎02 250 6359, ⓦbascarsija
.si. Immediately identifiable thanks to its pretty, green
shuttered windows, *Baščaršija* is named after the old bazaar
district in Sarajevo, and does a great job of aping a Bosnian
tavern. The menu is devoted to classic Bosnian dishes (€5–
8) like *sarma* (meat and rice rolled in cabbage), *pita* (a salty,

filled pastry) and *tufahija* (baked apples stuffed with
walnuts), all of which taste great washed down with a pint
of Sarajevsko beer. Cheap, cheerful and a lot of fun. Mon–
Thurs 8am–midnight, Fri & Sat 8am–midnight.
Bistro Arty Slovenska ulica 20 ☎031 365 316. With a
row of colourful potted plants lining the windowsill,

this delightful, veggie-oriented café serves the likes of dandelion soup and garlic pie (€5) at bargain prices. The agreeable old-fashioned interior, with its checked table-cloths, polka-dot cushions and recessed books, looks fab. Mon–Fri 7am–6pm, Sat 7am–3pm.

Čajek Slovenska ulica 4 ☎ 02 250 2986, ⓦ cajek.com. The cosy, wooden interior of this comely two-floored teahouse is a delightful spot to indulge in some of the many teas on offer – you even get given a timer to tell you when your brew is ready. Mon–Fri 7.30am–10pm, Sat 9am–10pm, Sun 3–9pm.

Gril Ranca Dravska ulica 10 ☎ 02 252 5550. Nothing's changed at *Ranca* for years – including the staff, it seems – and that's just the way the locals like it. This is fast food Balkan style, with a short menu exclusively listing gut-busting Serbian meats, *čevapčiči* and *pljeskavica*, typically served with raw onion and *kajmak* (cheese) wedged inside a deliciously doughy *lepinja* (bread roll); €6–8. Daily 8am–11pm.

Ilich Slovenska ulica 6 ☎ 02 250 2408. Venerable coffeehouse that has been doling out the city's best coffees, cakes and ices since 1909; the softly lit, old-world-style vaulted interior makes *Ilich* one of the most relaxing places to while away an hour or so, and in warmer weather the dinky terrace is the place to people-watch. Mon–Sat

7am–10pm, Sun 8am–10pm.

★**Mal'ca** Slovenska ulica 4 ☎ 059 100 397, ⓦ malcamimogrede.si. A fantastic lunchtime bolthole where five different dishes (€5–7) are prepared each day – two of them vegetarian. However, it would be remiss not to try the house speciality and the one constant on the menu – *žlikrofi* with beef and herbs served with cranberry sauce, best enjoyed with a cheeky glass of wine. Such is *Mal'ca's* popularity that you may have to wait a short while for a table. Mon–Fri 10am–5pm.

Pizzeria La Cantina Pohorska ulica 60, Zgornje Radvanje ☎ 02 614 5614, ⓦ la-cantina.si. Buzzy, and surprisingly accomplished, restaurant next to the cable-car station, which makes for a great pit stop either pre or post mountain hike. There's an extensive pizza menu and lots of other good stuff on offer, such as spinach fettuccini with shrimp tails or polenta gnocchi with goulash (€7.50). Daily 8am–midnight.

Gostilna pri Treh Ribnikih Ribniška ulica 9 ☎ 02 234 4170, ⓦ trijeribniki.si. Dating from 1825, this handsome inn-style restaurant enjoys an enviable position out by the Three Lakes and its food rates extremely highly too – smoked trout with horseradish yoghurt (€9.50), for example, or marinated lamb crowns with rosemary polenta (€20). Mon–Thurs 11am–10pm, Fri & Sat 11am–11pm, Sun 11am–7pm.

DRINKING

Maribor's main drinking strip, **Poštna ulica**, flaunts a colourful parade of cafés and bars packed cheek by jowl. Otherwise, on warm summer evenings, the many venues along the **Lent** waterfront spill out onto the street creating the hectic atmosphere of a mass open-air bar.

Dveri Pax Ulica Vita Kraigherja 3 ☎ 051 274 747, ⓦ dveri-pax.com. If you don't manage to get to one of Maribor's outlying wine roads, content yourself with a

little excursion to this classy wine bar, stocking a cornucopia of wines from the region. Mon–Thurs 7am–10pm, Fri 7am–midnight, Sat 10am–midnight.

MARIBOR FESTIVALS

Maribor puts on a great range of festivals and events throughout the year, the biggest and best of which is the **Festival Lent** (ⓦ festival-lent.si) at the end of June/beginning of July. Second only to Ljubljana's Summer Festival in size, this is arguably Slovenia's most exuberant gathering, comprising two fabulous weeks of street and puppet theatre, comedy, modern and classical dance and jazz, pop and classical music along the waterfront and in the squares and streets around town. The Old Vine is the site of the **Pruning of the Vine** at the beginning of March, and the **Old Vine Festival** throughout October, the latter entailing the harvesting of the grapes, though both are really little more than excuses for a good knees-up.

Musically, the key event is the **Festival Maribor** (ⓦ festival-maribor.si) at the beginning of September, with ten days of quality classical concerts (including numerous celebrated international artists) taking place in diverse venues. There's also the **International Choral Competition** in April (ⓦ jskd.si), and in September the **No Border Jam Festival**, a gathering of international punk acts. For kids (and adults too), the terrific **International Puppet Festival** in August features a huge variety of acts from all over Europe.

The **Golden Fox slalom race** (Zlata Lisica; ⓦ goldenfox.org) on the slopes of Maribor Pohorje at the end of January is one of the country's major sporting occasions, attracting the world's top women skiers, not to mention some 25,000 spectators, for a weekend of top-class sporting action and lots of drinking.

5

Isabella Poštna ulica 3 ☎059 959 450. There's little to choose between most bars along this feverishly busy street, but *Isabella* just about wins by virtue of its decor – spare, with white-painted brick walls and big bay windows – a terrific selection of craft beers, such as Humanfish and the local (well, Slovenian but brewed just across the border in Austria) Bevog, and a cool soundtrack. Mon–Thurs 8am–

midnight, Fri & Sat 8am–2am, Sun 10am–midnight.

Kibla Ulica Kneza Koclja 9 ☎059 076 377, ⓦkibla.org. On the ground floor of the stately Narodni Dom building, this large and relaxing venue is an internet café-cum-bar, bookshop and multimedia centre all rolled into one – the contemporary art exhibitions are highly regarded. Mon–Fri 9am–10pm, Sat 4–10pm.

NIGHTLIFE

KGB Vojašniški trg 5 ☎02 252 3077, ⓦklub-kgb.si. Opposite the Minorite church on a ramshackle square just west of Lent, this small but brilliant underground cellar bar/club (check out the fantastic door as you enter) is the funkiest place in town, with regular live music – hence its name, which aptly translates as "cultural musical lair". A guaranteed good time. Mon–Sat 7pm–2am.

MC Pekarna Ob železnici 16 ☎02 320 2018, ⓦpekarna .net. Located in a former military bakery factory (*Pekarna* means bakery), this grungey, Gothic-flavoured underground club/bar remains the venue of choice among the many scattered around this complex, which is a

(lower-key) riposte to Ljublana's Metelkova (see p.73). The club's four interconnected rooms (some of the original bakery fixtures and fittings have been retained) are used for a range of concerts, exhibitions and other innovative cultural happenings. Mon–Thurs 10am–1am, Fri 10am–4am, Sat 6pm–4am, Sun 6pm–1am.

Satchmo Jazz Klub Strossmayerjeva ulica 6 ☎04 454 779, ⓦsatchmo.si. Good-time jazz club with a top-class rota of gigs, though the summer programme is irregular – count on around one gig every two weeks during this period. Otherwise, ideal for a bout of mellow drinking. Tues–Thurs 7pm–3am, Fri & Sat 8pm–5am.

ENTERTAINMENT

Puppet Theatre (Lutkovno gledališče) Vojašniški trg 2a ☎02 228 1979, ⓦlg-ms.si. This delightful theatre puts on performances, in Slovene, every Sat at 10am (adults €10, children €5). Closed July.

Slovensko Narodno Gledališče (SNG) Slovenska ulica 27 ☎02 250 6115, ⓦsng-mb.si. With a top-class roster of

theatre, opera and ballet, the Slovenian National Theatre is the most highly regarded in the country; theatre tickets cost around €10–15, operatic and ballet performances €15–20. Box office Mon–Fri 10am–1pm & 3–7.30pm, Sat 10am–1pm; and 1hr before each performance.

Maribor Pohorje

Cable car Daily: April–Nov hourly 7am–10pm; Dec–March nonstop 7am–10pm • €4 one-way, €6 return • Bus #6 runs regularly from Maribor train station to Zgornje Radvanje

The suburb of **Zgornje Radvanje**, 7km southwest of the city, lies at the foot of the popular ski resort, **Maribor Pohorje** (ⓦvisitpohorje.si), which is worth visiting at any time of year. From the **cable-car** station (vzpenjača), small six-seater cabins transport skiers and hikers to the upper station (1042m) on **Bolfenk** in fifteen minutes; alternatively, you can walk up (or down), which should take around ninety minutes at a leisurely pace.

Skiing aside (see box opposite), there are plenty of exciting activities on offer at the **Adrenaline Park**, which is not a park as such, but rather the collective name for a range of **activities** available at different locations around the mountain; the main operation here is the superb **bike park** (Mon–Thurs €17 for half a day, €20/day; Fri–Sun €20 for half a day, €24/day; ☎059 250 041, ⓦbikeparkpohorje.si), which has three trails (easy, medium and difficult). Otherwise, Pohorje offers terrific woodland **cycling**, with numerous cycle paths carving their way across the massif; both downhill (for use in the bike park) and cross-country bikes can be rented from the Extreme Vital shop, next to the cable-car station (☎059 259 040; €15/4hr, €20/day). A free cycle map outlines numerous trails, and the 1:50,000 *Pohorje* **map** proves useful whether hiking or cycling – both are available from the tourist office in Maribor (see p.273).

ARRIVAL AND DEPARTURE   MARIBOR POHORJE

Note that if driving, or cycling, to **Bolfenk** from Maribor, you should take the road south to Ljubljana before turning at the village of Hoče, from where it's a further 10km uphill.

SKIING AND HIKING IN POHORJE

Rogla, in the heart of the Pohorje massif, and **Maribor Pohorje**, further east on the doorstep of Maribor, are two of the best **ski and snowboard** resorts in the country. Rogla has around 12km of ski trails, most of which are suited to intermediate skiers, though there are a few slopes for the less experienced. At 1347m, Mariborsko Pohorje is a slightly lower mountain range, but has one of the largest capacities of all Slovenia's ski resorts and far more tourist facilities, particularly accommodation, than Rogla. With more than 40km of trails, almost half of which are for beginners, it also has 10km of night-time (floodlit) slopes. The main piste is the venue for the women's World Cup slalom race, the "Golden Fox", at the end of January – not to be missed if you're in the region around this time.

The **ski season** at both resorts usually runs from December to March, and the presence of snow cannons along the main runs ensures that it's possible to ski throughout this period, regardless of snowfall. **Day passes** at both cost around €35 and **weekly passes** around €180.

The massif also has some excellent **hiking**. The trails on Rogla are numbered from PP1 to PP7, and range in distance from just a few kilometres to more than thirty. If you're short on time, try the nice and easy 45-minute walk north from the *Planja* hotel in Rogla to the *Koča na Pesku* mountain hut (☎ 03 757 7167; 1386m), which has accommodation and food year-round. From here, you can either continue northwest to the beautiful **Lovrenška jezera** (Lovrenc Marsh Lakes; 1hr), and then further on to the *Ribniška Koča na Pohorju* hut (1507m; 2hr), where there's more accommodation (☎ 02 876 8246; closed April & Nov); or east to **Osankarica** (1193m) and the *Dom na Osankarica* (☎ 02 845 0113), where there are refreshments only – the trail continues east to the **Črno jezero** (Black Lake), one of the largest lakes in the massif.

ACCOMMODATION, EATING AND DRINKING

There's stacks of accommodation on top of the mountain.

Bellevue Next to the upper cable-car station ☎ 02 234 4333, ⓦ hotelbellevue.si. A smart, glass-fronted chalet-type place with fabulous rooms and a fine restaurant and bar – it's also the best spot to refuel following any exertions. Good value outside the ski season. **€95**

Zelena Vas Ruševec Hočko Pohorje 36 ☎ 02 603 6300, ⓦ rusevec.com. Set among lush pine forests about 3km south of Bolfenk, this small eco-village comprises five chunky log cabins constructed from local spruce timber and insulated throughout with thick wool; each one sleeps four people – two downstairs and two upstairs – with bedding made from organic materials. Among the resort's many commendable sustainable initiatives are compost piles, a water reservoir and a small apiary. **€120**

Pohorje massif

The **Pohorje massif** is a 50km-long, sparsely populated plateau arcing between Maribor in the east and Dravograd in the west. Geologically, the massif is an extension of the Alps, although physically it's quite different, a series of gently rounded ridges – few peaks top 1500m – riddled with peat marshes and small swampy lakes, and where the only settlements are isolated farmsteads and tiny upland churches. The massif was once home to sawmills, forges and *glažute* (glass-making workshops), but today tourism rules the roost, with a major ski centre, **Rogla** (see box above), hiking paths and other recreational facilities complemented by a good number of mountain huts and tourist farms.

Ptuj and around

If you've only got time to visit one place in eastern Slovenia, make it **PTUJ**. Set 26km southeast of Maribor on the broad, flat Drava Plain between the Slovenske gorice and Haloze hills, Ptuj is the oldest continuously settled site in Slovenia and historically the most important settlement outside Ljubljana. The town and its surroundings are run through with two thousand years of history, its squares, streets and buildings rampant with architectural and archeological riches – Romanesque and medieval townhouses,

5

Roman monuments and tombstones, and ancient Mithras shrines. Although it's a compact town, you could quite easily spend a couple of days exploring the sights and admiring the wealth of architectural detail; it also lies close to the beautiful Church of the Holy Virgin in **Ptujska Gora**. Ptuj is also home to the wonderful Shrovetide **Kurent carnival**, Slovenia's most famous, and entertaining, folkloric event.

Brief history

Settled as far back as the late **Stone Age**, and later populated by the **Celts**, Ptuj began life around 69 AD, when a **Roman** legionary camp was established on the south bank of the Drava River. The result of expansion across the river was the creation of a self-governing civilian entity called Poetovio, which functioned as a major staging post linking the Roman provinces of Pannonia and Noricum. Occupied successively by **Avars**, **Magyars** and then **Slavs**, Ptuj received its town rights in 977 AD, at which point it passed into the hands of the **Salzburg** archdiocese, whose members grew rich from the trade between Pannonia and the Italian peninsula.

During the **Middle Ages**, Ptuj developed around the solidly fortified castle and established itself as a commercial centre of some considerable importance. Until the death of **Frederick XI** in 1438, it remained under the jurisdiction of the Ptuj nobility, vassals of the Salzburg archdiocese, though subsequent incursions by the Turks and wars with the Hungarians undermined the town's development. It recovered sufficiently to re-establish itself as a small provincial town, which it remains to this day.

Grad Ptuj

Lording it over the flutter of red roofs and cobbled streets below, **Grad Ptuj** (Ptuj Castle) is the town's showpiece attraction. It began life around 69 AD when the inhabitants of Roman Poetovio built a fortress and temple atop this very hill. The oldest archives date the present structure to some time in the twelfth century, when the castle was owned by the archbishops of Salzburg, who in turn leased it to the lords of Ptuj. Fortified ahead of

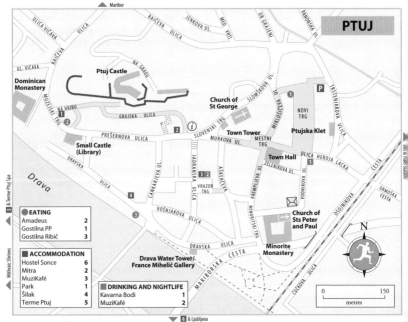

anticipated Turkish raids in the sixteenth century, the castle was further modified in Baroque fashion during the seventeenth century.

Whether approaching from the path opposite the Dominican Monastery, or via Grajska ulica, a narrow street just off Prešernova ulica near the *Mitra* hotel, you enter the castle grounds through the thick-set **Charles portal**, which opens up into the lower courtyard, once the location for the castle stables and military outbuildings, but now empty save for a weatherbeaten statue of a one-armed St Florian dousing a fire – the views from this platform, however, are fantastic. Walk on up through the fine Renaissance **Peruzzi portal** into the immaculate inner courtyard, enclosed by a horseshoe-shaped, three-tiered **residential palace**. Before entering the museum take a look at the splendid red Salzburg marble tombstone of Frederick IX, the last lord of Ptuj, embedded into the wall on the left-hand side of the courtyard.

Pokrajinski muzej

May, June & Sept to mid-Oct daily 9am–6pm; July & Aug Mon–Fri 9am–6pm Sat & Sun 9am–8pm; mid-Oct to April daily 9am–5pm • €5 • ☎ 02 748 0360, ⓦ pmpo.si

The castle's **Pokrajinksi muzej** (Regional Museum) comprises half a dozen different exhibitions, which take some getting through. By far the most worthwhile is the **Kurent** display, with carnival paraphernalia and a splendid array of masks and costumes, from the devil himself – clad in red or black – to the various members of the *Kurenti*, furnished with chunky sheepskin garments, feathered or horned caps, cow bells and wooden clubs, and the ploughers, typically attired in waistcoat, headscarf and black leather boots (see box, p.280). Next best is the display of **musical instruments** – the finest in the country – which charts the rich history of Ptuj's military and town brass bands; the most remarkable exhibit here (indeed, the museum's most important item) is a tibia fragment believed to have been used as a pipe to be played at funerals, social dances and the like. The main hall, meanwhile, holds a superb grouping of turqueries, seventeenth-century portraits of Turkish sultans, dignitaries, military commanders and the like. Having absorbed that little lot, savour the marvellous views of the Drava River and Haloze hills beyond.

Mestni trg and around

The ideal place to start a town tour is fourteenth-century **Mestni trg** (Town Square), a charming little square ringed by several stately buildings. Most prominent is the muddy-green **Town Hall**, a large neo-Gothic German pile raised in 1907 on the site of a late Renaissance structure built by the Dominicans in 1571. Remnants of this earlier building are still just visible in the form of a pair of dragon reliefs and a reclining nude on one of the corner prominences. The colourful, heavily stuccoed eighteenth-century **corner house**, opposite at no. 2, is now the *Café Evropa*; above the entrance a slender corner niche holds a statue of Mary with Child. At the heart of the square, the regulation **plague column**, featuring a posturing St Florian dressed in military attire, is a copy, erected in 1993.

There's more architecture to admire along **Krempljeva ulica** – the street heading south from Mestni trg – notably at no. 1, whose peeling paintwork can't detract from marvellous stuccowork, and in particular, the beehive relief between the windows on the prominence. At no. 7, the entrance to the old **Court House** is framed by a superb sixteenth-century Renaissance portal, either side of which sits a pair of lions holding escutcheons. West from Mestni trg, on **Murkova ulica**, check out the portal with griffins at no. 2, and the Patrician Mansion, opposite at no. 1.

Minoritski samostan and Cerkev Sv Petra in Pavla

Minoritski trg 1 • To visit the library you must contact the tourist office (see p.282)

Unlike the majority of Slovenia's monasteries, the late thirteenth-century **Minoritski samostan** (Minorite Monastery) wasn't closed under the reforms of Emperor Joseph II

5

THE KURENT

One of the oldest, most unusual and celebrated folklore events in the Slovene calendar is the **Kurent**, a kind of fertility rite and celebration of the awakening of spring, which takes place in the ten days up to Shrove Tuesday (late February/early March); from a spectator's point of view, the two main days are the Sunday before Shrove Tuesday, which is when the main procession takes place, and Shrove Tuesday itself, when the devil is executed and the carnival is "buried". Wearing spooky masks made of sheepskin and feathers with a coloured beak for a nose, white beads for teeth and long, bright red tongues, the *Kurenti* proceed from house to house, warding off evil spirits with the incessant din from the cowbells and other instruments tied to their weighty costumes. Leading the procession is the **Devil** (*Hudič*), pitchfork in hand and wrapped in a net to symbolize his capture: behind the *Kurenti*, the ploughers (*Orači*) pull a small wooden plough, scattering sand to represent the sowing of seed, while the other participants smash clay pots at their feet in return for good luck and health. Although several similar carnivals, known as Pust, take place in other towns throughout Slovenia – most famously in Cerkno and Cerknica – and in neighbouring countries such as Hungary and Croatia, most are pale imitations of the events that take place here in Ptuj.

---

at the end of the eighteenth century. Instead, it continued to prosper as a centre of learning until World War II, when it was confiscated by the Germans, then bombed by the Allies. The most feted part of the complex is the first-floor **summer refectory**, thanks to its thickly stuccoed ceiling, decorated by Italians Quadrio and Bettini, and oval and rectangular panels depicting scenes from the lives of the monastery's patrons, Sts Peter and Paul; it's normally open for a peek. Otherwise, the prize exhibit in the monastery's richly stocked **library** is one of three original copies of the New Testament translated into Slovene by Primož Trubar in 1561 – the other two reside in the National Library in Ljubljana, and in Vienna.

The adjoining **Cerkev Sv Petra in Pavla** (Church of Sts Peter and Paul) was one of Slovenia's greatest ecclesiastical losses during World War II. The only part of the church to survive the raids was the presbytery, slightly shortened after the war in order to accommodate, rather insensitively, a post office on the site of the bombed-out nave. Look out for the beautifully worked relief of a lamb on a keystone by the high altar, and the gargoyle-like animal heads on the exterior buttresses. Reconstructed in 2005, the nave stands in stark contrast, a large, austere space worked over in glass and marble.

Miheličeva galerija

Dravska ulica 4 • Tues–Fri 10am–4pm, Sat 10am–1pm • Free • ☎ 02 748 0359, ⊕ pmso.si

During the Middle Ages, **Dravska ulica** was known for its butchers' shops and tanneries, as indicated by the numerous portals embedded with the traditional tanners' symbols of a bucket with two crossed scrapers. The bulky **Drava stolp** (Drava Water Tower) is the largest of six former defensive towers that once formed the core of the town's fortification system; contrary to popular legend, the stone balls built into the upper section of the walls were not those fired by Turks, but rather were placed there by local enthusiasts who had a penchant for this kind of architecture. The tower now functions as the **Miheličeva galerija** (France Mihelič Gallery), the first two floors hosting temporary exhibitions, and the top floor a selection of works by the eponymous graphic artist. Many of the prints and paintings on display were completed during his time as a drawing teacher at a local grammar school between 1936 and 1941. They're strongly influenced by the landscape and characters of the region, for example *Wretches*, *Study of the Church Fair at Ptujska Gora* and, in particular, the figures of the Kurent, such as *Dead Kurent*, a typically oddball abstract piece.

Mestni stolp

The centre of triangular **Slovenski trg** is dominated by the chunky, five-storey **Mestni stolp** (Town Tower), originally a sixteenth-century bell tower, then a seventeenth-century watchtower, before retiring gracefully in the 1900s, when it was embellished with an onion-bulb spire. Embedded within the tower's lower reaches are numerous civil and military tombstones, relief votive slabs and sacrificial altars, though the most impressive tombstone is the freestanding **Orpheus Monument** in front of the tower (it's covered up in winter). Cut from Pohorje marble, the thick rectangular column commemorates Marcus Verus, former mayor of Poetovio, although during the Middle Ages it was used as a pillory, whereby petty criminals were chained to iron rings fastened to the bottom of the block – the poor state of the inscriptions is down to the wear and tear caused by the chains.

Cerkev Sv Jurij

Outwardly austere, the twelfth-century Gothic **Cerkev Sv Jurij** (Church of St George) conceals some exceptional works of art. The first thing you see as you enter is a small glass cabinet on the left, containing a fragile and rather foppish-looking fourteenth-century wooden **sculpture of St George** nonchalantly slaying a dragon. From here proceed into the central nave, arranged with incongruously placed frescoes, altars and chapels, such as the **Crucifixion**, framed with an elaborately decorated banner, immediately to the left, and, opposite, the **Altar of the Three Kings**, featuring a relief of the Coronation of St Mary inside a Baroque casing. The church's most renowned piece of work, **Laib's winged altar**, is at the rear of the south aisle. Dating from around 1460, the gilded paintings depict, in the centre, Mary's death, and to the left and right respectively, St Hieronymous with a church model in one hand and a book in the other, and St Mark writing the Gospel held by a lion.

Of the several chapels dotted around the church, the most important is the **Chapel of Our Lady of Sorrows** at the end of the north aisle, the centrepiece of which is a fifteenth-century stone pietà. Just to the right of the chapel, a splendid, high lancet-arch fronts the bright fourteenth-century cross-vaulted presbytery, and a magnificent long choir, lined either side by two long rows of oak-wood pews ornamented with figures of animals.

Prešernova ulica and around

The Old Town's central artery, **Prešernova ulica**, is an attractive, peaceful thoroughfare, lined with tightly packed ranks of medieval townhouses, almost every one furnished with a Renaissance stone portal or some other beautifully crafted feature. For starters take a look at house no. 1, whose corner prominence is supported by a so-called Parlerian mask, a black painted head of a grinning, curly-haired man; and, opposite, at no. 4, the Romanesque Bratonič house, the oldest tenement along the street and which now accommodates the tourist office. Before continuing, take a quick look down **Jadranska ulica**, and in particular nos. 4 and 6, the facades of which are decorated with Kurent-style masks worked in flat relief (see box opposite).

Back on Prešernova, beyond the colourful neo-Baroque *Mitra* hotel at no. 6, the house at no. 16 is notable for marble fragments jutting out of the passageway wall, which, on closer inspection, reveal themselves to be parts of dedication blocks or tombstones – there are more complete blocks embedded into the back wall of the run-down courtyard. On the opposite side of the road, at no. 27, take a peek inside the courtyard, where there's another grey marble relief, this one of a prostrate, headless lion.

Dominikanski samostan

Muzejski trg 1 • April–Oct daily 9am–4pm • €1 • ☎ 02 620 7342, ⓦ dominikanskisamostan.si

The **Dominikanski samostan** (Dominican Monastery) stands in a small park-like area, its bright pink facade hung with spidery stuccowork and pocked with five niches

5

containing statues of saints. Founded in 1230, the monastery was forced to disband as part of Joseph II's reforms in 1786, after which it was used alternately as a barracks and a residential building, before eventually falling into a state of disrepair.

There's little to see save for the monastery's gloriously dishevelled **cloisters** – painted with early fourteenth-century frescoes (restored during the interwar period) and vaulted around a century later – and which are now cluttered with an array of statuary and fragments, some of which were brought across from the demolished Minorite church after World War II. The **old refectory** is also worth a peek for its gorgeous vaulted and stuccoed ceiling – not dissimilar to that of the summer refectory in the Minorite Monastery (see p.280), and similarly painted with venerated saints. The shell of the old church, meanwhile, has been converted into a conference and concert hall, with tiers of chairs sweeping down over the main crypt in rather crass fashion; it's worth a look just to see how odd it all appears.

ARRIVAL AND INFORMATION PTUJ

By train Ptuj's train station is 500m northeast of the centre on Osojnikova cesta.
Destinations Ljubljana (2–3 daily; 2hr 30min); Maribor (Mon–Fri every 1–2hr, Sat & Sun 3–4 daily; 40–50min); Murska Sobota (7–8 daily; 50min–1hr 10min).
By bus The bus station is on the same road as the train station, 200m closer to town.
Destinations Ljutomer (Mon–Fri 2 daily; 1hr 10min);

Maribor (Mon–Sat every 45min–hourly, Sat 10 daily, Sun 6 daily; 30min); Ptujska Gora (Mon–Fri 7 daily; 20min).
Tourist office Slovenski trg 5 (daily: May–Sept 9am–8pm; Oct–April 9am–6pm; ☎02 779 6011, ⓦ ptuj.info), though you can get the same information at the welcoming Centre for Free Time Activities (CID), just across from the bus station in the modern building at Osojnikova 9 (Mon–Fri 9am–6pm; ☎02 780 5540, ⓦ cid.si). They offer free bike rental.

ACCOMMODATION

HOTELS AND B&BS

Mitra Prešernova ulica 6 ☎02 787 7455, ⓦ hotel-mitra.si. The seductive white and silver rooms in this first-rate hotel – each themed after historical characters (St George, Mithras, Lords of Ptuj, Habsburgs, etc) – are furnished with elegant drapes, gorgeous beds and thick duvets and pillows. There's also a brick-vaulted spa, atrium/courtyard, wine cellar and coffee house to enjoy. **€112**

★ MuziKafé Vrazov trg 1 ☎02 787 8860, ⓦ muzikafe.si. This arty bar/venue (see p.284) has seven beautifully conceived rooms brimming with colour and creativity; among the odd spotty painted cupboard or striped toilet seat there are custom-made upholstered chairs, artily framed mirrors and oversized lamps, as well as miniature radios and table games for wetter days. **€60**

Park Prešernova ulica 38 ☎02 749 3300, ⓦ parkhotel-ptuj.si. In much the same vein as the *Mitra*, this wonderfully renovated sixteenth-century house (which has retained much of its stunning original architectural features) conceals fifteen individually styled rooms, each of which is named for a historical character; breakfast in the old wine cellar is a treat. **€100**

Šilak Dravska ulica 13 ☎02 787 7447, ⓦ rooms-silak.com. Occupying one of the many erstwhile tannery buildings along this street, the family-run *Šilak* B&B is a delight; set around a pretty, cobbled courtyard, its dozen or so rooms have thick stone walls, chunky, cherry-wood furnishings and soft carpets. Breakfast (€5) is taken in the splendid brick-vaulted cellar. **€60**

HOSTELS AND CAMPING

Hostel Sonce Zagrebška cesta 10 ☎02 788 9331, ⓦ hostel-sonce.com. A 5min walk from the centre, across the river, this very neat and very bright family-run hostel puts many hotels to shame; all rooms (from singles up to five-bed dorms) are en suite and come with TV and a/c. Laundry and kitchen available, as well as a pleasant garden terrace. Breakfast €3. Dorms **€25**, doubles **€50**

Terme Ptuj Pot v Toplice ☎02 749 4100, ⓦ sava-hotels-resorts.com. Across the river, 2km west of town, this pleasant resort-style campsite also has enormous wine barrels that have been ingeniously converted into pod-like glamping options; guests can also use the on-site Thermal Park pools and saunas. Camping/person **€14.30**, wine barrels **€66**

EATING

Amadeus Prešernova ulica 36 ☎02 771 7051, ⓦ gostilna-amadeus.si. In truth, this good-looking place promises more than it delivers, but still, it's a decent option, the main draw being a lip-smacking steak menu (€14–18)

alongside some unusually appealing vegetarian options. Mon & Wed–Sat noon–10pm, Sun noon–4pm.
Gostilna PP Novi trg 2 ☎02 749 0622. For something cheap and filling, you can't beat this cheerful canteen-style

5

joint which knocks up fast and surprisingly tasty daily specials (around €6) – including vegetarian – though it's well known for its local chicken dishes, served every which way. Mon–Fri 9am–8pm, Sat noon–4pm.

★**Gostilna Ribič** Dravska ulica 9 ☎ 02 749 0635, ⓦ pan -restavracija.si. Enticingly positioned on the bank of the Drava, this smartly decorated restaurant (though you really must bag a table on the riverside terrace) has a menu almost exclusively devoted to fish (freshwater and sea) and shellfish – hence thoughtfully crafted dishes such as lobster tails with truffle purée and candied tomatoes, and marinated trout with sour anchovy salad (€16). Top-rate wines, too. Daily 10am–11pm.

DRINKING AND NIGHTLIFE

While no one could accuse Ptuj of being party central, there's no shortage of **cafés** around town, and for such a small place, its **cultural offerings** are surprisingly strong. It's worth checking out what's going on at the Centre for Free Time Activities (see p.282), which occasionally stages the odd gig in its basement bar.

Kavarna Bodi Ulica heroja Lacka 8 ☎ 040 890 086. Tucked away down an anonymous side street, this smashing little place has a good old-fashioned pub vibe, thanks to a random scattering of pubby paraphernalia and one hundred or so beers, many on tap, including some delicious Slovenian and Croatian craft versions. Mon–Thurs 9am–11.30pm, Fri & Sat 9am–1.30am, Sun 4–11pm.

★**MuziKafé** Vrazov trg 1 ☎ 02 787 8860, ⓦ muzikafe.si.

The town's fantastic cultural hub, *MuziKafé* combines a summery stone terrace with a loungey, richly painted interior (the retro/vintage furnishings, including flip-down cinema-style seats, are ace) where you can chill out to various sounds and dip into books and magazines. Both the stunning bare-brick cellar and pretty courtyard garden are used for a constant roster of events, of every stripe; Slovenia's finest musicians perform here on a regular basis. Mon–Thurs & Sun 8am–11pm, Fri & Sat 8am–midnight.

Mitrej III

Across the river in Zgornji Breg, 1km west of Ptuj • Call in advance if you wish to visit • €2 • ☎ 02 748 0360, ⓦ pmpo.si

Mitrej III (Mithra III) in **Zgornji Breg** is one of four shrines in Ptuj dedicated to the sun god and warrior **Mithra** (see box below). Discovered in 1913, the shrine – housed *in situ* inside a small pavilion – dates from 3 AD and comprises the remains of a three-naved temple, around which are scattered sacrificial altars carved with votive inscriptions. The plate on the far wall is a copy of an altar relief of the sacrificial bull from the Mithraeum in Osterburken, in Germany, though there are a few surviving fragments from the original in the right-hand corner. The rest of the room is neatly arranged with dedication blocks, chunky slabs of marble carved with reliefs from the Mithras cult – his birth from a rock, his slaying of a bull, and another that depicts him shooting water from a rock with an arrow. The most impressive stone, however, is positioned in front of the main altar, depicting two figures taking an oath over the fire on the sacrificial altar.

MITHRAISM

Mithraism, the ancient religion of Mithras the sun god, is believed to have originated in Persia before spreading west during the time of the Roman Empire. It was never officially recognized by the Romans, who weren't keen to acknowledge any elements of the religion of the Persians, their bitter enemies, and for this reason the first Mithras shrines, such as those in Ptuj, were built outside town boundaries. By the second half of the third century, however, Mithraism – with Ptuj as one of its leading centres – had almost established itself as the state religion, rivalling Christianity as the dominant faith. However, with Emperor Constantine's ascension to the throne in the fourth century, Mithraism, along with other pagan religions, was outlawed and most of its temples destroyed.

Little is known of its rituals and believers, although it's likely that meetings took place within confined religious communities, dominated exclusively by male members; Initiates were typically imperial administrators, slaves of the customs administration or soldiers, and would number around one hundred. Although stone dedication blocks and relief depictions of Mithras were widely distributed throughout the Roman Empire, few match the calibre of those in Ptuj. There's another excellent Mithraeum shrine in Rožanec, near Črnomelj (see p.239).

Mitrej I

Spodnja Hajdina, 2.5km southwest of Ptuj • Call in advance if you wish to visit • €2 • ☎ 02 748 0360, ⓦ pmpo.si

A twenty-minute walk southwest of Mithra III, across a dusty field in the tiny settlement of **Spodnja Hajdina**, a smaller building holds the remains of **Mitrej I** (Mithra I), discovered in 1898 and considered to be the oldest of the Mithra temples in the Roman Empire's northern province; this one dates from around the second half of the second century. The most interesting of the dozen or so haphazardly arranged stone dedication blocks are statues of Mithras dragging the sacrifical bull, and a snake coiled around a torso emerging from a rock mass.

Cerkev Sv Marija

Ptujska Gora, 12km southwest of Ptuj • Daily 7am–8pm • Free • Take one of the half a dozen or so buses (Mon–Fri) heading to Majšperk, and alight on the main road just below the church, from where it's a 5min walk

Prominently sited atop the not insubstantial **Črna Gora** (Black Hill), the Gothic **Cerkev Sv Marija** (Church of the Virgin Mary) ranks alongside the churches at Brezje and Sveta Gora as one of the country's premier pilgrimage destinations. Built some time around 1400, the church is entered via a rather fine Baroque stone staircase, flanked on either side by statues of St Nepomuk and St Florian, the latter doing what he does best, dousing fires. Its beautifully cool interior boasts some outstanding Gothic architecture, most notably in the form of the three arches, which presage the tripartite nave, whose aisles are separated by smooth slender columns. But nothing in this, or any other church in Slovenia, comes close to the splendour of the **high altar**, a majestic, towering work of art whose focal point is the *Virgin with Mantle* relief. This features seven angels lifting a dusky green cloak to reveal ranks of eighty figures, each carved in remarkable life-like detail; mingling among the cast of the rich and the poor are several of the counts of Celje. So compelling is this piece that it somewhat detracts from the rest of the altar's ornamentation, most notably some extraordinary sculptural work.

To the right of the high altar, in the southern aisle, the canopied **Celje Altar** pays further homage to the counts of Celje, its baldachin ceiling and pillars beautifully ornamented with sculpted flowers, animal figures and the counts' coats of arms. Also worthy of close inspection are the frescoes depicting scenes from *Christ's Passion* by John Bruneck, under the organ loft, and a fine statue of St James (minus his right hand) standing on the console of a pillar in the southern aisle. From the terrace outside, savour the marvellous wide-open views of the flat Drava Plain to the north and the lumpy Haloze hills to the south.

The Ljutomer wine road

Around 23km east of Ptuj, the anonymous town of **Ormož** is the starting point for the **Ljutomer wine road**, which extends north to Ljutomer, 20km distant. Despite being the smallest of Podravje's six wine-growing districts, the region possesses a high density of viticultural sites. Moreover, it vies with Goriška Brda in Primorje for the title of Slovenia's most beautiful wine-producing region, a fabulously picturesque and sunny landscape shaped by horizontal rows of curving, terraced vineyards set against the backdrop of *Klopotec*, wooden wind-powered rattles designed to scare off birds and, according to local superstition, to drive snakes out of the vineyards. Of the predominantly **white wines** harvested here, the smooth and slightly sweet Beli Pinot is regarded as the finest, followed by Laški Rizling, Šipon and Traminec; the blended wines Jeruzalemčan and Ljutomerčan are popular alternatives. The numerous **cellars** lining the route are marked by brown and cream signposts – although you can call in on the off-chance, most prefer advance notice; a couple of vintners worth considering are Hlebec, at Kog 108 (☎ 02 713 7060, ⓦ hlebec -kog.net), and, close by, Puklavec, at Zasavci 21 (☎ 041 916 343, ⓦ jeruzalempuklavec.si).

5

The route is made for **cycling**, and you may not have much choice anyway, as those buses that do travel between Ormož and Ljutomer take the main road running parallel to the east, passing through Ivanjkovci. If you're planning to cycle the entire route, you should allow for around four to five hours, or a little more, of course, if cellar-hopping is on the agenda. The stretch between Jeruzalem and Ljutomer is slightly tougher going than the stretch between Jeruzalem and Ormož, which flattens out markedly after Vinski Vir. **Bikes** can be rented at the tourist offices in both Jeruzalem and Ljutomer.

Jeruzalem

The midway point of the route is the delightful hilltop village of **JERUZALEM**, so-named after crusaders visiting here in the thirteenth century became so enamoured with the wine and the people that they decided to name the settlement after the holy city. At the centre of the village is the Baroque **Church of Our Lady of Sorrows**, whose painting of Our Lady of Sorrows on the high altar is a late seventeenth-century copy of the original, which was brought here by the crusaders but later stolen. Look out, too, for the imprint of a horse hoof, which, according to local legend, was left here by one of the marauding Turks during seventeenth-century raids.

ARRIVAL AND INFORMATION   JERUZALEM

By bus Buses from Ljutomer (Mon–Fri 2 daily; 30min) stop by the car park opposite the church.
Tourist office Just across from the church, the super-helpful tourist office (daily: April–Oct 10am–6pm;

Nov–March 10am–4pm; ☎ 02 719 4545, ⓦ jeruzalem.si) can advise on the best cellars to visit, and they also offer tastings (around €7 for five samples). They also have bikes for rent (€2/hr).

ACCOMMODATION AND EATING

Dvorec Jeruzalem 18 ☎ 02 719 4805. Next to the church, this fairly upmarket, ten-room hotel represents fair value; ample rooms come with parquet floors and beautifully crafted furnishings. Better still is the gravel terrace over-looking the sun-soaked vineyards, a lovely spot to pause with a glass, whether you're staying or not. €98
Vinski Hram 500m back down the road from the

church in the direction or Ormož ☎ 02 719 4504, ⓦ brenholc.com. Solid, unspectacular and fairly priced rooms. The extensive vine-covered terrace overlooking the hills is a terrific spot for lunch, and the food – perhaps venison steak, or cheese dumplings with mushrooms and tarragon (€8) – is on the button. Daily 9am–10pm. €60

Ljutomer

The economic and cultural centre of the region, **LJUTOMER** is the last town before you cross the Mura River into Prekmurje, and although it's unlikely you will need or want to stay here, there are a couple of interesting diversions.

Muzej Ljutomer

Glavni trg 1 • Mon–Fri 8am–3pm • €1.50 • ☎ 02 581 1295

Despite its limited scope, the small **Muzej Ljutomer** (Ljutomer Museum), in the town hall, is worth visiting to view original footage of the first-ever films to be produced in

---

HORSE-TROTTING

Wine connections aside, Ljutomer is best known for its **horse racing**, having staged trotting races since 1874. Today, the **hippodrome** – around 500m northwest of the centre – stages nine **horse-trotting races** a year. These usually take place on Sundays and public holidays between April and September (around €5), but check with the tourist office first for schedules. If you can't manage to get here for a race day, you can still visit the track and stables, and you may also get to see the horses in training; the tourist office (see opposite) should be able to fix something up for you.

5

Slovenia, *People Leaving the Church* and *The Fair at Ljutomer*, which were shot by Karol Grossmann in 1905 (see p.310). There's also an interesting exhibition on the so-called "Tabor Movement"; between 1868 and 1870, numerous groups of young intellectuals living in Slovene ethnic territories initiated regular mass open-air forums (*tabors*) to publicize and rally support for a united Slovenia, whose very existence as a national group around that time appeared seriously threatened. Although they were subsequently banned by Vienna, the influence of the *tabors* continued to be felt in later years whenever questions concerning the Slovene national movement were raised.

ARRIVAL AND INFORMATION   LJUTOMER

By train Ljutomer has two train stations: Ljutomer, and the smaller Ljutomer Mesto on Rajh Nade ulica, where you should alight for the town centre, a 10min walk south.
Destinations Murska Sobota (Mon–Fri 6 daily; 20min).
By bus The bus station is on Ormoška cesta, a hop away from the main square, Glavni trg.
Destinations Murska Sobota (Mon–Fri 6 daily; 40min);

Ormož (Mon–Fri 5 daily; 30min).
Tourist office A large kiosk in one corner of Glavni trg (Mon–Fri 8am–4pm, Sat 8am–noon; ☎02 584 3333, ⓦjeruzalem.si). As well as supplying information on the Ljutomer wine road (see p.285), staff can arrange accommodation along the route; there are also bikes for rent (€10/day).

ACCOMMODATION AND EATING

Enoteka Ljutomer Prešernova ulica 1 15 ☎031 229 778, ⓦenoteka.si. Sparkling wine bar/shop stocking the wines of some thirty or so local producers, all of which you can buy or taste (€1.20 a glass); there's also a small exhibition on the local wine industry with an enormous vintage press and some lovely footage from 1949 of villagers harvesting the fields. Mon–Fri 10am–6pm, Sat 10am–3pm.
Ozmec Tourist Farm Slamnjak 33, 2km south of Ljutomer back out on the road towards Jeruzalem

☎02 584 9666, ⓦfrank-ozmec.com. This large and busy working farm makes for a most agreeable stopover; snug rooms, delicious food straight from the farm and excellent domestic organic wine. **€50**
Stela Glavni trg 15 ☎059 308 130, ⓦstela.si. On the town's main square, this somewhat faceless hotel won't win any awards (for anything), but it is clean and cheap(ish); more exciting is its pastry shop, whose cabinets are well stocked with a delectable selection of home-made treats. **€60**

Prekmurje

Cut off by the fast-flowing Mura River to the south, and bounded on the remaining three sides by the Austrian, Hungarian and Croatian borders, **Prekmurje** (Pomurje) is a region quite apart from the rest of the country. Known as Slovenia's breadbasket, it is, for the most part, a relentlessly flat landscape, carved up by grids of smooth green fields, picturesque villages and little white churches. Prekmurje has one of the richest **culinary traditions** in Slovenia, and you shouldn't leave without trying *bograč*, a steaming goulash pot of mixed meats, onions and potatoes, or its most famous product, *gibanica*, a delicious sweet pie stuffed with cottage cheese, poppy seeds, walnut and apple; meanwhile, the local pumpkin seed oil is simply divine.

A fairly regular bus service links the region's two towns, **Murska Sobota** and **Lendava**, via most of the villages in between, including **Martjanci**, **Bogojina** and **Beltinci**. However, services are dramatically reduced (or nonexistent) at weekends, so try and visit on a weekday. Alternatively, the best way to explore the region is by bike (see box, p.290).

Brief history

Prekmurje's relative isolation is rooted in over a thousand years of **Magyar** rule, a situation that changed only after World War I when it was incorporated into Yugoslav lands, although there was another brief period of Hungarian imposition during World War II. Physically, economically and culturally distanced from the rest of the country prior to World War I – there was no bridge crossing the Mura until 1924 – Prekmurje is still regarded by many Slovenes as something of a backwater. However, thanks largely

5

to Hungary's long-term rule, the region remains one of Slovenia's most ethnically diverse, embracing a sizeable Hungarian minority, as well as the country's largest Roma community. Prior to World War II it also accounted for more than half of the country's Jewish population.

Murska Sobota

In the geographical centre of Prekmurje, **MURSKA SOBOTA** is the largest settlement in the province, a one-horse town where nothing very much happens. However, it is the region's main road and rail hub, so there's a good chance you'll wind up here if you're planning to explore the surrounding countryside. The town developed alongside the Ledava River, in the plains north of the Mura River, during the eleventh century, and was almost immediately incorporated into the Hungarian state, under whose administration it remained until 1920. Another period of Hungarian control during World War II was ended by the Red Army, who liberated the town in April 1945; the suitably dour **Liberation Monument** stands in recognition of this event in the centre of Trg Zmage, or Victory Square.

Pomurski muzej

Trubarjev drevored 5 • Tues–Fri 9am–5pm, Sat 9am–1pm, Sun 2–6pm • €3 • ☎ 02 527 1706, ⓦ pomurski-muzej.si

Housed inside an eighteenth-century Renaissance mansion in the centre of leafy **City Park**, the **Pomurski muzej** (Pomurje Museum) offers an impressive narrative of life in the town and Prekmurje from prehistory to the end of World War II. Highlights from the earliest periods include Roman burial mounds and the remnants of a medieval forge discovered in Grad na Goričkem in 1990. The medieval period is further represented by some superb Gothic architecture, including a stone tabernacle, as well as some fresco fragments.

Trades such as shoe-making, milling and wheel-making all make an appearance, though the greatest emphasis is on **pottery**, one of the region's most important nineteenth-century cottage industries, and a tradition that just about survives to this day in old potters' settlements such as Filovci (see p.291). The last few rooms document the town's struggles during World War II and its occupation first by Hungary and then by the Nazis, before it was liberated – with the help of the Prekmurje Partisan Brigade – by the Red Army in 1945. There's footage of the unveiling of the Liberation Monument (see above), erected on August 12, 1945, less than two months after the Red Army left Murska Sobota.

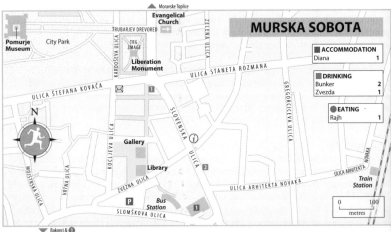

ARRIVAL AND INFORMATION

MURSKA SOBOTA

By bus The bus station is centrally located on Slomškova ulica. Destinations Bakovci Mon–Fri 12 daily, Sat 3 daily; 15min); Beltinci (Mon–Fri hourly, Sat 3 daily; 15min); Bogojina (Mon–Fri 9 daily; 20min); Filovci (Mon–Fri 9 daily; 25min); Lendava (Mon–Fri hourly, Sat 3 daily; 40min); Ljutomer (Mon–Fri 5 daily; 40min); Maribor (Mon–Fri 10 daily, Sat & Sun 3 daily; 1hr 10min); Moravske Toplice (Mon–Fri 10 daily; 10min).

By train The train station is on Ulica arhitekta novaka, from where it's a 5min walk west to the town centre. Destinations Ljubljana (Mon–Sat 2 daily, Sun 1; 3hr 15min); Ljutomer (Mon–Fri 7 daily, Sat & Sun 3 daily; 20min); Ptuj (Mon–Fri 7 daily, Sat & Sun 4–5 daily; 50min–1hr 10min). Budapest (1 daily; 5hr 15min).

Tourist office Slovenska ulica 41 (Mon–Fri 9am–5pm, Sat 9am–noon; ☎ 02 534 1130).

ACCOMMODATION

Diana Slovenska ulica 52 ☎ 02 514 1200, ⌨hotel -diana.si. The town's one hotel is a bit poky and plasticky in parts, but it does the job for a brief stopover, and there's a pool, sauna, solarium and gym on site, all of which are free to guests. **€86**

EATING

★Rajh Soboška ulica 32, Bakovci ☎ 02 543 9098, ⌨rajh.si. If you're prepared to travel for your food (and even if you're not), then make tracks for the exceptional *Rajh*, 5km south of town in the village of Bakovci. They don't serve Indian food, but rather exquisitely prepared Slovenian dishes with a solid local slant, like smoked goose breast with roasted pumpkin seed oil and poppy seeds (€11); tasting menu €38. Tues–Sat 10.30am–10pm, Sun 11.30am–4pm.

DRINKING

Bunker Slovenska ulica 47 ☎ 031 670 444. Murska Sobota is almost the last place you'd expect to find a "postapocalyptic steampunk bar" – think *Mad Max* and *The Terminator* rolled into one. Quite brilliant it is too; leather car seats and steel-backed chairs, aluminium piping, caged mannequins and that sort of thing – even the staff are togged up in futuristic garb. The beer, served from mini-gasoline pumps, is tremendous; you can soak it all up with burgers, wings and the like. Mon–Thurs 7am–11pm, Fri & Sat 7am–1am, Sun 9am–11pm.

Zvezda Trg zmage 8 ☎ 02 539 1572. While not quite as out there as *Bunker*, this popular place does brew its own selection of light and dark beers on site – before you enter, take a look at the stuccoed reliefs of moustachioed men on the facade. Mon–Thurs & Sun 7am–11pm, Fri & Sat 7am–1am.

Cerkev Sv Martina

Heading north out of Murska Sobota along the road to Moravske Toplice, it's worth taking a moment to stop off at the roadside **Cerkev Sv Martina** (Parish Church of St Martin) in the village of **MARTJANCI**. Distinguished by an elegant high Gothic belfry, the church was designed and painted by Janez Aquila, a frequent contributor to religious monuments in the Prekmurje region. Arguably the most beautifully frescoed church in Prekmurje, its gorgeous, cross-ribbed vaulted presbytery is smothered with some fine paintings – Apostles (including the *Masters of the Apostles*), saints and prophets, as well as a painting of the author himself (supposedly one of the oldest self-portraits known to exist in European art). On the inner wall of the triumphal arch there's a fabulous fresco of George and the Dragon. The simple high altar, meanwhile, featuring a statue of St Martin, is the work of Jože Plečnik, a modest contribution by the architect in comparison to his work at Bogojina (see p.290).

Moravske Toplice

MORAVSKE TOPLICE, 7km north of Murska Sobota, is dominated by the **Terme 3000 Spa** (daily 9am–9pm; daily ticket €13.90, after 3pm €10.90; ☎ 02 512 2200, ⌨sava-hotels-resorts.com), a sprawling, modern complex incorporating one of the largest recreational centres in the country. Starting out in the 1960s, when thermal springs were discovered during a search for oil, the spa now comprises fourteen separate

5

CYCLING IN PREKMURJE

Given the region's predominantly flat terrain, **cycling** around Prekmurje is a joy, and there's an excellent network of well-marked and well-maintained cycle paths to choose from. Moreover, with no two villages more than a few kilometres apart, there are plenty of places to rest up before pushing on to the next destination.

The best place for information and advice is the **Bike Center** (May–Sept daily 9am–noon & 2–7pm, out of season call a day in advance; ☎070 141 680, ⊛bike-center.si), whose shop is within the grounds of the Terme 3000 Spa in Moravske Toplice; as well as servicing and **renting bikes** (€11 for four hours, €14/day), they also organize bicycle excursions, though a minimum of five people is usually required.

The *Cycling Map of Prekmurje* (€3), available from the tourist office in Moravske Toplice, details eight routes, indicating sights of interest, places to sleep and eat as well as bike rental and repair shops; the 1:75,000 *Pomurje* map (€5) is also useful.

indoor and outdoor bathing areas featuring water and air massage pools, geysers and waterfalls, a diving pool, wave machines and enormous water slides; the highlight is Aqualoop, featuring a 360-degree loop.

ARRIVAL AND INFORMATION

By bus Buses stop on the main road by the entrance to the spa.

Destinations Bogojina and Filovci (Mon–Fri 8 daily; 10min); Lendava (Mon–Fri 3 daily; 30min); Murska Sobota (Mon–Fri 10 daily; 10min).

Tourist office Kranjčeva cesta 3, among the small complex of shops as you enter the village – if coming by bus, backtrack 200m from the bus stop (Mon–Fri 8am–6pm/8pm in summer, Sat 7am–3pm, Sun 8am–2pm;

MORAVSKE TOPLICE

☎02 538 1520, ⊛moravske-toplice.com).

Activities Bikes can be rented from the tourist office (€3/hr, €12/day) and the Bike Center (see box above). There's also tennis (€5 for 1hr) and a long and lovely eighteen-hole golf course (☎02 512 5066; €32 for nine holes, €45 for eighteen holes; club rental €8.50); reception is under the *Livada* hotel and there's a twenty percent discount for hotel guests.

ACCOMMODATION

There's plenty of accommodation here, though none of the spa's three adjoining hotels, all of which are inclined towards package visitors, is particularly inspiring. All hotel guests receive free access to the spa pools.

Bungalow Tourist Village Terme 3000 ☎02 538 2200, ⊛sava-hotels-resorts.com. A far more pleasant, and affordable, alternative to the on-site hotels, with a large spread of lovely thatch-roofed, Prekmurje-style bungalows sheltered among trees on the opposite side of the complex; they all have four double rooms, each with its own entrance. Guests receive free admission to the spa complex. **€96**

Camping Terme 3000 Kranjčeva cesta 12 ☎02 512 1200, ⊛camping-slovenia.com. Tacked onto the far side of the resort, this large, well-tended campsite is great if you

want easy access to a whole range of facilities. Without spa admission **€26**, with spa admission **€38**

Tremel Tourist Farm Bokrači 28 ☎02 545 1017, ⊛kmetija-tremel.si. Lovely renovated farmstead 10km north of Moravske Toplice in the village of Bokrači, which boasts more than thirty years of first-class hospitality. Both the wine and the food here are fantastic, not least the house's signature *gibanica* dish, which has won many awards. From Murska Sobota, follow signs for Hodoš, then Sebeborci. **€50**

Bogojina

Around 5km east of Moravske Toplice, **BOGOJINA** is the site of Prekmurje's best-known – and most important – church, the **Cerkev Vnebovhod** (Church of the Ascension). Visible from far and wide – owing to its slight elevation above the rest of the village – the church was redesigned by Slovenia's greatest architect, Jože Plečnik (see box, p.49), between 1925 and 1927, and clearly displays his trademark characteristics, from the high cylindrical tower to the columns, pillars and fanciful oddments gracing the interior. At the heart of this bright, single-nave hall-church is a monumental dark-grey marble column, from which four equally striking vaults emanate, built to help support the beautiful oak timber ceiling. Eight chunky grey pillars run down each side of the nave, while the circular marble pulpit and wooden balcony are classic Plečnik designs. In typically idiosyncratic fashion, Plečnik furnished the church with numerous flamboyant accessories, such as the ceramic plates and jugs ornamenting the ceiling and high altar; even if you're not a fan of Plečnik's work, this is not only Prekmurje's, but one of Slovenia's, most striking ecclesiastical monuments. The **village** itself is exceptionally pretty, and it's an enjoyable fifteen-minute walk from the bus stop on the main road to the church, past rows of colourful Prekmurje-style farmhouses – L-shaped homesteads built on narrow strips of land perpendicular to the traffic routes.

Filovci

The *Črna keramika*, or **black pottery**, industry flourished in several villages hereabouts from the late eighteenth century onwards, and especially in **FILOVCI**, 2km along the road from Bogojina. In the centre of the village, at no. 29 – walk across the small bridge and beyond the church – the Bojnec family offers pottery demonstrations in their workshop; they've also got a shop selling a wide range of earthenware. Contact the tourist office in Moravske Toplice (see opposite) to arrange a visit.

Beltinci

If you're around at the beginning of August, don't miss the **Beltinci International Folklore Festival**, which takes place in the large village of **BELTINCI**, about 10km south of Bogojina – it is actually easier to reach the village via the faster road from Murska Sobota to Lendava. For more than forty years this superb festival has consistently attracted a high-calibre roster of domestic and foreign folk groups, musicians and dance troupes, who perform over four days on several stages in the village's large and leafy manor park – Saturday is generally reckoned to be the best day. It's also a great opportunity to try out traditional Prekmurje dishes at the many stalls spread out around the grounds.

Dvorec Beltinci

Mladinska ulica 2 • Exhibitions May–Oct Mon–Fri 8am–3pm • Free

The focal point of the park itself is the seventeenth-century L-shaped **Dvorec Beltinci** (Beltinci Manor), which was owned by the noble Hungarian Zichy family until World War II, after which it fell into a terrible state of disrepair – it's now owned by the local authority, although this is still disputed by descendants of the family. In any case, the house is currently in the throes of a painstakingly long renovation programme, and while there's little of substance to see, you can view a couple of charming little exhibitions. First up is a **pharmacy exhibition**, featuring original early twentieth-century fixtures and fittings, including gorgeous wood-carved cabinets, painted ceramic jars and other vessels. Another couple of rooms hold a delightful collection of **vintage bicycles**; one of the most enchanting is a fireman's bike, complete with hose, dating from 1935. For more information, ask at the **tourist office**, which is on the ground floor (Mon–Fri 8am–3pm; ☏ 02 541 3580).

Selo

From the village of **Tešanovci**, 1km or so east of Moravske Toplice, a road breaks left and climbs slowly up to the scattered settlement of **SELO**, some 10km distant. Standing in a field below the main road is the pinkish **Rotunda Sv Nikolaj** (Chapel of St Nicholas; April–Oct Tues–Sat 10am–6pm – to visit, call in at the information hut on the main road; €2), a superb Romanesque rotunda built in the mid-thirteenth century, though much reworked over the years, most recently, and extensively, in the

5

middle of the nineteenth century. The exterior features a smooth shingle roof and a wooden bell tower, both of which mark it out as a particularly unique specimen in Slovenia. Its interior, meanwhile, is adorned with some exceptional, albeit badly effaced, wall paintings, the upper half covered in scenes from the Adoration of the Magi and the Passion Cycle, and the dome smothered with evangelical symbols.

EATING SELO

K Rotundi Selo 30a ☎ 02 544 1035. Located 1km back along the road (before the church), the roadside *gostilna* is one of the region's best restaurants; as well as Prekmurje specialities, it's known for its game and roast goat dishes. Mon–Sat 11am–10pm, Sun 10am–4pm.

Lendava

Wedged into the southeastern corner of Prekmurje, 31km from Murska Sobota and a stone's throw from the Croatian and Hungarian borders, **LENDAVA** (Lendva in Hungarian) is Slovenia's easternmost town and one of the largest bilingual settlements in the country, its sizeable Hungarian minority accounting for nearly half of the town's population. Despite this harmonized ethnic union, it's a fairly low-key place, its relative isolation ensuring that few visitors make it to this remote little corner of the country.

Lendava's major **festival** is the fun Bogračfest on the last Saturday in August, a culinary affair where dozens of teams line up along Glavna ulica to prepare the tastiest, meatiest goulash, accompanied by lots of wine and music.

Galerija-muzej Lendava

Banffyjev trg 1 • Mon–Fri 8am–4pm, Sat 10am–2pm • €2.50 • ☎ 02 578 9260, ⓦ gml.si

The town's major sight is the **castle**, reached via a steep path next to the Parish Church of St Catherine, midway along Glavna ulica. Although a fortification of sorts stood here as early as the twelfth century, the present **Lendavski Grad** (Lendava Castle) was rebuilt by the noble Hungarian Esterházy family between 1712 and 1717, and remained in their possession until the beginning of World War II. It now houses the modest **Galerija-muzej Lendava**, a more miss-than-hit affair that does at least contain a reasonably stimulating collection of Bronze Age artefacts, weaponry from battles with the Turks and, in the attic, a hoard of curious sculptures by Slovene and Hungarian artists. It's often most interesting for its ambitious temporary exhibitions – a recent show focused on Joan Miró.

Sinagoga

Župančičeva ulica • Tues–Sun 10am–2pm • €1.50 • ☎ 02 578 9260, ⓦ sinagoga-lendava.si

Built in 1866, the **sinagoga** (synagogue) was cleared out, along with the town's several-hundred-strong Jewish population, during World War II. Although there is no longer a Jewish community in town, the synagogue has been restored to something like its former self; the most notable things, architecturally, are six fluted iron pillars with Corinthian capitals, while the clock you see is the only remaining original item. The synagogue now accommodates a small exhibition – mainly photos and religious items – from the pre-World War II period.

Kulturni center

Trg Gyorgya Zale 1 • ☎ 02 577 6022

Across the square from the synagogue stands the extraordinary **Kulturni center** (Cultural Centre), designed by the renowned, and controversial, Hungarian architect **Imre Makovecz**, known for his anti-modernist, back-to-nature structures that can be found all over Hungary. The centre sports several wood-clad towers that resemble church-like steeples, while motifs inspired by Magyar art and folklore dot the facade. The interior is no less startling, its centrepiece a fine theatre with Slovene and Hungarian productions sharing equal billing; there's a decent café, too (see opposite).

Cerkev Sv Trojice

Nestled among the wine-growing **Lendava hills** (Lendavske gorice), less than 1km southeast of town, the **Cerkev Sv Trojice** (Church of the Holy Trinity) is a standard Baroque issue built in 1728. The church is notable, however, for holding the grisly, mummified body of local warrior Mihael Hadik, slain by the Turks in 1603, but whose immaculately preserved body – take a peek if you wish – was miraculously discovered in a casket during construction of the castle chapel in 1728. If you want to visit, contact the tourist office (see below); a member of staff will accompany you.

ARRIVAL AND INFORMATION   LENDAVA

By bus Arriving at the bus station on Kolodvorska ulica, make your way across the ugly concrete square towards the *Elizabeta* hotel, through the small complex of shops to the park; take a right here, up past the town hall to the triangle in the middle of the road. At this point turn left and you'll find yourself on the main street, Glavna ulica.

Destinations Moravske Toplice (Mon–Fri 4 daily; 30min); Murska Sobota (Mon–Fri hourly, Sat 2 daily; 40min).

Tourist office The (rather useless) office is at Glava ulica 38 (Mon–Fri 8am–4pm, Sat 9am–1pm; ☎ 02 578 8390, ⓦ turizem-lendava.si).

Activities If you fancy a wallow, head to the Terme Lendava Spa, 1km south of town at Tomšičeva 2 (Mon–Thurs & Sun 7am–8pm, Fri & Sat 7am–11pm; €10 for the day, €7 after 1pm; ☎ 02 577 4460, ⓦ sava-hotels-resorts .com); one of the country's warmest spas, it has two indoor and three outdoor (May–Sept) pools, with temperatures between 29 and 37 degrees centigrade.

ACCOMMODATION, EATING AND DRINKING

Banffy Glavna ulica 124 ☎ 02 577 6660. Just along from the tourist office, there's good coffee at this lovely old-style *kavarna*, whose rather stiff-looking interior belies a pleasantly restful atmosphere. Mon–Sat 7.30am–9pm, Sun 8am–noon.

Cuk Wine Cellar Lendavske gorice 217 ☎ 02 575 1815, ⓦ hisa-vina-cuk.si. Wine buffs may care to visit this pretty little hillside cellar 1km southeast of town on the fringe of the Lendava hills. As well as wine-tasting (five wines for €10), they've also got a handful of rooms and apartments. Cellar Fri–Sun 1–9pm; other times by arrangement. €70

Elizabeta Mlinska ulica 5 ☎ 02 577 4600, ⓦ hotel -elizabeta.si. Aimed at nonexistent business travellers, this gleaming glass block offers fairly priced, perfectly fine and comfortable rooms around a central atrium. €60

Teater Café Trg Gyorgya Zale 1 ☎ 02 577 6020. The best place for a drink is the café inside the Cultural Centre, with its high-backed, throne-like chairs; don't leave without trying some *dobos torta*, a traditional Hungarian layered cream cake topped with caramel. Mon–Sat 8am–10pm, Sun 9am–9pm.

Velika Polana

If you've got your own transport, you can visit two villages of interest a short way from Lendava. **VELIKA POLANA**, around 10km west, is one of Europe's officially designated **stork villages** thanks to the dozen or so storks that pitch up here each spring. Attracted by the abundance of food, especially frogs and toads, to be found in the nearby marshes and swamplands, the storks usually return to the same nests (improbably bulky constructions perched atop telegraph poles or chimneys) each year. Whether kicking back in their nests, or skulking around the fields foraging for food, they offer irresistible photo opportunities.

CHURCH FRESCO, TRIGLAV NATIONAL PARK, NEAR KRANJSKA GORA

Contexts

History

Although recorded history of the area now covered by Slovenia begins with the arrival of the Romans, archeological finds suggest that this territory was already settled in the Paleolithic and Neolithic eras. The most intriguing discovery from the Paleolithic era was a bone flute unearthed from a cave in Šebrelje near Cerkno in 1995, while the most compelling evidence of the existence of a Neolithic culture comes from the Ljubljana Marshes south of the capital. Here, the inhabitants built wooden huts on stilts, made coarse pottery and raised livestock.

Hallstatt period

The early Iron Age, or **Hallstatt**, period (eighth to fourth centuries BC) coincided with the arrival of the region's first identifiable peoples – Illyrian-speaking tribes, possibly called Veneti, who settled in the alpine region. The major Hallstatt settlements were in Most na Soči and throughout the region of Dolenjska – superb archeological finds in these areas have included armour, jewellery and *situlae* (ornately embossed pails or buckets). More generally, this was a period of great economic and cultural advancement. Around the third century BC, the Hallstatt cultures were superseded by the Celts who, led by the Norics, established a protostate called **Noricum**, the centre of which was located in the eastern Alps, while a second centre grew up in the area of present-day Celje, then called **Celeia**.

The Romans

Noricum was subsumed into the Roman Empire around 10 BC, which more or less marked the beginning of **Roman occupation** in this territory. Settled by colonists from Aquileia (a small town in the Gulf of Trieste established by the Romans in 181 BC), **Emona** (Ljubljana) was the first Roman town to develop on the territory of present-day Slovenia, followed by Poetovio (Ptuj) and Celeia (Celje). Trade, administration and culture grew up around these garrison towns and spread along the roads constructed to link the imperial heartland with Pannonia and beyond. Some of the country's best-preserved **Roman remains** include vestigial ruins in Ljubljana, a wealth of monuments in Ptuj and a superb Roman necropolis in Šempeter, just outside Celje. The most significant legacy of the Roman occupation was the partition of the Byzantine and Roman spheres into separate civilizations, a division that would later result in a critical split between the Eastern Orthodox and Roman Catholic churches. The disintegration of the Roman Empire in the fifth century corresponded with a series of incursions into the region by a multitude of warring tribes, such as the Huns, Ostrogoths and Lombards, and the all-powerful **Avars**, a Turkic people from Central Asia whose empire survived well into the eighth century, before it was crushed by the Franks.

8th–4th century BC	3rd century BC	181 BC
Illyrian-speaking tribes settle in alpine regions	Celts and Noric peoples establish a protostate in the eastern Alps, with a second centre in Celeia (Celje)	Foundation of Aquileia marks the beginning of Roman occupation on Slovene lands

From the first Slav state to Habsburg rule

Although there is no definitive record as to when, or from where, the ancestors of today's Slovenes first entered the territory of present-day Slovenia, the most widespread theory is that migrating Slav tribes (loosely divided into two different, but related, groups, Slaveni and Antes) arrived from the Carpathian Basin in the middle of the sixth century. As Avar power waned, these tribes, along with others, united into a loose confederation, resulting in the first Slav political entity, the **Duchy of Karantanija**, located near present-day Klagenfurt in Austria. This brief period of autonomy lasted until 745 AD, when the Duchy was subsumed into the Carolingian Empire of the Franks, thus subjecting the Karantanian Slav population to a Germanic domination that would continue for several centuries more. Around the same time, an influx of Western missionaries and the establishment of a formal church paved the way for the **Christianization of the Slovenes**.

In the tenth century, the **Magyars**, led by the feared Arpad clan, invaded and settled in the Slovenian regions of Pannonia. Before they were able to advance any further, however, they ran into the imperial forces of the German king, Otto I, who promptly routed them in a counteroffensive just outside Augsburg in 955 AD. **German victory** instigated the reorganization of Karantanian territory into frontier marches: Carinthia (Koroška), Carniola (Kranjska), Styria (Štajerska), Gorica (Goriška) and Bela Krajina, the boundaries of which would essentially remain the same for the next thousand years.

The first **chartered towns** on Slovene territory – Kamnik, Piran, Ptuj, Škofja Loka and the capital Ljubljana – began to develop a short while thereafter, around the beginning of the twelfth century. By the fourteenth century there would be some 27 chartered towns and countless other market towns, many of which developed trade and crafts industries as an adjunct to agricultural activity. Cultural life during this period, meanwhile, was mostly centred around the newly established **monasteries**, such as the Carthusian orders at Pleterje and Žiče, and the Cistercian orders at Kostanjevica and Stična. Meanwhile, the prominent ruling entities of this time – the Bamberg, Spanheim and Premysl dynasties – were confronted with the spectre of the Habsburgs who, by 1270, had already established a stronghold in the eastern Alps and would soon rule across most of the Slovene lands.

Habsburg rule, Turkish invasions and the Reformation

The **Habsburg dynasty** established its first feudal holdings in Slovene lands in 1282, holding sway across most of the territory until the end of World War I, while small geographical areas in the eastern and western peripheries were governed by Hungary and Venice respectively. The only serious political rivals to the Habsburgs at this time were the **counts of Celje**, an aristocratic dynasty who, through a combination of fortuitous politics and skilfully arranged marriages into distinguished European feudal houses, managed to acquire great swathes of territory and wield tremendous influence across the country. Although the assassination of Count Ulrik II in Belgrade in 1456 nullified this particular threat, the Habsburgs now had to contend with other problems.

Having already conquered much of the Balkan peninsula in the first half of the fifteenth century, the **Ottoman Turks** resumed their advance north towards Slovene territories around 1470. Despite repeated raids, which reached their peak during the reign of Sultan Suleyman I "the Magnificent" (1520–66), the defining moment was the **Battle of Sisak** in

c.550	745	c.900
Slav tribes arrive from the Carpathian Basin; the Duchy of Karantanija emerges as the first Slav political entity	Karantanija loses its independence; Christianization of the Slovenes	Magyars (Hungarians) settle in Slovene regions of Pannonia

1593, where the Turks were crushed by combined Habsburg-Croatian forces, an episode which effectively put the lid on Turkish aspirations in Habsburg-occupied lands.

The economic pressures engendered as a result of these assaults, coupled with the transformation of the old feudal tax system into less favourable forms, precipitated a series of violent and widespread **peasant revolts**. The most famous of these was the 1573 uprising, during which some ten thousand Slovene and Croatian peasants (*puntarji*) participated. In the event, the rebellion was crushed and its leader, Matija Gubec, met a somewhat ignominious fate (crowned with a red-hot metal rod in Zagreb Cathedral), while the peasants were bound to perpetual serfdom. There was little other economic activity to speak of around this time, though pockets of proto-industrialization existed in parts of the country, such as the Idrija mercury mine and the forges in Kropa.

The **Germanization** of culture, education and administration had been a key policy of Habsburg rule since the tenth century, yet despite this, Slovenes managed to preserve both their language and cultural identity. This was largely down to **Protestant reformers** such as **Primož Trubar** (the "Slovene Luther"), who wrote and published the first book in the Slovene language, and **Adam Bohorič**, who compiled the first Slovene grammar book. It would, however, be another two centuries before written Slovene would be appropriated for secular use. Having seen off the Turks, the Austrians, under Archduke Ferdinand, turned their attention to the religious revolts taking place throughout Habsburg lands, and by the end of the century the **Counter-Reformation** was in full swing. The ensuing period of recatholicization and absolutism resulted in a lengthy spell of political, economic and cultural regression for Slovenes.

The eighteenth century: reform and the Enlightenment

Prospects looked decidedly brighter at the turn of the eighteenth century owing to strong economic growth and modernization, manifest in the development of manufacturing industries – forges in Bohinj and Jesenice, textile mills in Ljubljana, improved transport links between Vienna and Trieste (via Maribor, Celje and Ljubljana) and the declaration of Trieste as a free port. These developments were taken a stage further under the centralized, state-building reforms of **Maria Theresa** and her son **Joseph II** during the second half of the century: judicial reforms were introduced, primary schooling was made compulsory and religious tolerance was decreed. More tendentiously, German replaced Latin as the language of government, a move that caused some alarm among the emerging national groups, many of whom preferred to use their own language.

Led by the cultural innovator **Baron Žiga Zois** and a small coterie of Slovene intellectuals (the so-called "Zois Circle"), the **Slovene Enlightenment** (roughly 1760–1820) was the first sustained period of cultural advancement since the work of the sixteenth-century Protestant reformers. This celebrated group featured the historian/playwright **Anton Linhart**, poet/journalist **Valentin Vodnik** – founder of the first Slovene newspaper, *Ljublanske Novice* (*The Ljubljana News*) – and the priest, **Marko Pohlin**, whose 1768 publication, *Kranjska gramatika* (*Carniolan Grammar*), was the forerunner to a modern Slovene literary language. In addition, theatres in Ljubljana, Maribor and Celje were built, public and private libraries became the focus for Slovene cultural life, and the establishment of assorted professional and cultural societies and institutions, including the Philharmonic Music Society (1794) and the literary and linguistic society, Academia

1144	**1160**	**1282**
First recorded mention of Ljubljana, known as Laibach	Žiče is the first Carthusian monastery established outside France	Habsburgs establish feudal holdings in Slovene lands, their main rivals being the counts of Celje

Operosorum, affirmed Slovenia's integration into the circle of cultured European nations. It was also a time of great **Baroque** extravagance, particularly in the fields of architecture, painting and sculpture. Nowhere was this more so than in Ljubljana, which acquired several beautiful churches, church paintings and buildings. Leading Baroque contributors included the painters Valentin Metzinger and Giulio Quaglio, architect Andrea Pozzo and sculptor Francesco Robba.

Illyrian Provinces and nationalism

Following **Napoleon**'s dissolution of the Venetian republic in 1797, the French were drawn into several wars against the Austrians, culminating in a hard-fought victory for the French at Wagram in 1809. Subsequent to this, Napoleon cut the Austrians off from the Adriatic and created a quasi-ethnic state, stretching from Graz in Austria down to the Bay of Kotor in Montenegro, a region known as the **Illyrian Provinces**. Over the next four years, and with Ljubljana designated as the provinces' administrative centre, Slovenes enjoyed a series of liberating French reforms, the most important of which was free use of the Slovene language in administration and schools. Following Napoleon's defeat in 1813, and the subsequent collapse of the French Empire, Slovene territory was reincorporated into the Habsburg domain and all the old political and feudal systems were restored. Nevertheless, four years of French rule was long enough for Slovene intellectuals to be made aware of their ethno-national identities; moreover, the inclusion of Croats, as well as a minority Serb population, within the same state gave rise to the notion that some form of common Slav union might one day be realized. These embryonic national sentiments were powerfully reinforced through the work of Slovenia's pre-eminent Romantic poet and greatest-ever literary figure, **France Prešeren** (see box, p.113), who refashioned Slovenian as a literary language and raised it to the level of other European languages. It was no surprise, therefore, when Prešeren's poem, *Zdravljica* (*A Toast*), was adopted as the Slovene national anthem in 1991.

The **1848 Revolution** was the catalyst for tremendous upheaval across continental Europe, including Austria, where the tenets of absolutism and serfdom had reigned since the demise of the Illyrian Provinces in 1813. Fired by the literary brilliance of Prešeren and the pedagogic reforms of **Anton Slomšek** (the bishop of Maribor), **Slovene nationalism** became increasingly vocal around this time, culminating in calls for a **United Slovenia programme** (*Zedinjena Slovenija*), whose prime objectives were to unite all ethnic Slovene territories within one autonomous region and to promulgate the use of the Slovene language. Although the programme was never realized, its basic tenets informed much of Slovene political life well into the next century. By and large, though, most Slovenes remained committed to Austria and few envisaged a future outside the Habsburg Empire.

Reform and Yugoslavism

According to the terms of the **Compromise of 1867**, the Habsburg state became the **Dual Monarchy of Austria-Hungary**, whereby the two became constitutionally separate entities, albeit with the same Habsburg ruler, Franz Jozef – emperor in Austria and king in Hungary. In practice this meant shared common foreign and defence policies, but internally each was governed by its own constitution. As a result of the compromise most Slovenes remained within Austria, though a small, yet significant, number were

1470	1511	1550
Ottoman Turks advance on Slovenia	Ljubljana almost completely destroyed by earthquake	Protestant reformer Primož Trubar publishes the first books in the Slovene language

incorporated into Hungarian and Italian sectors. Around this time Slovenes began to make important strides politically, organizing themselves into distinct and identifiable political groupings, and by the end of the century three core parties had been established: the liberal **National Progressive Party**, the conservative, or clerical, **Slovene People's Party** and the socialist **Yugoslav Democratic Party**.

Each presented alternative political philosophies, but they collectively espoused a common commitment to some form of pan-Slavism, or **Yugoslavism**, a political concept that had initially taken root earlier that century. However, despite adopting broadly nationalist agendas, all three parties remained firmly committed to their Austrian overlords, aware that they were too small and there were too few of them (even with their Slav allies) to go it alone. Instead, they concluded that **Trialism** – the notion that a third element, a South Slav component, would be created within the Habsburg Empire – could be the only possible framework for any form of Slovene self-determination. The latter part of the century was also a time of cultural efflorescence for Slovenes, with the establishment of **reading societies** (*iitalnice*), the **Slovene Literary Society** (Slovenska Matica) and the **Sokol** (Falcon) association, a patriotic gymnastic society that advocated the cult of the healthy body as well as Slavonic brotherhood.

In the two decades before World War I, Slovene political life became increasingly preoccupied with the idea of Yugoslavism, and while most Slovenes ostensibly remained loyal to Austria, there were those who felt increasingly uneasy with regard to Austria's domestic and foreign policies, and in particular its progressively cosy alliance with Germany. Championing the Yugoslav cause was the celebrated novelist **Ivan Cankar**, who posited that some form of linguistic and cultural merging was both practical and desirable. Cankar was closely associated with the avowedly anti-Austrian student organization **Preporod** (Rebirth), which, along with other South Slav groups, including the ultranationalist Young Bosnian movement from Sarajevo, advocated an independent Yugoslav state. Following the **assassination of Archduke Franz Ferdinand** in Sarajevo in 1914 by Gavrilo Princip (a member of the Young Bosnians), Austria declared war on Serbia. Within a matter of days, Europe's major alliance systems had been activated – Germany joined forces with Austria, while their opponents, who supported Serbia, were the Entente powers of Russia, France and Britain.

World War I and the Kingdom of Serbs, Croats and Slovenes

During the formative stages of **World War I**, Slovenes fought in several arenas on behalf of the Austrian crown, including the Serbian and Russian fronts, though the prospect of fighting fellow Slavs appealed to few Slovenes and defections were common. The single most important factor affecting Slovenia during the war was the **1915 London Pact**, which persuaded Italians to join the Entente forces in return for promises of land populated by Slovenes and Croats. Galvanized into action, Slovenes pitched in with the Austrians along the Western **Soča front**, which extended for some 90km from Mount Rombon, near Bovec, along the course of the Soča River down to a position just north of Trieste on the Adriatic coast. The Soča Front was one of the bloodiest battlegrounds of the entire war, with catastrophic losses on both sides, though particularly for the Italians who were routed during the famous twelfth and final offensive in the Krn mountain range above Kobarid in October 1917.

1573	**1760–1820**	**1800**
Peasant revolts	Period of Slovene Enlightenment	Slovenia's greatest poet, France Prešeren, born

With an increasingly mutinous Slovene military, and the Habsburg Empire on the verge of collapse, a group of South Slav delegates, led by Slovene Anton Korošec, presented the **May 1917 declaration** to Vienna demanding the creation of an autonomous, democratic Slav state within the Habsburg monarchy. The demand was dismissed, but support for a unitary state continued apace and in October 1918, Serb, Croat and Slovene political leaders convened in Zagreb to form the **National Council**, at the same time declaring their independence from Budapest and Vienna. Little more than a month later, on December 1, 1918, in Belgrade, Serbian Prince Alexander Karađorđević declared the establishment of the **Kingdom of Serbs, Croats and Slovenes**, which also incorporated the territories of Bosnia, Montenegro and Macedonia.

At the end of the war, Slovenia's ethnic territory was subject to widescale dismemberment: while the greater part of Slovenia was incorporated into the kingdom, a significant portion of southern Carinthia was ceded to Austria and, under the terms of the **1920 Treaty of Rapallo**, almost a third of Slovene territory – which included the economically important cities of Trieste and Gorizia – was annexed to Italy. The first few years under Italian jurisdiction were bearable, but the situation worsened considerably following Mussolini's ascent to power: political and cultural institutions were banned, public use of the Slovene language was abolished (except in Catholic churches) and all Slavic geographical names were Italianized. While large numbers of Slovenes chose to emigrate during this heightened period of Italian irredentism, many more established political, social and cultural organizations and underground movements, in order to fight for minority rights – some, such as the terror group, **TIRG** (Trst, Istra, Reka, Gorica), had several of its members executed.

For Slovenes living within the new kingdom, the situation was not much better than it was for those in Italy or Austria, and certainly not what they had in mind when they cast their lot with that of their fellow southern Slavs. The centralistic **1921 Vidovdan Constitution**, which established a parliamentary, constitutional monarchy for the kingdom, with Belgrade as its capital and Karađorđević as head of state, immediately buried any aspirations Slovenes (and other constituent groups within the state) may have had for political autonomy. Although traditional liberties were largely protected by the constitution, the rights of liberals and Communists were frequently infringed and the king wielded almost absolute power. Years of political chaos – ineffectual governments, high-profile assassinations and persistent attempts to undermine Serb rule – culminated in the suspension of the constitution in January 1929.

Kingdom of Yugoslavia

A **royal dictatorship** was imposed and the Kingdom of Serbs, Croats and Slovenes was recast as the **Kingdom of Yugoslavia**, ostensibly to foster Yugoslav political unitarism but which was ultimately a disaster for all non-Serbs. Increasingly violent nationalist strains began to emerge among the constituent groups, particularly in Croatia, where the ultranationalist, proto-fascist **Ustaše** movement were particularly prominent – it was they who masterminded the assassination of King Alexander Karađorđević in Marseille in 1934. Authority, thereafter, passed to Prince Paul, whose regime merely escalated anti-Serb sentiment.

Another organization opposed to the unitary Yugoslav state was the **Communist Party of Yugoslavia** (CPY), which, from the time of its formation in 1919 until the mid-1930s,

1809	**1813**	**1848**
Ljubljana designated the administrative centre of the Illyrian Provinces	Slovenian territory reincorporated into Habsburg lands following Napoleon's defeat	Revolutions around Europe; Slovene nationalism on the rise

had remained a largely underground movement, with many of its congresses held abroad and most of its activity supervised from Moscow. With the appointment, in 1937, of **Josip Broz Tito** as its leader, the party began to reorganize itself into a federation of national units – hence the birth of the **Communist Party of Slovenia** (CPS). Of immediate concern to Slovenia was the menacing presence of Italian Fascism and German imperialism, for both Italy and Germany had territorial designs on Slovene lands.

World War II

Whereas in World War I Slovenia and the other Slav states found themselves embroiled in combat from the very start, it was more than eighteen months after the start of **World War II** before Yugoslavia (and by implication, Slovenia) became involved. By this time much of continental Europe had already fallen under the sway of Germany and Italy. After initially being cowed into joining the Axis powers' orbit, Yugoslavia renounced the decision following a governmental coup, a decision they paid for on April 6, 1941, when Germany blitzed Belgrade. The king fled in exile to London and within a matter of days the country had capitulated. For its part, Slovenia was partitioned between Germany, which claimed the northern and eastern areas, Hungary, which took Prekmurje, and Italy, which annexed the rest. While the Italians were more or less sympathetic to Slovenes, allowing them a measure of cultural autonomy, those in the German and Hungarian occupied territories were subject to aggressive denaturalizing policies – arrests, torture, execution and deportation.

In response, **resistance groups** took up arms almost immediately. Organized by the CPY, with Tito as chief military commander, a **Yugoslav Partisan resistance** movement was established. In Slovenia, the **Liberation Front** (OF – Osvobodilna Fronta) was formed, organized and controlled by the CPS; it comprised Christian Socialists, the liberal Sokols and leftist intellectuals, as well as party members. The Liberation Front was broken up into smaller Partisan units, dispersed throughout the cities and countryside – circumstances, however, dictated that in the early stages at least, the Slovenes and Tito's Partisans were mostly detached from each other. The Slovene Partisan army continued in a fairly independent manner until 1944, when they joined forces in a wider pan-Yugoslav resistance movement, which had by now received official recognition from the Allies. By this stage Tito had already moved to establish a provisional government, the **Anti-Fascist Assembly for the National Liberation of Yugoslavia** (AVNOJ), which laid down the principles for the eventual Yugoslav state. For the most part, the terms of the programme – one of which made provision for a republic's right to self-determination (this was later dropped) – were welcomed by the Slovenes, as confirmed by their participation at the second AVNOJ meeting in Jajce, Bosnia, in 1943.

Communist resistance was complicated by conflicting political ideologies within Slovenia, demonstrated by the emergence of several armed organizations. The most prominent of these was the **Home Guard** (Domobranci), a major anti-Communist organization formed in Ljubljana in September 1943 with the approval and assistance of the Germans. Its resistance, however, didn't last long. Faced by overwhelming Partisan force, the Guard was forced to retreat into Austrian Carinthia, where it was met by the British and disarmed as German collaborators. Following their repatriation to Slovenia and the waiting Partisans, thousands of guardists and anti-Communist civilians (estimates suggest up to ten thousand in total) were executed and thrown into

1857	1914	1915–17
Vienna to Trieste railway line opens	Assassination of Archduke Franz Ferdinand in Sarajevo sparks World War I	Fighting on the Soča Front during World War I leaves around a million dead

pits close to the Liberation Fronts' wartime headquarters in the forests of **Kočevski Rog** in southern Slovenia. The grisly secrets were only revealed to the wider Slovene public some thirty years later, when politician and writer Edvard Kocbek spilled the beans in an interview with a Trieste newspaper.

Having finally driven the occupying forces from Slovene territory in May 1945, the Partisans liberated Trieste that same month, but just two months later the Western Allies issued an ultimatum requiring Yugoslav forces to leave. At the 1946 Paris Peace Conference the region was partitioned into two zones: Zone A (Trieste and hinterland), controlled by the Allies, and Zone B (Slovene coast and Istria), controlled by Yugoslavia. The **1954 London Agreement** restored Zone A to Italy, thus bringing an end to a bitter and long-standing dispute, though many Italians returned to Italy, as others had done at the end of the war.

The second Yugoslavia: Tito and socialism

Following the émigré government's recognition of Tito as *de facto* leader, **elections** were held towards the end of 1945, though given that the only party standing was the **People's Front**, an organization dominated by the Communist Party, these were something of a foregone conclusion. Following these elections, the monarchy was abolished and in November the **Federal People's Republic of Yugoslavia** was proclaimed, comprising six federal republics – Serbia, Croatia, Bosnia, Macedonia, Montenegro and Slovenia.

Power was now incontrovertibly held in the hands of the Communists, who sought to emulate the Soviet model of control, a system shaped by central planning, nationalization of property and ideological conformity – this also included a substantial amount of **forced industrialization** throughout the entire country, although the speed with which this was done created numerous problems, not least the decline in agricultural practices, as individual and large institutional landowners were expropriated without compensation. A critical rift over political and ideological differences between the Soviet Union and Yugoslavia in 1948 resulted in the latter's **expulsion from the Cominform**, the Soviet-controlled organization of European communist countries. The split effected an almost immediate (albeit cosmetic) change in name of both the Communist Party of Yugoslavia, renamed the **League of Communists of Yugoslavia** (LCY), and the Communist Party of Slovenia, renamed the **League of Communists of Slovenia** (LCS).

More importantly, it presented Tito with an opportunity to fashion his own, alternative brand of communism, one that featured a mix of socialist and capitalist ideals. The basic institution at the heart of "Titoism", as it was known, was a system of **workers' self-management** with the slogan "Factories to the workers!" Such an approach, however, invited dissent in the form of strikes and political criticism, particularly in Slovenia. In the international arena, Tito manoeuvred carefully, his policy of **non-alignment** enabling Yugoslavia to secure prestigious international endorsement. Meanwhile, those party members suspected of collaborating with Stalin (known as "Conformists") were immediately purged and packed off to concentration camps, such as the notorious Goli Otok (Bare Island) camp in the Adriatic. With regard to this, there were few dissidents on the Slovene side, the Slovene Communists well aware that supporting a federal Yugoslav republic was their only option, especially given that such a Yugoslavia would support Slovenia's claims to ethnic territory in Italy and Austria.

1918	**1920**	**1929**
Kingdom of Serbs, Croats and Slovenes established	Treaty of Rapallo sees a third of Slovene lands annexed to Italy	Kingdom of Yugoslavia formed

The 1960s and 1970s

Yugoslavia in the **1960s** was characterized by strong economic growth and improved living conditions, particularly for Slovenes, many of whom could travel freely abroad, a liberty denied to citizens of most other countries in the Eastern bloc, including many within the Yugoslav federation itself. That said, Slovenes were becoming increasingly resentful at the federal bureau's centrally planned means of redistribution, whereby money was siphoned off to support the less wealthy republics in the federation, thereby stifling their own economic development.

The so-called **Road Affair** of 1969 was indicative of such problems. Having solicited funds from the World Bank for the development of its road network – in order to better facilitate trade and increase tourism opportunities – the federal authorities redistributed the money to road projects in other republics instead, triggering widespread protests throughout Slovenia. The federal bureau merely dismissed the protest as nothing more than the work of a bunch of renegade Slovene nationalists. In any case, the Road Affair signalled the end of the **liberalization movement** of the 1960s, whose members had pushed for major market economic reforms throughout Yugoslavia. Fearful of losing control, the conservative Communists purged the party of its stronger liberal elements, before turning their attention to those in other institutions – universities, intellectual journals and the media.

Numerous **constitutional amendments and changes** repeatedly brought to the surface old arguments about decentralization and the need for greater autonomy, with Slovenia invariably at the forefront of these disputes. The **1974 constitution** went a stage further than previous ones, giving more autonomy to Vojvodina and Kosovo, and making provision for each republic to assume greater responsibility for its own internal affairs. However, the issue of centralism versus federalism, a recurring theme since the formation of the Kingdom of Serbs, Croats and Slovenes back in 1918, remained at the forefront of Slovene and Yugoslav political life up to and following **Tito's death** in 1980.

The 1980s

With the death of its founding father, the federal construct began to fall apart in dramatic fashion: Yugoslavia had racked up enormous foreign debt and unemployment, inflation had reached unacceptably high levels and **inter-republic relations** were at an all-time low. Of particular concern were the worsening relations between the Serbs and the Albanian majority in the autonomous province of Kosovo in southern Serbia, where riots in 1981 were followed by further draconian anti-Albanian measures, culminating in the annulment of the province's autonomy in 1989. On the domestic front, in 1986, **Milan Kučan** was elected president of the League of Communists of Slovenia, who were by now struggling to reconcile the political and ideological doctrines of the Yugoslav League of Communists with the increasingly widespread pluralistic inclinations pervading Slovenian society around this time.

In particular, it was the emergence of **avant-garde and alternative movements** (also known as new social movements) – foremost among these were the arts collective **Neue Slowenische Kunst** (New Slovene Art), one of whose members was the legendary punk rock group Laibach (see p.312) – that paved the way for the democratization of Slovene society. No less influential were the countercultural **magazines** *Nova Revija*

1937	1941	1945
Birth of the Communist Party of Slovenia	Slovenia occupied by German, Italian and Hungarian forces; anti-fascist resistance groups (Partisans) formed	Slovenia becomes a constituent state within the Federal People's Republic of Yugoslavia, with Tito as president

(*New Review*) and *Mladina* (*Youth*), both of which provided broad-based platforms for cultural and intellectual expression and exchange, as well as political dialogue and debate. In *Nova Revija*'s infamous issue no. 57 (February 1987), the magazine published "Contributions to a Slovene National Programme", a collection of papers that outlined provisions for Slovenian self-determination (this essentially echoed and amplified the content of Revija 57, a document that had appeared exactly thirty years earlier). Despite intense pressure from the federal government, the Slovene authorities refused to acquiesce to Belgrade's demands for those responsible to be prosecuted.

Mladina, meanwhile, continued to provoke with its fearless and often humorous attacks on key groups and individuals within the Yugoslav federation, and articles on social taboos such as homosexuality and World War II massacres. In 1988, three of the magazine's members, along with an officer, were hauled up before a military court on trumped-up charges of betraying state secrets (widely believed to be a plan for military intervention in Slovenia), an affair known as the **Ljubljana Four Trial**. Conducted entirely in secret and in Serbo-Croatian, the trial was considered unconstitutional by most Slovenes, and served only to radicalize political opinion towards Belgrade. The trial, and the mass rallies that it inspired, represented the last hurrah for these movements, which became increasingly marginalized thereafter. However, despite fewer and less obvious targets these days, *Mladina* remains an influential and topical political journal.

The **fall of the Berlin Wall** in November 1989 set in motion a chain of events that convulsed Eastern Europe, culminating in the bloody overthrow of Ceaușescu in Romania. These events, though, had little direct effect on Yugoslavia, which was readying itself for its own, spectacular, implosion.

The road to independence

At the fourteenth and final **Congress of the Yugoslav League of Communists** in January 1990, Slovenian calls for absolute independence for the respective communist parties were given short shrift by the Serbs. In response, the Slovene delegation walked out of the assembly, an incident that effectively spelled the end of the Yugoslav Communist Party. Just three months later, in April 1990, the country's first ever multiparty elections were won by the coalition Demos Party (Democratic Opposition of Slovenia), while **Milan Kučan**, the reformed Communist leader of the Party of Democratic Renewal (SDP) – formerly the League of Communists of Slovenia – was sworn in as president. Immediately after the elections, a number of constitutional amendments were implemented, thus paving the way for eventual separation from the Yugoslav federation.

The one remaining obstacle was **Serbia**, which, with Slobodan Milošević in charge and championing a greater Serbia, now had control of four of the eight votes on the federal presidency (those of Vojvodina, Kosovo and Montenegro, in addition to its own), prompting Slovenes to coin the phrase "Serboslavia". Undaunted, Slovenia pressed on, and in December that year a **plebiscite for independence** was held, the result of which was an overwhelming 88 percent vote (the turn-out was 93 percent) for a split with the federation. Six months later, on June 25, 1991, the Slovene Parliament passed a constitutional law declaring independence, thus triggering the **Ten-Day War** (see box opposite). **Slovene independence** was formally recognized by the European Union on January 15, 1992, and the country was officially admitted into the United Nations on May 22.

1948	1954	1969
Yugoslavia expelled from the Cominform, leading to a policy of non-alignment	London Agreement sees Trieste restored to Italy and Slovenia gain northern Istria	The Road Affair fuels widespread protests throughout Slovenia

THE TEN-DAY WAR

Even as Slovenes were celebrating the declaration of independence in Ljubljana on the night of June 26, 1991, the Serb-dominated **Yugoslav army** (JNA) had begun manoeuvring tank units towards Ljubljana's Brnik airport, and some thirty border posts that Slovenia had taken over following the declaration. The well-drilled Slovenian defence comprised the Territorial Defence (which itself was removed from the JNA's jurisdiction in a constitutional amendment the previous year) and the police, and was orchestrated by Minister of Defence Janez Janša – ironically one of those implicated in the Ljubljana Four Trial three years earlier.

As Slovene soldiers and officers began **deserting** the Yugoslav army in droves, the first strikes took place, though the capture of Brnik and threatened assault on the capital itself never materialized. In the end, there were few major clashes, with the majority of engagements being small-scale skirmishes at key traffic points and border positions. Nevertheless, and much to the surprise of the Yugoslav army – as well as neutral observers and many Slovenes themselves – the Slovene forces proved themselves to be more than competent adversaries, forcing around 2500 JNA troops to desert or **surrender**, while many more were captured. Following a flurry of diplomatic activity and several attempts to mediate by European Union representatives, the ten-day conflict was brought to an end on July 7, following the brokering of the Brioni Agreement, which provided for an **immediate ceasefire** and **withdrawal** of the Yugoslav army. Moreover, it stipulated that Slovenia put its declaration of independence on hold for a further three months. In human terms, the price was relatively low: officially, 21 Slovenes (military and civilian) were killed and a further 100 wounded, while 39 Yugoslav troops were killed and around 160 wounded.

The reason for Belgrade's confused and rather diffident policy in Slovenia was unclear, though most analysts concurred that it was based on an (ill-founded) assumption that a short, sharp show of force would be enough to cow the Slovenes into submission – failing that, they could resort to a policy of escalation. Their humiliating climbdown, meanwhile, was attributed to the fact that Serbia had no strong territorial or ethnic claims to Slovenia.

The 1990s

While the war continued to savage effect in Croatia and Bosnia, Slovenia was facing up to the difficult transition from communist to **market economy**. Despite possessing an already relatively sound economy, Slovenia still faced considerable problems: namely, rising unemployment, low salaries and high inflation, while additional strains were being placed on the economy as a result of the influx of refugees fleeing the chaos in Croatia and Bosnia. The task of economic restructuring was further complicated by the necessary imposition of **trade barriers** with the other republics, hitherto its most important markets. Moreover, potential foreign investors were frightened off by the perceived political risks associated with the ongoing **hostilities in the region**. It was for this reason that tourist numbers remained well below the levels the country experienced prior to the war, when it was one of the most popular destinations in Yugoslavia. However, the introduction of a **new currency** (the tolar), coupled with reforms in the banking and public service sectors and the creation of new institutions, gradually smoothed the path to economic stability.

Slovenia's first **multiparty elections** as an independent nation took place in December 1992, by which stage internal discord within the Demos coalition had seen that party disband. Of the eight parties to win seats in the ninety-member parliament, it was the reform-oriented centre-left Liberal Democratic Party, led by the introverted yet competent

1980	Mid-1980s	1990
Tito dies in Ljubljana	New social movements, such as the influential New Slowenische Kunst, emerge	First multiparty elections; Milan Kučan becomes president

Janez Drnovšek (he was also president of the Yugoslav Federation from May 1989 to May 1990), who secured the greatest number of votes (22 percent), followed by the centre-right Slovene Christian Democrats. Drnovšek himself was elected head of the coalition government. That same month saw the popular and avuncular Kučan returned as president, thus cementing his considerable standing in Slovene politics. Four years down the line, the 1996 elections yielded similar results, with the Liberal Democrats once again topping the polls, leaving Drnovšek to form a coalition government with seven other parties, despite the clear ideological differences between them. In November the following year, the unassailable Kučan was re-elected president for a second and final term.

Europe and the new millennium

Since the early 1990s Slovenia had been regarded as one of the outstanding candidates for EU accession among the Central and East European countries, which was in part a reflection of the country's relatively strong economic and political standing. Obstacles remained, however, not least a simmering feud between Slovenia and **Italy** over disputed property rights, and in particular the issue of **restitution of property** to Italian owners who had emigrated from Yugoslavia after World War II, an issue Slovenes claimed had been resolved in 1983 following the Treaty of Rome.

Relations with **Croatia** were no less troubled, by far the thorniest issue concerning the long-standing dispute over **sea borders** in the Bay of Piran. The initial problem arose because no sea border ever existed during the time of Yugoslavia, and neither was one defined once the two countries had seceded from the federation. Following a series of incidents in the disputed waters, the situation reached crisis point in the summer of 2003, when Croatia unilaterally announced its intention to declare an Exclusive Economic Zone (EEZ), a move vehemently opposed by Slovenia, which argued that it would be impossible to create such a zone if the boundaries of the territorial waters hadn't been defined. Moreover, any such zone would effectively invalidate Slovenia's right to access international waters. In 2009, an internationally brokered solution was endorsed by both sides, with Slovenia simultaneously stating that it would no longer block Croatia's negotiations to join the European Union. However, as of 2017, issues still remained, thus ensuring this is one dispute that seems destined to run and run.

During **parliamentary elections** in October 2000, the ruling Liberal Democrats, with Drnovšek still firmly in command, once again eased to victory, their third in succession. Two years later, in December 2002, the **presidential elections** saw an end to the decade-long Kučan-Drnovšek union, for Kučan was obliged to stand down, having served the maximum two terms allowed in the constitution. His retirement paved the way for Drnovšek as his successor and opened the door for a new prime minister, a post duly taken up by finance minister and vice-president of the senior coalition party (Liberal Democrats), Anton Rop. Rop was immediately assigned the task of forming a new government from a broad-based coalition of four parties.

On the international front, **NATO membership** was finally confirmed in March 2004, and was followed on May 1 by the country's **admission into the European Union** alongside nine other central-eastern European countries. Slovenia also claimed a minor coup when it became the first of the ten new member states to **introduce the euro currency**, in January 2007.

1991	2004	2007
Slovenia declares independence, triggering the Ten-Day War	Slovenia joins NATO and the European Union	Slovenia becomes the first former communist state to adopt the euro

Parliamentary elections in October 2004 – the fourth since independence, which also saw the lowest-ever turnout – resulted in a surprisingly comfortable victory for the opposition Slovenian Democratic Party (SDS) over the Liberal Democrats, the first time that the latter had been ousted since independence. Anton Rop was replaced as prime minister by **Janez Janša**, best known as one of the defendants in the infamous Ljubljana Four Trial in 1988 (see p.304), which resulted in his imprisonment for six months. Following his release, Janša helped found the Slovenian Democratic Union (SDZ), after which he became defence minister, a position he held during the Ten-Day War of independence.

Owing to increasing ill-health, Drnovšek did not run for the 2007 presidential elections, and was succeeded by the leftist former diplomat, **Danilo Tuerk**. Having since turned his attention to environmental issues, Drnovšek – one of the key figures in Slovenia's drive for both independence and EU membership – died in February 2008. Tuerk, meanwhile, was sworn in just in time for Slovenia's assumption of the EU presidency in January 2008, the first former communist state to have had this honour bestowed. Parliamentary elections later that year saw Janša and his Slovenian Democratic Party narrowly defeated by the Social Democrats, led by the hitherto little-known **Borut Pahor**, who headed up a centre-left coalition comprising three other parties.

From 2010

Since the 2008 election, the country's political landscape has been pretty turbulent by Slovenian standards. In September 2011, Pahor's coalition government collapsed after losing a confidence vote in parliament. This was followed, two months later, by a surprising victory for the newly formed **Positive Slovenia** party, led by the mayor of Ljubljana, **Zoran Janković**; however, parliament summarily rejected Janković's candidacy as prime minister, which paved the way for Janez Janša to return to office as head of a centre-right coalition. At the same time, widespread disillusionment with increased austerity measures, allied to further allegations of corruption at the highest levels, led to protests – occasionally violent – in the major cities. Meanwhile, the merry-go-round continued in 2012 when Tuerk was replaced as president by Pahor, a post he still held as of 2017. In 2013, allegations of impropriety against Janša saw him not only shoved out of office, but later that year (in what must have been a familiar feeling) imprisoned, where he remained for six months. In the meantime, the role of prime minister had been taken up by Alenka Bratušek of the Positive Slovenia party, the first woman to hold this position. She lasted until May 2014, before a snap election saw **Miro Cerar** (whose Modern Centre party had only been formed one month earlier) assume the mantle.

In the meantime, Janković – who, as of 2017, was serving his second term as mayor of Ljubljana – has set about transforming the cityscape, which has included funding the construction of the Stožice national stadium and pedestrianizing huge swathes of the city centre; it was this, among many other initiatives, that helped secure Ljubljana the title of **European Green Capital** in 2016. However, allegations of corruption continue to swirl around Janković, as they have done for much of his business and political life. Notwithstanding all this political upheaval, the economy is in recovery, while Slovenia's reputation as a safe, welcoming – and green – country means that its stock as a **tourist destination** continues to rise.

2012	2014	2016
Protests staged against government corruption and austerity measures	Miro Cerar becomes the third prime minister in three years	Ljubljana is European Green Capital

Books and film

There's a dearth of books about Slovenia in the English language, in every genre. What recent titles there are – particularly travelogues and historical or political publications – tend to revolve almost exclusively around the other countries of the former Yugoslavia. Slovenia's literary heritage, however, is strong, and while there's little available in translation, there are several impressive anthologies to choose from. Similarly, Slovenia has yielded some terrific, and influential, filmmakers in recent years, though few are known beyond the country's borders.

Books

The number of publications dedicated to the **break-up of Yugoslavia** is considerable, yet in most cases there is scant coverage of Slovenia's involvement in the conflict. While you'll find some reference to Slovenia in the titles reviewed in our bibliography, the following are excellent reads in their own right, and well worth dipping into if you're travelling more widely around the region: Misha Glenny, *The Fall of Yugoslavia*; John Allcock, *Explaining Yugoslavia*; John Lampe, *Yugoslavia as History – Twice There Was a Country* and *Balkans into Southeastern Europe 1914–2014*; Patrick Hyder Patterson, *Bought and Sold: Living and Losing the Good Life in Socialist Yugoslavia*; Branka Magas and Ivo Žanič, *The War in Croatia and Bosnia-Herzegovina 1991–1995*; and Dejan Djokič, *Elusive Compromise: A History of Interwar Yugoslavia*.

Literature

Although written records in Slovenian appeared as early as the tenth century, **Slovenian literature** began systematically to develop during the **sixteenth-century Reformation**. This development was thanks to leading reformers Primož Trubar (writer of the first Slovene book, the primer *Abecedarium*, in 1550), Jurij Dalmatin (the first Slovene translation of the Bible, in 1584) and linguist Adam Bohorič, whose *Arcticae Horulae* (*Winter Hours*) was the first Slovene grammar book, written in Latin and published the same year as Dalmatin's Bible. Around a century later Janez Vajkard Valvasor (see box, p.223) wrote and published (in German) the seminal *Glory of the Duchy of Carniola*, which synthesized the country's history, sights and peoples in one encyclopedic, four-volume work; to this day it remains the single most important document written about the Slovene lands.

Slovene literature reached its first peak during the period of **Romanticism** in the early nineteenth century, thanks to the poet France Prešeren (see box, p.113), the most iconic literary figure in Slovenia's history. Very little of Prešeren's work has been translated into English, but the audio CD *Sonnets of Unhappiness* is a beautifully read (by Vanessa Redgrave, Katrin Cartlidge and Simon Callow) collection of the poet's key works. The next writers to make their mark were the **Realists**, led by the playwright Josip Juričič, whose enduringly popular *Deseti Brat* (*The Tenth Brother*) was the first full-length Slovene novel to be published (1866) – an abridged version is available in English. Literary trends at the start of the twentieth century were shaped by the so-called **Moderna movement**, whose main representatives were Oton Župančič and Ivan Cankar, the second of whom is regarded as Slovenia's finest prose writer; one of the few novels available in English translation, *Martin Kačur: The Biography of an Idealist*, is Cankar's expressive tale of a young schoolteacher and his misguided attempts to enlighten his fellow countrymen as he travels around provincial Slovenia. A prolific and highly politicized essayist and polemicist, Cankar was also one of the first to champion a southern Slav union.

The coexistent movements of Expressionism and Social Realism that had dominated both the artistic and literary landscape prior to, and just after, World War II eventually gave way to Western literary trends, notably **Symbolism** and **Existentialism**. Foremost among these writers was the dissident politician and ex-Partisan Edvard Kocbek, whose opposition to communist ideology and socialist repression manifested itself in a short-story collection, *Strah in Pogum* (*Fear and Courage*), and the diaries *Tovarišija* (*Comrades*) and *Listina* (*The Document*) – it also landed him a spell in prison. Similar critiques of the resistance movement were put forward by other commentators at that time, including Dane Zajc and Tomaž Šalamun, the doyens of Slovene postwar poets.

Prominent among the **new generation** of writers are postmodern fiction writer Andrej Blatnik, whose collection of short stories, *Skinswaps*, is a good introduction to his work; and poet and gay rights activist Brane Mozetič. Also worth seeking out is the late Aleš Debeljak, whose *The City and the Child* is one of his best volumes of poetry. Given that there's only a limited amount of Slovenian **literature in translation**, you're best off starting with one of the several excellent anthologies available: *A Bilingual Anthology of Slovene Literature* includes poems and prose by a panoply of Slovenia's literary greats, from Trubar and Prešeren to Kocbek and Šalamun, while *The Imagination of Terra Incognita: Slovenian Writing 1945–1995* is the best available anthology of essays, poems and fiction by authors from the second half of the last century. A useful reference book is *Key Slovenia: Contemporary Slovenian Literature in Translation*.

BIBLIOGRAPHY

★**Jill Benderley and Evan Craft** *Independent Slovenia: Origins, Movements, Prospects.* Enjoyable and wide-ranging collection of essays pertaining to the country's historical development up to and including independence. The most interesting accounts chart the development of the so-called new social movements of the 1980s (trade unions, women's organizations and the local punk scene), all of which helped fashion a strong and independent civil society in the run-up to independence.

Janez Bogotaj *Handicrafts of Slovenia: Encounters with Contemporary Slovene Craftsmen.* Beautifully illustrated work covering Slovenia's rich tradition of crafts, including ceramicists, potters, lace-makers, weavers and glass-painters.

Justi Carey and Roy Clark *The Julian Alps of Slovenia.* Cicerone's useful pocket-sized book, updated in 2015, detailing nearly sixty trails throughout the Julian Alps, with treks starting from Bled, Bohinj, Bovec, Kobarid and Kranjska Gora. Cicerone also publishes *Mountain Biking in Slovenia*, which covers 35 full- and half-day bike trips throughout the country.

★**John Corsellis and Marcus Ferrar** *Slovenia 1945: Memories of Death and Survival after World War II.* Sympathetic and superbly accomplished account documenting the fate of the large Catholic, non-Communist Slovene migrant community (including members of the anti-Communist Home Guard) during and after World War II.

Aleš Debeljak *Twilight of the Idols: Recollections of a Lost Yugoslavia.* Better known for fiction and poetry (see above), the late Slovene novelist turns his attention to politics in this critical reflection on the disintegration of

Yugoslavia, though his portrayal of the Serbs as outright aggressors is overly subjective.

★**James Gow and Cathie Carmichael** *Slovenia and the Slovenes: A Small State and the New Europe.* The most thoroughgoing assessment of twentieth-century Slovenian history currently available. The introductory chapter sets the tone with an illuminating overview of the country, and is followed by very readable accounts of Slovenia's cultural, economic and political maturation; the book concludes with a revealing insight into the events surrounding the country's drive for independence and the Ten-Day War. Updated in 2010.

Andrej Hrausky and Janez Koželj *Architectural Guide to Ljubljana.* Insightful guide to one hundred of the capital's buildings, from its castles and churches to its many Baroque and Secessionist splendours, as well as most of the projects conceived by Slovenia's greatest urban planner, Jože Plečnik. For more on Plečnik, try the more detailed *Plečnik's Ljubljana* and *National and University Library Ljubljana*.

Lojze Kovačič *Newcomers.* This acclaimed author's richly detailed novel – the first volume of an autobiographical trilogy – chronicles his harrowing experiences as a 10-year-old boy after his family's 1938 expulsion from Switzerland (the country of his birth) to Slovenia. The translation, by Michael Biggins, is wonderful.

Oto Luthar (ed) *The Land Between: A History of Slovenia.* Written by a team of Slovene scholars, this is a solid, well-researched history of the country, with particularly enlightening chapters on the early Slav settlements through to the Middle Ages.

Tine Mihelič *Mountaineering in Slovenia*. Excellent and easy-to-follow guide to tackling Slovenia's most important summits, in the Julian, Kamnik and Savinja Alps and the Karavanke mountains. Complete with diagrams and lots of glossy pictures.

★**Alexei Monroe** *Interrogation Machine: Laibach and NSK*. Thorough and fascinating insight into the workings of the provocative avant-garde Slovene collective NSK, the most famous and controversial component of which was the rock band Laibach (see p.312).

Julij Nemanič and Janez Bogataj *Wines of Slovenia*. This comprehensive handbook, featuring some beautifully illustrated pictures, is the definitive guide to the country's wines (with ratings for each) and wine-growing districts; a must for anyone serious about Slovenian wine.

Nigel Thomas *The Yugoslav Wars: Slovenia and Croatia 1991–95*. Authoritative and well-illustrated guide – including some rare photos – documenting the roles played by the various combatant armies on Slovenian and Croatian territory during the wars of the early 1990s.

Slavoj Žižek and Glyn Daly *Conversations with Žižek*. In this entertaining series of conversations, the renowned Slovene theorist elaborates on various aspects of popular culture and politics, including Marxism, Nazism and the films of Stanley Kubrick; a far more accessible introduction to the mindset of Žižek than his other work.

Film

Cinematography in Slovenia made its mark as early as 1905, with the short documentaries *The Fair at Ljutomer* and *People Leaving the Church*, shot by the pioneer of Slovene film, Karol Grossman. The development of the industry continued apace after World War II – a golden period for Slovene cinema, thanks to the state-financed Triglav Film studio, which produced several classics, such as *Kekec*, Jože Gale's enduringly popular 1952 film about a clever shepherd boy, and France Štiglič's 1956 *Dolina Miru* (*Valley of Peace*).

Today, despite the fact that it has one of the lowest cinematic outputs among central-eastern European countries, Slovenia is producing some fine movies, and some fine directors. By far the most successful and celebrated film in recent years – it was actually a joint Belgian-French-Italian-Slovenian project, and shot in the village of Bač near Postojna – was **Nikogaršnje Ozemlje** (**No Man's Land**) by Bosnian director Danis Tanovič, which won an Oscar for Best Foreign Film in 2001. Featuring a Bosnian and a Serb as the two protagonists trapped together in a trench somewhere between enemy lines, it's an acute, compassionate and darkly comic dissection of a pitiless conflict, and without doubt one of the most affecting movies ever made about the Yugoslav wars. Another landmark Slovenian film, and winner of the prestigious Golden Lion award at the 2001 Venice Film festival, **Kruh in Mleko** (**Bread and Milk**) is the outstanding debut by Jan Cvetkovič, a brooding social commentary on the effects of alcoholism and alienation in small-town Slovenia.

Other films to look out for include Damjan Kožole's *Rezervni Deli* (*Spare Parts*), a gritty, sobering drama about human trafficking across Slovenia; the humorous *Kajmak in Marmelada* (*Cheese and Jam*), which explores race, immigration and happiness in contemporary Slovenia – directed by and starring the respected Bosnian actor Branko Djurič (also the lead actor in *No Man's Land*); *Varuh Meje* (*Guardians of the Frontier*), a creepy, atmospheric tale of sexual discovery down on the Kolpa River; *Petelinji Zajtrk* (*Rooster's Breakfast*), a sympathetic love story set in a village in Prekmurje; and the dense, moody thriller, *9:06*. The most intriguing film of recent years, however, is 2015's action-horror, **Idila** (**Idyll**), which is anything but; a tale of abduction and hoped-for survival, it touches upon many of modern-day Slovenia's social ills.

Music

As in other spheres of the arts and culture, Slovenia's musical heritage is surprisingly strong, from ancient folk traditions to a punk/rock scene that, during the 1980s, spawned some of the most exciting and controversial music in the former Yugoslavia. Although Slovenia has few jazz artists of its own, the genre has a small yet devout following, as shown by the increasing number of bars with live music and a world-class summer jazz festival in Ljubljana (see box, p.74). In general, Slovenia has no shortage of music events, chief among which is the world music festival, Druga Godba (see box, p.74), and some superb classical music gatherings around the country each summer, notably in Brežice, Piran and Radovljica.

Folk music

The most traditional forms of **Slovenian folk music** are based on age-old folk literature and poems and utilize instruments such as the *okarina* (clay flute), *trstenka* (panpipe), *drumlja* (Jew's harp) and *gudalo*, a small clay pot over the top of which a pig's bladder is stretched – the bass sound emitted is made by rubbing the straw rod that extends up through the membrane. Although its role in everyday life has largely diminished, you are likely to come across traditional music during local festivals.

Some of the best Slovene folk music in recent years has come out of the small village of Beltinci in Prekmurje, in particular from the remarkable **Beltinška Banda Kociper**, a kind of Mitteleuropean Buena Vista Social Club, whose members, playing the fiddle (a stock Prekmurje instrument), violin, clarinet, cimbalom, double bass and accordion, have been delighting audiences for more than half a century. The baton has now been passed down to a new generation of musicians from the same village, namely the five-strong **Mlada Beltinška Banda**. Another folk band to listen out for are the stunning all-female vocal group **Katice**, who specialize in interpreting classic harmonies from the Rezija mountain valley region on the Italian side of the Julian Alps.

No self-respecting gathering is complete without some form of **dancing**, which, like songs, varies greatly from region to region. The oldest dances developed in Bela Krajina during the sixteenth century and were heavily influenced by the Uskoks, bands of renegades from Serbia and Croatia who fled the Turks and settled in the region. The most popular dance is the *kolo*, an energetic, circular group dance performed to musical and vocal accompaniment. The dances of Prekmurje are less exuberant affairs – typical is the *tkalecka* (weaver's dance), a kind of skipping dance whereby handkerchiefs are waved under the knees (reminiscent of an English Morris dance) – while those of Primorska are altogether more refined, having been established in bourgeois circles.

Although not strictly folk, **Terrafolk** is a group of four academically and classically trained musicians whose free-ranging repertoire of Balkan, Gypsy, folk, klezmer, Irish and classical pretty much defies categorization. Featuring an eclectic set of violin, flute, guitar, drums, accordion and double bass, Terrafolk's reputation has largely been built on their entertaining live shows, which combine ebullient musicianship with roguish humour. A former member of the group, accordionist **Marko Hatlak**, now fronts his own band, who deliver a dizzying fusion of pop, jazz, funk, Latin and blues. Another fine live prospect is the marvellous six-piece **Katalena**, another slightly unorthodox outfit who marry traditional folk forms with souped-up jazz and blues to beautiful effect.

Rock and pop

Although a number of creative bands emerged throughout Yugoslavia in the 1970s, Ljubljana was the first of the Yugoslav cities to develop an authentic, home-grown musical scene of its own. In particular, it was the emergence of a local punk subculture in the late 1970s, alongside other so-called new social movements, that set the tone for the next few years. The most prominent of the first generation of punk bands were **Pankrti** (The Bastards). They, like the majority of punk groups and their followers at that time, were deemed a threat to civil society by the authorities, who attempted to associate the movement with Nazism; concerts were prohibited and persecution by the police was commonplace. Dismantled by the state in the early 1980s, the punk scene was eventually supplanted by other social movements, most notably an avant-garde collective called **Neue Slowenische Kunst** (New Slovene Art, or NSK), whose core members included the rock group Laibach.

Conceived in the industrial mining town of Trbovlje in 1980, **Laibach** produced some of the most uncompromising music and art ever to come out of the former Yugoslavia. Following an interview on national television in June 1983 – six months after the band's original singer, Tomaž Hostnik, committed suicide – Laibach were summarily banned from appearing in public. The authorities argued that the band's use of the German language (Laibach is the German name for Ljubljana, used during both Habsburg rule and the Nazi occupation) and their apparent appropriation of Nazi images was just a cover for the resurgence of fascism. Laibach, meanwhile, maintained that, rather than espousing totalitarianism, they were in fact exposing its ugliest facets. Ostracized, the group embarked on the "Occupied Europe Tour" later that year, a tour that took them to countries on both sides of the Iron Curtain and exposed them for the first time to audiences outside their own country. In 1987, Laibach marked the lifting of the ban with a series of homecoming gigs (the "Bloody Ground-Fertile Soil" tour) in several Yugoslav cities, including Zagreb and Belgrade. Returning to Belgrade two years later, the group delivered a typically incendiary speech, warning against the inflammatory rhetoric of Slobodan Milošević, alongside a screening of a 1941 German propaganda film on the bombing of the Serbian capital.

Since their eponymously titled debut in 1985, Laibach have released more than a dozen albums. Their earlier recordings were wilfully experimental, avant-garde exercises, which drew heavily on the electronic minimalism of Kraftwerk and DAF – as a result they do not make for easy listening. Towards the end of the 1980s the group moved towards a more accessible rock sound, thanks in part to their predilection for doing cover albums, namely the Beatles' *Let it Be*, and the Stones' *Sympathy for the Devil*, neither of which will sound quite the same again once you've heard Laibach's version. The group returned to familiar ground with the 1994 release, *NATO*, which anticipated the expansion of Western influence in the region, while 1996's metal-driven *Jesus Christ Superstars* marked another shift in musical direction.

After a seven-year hiatus, Laibach returned with *WAT* (We Are Time), marking a return to the heavy techno/industrial rhythms of earlier albums – which was followed by *Volk* and *LaiBachKunstDerFuge*, the former a collection of surprisingly melodic interpretations of national anthems, the latter an uncompromising reworking of Bach's *The Art of Fugue*. Their most recent record, *Spectre*, saw the band re-engage politically, with prescient tracks like *Eurovision*, in which frontman Milan Fras sings, in trademark guttural fashion, that "Europe is Falling Apart". In 2015 Laibach became the first foreign band to play in North Korea, albeit to a slightly bemused audience.

Spearheading Slovenian **pop music** these days is **Siddharta**, whose melodic brand of stadium rock has made them the most successful and popular home-grown outfit since Laibach. Other current pop acts range from mainstream groups (**The Elevators** and **Big Foot Mama**) to dance and techno-inspired performers like **DJ Umek**, a regular on the European house circuit. One of the newest and most impressive bands on the block is **Jardier**, a melodic Ljubljana five-piece.

Two stalwarts of the Slovenian music scene are the singer-songwriter **Vlado Kreslin**, who has kept legions of fans in thrall for nearly two decades with his folksy brand of guitar-based rock, and the perennially popular poet and songwriter **Zoran Predin**, who first came to prominence some twenty years ago as the founder of the rock group Lačni Franz (Hungry Franz).

Discography

The following list is a pointer to some of the recordings available, a few, but not many of them, internationally; rooting around stores and record shops in Slovenia will yield the many more CDs that don't have international distribution.

FOLK MUSIC

Katalena *(Z)godbe* (RTV Slovenia). Luscious-sounding album of traditional songs from Slovenia's most important folk regions, Prekmurje, Istria and Bela Krajina. While remaining faithful to their folk roots, the two subsequent releases, *Babje Leto* and *Kmečka ohcet* (Dallas), feature a denser, rockier sound, while *Cvik Cvak!* (Dallas) is exclusively dedicated to the musical heritage of the Rezija Valley in Italy. Their two most recent albums are *Noč Čarovnic* and *Enci Benci Katalenci,* the latter, entertainingly, based on children's counting rhymes.

Mlada Beltinska Banda *Prekmurje Musical Heritage* (KUD Beltinci). Traditional folk music from the Prekmurje region, as performed by the young Beltinci Band.

Modern Folk Music in Slovenia Volumes I & II (Folk Slovenia Cultural Society). This enjoyable two-disc set is the best introduction to Slovenia's contemporary folk artists, including the female vocal group Katice, Styrian folk trio Kurja Koža and the Marko Banda from Prekmurje.

Slovenian Folk Songs (RTV Slovenia). Four-disc set of narrative folk music recorded on site by the Institute of Ethnomusicology in Ljubljana. Drawing on themes of heroes, legends and love, this voluminous collection brings together poems, songs and instruments from the country's many regions. The excellent sleeve notes help make some sense of it all.

Terrafolk Packed with their trademark effervescent tunes, the band's first two releases, *StereoFolk Live* and *Jumper of Love*, are both live outings recorded in clubs across Slovenia. The third (studio) album, *N'taka*, in a similar vein, features the gorgeous female voices of Katice. Following a return to the live arena with *Live at Queen's Hall*, the diverse and entertaining *Full Circle* features a rather novel reworking of *You Are My Sunshine*. Their most recent release was 2011's *Ice Harvest* (All Music Net).

ROCK/POP MUSIC

Jardier *Jardier* (Spinnup). The band's debut album is packed with lush, guitar-based tunes, with lyrics sung in English throughout.

Laibach The band's earliest works are cassette-only affairs, and very difficult to get hold of. Selected albums available on CD include: *Laibach* (Ropot, 1985); the double box-set *Rekapitulacija 1980–1984* (Mute, 2002); *Nova Akropola* (Cherry Red, 1987); *Opus Dei* (Mute, 1987); *Krst Pod Triglavom* (the soundtrack to NSK's theatre performance that same year; Sub Rosa, 1987); *Let it Be* (Mute, 1988); *Sympathy for the Devil* (Mute, 1990); *Nato* (Mute, 1994); *Jesus Christ Superstars* (Mute, 1996); *The John Peel Sessions* (recordings from two sessions, in 1986 and 1987, with the legendary DJ; Strange Fruit, 2002); *WAT* (Mute, 2003); *Volk* (Mute, 2006); *LaiBachKunstDerFuge* (Mute, 2008); *Spectre* (Mute, 2014). *Anthems* (Mute, 2004) is a best-of album that also contains a superb forty-page booklet, while *Monumental Retro-Avant-Garde* (Mute, 2012) is a recording of their performance at the Tate Modern in London.

Siddharta *ID, Nord and Rh-* (Menart). Released between 1999 and 2003, these are the band's first three albums, the last (and best) of which is available in a limited edition English version. The more garagey-sounding *Petrolea* (2006) was followed by *Saga*, in 2009, while sister albums *Infra* and *Ultra* were released just months apart in 2015.

ROMANY MUSIC

Šukar *Prvo Ti (First Snow;* Nika) and *En Concert 1990–2002* (Etno Karavana). These two offerings (the second a live album) by this five-piece ensemble from Ljubljana feature sumptuous reworkings of traditional Gypsy dance songs and ballads. *Mentol Bombon* is an album of songs recorded with singer songwriter, Zoran Predin.

Slovenian

Although the earliest written records in Slovene date from around 1000 AD, it has existed as a literary language since the middle of the sixteenth century, when the first printed books – including a translation of the Bible – came into being. Today it's spoken by nearly two million people within Slovenia, and around half a million more outside the country's borders. Slovenian is **a Slavic language**, a branch of the Indo-European linguistic family, and is most closely related to Croatian and Serbian, with which it shares quite a few identical words and phrases.

While attempting the odd word or phrase of Slovenian will be appreciated, and can be a fun experience in itself, generally speaking there will be little call for it, as the standard of English among Slovenes – especially the young – is exceptionally high. Many older Slovenes speak **Serbo-Croatian** (as it was formerly called), while **Italian** is widely spoken in the Primorska region, and **Hungarian** in Prekmurje. Regional variations of Slovene abound, and the language is characterized by nearly fifty **dialects** and subdialects.

Pronunciation

Slovenian has **free stress** – it may fall on any syllable of a word. Like English, there are different values for vowels; vowels can be stressed or unstressed, long or short, open or closed, with further subtle variations in the pronunciation. The Slovenian consonants are mostly pronounced as they are spelt. Letters not included below are pronounced as in English. There are no explosive or aspirated consonants.

A short **a** as in cat, long **a** as in father
C ts as in bats
Č ch as in church
D d as in dog (dan), **t** as in sit (grad)
E short **e** as in met (več), **ea** as in pear (mleko)
I short **i** as in hit (ris), long **ee** as in been (sin)
J y as in yet
L l as in leap

O short **o** as in hot (voda), long **o** as in short (sok)
R r pronounced with the tip of the tongue like a
  Scottish "r"
Š sh as in shop
U oo as in foot (kruh)
V v as in vat (voda), **w** as in word (avto)
Ž zh as in measure

WORDS AND PHRASES

Slovenian distinguishes between **formal** and **informal** means of address. The formal (polite) way is very often used. The informal way is used among friends and people you know well. The phrases below use the polite form of address.

BASICS		Slovenian language	Slovenščina
Yes	Ja	Do you speak...?	Govorite...?
No	Ne	English	Angleško
I am from	Sem iz	German	Nemško
Britain/Ireland/	Velike Britanije/Irske/	French	Francosko
America/Canada/	Amerike/Kanade/	What's your name?	Kako ti je ime?
Australia/New Zealand	Avstralije/Nove Zelandije	My name is	Ime mi je
Slovenian	Slovensko	I (don't) understand	(Ne) Razumem
Slovenian person	Slovenec (male)/	Please	Prosim
	Slovenka (female)	Excuse me	Oprostite

Two beers, please	Dve pivi, prosim	**Open**	Odprto
Thank you (very much)	Hvala (lepa)	**Closed**	Zaprto
You're welcome	Prosim/ni za kaj	**Free admission**	Prost vstop
Hello (informal)	Živijo	**Toilet**	Stranišče/WC (women's –
Goodbye	Nasvidenje		ženske, men's – moški)
See you later (informal)	Adijo	**Shop**	Trgovina
Good morning	Dobro jutro	**Market**	Trg
Good day	Dober dan	**Hospital**	Bolnica/bolnišnica
Good evening	Dober večer	**Pharmacy**	Lekarna
Good night	Lahko noč	**Police**	Policija
How are you?	Kako ste?	**Caution/beware**	Previdno/pozor
Could you speak	Lahko govorite	**Help!**	Na pomoč!
more slowly?	počasneje?	**I'm ill**	Bolan (bolna) sem
What do you call…?	Kako se reče…?	**No smoking**	Kajenje prepovedano
Please write it down	Lahko prosim napišete	**No bathing**	Kopanje prepovedano
Hurry up!	Pohitite!	**Where is/are?**	Kje je/so?
Entrance	Vhod	**What?**	Kaj?
Exit	Izhod	**Why?**	Zakaj?
Arrival	Prihod	**When?**	Kdaj?
Departure	Odhod	**Who?**	Kdo?

ACCOMMODATION

I'd like/we'd like	Rad(a)**/radi bi	Do you have a student	Ali imate študentski
when speaker is male	**rad	discount?	popust?
when speaker is female	**rada	Is everything included?	Je vse vključeno v ceno?
How much is it?	Koliko stane?	Is breakfast included?	Ali je zajtrk vključen
Per night	Na noč		v ceno?
Per week	Na teden	Full board	Polni penzion
Single room	Enoposteljna soba	Half board	Pol penzion
Double room	Dvoposteljna soba	Can we camp here?	Ali lahko tukaj
Rooms for rent	Sobe/oddaja sob		kampiramo?
Hot (cold) water	Topla (mrzla) voda	Can I see the room?	Ali lahko vidim sobo?
Shower	Tuš	I have a reservation	Imam rezervacijo
It's very expensive	Zelo drago je	The bill please	Račun prosim
Do you have anything	Ali imate kaj	We're paying separately	Plačamo posebej
cheaper?	cenejšega?		

GETTING AROUND

Where's the…?	Kje je…?	When does the next train/	Kdaj odpelje naslednji
Campsite	Kamp	bus leave for…?	vlak/avtobus v…?
Hotel	Hotel	Do I have to change trains?	Ali moram prestopiti?
Railway station	Železniška postaja	Towards	Proti
Bus station	Avtobusna postaja	On the right (left)	Na desni (levi)
Bus stop	Avtobusno postajališče	Straight ahead	Naravnost
Inland	Notranji promet	(Over) There/here	Tam/tukaj
International	Mednarodni promet	Where are you going?	Kam greste?
Is it near (far)?	Ali je blizu (daleč)?	Is that on the way to…?	Ali je to na poti v…?
Which bus goes to…?	Kateri avtobus pelje v…?	I want to get out at…	Rad(a) bi izstopil(a) v…
A one-way ticket	Enosmerno vozovnico	Please stop here	Prosim ustavite tukaj
to… please	za… prosim	I'm lost	Izgubil(a) sem se
A return ticket to…	Povratno vozovnico za…	Arrivals	Prihodi
Can I reserve a seat?	Ali lahko rezerviram sedež?	Departures	Odhodi
What time does the train/	Kdaj odpelje vlak/	To/from	V/iz
bus leave…?	avtobus…?	Change	Prestop

NUMBERS

1	Ena	17	Sedemnajst
2	Dva	18	Osemnajst
3	Tri	19	Devetnajst
4	Štiri	20	Dvajset
5	Pet	21	Enaindvajset
6	Šest	30	Trideset
7	Sedem	40	Štirideset
8	Osem	50	Petdeset
9	Devet	60	Šestdeset
10	Deset	70	Sedemdeset
11	Enajst	80	Osemdeset
12	Dvanajst	90	Devetdeset
13	Trinajst	100	Sto
14	Štirinajst	Half	Pol
15	Petnajst	Quarter	Četrt
16	Šestnajst		

TIME, DAYS AND DATES

Either the 24- or 12-hour clock is used. When the 12-hour clock is used, "in the morning" (*dopoldan*), or "in the afternoon" (*popoldan*), is usually added. Halves and quarters are used: 4.30 is either *štiri trideset* or *pol petih*, the latter being more common; 4.15 is either *štiri petnajst* or *četrt čez štiri*. Duration is expressed by the prepositions *od* (from) and *do* (to). To **ask the time**, say: *Koliko je ura?*

Day	Dan	Wednesday	Sreda
Week	Teden	Thursday	Četrtek
Month	Mesec	Friday	Petek
Year	Leto	Saturday	Sobota
Today	Danes	January	Januar
Tomorrow	Jutri	February	Februar
The day after tomorrow	Pojutrišnjem	March	Marec
Yesterday	Včeraj	April	April
The day before yesterday	Predvčerajšnjim	May	Maj
In the morning	Zjutraj	June	Junij
Before noon	Dopoldan	July	Julij
Noon	Opoldan	August	Avgust
Afternoon	Popoldan	September	September
In the evening	Zvečer	October	Oktober
At midnight	Ob polnoči	November	November
At night	Ponoči	December	December
What is the time?	Koliko je ura?	Spring	Pomlad
Sunday	Nedelja	Summer	Poletje
Monday	Ponedeljek	Autumn	Jesen
Tuesday	Torek	Winter	Zima

FOOD AND DRINK

BASICS

		Kis	Vinegar
Bedro	Leg	Kisla smetana	Sour cream
Bučno olje	Pumpkin seed oil	Kruh	Bread
Dober tek!	Bon appétit!	Kuhano	Boiled
Dunajsko	Vienna-style (deep-fried in breadcrumbs)	Malo krvavo	Underdone/rare
		Maslo	Butter
Dušeno	Steamed	Med	Honey
Gorčica/senf	Mustard	Na žaru	Grilled

Na zdravje!	Cheers!
Ocvrto	Fried
Pariško	à la Parisienne (deep-fried without breadcrumbs)
Pečeno	Baked
Poper	Pepper
Praženo	Roasted
Prsi	Breast
Sladkor	Sugar
Smetana	Cream
Sol	Salt
Žemlja/Štrucka	Bread roll
Zapečeno	Well done (fried)

SOUPS (*JUHE*) AND STEWS (*ENOLONČNICE*)

Bograč	Meats, spices, peppers and tomatoes stewed in a copper pot
Fižolova juha	Bean soup
Gobova juha	Mushroom soup
Golaž	Hungarian-style goulash
Goveja juha	Beef broth
Jota	Bean and sauerkraut soup
Kisla juha	Soup made with sour cream and pigs' knuckles and head
Krompirjeva juha	Potato soup
Mineštra	Minestrone (mixed vegetable stew)
Paradižnikova juha	Tomato soup
Prežganka	Soup made by browning flour on lard and adding water
Ribji brodet	Istrian fish soup
Ričet	Barley and pork broth
Telečja obara	Veal stew
Zelenjavna juha	Vegetable soup

APPETIZERS – COLD OR HOT (*PREDJEDI – HLADNE ALI TOPLE*)

Narezek	Slices of cold meats
Olive	Olives
Pašteta (jetrna, račja, ribja)	Pâté (liver, duck, fish)
Pršut	Dry-cured Italian ham/ smoked ham
Rižota	Risotto
Sir (kozji, kravji, ovčji)	Cheese (goat, cow, sheep)
Šunka	Ham
Tatarski biftek	Raw mince with spices spread on toast

SALADS (*SOLATE*)

Fižolova solata	Bean salad
Hobotnica v solati	Octopus salad
Krompirjeva solata	Potato salad
Kumarična solata	Cucumber salad
Mešana solata	Mixed salad
Motovilec	Lamb's lettuce
Paradižnikova solata	Tomato salad
Radič	Radicchio
Rdeča pesa	Beetroot
Regrad	Dandelion
Sezonska solata	Fresh salad or whatever is in season
Šopska solata	Mixed tomatoes, cucumbers, red/green peppers and cheese
Zelena solata	Lettuce
Zeljnata solata	Cabbage salad

FISH DISHES (*RIBJE JEDI*) AND SEAFOOD (*MORSKI SADEŽI*)

Brancin	Seabass
Lignji	Squid
Losos	Salmon
Morski list	Sole
Ocvrta riba	Fried fish
Orada	Dorada
Oslič	Variety of cod
Postrvi	Trout
Rakci	Prawns
Sardele	Anchovies
Škampi	Shrimps
Školjke	Mussels
Skuša	Mackerel
Tuna	Tuna

MEAT DISHES (*MESNE JEDI*)

Čevapčiči	Minced meat, grilled in rolled pieces
Divjačina	Venison
Dunajski zrezek	Wiener schnitzel
Fazan	Pheasant
Gos	Goose
Govedina	Beef
Goveji zrezek	Rumpsteak
Jagnjetina	Lamb
Jetra	Liver
Kranjska klobasa s kislim zeljem	Smoked sausage with sauerkraut
Medved	Bear
Mesne kroglice	Meatballs
Meso na žaru	Assorted grilled meat
Možgani	Fried brains
Ovčetina	Mutton

Perutnina	Poultry
Piščanec	Chicken
Polnjene paprike	Peppers stuffed with meat and rice
Puran	Turkey
Raca	Duck
Sarma	Cabbage stuffed with meat and rice
Srna	Venison
Svinjina	Pork
Svinjski kotlet	Pork chop
Telečja (svinjska) krača	Veal (pork) shank
Telečja (svinjska) pečenka	Roast veal (pork)
Telečji zrezek	Roast cutlet
Teletina	Veal
Vampi	Tripe
Zajec	Rabbit
Žrebičkov zrezek	Horse steak

SAUCES (*OMAKE*)

Gobova omaka	Mushroom sauce
Paradižnikova omaka	Tomato sauce
Sirova omaka	Cheese sauce
Smetanova omaka	Cream sauce
Tatarska omaka	Sauce made of mayonnaise, mustard, garlic and parsley
Vinska omaka	Wine sauce

ACCOMPANIMENTS (*PRILOGE*)

Ajdovi žganci	Buckwheat porridge
Burek	Oily pastry with cheese or meat filling
Frika	Fried potato and cheese pie
Krompir	Potatoes
Krompirjevi cmoki	Potato dumplings
Kruhovi cmoki	Bread dumplings
Kuhan	Boiled
Kuhana zelenjava	Boiled vegetables
Njoki	Gnocchi
Ocvrti sir	Cheese fried in breadcrumbs
Pečen	Roasted
Pire	Mashed
Pommes frites (pomfri)	French fries
Riž	Rice
Testenine	Pasta
Žlikrofi	Slovene type of ravioli

VEGETABLES (*ZELENJAVA*)

Artičoka	Artichoke
Beluši/šparglji	Asparagus
Brstični ohrovt	Brussels sprouts

Bučke	Courgette
Čebula	Onions
Česen	Garlic
Cvetača	Cauliflower
Fižol	Beans
Gobe	Mushrooms
Grah	Peas
Hren	Horseradish
Jajčevec/melancana	Aubergine/eggplant
Korenje	Carrots
Koruza	Sweetcorn
Krompir	Potatoes
Kumara	Cucumber
Paprika	Red/green peppers
Paradižnik	Tomato
Peteršilj	Parsley
Por	Leek
Rdeča pesa	Beetroot
Redkev	Radish
Repa	Turnip
Špinača	Spinach
Zelena	Celery
Zelje	Cabbage

FRUIT (*SADJE*) AND NUTS (*ORESKI*)

Ananas	Pineapple
Breskev	Peach
Češnja	Cherry
Figa/smokva	Fig
Grozdje	Grapes
Hruška	Pear
Jabolko	Apple
Jagoda	Strawberry
Lešnik	Hazelnut
Limona	Lemon
Lubenica	Watermelon
Malina	Raspberry
Mandelj	Almond
Marelica	Apricot
Melona	Melon
Oreh	Walnut
Pomaranča	Orange
Ribez	Currant
Sliva	Plum

DESSERTS (*SLADICE*)

Gibanica	Pastry stuffed with apples, walnuts, cream and poppy seeds
Kremšnita	Cream cake with vanilla and whipped cream
Palačinke z orehi, čokolado ali marmelado	Pancakes with walnuts, chocolate or jam

Potica (orehova ali pehtranova)	Sweet roll flavoured with nuts, tarragon and honey	**Kava**	Coffee
Sladoled	Ice cream	**Kava z mlekom**	Coffee with milk
Štruklji (ajdovi, orehovi ali sirovi)	Dumplings with savoury (buckwheat, for example) or sweet (walnut or sweet cheese) fillings	**Medica**	Honey liqueur
		Mineralna voda	Mineral water, usually with gas
		Pivo	Beer
		Sadjevec	Fruit brandy
Zavitek (jabolčni ali sirov)	Strudel (apple or cheese)	**Slivovka**	Plum brandy
		Sok	Juice
		Temno pivo	Dark beer
DRINKS (*PIJACE*)		**Viljamovka**	Pear brandy
Brinovec	Juniper brandy	**Vino (belo, rdeče)**	Wine (white, red)
Čaj	Tea	**Voda**	Water

Glossary of Slovenian words and terms

Avto Car
Avtobusna postaja Bus station
Avtobusna postajališče Bus stop
Avtocesta Highway
Banka Bank
Bolnica Hospital
Center Centre
Cerkev Church
Cesta Road
DDV Goods tax, equivalent to VAT
Denar Money
Dolina Valley
Dom/Koča Mountain hut
Gledališče Theatre
Gora Mountain
Gostilna Inn, primarily serving food but which sometimes has accommodation
Gostišče Inn, typically offering both accommodation and food
Gozd Forest
Grad Castle
Hiša House
Hrib Hill
Jama Cave
Jezero Lake
Kino Cinema
Kmečki turizem Farm tourism
Letališče Airport
Mestna hiša Town hall
Mesto Town, city
Morje Sea
Most Bridge
Muzej Museum

Nakupovalni center Shopping centre
Optik Optician
Otok Island
Pekarna Bakery
Peron Platform (at the station)
Plavalni bazen Swimming pool
Plaža Beach
Pokopališče Cemetery
Polje Field
Pošta Post office
Pot Path/way/trail
Pristanišče Port
Reka River
Restavracija Restaurant
Samostan Monastery
Sejem Fair
Slap Waterfall
Slaščičarna Patisserie
Šola School
Stadion Stadium
Toplice Spa or mineral baths
Trajekt Ferry
Trg Square, market
Trgovina Shop/supermarket
Ulica Street
Vas Village
Veloposlaništvo Embassy
Vodnjak Fountain
Vozni red Timetable (bus and train)
Vrt Garden
Zdravnik Doctor
Železniška postaja Railway station
Zemljevid Map

Small print and index

Rough Guide credits

Editor: Samantha Cook
Layout: Nikhil Agarwal
Cartography: Animesh Pathak
Picture editor: Phoebe Lowndes
Proofreader: Jan McCann
Managing editor: Monica Woods
Assistant editor: Payal Sharotri

Production: Jimmy Lao
Cover photo research: Sarah Stewart-Richardson
Editorial assistant: Aimee White
Senior DTP coordinator: Dan May
Programme manager: Gareth Lowe
Publishing director: Georgina Dee

Publishing information

This fourth edition published June 2017 by
Rough Guides Ltd,
80 Strand, London WC2R 0RL
11, Community Centre, Panchsheel Park,
New Delhi 110017, India
Distributed by Penguin Random House
Penguin Books Ltd, 80 Strand, London WC2R 0RL
Penguin Group (USA), 345 Hudson Street, NY 10014, USA
Penguin Group (Australia), 250 Camberwell Road,
Camberwell, Victoria 3124, Australia
Penguin Group (NZ), 67 Apollo Drive, Mairangi Bay,
Auckland 1310, New Zealand
Penguin Group (South Africa), Block D, Rosebank Office
Park, 181 Jan Smuts Avenue, Parktown North, Gauteng,
South Africa 2193
Rough Guides is represented in Canada by DK Canada, 320
Front Street West, Suite 1400, Toronto, Ontario M5V 3B6
Printed in Singapore
© Rough Guides 2017
Maps © Rough Guides

328pp includes index
A catalogue record for this book is available from the
British Library
ISBN: 978-0-24128-299-1
The publishers and authors have done their best to
ensure the accuracy and currency of all the information in
The Rough Guide to Slovenia, however, they can accept
no responsibility for any loss, injury, or inconvenience
sustained by any traveller as a result of information or
advice contained in the guide.
1 3 5 7 9 8 6 4 2

Help us update

We've gone to a lot of effort to ensure that the fourth
edition of **The Rough Guide to Slovenia** is accurate
and up-to-date. However, things change – places get
"discovered", opening hours are notoriously fickle,
restaurants and rooms raise prices or lower standards.
If you feel we've got it wrong or left something out,
we'd like to know, and if you can remember the
address, the price, the hours, the phone number, so
much the better.

Please send your comments with the subject line
"**Rough Guide Slovenia Update**" to mail@uk.roughguides
.com. We'll credit all contributions and send a copy of the
next edition (or any other Rough Guide if you prefer) for
the very best emails.

A ROUGH GUIDE TO ROUGH GUIDES

Published in 1982, the first Rough Guide – to Greece – was a student scheme that became a
publishing phenomenon. Mark Ellingham, a recent graduate in English from Bristol University,
had been travelling in Greece the previous summer and couldn't find the right guidebook.
With a small group of friends he wrote his own guide, combining a contemporary, journalistic
style with a thoroughly practical approach to travellers' needs.

The immediate success of the book spawned a series that rapidly covered dozens of
destinations. And, in addition to impecunious backpackers, Rough Guides soon acquired a
much broader readership that relished the guides' wit and inquisitiveness as much as their
enthusiastic, critical approach and value-for-money ethos. These days, Rough Guides include
recommendations from budget to luxury and cover more than 120 destinations around the
globe, from Amsterdam to Zanzibar, all regularly updated by our team of roaming writers.

Browse all our latest guides, read inspirational features and book your trip at **roughguides.com**.

ABOUT THE AUTHOR

Norm Longley has been visiting Slovenia for the best part of twenty years, and has spent most of his working life in central/eastern Europe – he is also the author of the Rough Guides to Romania and Budapest. More recently he has turned his hand to home shores, contributing to the Scotland, Wales and Ireland guides. He lives in Somerset and can occasionally be seen erecting marquees on The Rec in Bath.

Acknowledgements

Norm would like to thank Monica, without whom this project would not have happened, and Sam for her first-class editing, kindness and extraordinary patience in the process of updating this book. Very special thanks are due to Tine Murn, whose assistance throughout has been nothing short of spectacular; to Renata and Vesna at the Association of Slovenian Tourist Farms for their continued support; and Jani Peljhan, for some truly memorable (mostly gastronomic) experiences in the Vipava Valley. Thanks are also due to Gerry Copsey and the team in Mells; Matej and Mitja in Ljubljana; Nika Pirnar and Petra Stušek in Ljubljana; Tjaša Ohojak in Bovec; Grega Ugovšek in Kamnik;

Dejan Iskra and Boštjan Kurent in Pivka; Marko Habjan in Novo Mesto; Lara Pirc in Izola; Lea Šuligoj in Portorož; Tatjana Humar in Kobarid; Lidija and the team at *Camp Koren*; Tanja Srečkovič Bolseč in Maribor; Peter Črnič in Črnomelj; Nikolaš Borut in Tolmin; Katja Gonc in Ptuj; Maja Lakota in Bled; Tina Čič at Lipica; Matej Tomažič in Slap; Manca Strugar and Iztok Loborec in Kranj; Nina Peternel in Kranjska Gora; Dragan Barbutovski in Ljubljana; Peter Lisjak in Dornberk; Janez Fajfar in Bled; Frank Marr; Marc Ožbej; and Igor and Stanka at the wonderful *MuziKafé* in Ptuj.

Most importantly, thank you to Christian, Luka, Patrick and Anna, and finally, to Tatjana Radovič, a most special friend.

Photo credits

All photos © Rough Guides, except the following:
(Key: t-top; c-centre; b-bottom; l-left; r-right)

1 Alamy Stock Photo: age fotostock
2 Alamy Stock Photo: Westend61 GmbH
4 Alamy Stock Photo: funkyfood London
7 Alamy Stock Photo: E9JK5F (c); robertharding (t).
Dreamstime.com: Jessamine (b)
8 Alamy Stock Photo: Tibor Bognar
9 AWL Images: Alan Copson
11 Alamy Stock Photo: imageBROKER (b); YAY Media AS (t)
12 Dreamstime.com: Jay Beiler
13 Alamy Stock Photo: INSADCO Photography (b).
AWL Images: Michele Falzone (c); Amar Grover (tr).
Getty Images: Jan Hetfleischc (tl)
14 Alamy Stock Photo: Sasa Huzjak (tl); Matthew
Williams-Ellis (b); Jan Wlodarczyk (tr). **AWL Images:**
Alan Copson
15 Alamy Stock Photo: F.J. Fdez. Bordonada (b);
Graham Lawrence (t)
16 Alamy Stock Photo: Nino Marcutti (t); Tuul and
Bruno Morandi (c); Realy Easy Star/Tullio Valente (bl)
17 Alamy Stock Photo: Marco Secchi (b); Adrian
Sherratt (t)
18 AWL Images: Hemis (l). **Dreamstime.com:** Sergii
Figurnyi (r)
20 Alamy Stock Photo: Iris Kürschner
38–39 AWL Images: Alan Copson
41 Alamy Stock Photo: Realy Easy Star/Toni Spagone
53 Alamy Stock Photo: allOver – Collection 148 (tr);
Xinhua (b). **SuperStock:** Cubo Images (tl)

65 Alamy Stock Photo: Realy Easy Star/Toni Spagone (b).
Dreamstime.com: Matic Štojs (t)
76–77 Dreamstime.com: Roman Smirnov
79 AWL Images: Marco Bottigelli
99 Alamy Stock Photo: David Robertson (t). **AWL Images:**
Alan Copson (b)
125 Alamy Stock Photo: Roger Bacon Valente (b);
parkerphotography (tl); Ken Welsh (tr)
136–137 Alamy Stock Photo: Nicholas Pitt
139 Alamy Stock Photo: Matthew Williams-Ellis
155 Alamy Stock Photo: hemis.fr/GARDEL Bertrand (b);
LianeM (t)
175 AWL Images: Nick Ledger
198–199 Alamy Stock Photo: Marko Trebusak
201 SuperStock: age footstock/F.J. Fdez. Bordonada
215 Alamy Stock Photo: Karol Czinege
231 Alamy Stock Photo: Erin Babnik (tr); Ivan Batinic (br);
Graham Lawrence (tl). **SuperStock:** age fotostock/Juan
Carlos Muñoz (bl)
244–245 Alamy Stock Photo: parkerphotography
247 Getty Images: Jure Makovec
265 Alamy Stock Photo: Sasa Huzjak (b). **SuperStock:**
imageBROKER (t)
283 Alamy Stock Photo: East Images (bl); Realy Easy Star/
Toni Spagone (tl); Daniel Simon (tr); Matic Štojs (br)
294 Alamy Stock Photo: parkerphotography

Cover *Julian Alps, Slovenia* **Getty Images:** Guy Edwardes

Index

Maps are marked in grey

Map symbols

The symbols below are used on maps throughout the book

▬ ▬ ▪ ▪	International boundary	⛴	Boat	🔫	Waterfall	♟	Museum
▬ ▬ ▬	Chapter division boundary	@	Internet access	/|\\	Hill	♟	Fortress
▬▬▬▬	Motorway	ⓘ	Information office		Gorge	♜	Castle
▬▬▬▬	Pedestrianized road	⊤	Gardens	🌳	Arboretum	⛪	Monastery
▬▬▬	Road	P	Parking	🏠	Mountain refuge	✝	Church (regional maps)
▬▬▬▬	Steps	⊠	Post office	⛊	Border post		Building
▬▬▬▬	Funicular line	⊠	Gate	◠	Cave		Church (town maps)
●▬▬▬●	Cable car	◆	Place of interest	⌣	Bridge	⬭	Stadium
▬ ▬ ▬	Footpath	⸫	Ruin	▲	Mountain peak	▢	Park
▬▬▬▬	Wall	✡	Synagogue	⌢	Mountain range	▢	Beach
▭▭▭	Railway	◠	Arch	⛷	Ski resort	⊞	Cemetery
✈	Airport	🍇	Vineyard/winery	🏛	Stately home/palace	▱	Marsh
★	Bus stop	⋇	Lighthouse	🏛	Monument	▭	Saltpan

Listings key

■	Accommodation
●	Eating
■	Drinking/nightlife
●	Shopping

HOLIDAYS ON FARMS IN SLOVENIA
AN UNFORGETTABLE EXPERIENCE

Wake up to the countryside and discover what makes the perfect holiday experience for you. This idyllic setting offers numerous opportunities for hiking, cycling, horseback riding, watersports and more, while farms are excellent starting points for excursions around Slovenia. You can start the day with an excellent breakfast, freshly-cooked from local or home-grown produce and finish it with delicious dinner accompanied by excellent wines.

To discover more about your perfect farm holiday, visit the official page www.farmtourism.si, Facebook (Tourist farms of Slovenia) or Instagram (farmstayslovenia).